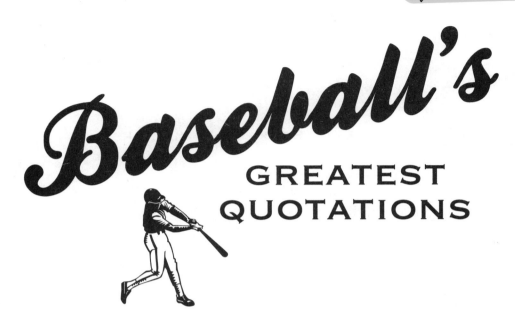

Baseball's

GREATEST
QUOTATIONS

BAT AND BALL BOOKS BY PAUL DICKSON

The Dickson Baseball Dictionary (1989)

Baseball's Greatest Quotations—First Compilation (1991)

Baseball: The President's Game (with William B. Mead) (1993)

The Worth Book of Softball (1994)

The Joy of Keeping Score (1996)

The New Dickson Baseball Dictionary (1999)

The Hidden Language of Baseball (2003)

Baseball's GREATEST QUOTATIONS

———⊷◆⊶———

AN ILLUSTRATED TREASURY
OF BASEBALL QUOTATIONS
AND HISTORICAL LORE

———⊷◆⊶———

PAUL DICKSON

Collins
An Imprint of HarperCollins*Publishers*

Copyright acknowledgments for this book may be found on page 625.

BASEBALL'S GREATEST QUOTATIONS, REVISED EDITION. Copyright © 2008 by Paul Dickson. All rights reserved. Printed in the United States of America. No part of this book may be used or reproduced in any manner whatsoever without written permission except in the case of brief quotations embodied in critical articles or reviews. For information, address Harper-Collins Publishers, 10 East 53rd Street, New York, NY 10022.

HarperCollins books may be purchased for educational, business, or sales promotional use. For information, please write: Special Markets Department, HarperCollins Publishers, 10 East 53rd Street, New York, NY 10022.

Library of Congress Cataloging-in-Publication Data

Baseball's greatest quotations / [compiled by] Paul Dickson. — Rev. ed.
       p. cm.
    Includes bibliographical references and index.
    ISBN 978-0-06-126060-5 (pb) 1. Baseball—Quotations, maxims, etc.
I. Dickson, Paul. II. Title.

GV867.3.B366 2008
793.357—dc22

2007034389

08 09 10 11 12 ISPN/RRD 10 9 8 7 6 5 4 3 2 1

To the late Charles D. Poe, who caught on to this idea immediately and helped me with it on a daily basis. If this book flies, credit him with the navigation . . . and a lot of the fuel. Also to Isabelle C. Dickson, who got the quote-collecting engine started, and Nancy Dickson, who keeps the engine purring: with more thanks than words can express. Then there is Tom Mellers, who has been advising me on this project since dinosaurs roamed the earth, and Joseph C. Goulden, with his uncanny ability to spot classic quotations. And, last but not least, to Skip McAfee, for his incredible generosity in collecting and sharing quotations from his collection of classic baseball quotations.

"I can remember a reporter asking for a quote, and I didn't know what a quote was. I thought it was some kind of a soft drink."
—Joe DiMaggio on his first season in the majors

⟫⟪

"*Quotes.* That which a player says immediately after the game but is sure he didn't say when it appears in print the next day."
—Jerry Howarth in *Baseball Lite*

CONTENTS

INTRODUCTION

———————

Quotations are extremely important to baseball. They are, in fact, integral to the charm and appeal of the game. They are not, of course, the game itself, but giving and recording them is an important baseball ritual. Simply put: other than politics, it is hard to think of any other American realm where quotation marks are as significant.

Indeed, there are even times when they come close to being the game itself. For example, the lore of the game says that a mere ten seemingly innocuous words—six from Bill Terry and four from Charlie Dressen—greatly affected the seasons of 1934 and 1953, respectively, and still define the Giants-Dodgers rivalry on two coasts. Terry's "Is Brooklyn still in the league?" goaded the Dodgers to a pennant, while Dressen's "The Giants is dead" profoundly irked the fifth-place Giants and motivate them to win the 1954 National League pennant and World Series. Both are still recalled vividly by fans born after the lines were uttered.

Or think about the mere eight words which may forever prevent Mark McGwire's election to the Baseball Hall of Fame, when he told a congressional committee looking into steroid use, "I'm not here to talk about the past." If nothing else, baseball, which has turned records and statistics into a sacrament, is totally absorbed by the past.

Consider for a moment what the game would be like if it were suddenly stripped of the pre- and postgame quote, the off-season quote, the spring training quote, the Hall of Fame induction quote, the home run "call," the old-timer quote, and the other species and subspecies of baseball quotations. It would of course still be a game, but it would lose its off-the-field color and zest. Columns would flounder and die, and sportscasting would dwindle to described action and statistics.

It would also lose its context in the culture, where it can be heard in such components of Americana as Satchel Paige's Rules, the many lines attributed to Yogi Berra, Babe Ruth's comments on the president's salary, Lou Gehrig's "luckiest man" speech, "Casey at the Bat," Russ Hodges's call of Bobby Thomson's home run, and so many more.

This is, after all, a game in which Walter Johnson could "throw a lamb chop past a wolf," a game played on a planet two-thirds covered by water "and one-third covered by Garry Maddox."

What's more, baseball quotations are popular and seem to crowd out quotations from other fields. Consider this: In 1979 *Sports Illustrated* ran a list, compiled by Phil Pepe and Zander Hollander, of the fifteen all-time most famous American sports quotations. Two came from football, three from boxing, and the other ten were from baseball. Fact is, it would have been easy to make the baseball total higher if they had included "Say it ain't so, Joe" and a line or two from "Casey at the Bat"—the most repeated and recited poem in the history of the Republic.

A real reason for this popularity is that quotes are integral to reporting the game. "Hours at a time," Dan Connolly wrote in the *Baltimore Sun* in 2006, "baseball writers stand in clubhouses with notebooks and tape recorders waiting for players to offer pearls of wisdom. Most times, we get nothing. Clichés. Brief answers. Nasty stares if the questions are particularly stupid or the one being interviewed is particularly surly. Occasionally, though, ballplayers and managers fill it up with introspective stuff, funny stuff, bizarre stuff."

Baseball is played and managed by a changing cast of characters who leave two things in their wake: numbers and strings of words. The strings of words are such a factor in baseball that names have been given to various individuals' lifetime utterances. There are Deanisms, Berraisms (also known as Yogisms to those who like the mystical sound), Weaverisms, Ozarkisms, and Rickeyisms (or what one writer dubbed "Gem Rickeys"). Of course, there is also that vast body of sayings from Casey Stengel—"Stengelisms"—which were long ago delivered in a one-man dialect known as Stengelese.

And these very sayings have gone a long way to giving baseball its own set of stock characters, filling all sorts of roles which live on after them. Some of the dramatis personae:

The Boy King. Who else but the Babe could turn to the chief executive and say "Hot as hell, ain't it, Prez?"

The Wise Fool; quoted by presidents, CEOs, and commencement speakers alike, what he says sounds goofy, but just for the moment. Yogi Berra has his own pack of interpreters who will entertain at a banquet by quoting his best lines.

The Ruthless Warrior. Defined in the twentieth century by the likes of Ty Cobb and headhunter Early Wynn, who we all know would bounce one off his mama's noggin on Mother's Day if she were crowding the plate.

The Incorruptible Czar. Judge Landis.

The Intellectual Czar. Bart Giamatti.

The Prodigal Sons. Joe Pepitone, Billy Martin, Denny McLain, Pete Rose, José Canseco, and more.

The Worldly Philosopher Hisself. Casey Stengel, who was never more or less clear in what he actually meant than a pack of academically approved existentialists. He has had reincarnations, perhaps none as direct as George "Sparky" Anderson.

The Chorus of Narrators and Commentators. Red Barber, Vin Scully, Ring and John Lardner, Red Smith, Dizzy Dean, Jim Murray, Gaylord Perry, Roger Angell, Roger Kahn, Red Smith, Pat Jordan, Tom Boswell, George Will, Jim Brosnan, Satchel Paige and Lefty Gomez, to name a few.

There are more—many more in fact—but the point is made.

Baseball is unusual among sports in the sense that at any given moment one or two players or managers may wear the mantle of "quote machine," that is, one who is always good for a one-liner or an edgy comment in those Sunday baseball wrap-ups favored by the major papers. Andy Van Slyke, Sparky Anderson, Dick Howser, David Wells, and Don Zimmer have all filled this role.

The most recent heir apparent as quote machine is pitcher Todd Jones. Jack Curry of the *New York Times,* on October 27, 2006, called him "the king of quotations, the sultan of sound bites, the emperor of one-liners." He added, "When Jones, the closer for the Detroit Tigers, is talking, which is often, there is almost always a crowd of reporters around him waiting for his next verbal gem."

More often than not; quote machines attract more ink than Hall of Fame votes, and more often than not, the really great players do not take on the role of jester or cosmic observer.

Besides the famous and familiar quotations from those who are tied directly to the game, there are a surprising number of outside observers who have had their say in the matter. Individuals as diverse as Ralph Nader, H. L. Mencken, Bob Dylan, Truman Capote, George Bernard Shaw, Jane Austen, Walt Whitman, and Mark Twain have weighed in on baseball topics, and it is hard to find a modern president who did not come up with some sweeping pronouncement on the game. The nature of the commentary is diverse, ranging from those who adore the game (James T. Farrell, Carl Sandburg, William Saroyan) to those who detest it (F. Scott Fitzgerald, Shaw). For a compiler of quotations, it is a realm of great riches.

ABOUT THE SECOND EDITION

The first version of this work was published in 1991, and since then more quotations have been collected, relating to a host of developments—the Pete Rose vs. Bart Giamatti confrontation, the long strike of 1994–95, the deaths of Mickey Mantle, Joe DiMaggio, Ted Williams, Dan Quisenberry, and so many others, the rise (and fall) of Mark McGwire, Cal Ripken's 2,131-game streak, and so much more. Readers of the first book have not only sent me new lines but those omitted from the past—many from the nineteenth century.

Since the first edition, the Internet has blossomed and with it scads of Web sites containing baseball quotations—more than a thousand containing quotations by Casey Stengel in his own lingo, Stengelese. This is as it should be; the pity is that almost without exception these collections are presented without benefit of context or source, immediately diminishing their value.

As this new and improved version of the 1991 book was prepared I became more and more aware of something troubling, which is that baseball is not producing memorable quotes at anything like the rate it did prior to 1990, when work on the last collection was completed.

What first alerted me to this was an article by Lee Green in the September 1993 *American Way* magazine entitled "Whatever Happened to Sports Quotes?" the gist of which was that a sudden and inexplicable shortage of good pithy sports quotes had set upon the land, especially those (to quote Green) "zippy one liners that used to distract us from the troubling notion that 'Winning isn't everything. it's the only thing' which incidentally Vince Lombardi swore he never said."

The drought, Bob Costas told Green, was because "there seem to be fewer genuinely colorful characters these days," and columnist Scott Osler opined, "You'd think that the law of averages would drop a few more really clever, witty guys on us now and then, but it just doesn't seem to happen."

All of this is sadly true. The quotable Bart Giamatti gave way to the turgid voice of Bud Selig; Casey Stengel's "perfessorial" pinstripe leadership role was ceded to the most likeable but seldom quotable Joe Torre. There is no new Branch Rickey, no new maverick like Bill Veeck, and no new lexical phenom on the order of Dizzy Dean or a new Berra of one one-liners. The great late-twentieth century aphorist Dan Quisenberry died at the height of his powers at age forty-five.

There are a few real reasons for this. The number of players whose native language is other than English has skyrocketed, and players who learned the game in the Dominican Republic, Korea, or Japan (Ichiro notwithstanding) may be the soul of wit speaking their native tongue but not in English. Then there is a certain change in the atmosphere of the game which works against wit and subtlety—steroids, reporters with an ear set for anger and hostility, clubhouses where the number of iPods is equal to the number of jockstraps. Some clubhouses are that in name only and have turned into locker rooms for baseball players who sort themselves into cliques—Christian athletes, Spanish speakers, etc. There is nothing wrong with any of this save for the fact that it generates fewer good quotes.

There are exceptions among players (Todd Jones and Mark Grace for starters). It is true that as of this writing quotemeisters Yogi Berra, Don Zimmer, Bob Uecker, and Joe Garagiola are still hitting doubles and triples, but they are old-school echoes of the past showing up for the verbal equivalent of old-timers games.

As for the voices of the game, Vin Scully, Red Barber, Mel Allen, and their ilk have not been replaced—although Bob Costas and Jon Miller, especially in tandem with Joe Morgan, are working their up to broadcasting Olympus. But this is partially due to the fact that radio has yielded to television as the medium of choice.

I CALL 'EM AS I SEE 'EM

(A FEW WORDS ON THE DEMONSTRABLE
VERACITY OF THESE QUOTES)

When Dizzy Dean died in July 1974 the *St. Louis Post-Dispatch* carried an immense obituary on the man who had dazzled and entertained that city for decades. Before running a long list of "Deanisms" as part of its tribute, the paper made this disclaimer: "Stories about Dean became baseball legend; in the retelling the exact quotes attributed to him often changed."

Old Diz would have loved that stuffy disclaimer because the quotes changed mostly because it was he—Jay Hanna Dean—who gave different versions of the same quote. Polished 'em up, as he liked to say.

For instance, he puckishly told different reporters about different birthplaces. Depending on his mood and the last person he talked to with a pad and pencil, Diz would look you straight in the eye and say he hailed from Lucas, Arkansas . . . or Holdenville, Oklahoma . . . or Bond, Mississippi, or somewhere else in the general vicinity—the vicinity being someplace in 'Merica. When he was pressed on the matter of his ever-changing place of birth, Dean replied, "I was helpin' the writers out. Them ain't lies; them's scoops."

The question that this begs is whether or not the quotes were valid when first recorded. The answer is an unequivocal "maybe, maybe not."

Early in my collecting I wrote to the late Robert Smith of Lenox, Massachusetts, one of my favorite writers and a veteran of baseball books, to ask if he had any thoughts on the matter of baseball quotations. His reply in part: "One thing I can do is offer some advice you probably by this time do not need: about 75 percent of the quotations offered by many of the old-time sportswriters as being taken right from a ballplayer's lips are fictitious." Smith then went on to name some names of "fiction writers."

One might quibble with Smith's number of 75 percent, but there is no question that many quotes were tailored to the player in question. There is little one can do other than toss out the most obviously bogus quotations and hope that one has picked a large percentage of the legitimate ones.

Was Casey Stengel's wise man/fool persona, with his own style of doubletalk, an act? Howard Rosenthal, who covered the Yankees for nine of the twelve years that Stengel managed them, insisted that it was in his book, *The 10 Best Years of Baseball:* "The clown image was a façade for Casey. He knew what was going on. In fact, he was quite a bright guy, especially when it came to real estate and finance."

As for Yogi Berra, Ralph Keyes in his masterful work on attribution, *The Quote Verifier* (St. Martin's, 2006), shows that many of the quotes credited to Berra have precedents elsewhere and may not be his at all—echoing one of his better lines, "I really didn't say everything I said."

Then there are the celebrity quotes. "They will have to wait a few minutes till I get my time at bat," is what Abraham Lincoln was supposed to have said when informed of his nomination for president. In another version, he is alleged to have said, "Tell the gentlemen I am glad to hear of their coming but they will have to wait a few minutes till I make another base hit."

He is also supposed to have turned, while dying from an assassin's bullet, to one Abner Doubleday and whispered the immortal line "Don't let baseball die." Several people told me that F. Scott Fitzgerald once said, "Baseball has destroyed more good writers than liquor." This was alleged to be a rap against Ring Lardner. Fitzgerald did not like the game and thought Lardner was squandering his talents, but there is no evidence that I could find to support the quote in question.

Neither the two Lincoln quotes nor the Fitzgerald quote appears in the body of the book.

Another point. Several people have asked if these quotes will be "original," or if any will be filtered through collaborators in "as told to" autobiographies. The fact is that after several months of wrestling with this question I discovered that in almost all cases a good line uttered in the clubhouse in front of a microphone is likely to emerge intact in a book written in most cases by beat sports reporters. These may not be the original quotations, but they are as close as one is likely to get to the original. It is something like the voice of legislators whose words are filtered through the cleansing process which takes place between the time something is said and when it appears in the *Congressional Record.*

A GUIDE TO THE COLLECTION AND THE ARRANGEMENT OF ENTRIES

Lest there be any doubt, only a small percentage of the quotations in this book will be "familiar quotations." The aim has been to make most of them fresh and surprising. But, by the same token, I have striven to make sure that all of the most quoted lines are repeated here, and I have tried to surround those familiar quotations with an extra dollop of background and objectivity.

I also tried to achieve a certain objectivity in selecting quotations, but subjectivity quickly came into play as I outlined a group of subjects that would have limits imposed on them. These were simply things that I felt had become clichéd, overworked, and boring. I made a list of themes which I posted on the wall over my desk for the first edition of the book and about which I felt I had to be highly selective. That list included:

- free agency
- the lively ball (along with extended metaphors involving rabbits, lettuce-eating balls, etc.)
- owners whining about free agency, compensation, and fan loyalty
- players whining about the stinginess of owners
- to DH or not to DH
- baseball strikes (not the kind at the plate)
- old-timers decrying $$$$ paid to young-timers
- why "the numbers" are misleading
- the game is far more than a game but a metaphor for life on earth, all that is sublime, the order of the cosmos, etc.

For this edition, I have added to that list:

- inordinate speculation on who is, was, and still uses performance-enhancing drugs.
- quotes from young players who by dint of background or education are not fully apprised of baseball history and admit they are not aware of players past, along the lines of the rookie Ruben Rivera, who, when compared by a journalist to two Yankee greats, responded, "I don't know anything about Mantle or DiMaggio. Were they as good as Ken Griffey Jr.?"

FORMAT

The entries in this book are listed by speaker rather than by topic. The beauty of this system is that it allows the character—or at least an impression of the character—of the person being quoted to be shown off in one place. This is the classic approach followed by, for example, *Bartlett's Familiar Quotations.*

The drawback to this system is that it is not topical. To compensate for this I have used a system of cross-references and indexing which works as follows:

1. If there is a quote about a person by another person, it is cross-referenced. If Casey Stengel had something memorable to say about Yogi Berra, this will be mentioned at the end of the section of Berra quotations.
2. The quotations are also arranged alphabetically within entries—Yogi Berra's "It ain't over 'til it's over" comes after "It ain't like football. You can't make up no trick plays."
3. The index has been reserved for topics and broad themes. This is where one should head to find, for example, all the critics of the game or all of the book's quotations on rookies. The advantage of this system is that it allows a given quote to be listed under several topics in the index. To make this an easy book to use, I have divided it up into indexed themes. I have based the index on the thematic filing system at the National Baseball Library.
4. With one notable exception, it has been the custom of sports-quotations books to be long on color and short on attribution. There is good reason for this. Unlike the words of people in the real world (statesmen or perhaps lawyers), the words of athletes and people

who write about athletic contests tend to be recalled with a determined lack of precision along the lines of "as Connie Mack once said" or "as Casey Stengel was fond of saying."

I have done the best I can in dating and attributing the quotations; however, there are limits to what can be done. In many cases I have simply noted that a quote is "widely quoted" or "widely attributed," which is a shorthand way of saying that the line or lines in question have appeared in two or more previous collections of quotations and one or more of the five major periodical carriers of sports wit and wisdom (*Baseball Digest, Inside Sports, Sport, Sports Illustrated,* and the *Sporting News*). In other words, these are the quotes which have become the standards.

I have also credited several collections. Those noted as coming from SABR (Society of American Baseball Research) or from a SABR collector come from members who collect quotations and responded to my plea for favorite items. The several dozen quotes which are attributed to the "Hall of Fame" come from a file of quotations in the National Baseball Library in Cooperstown.

On to the collection!

A

AARON, ESTELLA

"My boy has a chance to do it. He takes care of himself and nothing comes in front of baseball for Henry. Nothing. On days when he is feeling good, it's just too bad for the pitchers."

> —On her son Hank and the home run record; quoted in *Hank Aaron . . . 714 and Beyond* by Jerry Brondfield

AARON, HANK

"Babe Ruth never had to contend with anything like that when he was establishing his record."

> —On the threats by racists vexed by his closing in on Babe Ruth's record; quoted by Fred Lieb in *Baseball as I Have Known It*. Lieb added: "Hank Aaron was wrong in thinking that Ruth had no race problem. Many players, including fellow members of his old Red Sox team, thought that Ruth was part Negro. When he was pitching and batting, nothing would enrage him more than to have some coach or rookie, hiding in the obscurity of the bench, yell nigger at him.

"Can I smoke now without someone taking my picture?"

> —To the press after one of his milestone home runs

"Guessing what the pitcher is going to throw is 80 per cent of being a successful hitter. The other 20 percent is just execution."

> —On hitting in *Hank Aaron . . . 714 and Beyond* by Jerry Brondfield

"I can't recall a day this year or last when I did not hear the name of Babe Ruth."

> —As he moved toward Ruth's record of 714 home runs; quoted in *Babe: The Legend Comes to Life* by Robert W. Creamer

"I don't see pitches down the middle anymore—not even in batting practice."

> —During the 1973 season; quoted widely

"I don't want them to forget Ruth. I just want them to remember me!"

> —Widely quoted during the latter days of his home run drive, first stated by Aaron late in the 1973 season

1

"I like those lefties, but when you're hitting, all pitchers look alike. I don't care much who's throwing or what he throws."

—In 1957 from *The Sporting News Chronicle of 20th Century Sport*

"I never smile when I have a bat in my hands. That's when you've got to be serious. When I get out on the field, nothing's a joke to me. I don't feel I should walk around with a smile on my face."

—Quoted in the *Milwaukee Journal,* July 31, 1956

"I used to love to come to the ballpark. Now I hate it. Every day becomes a little tougher because of all this. Writers, tape recorders, microphones, cameras, questions and more questions. Roger Maris lost his hair the season he hit sixty-one. I still have all my hair, but when it's over, I'm going home to Mobile and fish for a long time."

—During the later days of his campaign to break Babe Ruth's home run record; quoted in *Hammerin' Hank* by Dan Schlossberg

"If I had to pay to go see somebody play for one game, I wouldn't pay to see Hank Aaron. I wasn't flashy. I didn't start fights. I didn't rush out to the mound every time a pitch came near me. I didn't hustle after fly balls that were 20 rows back in the seats. But if I had to pay to see someone play a three-game series, I'd rather see myself."

—As a former player; quoted in the *New York Times,* April 21, 1982, the year he was inducted into the National Baseball Hall of Fame

Hank Aaron (*Author's Collection*)

"If I knew exactly what I know now and had it to do over, I'd be a switch hitter. No telling what I could have done."

—Quoted in *Hank Aaron . . . 714 and Beyond* by Jerry Brondfield

"In baseball, there is something electrifying about the big leagues. I had read so much about Musial, Williams and Robinson . . . I had put those guys on a pedestal. They were something special. . . . I really thought that they put their pants on different, rather than one leg at a time."

—Widely attributed

"It may sound silly, but I don't hear a thing when I'm up at bat. Someone can be standing and hollering right by the dugout, but I don't hear it. I'm concentrating on the pitcher. I don't worry about what's happening in the stands."

— Quoted in *Hammerin' Hank* by Dan Schlossberg

"It would be a great thing for blacks, giving black children hope that no matter how high the mountain, they can climb it.

"I'm hoping someday that some kid, black or white, will hit more home runs than myself. Whoever it is, I'd be pulling for him."

— In answer to a banquet-speech question about the importance of breaking Ruth's record to blacks; quoted in the *Sporting News,* January 5, 1974

"It's a long way off, I'll just try to get one home run at a time. I'm not really a home run hitter. I like to think of myself as a complete ballplayer. I'd like to be remembered as a good all-around player, not just as a fellow who hit home runs."

— To the press after hitting home run 600 on April 20, 1971; he was asked about his chances of besting Babe Ruth's record

"I've tried a lot of things in the off-season, but the only thing I really know is baseball."

— *Milwaukee Journal,* July 31, 1956

"Last year, I was a sort of kid and I was a little scared. I ain't scared any more."

— Quoted in the *Sporting News,* May 4, 1955

"My arrival in the major leagues was pretty dull. No drama, no excitement, absolutely none. I just arrived, and that was all."

— Quoted in the *Sporting News,* May 23, 1970

"On the field, blacks have been able to be super giants. But once our playing days are over, this is the end of it and we go back to the back of the bus again."

— Quoted in *Hammerin' Hank* by Dan Schlossberg

"714, 715, I've forgotten them already."

— On home run 716 (just another home run) in Atlanta on April 11, 1974; quoted by Tom Saladino in the *New York Post,* April 12

"That's something for the men with the pencils to worry about. I'll hit as many as I can and you guys figure out what it comes to."

— On his numbers; quoted in *Hammerin' Hank* by Dan Schlossberg

"The average person can't realize what a nightmare this has been. The last 10 days of the season, all winter, spring training, right up till today. Now I'm just tired. Not let down— just tired. I'm beat."

— After hitting his 715th career home run to break Babe Ruth's record, as quoted in the *New York Times,* April 14, 1974.

"The pitcher has got only a ball. I've got a bat. So the percentage in weapons is in my favor and I let the fellow with the ball do the fretting."

— Quoted in the *Milwaukee Journal,* July 31, 1956. This was later widely quoted as Aaron's "batting philosophy" and shortened to: "The pitcher has got only a ball. I've got a bat. The percentage of weapons is in my favor."

AARON, HANK (CONTINUED)

"The triple is the most exciting thing in baseball. . . . Home runs win a lot of games, but I never understood why fans are so obsessed with them."

—*Time,* July 20, 1998

"Throughout the past century, the home run has held a special place in baseball and I have been privileged to hold this record for 33 of those years. I move over now and offer my best wishes to Barry and his family on this historic achievement. My hope today, as it was on that April evening in 1974, is that the achievement of this record will inspire others to chase their own dreams."

—In a surprise taped message played on the big video scoreboard at AT&T Park in San Francisco seconds after Barry Bonds hit No. 756 on August 7, 2007

"Well, it took me 17 years to get 3,000 hits in baseball, and I did it in one afternoon on the golf course."

—In 1971, from *The Sporting News Chronicle of 20th Century Sport*

"Yogi, I came up here to hit, not to read."

—On coming to bat in the '58 Series, and answering Yankee catcher Yogi Berra's "Henry, you'd better turn the trademark around so you can read it. Otherwise you'll break your bat"; widely quoted

"You can only milk a cow so long, then you're left holding the pail."

—Announcing his retirement; widely attributed

AARON, HERBERT SR.

"When Henry came up, I heard the fans yell 'Hit that nigger. Hit that nigger.' Henry hit the ball up against the clock. The next time he came up, they said 'Walk him, walk him.'"

—Hank Aaron's father recalling first seeing his son play in Montgomery, Alabama; quoted in *Hammerin' Hank* by Dan Schlossberg

AASE, DON

"I'm like a whale. Every once in a while, I resurface."

—On his return to the big leagues in 1989; quoted in the *Major League Baseball Newsletter,* May 1989

ABBOTT, ANGUS EVAN

"The Americans have a genius for taking a thing, examining its every part, and developing each part to the utmost. This they have done with the game of rounders, and, from a clumsy, primitive pastime, have so tightened its joints and put such a fine finish on its points that it stands forth a complicated machine of infinite exactitude."

—English commentator, on baseball, in the early 1900s; quoted by Thomas Boswell, "Baseball: Sport of Myth in the Age of Reason," *Washington Post,* September 5, 1982

ABBOTT, JIM

"For a time, there's going to be a certain novelty about me pitching. But I wonder how

Jim Abbott (*California Angels*)

long I'll keep getting cheered at opponents' ballparks."

—As an Angels rookie early in the 1989 season. The novelty he alludes to is a deformed hand.

"I wanted to be like Nolan Ryan. I didn't want to be like Pete Gray. It's that kind of feeling. And I don't want kids to be like me because I have one hand. I want kids to be like Jim Abbott because he's a baseball pitcher at Michigan and he won the Big Ten championship game, and not because I can field a bunt and throw to first."

—As a Michigan left-hander in the June 10, 1988, *Baseball America*

ACKERMAN, AL

"Sparky came here two years ago promising to build a team in his own image, and now the club is looking for small, white-haired infielders with .212 batting averages."

—As Tiger announcer, 1981

ADAIR, ROBERT KEMP

"Though the right leg bears more of a burden than the left for a batter who swings from the right side, the arms share the forces nearly equally. Hence, there is no natural advantage for a right-handed man in batting right-handed. Indeed, since the left-handed batter is favored in many ways, many players who throw right bat left: the batter who swings from the left side is closer to first base and moves in that direction as he finishes his swing. For some reason right-field fences tend to be closer than left-field fences, and there are more right-handed pitchers (whose slants are easier for a left-handed batter) than left-handed pitchers. There are, however, two famous first basemen who threw left and batted right, Hal Chase and George Bush. Chase, a great-fielding first baseman, was considered the best ever at the position by Walter Johnson and Babe Ruth while Bush, captain of a fine Yale team that went to the finals of the NCAA tournament, has done an exemplary job recently of throwing out the first ball on opening day."

—*The Physics of Baseball* (New York: HarperPerennial, 1990)

Adams, Franklin P.

A Ballplayer's Day

"Sweet are the uses of advertisement."
—*Old Song*

The famous pitcher woke at eight
    To one of GUFF'S ALARUM CLOCKS,
Put on a suit of AERO-GREAT,
    And donned a pair of SILKO-SOX.
Then, lathered well with SMEAREM'S SOAP,
    He shaved with BORKEM'S RUSTLESS
    BLADE;
Did on a suit of heliotrope—
    THE KAMPUS KUT in every shade.
Then berries served with JORDAN'S CREAM
    And eggs from BUNKEM'S DAIRY
    FARM;
Then, as he read THE MORNING SCREAM,
    He smoked a pipe of LUCKY CHARM.
Then, donning one of BEANEM'S HATS,
    He rode out in his WHATSTHECAR;
Played ball; then home to RENTEM'S FLATS
    To smoke a SHUTEMOUNT CIGAR.
He listened to his WAXAPHONE,
    Then lay—ending his day so rough—
Upon a mattress widely known.

———

"But, as the price, I've said enough."
—*In Other Words*, 1912

Baseball Note

In winter, when it's cold out,
Appears the baseball holdout;
In spring, when it is warm out,
He gets his uniform out.

—From *Nods & Becks*

"He was the guy who hit all those home runs
the year Ruth broke the record."

    —On Lou Gehrig, a line that became a bitter
    epitaph for Gehrig at the time of his death;
    quoted in *Sport Magazine's All-Time All Stars*,
    edited by Tom Murray

On the 18th of April '28
My Tim began to be corporate.
Be brave, my son, and speak the trut',
And I hope you'll like your baseball suit.

    —"Happy Lifetime to You"

Baseball's Sad Lexicon

These are the saddest of possible words:
    "Tinker to Evers to Chance."
Trio of bear cubs, and fleeter than birds,
    Tinker and Evers and Chance.
Ruthlessly pricking our gonfalon bubble,
    Making a Giant hit into a double—
Words that are heavy with nothing but trouble:
    "Tinker to Evers to Chance."

    —Poem originally appeared in the *New York
    Evening Mail*, July 12, 1910, as "That Double
    Play Again" and reprinted under the title
    "Baseball's Sad Lexicon," July 18, 1910

To Myrtilla, on Opening Day

Myrtilla, ere the season starts,
    Or e'er the primal ball be thrown
If you would win this callous heart's
    Affection for your very own,
This counsel, blooming, fresh and frondent—
Accept it from your correspondent.
Back in the days of Old Cap Anse
    'Twas reconed cute to spoof a dame,

And famed was her incognitance
    About the so-called national game;
And comment feminine was silly.
That was before your day, Myrtilly.
For, now, Myrtilla, I admit
    Your knowledge far transcends mine own;
You know an error from a hit—
    A quaver from a semitone;
You never say 'How small the bat is!'
You never have to ask who that is.
Nay, Myrt, too well you like the game;
    You are too true a devotee;
My Blue-Print is the kind of dame
    Whose love is less for ball than me;
And so, my Myrt, that is the reason
I think I'll go alone this season.

    —*In Other Words,* 1912

"We would like to live long enough to read the statement of the manager of the team that lost the first game of the World Series which would not be to the effect that the loss of the game was the most encouraging thing that could have happened, and that it was a sign his team would win."

    —From his column "The Conning Tower"

ADAMS, JOHN

"Mornings, noon and nights, making and sailing boats, in swimming, in skating, flying kites and shooting, in marbles, ninepins, bat and ball, football; quoits and wrestling."

    —In a letter to Dr. Benjamin West

ADATOV, ALEKSANDR

"Throw to second, not first. Second is the one in the middle."

    —The coach of the Soviet national baseball team, during the team's debut game against a United States Naval Academy squad, which won 21–1; quoted in *Parade* magazine, December 31, 1989

ADCOCK, JOE

"Trying to sneak a pitch past Hank Aaron is like trying to sneak the sunrise past a rooster."

    —His most famous line, uttered as Aaron's teammate on the Braves

ADDIE, BOB

"Carl Yastrzemski—The fellow who has the lead in the road company version of 'The Music Man.'
"Willie Mays—The good guy's pal in one of those Western movies. . . .
"Brooks Robinson—The mild-mannered Secret Service agent who is a black belt in karate. . . .
"Hank Aaron—The quiet, soft-spoken fellow that department stores put in complaint departments. . . ."

    —One of many descriptions of "What They Look Like out of Their Baseball Uniforms" from his *Sporting News* column of April 20, 1968

"These are the days when the Yanks are leading both leagues—the American and Pacific."

    —In the *Washington Times-Herald;* quoted in *Baseball Digest,* October 1942

ADDIE, BOB (CONTINUED)

"We seem to have reached a strange economic impasse with Japan.... We can't compete with the Japanese goods brought in because they're too cheap, and we can't compete for Japanese ball players. The reason? Too expensive."

> —His column in the *Sporting News,* December 8, 1962. Addie goes on to quote Bob Scheffing, Detroit manager. who had just returned from Japan and mentioned some players he wanted to sign. "We'd have no chance getting those Japanese players," Bob sighed. "In the first place, we'd never be able to pay them the salaries they get back home."

ADDIS, DON

"Do you realize that if Babe Ruth had used steroids, he would have far surpassed his own record—or died before he reached it."

> —*St. Petersburg Times,* September 27, 1998

ADELIS, PETE, "THE IRON LUNG OF SHIBE PARK"

1. No profanity.
2. Nothing purely personal.
3. Keep pouring it on.
4. Know your players.
5. Don't be shouted down.
6. Take it as well as give it.
7. Give the old-timer a chance—he was a rookie once.

> —Rules of "scientific heckling" by one of the most famous razzers in the history of the game. These rules first appeared in the *Sporting News* in 1948.

ADVERTISEMENTS

9 programs: $27
5 hot dogs, 6 pennants: $45
1 big puffy hand: $6
Their first big league ballgame: priceless.
There are some things money can't buy.
For everything else, there's MasterCard.
The card of the heart of Major League Baseball.

> —Television ad during 1998 Division Series, League Championships, and World Series

"HOME RUN IN YOUR LIVING ROOM— BY TELEVISION!

"From the comfort of your living room, you'll watch the runs that win the pennant, the champ's knock-out punch, close-ups of the great moments of sport, news and entertainment—brought to you by a Capehart or Farnsworth electronic television receiver."

> —Farnsworth Television & Radio Corp. ad in the *Saturday Evening Post,* September 15, 1945

"Pity the Poor Baseball. . . . Look what it has to go through to be a hit!"

—Rawlings glove ad, 1962

"United Air Lines flies more twenty-game winners, more .300 hitters, more RBI leaders, more southpaws, knuckleballers and relief hurlers, more bonus-babies and bullpen fire-men, more pinch-hitters, clutch-hitters and switch-hitters than any other airline. In fact, United flies 17 out of the 24 professional baseball teams. And if we can handle the Pros, just think what we can do for you."

—United Airlines ad, ca. 1965, from the *New York Post*

AKER, JACK

"It's the underground nuclear testing. Because of that, all gravity is leaving the earth. And so are the baseballs."

—As Cleveland pitching coach, on the proliferation of home runs, 1973: SABR Collector

ALBOM, MITCH

"The end of summer, a chilling breeze swirled through Yankee Stadium and danced across the infield and out into the area by the left-field bleachers, the area they call Monument Park. . . .

"It is a place for heroes, for memories, and for ghosts. One of those ghosts actually moved last night. Sometime after nine o'clock, unnoticed by fans watching the Yankees play the Mariners, the skies opened with a quiet thunder, and Lou Gehrig, the great Lou Gehrig, the Captain, the Iron Horse, maybe the finest first baseman in the history of the game, took one step backward. And in so doing, he was suddenly out of sync with the words on his plaque, as if someone had tilted his tombstone."

—Sportswriter for *Detroit Free Press,* September 7, 1995, after Cal Ripken played in his 2131st consecutive game, September 6, 1995; quoted in the *Baltimore Sun,* September 7, 1995

ALBORN, TIM

"Americans sometimes don't recognize this, but for Britain to move away from the monarchy is like us moving away from baseball."

—Quoted by John Yemma, September 9, 1997, "Monarchy Stumbles, but a Fall Is Unlikely," *Boston Globe,* September 9, 1997. Alborn is a Harvard historian who specializes in Great Britain.

ALDERSON, SANDY

"Our tongues are in the water, and we're trying to decide if it's cold or hot."

—A's GM beginning contract negotiations with Jose Canseco; quoted in the *Sporting News,* January 9, 1989

"The beauty of the game is that there are no absolutes. It's all nuances and anticipation, not like football, which is all about vectors and forces."

—Quoted in *Men at Work,* by George F. Will (New York: Macmillan, 1990)

ALEXANDER, GROVER CLEVELAND

"Less than a foot made the difference between a hero and a bum."

> —On Tony Lazzeri, whom he struck out to end the seventh inning and save the seventh and deciding game of the 1926 World Series, after Lazzeri had hit a long foul into the stands the pitch before. Bob O'Farrell's cutting down Babe Ruth trying to steal second was the last out of the game in the bottom of the ninth. With Lou Gehrig batting, this was probably the worst single mistake of Ruth's career. O'Farrell was the MVP of the 1926 Serie, and Lazzeri and Ruth the goats.

"You know I can't eat tablets or nicely framed awards. Neither can my wife. But they don't think of things like that."

> —On the replica tablet he took away from Cooperstown on his induction in 1939; quoted by Fred Lieb in *Baseball as I Have Known It*

Grover Cleveland Alexander (*Library of Congress Prints and Photographs, Bain Collection*)

"What, and give him a chance to think on my time?"

> —The St. Louis Cardinals pitcher on why he didn't take more time on the mound; widely attributed

"What do you want me to do? Let those sons of bitches stand up there and think on my time?"

> —On why he pitched so fast

ALGREN, NELSON

"Benedict Arnold Betrayers of American boyhood. Not to mention American Girlhood and American Womanhood and American Hoodhood."

> —On the 1919 Chicago "Black Sox"

ALLEN, DICK (ALSO KNOWN AS RICHIE)

"I once loved this game. But after being traded four times, I realized that it's nothing but a business. I treat my horses better than the owners treat us. It's a shame they've destroyed my love for the game."

> —As a Chicago White Sox infielder; widely attributed

"I wish they'd shut the gates, and let us play ball with no press and no fans."

> —As a Philly

"If a horse won't eat it, I don't want to play on it."

> —On artificial turf; *Esquire*, March 1978

Dick Allen (*Author's Collection*)

"Flick reported with a bat that he had turned out for himself on a lathe and kept in a canvas bag."

> —On Hall of Famer Elmer Flick; quoted in the 1989 Fiftieth Anniversary Hall of Fame *Yearbook*

"The home run, once as exotic and mysterious as the orchid, has become as commonplace and monotonous as the dandelion. The continual bombardment has resulted in the lengthening of games, the establishment of numerous records and the ruination of some pitchers. The spectator who once thrilled to the homer is now in much the same state of mind and body as the man who tried to eat quail every day for a month."

> —*The Hot Stove League* (New York: A. S. Barnes, 1955)

ALLEN, MAURY

"Extramarital sex is a proven, harmless pastime for most players: what the little woman doesn't know doesn't hurt her. But card losses are a lot harder to hide. Johnny Superstar has an awful tough time convincing the old lady his pay is a thousand dollars short because he was fined for not running out a ground ball."

> —*Bo: Pitching and Wooing*

"I'll play first, third, left. I'll play anywhere—except Philadelphia."

> —Asked, as a Cardinal, what position he'd most like to play; the *Sporting News,* April 11, 1970

"You gotta be careful with your body. Your body is like a bar of soap. The more you use it, the more it wears down."

> —As a White Sox infielder; widely attributed

ALLEN, LEE

"A chunky, unshaven hobo who ran the bases like a berserk locomotive, slept in the raw, and swore at pitchers in his sleep."

> —On Pepper Martin; SABR Collection

ALLEN, MAURY (CONTINUED)

"[Ruth] never played a night game, he never hit against fireball relief pitching (relief pitchers in his day were worn-out old starters), he never traveled cross-country for a night game and played a day game the next day, he never performed before millions of television viewers, he never had to run on artificial turf. It is the changes in the game, the modern factors that have made the game more difficult, that bring Babe in here as number three, behind Mays and Aaron. His feats were heroic. So were theirs. They simply did them under tougher conditions."

—On why he ranked Babe Ruth #3, after Willie Mays #1 and Hank Aaron #2 in *Baseball's 100: A Personal Ranking*

"Sex is very significant aspect of athletes' lives. If you think about it, you realize right away that athletic performance and sexual performance always go hand in hand."

—Quoted by Roger Angell in *Late Innings*

"There are 499 Major League ballplayers. Then there's Willie Mays."

—SABR Collection, 1964

ALLEN, MEL

"How 'bout that, sports fans?"

—Signature line; widely attributed

"The Yankees have all the hits in the game."

—How he dealt as a sportscaster with the fact that Don Larsen was throwing a perfect game on October 8, 1956. It was his way of handling the taboo against mentioning a no-hitter in progress.

ALLEN, RICHIE (SEE ALLEN, DICK)

ALLEN, WOODY

"I love baseball, you know it doesn't have to mean anything, it's just very beautiful to watch."

—*Zelig*

"When we played softball, I'd steal second, then feel guilty and go back."

—*Time* magazine interview of July 3, 1972. In this interview he also said, "I don't believe in an afterlife, although I am bringing a change of underwear."

ALOU, FELIPE

"It was one of the worst innings I've seen since I put on a uniform, and my first uniform was made out of an onion bag in the Dominican."

—Giants manager on an eight-run inning against the giants; from MLB.com, cited by John Erhardt on the Baseball Prospectus Web site in the "Year in Quotes, 2006"

ALSTON, WALTER

"I'm happy for him, that is, if you think becoming a big-league manager is a good thing to have happen to you."

—About Gil Hodges when he was named manager of the Senators; quoted by Bob Uecker in *Catcher in the Wry*

"It's not the winters that bother me. It's the summers."

> —When, as Dodger manager, he was asked if he had had a good winter

"I've never been in favor of long win streaks. I'd rather win two or three, lose one, win two or three more. I'm a great believer in things evening out. If you win a whole bunch in a row, somewhere along the line you're going to lose some, too. Fans tend to get too excited by streaks of either kind. I think the press does, too. There should be a happy medium."

> —On streaks; in the *Los Angeles Times*, May 7, 1976

"Look at misfortune the same way you look at success: Don't panic. Do your best and forget the consequences."

> —His playing credo; SABR Collection

"Perhaps the truest axiom in baseball is that the toughest thing to do is repeat. The tendency is to relax without even knowing it, the feeling being, 'we did it last year, so we can do it again.'"

> —Quoted in the *Los Angeles Herald-Examiner*, February 27, 1975

ALTOBELLI, JOE

"Roger Craig is so optimistic he could find good in a tornado."

> —As Orioles manager; from Robert Craig's *Inside Pitch*

ANDERSON, BRUCE

"When Pipp retired, there was little ado about his adieu."

> — On Wally Pipp, the man who came out of the Yankee batting order to be replaced by Lou Gehrig; in "Just a Pipp of a Legend," *Sports Illustrated*, June 29, 1987

ANDERSON, DAVE

"Today I told my little girl I'm going to the ballpark, and she asked, 'What for?'"

> —As a Dodger on his lack of playing time; quoted in *Sports Illustrated*, June 22, 1987

ANDERSON, GEORGE "SPARKY"

"A baseball manager is a necessary evil."

> —As Reds manager; widely attributed

"Babe Ruth is dead and buried in Baltimore, but the game is bigger and better than ever."

> —On the fact that Kirk Gibson had signed with the Dodgers, February 1988

"Baseball is a simple game. If you have good players, and if you keep them in the right frame of mind, then the manager is a success. The players make the manager; it's never the other way."

> —As Cincinnati Reds manager; widely attributed

"He is Cincinnati. He's the Reds."

> —On Pete Rose to the press as his manager; quoted in *Heavy Hitters: Lynn, Parker, Carew, Rose* by Bill Gutman

ANDERSON, GEORGE "SPARKY" (CONTINUED)

"He's such a big, strong guy he should love that porch. He's got power enough to hit home runs in any park, including Yellowstone."

> —On Willie Stargell batting in Tiger Stadium for an All-Star Game

"I didn't ever want to go into the most precious place in the world unless I belonged there. But I would have been sorry if I hadn't come here."

> —On being inducted into the Baseball Hall of Fame; quoted in the *Chicago Sun-Times*, April 19, 2000

"I don't want to embarrass any other catcher by comparing him with Johnny Bench."

> —Quoted for the 1989 Hall of Fame *Yearbook*

"I know what the guy in the other dugout is feeling because I've been there myself. My God, what an awful feeling it is. I understand that. But understanding is something you'll never truly understand."

> —*Baltimore Sun*, May 20, 1994

"I wish every athlete in all of sports, not just baseball, could act like this man. Never once in his career did I see him throw a helmet. He never once threw a bat. He never once made an alibi."

> —As former Reds manager on new Hall of Famer Tony Perez, *Chicago Sun-Times*, January 13, 2000

Sparky Anderson (*Detroit Tigers*)

"If you have to choose between power and speed—and it often turns out you have to make that choice—you've got to go for speed. In today's baseball, pitching is getting so special that a team at bat doesn't dare consider the big inning. You have to score piecemeal with your legs. You must go for the guys who steal and who take the extra base on a hit."

> —Quoted in *TV Guide*, April 3, 1982

"If you've got a group that wants to win, you've got to let them."

—Anderson adage which has been turned into a sign that hangs in various managers' and coaches' offices at all level of sports. According to the *Phoenix Gazette,* January 16, 1996, it hung in the coach's office at the America West Arena, home of the Phoenix Suns basketball team.

"It's a terrible thing to have to tell your fans, who have waited like Detroit's have, that their team won't win it this year. But it's better than lying to them."

—On being new manager of the Tigers; quoted in *Sports Illustrated,* July 9, 1979

"It's all kind of crazy, and it all started with a fellow named Catfish Hunter. He showed the world how foolish some owners can be. Catfish went home to Ahoskie, North Carolina, and did nothing but sit there, holding court. The owners came to him with fortunes. This is how the madness began. If a guy wants to get drunk and wrap his car around a pole, that's his business; but when he hurts others, you've got another story. Everyone got drawn into the spending, and that's why all you hear in spring camps today are arguments over money."

—Quoted in the *Los Angeles Herald-Examiner,* March 10, 1977

"I've changed my mind about it. Instead of being bad, it stinks."

—On the designated hitter

"I've got my faults, but living in the past isn't one of them—there's no future in it."

—Quoted in Steve Rushin, "The New Perfesser," *Sports Illustrated,* June 28, 1993

"If I hear him say just once more he's doing something for the betterment of baseball, I'm going to throw up."

—As Reds manager; quoted in the *Sporting News,* spring 1978, on Commissioner Bowie Kuhn

"My idea of managing is giving the ball to Tom Seaver and sitting down and watching him work."

—Quoted in *Late Innings* by Roger Angell

"Power should never be used. The manager who uses power has lost control. Common sense—that's the key. It's what I talk to them about. I have no rules, but they know how I feel about long hair and a number of other things. I can't count how many times I've told them that I think it's a disgrace when you see a guy who's a hell of a player who isn't also a hell of a person."

—As Reds manager on managing; quoted in the *Los Angeles Times,* August 1, 1975

"Some teams never win. They've got four or five guys who never care about anything. They don't want the grind of the full six months. As soon as things start to go bad, they crack and just go for themselves. Talent is one thing. Being able to go from spring to October is another."

—As Cincinnati manager; widely attributed

ANDERSON, GEORGE "SPARKY" (CONTINUED)

"The great thing about baseball is when you're done, you'll only tell your grandchildren the good things. If they ask me about 1989, I'll tell them I had amnesia."

—As Detroit manager; quoted in the September 1989 *Major League Baseball Newsletter*

"The man I marvel at is the one that's in there day after day and night after night and still puts the figures on the board. I'm talking about Pete Rose, Stan Musial, the real stars. Believe me, especially the way we travel today, flying all night with a game the next night and then the next afternoon, if you can play 162 games, you're a man."

—*New York Times,* March 29, 1976

"The only reason I'm coming out here tomorrow is the schedule says I have to."

—Tigers manager after losing, 16–4, to Minnesota in April 1990; quoted by Steve Fainaru, the *Boston Globe,* April 29, 1990

"The only thing I believe is this: A player does not have to like a manager and he does not have to respect a manager. All he has to do is obey the rules."

—As Reds manager; widely attributed

"There ain't no way that no Jack Morris ain't gonna win no 20 games."

—Manager of the Detroit Tigers, 1986 spring training; quoted in the *Baltimore Sun,* March 5, 2006. A rare quintuple negative

"They're a necessary evil. I don't believe a manager ever won a pennant. Casey Stengel won all those pennants with the *Yankees*. How many did he win with the Boston *Braves* and *Mets*? I've never seen a team win a pennant without players. . . . I think the only thing the manager has to do is keep things within certain boundaries."

—Quoted on managers in the *Los Angeles Times,* August 8, 1974

"This game has taken a lot of guys over the years, who would have had to work in factories and gas stations, and made them prominent people. I only had a high-school education and, believe me, I had to cheat to get that. There isn't a college in the world that would have me. And yet in this business you can walk into a room with millionaires, doctors, professional people and get more attention than they get. I don't know any other business where you can do that."

—Quoted in the *Los Angeles Times,* December 26, 1975

ANDUJAR, JOAQUIN

"I win or I die."

—Before the seventh game of the 1982 World Series, when asked about pressure

"There are 300,000 sportswriters and they're all against me. Every one of them."

—Quoted in the July 3, 1988 *Boston Herald*

Joaquin Andujar (*St. Louis Cardinals*)

"There is one word in America that says it all, and that one word is 'You never know.'"

> —He would often preface his remarks with "You never know" or "You never know in this game." Quoted in the *Los Angeles Times* on June 21, 1984: "You never know in this game. Sometimes you don't pitch too well and they score. I've learned to just go out there, work hard and keep your head up"; *Sports Illustrated,* June 22, 1987, among other places

"You can't worry if it's cold; you can't worry if it's hot; you only worry if you get sick. Because then if you don't get well, you die."

> —Widely attributed

ANGELL, ROGER

"Any baseball is beautiful. No other small package comes as close to the ideal in design and utility. It is a perfect object for a man's hand. Pick it up and it instantly suggests its purpose; it is meant to be thrown a considerable distance—thrown hard and with precision. Its feel and heft are the beginning of the sport's critical dimensions; if it were a fraction of an inch larger or smaller, a few centigrams heavier or lighter, the game of baseball would be utterly different. Hold a baseball in your hand. As it happens, this one is not brand-new. Here, just to one side of the curved surgical welt of stitches, there is a pale-green grass smudge, darkening on one edge almost to black—the mark of an old infield play, a tough grounder now lost in memory. Feel the ball, turn it over in your hand; hold it across the seam or the other way, with the seam just to the side of your middle finger. Speculation stirs. You want to get outdoors and throw this spare and sensual object to somebody or, at the very least, watch somebody else throw it. The game has begun."

> —*On the Ball*

"Back when I was nine or ten years old, what I loved best in the sports pages were box scores and, above all, names. . . . I . . . found rafts of names that prickled or sang in one's mind. Eppa Rixey, Goose Goslin, Firpo Marberry, Jack Rothrock, Eldon Auker, Luck [sic] Appling, Mule Haas, Adolfo Luque . . .— Dickens couldn't have done better. Paul Derringer was exciting: a man named for a pistol! I lingered over Heinie Manush (sort of like sitting on a cereal) and Van Lingle Mungo, the Dodger ace. When I exchanged baseball celebrities with pals at school, we used last names, to show a suave familiarity, but no one ever just said 'Mungo,' or even 'Van Mungo.' When he came up in conversation, it was obligatory to roll out the full name, as if it were a royal title, and everyone in the group would join in at the end, in chorus: 'Van Lingle MUN-go!'"

—"Early Innings," in Ron Fimrite, ed., *Birth of a Fan* (New York: Macmillan, 1993)

"Baseball, we understand once again, is spare and rigorous by nature, and is also somehow right. We can ignore it or hate it, if that is our choice, but we must take it as it is. It cannot be better."

—*Baseball* (New York: Harry N. Abrams, 1984)

"Baseball's time is seamless and invisible, a bubble within which players move at exactly the same pace and rhythms as all their predecessors. This is the way the game was played in our youth and in our fathers' youth, and even back then—back in the country days—

there must have been the same feeling that time could be stopped. Since baseball time is measured only in outs, all you have to do is succeed utterly; keep hitting, keep the rally alive, and you have defeated time. You remain forever young. Sitting in the stands, we sense this, if only dimly. The players below us— Mays, DiMaggio, Ruth, Snodgrass—swim and blur in memory, the ball floats over to Terry Turner, and the end of this game may never come."

—*The Interior Stadium*

"Brilliance in the front office is rarer than a triple play."

—Jonathan Fraser Light, *The Cultural Encyclopedia of Baseball* (Jefferson NC: McFarland, 1997)

"Consider the catcher. Bulky, thought-burdened, unclean, he retrieves his cap and mask from the ground (where he has flung them, moments ago, in mid-crisis) and moves slowly again to his workplace. He whacks the cap against his leg, producing a puff of dust, and settles it in place, its bill astern, with an oddly feminine gesture and then, reversing the movement, pulls on the mask and firms it with a soldierly downward tug. Armored, he sinks into his squat, punches his mitt, and becomes wary, balanced, and ominous; his bare right hand rests casually on his thigh while he regards, through the portcullis, the field and deployed fielders, the batter, the base runner, his pitcher, and the state of the world, which he now, for a waiting instant, holds in sway."

—*In the Fire*

"Glooming in print about the dire fate of the Sox and their oppressed devotees has become such a popular art form that it verges on a new Hellenistic age of mannered excess. Everyone east of the Hudson with a Selectric or a word processor has had his or her say, it seems (the *Globe* actually published a special twenty-four-page section entitled 'Literati on the Red Sox' before the Series, with essays by George Will, John Updike, Bart Giamatti—the new National League president, but for all that a Boston fan through and through—Stephen King, Doris Kearns Goodwin, and other worthies), and one begins to see at last that the true function of the Red Sox may be not to win but to provide New England authors with a theme, now that guilt and whaling have gone out of style."

—"Not So, Boston" in *Once More Around The Park: A Baseball Reader* (New York: Ballantine Books, 1991)

"Front-office brilliance is rarer in baseball than the triple play."

—*Late Innings*

"I continued pitching on into high school . . . but I didn't make the big team; by that time, the batters I faced were smarter and did frightful things to my trusty roundhouse. I fanned a batter here and there, but took up smoking and irony in self-defense. A short career."

—"Early Innings"

"Suddenly I saw that from my seat behind first base the two pitchers—the two best left-handers in baseball, the two best left- *or* right-handers in baseball—were in a direct line with each other, Ford exactly superimposed on Spahn, throwing baseballs in the same fragment of space. Ford, with his short, business-like windup, was shoulders and quickness, while, behind him, Spahn would slowly kick his right leg up high and to the left, peering over his shoulder as he leaned back, and then deliver the ball with an easy, explosive sweep. It excited me to a ridiculous extent."

—"The Old Folks Behind Home," about covering his first game in Spring Training 1962 which re-appeared in *A Baseball Companion* (Orlando, FL: Harcourt, 2003)

"Suddenly the Mets fans made sense to me. What we were witnessing was precisely the opposite of the kind of rooting that goes on across the river. This was the losing cheer, the gallant yell for a good try—antimatter to the sounds of Yankee Stadium. This was a new recognition that perfection is admirable but a trifle inhuman, and that a stumbling kind of semi-success can be much more warming. Most of all, perhaps, these exultant yells for the Mets were also yells for ourselves, and came from a wry, half-understood recognition that there is more Met than Yankee in every one of us. I knew for whom that foghorn blew, it blew for me."

—*The "Go!" Shouters*

"The stuff about the connection between baseball and American life, the 'Field of Dreams' thing, gives me a pain. I hated that movie. It's mostly fake. You look back into the meaning of old-time baseball, and really in the early days it was full of roughnecks and drunks. They beat up the umpires and played near saloons. In 'Field of Dreams' there's a line at the end that says the game of baseball was good when America was good, and they're talking about the time of the biggest riots in the country and Prohibition. What is that? The dreaminess, I really hated that."

—Quoted by Steve Kettmann in *Salon*, August 29, 2000, the year Angell turned 80

"We would never be a part of that golden company on the field, which each of us, certainly for one moment of his life, had wanted more than anything else in the world to join."

—Sitting with three old timers as a spring training game in Sarasota watching players in the field; from *Game Time* (San Diego: Harcourt, 2003). The quote appeared in the *Time* review of the book which Lev Grossman said "It's like being a Muggle with your nose pressed up against the gates of Hogwarts." (May 13, 2003)

"What I do know is that this belonging and caring is what our games are all about; this is what we come for. It is foolish and childish, on the face of it, to affiliate ourselves with anything so insignificant and patently contrived and commercially exploitative as a professional sports team, and the amused superiority and icy scorn that the non-fan directs at the sports nut (I know this look—I know it by heart) is understandable and almost unanswerable. Almost. What is left out of this calculation, it seems to me, is the business of caring—caring deeply and passionately, really *caring*—which is a capacity or an emotion that has almost gone out of our lives. And so it seems possible that we have come to a time when it no longer matters so much what the caring is about, how frail or foolish is the object of that concern, as long as the feeling itself can be saved. Naiveté—the infantile and ignoble joy that sends a grown man or woman to dancing and shouting with joy in the middle of the night over the haphazardous flight of a distant ball— seems a small price to pay for such a gift."

—*Agincourt and After*

ANGELOS, PETER

"I understand that Edward Bennett Williams really got into this, that he attended as many games as he could and raised holy hell when things weren't going well. I have said to people who related that to me, 'That's not going to happen to me.' I really don't think it will. I can be pretty detached."

—After buying the Baltimore Orioles in 1993; quoted by Thom Loverro in the *Washington Times*, January 2, 2000, on the best and funniest quotes that had appeared in sports pages over the course of the previous century

"A new column titled 'Dollar Evaluation' has been added to your prospect-summary sheet. Your dollar evaluation should be the highest figure you would go in order to sign a player if he were on the open market. The figure would be based solely on the player's ability. Other factors, such as what the player is asking for, or what you think you can sign him for, would not be considered when determining a dollar evaluation. (It is likely that you would sign the player at a smaller figure.) Boiled down, it is the 'dollar sign on the muscle' and no more."

> —Philadelphia Phillies' *Scouting Manual,* used by author Kevin Kerrane in titling his book on scouts *Dollar Sign on the Muscle.* It also invokes Branch Rickey's famous line: "It is indeed a risky business to put the dollar mark on the individual muscle."

"Alan Sutton Sothoron pitched his initials off today."

> —Lead in a baseball story in a St. Louis newspaper of the 1920s; quoted in *The Pitchers,* by John Thorn and John Holway

"Babe Ruth struck out 1,330 times."

> —New York City graffiti; Hall of Fame Collection

"BASE-BALL. The national game of America, is an evolution of the old English schoolboy pastime known as 'rounders.' It was but a boy's game in this country prior to about 1860, but has been extended throughout the United States, and has secured a strong foothold in Canada. The game needs little introduction to the American reader."

> —*Encyclopaedia Britannica,* 1891

"Baseball is . . . packing alone, driving 1,500 miles across the country alone with three children (all under six) to join your husband's new team."

"Baseball is . . . buying your World Series wardrobe a week before the season ends—only to be beaten out in the last game of the year by the Dodgers."

"Baseball is . . . watching your husband sing 'Happy Birthday' to Charlie Finley's mule."

"Baseball is . . . hearing the man behind you call your husband a bum."

"Baseball is . . . the weeks and months following your husband's injury, wondering if he'll be able to play again."

> —From a much longer list of "Baseball is . . ." one-liners composed by Atlanta Braves' wives; quoted in the *Sporting News,* August 7, 1971

"Bess Truman enjoyed hunting, fishing, skating, riding, tennis, and swimming. She played a crackerjack third base and could beat all the boys at mumblety-peg. She was the star forward in the Barstow School's 22–10 baseball triumph over Independence, Mo. . . . One contemporary remembered Bess Truman as 'the first girl I ever knew who could whistle through her teeth.'"

> —*WomenSports;* quoted in *Say It Again* by Dorothy Uris

"By standing up to the Red aggressors from Cincinnati, silencing the majority of their sluggers, and denying the radic-libs from middle America a chance to do their thing, the Orioles proved that clean living and thinking plus Brooks Robinson at third base can bring victory with honor."

—*New York Times* editorial, October 16, 1976

"Competition to determine what team of baseball players in the upper right-hand corner of the U.S.A., North America, Western Hemisphere, the world, wins the most games."

—On the World Series

"Did you hear that Waite Hert was hoit?"

—Oft-quoted Brooklyn fan hearing that Waite Hoyt was injured; quoted by Bob Broeg in his November 27, 1976, *Sporting News* column and elsewhere

"Does that mean you too?"

—From a fan letter to Angel first baseman Steve Bilko regarding the PA warning about spectators touching a ball in play; *Sport*, December 1961

"Fans May Keep Baseballs"

"Pittsburgh, July 9 (1921)—Fans who attend games at the National League baseball park here may keep balls knocked into the stands without fear of being molested by policemen, according to an order issued by Robert J. Alderdice, Director of Public Safety. Director Alderdice made the ruling following threatened damage suits against policemen who placed three fans under arrest for refusing to throw balls back onto the diamond."

—*The New York Times Book of Baseball History*

"Fielding—He can't stop quickly and throw hard. You can take the extra base on him if he's in motion away from line of throw. He won't throw on questionable plays and I would challenge him even though he threw a man or so out.

"Speed—He can't run and he won't bunt.

"Hitting vs. right-handed pitcher—His reflexes are very slow and he can't pull a good fastball at all. The fastball is better thrown high, but that is not too important as long as it is fast. Throw him nothing but good fastballs and fast curveballs. Don't slow up on him.

"Hitting vs. left-handed pitcher—Will pull left-hand pitcher a little more than right-hand pitcher. Pitch him the same. Don't slow up on him. He will go for a bad pitch once in a while with two strikes."

—The Brooklyn Dodgers' scouting report on Joe DiMaggio for the 1951 World Series; quoted by William B. Mead in *The Official Yankee Hater's Handbook*

"He can speak ten languages but he can't hit in any of them."

—Assessment of Moe Berg, Princeton scholar and catcher, by a teammate; quoted long after his playing days and mentioned in his various obituaries

"His legs are buckled into clumsy shin guards; his face is hidden by the metal grille of a heavy mask. . . . His chest is covered with a corrugated protective pad, and his big mitt is thrust out as if to fend off destruction. . . . his field of vision gives him his own special view of the vast ballpark. In a sense, the game belongs to him. He is the catcher."

—*Time;* on the role of catcher in baseball, August 8, 1955

"I don't know if this is what you're asking. But I feel closest to God, like after I'm rounding second base after I hit a double."

—Eight-year-old Jewish boy; quoted in "The Children's God," *Psychology Today,* December 1985; SABR Collection

"I don't know that it's so important to have Tug McGraw's autograph. It's not like he's Donald Duck or something."

—Elementary-school girl on McGraw's appearance at his children's school; quoted in *Sports Illustrated,* November 20, 1978

"Ideally, the umpire should combine the integrity of a Supreme Court justice, the physical agility of an acrobat, the endurance of Job and the imperturbability of Buddha."

— "The Villains in Blue," *Time,* August 25, 1961

"In earlier days of baseball there was a sentiment attached to the national game that made games take on the appearance of real battles between cities and sections, but sentiment no longer figures in the sport. It is now only a battle of dollars."

—Editorial, *New York Evening Journal,* October 7, 1908, and repeated in G. H. Fleming's *The Unforgettable Season*

"Indians Wear Numbers"

"Cleveland, Ohio, June 26 (1916)—Cleveland American League players wore numbers on the sleeves of their uniforms in today's game with Chicago for the first time in the history of baseball, so far as is known. The numbers corresponded to similar numbers set opposite the players' names on the scorecards, so that all fans in the stands might easily identify the members of the home club."

—*The New York Times Book of Baseball History*

"It is, as a rule, a man's own business how he spends his money. But nevertheless we wish to call attention to the fact that many men do so in a very unwise manner. A very glaring instance of this among baseball players is the recent evil tendency to purchase and maintain automobiles. Put the money away, boys, where it will be safe. You don't need these automobiles. The money will look mighty good later on in life. Think it over, boys."

—1914 *Baseball* magazine editorial; quoted by George Will in *Men at Work: The Craft of Baseball*

"It's worth remembering, that under Steinbrenner we tend to operate on the theory that no one is unsignable."

> —A Yankees scout, while trying to lure John Elway away from football; *All-America Baseball News,* September 10, 1982

"Let me put it this way—if Mary Poppins played baseball, she'd have B. Robinson stenciled across the back of her uniform."

> —Anonymous fellow Oriole; quoted in *Third Base Is My Home* by Brooks Robinson

"Man Bites Dog"

> —Headline in a Boston newspaper when the Red Sox bought a player from the Yankees in 1934; quoted by William B. Mead in *The Official Yankee Hater's Handbook*

"Negroes Allowed In"

"St. Louis, May 4 [1944] [AP]—The St. Louis major league baseball teams, the Cardinals and Browns, have discontinued their old policy of restricting Negroes to the bleachers and pavilion at Sportsman's Park. Negroes now may purchase seats in the grandstand."

> —*The New York Times Book of Baseball History*

"Only the rigors of winter apparently can avail to put an end to the long season of base-ball. As far as outward indications serve as a guide, the interest of the people in the game itself is as wide-spread and as well sustained as in the height of the season, and possibly, if the managers could have their way, the approach of a settled period of cold weather would be made extremely remote and indefinite. The weather, however, is not to be put off, and the season for the base-ball player and the base-ball enthusiast—for whom, by-the-way, no appropriate term of designation has yet been invented—has practically come to an end, the final game in the League series having been played on Saturday. The last lingering contests of the Association nines will be determined this week.

> —"The Base-Ball Season," *Harper's Weekly,* October 20, 1988

"Playing ball is among the very first of the 'sports' of our early years. . . . Who has not played 'barnball' in his boyhood, 'base' in his youth, and 'wicket' in his manhood?"

> —*New Orleans Daily Picayune,* May 1841

"Say it ain't so, Joe."

> —A little boy who accosted "Shoeless Joe" Jackson on the street after the airing of the "Black Sox" scandal in 1920, and begged him to say that he and other White Sox players had not received money to "throw" the World Series of 1919. Although it has been venerated as one of the classic lines of baseball fact, it is almost certainly apocryphal. Regardless, it is part of the lore of the game.

SCOUTING REPORT

"He showed very good power at the plate, especially hitting the fast ball well. He did have considerable trouble with the 'breaking stuff,' particularly when hitting against right-handed pitching. A problem with most young players. Joe has a little better than average speed and uses it to good advantage in the outfield. A pretty good outfielder, going back well after balls hit over the head. He also gets a better-than-average jump on the ball.

"His arm is adequate from right and center field, but a bit better from left. He is a good athlete with good baseball sense. Has an outside chance to majors, dependent on his ultimate ability to hit the breaking pitches effectively. I spoke to him in reference to signing a contract with an average Class C salary, plus an approximately $5,000 bonus. But his college scholarship offers no doubt were better and he is matriculating at Alabama. Perhaps if he were offered quite a bit more, he might accept a baseball contract. But his lack of consistent hitting ability does not warrant a much larger bonus offer."

> —1961 Mets prospect report on Joe Namath of Beaver Falls, Pennsylvania

"Scratch an intellectual and you'll find a baseball fan."

> —Anonymous

"So the 49'ers played a dull game. Good heavens, it is not the 49'ers, it is the game."

> —A sports fan's letter to the *San Francisco Chronicle* in response to an article in that paper

"Stop sending stories about European politics this wk. Public not interested. World Series started."

> —Editor to European correspondent on eve of world war (take your pick). Almost certainly apocryphal

"The artist who says there is no beauty in straight lines never has seen a white sphere describing one just over second base."

> —Traditional

"The baseball mania has run its course. It has no future as a professional endeavor."

> —*Cincinnati Gazette*, 1879; quoted in *Cooperstown Corner: Columns from the Sporting News 1962–1969* by Lee Allen

The good time is approaching.
The season is at hand.
When the merry click of the two-base lick
Will be heard throughout the land.
The frost still lingers on the earth, and
Budless are the trees.
But the merry ring of the voice of spring
Is borne upon the breeze.

> —An item appearing in the premiere issue of the *Sporting News*, 1886

"The rivalry between New York and Brooklyn as regards baseball is unparalleled in the history of the national game."

> —*New York Times*, 1889; quoted by Noel Hynd in *The Giants of the Polo Grounds*

"This is truly a national game and is played by the school boys in every country village in New England, as well as in the parks of many of our New England cities. . . . Base used to be a favorite game with the students of the English High and Latin Schools of Boston, a few years ago . . . Base is also a favorite game upon the ground in front of village school-houses in the country throughout New England; and in this city, on Fast Day . . . Boston Common is covered with amateur parties of men and boys playing Base."

—*Porter's Spirit of the Times*, December 27, 1856

"This latest protection for catchers looks rather clumsy, besides delaying a game while the guards are strapped above the knee and around the ankle, and it is doubtful if the fad will ever become popular."

—*New York Sun*, 1907; on the use of shin guards by catcher Roger Bresnahan

"Verily, the National Game is great!"

—*Sporting Life*, 1884

"We do not trust cashiers half so much, or diplomats, or policemen, or physicians, as we trust an outfielder or shortstop. The light which beats upon him would do very well for a throne. The one thing which he is not called—many things as he may be called for his blunders—is sneak or traitor. The man at the bat, cheer him or hoot at him as we may, is supposed to be doing his best. . . . All may

be fair in love and war, but in sport nothing is fair but the rules."

—*The Nation*, 1920; quoted in Raymond Mungo's *Confessions from Left Field*

"We were just so happy to be in the World Series that we forgot what to do until it was too late."

—An anonymous Yankee after his team was swept by Cincinnati in the 1976 World Series; quoted in the *Official Yankee Hater's Handbook* by William Mead

"Wes Farrell, recently of the New York Yankees, during a round of golf resorted to a drastic remedy to regain effectiveness of his pitching arm.

"He caught honey bees from flowers and held them to his arms until they stung him. When Farrell finished the round his arm was swollen to almost twice normal size. 'It is the only way you can get that arthritis out of your arm when it's sore,' Farrell replied when asked for an explanation."

—From a 1939 issue of *the Fargo Forum*, supplied to the *SABR Bulletin* by David Kemp

"We've got the Rock 'n' Roll Hall of Fame and the Indians are in the World Series."

—On Cleveland from the *Washington Post*, October 22, 1995

"When the Yankees go out for dinner, they reserve twenty-five tables for one."

—Traditional rap on lack of pinstripe team spirit; hauled out when there is clubhouse turmoil

"Why a .353 hitter like George Brett would lumber along with a Marvelous Throneberry model [lifetime .237] is the sort of paradox that, scientists say, has trees talking to themselves."

> —On George Brett losing a home run against the Yankees when the umpires discovered that his bat had pine tar more than eighteen inches from the end of the bat. That bat!; *Time*, August 8, 1983

"Why is it that Jack Clark can find God but not the cutoff man?"

> —A fan asks a penetrating question about the born-again outfielder

"William Wrigley was in attendance for the second day in a row. That is believed to be a new Wrigley family record."

> —A Chicago sportswriter comments on the devotion of the Wrigley family to their Chicago Cubs

"Yankees Training on Scotch"

> —Headline in a New York newspaper during spring training, 1922; quoted by William Mead in *The Official Yankee Hater's Handbook*

ANONYMOUS—PRESS BOX

"Cy Young and his sister have still got them all beat."

> —Settling the argument as to who had been or was the greatest set of sibling pitchers in the history of the game; quoted in *Five Seasons* by Roger Angell

"Ellis is a better *doctor* than this guy!"

> —On Gabe Paul's trade of Dock Ellis for Doc Medich, a medical student, after watching Medich struggle for several innings. Medich played his first Major League game on September 5, 1972 and began his first year of medical school at Pitt the next day.

"He's a Williams type player. He bats like Ted and fields like Esther."

> —On Dick Stuart after seeing him bash the ball for fantastic distances and then butcher the easiest kind of ground balls at first base;

from *Scholastic Coach*; quoted in the July, 1962 *Baseball Digest*

"He's lost a yard off his heater."

> —On a pitcher whose fastball is slowing, *Washington Post*, October 4, 1994

"I don't see how either team can possibly win."

> —On the inferior (by prewar standards) teams—the Tigers and Cubs—in the 1945 World Series; quoted in *The Mutual Baseball Almanac*

"I'll be home soon, Ma. The pitchers are starting to curve me."

> —Traditional line of the rookie who will not last his first spring training camp

"In the whole history of the major leagues there has never been a single case of umpire dishonesty!"

> —Overheard by Ford C. Frick and quoted in his *Games, Asterisks, and People*

"Is that the best game you ever pitched?"

> —Reporter to Don Larsen after pitching his perfect game in the 1956 World Series

"Just so-so in center field."

> —Assessing the talents of the New York Giants' "latest phenom," Willie Mays, after his major-league debut, *New York Daily News*, May 26, 1951

"Look, Mays just lost his halo."

> —On Willie Mays in 1954, when a reporter saw a shining object lying next to Mays in the outfield. Mays had achieved certain supremacy that season, and the line put things into perspective.

"MOSCOW, Sept. 15—The magazine *Smena*, under the title 'Beizbol,' explained to its readers today that baseball, the American national sport, was a 'beastly battle, a bloody fight with mayhem and murder' and furthermore nothing but a Yankee perversion of an ancient Russian village sport called 'lapta.'

"*Smena* presented a vivid description of the American national sport for its readers, declaring that far from being 'amusing,' 'noble' or 'safe' beizbol actually was a dangerous game in which both players and spectators frequently suffered terrible wounds or even death."

> —*New York Times*, September 16, 1952, under the headline "Russians Say U.S. Stole 'Beizbol,' Made It a Game of Bloody Murder." It goes on to identify "Babis Rut" and "Tai Koph" as "baseball slaves." Tom Heitz, former librarian at the National Baseball Library in Cooperstown, says that he was often asked for copies of the article in question.

"My God! The place is haunted!"

> —A reporter from the *New York Herald Tribune*, on entering a World Series press box to find a group of reporters who had also recently ghosted player autobiographies

"The only thing the Mets have to fear is mediocrity."

> —On becoming an ordinary second-division team during the early years

"Well, Bill Terry is right at last. Brooklyn is no longer in the league."

> —Reporter the day the Dodgers departed Ebbets Field; quoted by Curley Grieve in the *Sporting News*, October 9, 1957

"We've seen history made here today, a performance which probably never will be duplicated."

> —On Babe Ruth hitting three home runs in Sportsman's Park during the 1926 World Series; quoted in *The Babe Ruth Story* by Babe Ruth as told to Bob Considine

"When Kent Tekulve was born, the doctor slapped his mother."

> —Unidentified press-box writer, Portland, Oregon

"You can't afford to give the Mets an opening. Make four or five mistakes against them and they can kill you."

— Reporter on the early Mets

"You've got an arm like a leg."

— Heckler to a relief pitcher; quoted in *Sport* magazine, September 1963

ANONYMOUS—VERSE

EPITAPH ON A BASE-BALLIST

Fear not, Jim.
You have made a good hit.
And though the World pitched,
And the Devil played behind,
And the Seven Deadly Sins were alive
In the field;
Yet you have reached the Home-Plate of
    Heaven,
And, amid cries of Judgment
From the World, and How's That?
From the Devil,
Are proclaimed by the Great Umpire
Of the Universe,
NOT OUT.

> — This poem copied from issue of *Louisville* (KY) *Courier-Journal* by Louis T. Moore, chairman of New Hanover (Wilmington, NC) Historical Commission, and donated to the Hall of Fame, is believed to have been written in 1872.

"Eve stole first and Adam second,
St. Peter umpired the game.
Rebecca went to the well with a pitcher,
And Ruth in the field won fame.
Goliath was struck out by David,
A base hit on Abel was made by Cain.
The Prodigal Son made one home run,
And Brother Noah gave out checks for rain."

> — Quoted in the *Sporting News*, August 22, 1981

ODE TO A PITCHER

Truett Sewell
T'rew it swell.

> — Widely quoted, 1940s

The *Ball* once struck off,
Away flies the *Boy*
To the next destin'd Post,
And then Home with Joy.

> — *A Little Pretty Pocket Book*, 1744. The quatrain is headed "Base Ball." This is supposed to be the first mention of baseball in print.

THEY LIVED TOO SOON

George Washington was President
    and honored in his day,
He was the father of the land and
    all things came his way;
He had a basketful of fun, a wagon
    load of fame—
But he never was a rooter at a base-
    ball game.
Napoleon conquered half the world
    and had a crown of gold,
And in his time his cup was just
    as full as it could hold.
It looks from here as though he
    should have had his share of fun—
But he never strained his vocals
    when the home team won.

And also Julius Caesar, who had his
    share of sport,
He won his share of battles, and
    always held the fort.
He killed off lots of people, regard-
    less of the cost—
But he never booed the umpire
    when the home team lost.
And also Alexander, he turned most
    every trick,
And then shed tears because there
    were no more worlds to lick,

He climbed 'way up the ladder, as
    high as people get—
But he never pawned his scepter to pay a
    baseball bet.
—*Chicago Record*, 1896

TO CRITICIZE MIZE IS UNWISE;
HIS BAT SUPPLIES HIS BEST REPLIES.

    —*Boston Traveler* headline; quoted in the
    January 1950 *Baseball* magazine

ANSON, CAP

"'Baseball as at present conducted is a gigantic monopoly,' stated Anson, 'intolerant of opposition, and run on a grab-all-that-there-is-in-sight basis that is alienating its friends and disgusting the very public that has so long and cheerfully given to it the support that it has withheld from other forms of amusement.'"

    —From his autobiography, *A Ball Player's Career*, 1890

"Don't go gentlemen! The game is not finished."

    — "Not Done Till Ended," by O. P. Caylor in the *Atchison Daily Globe*, August 6, 1897. Bellowed to a departing crowd in a June 1897 game at the Polo Grounds in which the Giants led Anson's Chicago team by a number of runs at the end of the eighth inning. Anson's team came back to win, and the line became quoted in reference to other games won in the final inning. It was the nineteenth-century equivalent to "It ain't over, till it's over."

Cap Anson (*Library of Congress Prints and Photographs, Bain Collection.*)

APPLE, MAX

"Pitching really is like writing. How your arm feels. Change that to imagination and you have writing."

    —*Houston Post,* June 24, 1987

"Zloto came to Havana, showed Fidel his hands, talked about the '50s. Fidel said, 'They took our good men and put them in Yankee uniforms, in Bosox, Chisox, Dodgers, Birds. They took our manhood, Zloto. They took our Achilles and called him 'Archie'. Hector Gonzalez they called 'Ramrod,' Jess Ortiz they made a 'Jayo.' They treated Cuban manhood like a bowl of chicos and ricos. Yes, we have no bananas but we got vine-ripened Latinos who play good ball all year, stick their heads over the plate and wait for the Revolution. Fidel Castro gave it to them.'"

    —"Understanding Alvarado," in *The Oranging of America,* 1975

APPLING, LUKE

"I'm sure glad the season is over."

    —At seventy-five, after hitting a home run in the Old-Timers' Classic in Washington, *Sports Illustrated,* August 2, 1982

"The fans may be surprised to know that during my freshman year at Oglethorpe, I waited on table and never made an error, never dropped a tray nor broke a dish."

    —In the clubhouse after an early appearance at shortstop for the White Sox when his fielding abilities were yet to be proved; quoted by Lee Allen in *Cooperstown Corner*

Luke Appling (*Society for American Baseball Research; SABR*)

"The spitter wasn't hard to hit when you knew a pitcher could throw it legally. But the guys to worry about were the pitchers who sneaked over the illegal spitter after the pitch was outlawed."

    —As manager at Richmond of the International League; quoted in the *Sporting News,* April 13, 1955

"You can't let any team awe you. If you do, you'll wind up a horseshit player."

    —The Hall of Famer on his attitude toward the Yankees during twenty seasons with the Chicago White Sox; quoted by William B. Mead in *The Official Yankee Hater's Handbook*

ARATON, HARVEY

"Critics who howled about pitch-calling during the last post-season . . . make the sweeping charge that the umpires won't call the high strike and will call the wide strike.

"Why umpires would have arbitrarily decided in a secret meeting at a terrorist camp deep inside Afghanistan to shrink one part of the strike zone and grow another is one of the unsolved mysteries of the late 20th century."

—"Any Way One Tosses It, No Strike Zone Can Be Treated Equally," the *New York Times,* February 26, 1999 (Sports of the Times)

ARONSON, HARVEY

"I don't know how Abner Doubleday would have felt about the game, but Laurel and Hardy would have loved it."

"We will be out again next Sunday as every Sunday—old people reaching for youth and young people reaching for line drives. And everybody catching something."

"Laughs, not hits, are essentials of what the game is all about."

"The philosophic thrust of the game is inherent in the pitcher's obligation to make a hitter of the batter. It is a choose-up game and the sides are different each week."

—*New York Times;* quoted in *Say It Again* by Dorothy Uris

ARTHUR, CHESTER A.

"Good ballplayers make good citizens."

—On greeting a delegation of ballplayers at the White House on April 3, 1883

ASHBURN, RICHIE

"After 15 years of facing them, you don't really get over them. They're devious. They're the only players in the game allowed to cheat. They throw illegal pitches and they sneak foreign substances on the ball. They can inflict pain whenever they wish. And they're the only ones on the diamond who have high ground. That's symbolic. You know what they tell you in a war: 'Take the high ground first.'"

—On pitchers; quoted in the *Los Angeles Times,* June 16, 1975

"I wish I'd known early what I had to learn late."

—On the fact that when he was young he was so fast that he didn't have to learn to hit; quoted in *Late Innings* by Roger Angell

"I'm flattered that so many baseball people think I'm a Hall of Famer. But what's hard to believe is how 150-plus people have changed their minds about me since I became eligible, because I haven't had a base hit since then."

—The former Phillies outfielder, after receiving 158 votes in the Hall of Fame balloting, up from 6 the previous year. He was inducted into the Hall of Fame in 1995.

"The Kid doesn't chew tobacco, smoke, drink, curse or chase broads. I don't see how he can possibly make it."

—As an announcer on a rookie; widely attributed

"They should've called a welder."

—As a Phillies announcer on watching Met
Dave Kingman's glove being mended; quoted
in *Sports Illustrated*, October 11, 1982

ASINOF, ELIOT

"There was something almost prophetic
about the scandal. The 1920's, a decade of
unprecedented crime, corruption and immo-
rality, were just beginning.

"'Say it ain't so, Joe . . . say it ain't so.'

"It was like a last, desperate plea for faith
itself.

"A week later, Chicago kids were hollering
derisively: 'Play bail!' in lieu of the usual cry
to begin a game."

—*Eight Men Out* (New York: Holt, Rinehart,
and Winston)

ASPROMONTE, BOB

"I've heard of guys going 0-for-15, or 0-for-
25, but I was 0-for-July."

—As an Astro; widely attributed

ASPROMONTE, KEN

"The biggest thing in managing a major
league team is to establish some sort of
authority without making it smothering discipline."

—As Cleveland Indians manager; widely
attributed

SAINT AUGUSTINE

"For we wanted not, O Lord, memory or
capacity, whereof Thy will gave enough for
our age; but our sole delight was play; and
for this we were punished by those who yet
themselves were doing the like. But elder
folks' idleness is called 'business,' that of boys,
being really the same, is punished by those
elders; and none commiserates either boys or
men. For will any of sound discretion approve
of my being beaten as a boy because, by playing at ball, I made less progress in studies
which I was to learn only that, as a man, I
might play more unbeseemingly? And what
else did he who beat me? Who, if worsted in
some trifling discussion with his fellow-tutor,
was more embittered and jealous than I, when
beaten at ball by a play-fellow?"

—*Confessions*, book 1, 9; 15. At age fifteen.

AUSTEN, JANE

"It was not very wonderful that Catherine
[Morland], who had by nature nothing heroic
about her, should prefer cricket, base ball,
riding on horseback, and running about the
country, at the age of fourteen, to books."

—The first recorded literary reference to
baseball, in *Northanger Abbey*, written in 1794
and published in December, 1817 (dated
1818), depending on the source. David
Block's definitive work *Baseball Before We
Knew It* (2005) gives the 1818 date.

AUTRY, GENE

"Grantland Rice, the great sports writer, once said, 'It's not whether you win or lose, it's how you play the game.' Well, Grantland Rice can go to hell as far as I'm concerned."

> —The Angels owner on those who criticized his free-agent purchases; *Los Angeles Times,* May 10, 1984

"I have a lot of money to spend and not a lot of time [to live] and I want a World Series ring."

> —At eighty-one, on why he was relying on free agents; from a list of "Memorable Quotes of 1988" from the *Tampa Tribune,* December 25, 1988

AVERILL, EARL

"I thank those who supported my election. However, I'm convinced my record speaks for itself and that I was qualified to become a member. Not that I think of myself walking in the light of Babe Ruth, Ty Cobb or Rogers Hornsby; but then who else could stand beside those giants?

"My disagreement with how Hall of Fame elections are held and who is elected is not based on bitterness, that I had to wait 34 years after retirement to receive this honor. It is based on the fact that statistics alone are not enough to gain a player such recognition.

"What rights does anyone have to ignore cold hard facts in favor of looking for some intangible item to keep a person out of Cooperstown? An excellent example would be my old teammate, Joe Sewell. His .312 lifetime batting average for a shortstop with 2,000 hits is still

the American League record. He made 2,226 lifetime hits and batted home 1,011 runs. He ranks among the best hitters of any era. But after forty-two years, he still is not a member."

> —On being inducted into the Hall of Fame at age seventy-three, August 18, 1975

"There's no meaning to this honor if you're not alive."

> —On being inducted into the Hall of Fame; widely attributed

B

BABITZ, EVE

"Baseball is easy to fathom, not like football, which people explain to me at great length and I understand for one brief moment before it all falls apart in my brain and looks like an ominous calculus problem. The tension in baseball comes in spurts between long waits where everyone can forget about it, a perfectly lifelike rhythm."

—*Slow Days, Fast Company: the World, the Flesh, and L.A.* (New York: Knopf, 1977)

BACKMAN, WALLY

"If I hit eight home runs there, the place should be condemned. If I don't, I should be condemned."

—On the prospect of hitting in the Metrodome; quoted in the *Sporting News*, January 2, 1989.

BAER TRUTHS

Arthur "Bugs" Baer (1886–1969) was once read by fifteen million people daily, and he was considered to be the great popular aphorist of his day—a day which lasted a long time. He was known for the truths and observations which appeared in his column. Many were about baseball, most were not. It would be a shame to invoke his name without offering a few of his many lines, culled from fifty years of column writing. A few that the compiler has collected over the years:

"Cobb stopped off at a barbershop on the way to the ballpark to have his spikes sharpened."

—Written after a spiking incident involving Ty Cobb. According to Bob Considine of the *Washington Post*, who recalled it many years later (August 14, 1955), the quote prompted Cobb to compose a fourteen-page longhand letter to Baer beginning with the salutation "You dirty rat."

"DiMaggio could have done all of his hitting in a chimney."

> —After DiMaggio popped up to the catcher his first four times at bat in the 1950 World Series

"He had the greatest day since Lizzie Borden got 2 for 2 in Fall River, Massachusetts."

> —On a hot batter

"His head was full of larceny, but his feet were honest."

> —On Ping Bodie's inability to steal second base, 1917. One of those quotations that appear in many places and with many variations, such as "He had larceny in his heart, but his feet were honest," and "His heart was full of larceny, but his feet were honest." The line

so amused press baron William Randolph Hearst Sr. that he hired Baer to write for his *New York American*.

"He would climb a mountain to take a punch at an echo."

> —On Ty Cobb

"McGraw wouldn't pay that for a kid who could throw a lamb chop past a wolf."

> —On the salary demands of a New York pitcher

"Pratt slid home on his surname."

> —About one of the several Pratts in the game during his writing years. The quote is recalled while the Pratt is not.

"World Series week indicates that baseball is one of America's major disturbances."

> —From his syndicated column October 8, 1947

BAGLEY, ELI, AND OTHERS

A CHALLENGE

"The undersigned, all residents of the new town of Hamden, with the exception of Asa C. Rowland, who has recently removed to Delhi, challenge an equal number of persons of any town in the County of Delaware, to meet them at any time at the house of Edward B. Chace, in said town, to play the game of BASE-BALL, for the sum of one dollar each per game. If no town can be found that will produce the required number, they have no objection to play against any selection that can be made from the several towns in the county."

Eli Bagley,
Edward B. Chace,
Harry P. Chace,
Ira Peak
Walter C. Peak,
H. B. Groodrich,
R .F. Thurber,
Asa C. Howland,
M. L. Bostwick.

Hamden, July 12, 1825."

> —One of the earliest known journalistic references to baseball, published in the *Delhi* [NY] *Gazette*, July 13, 1825

BAKER, KEVIN

"Ballplayers call a manager 'skip' when they like him. Makes him feel like Casey Stengel."

> —Spoken by Rapid Ricky "the Old Swizzlehead" Falls to manager Ol' Cal Rigby, in *Sometimes You See It Coming* (New York: Crown Publishers, 1993)

BAKER, RUSSELL

"Every day in every way, baseball gets fancier. A few more years and they'll be playing on oriental rugs."

> —Widely quoted

"Joe DiMaggio is not selling panty hose, but Joe Namath is. DiMaggio is selling coffee pots. Mickey Mantle, who replaced him in center field for the Yankees, is selling beer, with the help of Whitey Ford, who was to left-handed pitching what Edward G. Robinson was to the .45-caliber automatic."

> —On endorsements; *New York Times*, June 29, 1975

BALLARD, JEFF

"The only way to learn to play in the big leagues is to play in the big leagues. That's the best saying ever."

> —As an Orioles pitcher; quoted in the *Washington Post* March 6, 1989

BAMBERGER, GEORGE

"The best way to hide the spitter is to fake all the tricky stuff—Vaseline behind the knee

or under the bill of your cap—then just spit on your hand when they're looking at you. I never did it any other way."

> —As Milwaukee Brewers manager, 1981

"Times are different. The kids [players] today . . . well, you can't yell at them. When I was a kid, they yelled at me and I accepted it. Today they go into a shell if you do that and so you have to do a lot more talking to them. That's what they mean by communicating. Some [managers] can communicate and some can't."

> —*Dallas Times-Herald,* April 23, 1978

"We do not play baseball. We play professional baseball. Amateurs play games. We are paid to win games. There are rules, and there are consequences if you break them. If you are a pro, then you often don't decide whether to cheat based on if it's 'right or wrong.' You base it on whether or not you can get away with it, and what the penalty might be. A guy who cheats in a friendly game of cards is a cheater. A pro who throws a spitball to support his family is a competitor."

> —Quoted in Thomas Boswell's column, the *Washington Post*, August 6, 1987

BANDO, SAL

"I've learned to enjoy it because of the rest it provides. It enables you to give 100 per cent, mentally, to hitting. I'm a firm believer in, if that's what they ask you to do, go do it 100 per cent and learn to enjoy it."

> —On being the Brewers' DH; quoted in the *Los Angeles Times*, August 13, 1978

BANDO, SAL (CONTINUED)

"Was it difficult leaving the *Titanic*?"

> —In response to a question about how he felt
> leaving the Oakland A's

BANE, EDDIE

"I think I throw the ball as hard as anyone.
The ball just doesn't get there as fast."

> —As a Minnesota pitcher; *The Sporting News
> Chronicle of 20th Century Sport.*

BANKHEAD, TALLULAH

"Dahling, I am the national pastime."

> —Response to Milton Berle's comment, "I
> didn't realize you were so interested in the
> national pastime"; quoted in Bennett Cerf's
> *Life of the Party*

"I just die when his little cap falls off when he
runs around the bases. He is like a gazelle."

> —On Willie Mays, in the *Chicago Defender,*
> December 1, 1958

"I was hoping they would move 200 miles
farther West."

> —On the Dodgers' move from Brooklyn to
> Los Angeles; quoted in the *San Francisco
> Chronicle,* 1958

"I wish I'd been born a second baseman."

> —The rabid Giants fan; quoted in a 1950 issue
> of *Holiday*

"There have been only two authentic geniuses
in the world, Willie Mays and Willie Shakespeare."

> —*The Baseball Card Engagement Book,* Michael
> Gershman, 1987

BANKS, ERNIE

"Did you hear that? I didn't hear anything.
Put that question another way."

> —As a former Cub, when asked why his team
> was so bad during the 1982 season; quoted in
> *Sports Illustrated,* August 23, 1982

"I like my players to be married and in debt.
That's the way you motivate them."

> —As a minor-league instructor for the Cubs,
> *New York Times,* April 11, 1976

"I once read that success depends on talents
God gave you and also on the people who
believe in you. This honor belongs to those
people who believed in me—my parents, my
wife and children, and those individuals, such
as Monte Irvin and 'Cool Papa' Bell, who
helped teach me. And then, of course, there
are the fans."

> —On being inducted into the Hall of Fame,
> August 8, 1977

"Isn't it a beautiful day? . . . The Cubs of
Chicago versus the Phillies of Philadelphia,
in beautiful, historic Wrigley Field. Let's go,
let's go. It's Sunday in America."

> —Pregame chatter; quoted in *Sport,* December
> 1971

"It's a great day for a ballgame; let's play two."

> —His signature line, which defined his attitude toward the game. It would be amended to "Let's play three" when a doubleheader was scheduled.

"Mr. Grand Slam Himself, Ernie Banks, is available for a limited number of selected talks and appearances at luncheons, dinners and Christmas parties during December and January."

> —Ad in the *Chicago American*, fall, 1955

"Spring training means flowers, people coming outdoors, sunshine, optimism and baseball. Spring training is a time to think about being young again."

> —*New York Times*, February 22, 1986

"The Cubs are due in sixty-two. The Cubs are gonna shine in sixty-nine."

> —His own mottoes for the Cubs

"The riches of the game are in the thrills, not the money."

> —After hitting his 500th home run on May 12, 1970. According to the *Sporting News*, he jumped on a chair in the clubhouse after the game and yelled this out.

"Welcome to Wrigley Field."

> —What he was given to singing out to the crowd before games began

"You must try to generate happiness within yourself. If you aren't happy in one place, chances are you won't be happy any place."

> —Widely attributed

BANNERS, BUMPER STICKERS, AND BUTTONS

In 1962, when Casey Stengel was fielding the first Mets team at the Polo Grounds in New York, the fans began showing up with odd messages and words of encouragement, usually written on old bedsheets. It was something new, and the first reaction of the Mets' front office was to have them torn down. But as George Vecsey later reported, "The spirit of the people prevailed, and by the end of the season, the Mets were holding their first Banner Day."

It would be impossible to list more than a sampling of this American haiku, but here is a good sampling along with a smattering of bumper sticker slogans and buttons, banners, etc.

BASEBALL, THE GREAT CANADIAN PASTIME

> —Exhibition Stadium, Toronto, 1985 ALCS

BEATLES, SHMEETLES, WE HAVE THE METS

> —Early Shea Stadium example; cited by Maury Allen in *The Incredible Mets*

BRING BASEBALL TO ATLANTA

> —Bumper sticker traditional during years in which the Braves have fared poorly

CALVIN IS OUR DH . . . DESIGNATED HALF-WIT

> —Metropolitan Stadium, Twins fans expressing their dissatisfaction with owner Calvin Griffith, 1978

DEWEY BEATS TRUMAN
THE CARDS IN FIVE

—By a Kansas City Royals fan during the sixth
game of the '85 World Series

**EXTREMISM IN DEFENSE OF THE METS IS
NO VICE**

—An allusion to Barry Goldwater's 1964
"Extremism in the defense of liberty is no
vice" hung for the Mets that same year

**GIVE ME A LOAF OF BRETT, A POUND OF BIAN-
CALANA, AND A SLICE OF BALBONI**

—In Royals Stadium; quoted in *Baseball . . . a
Laughing Matter* by Warner Fusselle

GREATEST JOE ON EARTH

—Button for Joe DiMaggio at an old-timers' game

**HEY, CHICAGO, GOOD THING YOUR CITY
IS WINDY, BECAUSE YOUR SOX SMELL**

—Baltimore's Memorial Stadium; at the outset
of the 1983 ALCS

HONK IF YOU HAVE GROCERIES

—Bumper sticker allegedly found on Tommy
Lasorda's car, ca. 1986; widely reported and
almost certainly apocryphal

**HEY METS AND GIANTS—HOW'S THE TV
RECEPTION?**

—Busch Stadium during the 1987 World Series

**HEY WADE WE'RE NOT WEARING ANY UNDER-
WEAR.**

—Banner held up for Wade Boggs at
Baltimore's Memorial Stadium, Opening
Day, 1989

I'VE BEEN A METS FAN ALL MY LIFE.

—Banner unfurled at the Polo Grounds
when the New York Mets played their first
Opening Day, 1962

M IS FOR MIGHTY
E IS FOR EXCITING
T IS FOR TERRIFIC
S IS FOR SO LOVABLE.

—Shea Stadium banner, 1969; cited in *The
Summer Game* by Roger Angell

NIGHT OF THE LIVING DEAD

—"The Sign Man of Shea" on the Mets' first
night game of 1976

PRAY

—Mets banner, Polo Grounds, 1962

**SELL CAMPBELL AND BRING BACK THE $1.50
BLEACHER SEATS!**

—Fenway banner greeting Bill Campbell after
being one of the first free agents to sign a
million-dollar contract, 1977

SOX 2, METS 0, YANKEES—NO GAME TODAY

—Fenway Park after the first game of the 1986
World Series

THE SOX ARE BETTER THAN SEX

—Fenway Park perennial

TO ERR IS HUMAN, TO FORGIVE IS A METS FAN

—Polo Grounds, 1962

WASHINGTON SLEPT HERE

—Comiskey Park banner aimed at Claudell Washington and, as Bill Veeck once put it, "the casual attitude he took toward ground balls."

WE CAME TO BURY SEAVER

—The "Sign Man of Shea," after, he claims, he was snubbed by Tom Seaver; cited in the *New York Times* April 8, 1976

WE DON'T WANT TO SET THE WORLD ON FIRE . . . WE JUST WANT TO FINISH NINTH

—Early Shea Stadium example; cited by Maury Allen in *The Incredible Mets*

WE WHO ARE ABOUT TO CRY SALUTE YOU

—At Shea Stadium for Willie Mays's farewell. Also noted that night:
"A giant among Mets."
"Bye, Willy, we hate to see you go."
"Thanks for the excitement through the years."
"Shalom."

WELCOME, ANNUAL PENNANT CHOKERS

—Hung in Comiskey Park for the Royals, 1978. It so infuriated pitcher Doug Bird than he went out and pulled it down.

WELCOME TO GRANT'S TOMB

—Ibid., an allusion to Donald Grant.

WHY ARE THE METS THE BEST LOSERS? PRACTICE MAKES PERFECT

—Shea Stadium, 1963

WILL THE LAST PERSON TO LEAVE THE STADIUM PLEASE TURN OUT THE LIGHTS

—Sign held up by a fan in the bleachers at the end of the first complete night game at Chicago's Wrigley Field, August 9, 1988

BARBERISMS—RED BARBER

His manner of speaking set him apart, especially with a certain set of expressions including these:

"He's sittin' in the catbird seat!" (Sitting on a lead.)

"Hold the phone!" (Manager is headed for the mound.)

"Oh, Doctor!" (A sudden turn of events.)

"Runnin' like a bunny with his tail on fire!" (Really moving.)

"The bases are F.O.B.'s" (Full of Brooklyns.)

"The fat's in the fire." (Things have come to a critical juncture.)

"They're tearin' up the pea patch!" (The Dodgers are scoring.)

"There's fever in Flatbush!" (During a Dodger rally.)

"This ol' country boy." (Himself.)

Some of his many baseball quotations:

"Baseball is my favorite sport . . . because it is orderly. Football is organized confusion. Even the coaches don't know anything about it until they get it on film. And basketball is just fellows running up and down in their undershorts."

> —*Red Barber* by Barbara Grizzuti Harrison, 1991; quoted in Elinor Nauen, ed., *Diamonds Are a Girl's Best Friend: Women Writers on Baseball* (Boston: Faber & Faber, 1994)

"First a famine. Now a feast."

> —On baseball books, comparing the 1930s to the 1980s, in the *Boston Globe,* June 18, 1989

"On TV it's the director's show, and the broadcaster is an instrument of his, like a camera. On radio, it's my show, where my knowledge and experience and taste and judgment decide what goes and what doesn't. On radio, you're an artist. On TV, you're a servant."

> —On his preference for radio over television, from *Rhubarb in the Catbird Seat*

"The sky overhead is a very beautiful robin's egg blue with, as the boys say, very few angels [clouds]. It's a very tough sky for the players

Red Barber (*Library of Congress Prints and Photographs Division*)

to look into and left field in Yankee stadium is the sun garden."

> —Description of field conditions during one of the thirteen World Series he broadcast; quoted by the *St. Petersburg Times,* April 3, 1990

"This is Red Barber speaking. Let me say hello to you all."

> —First words on the debut TV broadcast of major-league baseball, August 26, 1939

"When I was in baseball and you went into the clubhouse, you didn't see ball players with curling irons."

> —*USA Today,* February 17, 1988, on his eightieth birthday.

"Whenever you have a tight situation and there's a close pitch, the umpire gets a squawk no matter how he calls it. You wonder why men take a job in which they get so much abuse."

> —Quoted by Edward F. Murphy in the *New York Times,* April 25, 1976.

"Why is baseball the best sport to broadcast? The baseball announcer must know the game thoroughly, because the game is so open and the fans so knowledgeable. The slightest mistake is glaringly obvious."

> —*Christian Science Monitor,* August 27, 1987

BARFIELD, JESSE

"I'm ecstatic for him. And the good thing about it is there's more where it came from."

> —The Yankees right fielder Jesse Barfield, who was beginning a three-year, $5.4 million contract, about Don Mattingly's new five-year, $19.3 million contract; quoted in *USA Today,* April 10, 1990.

BARNEY, REX

"Give that fan a contract."

> —Baltimore Orioles public address announcer, said whenever a fan made a nice catch of a foul ball at Memorial Stadium and Oriole Park at Camden Yards; original idea for announcement came from Jack Dunn III

BARNICLE, MIKE

"I am a great success dealing with failure. I handle death, termination, dismissal, tragedies of all kind with marvelous skill. I stink when it comes to good news.

"And this morning, looking at the standings in the American League East, I know. I simply know. And if you're at all like me you know what I know too.

"Today, the Red Sox are doing to us what Michelle Pfeiffer does to me while I'm sound asleep. June is foreplay month, one long, hot, humid tease."

> —On the Red Sox being in first place at the end of June, in the *Boston Globe,* June 28, 1990

"We should have a place where the victims of this dreaded regional illness can be cared for by professionals. Following the Red Sox is a form of substance abuse, you know. They will get the best of you."

> —On the Red Sox, in his *Boston Globe* column August 3, 1989

BARROW, ED

"This is exactly what you were hired not to do."

> —The Yankee GM, infuriated because farm-system director George Weiss (whom he had hired "to develop players, not to buy them") wanted permission to purchase minor-leaguer Joe DiMaggio from the San Francisco Seals, 1935; quoted in, among other places, *The Experts Speak: The Definitive Compendium of Authoritative Misinformation* by Christopher Cerf and Victor S. Bavasky (New York: Random House, 1990)

BARRY, DAVE

"If a woman has to choose between catching a fly ball and saving an infant's life, she will choose to save the infant's life without even considering if there is a man on base."

> —This is one of the humorist's most quoted lines, along with "Skiing combines outdoor fun with knocking down trees with your face."

BARRY, JACK

"'It makes me laugh when I read where a club has given an untried youngster $50,000 or more to sign a contract,' he would remark. 'They called us the "$100,000 infield" when I played with McInnis, Collins and Baker, but I'll bet it didn't cost Connie Mack more than $50 to land us all. I know that all it cost him to get Collins and myself was carfare.'"

> —Member of the fabled $100,000 infield of the second decade of the twentieth century; quoted in his *Sporting News* obituary. Barry died on April 23, 1951, at age seventy-three.

BARRYMORE, ETHEL

"Isn't Willie Mays wonderful?"

> —From an interview on her seventy-fifth birthday, 1954; quoted in Arnold Hano's *Willie Mays*

"Shut up, kid, I'm listening to the ballgame."

> —According to actress Barbara Bel Geddes, these were the first words she ever heard from the great Barrymore. Both were in the play *School for Scandal;* originally quoted by Leonard Lyons of the *New York Post*

BARTELME, PHIL G.

"Bigger and better release notices."

> —This was one of eight "Famous Baseball Sayings" collected by Ernest J. Lanigan of the Hall of Fame when he identified himself as "Historian and authority on the game for sixty-five years."

BARZUN, JACQUES

"Happy the man in the bleachers. He is enjoying the spectacle that the gods on Olympus contrived only with difficulty when they sent Helen to Troy and picked their teams. And the gods missed the fun of doing this by catching a bat near the narrow end and measuring hand over hand for first pick. In Troy, New York, the game scheduled for 2 p.m. will break no bones, yet it will be a real fight between Southpaw Dick and Red Larsen. . . .

"And the next day in the paper: learned comment, statistical summaries, and the verbal imagery of meta-euphoric experts. In the face of so much joy, one can only ask, Were you there when Dogface Joe parked the pellet beyond the pale?"

> —*God's Country and Mine: A Declaration of Love Spiced with a Few Harsh Words* (Boston: Little, Brown, 1954)

"Whoever wants to know the heart and mind of America had better learn baseball, the rules and realities of the game—and do it by watching first some high school or small-town teams."

> —*God's Country and Mine.* This may well be the most requoted line on the game in the years since World War II. Barzun later had harsh

words for the game such as these from the *Baltimore Sun,* April 4, 1993:

"I've gotten so disgusted with baseball, I don't follow it anymore. I just see the headlines and turn my head away in shame from what we have done with our most interesting game and best, healthiest pastime.

"The commercialization is beyond anything that was ever thought of, the overvaluing, really, of the game itself. It's out of proportion to the place an entertainment ought to have.

"Other things are similarly commercialized and out of proportion. But for baseball, which is so intimately connected with the nation's spirit and tradition, it's a disaster."

THE BASEBALL BIBLE

The Bible may have preceded America's leading pastime, baseball, by centuries, but an industrious rabbi, Bernard S. Raskas of Temple Aaronin Cincinnati, has demonstrated that it could be said to have anticipated at least the vernacular of the game.

PITCHER—"Rebekah came out . . . with her pitcher" (Gen. 24:15).

CATCHER—"And he received them at their hand" (Exod. 32:4).

OUTFIELDERS—"He sent among them swarms of flies." (Ps. 78:45).

SACRIFICE PLAY—"And Amon sacrificed" (2 Chron. 33:22) "and Noah went in" (Gen. 7:7).

HIT AND RUN—"And they ran as soon as he had stretched out his hand" (Josh 8:19).

HOME RUN—"And all the people shouted with a great shout" (Ezra 3:11).

VISITING TEAM—"Then the Philistines went up and pitched in Judah" (Judges 5:9).

UMPIRE—"The Lord openeth the eyes of the blind" (Ps. 146:8).

SPORTSWRITER AFTER THE GAME—"Who can discern errors" (Ps. 19:13).

TEAM MANAGER TO TALENT SCOUT—"Do I lack madmen that they have brought this fellow to play?" (1 Sam. 21:16).

—*National Jewish Post;* quoted widely, including in the April 1961 *Baseball Digest.* Such lists have been circulating for more than a hundred years. The earliest which has come to this compiler's attention showed up in the *Chicago Tribune* for February 20, 1898, and began with "Hast thou not signed." (Dan. 6:12).

BAUER, HANK

"For the benefit of you younger fellows, we have a lot of rules on this club. Midnight curfew, stay out of the bar at the hotel where we're staying, wear a shirt and sweater to breakfast and a coat and tie to dinner. Think you can remember all that?"

—As Orioles manager, spring training 1967; quoted in the *Sporting News,* April 1, 1967

"It's no fun playing if you don't make somebody else unhappy. I do everything hard."

—Recalled in his *New York Times* obituary, February 10, 2007

BAVASI, BUZZIE

"I'd rather be an attendant in a gas station. You wipe a windshield and they say, 'Thank you.' Nobody ever says thank you to the commissioner of baseball."

—The San Diego Padres president, on being the commissioner of baseball; widely attributed.

"Players have lost all loyalty to a club, to their teammates, and perhaps even to themselves."

—On the modern player; widely attributed

"They ridicule the modern ball player and tell you pitching is ruining baseball but Sandy Koufax was the biggest drawing card in the last 10 years—and they didn't come out to see him hit home runs."

—As Padres president; quoted in *Baseball Digest,* February 1969

Hank Bauer (*Author's Collection*)

"You keep defying major-league hitters to hit you and they will."

—*The Baseball Life of Sandy Koufax*

BAVASI, PETER

"When the one great scorer comes to mark against your name, it's not whether you won or lost but how many paid to see the game."

—As Blue Jays general manager; widely attributed

BAYLOR, DON

"I came into this game sane, and I want to leave it sane."

—As to why he would say no if George Steinbrenner offered him the Yankees' managing job, *Sports Illustrated*, October 14, 1987

"That's a bleeping disgrace. Bleeping bleep. Absolute bleeping bleep. We bleeping get two strikes on guys. We walk a guy hitting bleeping .200 (Jeff Blauser). They do us a bleeping favor and leave him bleeping in, and we bleeping walk him. You've got to be bleeping bleeping me. The bleeping guy pitches his bleeping heart out, and we go out and bleep up the game like that. They're bleeping worried about him being a replacement player? You have to be bleeping bleeping me. He bleeping pitches against one of the best bleeping pitchers in the history of the bleeping game [Greg Maddux]. He bleeping battled his bleeping bleep off, and he's got to watch that bleeping bleep. He had to bleeping wait to get here and bleeping pitch. He bleeping pitches his bleep off on a bleeping night he has no bleeping chance because bleeping Maddux is pitching."

—Colorado Rockies manager's critique of 6–5, ten-inning loss on May 7, 1996, to the Atlanta Braves, despite a two-hit, seven-inning performance by Mike Farmer, a one-time replacement pitcher making his first big-league start, as relievers Bruce Ruffin and Curtis Leskanic combined to blow a 5–2 lead; quoted in *Sports Illustrated*, May 20, 1996

Don Baylor (*California Angels*)

BEARD, GORDON

"Brooks never asked anyone to name a candy bar after him. In Baltimore people name their children after him."

—On Brooks Robinson, 1973

BEAUMONT, GERALD

"Baseball is a peculiar profession, possibly the only one which capitalized a boyhood pleasure, unfits the athlete for any other career, keeps him young in mind and spirit, and then rejects him as too old before he has yet attained the prime of life."

—*Hearts and the Diamond* (New York: Dodd Mead, 1921)

BELINSKY, BO

"He who plays and runs away lives to play some other day."

—Quoted in *Bo: Pitching and Wooing* by Maury Allen

"I figured baseball would be just as good as the overalls factory. I knew I would go as far as my arm would take me. Nobody would help me. I knew that if you want a helping hand in this world look at the end of your arm."

—Quoted in *Bo: Pitching and Wooing*

"I think I have gotten more publicity for doing less than any player who ever lived."

— *Catcher in the Wry* by Bob Uecker

"If I'd known I was gonna pitch a no-hitter today I would have gotten a haircut."

— *The Suitors of Spring* by Pat Jordan

"I'm not going to ask for more money, I'll just wait and let them come and insist I take a raise."

—As a rookie; quoted in *No-Hitter* by Phil Pepe

"In baseball you have to do your job today. You can't worry about mañana. If you don't win, you're gone. The reason so many guys are popping greenies is because they need that extra lift."

—Quoted in *Bo: Pitching and Wooing* by Maury Allen

"My only regret in life is that I can't sit in the stands and watch me pitch."

—Quoted in *The Suitors of Spring* by Pat Jordan

Bo Belinsky (*Author's Collection*)

"Never try to snow a snowman."

—Quoted in *Bo: Pitching and Wooing* by Maury Allen

"No regrets, not a single one. Maybe the only thing I'm truly sorry about is hitting one guy in the face with a pitch. It was Jimmie Hall and he was with Minnesota and it was a damn accident. He never was the same again. A thing like that stays with you. I almost cost a guy his life."

—After fifteen years in baseball; quoted in *Bo: Pitching and Wooing* by Maury Allen

"Philadelphia fans would boo funerals, an Easter egg hunt, a parade of armless war vets, and the Liberty Bell."

>—1972, Hall of Fame collection

"Rigney made a big deal of it. Everybody has bad games and nothing is said. If I had a bad game he would mention Mamie's name and suggest that if I didn't go out with Mamie maybe I would win more games. I felt like telling him if I got more runs and the guys behind me played better, maybe I'd win more games."

>—On his relationship with Mamie Van Doren; quoted in *Bo: Pitching and Wooing* by Maury Allen

"Some day, I would like to go up in the stands and boo some fans."

>—*Bo: Pitching and Wooing* by Maury Allen

"The no-hitter I pitched actually cost me money. I had to buy drinks for everyone. It was like making a hole-in-one."

>— *Catcher in the Wry* by Bob Uecker

"These guys didn't want the truth. That wasn't as good a story as something I could make up. So I went along with them. I answered all their questions the way they wanted. When they asked about broadies, I built it up. When they asked about pool, I made out to be the best player that ever picked up a cue. When they asked about my contract, I made it sound like I wouldn't sign under any conditions unless Autry begged me personally."

>—On the media; quoted in *Bo: Pitching and Wooing* by Maury Allen

"The spitter was a lot of help. It kept me in the big leagues when all else failed."

>—*Bo: Pitching and Wooing* by Maury Allen

"They would even boo a funeral."

>—On the Philadelphia fans; quoted in *Bo: Pitching and Wooing* by Maury Allen; and often and widely, perhaps his most famous line

"When I lose, I drink, and when I win I celebrate."

>—Torrez in *High Inside: Memoirs of a Baseball Wife* by Danielle Gagnon

BELL, BUDDY

"None of us loves having it. And, as much as you want to knock down the ignorant misconceptions of those who think it's freaky and weird, you don't want epilepsy to be read into every argument you have with the umpires. 'Look at Buddy. Is he going to lose it?' One reason I never wanted people to know was just that I didn't want them to worry about me. I don't think about it every day. I don't think about it every month. I'd be the same way without it."

>—Revealing his epilepsy after playing with it for fifteen years; quoted by Tom Callahan, the *Washington Post*, November 5, 1989

"We're not so bad as people thought, although that's not saying much."

>—On the Rangers' moderately strong start in 1983; quoted in *Sports Illustrated*, June 6, 1983

BELL, JAMES "COOL PAPA"

"I remember one game I got five hits and stole five bases, but none of it was written down because they forgot to bring the scorebook to the game that day."

—Quoted in the 1981 50th Anniversary Hall of Fame *Yearbook*

"We would frequently play two and three games a day. We'd play a twilight game, ride 40 miles, and play another game, under the lights. This was in the 1940's. On Sundays you'd play three games—a doubleheader in one town and a single night game in another. Or three single games in three different towns. One game would start about one o'clock, a second about four, and a third at about eight. Three different towns, mind you. Same uniform all day, too. We'd change socks and sweat shirts, but that's about all. When you got to the town, they'd be waiting for you, and all you'd have time to do would be to warm your pitcher up. Many a time I put on my uniform at eight o'clock in the morning and wouldn't take it off till three or four the next morning."

—On barnstorming in the Negro leagues, from Donald Honig's *Baseball When the Grass Was Real: Baseball from the Twenties to the Forties Told by the Men Who Played It* (1993)

"You try to get that game out of your mind, but it never leaves you."

— "A Loss for Baseball," by Richard Demak, *Sports Illustrated*, March 18, 1991

BELL, GEORGE

"If they don't know the game after 11 or 12 years of the Toronto Blue Jays . . . The people booing me are 21, 23, 25, 26 years old. I'm 28 years old, I make $2 million a year and I don't have to get up at 6 in the morning to go to work."

—*Portsmouth Herald,* July 16, 1989

BELTAIRE, MARK

"Almost the only place in life where a sacrifice is really appreciated."

—*Webster's New World Dictionary of Quotable Definitions*

BENCH, JOHNNY

"He looks like a pair of pliers."

—As a broadcaster on the lanky Von Hayes, *Sports Illustrated*, August 18, 1988

"I want to win, but there's the grind. There's so much responsibility for a catcher. I have to contribute on offense and work with the pitching, too. I've got a fine contract. I should play for five more years. But then I ask myself if that's what I really want. My arm feels good. My legs will be all right. How long will I go on? How long can I go on? How long do I want to go on playing baseball? Is this what it's like to be 30?"

—On playing at thirty; quoted in the *New York Times*, March 27, 1978

Johnny Bench (*National Baseball Library*)

"Jimmy Conners plays two tennis matches and winds up with $850,000, and Muhammad Ali fights one bout and winds up with five million bucks. Me, I play 190 games—if you count exhibitions—and I'm overpaid!"

　　—On his $175,000 salary; quoted in the *New York Times*, May 25, 1975

"They are as greedy as we are. They want to win the pennant. They want recognition. They want to put people in the ballpark."

　　—On owners and the advent of multimillion-dollar contracts; quoted in the *Dallas Times-Herald*, January 6, 1977

"They're like sleeping in a soft bed. Easy to get into and hard to get out of."

　　—On slumps; widely attributed

BENCHLEY, ROBERT

"An ardent supporter of the home town team should go to a game prepared to take offense, no matter what happens."

　　—Widely attributed.

"One of the chief duties of the fan is to engage in arguments with the man behind him. This department has been allowed to run down fearfully."

　　—Quoted in *The Baseball Reader*, ed., Ralph S. Graber

BENDER, CHARLES ALBERT "CHIEF"

"BASEBALL'S TEN COMMANDMENTS"

1. Nobody ever becomes a ballplayer by walking after a ball.
2. You will never become a .300 hitter unless you take the bat off your shoulder.
3. If what you did yesterday still looks big to you, you haven't done much today.
4. Keep your head up and you may not have to keep it down.
5. When you start to slide, SLIDE. He who changes his mind may have to change a good leg for a bad one.
6. Do not alibi on bad hops. Anybody can field the good ones.
7. Always run them out. You never can tell.
8. Never quit.
9. Do not find too much fault with the umpires. You cannot expect them to be as perfect as you are.
10. A pitcher who hasn't control hasn't anything.

　　—Quoted in the *Baseball Digest*, April 1970

BENDER, CHARLES ALBERT "CHIEF" (CONTINUED)

"You ignorant, ill-bred foreigners! If you don't like the way I'm doing things out there, why don't you just pack up and go back to your own countries!"

—This American Indian, to jeering fans (ca. 1910); SABR Collection

BENJAMIN, ROBERT B.

"Baseball will become the national game of England and of the entire British empire within a short time after the Allies have settled with the Kaiser and the Potsdam maniacs. The American national game will replace cricket in the hearts of the Britishers. Baseball or cricket as the world game, you ask? Baseball every time!"

—The head of the Australian national cricket team in 1913; quoted in the *Sporting News*, October 17, 1925

BERG, MOE

"The players are not interested in the score, but merely in how many runs are necessary to tie and to win. They take nothing for granted in baseball. The idea is to win. The game's the thing."

— "Pitchers and Catchers," *Atlantic Monthly*, September 1941

BERKOW, IRA

"Baseball is a pleasant pastime, a genial undertaking, a civil essay. Football is war.

"Baseball is a kid's game. You put on a beanie and knickers to play it. In football, you don armor.

"When you put on a baseball cap, it shields the sun. When you tug on a football helmet, it burns your ears. When it rains in baseball, you seek shelter. People usually have the good sense to go indoors and eat hot dogs. In football, people sit outside in thunderstorms, in lightning, in snow and sleet. Of course, they must come equipped with medicinal jugs to get them through the struggle.

"When the field gets muddy in baseball, they stop the game. When the field gets muddy in football, the players roll around in it like board hogs.

"Baseball is leisurely, if not in fact soporific. Football is, well, as the great Red Grange said: 'Football is work. Baseball is fun.'"

—"For Jackson, What Choice?" *New York Times*, June 24, 1986 ("Sports of the Times")

BERKOWITZ, STEVE

"Five years together. It was the Pete and Marge Show, and we had a lot of fun."

—The *Washington Post* writer on Pete Rose's departure from the Reds, August 25, 1989

BERMAN, CHRIS

"There are three things that a male cannot change in our society. . . . They are: his date of birth, social security number, and baseball team. Oh, you can change allegiances in football or basketball. But not baseball. . . . I was a lifelong San Francisco Giants fan."

> —"A Look Back, Back, Back, Back . . . ," *Giants Magazine*, 1989 (Guest column)

BERRA, DALE

"Our similarities are different."

> —On comparisons to his father, *Sports Illustrated*, August 1, 1982

BERRAISMS/YOGISMS—YOGI BERRA

In the March 17, 1986, edition of the *Sporting News* Yogi Berra puts it bluntly: "I really didn't say everything I said." It is at once the glory and dilemma of assembling Berra quotes. The line is both a perfect Berraism and a repudiation of Berraisms.

His ability to get quoted is remarkable. *The New Yorker* has observed, "Hardly anybody would quarrel that Winston Churchill has been replaced by Yogi Berra as the . . . favorite source of quotations," and the *New York Times* proclaimed him the most commonly quoted American in graduation speeches. "Talking to Yogi Berra about baseball is like talking to Homer about the gods," the late Bart Giamatti said.

What follows is a major collection of them.

"A lot of guys have that many all by themselves."

> —On his 1974 Met bullpen, which saved a scant fourteen games

"A nickel ain't worth a dime anymore."

> —Quoted in *Baseball Digest*, June 1987

"All pitchers are liars and crybabies."

> —SABR Collection

"Anybody who can't tell the difference between a ball hitting wood and a ball hitting concrete must be blind."

> —In an argument with an umpire, who ruled that a ball hit a concrete outfield wall and was thus in play, while Berra said it hit a wooden barricade beyond the wall and was thus a home run; quoted in *Sports Illustrated*, April 30, 1979

Yogi Berra (*New York Yankees*)

"Baseball is ninety percent mental. The other half is physical."

—One of the most often stated Berraisms, Berra has stood by this one. "It may be 95 per cent or it may be only 80, but anybody who plays golf, tennis, or any other sport knows what I mean," is how he put it in *Yogi: It Ain't Over...* See also Jim Wohlford, who probably first uttered those words.

"Baseball is the champ of them all. Like somebody said, the pay is good and the hours are short."

—Quoted in the *Sporting News,* November 21, 1951

"Bill Dickey learned me all his experiences."

—Widely quoted

"Boy, I'm glad I don't live in them days."

—Impromptu review of the bloody movie *The Vikings;* quoted by Leonard Koppett in the *Sporting News,* July 18, 1970

"Come over here and show me how to work this thing!"

—Calling a teammate about his new piano; widely attributed

"Congratulations on breaking my record. I always thought the record would stand until it was broken."

—The telegram he was reported to have sent to Reds catcher Johnny Bench, the day after Bench broke Berra's all-time home run record for catchers. Good story, but in *Yogi: It Ain't Over...*" Berra says that the telegram was a "public relations stunt."

"Dr. Zhivago, again. What's the matter with you now?"

—After his wife came back to the hotel where the Mets were staying and mentioned that she had just seen *Dr. Zhivago* for the second time. Almost certainly a joke into which Berra's name has been inserted, it has been widely retold as gospel.

"Don't know, they were wearing a bag over their head."

—When, after seeing his first streaker, he was asked if the person was male or female; quoted by Ron Luciano in *Strike Two*

"Everyone I know drinks Miller Lite. And if they don't I probably don't know them."

—1981 Beer advertisement featuring Berra. One can only assume that this Berraism was written for him.

"He can run anytime he wants. I'm giving him the red light."

—As Yankee manager on the acquisition of Rickey Henderson; quoted in *Sports Illustrated,* March 25, 1985

"He is a big clog in their machine."

—On Ted Williams (although he allegedly also said it about Tony Perez with the Reds)

"He must have made that before he died."

—On a Steve McQueen movie, 1982

"He was a hard out."

—Speaking of the late Jackie Robinson; quoted in the *New York Times*, October 25, 1972

"How did yours come out?"

—After laying down his comic book, to infielder Bobby Brown, later an MD, who was reading *Gray's Anatomy*. If this seems bogus, consider the fact that Brown confirmed the story at a dinner on June 24, 1981, at the annual convention of the Society for American Baseball Research (SABR).

"I don't know if we're the oldest battery, but we're certainly the ugliest."

—When brought back by the Mets to catch for Warren Spahn; widely attributed

"I don't know. I'm not in shape yet."

—When asked his cap size by the clubhouse man when he checked into spring training as a coach for the Houston Astros; quoted in *Baseball Digest*, August 1986

"I don't see how he lost five games during the season."

—On Sandy Koufax during the 1963 World Series. Koufax's regular-season record for the year was 25–5.

"I got a touch of pantomime poisoning."

—Why he couldn't play in a game for Yankee manager Casey Stengel; from a collection of Jimmy Powers *Berraisms* in the November 6, 1957, *Sporting News*

"I love movies—if you like them."

—On his role as critic in the short-lived "Yogi at the Movies" television feature, *Newsweek*, December 14, 1997

"I want to thank you for making this day necessary."

—As hometown fans in St. Louis were throwing a "day" for him in 1947 at Sportsman's Park. He revived the line at his induction into the Baseball Hall of Fame in 1972 (*Sporting News*, August 19, 1972) and again in giving the commencement address to the class of '96 at Montclair State (*USA Today*, May 17, 1996).

"I usually take a two-hour nap, from one o'clock to four."

—When asked what he does the afternoon of a night game; from *The Wit and Wisdom of Yogi Berra* by Phil Pepe

"I wish I had an answer to that because I'm getting tired of answering that question."

—When asked about the sad record of his 1984 Yankees; quoted in *Sports Illustrated*, June 11, 1984

"If the fellow who lost it was poor, I'd return it."

—In response to Casey Stengel's question of what he would do if he found a million dollars. This story was told by Jimmy Powers in 1962 in the *New York News* after this introduction: "Most of the stories attributed to Yogi are the products of the fertile minds of witty correspondents traveling with him. It goes without saying that they are extremely fond of him. Casey himself added to the Berra legend."

"If the people don't want to come out to the park, nobody's going to stop them."

—Explaining declining attendance in Kansas City; SABR Collection

"If the world were perfect, it wouldn't be."

—From *The Yogi Book: I Really Didn't Say Everything I Said*

"If you ain't got a bullpen, you ain't got nothin'."

—As Mets manager as his relievers failed him during the 1975 season, when he was on his way out

"If you can't imitate him, don't copy him."

—When Ron Swoboda told Yogi, then a Mets coach, that he liked to crowd the plate like Frank Robinson; quoted in the August 1969 *Baseball Digest*

"If you come to a fork in the road, take it."

—Berra himself is not sure if he actually said this or not, but according to his statement in *Yogi: It Ain't Over . . .* he is amused by the fact that it is being used and attributed to him in commencement speeches.

"In baseball, you don't know nothing."

—This quotation, which was first collected in the 1970s, has shown up in many places including books by Roger Angell and George Will.

"In one of his salary disputes with George Weiss, Berra contended he would be named the league's most valuable player. 'That isn't official yet,' Weiss said. 'Some of the papers say there were players more valuable than you.' That didn't register with Yogi, who merely shook his head and replied, 'I read only them papers which say I'm the most valuable.'"

—From a collection of Berraisms which appeared in the *Sporting News,* November 6, 1957

"It ain't like football. You can't make up no trick plays."

—When asked in 1964 if he had new plans for the World Series

"It ain't over 'til it's over."

—Talking about the 1973 pennant race, when the Mets were bouncing all over the place and finally won their division by winning 82 games and losing 79. There are many versions of this quote, as there are of other important quotations. One early version has Yogi saying, "It's never over till it's over."

"It could only happen in America."

—On being told about Robert Briscoe, the first Jewish mayor of Dublin, on his first visit to the United States; quoted in Herbert L. Maslin's *Baseball Laughs*

"It gets late early out here."

—While explaining why the sun makes Yankee Stadium's left field difficult to play during day games in October; SABR Collection

"It was hard to have a conversation with anyone, there were so many people talking."

> —On a White House dinner he attended; quoted in *Sports Illustrated,* April 8, 1985

"It's déjà vu all over again."

> —One of his most popular lines, despite the fact that he insists in *Yogi: It Ain't Over . . .* that he didn't say it

"It's so crowded nobody goes there anymore."

> —On Toots Shor's restaurant. In his book of sports quotations, Burt Sugar says that this line originally appeared in a John McNulty short story.

"Little League baseball is a very good thing because it keeps the parents off the streets."

> — *Catcher in the Wry* by Bob Uecker

"Ninety percent of this game is half mental."

> —Explaining baseball; quoted in *Sports Illustrated,* May 14, 1979

"Slump? I ain't in no slump. I just ain't hitting."

> —*Sports Illustrated,* March 17, 1986

"So I'm ugly. So what? I never saw anyone hit with his face."

> —The classic Berraism

"That restaurant served the biggest shrimp I ever saw."

> —When Dave Kaplan, head of the Yogi Berra Museum in Montclair, New Jersey, asked Berra what he remembered of his lunch with Marilyn Monroe and Joe DiMaggio after the two had gotten married; quoted in the *Times-Picayune,* September 2, 1999

"The knee is not for sale. It's going in my museum."

> —Before knee-replacement surgery at age seventy-four; from the *Chicago Sun-Times,* November 18, 1999

"The other teams could make trouble for us if they win."

> —As Yankees manager; widely attributed

"They asked me to take it for a year and see if I liked it. Sometimes I did and sometimes I didn't."

> —After he had managed the Yankees one season, won the pennant, and was fired; quoted by William B. Mead in *The Official Yankee Hater's Handbook*

"Think! How the hell are you gonna think and hit at the same time?"

> —On being told as a young Yankee by Bucky Harris to think about what was being thrown to him as a batter. An early article on Berra in *Sport* ("The Fabulous Yogi Berra") by Ed Fitzgerald shows that Yogi never said this, but it was put in his mouth by a sportswriter. Despite this and denials from Berra, it is still widely attributed to him.

"Third ain't so bad if nothin' is hit to you."

> —On Casey Stengel's experiment using him as a third baseman, *Sport,* June 1960

"This ain't the way to spell my name."

—From the old tale in which it was claimed that Berra was handed a check reading, "Pay to bearer"; widely attributed

Tom Seaver: "Hey, Yogi, what time is it?"
Yogi Berra: "You mean now?"

—From Jon Winokur's *Zen to Go.* Berra himself does not deny that he said this, but the question is whom he said it to. As he put it in *Yogi: It Ain't Over . .* "So many people claim that they have asked me what time it was and I said, 'Do you mean now?' that if I listed them all, this would be a very fat book."

"Wait a minute. These people came all the way from Texas."

—Holding up his party after a banquet in Houston so that he could sign a program for a Dallas couple. This line has been quoted in several issues of *Baseball Digest.*

"We don't throw at .200 hitters!"

—Said in a game between the New York Yankees and the Boston Red Sox during the 1957 season, Jimmy Piersall in the midst of a batting slump, said to Berra, "If you tell that blankety-blank pitcher to throw at me I'll bash your head with this bat—and plead temporary insanity"; quoted in *Baseball Digest,* August 1972

"We have deep depth."

—SABR Collector

"We made too many wrong mistakes."

—His reason for the Yankees losing the 1960 World Series to the Pittsburgh Pirates. George Bush used this quote on various occasions, saying that the nation could ill-afford "wrong mistakes"; from *The Wit and Wisdom of Yogi Berra* by Phil Pepe

"Well, who's in it?"

—On being asked by a reporter if he wanted to go see a dirty movie; quoted by Leonard Koppett in the *Sporting News,* July 18, 1970

"Well, I used to look like this when I was young and now I still do."

—As a Mets coach explaining how he had kept his youthful appearance; the *Sporting News,* July 11, 1970

"We're not exactly hitting the ball off the cover."

—When asked what was the problem with New York Mets hitters

"What for? The only time I ever use it is when I travel."

—In response to the question of why he didn't buy himself a new suitcase; quoted by Bennett Cerf in his *Good for a Laugh*

"When we followed Detroit into a city, we could always tell how Hutch fared. If we got stools in the dressing room, we knew he had won. If we got kindling, we knew he had lost."

—On the late Fred Hutchinson of the Tigers; quoted in *Baseball Digest,* March 1965

"Why buy good luggage? You only use it when you travel."

—An opinion (since changed) that he admits to in *Yogi: It Ain't Over . . .*

"Why, they was as close as Damon and Runyon!"

—Describing two Yankee infielders; quoted in Bennett Cerf's *Life of the Party*

"Yeah, for what paper?"

—On someone's remark that Ernest Hemingway was a "great writer"; widely attributed

"You can observe a lot by watching."

—Explaining why, on being appointed rookie Yankee manager in 1964, he would do well despite a lack of full managerial experience (he had assisted Stengel the previous year). First quoted in the *New York Times*, October 25, 1963. This line has been requoted by people in all walks of life. For instance, when pressed for comments after the 1985 Hall of Fame Game in Cooperstown, then-vice president George Bush said, "As Yogi Berra once said, you can observe a lot by watching. I want to watch."

"You don't look so hot yourself."

—When told by Mary Lindsay, wife of then-New York mayor John Lindsay, that he looked nice and cool. Although some claim that this never happened, Berra says it did.

"You guys make a fine pair."

—On approaching a group of three players; quoted by Alan Truax of the *Houston Chronicle* in *Baseball Digest*, June 1987

"You'd better make it four. I don't think I can eat six pieces."

—When asked if he wanted his pizza cut into four or six pieces; Hall of Fame Collection

"You can't win all of the time. There are guys out there who are better than you."

—"More Yogi-isms," *USA Weekend*, July 8–10, 1988

"You dead yet?"

—Concerned about reports that Whitey Ford had a recurrence of cancer, he asked this question of his former Yankee battery mate when reaching him by phone. "I'm still here," Ford assured him; *New York Times*, May 10, 2000

"You give 100 percent in the first half of the game, and if that isn't enough, in the second half you give what's left."

—As a Yankees coach in 1982

"You guys are trying to stop Musial in fifteen minutes when the National League ain't stopped him in fifteen years."

—His comment on an All-Star pregame meeting designed to analyze strengths of National League batters

"You're never out of it till you're out of it."

—Occasionally uttered version on his "It ain't over . . ." line

"You've got to be careful if you don't know where you're going, because you might not get there."

—SABR Collection

BERRY, ELMER

"Baseball is peculiarly American, in its temperament and psychology. . . . It is our national game not alone because of history and development but by nature and characteristics as well. The game 'fits' Americans; it pleases, satisfies, represents us."

—*The Philosophy of Athletics* (New York: A. S. Barnes, 1930)

BICHETTE, DANTE

"He's the kid who, when he played Little League, all the parents called the president of the league and said, 'Get him out of there. I don't want him to hurt my son.' I had my mom call the National League office to see if she could do it for me."

—As a Rockies outfielder, on Mark McGwire; quoted in the *St. Louis Post-Dispatch*, October 4, 1998

"If I knew I was battling for a job, my whole preparation would have been better."

—Reacting to manager Jimy Williams's decision to bump him from the Red Sox lineup, *Boston Herald*, April 1, 2001

BIGGIO, CRAIG

"He probably hurt it from having to signal 'safe' so many times."

—In a 1981 game as Houston Astros catcher after a shoulder injury forced second-base umpire Mark Hirschbeck to leave a game after the Astros and Pittsburgh Pirates combined for twelve stolen bases

BIITTNER, LARRY

"I'd be hitting about .950 if they'd get rid of the second baseman."

—Onetime Washington Senator on his frequent ground outs and .161 springtime batting average for the Cincinnati Reds, *Washington Star*, April 2, 1981

BJARKMAN, PETER C.

"It seems, indeed, that baseball may well have . . . been fortuitously invented just to remind us of all other things in life. Things like our lost childhoods, and like our endlessly repeated emotional trips through the travails of our own private base paths, in hopeless search for a misplaced route back home. It is a grand game, a thinking man's game, and a thinking woman's game as well. It is a game which surely does not mean half of the things we take it to mean. Then again, it probably means so much more."

—Peter C. Bjarkman, ed., *Baseball and the Game of Ideas: Essays for the Serious Fan* (Delhi, N.Y.: Birch Brook Press, 1993)

BLACK, JOE

blackball,

black book,

black eye,

black Friday,

black hand,

black heart,

blackjack,

black magic,

blackmail,

black market,

black maria,

black mark,

little black sambo,

white lies.

Black is Beautiful.

> —Quoted in Roger Kahn, *The Boys of Summer*
> (New York: Harper & Row, 1971)

BLACKMUN, HARRY

"Professional baseball is a business and it is engaged in interstate commerce—and thus normally subject to federal business law. But it is in a very distinct sense an exception and an anomaly. The aberration is an established one."

> —Supreme Court justice delivering the 5–3 majority opinion that upheld the owners in a suit brought by Cardinal outfielder Curt Flood, 1972

BLAIR, PAUL

"A mystique of history and heritage surrounds the New York Yankees. It's like the old days revived. We're loved and hated, but always in larger doses than any other team. We're the only team in any sport whose name and uniform and insignia are synonymous with their entire sport all over the world. When you're with another team, you have to accept it, but the Yankees mean baseball to more people than all the other teams combined.

"Heck, we draw standing-room-only in spring training."

> —*Washington Post* as a Yankee, June 22, 1978

BLAKELY, MARY KAY

"Spooky things happen in houses densely occupied by adolescent boys. When I checked out a four-inch dent in the living room ceiling one afternoon, even the kid still holding the baseball bat looked genuinely baffled about how he possibly could have done it."

> —*American Mom*, 1994

BLANKENSHIP, CLIFF

"You can't hit what you can't see. I've signed him and he's leaving today."

> —The Washington Senator catcher who in 1908 was sent to Weiser, Idaho, to scout Walter Johnson

BLEDSOE, LUCY JANE

"The crack of the bat against a ball has been my mantra, a sound I hear in desperate moments, at times when I crave total satisfaction, a sound I hear over and over when I want something very badly but can't express what it is."

> —"State of Grace," in Naomi Holoch and Joan Nestle, eds., *Women on Women*, (NewYork: Plume, 1993)

BLEFARY, CURT

"Homers are the root of all evil. You hit a couple and every time up you're looking to hit the ball out. First thing you know, you're in a slump."

—As an Oriole outfielder; widely attributed.

BLITZ, ANDY

"I was sitting on the first-base side of the upper deck at Shea Stadium when a Gooden fastball was hit to deep right field by Barry Larkin. Keith Miller drifted back and picked the ball out of the air and in one fluid motion hurled it toward third. The runner, tagged and ready at second, had to hold.

"It was not the most glamorous or dramatic play in baseball; not one made by a legend, or even an everyday player. It was just a good catch followed by a good throw. I don't know why, but I stood and cheered Miller's play so loud that the fans sitting around me turned and seemed to wonder whether I was watching a different game."

—In Mike Schacht, *Mudville Diaries: A Book of Baseball Memories* (New York: Avon Books, 1996)

BLOMBERG, RON

"With Bobby Bonds in right field and three first basemen, I might as well donate my glove to charity."

—On becoming baseball's first designated hitter; quoted in the *Los Angeles Times,* March 3, 1973

BLOUNT, ROY JR.

"Great demands were not made on Little League outfielders in my time. . . . Nothing throws off the tempo of a game more than a winded and perhaps even tearful outfielder still scrambling, long after the bases have cleared, to retrieve the horsehide from a crowd of slightly smaller children under a jungle gym, as he half-hears distant cries from the game he had been involved in; 'Use another ball. Let's go on without him.'"

—"Baseball in My Blood," in Ron Fimrite, ed., *Birth of a Fan* (New York: Macmillan, 1993)

"In 1951 Marilyn Monroe was a starlet, Bobby Orr a baby, Hubert Humphrey a comer—and Willie Mays very nearly the same phenomenon he was last week. In harsh heat and foggy chill, and under the intense scrutiny such a situation demanded, he chased after his 3,000th hit—and seemed to blossom rather than wilt under the pressure."

—*Sports Illustrated,* July 27, 1970

"The DH is unnatural, like beer with fruit in it."

—*Sports Illustrated,* April 5, 2004

BLUE, VIDA

"Baseball is fine and it's been good to me and my family, but honestly, the only sport that gets me really fired up is football. It's ridiculous to think some club would give me a tryout, but I'll tell you this, if one came along with an invitation, I wouldn't turn it down.

Vida Blue (*San Francisco Giants*)

That's right, I'd walk right out of here and give it my best."

—On his desire to quarterback while pitching for the Athletics; quoted in the *Los Angeles Times,* July 13, 1975

"Finley treated me like a colored boy."

—After negotiating his '72 contract; quoted in *Sport.* In *Vida: His Own Story* he proves he did not just say this in the heat of the moment: "Charlie Finley has soured my stomach for baseball. He treated me like a damn colored boy."

"I just pick it up and throw it. He hit it. They scored. We didn't. That's it. It's over. It's history. OK?"

—Explaining a game to a reporter; from *Vida: His Own Story* by Bill Libby and Vida Blue

"I keep telling myself, don't get cocky. Give your services to the press and the media, be nice to the kids, throw a baseball into the stands once in a while. I've got to be modest about the whole thing."

—On being a celebrity; quoted in *Vida* by Richard Deming

"I think I have already signed some scrap of paper for every man, woman and child in the United States. What do they do with all those scraps of paper with my signature on it?"

—*Vida: His Own Story* by Bill Libby and Vida Blue

"I want to answer all their questions. I guess I just got to hope they don't twist my answers. But it's like giving little pieces of me away each time. If I keep giving pieces of myself away, after a while what will I have left?"

—After an interview, recalled in *Vida: His Own Story*

"If he thinks it's such a great name, why doesn't he call himself True O. Finley?"

—To teammates after Finley was unable to convince Blue that he should be called "True" Blue; quoted in *Vida* by Richard Deming

"I'm tired of seeing my name in big print. I don't like being a bumper sticker. You know, 'If You Drink, Don't Drive,' that kind of stuff: 'Vida Blue is Beautiful!'"

—*Vida: His Own Story*

BLUE, VIDA (CONTINUED)

"It's a weird scene. You win a few baseball games and all of a sudden you're surrounded by reporters and TV men with camera asking you about Vietnam and race relations."

—*Los Angeles Times,* April 14, 1982

"It's easy, man. I just take the ball and throw. Hard! It's a God given talent. No one can teach it to you. They either hit it or they don't. They haven't been hitting it, that's all. No sweat."

—As a rookie in 1971, recalled in *Vida: His Own Story*

"Sometimes in this game it's as good to be lucky as it is to be good."

—*Vida: His Own Story*

"When I'm throwing good, I don't think there's a man in the world who can hit me."

—*Vida: His Own Story.* An earlier version of this famous line appeared in *Time:* "When I'm going good, I don't believe there's a batter who can hit me."

BLUEGE, OSSIE

"You should have been in the old St. Louis ballpark. It was a rat hole, that's what it was. You couldn't leave your shoes or gloves on the floor because rats would come up and chew them up. They had no shower stalls, one pipe in the middle of the room, hot and cold water, but it never got real cold because it was beastly hot in St. Louis. So you got tepid water coming out and still you had to wait in line, it was terrible, just terrible."

—As a Washington Senator

BLYLEVEN, BERT

"When I started to throw the ball back to the pitcher harder than he was throwing to me, we changed positions."

—Why he became a pitcher instead of a catcher

BODDICKER, MIKE

"The whole concept is to know what the guy up at bat is looking for but throw it a different speed than he expects."

—*The Baseball Card Engagement Book,* 1990

BODIE, PING

"I don't know. I never see him. I room with a suitcase."

—When asked what it was like to room with Babe Ruth; quoted in Harold Seymour, *Baseball: The Early Years* (New York and Oxford, U.K.: Oxford U. Press, 1960) and repeated forever after by roommates of players who devote their evenings to courtship

"When you're on the sleeper at night, take your pocketbook and put it in a sock under your pillow. That way, the next morning you won't forget your pocketbook, 'cause you're looking for your sock."

—Advice to New York Yankee rookie George Halas in 1919

Ping Bodie (*Society for American Baseball Research; SABR*)

BOEVER, JOE

"I feel like someone has a voodoo doll of me."

—This line from the Atlanta Brave was picked as "Quote of the Week," *Washington Post,* September 24, 1989

"BOGART, HUMPHREY

"A hot dog at the game beats roast beef at the Ritz."

—Line which he uttered in a commercial made for use in movie theaters in the early 1950s. It appears in the PBS 1989 *American Experience* show *Forever Baseball.* This has been widely quoted incorrectly (including in the first

edition of this book) as "A hot dog at the ball park is better than steak at the Ritz."

"You know, you take your worries to the park and you leave them there."

—From the same series of commercials, which were created at a time when the game's executives feared the newly emerging medium of television would hurt gate receipts

BOGGS, WADE

"Everyone asks me 'why' about everything. I have no idea. I see it. I swing. I hit it."

—On his superior 20/10 eyesight, the *Washington Post,* July 26, 1987

"How did they ever catch a ball back then? Absolutely amazing."

—On a tour of the Baseball Hall of Fame and seeing the gloves of Babe Ruth and Lou Gehrig, *Washington Post,* May 5, 2005

"I hit too many times a year to hit .400. I'd like to hit once a week—like the NFL where you play 16 games. The day I play 120 games in a season is when I'll have a chance to hit .400."

—*Washington Post,* July 26, 1987

BOMBECK, ERMA

"Call me a traditionalist, but there's something not right about going to a baseball game and eating crab soup and a Caesar salad.

"A ballpark hot dog is America. It goes with the crack of the bat, the organ music, and the guys in the dugout who are either spitting something brown and disgusting or blowing bubbles the size of the Hindenburg."

> —"Ballpark: Fast-Fading Bastion of Fast Food," the *Baltimore Sun*, June 28, 1994

"Nearly everyone's son wants to be a baseball player.

"Why not? What other profession could he choose where he can slide around in the dirt, never work when it rains and spit whenever he wants?"

> —"A Mouthful on Baseball's Spitting Image," *Baltimore Sun*, July 15, 1993

BONDS, BARRY

He makes his living running fast and I make mine running slow."

> —The Pirates slugger comparing himself to Carl Lewis and alluding to his home run trot, *Major League Baseball Newsletter*, June 1990

"I knew I hit it. I knew I got it. I was like, phew, finally."

> —On hitting home run 756 on August 7, 2007

"Only air is invincible. Last time I checked, we're not."

> —Explaining a 1999 elbow injury that put him on the disabled list for the second time in his career, *New Orleans Times-Picayune* April 22, 1999

"Their final offer was $70,000. I only wanted $75,000. If they'd given me $75,000, I'd have been gone. They kept saying, 'Your dad only signed for so much.' Hey, this is 1982."

> —The son of former major leaguer Bobby Bonds, on his decision to attend Arizona State instead of signing with the San Francisco Giants, who had selected him in the second round; quoted in *Baseball America*, December 15, 1982

"Walk him."

> —On pitching to Mark McGwire, *St. Louis Post-Dispatch*, October 4, 1998

BONDS, BOBBY

"If you get 200 hits a season, you're going to hit .333 and you'll still have 400 outs. I don't see why you have to run down to first base every time to make an out."

> —As a New York Yankees outfielder, on striking out; widely attributed.

BONILLA, BOBBY

"Kids today are looking for idols, but sometimes they look too far. . . . They don't have to look any farther than their home because those are the people that love you. They are the real heroes."

> —*USA Today*, March 30, 1989

BONURA, ZEKE

"Now I won't be able to sign my letters Senator Henry J. Bonura, Democrat, Louisiana."

> —On being asked why he was so downcast at being traded from lowly Washington to a better club in the National League *Baseball* magazine, August 1948

BOONE, BOB

"Catching is much like managing. Managers don't really win games, but they can lose plenty of them. The same way with catching. If you're doing a quality job, you should be almost anonymous."

> —The Kansas City catcher on catchers; quoted in the 1981 season opener issue of *AstroSports*

Bob Boone (*Kansas City Royals*)

BORDAGARAY, FRENCHY

"The penalty is a little more than I expectorated."

> —After being fined $500 for arguing with and spitting in the face of an umpire; recalled by Joe Falls in the September 1986, *Baseball Digest*

BORSCH, FRED

"On any given day . . . come out to the ballpark and you'll see something different."

> —The sportswriter, 1965, on a flight between San Francisco and Hawaii for a Pacific Coast League game

BOSWELL, THOMAS

"All baseball fans can be divided into two groups: those who come to batting practice and the others. Only those in the first category have much chance of amounting to anything."

> —"Those Who Watch Batting Practice and Those Who Don't," in *How Life Imitates the World Series* (Garden City, N.Y.: Doubleday, 1982)

"An almost inexorable baseball law: A Red Sox ship with a single leak will always find a way to sink. . . . No team is worshiped with such a perverse sense of fatality."

> —SABR Collection

BOSWELL, THOMAS (CONTINUED)

"Any person claiming to be a baseball fan who does not also claim to have invented the quickest, simplest and most complete method of keeping score probably is a fraud."

—From his column in the *Washington Post*, September 23, 1979

"Baseball is not necessarily an obsessive-compulsive disorder, like washing your hands 100 times a day, but it's beginning to seem that way. We're reaching the point where you can be a truly dedicated, state-of-the-art fan or you can have a life. Take your pick.

"These days, long-time baseball lovers face tough questions. 'Do you have to be in a Rotisserie league? Is it mandatory to read the *Elias Baseball Analyst* cover to cover with a highlight pen? If you haven't digested Bill James's latest 598-pager, are you still allowed to express an opinion while in the park?'"

—*Washington Post*, April 13, 1990

"Baseball is really two sports—the Summer Game and the Autumn Game. One is the leisurely pastime of our national mythology. The other is not so gentle."

—*How Life Imitates the World Series*

"Cheating is baseball's oldest profession. No other game is so rich in skullduggery, so suited to it or so proud of it."

—On doctored balls, *Inside Sports*, 1981

"More than any other American sport, baseball creates the magnetic, addictive illusion that it can almost be understood."

—*Inside Sports*, 1980

"Several rules of stadium building should be carved on every owner's forehead. Old, if properly refurbished, is always better than new. Smaller is better than bigger. Open is better than closed. Near beats far. Silent visual effects are better than loud ones. Eye pollution hurts attendance. Inside should look as good as outside. Domed stadiums are criminal."

—*How Life Imitates the World Series*

"The responsibilities of democracy are heavy. Voting, while a privilege, is still more a job than a pleasure. Especially when you're voting for the Baseball Hall of Fame.

"All my life I've enjoyed berating the thousand-or-so dolts who vote for Cooperstown. Now, the shoe is on the other foot. And it pinches."

—*Washington Post*, January 2, 1988. His column on Hall of Fame voting ended with this: "After this, voting for president will be a can of corn."

"This verbal tradition—the way the game has taken on the ambiance of the frontier campfire or the farmer's cracker barrel and moved it into the dugout—is what marks baseball so distinctively, not only among our games but also among all our endeavors. Baseball remains, in the best sense, archaic. This passion for language and the telling detail is what makes baseball the writer's game."

—*Esquire*, May, 1982

"Whoever dreamed that Pete Rose, who's given us such childish pleasure, would now give us such deeply adult pain?"

—*Washington Post*, March 24, 1989

BOUDREAU, LOU

"I'm really humbled by this because I never considered myself a superstar like Williams, DiMaggio, or Aaron."

—On his induction into the Hall of Fame

"This is reaching the top. That's what we all strive for no matter what profession we're in. I feel that my life is fulfilled now."

—On his induction into the Hall of Fame; widely attributed

BOUTON, JIM

4. A baseball feels better in your hand than a football.

Jim Bouton (*Andy Morsund Collection*)

5. Football has that ridiculous "instant replay" where officials up in a booth can overrule the umpires on the field. In baseball, the umpires get plenty of help from players and coaches who run onto the field and explain exactly what happened.
6. Baseball has spring training.
7. Baseball players are smarter than football players. How often do you see a baseball team penalized for having too many players on the field?
15. My wife says there is that sexy moment in baseball when the pitcher and the batter size each other up. She says football is just herds of buffalo running together into head-on collisions for no good reason.

—"Why Baseball Is Better Than Football: 15 Reasons," *Philip Morris Magazine,* Spring 1988

"A clubhouse is not a CIA office. If what happens in a clubhouse gets out, nobody will be shot, no wars will be caused, no one will die, no one will even get sick, except maybe from laughing."

—*I'm Glad You Didn't Take It Personally*

"A lot of long relievers are ashamed to tell their parents what they do. The only nice thing about it is that you get to wear a uniform like everybody else."

—SABR Collection

"All right, you guys, look horny."

—Oft-quoted advice to teammates returning from a long road trip

"Baseball players and their wives are very good packers."

—*Ball Four*

"Batting practice is the time to stand around in the outfield and tell each other stories."

—*Ball Four*

"Being a coach requires only showing up at the ballpark, hollering clichés and being able to play false sorrow when you lose."

—*Ball Four*

"Bowie is the best commissioner in baseball today."

—As a minor-league pitcher, on Bowie Kuhn; quoted in *Sports Illustrated*, July 24, 1978

"Bowie Kuhn is famous for not getting angry or anything."

—*I'm Glad You Didn't Take It Personally*

"Cosell is always lecturing about the absurd over-emphasis on sports in our society and yet nobody gets more excited about week-old football highlights than Cosell."

—*Ball Four Plus Five*

"I always liked to chew when I played ball. When you slide head first, you're liable to swallow a little juice, though."

—*I Managed Good, but Boy Did They Play Bad*

"I guess to really like baseball as a fan you've got to have some Richard Nixon in you."

—*Ball Four*

"I have always thought that baseball was a strange and inefficiently run business, shot through with stupidity, bullheadedness, nepotism and, yes, even dishonesty. The reason baseball calls itself a game, I believe, is that it's too screwed up to be a business."

—*I'm Glad You Didn't Take It Personally*

"It's a boring job. But people who become coaches are not easily bored. You ever see a baby play with a rattle for two hours?"

—*Ball Four*

"I really think that what blew so many minds was that I wrote a book about sports that was funny, irreverent, even grammatical."

—On *Ball Four* in *I'm Glad You Didn't Take It Personally*

"If you had a pill that would guarantee a pitcher 20 wins but might take five years off his life, he'd take it."

—*Ball Four*

"I've been tempted sometimes to say into a microphone that I feel I won tonight because I don't believe in God."

—*Ball Four*

"Looking and acting like a big-leaguer is very important to baseball people. If Jerry Rubin could hit .400, he'd still have trouble making the cut."

—*I Managed Good, but Boy Did They Play Bad*

"Maybe being a minor-league baseball player makes you insane. Maybe you just have to be crazy to be a minor-league baseball player."

—*I'm Glad You Didn't Take It Personally*

"The older they get the better they were when they were younger."

—On old-timers' days, in *Ball Four*

"The trouble with throwing knuckleballs is that 95 out of 100 pitches have to be right. If you get only 85 out of 100, the 15 that miss are going to turn into eight triples, five doubles and a home run or two."

—As a former pitcher, *Los Angeles Times*, June 2, 1971

"There's pettiness in baseball, and meanness and stupidity beyond belief, and everything else bad that you'll find outside of baseball."

—*Ball Four*

"This winter I'm working out every day, throwing at a wall. I'm 11 and 0 against the wall."

—As a former major-league pitcher

"That's the way things go in baseball. You could be North American dum-dum one and if your batting average is over .300, people listen to you like you were Secretary of State."

—*I'm Glad You Didn't Take It Personally*

"To the fierce, ardent leather-lunged professional fan, baseball is life itself, a motive for breathing, the yeast that helps his spirit, as well as his gorge, rise."

—"The Fantasy World of Baseball," *Atlantic Monthly*, April 1964

"What could be better than a Fourth of July doubleheader in Kansas City? Anything up to and including a kick in the ass."

—*Ball Four*

"With a sore arm? No more than a million."

—Asked what he would be drawing in late-1980s pay if he were still pitching. Obtained by baseball historian Robert Smith

"You see losing clubs bicker, and you think maybe if they pulled together they would win. No. That's not it. If they won, they would pull together."

—Dispelling the myth that clubs could "turn around if the players didn't quarrel"; quoted in the book Peter Golenbach's *Dynasty: The New York Yankees 1949–1964* (New York: McGraw Hill, 2000)

"You see, you spend a good piece of your life gripping a baseball, and in the end it turns out that it was the other way around all the time."

—*Ball Four*

"You're only as smart as your ERA."

—*I'm Glad You Didn't Take It Personally*

BOWA, LARRY

"Everybody in the park knows he's going to run and he makes it anyway."

—On Lou Brock; quoted by Edward F. Murphy in the *New York Times*, April 25, 1976

"Kansas City fans don't know how to be mean. They know how to be mean in Philadelphia."

—During the Philadelphia/Kansas City World Series of 1980; widely attributed

BOYD, BRENDAN

"He [Arnold Rothstein] . . . enjoyed dealing on the phone, conning a mark he couldn't even see.

"'With one black telephone, and a pot of heavy Java,' he'd tell dinner guests, 'I could make a running start at taking over the universe.'

"He strutted to his sideboard then and lit himself a stogie. It felt stimulating to be trying something new again, something cheekier, in a sense, than anything he'd ever tried before. He was manipulating an event the whole country cared about, queering it without precedent or sponsorship, from one tiny room in a tiny town in the Adirondacks.

"And nobody knew."

> —*Blue Ruin: A Novel of the 1919 World Series* (New York: W. W. Norton, 1991)

BOYD, DENNIS "OIL CAN"

"I'm cocky, I guess. Yes, I am. . . . Baseball got in me when I was little. It runs in my family, and it rubbed off on me. It's a disease. I'm never gonna get discouraged. Puzzled sometimes, but never down. Never."

> —While pitching at Double-A Bristol; quoted in the July 10, 1982, *All-America Baseball News*

"They keep me pretty much in the dark about everything. If it had blown up, I wouldn't have known anything about it."

> —On not being told about a bomb threat on a flight to Baltimore, *Sports Illustrated*, May 1, 1989

Cletis Boyer (*New York Yankees*)

BOYER, CLETE

"Mickey Mantle is the kind of man we all want to be like."

> —SABR Collection

"The line I'll remember as long as I live about Mantle is the one some writer wrote: 'Mickey Mantle is a celebrity in his own clubhouse.' He was super in everything."

> —At the time of Mantle's retirement; quoted by Clark Nelson of the *Boston Post*

BRADFORD, WILLIAM

"On ye day called Christmasday, ye Govr. caled them out to worke . . . but ye most of this new-company excused them selves and said it wente against their consciences to work on that day. So ye Govr tould them that if they made it mater of conscience, he would spare them till they were better informed. So he led away ye rest and left them; but when they came home at noone from their vorke, he found them in ye streets at play, openly; some pitching ye barr [ball], & some at stoole-ball, and shuch like sports. So he went to them, and took away their implements, and tould them that was against his conscience that they should play and others worke. If they made ye keeping of it a mater of devotion, let them kepe their houses, but ther should be no gameing or revelling in ye streets. Since

which time nothing has been attempted that way, at least openly."

> –Governor of Plymouth Plantation, taking a work crew out on Christmas morning, December 25, 1621. Bradford's *History of Plimouth Plantation,* published in 1898 from the original manuscript.

BRADLEY, OMAR

"Every member of our baseball team at West Point became a general: this proves the value of team sports for the military."

> —The great general; quoted in the *New York Times,* 1937, on the value of baseball to the military

BRAGAN, BOBBY

"Say you were standing with one foot in the oven and one foot in an ice bucket. According to the percentage people, you should be about perfectly comfortable."

> —As Milwaukee Braves manager on the reliance on statistics in baseball

BREADON, SAM

"Robinson is a good player. There may even be three or four other blacks in the country who can play well enough to get a chance in the big leagues."

> —The president of the St. Louis Cardinals at the time Jackie Robinson came up with the Dodgers, to Fred Lieb, who recalled it in *Baseball As I Have Known It*

Omar Bradley (*Library of Congress Prints and Photographs Division*)

BRENLY, BOB

"By the end of the season, I feel like a used car."

—The catcher; quoted in *American Way* magazine, May 14, 1985

BRENNAN, GERALD

"Partial inventory of the ballpark in Baltimore: mitts, balls, spikes, mound, rake, hose, cage, coach, masks, flag, slab, tarp, stubs, box, bucket, bullpen, alley, stirrups, on-deck circle, bags, fence, bench, fungo, plate, towels, shower, sweat, dirt, sky."

—"The Ballpark in Baltimore," in Mike Shannon, ed., *The Best of Spitball, the Literary Baseball Magazine* (New York: Pocket Books, 1988)

BRESLIN, JIMMY

"Baseball isn't statistics, it's Joe DiMaggio rounding second base."

—Quoted by Herb Caen in the *San Francisco Chronicle*, June 3, 1975

"Having Marv Throneberry play for your team is like having Willie Sutton work for your bank."

—SABR Collection. This quote also circulates in variant forms. for instance: "Having Marv Throneberry play for your team is like having Willie Sutton play for your bank."

"The bartender put a couple of fistfuls of ice chunks into a big, thick mixing glass and then proceeded to make a Tom Collins that had so much gin in it that the other people at the bar started to laugh. He served the drink to the Babe just as it was made, right in the mixing glass.

"Ruth said something abut how heavens to Betsy hot he was, and then he picked up the glass and opened his mouth, and there went everything. In one shot he swallowed the drink, the orange slice and the rest of the garbage, and the ice chunks too. He stopped for nothing. There is not a single man I have ever seen in a saloon who does not bring his teeth together a little bit and stop those ice chunks from going in. A man has to have a pipe the size of a trombone to take ice in one shot. But I saw Ruth do it, and whenever somebody tells me about how the Babe used to drink and eat when he was playing ball, I believe every word of it."

—*Can't Anybody Here Play This Game?*

"When you tell the story of this year's American League race . . . you go with a little thing called money, because money gets the job done better than all the pride and guts and whatever it is they talk about when an athlete does well."

—"The Other Check," *New York Herald Tribune*, July 26, 1963

"You see, the Mets are losers, just like nearly everybody else in life. This is a team for the cab driver who gets held up and the guy who loses out on a promotion because he didn't maneuver himself to lunch with the boss enough. It is the team for every guy who has to get out of bed in the morning and go to work for short money on a job he does not like. And it is the team for every woman who looks up ten years later and sees her husband eating dinner in a T-shirt and wonders how the hell she ever

George Brett (*Kansas City Royals*)

let this guy talk her into getting married. The Yankees? Who does well enough to root for them, Laurence Rockefeller?"

—*Can't Anybody Here Play This Game?*

BRETT, GEORGE

"He looks like a greyhound, but he runs like a bus."

> —On Royal third baseman Jamie Quirk; quoted in the September 3, 1971, *Sports Illustrated*

"I am not too serious about anything. I believe you have to enjoy yourself to get the most out of your ability."

> —Quoted in Ron Fimrite, "The Hits Keep Coming," *Sports Illustrated*, October 5, 1992

"If anyone stays away, my response is this: Those people had no right to ever come to the park, because they aren't true baseball fans."

> —On those fans who stayed away from the park after the 1981 player strike; widely attributed

"I've only read two books in my life: *Basketball Sparkplug* and *Love Story*."

> —In response to a reporter's question about his favorite books; quoted in *High Inside: Memoirs of a Baseball Wife* by Danielle Gagnon Torrez

BRETT, KEN

"The worst curse in life is 'unlimited potential.'"

> —The pitcher, 1977

BRICKER, CHARLES

"Being named manager of the Seattle Mariners is like becoming the head chef at McDonald's."

> —SABR Collection

BRIDGES, ROCKY

"An hour after the game you want to go out and play them again."

> —On what it was like to play a Japanese team; quoted by Jim Bouton in *I Managed Good, but Boy Did They Play Bad*

"I didn't try too hard. I was afraid I'd get emotionally involved with the cow."

> —As a minor-league manager, after finishing second in a pregame cow-milking contest

"I got a charge out of seeing Ted Williams hit. Once in a while they let me try and field some of them, which sort of dimmed my enthusiasm."

> —SABR Collection

"I prefer fast food."

> —As manager of the Salem Buccaneers, rejecting a waiter's suggestion of snails. *Sporting News*, July 3, 1989

"If you don't catch the ball, you catch the bus."

> —To an inept defensive player recalled by Yogi Berra in *Yogi: It Ain't Over*

"It's easier to spit on the floor in the clubhouse than in your hotel room or living room. My wife is fussy about those things."

> —*Saturday Evening Post*, June 11, 1960

"It's not to manage in the majors. I'd like to have my name in the *New York Times* Sunday crossword puzzle. That would be the pinnacle."

> —On his greatest ambition, interviewed as manager of the Phoenix Giants

"I've had more numbers on my back than a bingo board. My wife used to write to me care of Ford Frick [the former commissioner]. He was the only one who knew where I was. It's a good thing I stayed in Cincinnati for four years—it took me that long to learn how to spell it."

> —*Sporting News*, December 12, 1970

"I've seen a lot of bad weather in my time, but if Admiral Byrd were here tonight, he'd turn around and go back."

> —On the night of April 16, 1988, at Buffalo, where he managed the Bisons; quoted in the May 9, 1988, issue of the *Sporting News*

"José truly was the player to be named later in the trade."

> —As a Giants coach on shortstop José Gonzalez, who that spring changed his name to Uribe Gonzalez and then decided he wanted to be known as José Uribe; quoted in *USA Today*, April 4, 1985

"Nah. Somebody will think of something and designate it to a spokee to be named later."

> —When asked if he had said all that had been attributed to him; quoted in *Sports Illustrated*, July 3, 1985

"Whoever said that New Mexico is the Land of Enchantment was easily enchanted."

> —Manager, Phoenix Giants; quoted in Edwin Howsam's *Baseball Graffiti*, 1985

"That's for birds to eat. I'm afraid my players might start molting or going to the bathroom on newspapers."

> —As Vancouver manager on players nibbling on sunflower seeds

"The more I played with them, the more I found that no one could take a joke—my batting average."

> —On his two seasons with the Dodgers and his .237 batting average; quoted in *Sports Illustrated*, April 27, 1987

"The players are too serious. They don't have any fun any more. They come to camp with a financial adviser and they read the stock market page before the sport pages. They concern themselves with statistics rather than simply playing the game and enjoying it for what it is. Sure, I've got a job to do, but I also try to give them a little humor. They play better when they relax, and when they play better I can relax."

—Quoted in the *Sporting News,* December 12, 1970

"You mix two jiggers of scotch to one jigger of Metrecal. So far I've lost five pounds and my driver's license."

—On his diet as a minor-league manager; widely attributed

"We have throw-away beer bottles and throw-away pop bottles. Why we even have throw-away baby bottles. It's obvious our society has reached the point of no return."

—Quoted in the *Sporting News,* May 1, 1971

"We may lose again tomorrow, but not with the same guys."

—To a reporter on a minor-league team making a lot of errors; quoted by Yogi Berra in *Yogi: It Ain't Over*

"Well, there are three things that the average man thinks he can do better than anybody else. Build a fire, run a hotel and manage a baseball team. I hope the average man is right in his thinking. But I'm not cocky about my job."

—When asked how he would fare as a manager in the minors, 1963

BRIDGES, TOMMY

"The past is nice. I enjoyed my playing days and the memories are priceless. But you must live in the present."

—"Epitaph" line; quoted in his 1968 *Sporting News* obituary. He died on April 19, 1968.

"Why, Mr. Summers, don't you know the spitter has been outlawed for years? How would I ever learn to throw one?"

—After being accused by plate umpire Bill Summers of throwing spitters; widely quoted

BRIDWELL, AL

"I got along with him fine. He only suspended me once for two weeks. It was on account of I socked him."

—The shortstop tells about his fine relationship with John McGraw of the Giants

"I with I'd never gotten that hit that set off the Merkle incident. I wish I'd struck out . . . It would have been better all around."

—Said in 1966 and requoted in *The Giants of the Polo Grounds* by Noel Hynd

BRIGGS, DR. LYMAN J.

"What makes the ball curve? To answer this question, let us imagine that the spinning ball with its rough seams creates around itself a kind of whirlpool of air, that stays with the ball when it is thrown forward into still air. But the picture is easier to follow if we imagine that the ball is not moving forward, but that the wind is blowing past it. The relative motions are the same. Then on one side of the ball, the motions of the wind and the whirlpool are in the same direction and the whirlpool is speeded up. On the opposite side of the ball, the whirlpool is moving against the wind and is slowed down. Now it is well known from experiments with water flowing through a pipe that has a constriction in it that the pressure in the constriction is actually *less* than in front of or behind it; the velocity is of course higher. Hence on the side of the spinning ball where the velocity of the whirlpool has been increased, the air pressure has been reduced; and on the opposite side, it has been increased. This difference in pressure tends to push the ball sidewise or to make it curve. It moves toward that side of the ball where the wind and the whirlpool are traveling together."

> —The eighty-four-year old director emeritus of the National Bureau of Standards on March 29, 1959. The statement on why baseballs curve was based on two years of research using a gigantic mounted air gun to shoot balls into a paper target.

BRINKMAN, JOE

"They can holler at the uniform all they want, but when they start hollering at the man wearing the uniform, they're going to be in trouble."

> —The umpire; quoted by Ron Luciano in *Strike Two*

BRISSIE, LOU

"Oh, no. You can't take my leg off. I'm going to need it to play baseball."

> —In the army after he was told that his injured left leg would have to be amputated. It was not amputated, and he returned to baseball after more than twenty operations; quoted by Connie Mack in *From Sandlot to Big League: Connie Mack's Baseball Book.*

BRISTOL, DAVE

"A win in April is just as important as a win in September."

> —As Reds manager; widely attributed

BRITT, JIMMY

"I merely said that more than 34,000 people in the stands and the Red Sox players seemed to think it was a beanball."

> —In denying that he had accused Yankee Joe Page of throwing a beanball, May 2, 1948

BROCK, LOU

"He seems to have an obligation to hit."

> —On Pete Rose; quoted by Roger Angell in *Late Innings*

"I don't think about goals and records. Competition is what keeps me playing—the psychological warfare of matching skill against skill and wit against wit. If you're successful in what you do over a period of time, you'll start approaching records, but that's not what you're playing for. You're playing to challenge and be challenged."

> —Quoted in a *Christian Science Monitor* interview, January 20, 1975

"I was probably as big a fan of the event as anyone else there. After all, I'd never seen anybody get three thousand hits, either."

> —On his 3,000th hit; quoted in *Late Seasons* by Roger Angell

"If you aim to steal 30 or 40 bases a year, you do it by surprising the other side. But if your goal is 50 to 100 bases, the element of surprise doesn't matter. You go even though they know you're going to go. Then each steal becomes a contest, matching your skills against theirs."

> —As a Cardinal; quoted in the *Los Angeles Herald-Examiner*, June 13, 1974

"When you steal a base, 99 per cent of the time you steal on a pitcher. You actually never steal on a catcher. In order to be a good base stealer, you must study the mechanics of a pitcher's style—how he delivers it to the hitter. Most important, you have to run when you get your best jump. No, I've never stolen

Lou Brock (*St. Louis Cardinals*)

home and never will. I don't think the percentage is good."

> —Ray Grody in the *Milwaukee Sentinel;* quoted in *Baseball Digest,* February 1969

"You always have to know your purpose in playing. You have to have a premise, and the premise can change. Think about all the money ballplayers are making now. The money is asking for a Superman performance. The player can't reach that level, and he's in anguish. Every error he makes feels worse to him now, because of the money. But you can't be afraid to make errors! You can't be afraid to be naked before the crowd, because no one can ever master the game of baseball, or conquer it. You can only challenge it."

> —*Late Innings* by Roger Angell

BROCK, LOU (CONTINUED)

"Your bat is your life. It's your weapon. You don't want to go into battle with anything that feels less than perfect."

—Quoted in *American Way*, April 29, 1986

BRODERICK, BISHOP EDWIN

"I'm still a Yankee fan and God knows that's a hard thing to be these days."

—1969; widely attributed

BRODKEY, HAROLD

"An American image of the desolation of men, while suggesting a rather sorry moral loneliness, is . . . a baseball team on the field, nine men set widely apart, waiting, galvanized briefly by a ball in play, and then waiting again in the sunlight; widely separate and with their own territories and their own thoughts."

—"Variations on Sex," *New Yorker*, March 21, 1994

BROEG, BOB

"A well-written narrative, not peppered with quotes, can be an excellent change-of-pace."

—Writing in the fall 1982 *National Pastime*

"I look back in amazement now that we ever tolerated a day without the blacks in the big leagues. Looking back, I can't understand how it never struck me as odd that I went through school without ever having a black in class. And I'd competed against just one, who

couldn't hit a curve ball . . . but, then, hell, I couldn't, either."

—Writing in the fall 1982 *National Pastime* as sports editor of the *St. Louis Post-Dispatch* and author of *Super Stars of Baseball* and other sports books

"If cancer hadn't done him in, the Babe certainly would have become ill from the hearts-and-flowers movie based on his life."

—From his *Sporting News* column "Broeg on Baseball"

"1941. That was the season DiMaggio put together the incredible 56-game hitting streak, perhaps the most amazing feat of sustained excellence in baseball history."

—"Broeg on Baseball"

"If Casey Stengel really is dead, which, as he once said, most people his age really are, I'd like to bet his liver still is quivering. His personal filter was so marvelous that he gave us younger guys an inferiority complex as well as a hangover."

— *Sporting News*, November 1, 1975

"Ted hadn't forgotten the cruel coincidence by which the same year he'd become the LAST guy to hit .400, the other guy had become the ONLY fella to hit in 56 straight."

—On Ted Williams and Joe DiMaggio, at baseball's 1969 centennial. As Broeg put it in his column, Joseph Paul DiMaggio was decreed the greatest living player. Ted Williams, then managing in Washington, wasn't at the dinner.

BROOKE, RUPERT

"There is excitement in the game, but little beauty except in the long-limbed pitcher, whose duty it is to hurl the ball rather further than the length of a cricket-pitch, as bewilderingly as possible. In his efforts to combine speed, mystery, and curve, he gets into attitudes of a very novel and fantastic, but quite obvious beauty."

—*Letters from America*

BROSNAN, JIM

"After the batters usurped control of baseball all foreign aids to pitchers were declared illegal. They now must battle bare-handed in the arena, and working on a new pitch takes research and patience."

—*Pennant Race*

"All coaches religiously carry fungo bats in the spring to ward off suggestions that they are not working."

—*The Long Season*

"Ballplayers are notoriously slow getting dressed after a ball game. Between the end of a game and the moment the bus carries us to the hotel, enough time usually elapsed to play another ball game. Or replay the one just ended over several cans of refreshing suds."

—*Pennant Race*

"Beer makes some players happy. Winning ballgames makes some players happy. Cashing checks makes me delirious with joy."

—Quoted by Arnold Hano in "I'm for Me,"
Sport, December 1963

Jim Brosnan (*Author's Collection*)

"Bullpen conversations cover the gambit of male bull sessions. Sex, religion, politics, sex. Full circle. Occasionally, the game—or business—of baseball intrudes."

—*The Long Season*

"Buy a home in the town in which you play, and you'll be traded before your first lawn blows away."

—*The Long Season*

"Candlestick Park is the gross error in the history of major league baseball. Designed, at a corner table in Lefty O'Doul's, a Frisco saloon, by two politicians and an itinerant ditch digger, the ballpark slants toward the bay—in fact, it slides toward the bay and before long will be under water, which is the best place for it."

—*Pennant Race*

"Joe is considered something of a humorist, and, like Mark Twain, is from Missouri. The resemblance is strictly residential."

—On Joe Garagiola, in *The Long Season*

"Nothing is more likely to give a pitcher a positive, confident attitude than eight big ones on his side of the scoreboard."

—*The Long Season*

"Nothing makes a pitcher feel more secure than the sight of his teammates circling the bases during a ball game."

—*Pennant Race*

"One of the seemingly endless attractions of baseball that fans invent is the short work-day, the easy hours. One of the most common gripes of baseball players is the irregular, sometimes intolerable, hours they keep. Somehow the word isn't getting through to someone."

—*The Long Season*

"Otis Douglas played professional football until he was forty-four years old, and his tales of the mayhem and violence that pass for sport on the pro gridiron are enough to make my blood turn and run the other way. He sneers at the plaintive cries of baseball's babied batters who are afraid of a pitched ball."

—*Pennant Race*

"Sundays on which ballplayers rest from their labors are either cold because it's win-ter or miserable because it's raining and the scheduled game, or games, had to be postponed."

—*The Long Season*

"The baseball fan comes in every emotional size and shape. It is not surprising that in Los Angeles, where religious sects of outrageous and neurotic extremes are embarrassingly common, some baseball fans go batty."

—*Pennant Race*

"The human errors of the veteran ballplayers are so readily excused whereas the same errors of a rookie are savagely condemned."

—*The Long Season*

"The lethargy and dull despair that accompany a losing streak can't be dismissed completely except by winning."

—*The Long Season*

"The most grievous fault of a ballplayer is to give a ball game away."

—*The Long Season*

"The only good thing about a cold spring day at the ball park is the pitcher's heart-warming sight of the flag blowing in from center field. Takes a brisk wind to hold today's lively ball inside the park. So, blow nor'easter, blow."

—*Pennant Race*

"When a ballplayer is winning, even his sweat smells good."

—*The Long Season*

"When twenty thousand people applaud as you walk out to do your job, it should be an inspiration."

—*The Long Season*

"You can't win 'em in the clubhouse."

—*The Long Season*

BROUN, HEYWOOD

"His career typifies the heights to which dramatic talent may carry a man in America if only he has the foresight not to go on the stage."

—On Judge Landis; quoted in Harold Seymour's *Baseball: The Golden Age"*

"I suppose it was an important part of McGraw's great capacity for leadership that he would take kids out of the coal mines and out of the wheat fields and make them walk and talk and chatter and play ball with the look of eagles."

—On John McGraw in the *New York World Telegram*

"If Cobb sticks his cap on three hairs, as the Irish say, laughs in the faces of his opponents and steals bases while they stand with the ball in their hands, is he to be damned by the populace?

"With the curious crassity which always leads the mob to rend that hand that feeds it and to lick that which whips it, spectators at baseball games do not like this boy who gives them more for their hard-earned ticket than any man alive or dead ever gave them. When humanity put to death its Greatest Servant, all that he could say in condemnation was 'Father, forgive them, for they know not what they do.'

"That was the biggest and truest thing He

ever said. Humanity, the mob, never knows what it is doing. It always prefers guile and gaud to honesty and worth. No man who ever did anything for it ever got anything but its worst.

"Humanity is asinine."

—"It Seems to Me," *New York Morning Telegraph,* 1910; quoted in Ty Cobb with Al Stump (1961) *My Life in Baseball: The True Record* (Garden City N.Y.: Doubleday, 1961)

"Leo Durocher, whose lectures often made up in energy what they lacked in clarity."

—*Tumultuous Merriment*

"The Ruth is mighty and shall prevail."

—Widely quoted lead to his article in the *New York World* of October 12, 1923, entitled "The Sultan of Swat Steals a World Series Show." Seldom heard is Broun's second sentence, which was, "He did yesterday."

"The tradition of professional baseball always has been agreeably free of chivalry. The rule is, 'Do anything you can get away with.'"

—In the *World* (New York), 1923; quoted by Thomas Boswell in his August 6, 1987, column

BROWN, BOBBY

"It's a good color combination, to say the least."

—The AL president on being told that Bill White had been made National League President

BROWN, CHESTER A.

"Drugs take you further than you want to go, Keep you there longer than you want to stay, And cost you more than you can ever pay."

—As a former Negro League star

BROWN, JOE

"You can't make chicken salad out of chicken shit."

—General manager of Pittsburgh Pirates, 1973; from James T. Wooten, "Rookies" in *Playing Around*, ed., Donald Hall and others.

BROWNING, PETE

"Yeah? What league was he in?"

—Supposed to have been said upon hearing of the assassination of James A. Garfield; quoted in Lee Allen's *The Hot Stove League* (1955); similar quote in Ira L. Smith and H. Allen Smith, *Low and Inside* (1949)

BRUNDAGE, AVERY

"I suspect that if a professional baseball player discovered one day that he could make more money by going back home and laying bricks for a living, he'd go home and lay bricks."

—As Olympic president; widely attributed

BRUNDIDGE, HARRY

"Jesse, a power on the Phillipsburg, Ohio, town team, found it necessary to hide his uniform in a corncrib and on playing days, carry it to a convenient cornfield where he shed his overalls in favor of the wool stockings, spiked shoes and gaudily colored uniform. After the game he would return to the spot to change his clothing again, for Jesse's parents frowned on Sunday baseball."

—On Hall of Famer Jesse Haines in the *St. Louis Star*, June 12, 1929

BUCK, JACK

"It's a beautiful thing to behold with all 36 oars working in unison."

—At a 1981 sports banquet saying how much he admired George Steinbrenner's new yacht

BUCKLEY, WILLIAM F.

"I've never seen a major-league baseball game. I've never seen a professional football game. And that's not an affectation. I just happen never to have seen one."

—Quoted in the *Los Angeles Times*, December 13, 1976. On another occasion he was asked about baseball and replied, "There used to be two leagues, I know that, but now I think there are more, right?"

"To really enjoy the game, you have to study it, follow a team. . . . That's a tremendous investment of time. . . . It's sort of like learning Russian."

—Quoted on Charlie Rose's PBS show, October 1993; quoted in the *Baltimore Sun*, October 15, 1993

BUCKNER, BILL

"It bounced and bounced and then didn't bounce: it just skipped."

—The Red Sox first baseman describing the ground ball that went through his legs and allowed the winning run to score for the New York Mets in Game 6 of the 1986 World Series, "The Year in Quotations," *New York Times*, December 28, 1986

BUFFETT, WARREN

"Investing is like batting in baseball, except that you get as many pitches as you want and you never have to swing. Wait for the home run before investing."

—Billionaire investor, who is a quarter owner of the Omaha Royals, *Sports Illustrated*, June 14, 2004

BULGER, BOZEMAN

"He was possessed by the Furies."

—The *New York World* writer on Ty Cobb

BURDETTE, LEW

"I exploit the greed of all hitters."

—Widely attributed

"If I could get one of the first three hitters in the first inning to go back to the dugout saying I was cheating, by the fifth inning everybody on the team wanted to see the ball when they batted."

—Recalled in Danny Peary, ed., *We Played the Game* (New York: Hyperion, 1994)

"'If I made any motion to my mouth,' he continued, 'they became suspicious. So I'd go through my ritual, going to my hat and then crossing my chest. I got so many Catholic medals and Sacred Heart medals in the mail. I had a whole drawer of mementos which fans sent to me "from one good Catholic to another." I was a Southern Baptist.'"

—From his February 7, 2007, *New York Times* obituary

Lew Burdette (*Author's Collection*)

"Let them think I throw it. That gives me an edge because it's another pitch they have to worry about."

—On the spitter; quoted in *No-Hitter* by Phil Pepe

"They talk as if all you had to do to throw a spitball was to crank up and throw one. Don't they know it's the hardest pitch there is to control? It takes a lot of practice and you don't just throw one when you figure it might get the hitter out.

"I'd love to use it, if I knew how. Burleigh Grimes told me five years ago not to monkey around with it, but to let them think I threw it. That's what I've done."

—*Sporting News*, October 16, 1957

BURKE, MICHAEL

"A baseball club is part of the chemistry of the city. A game isn't just an athletic contest. It's a picnic, a kind of town meeting."

> —As president of the New York Yankees, testifying at a New York City Council committee hearing, March 25, 1971

"We are out to win ball games. We are out to fill Yankee Stadium. We believe we have charted a course for ourselves, both on the field and in the front office, that will do both."

> —The then-president of the Yankees, writing in *Dun's Review,* May 1967. The Yanks finished ninth; quoted by William B. Mead in *The Official Yankee Hater's Handbook*

BURNES, BOB

"Quickest Thinking of the Year. Pulled by Dizzy Dean the day in June when Babe Ruth made a personal appearance at Sportsman's Park. Diz was supposed to pitch to the Babe. Ruth stepped to the plate, but, in his weakened condition, the bat dropped off his shoulder. Sensing danger in the situation, Diz stepped off the mound, strode to the plate and pointed to right field—where the Babe used to clout them. Everybody recognized the gesture immediately."

> —*Sporting News,* October 13, 1948

BURNETT, W. R.

"The true fan is not only violently partisan, but very noisy, and an expert at offering advice to the home team, sometimes in not very polite terms. I used to amuse myself with wondering what would happen if a group of fans of this order would turn up at a tennis match or a golf meet."

> —*The Roar of the Crowd*

BURNS, BRITT

"I think too much on the mound sometimes, and I get brain cramps."

> —As a Chicago White Sox pitcher; quoted in *Grand Slams and Fumbles*

BURNS, GEORGE

"My last miracle was the sixty-nine Mets."

> —Line in the movie *Oh, God!*

BURNS, KEN

"Baseball is about the age-old struggle between labor and management, about the role of women, about popular culture, about how we invent ourselves. . . . This is the narrative of a country, of who we are as a people. But ultimately these broad social [themes] don't stick, don't have enduring meaning unless there's something very emotional about them. That's the key to baseball. Baseball touches our hearts. . . . It's not only about great sociological themes, it's about time and family and memory and home, and besides love, which the game engenders in any true fan, I can't think of any themes more important to Americans. . . .

"This is a story of people and of human drama—of a sport that is so much like life, in its tragic as well as glorious forms, that we get swept into its emotional drama whether we're fans or not. This is a game in which defense has the ball. This is a game that has no clock. This is a game that's incredibly regulated and yet every field is different. This is a game in which the greatest heroes fail 7 times out of 10—much like life. This is a game in which we can play forever—it reminds us of the rhythms of our own life. This is a game that begins in spring and ends in the fall, as our life does."

> —Interview in *Book-of-the-Month Club News*, November 1994

"Baseball tells us who we are; it is a barometer of our country."

> —The filmmaker; quoted in the *Boston Globe*, July 2, 1991

"If the Civil War was America's *Iliad*, a battle defining who we are, then baseball is its *Odyssey*. The object of *The Odyssey* is to come home, and the theme and object of this extraordinary game is to find home—literally and figuratively. I am for union, for home."

> —Quoted in Robert Sullivan, "Visions of Glory," *Life*, September 1994

BURNS, KEN, AND LYNN NOVICK

"Nothing in our daily life offers more of the comfort of continuity, the generational connection of belonging to a vast and complicated American family, the powerful sense of home, the freedom from time's constraints and the great gift of accumulated memory than does our National Pastime."

> —"A Sequel to *The Civil War*," *WETA Magazine*, September 1994

BUSBY, JIM

"Mickey Mantle is the strongest hitter in the game. He's the only one who hits the ball so hard, he knocks the spin off it. Catching a liner from him is like catching a knuckleball. It flutters all over."

> —As a Washington Senator, *Sporting News*, March 30, 1955

BUSBY, STEVE

"Baseball, to me, is still the national pastime because it is a summer game. I feel that almost all Americans are summer people, that summer is what they think of when they think of their childhood. I think it stirs up an incredible emotion within people."

> —As a Kansas City Royals pitcher; from a *Washington Post* interview, July 8, 1974

"You may go a long time without winning, but you never forget that scent."

> —As a Kansas City Royals pitcher

BUSCH, NOEL F.

"Unfortunately for the DiMaggios, the U.S. national game is run according to strictly Fascist lines. Its dictator is Judge Kenesaw Mountain Landis. Solidarity among baseball players is impossible since, in the nature of the sport, rival teams are supposed to hate each other bitterly and any co-operation between them would remove their reason for existence."

> —On the plan of Joe DiMaggio and his brother Tom (a union leader) to have Joe hold out for more than $25,000. The quote appears in *Joshua Then and Now* by Mordecai Richler.

BUSH, BARBARA

"George . . . was a great fielding first baseman. There are lots of jokes about his hitting ability, but the truth is, George hit when the chips were down. I should know—I kept score. He never missed playing in a game the three seasons we were there, and his team won the Eastern Championship for two of the years."

> —*Barbara Bush: A Memoir,* on her husband playing for Yale after World War II

BUSH, GEORGE HERBERT WALKER

"Baseball is just the great American pastime. I try to figure out what it is. I think its the joy of feeling part of [the game] more than other sports—wondering whether the guy is going to walk the hitter on purpose, wondering if the steal sign is on, wondering if he's going to bring in the relief pitcher. The fan somehow feels more a part of the game sitting in the stands. A lot of them are faster moving, but, in baseball, I get caught up in what I'd do if I were managing."

> —Quoted by Tom Boswell in the *Washington Post,* March 31, 1989

"If anyone figures that out, call me."

> —After seeing the movie *Field of Dreams;* quoted in *Newsweek,* May 14, 1990

"I'll bet it's not often that the Oakland A's are honored by an unofficial scout for the Texas Rangers."

> —To the Oakland A's Tony La Russa honoring the world champions, November 7, 1989. The president's oldest son, George W. Bush, was an owner of the Texas franchise.

George H.W. Bush, Yale baseballer, 1948 (*The White House*)

"I was captain of the ball club, so I got to receive him there. He was dying. He was hoarse and could hardly talk. He kind of croaked when they set up the mike by the pitcher's mound. It was tragic. He was hollow. His whole great shape was gaunt and hollowed out. I remember he complimented the Yale ball field. It was like a putting green, it was so beautiful. I don't remember too much more about it."

> —On meeting Babe Ruth in 1948, as captain of the Yale baseball team. Ruth was donating his papers to the university; quoted by Dan Shaughnessy in the *Boston Globe,* October 3, 1989

"It's just got everything."

> —On his fascination with the game; quoted in *USA Today,* October 6, 1989

"Nolan says throw it high because amateurs get out there, no matter how good they are, and throw it into the dirt. You get more of an 'ooooh' [from the crowd] if you heave it over the [catcher's] head instead of going with the fast-breaking deuce into the dirt."

—On advice he got from Nolan Ryan on throwing out the first ball; quoted by Tom Boswell in the *Washington Post*, March 31, 1989

"Normally, they boo politicians at baseball parks; that kind of goes with the territory."

—As vice president; quoted in *USA Today*, April 4, 1986

"Q: The delay of baseball's opening day is imminent. Is there anything that you as the 'First Fan' can do—[laughter]—to bring the sides closer together to prevent a tragic delay of the baseball season?

"A: Yes, I'm a ball fan and I want to go to the opening game someplace. Last year I went to the American League. This year I would like to go to the National League, if possible. I don't know whether it's going to work, maybe going to end up in Baltimore.

"But I want to see—I don't want to intervene. . . . I would simply appeal to both sides to get the matter resolved so the American people can hear that cry, 'Play ball,' again."

—Press conference, March 13, 1990

"The pros tell me that a lot of amateurs go out and they throw it into the dirt even though they have great arms."

—After an Opening Day throw fell short, as president, April 7, 1992

BUSH, GEORGE W.

"Baseball is the style of a Willie Mays or the determination of a Hank Aaron or the endurance of a Mickey Mantle, the discipline of a Carl Yastrzemski, the drive of Eddie Mathews, the reliability of a [Al] Kaline, the grace of a Joe DiMaggio, the kindness of a Harmon Killebrew, and the class of Stan Musial, the courage of a Jackie Robinson, or the heroism of Lou Gehrig."

—At an event at the While House to promote T-ball during which Hank Aaron, Yogi Berra, Ernie Banks, and other Hall of Famers lunched at the White House with the country's baseball fan-in-chief, *Milwaukee Journal Sentinel*, March 31, 2001.

"I got the dish at home now and when I work, I like to keep a game on."

—Quoted on Opening Day in Cincinnati, *Dayton Daily News*, April 4, 2006

"I slipped on a baseball cap, pulled 'er down, as did Condi. We looked like a normal couple."

—On his secrecy-laden trip to Baghdad to have Thanksgiving dinner with U.S. troops; reported in *Time*, December 8, 2003.

"Yogi's been an inspiration to me—not only because of his baseball skills but of course for the enduring mark he left on the English language. Some of the press corps even think he might be my speechwriter."

—In the presence of Yogi Berra at the aforementioned White House event, *Milwaukee Journal Sentinel*, March 31, 2001

BUSH, GUY

"Baseball was an experience you couldn't buy for money. Once you get established as a regular, you couldn't buy that. There's no way in the world I could explain it to you. It teaches you so much and broadens your mind. It makes you feel like you are somebody."

—Widely attributed

"He came up again in the ninth. I was a little mad. I told my catcher, Tommy Padden, he was not good enough to hit my fastball. I came through with a fastball for strike one. I missed with the second. The next pitch I nodded to Tommy. I was going to throw the ball past Mr. Ruth. It was on the outside corner.

"As he went around third, Ruth gave me the hand sign meaning 'to hell with you. He was better than me. He was the best that ever lived.

"That big joker hit it clear out of the ball park for his third home run of the game. It was the longest homer I'd ever seen in baseball."

—Recalling his giving up Babe Ruth's final home run. Despite a 176–136 record, he was primarily remembered for Babe's number 714. This version appeared in Bush's *Sporting News* obituary, which appeared after his death on July 2, 1986.

BUSH, VANNEVAR

"Baseball is like air travel; things move fast for a small part of the time. But they do not move so fast that the fans cannot follow them. And the fans participate vicariously in the strategy involved, more so than in any other sport. This is what keeps them coming and paying for tickets. It is why they learn, and keep up to date on, reams of statistics, many of them faulty or misleading. It is why they are relatively uninterested in any sport of analysis other than their own.

"It is a grand game, even if it could be a lot better, even if its use of statistics is foggy and its management occasionally dumb, even if the sports writers and the broadcasters tell us little about it that they have not repeated a thousand times. It is still a grand game because it exemplifies strategy in the raw, and because it has about it an air of mystery."

—"When Bat Meets Ball," *Science Is Not Enough* (New York: William Morrow, 1967)

"Is baseball a scientific game? It certainly is not. It probably never will be. In fact, if it became fully analyzed, it would probably destroy itself."

—"When Bat Meets Ball"

BUTCHER, JOHN

"I threw about 90 percent fastballs and sliders, 50 percent fastballs, 50 percent sliders. . . . wait, I'm starting to sound like Mickey Rivers."

—After throwing a one-hitter

C

CADORE, LEON

"That's your prerogative, nurse. I never cared much for hospitals, either."

> —Reply to a nurse who said to him on his deathbed, "So you're the famous pitcher. You know, I never cared much for baseball"; related by Fred Lieb in Cadore's *Sporting News* obituary. He died on March 16, 1958.

CADY, STEVE

"The line on Lemon is that the next person to say something bad about him will be the first."

> —On Bob Lemon, in the *New York Times*, July 29, 1978

CAEN, HERB

"Tyrus Raymond Cobb was, many experts believe, the greatest baseball player in history. Maybe this incident explains why. About ten years ago, Ty agreed to play in a sandlot game.

Playing first base for the opposing team was Lewis Lapham, son of the ex-mayor. His first time at bat, Cobb hit a tiny dribbler down third base—and the throw to Lapham had Ty beaten by a full stride. But as he crossed the bag, Cobb hit Lapham's arm so hard Lapham dropped the ball. 'Safe!' yelled the umpire. 'Look, Ty,' grimaced Lewis as Cobb stood grinning on first base, 'Take it easy. This is just a friendly game, y'know.' The grin disappeared from Cobb's face. 'When I play,' he snapped, 'I play to win.'"

> —*San Francisco Chronicle*, ca. 1950

CAHAN, ABRAHAM

"Let your boy play baseball and become excellent in playing the game."

> —Advice to the readers of the *Jewish Daily Forward*; quoted by Harold Seymour in *Baseball: The People's Game*

CALLAHAN, TOM

"A year is just an instant in baseball, but an inning is a long time ago, and before anyone could finish gulping or sighing, the World Series was on."

>—*Time,* October 27, 1986

"Looking as he [Yogi Berra] has always looked, like a taxicab with the doors open . . ."

>—"Saddling Losers," *Time,* May 13, 1985

CAMBRIA, JOE

"Lots of enthusiasm, not much of an arm. Suggest he go into another business."

>—Scouting report on Cuban pitcher Fidel
>Castro; quoted in *Orioles Gazette,* July 30, 1993

CAMERON, MIKE

"Stuff is going to happen sometimes. The sun has been there for 500, 600 years."

>—New York Mets outfielder, said in defense
>of a teammate who lost a fly ball in the sun;
>quoted by George F. Will, in *Newsweek,*
>September 19, 2005

CAMILLI, LOU

"They ought to change our name to the Cleveland Light Company. We don't have anything but utility men."

>—As an Indian; widely quoted

CAMP, WALTER

"Base-ball is for every boy a good, wholesome sport. It brings him out of the close confinement of the schoolroom. It takes the stoop from his shoulders and puts hard honest muscle all over his frame. It rests his eyes, strengthens his lungs, and teaches him self-reliance and courage. Every mother ought to rejoice when her boy says he is on the school or college nine."

>—In his classic nineteenth-century work *The
>Book of American Sports*

CAMPANELLA, ROY

"A baseball hasn't got any sense."

>—Summarizing the game, *New York Times,*
>October 14, 1951

"From the start catching appealed to me as a chance to be in the thick of the game continuously. I never had to be lonely behind the plate where I could talk to the hitters. I also learned that by engaging them in conversation I could sometimes distract them."

>—*It's Good to Be Alive*

"I never want to quit playing ball. They'll have to cut this uniform off me to get me out of it."

>—Quoted in *It Takes Heart* by Mel Allen with
>Frank Graham Jr.

"If life in general was a baseball game in the National or American League, this country wouldn't have these problems today."

>—On integration; widely quoted

Willie Mays, standing with Roy Campanella (*Andy Moresund*)

"My head ain't his bread and butter."

> —In response to Sal Maglie's defense of the beanball: "I gotta throw 'em. Hell, it's my bread and butter"; quoted by Roger Kahn in *Sport*, January 1956.

"Newk, you better do somethin', because when I signal for the express you throws me the local."

> —To Don Newcombe

"Secrecy is the idea behind the signs a catcher gives a pitcher, but a few catchers are so bad at keeping secrets that you can discover what the next pitch is going to be from a seat in the stands."

> —*The Mutual Baseball Almanac*, by Roger Kahn and Al Hoffer, eds., 1954

"They scouted me and were about to sign me. I went into Mr. [Branch] Rickey's office and sat across the table from him. He told me he had scouts watching me for months. There was no question I could play. What he couldn't tell was my habits. Did I drink? Did I run around with women? Would I embarrass the club with my conduct? That's what they had to be sure of before they signed any Negro player."

> —*Bo: Pitching and Wooing* by Maury Allen

"When you're hitting, you hit, and when you're not hitting—well, you just don't hit."

> —Quoted in *Life,* January 8, 1953, and described as Campy's "indisputable theory"

"You have to have a lot of the little boy in you to play baseball for a living."

> —1957; quoted in *Baseball: The Early Years* by Harold Seymour and in many other places. A longer variant: "To be good, you've got to have a lot of little boy in you. When you see Willie Mays and Ted Williams jumping and hopping around the bases after hitting a home run, and the kissing and hugging that goes on at home plate, you realize they have to be little boys." And still another direct quote, from the *New York Journal-American*, April 12, 1957: "You gotta be a man to play baseball for a living but you gotta have a lot of little boy in you." And just one more:

"Pro sports are a tough business—whether you're in baseball, football or something else. But when you're running around the bases after hitting a home run or jumping up and down after a touchdown, a little boy comes to the surface." (*San Francisco Examiner & Chronicle,* February 17, 1974) Regardless of

CAMPANELLA, ROY (CONTINUED)

the version, the "little boy" quote is one of the most popular of the modern era, as it clearly suggests a certain innocence.

CAMPANIS, AL

"He brought new dimension into baseball. He brought stealing back to the days of the twenties whereas up until that time baseball had become a long-ball hitting game."

—On Jackie Robinson, *Sporting News,* September 17, 1947

"I truly believe that they may not have some of the necessities to be, let's say, a field manager, or perhaps a general manager . . . Well, I don't say all of them, buy they certainly are short. How many quarterbacks do you have—how many pitchers do you have—that are black?"

—On African-Americans in baseball as a Dodgers official appearing as a guest on Ted Koppel's "Nightline" in April 1987. The show is a tribute to Jackie Robinson, who broke baseball's color barrier after forty years with the support of Campanis. There are various versions of the exact statement—this one is the one quoted by Tom Callahan in *Time,* April 20, 1987. This statement became one of the most notorious episodes of "typing" in the post-Robinson era, especially coming from a major-league baseball official. The controversy was especially heated when it was pointed out that Campanis had participated in the decision over who would replace Walter Alston as the manager of the Dodgers. It had been a choice between the two coaches at the time,

Tom Lasorda and Jim Gilliam, and raised the question of whether Gilliam had been passed over for racial reasons.

"The hairs on my arms rose."

—On scouting Sandy Koufax, *Time,* September 22, 2002

CANEL, BUCK

"'He wanted to know why Fred Haney used Lew Burdette in the seventh game of the World Series instead of Warren Spahn.'

"It was late in 1958 and I was down there covering the revolution. I knew Castro quite well. One day I had hired a car with four other correspondents and we went up to see him. I was the only one of us who spoke Spanish. We got to Castro and he greeted us warmly and then started jabbering rapidly in Spanish while my colleagues listened intently to see if they could pick up a word. Finally he finished and turned to talk to someone else.

"'What did he say? What did he say?' the other correspondents asked, certain they were on the threshold of a big scoop."

—The Spanish-language sportscaster on his 1958 stay in Cuba, shortly before Fidel Castro became premier; quoted by Maury Allen in *Baseball Digest,* December 1971

CANNON, JIMMY

"A curve ball that doesn't give a damn."

—His oft-quoted definition of a knuckleball

"Baseball, gentlemen, baseball!"

—Said to stop a press-box pro football conversation in the midst of a pennant race; quoted by Stan Isaacs in *Newsday*, April 9, 1990

"Baseball survives because guys like Clemente still play it."

—*New York Journal-American*

"I imagine rooting for the Yankees is like owning a yacht."

—Widely attributed; an alternate is Joe E. Lewis's "Rooting for the Yankees is like rooting for U.S. Steel."

"It is part of our national history that all boys dream of being Babe Ruth before they are anyone else."

—*New York Post;* quoted in *Great Sports Reporting* by Allen Kirschner

"It is the best of all games for me. It frequently escapes from the pattern of sport and assumes the form of a virile ballet. It is purer than any dance because the actions of the players are not governed by music or crowded into a formula by a director. The movement is natural and unrehearsed and controlled only by the unexpected flight of the ball."

—SABR Collection

"'Nice guys must finish last,' Durocher says. If that's the case, the Giants will win the pennant every year he manages them."

—On Leo Durocher moving from the Dodgers to the Giants on July 16, 1948, from the *New York Post* of that date

"Robinson is the loneliest man I have ever seen in sports."

—1947; quoted by Roger Kahn in *The Boys of Summer*. In that year Robinson became the first black to play in the major leagues.

"The cruelty of Cobb's style fascinated the multitudes, but it also alienated them. He played in a climate of hostility, friendless by choice in a violent world he populated with enemies. Other players resented his calculated meanness. Their respect was reluctant but they were forced to present him with the trophy of their crabbed admiration. He was the strangest of all our national sports idols. But not even his disagreeable character could destroy the image of his greatness as a ballplayer. Ty Cobb was the best. That seemed to be all he wanted."

—On Ty Cobb; quoted in the 1989 Fiftieth Anniversary Hall of Fame *Yearbook*.

"The Giants were our team. We left the tourists to the Yankees."

—As a columnist for *New York Journal-American;* quoted in *The Giants of the Polo Grounds* by Noel Hynd

"You're Yogi Berra, who wanted to be like the other guys. Now they want to be like you."

—*New York Journal-American*, January 19, 1955

CANSECO, ESTHER

"Let 'em sweep us. I should have worn a red dress."

> —On the benching of her husband, José, for Game 4 of the 1990 World Series, in which Canseco's A's were swept by the Cincinnati Reds

CANSECO, JOSÉ

"Fans always get on me. It's not a big deal. But tonight was different because it's usually teenagers or middle-aged men who've had a few beers. This was the first time I've ever heard it from a 50- or 60-year-old woman. The funny thing was I told her to shut up and her son or whoever was beside her, screamed, 'José, have some class.'"

> —October 27, 1989, during the World Series; quoted in the *Washington Post*, October 29, 1989

"I was standing in right field. At first I thought it was another of my migraines, but it was just an earthquake."

> —On the 1989 World Series earthquake; quoted by Ira Berkow in the *New York Times*, November 1, 1989

"If I played all of my career in the outfield, I'd have 500 homers and 600 errors."

> —*New Orleans Times-Picayune*, June 11, 1999

"Those people [in the entertainment field] get $20 million, $30 million a movie. But it's all positive because nobody sees their mistakes. After I strike out, I'd like to be able to say, 'cut, try that again.'"

> —Seeking to put his wealth in perspective after signing a five-year, $23.5 million contract that made him baseball's highest-paid player, in *USA Today*, July 11, 1990

CANTWELL, MARY

"To me [Ted] Williams was human only when he opened his mouth and confirmed—again and again—my conviction that idols should seldom, if ever, speak."

> —"Hating Doris," in Ron Fimrite, ed., *Birth of a Fan* (New York: Macmillan, 1993)

CAPOTE, TRUMAN

"They're going to win a pennant or something. That's nice."

> —On the 1969 Mets; quoted in *The Incredible Mets* by Maury Allen

CARAY, HARRY

"Aw, how could he lose the ball in the sun. He's from Mexico."

> —On Jorge Orta; quoted in *Sox: From Lane and Fain to Zisk and Fisk* by Bob Vanderberg

"It might be, it could be, it is . . . Harry Caray."

> —What he claimed an eyewitness said when he was hit by a car and knocked into the air in 1968, *St. Louis Post-Dispatch*, February 19, 1998

"It's the fans that need spring training. You gotta get 'em interested. Wake 'em up. Let 'em know that their season is coming, the good times are gonna roll."

> —Hall of Fame Collection

Harry Caray interviews President Reagan, 1988 (*Ronald Reagan Library*)

"Oh, I get a little tired now and then, but knowing my lifestyle, that's only natural."

> —On his 1987 stroke; quoted in the *Sporting News*, February 13, 1989

"This has been the remarkable thing about the fans in Chicago. They keep drawing an average of a million-three a year. And when the season's over and they've won their usual 71 games, you feel that those fans deserve a medal."

> —*Sox: From Lane and Fain to Zisk and Fisk* by Bob Vanderberg

CAREW, ROD

"Hitting is an art, but not an exact science."

> —*Heavy Hitters: Lynn, Parker, Carew, Rose* by Bill Gutman

"I get a kick out of watching a team defense me. A player moves two steps in one direction and I hit it two steps the other way. It goes right by his glove. And I laugh."

> —*New York Daily News*, July 25, 1979

CARLIN, GEORGE

"In football the object is to march into enemy territory and cross his goal. In baseball the object is to go home."

> —Hall of Fame Collection; from his famous comparison of the two sports.

CARLTON, STEVE

"If I was assured that there might be a job out there, I'd continue to throw. Because I love it. It's what I'm good at. It's what I like to do. But nobody's really calling. . . .

"I know I can still pitch. I know I still have the ability to win. But you can't make them take you."

> —Quoted by Paul Domowitz of Knight-Ridder in the *Lewiston* (Maine) *Daily Sun*, July 16, 1988, at the end of Carlton's career

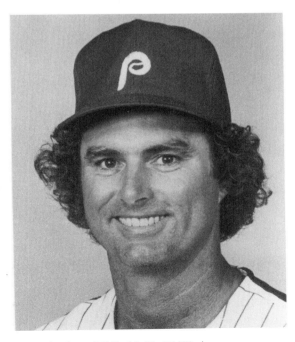

Steve Carlton (*Philadelphia Phillies*)

CARPENTER, RULY

"I'm going to write a book: *How to Make a Small Fortune in Baseball*—you start with a large fortune."

— As president and owner of the Phillies

CARROLL, CLAY

"[Baseball is] a hitter's game. They have pitchers because somebody has to go out there and throw the ball up to the plate."

— As Reds pitcher; widely quoted

CARSON, JOHNNY

"If the World series goes seven games, it will be NBC's longest-running show this fall."

— On NBC's poor ratings; quoted in *Sports Illustrated*, October 23, 1978

"The champagne they have stored is getting more valuable every year."

— On the inability of the California Angels to win the World Series

"There are close to 11 million unemployed and half of them are New York Yankee managers."

— *Sports Illustrated*, August 23, 1982

CARTER, GARY

"If the Expos come up with an offer I can't refuse, I wouldn't turn it down."

— Widely quoted

Gary Carter (*Montreal Expos*)

"That has to be the greatest game that ever lived."

— On the Mets' thrilling sixteen-inning, 7–6 win over the Astros for the 1986 National League pennant; widely attributed

CARTER, JIMMY

"I personally don't think that frequent playing for the national anthem down plays its importance. No matter how often I hear the national anthem, I'm always stirred within myself toward more intense feelings of patriotism and a realization of what our nation stands for. And I think for audiences at sports events to hear the national anthem played is

Softballer Jimmy Carter (*Jimmy Carter Library*)

good and not contrary to the influence that the national anthem has on all of us."

—Presidential news conference, December 12, 1978

"I was on the varsity basketball team in high school and, when I was in submarines, I was the pitcher of our baseball team. I learned there, obviously, that you have to be mutually dependent to achieve an identifiable goal, and you have to learn how to accept either defeat or victory with some degree of equanimity and look to the next contest with hope and anticipation, I think you have to yield sometimes your own selfish aspirations for the common good and be able to deal with one another in an open, sometimes competitive way, but not a personally antagonistic

way. I think those are some of the lessons that you learn from team sports an I hope that I remember them."

—As Democratic presidential nominee; quoted in the *Los Angeles Times*, August 24, 1976

CARTER, JOE

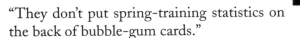

"They don't put spring-training statistics on the back of bubble-gum cards."

—The Blue Jays slugger on getting just one extra-base hit in 59 spring training at bats, *St. Louis Post-Dispatch*, April 21, 1993

CARTWRIGHT, ALEXANDER

"Let him hit it, you've got fielders behind you."

—Attributed to the baseball pioneer as an 1846 quotation by Bob Chieger in *Voices of Baseball*

"During the past week we have passed the

Alexander Cartwright (*National Baseball Library*)

CARTWRIGHT, ALEXANDER
(CONTINUED)

time in fixing wagon-covers, stowing property, etc., varied by hunting and fishing and playing base ball. It is comical to see mountain men and Indians playing the new game. I have the ball with me that we used back home [New York]."

—On his way to the goldfields in California, from a diary entry of April 23, 1849, from Independence, Missouri, and quoted by Harvey Frommer in *Primitive Baseball*

CARTY, RICO

"They say you have to be good to be lucky, but I think you have to be lucky to be good."

—As a Braves outfielder; widely quoted

CASE, GEORGE

"If I get hit on the knee, head or side with any more pitches, I'll begin to think that batting .370 isn't worth it."

—*The Sporting News Chronicle of 20th Century Sport*

"I'm licked when that pitcher takes the ball to his chest and just holds it there, just staring at you. You're tense out there on your toes, and this drains you and kills your speed. Not all pitchers know that, though."

—The former Washington Senator and dazzling base stealer on testing the pitcher

Norm Cash (*Author's Collection*)

CASH, NORM

"Pro-rated at 500 at-bats a year that means that for two years out of the fourteen I played, I never even touched the ball."

—Reflecting on his 1,081 strikeouts as a Tiger first baseman

"The only mistake I made in my whole baseball career was hitting .361 that one year, because ever since then people have expected me to keep on doing it."

—On his 1961 season; quoted by Bill Freehan in *Behind the Mask.*

CASHEN, FRANK

"The way I see it, the first thing you want in a catcher is ability to handle the pitchers. Then you want defensive skill, and, of course, the good arm. Last of all, if he can hit with power, well, then you've got a Johnny Bench. Very few good teams that win year after year have done so without a top catcher."

—As Orioles general manager; quoted in the *New York Times,* March 9, 1975

"Never in the history of baseball have so many refused to play for so much."

—As a Baltimore Orioles executive bewildered by the number of holdouts just prior to spring training in 1972

"You always dream of trading for the perfect player. But you can't, because if an excellent player isn't scarred in some way, you don't get a chance to trade for them."

—As Met general manager; quoted in the *Washington Post,* March 17, 1982

CATTON, BRUCE

"Say this much for big league baseball—it is beyond any question the greatest conversation piece ever invented in America."

—"Book Week," *New York Herald Tribune,* April 12, 1964

"The neat green field looks greener and cleaner under the lights, the moving players are silhouetted more sharply, and the enduring visual fascination of the game—the immobile pattern of nine men, grouped according to ancient formula and then, suddenly, to the sound of a wooden bat whacking a round ball, breaking into swift ritualized movement, movement so standardized that even the tyro in the bleachers can tell when someone goes off in the wrong direction—this is as it was in the old days. A gaffer from the era of William McKinley, abruptly brought back to the second half of the twentieth century, would find very little in modern life that would not seem new, strange, and rather bewildering, but put in a good grandstand seat back of first base he would see nothing that was not completely familiar."

—"The Great American Game," *American Heritage,* April, 1959

CAUSEY, WAYNE

"First guy in checks the dugout for alligators."

—As a Kansas City A's shortstop, on owner Charlie Finley's promotional animals; widely quoted

CAVARRETTA, PHIL

"After he hits a homer, he comes back to the bench looking as if he did something wrong."

—On Ernie Banks, as his first manager; widely attributed

CEPEDA, ORLANDO

"[Baseball manager] Alvin Dark is a baseball genius, but he can't communicate with his players. That's why he gets fired every time. But [manager] Billy Martin—he feels like a ballplayer himself. That's why he's such a good manager. So many managers forget they were players themselves. To respect your ballplayers is the main thing. The problem of managing is human relations."

—As a manager in Puerto Rico; quoted in the *Los Angeles Times,* April 9, 1978

"Once he threw me a spitter at first base to pick off a runner. The ball sank a foot and I dropped it. When I threw it back to him it was still wet and sank again. The runners advanced a base and I got an error!"

—On Gaylord Perry, from the jacket copy of Perry's *Me and the Spitter*

CEY, RON

"There are a lot of egotistical people in baseball, and I understand and totally accept and tolerate them. But that doesn't mean I have to like them. If I had to do it over again and say I was the best, I couldn't. That's not me. It would be a waste of my time. I have never solicited publicity."

—*Los Angeles Times,* July 19, 1977

CHABOT, DAN

"Lemmings head for the sea. The swallows come back to Capistrano. The buzzards somehow find their way to Hinckley, Ohio. The geese follow their instincts south. And baseball fans go to Cooperstown and the National Baseball Hall of Fame and Museum."

—As writer for the *Milwaukee Journal;* quoted in the 1989 50th Anniversary Baseball Hall of Fame *Yearbook*

CHADWICK, HENRY

"[Baseball] requires the possession of muscular strength, great agility, quickness of eye, readiness of hand, and many other faculties of mind and body that mark a man of nerve. . . . Suffice it to say that it is a recreation that anyone may be proud to excel in, as in order to do so, he must possess the characteristics of true manhood to a considerable degree."

—*Beadle's Dime Base-Ball Player,* New York, 1860

Henry Chadwick (*National Baseball Library*)

"Long hits are showy, but they do not pay in the long run. Sharp grounders insuring the first-base certain and sometimes the second-base easily, are worth all the hits made for home-runs."

—1868

CHAMBLISS, AUDREY

"We have no way to release our pent-up emotions. The men on the field can run and curse. We have to sit here and grin."

—The wife of Chris Chambliss on being a baseball wife; quoted in *High Inside: Memoirs of a Baseball Wife* by Danielle Gagnon Torrez; from a *New York Times* article

CHANCE, DEAN

"One day you can throw tomatoes through brick walls. The next day you can't dent a pane of glass with a rock. It hurts but you hang on hoping it'll come back. Oh, well, it's a helluva ride, the one on the way up."

—Quoted in *Vida: His Own Story* by Bill Libby and Vida Blue

"When we got caught out at five o'clock in the morning with those crazy broads, Bo took all the blame. He said, 'The kid here had nothing to do with it.' That's what I call a friend."

—On Bo Belinsky in *Bo: Pitching and Wooing* by Maury Allen

CHANDLER, HAPPY

"Baseball owners are the toughest set of ignoramuses anyone could ever come up against.

Dean Chance (*California Angels*)

Refreshingly dumb fellows. Greedy, short-sighted and stupid."

— *Sports Illustrated*, September 21, 1992; quote from 1951, after Chandler was removed as baseball commissioner

CHAPMAN, RAY

"John, for God's sake, don't call Kate. But if you do, tell her I'm all right."

—Cleveland Indians shortstop to friend John Henry, after being struck by a pitch thrown by New York Yankee Carl Mays, in the Polo Grounds, New Yok, August 16, 1920, before lapsing into unconsciousness at St. Lawrence Hospital (Kate was his wife); he died the following morning; quoted in Mike Sowell, *The Pitch that Killed* (New York: Macmillan, 1989)

CHAPMAN, RAY (CONTINUED)

"You can have it. It wouldn't do me any good."

> —To umpire Billy Evans after leaving the batter's box after taking two strikes from Walter Johnson in 1920. As he headed toward the dugout, Evans had informed Chapman that he still had another strike coming. Later in the season Chapman was killed by Carl Mays's fastball; quoted by Rich Marazzi in *The Rules and Love of Baseball.*

CHARLES, ED

"I was thirteen years old and Jackie Robinson came to town to play an exhibition with the Dodgers. All the black folks in town turned out to see him. The old people, who could hardly walk, paraded down the main street with their heads high and the kids were dancing and a few people were being taken to the game in wheelchairs and even some blind people and the very sick. Nobody wanted to miss it. And I sat up there in the bleachers watching him and saying that would be me someday and when the train with the Dodgers pulled out, Jackie stood on the back platform like a political campaigner waving and smiling and making everybody feel good. I followed that train all the way down those tracks as far as I could run until the sound was gone and the tracks didn't rattle any more."

> —On the day he decided to become a ballplayer; quoted in *The Incredible Mets* by Maury Allen

"I'm sure, I'm positive, I know there were people who changed their lives because of the Miracle Mets. People felt better. It was a good thing."

> —As former Met infielder, on the 1969 Miracle Mets; widely attributed

CHARLES, RAY

"You know who I'd really like to meet? Vin Scully. Because to me, the picture doesn't mean anything. It's all about the sound. And his broadcast is almost musical. Would you introduce me to Vin?"

> —To Bob Costas, recalled at the time of Charles's death in the *Boston Globe,* November 25, 2003

CHASE, HAL

"I am an outcast and I haven't a good name. I'm the loser just like all gamblers are. I lived to make great plays. What did I gain? Nothing. Everything was lost because I raised hell after hours. I was a wise guy, a know-it-all, I guess."

> —On his deathbed, 1947; quoted in Neal McCabe and Constance McCabe *Baseball's Golden Age: The Photographs of Charles M. Gordon* (New York: Harry N. Abrams, 1993)

CHEEVER, JOHN

"All literary men are Red Sox fans. To be a Yankee fan in literary society is to endanger your life."

> —Born in Massachusetts, Cheever lived most of his life in New York. This quotation has been used by many, including Stephen King who has

added, "All literary men are *not* baseball fans."
As he told *USA Today* on October 10, 2004, he
agrees that most writers who like baseball like
the Red Sox: "Maybe, because they know in
their hearts that books are lost causes?"

"The poet or storyteller who feels that he is
competing with a superb double play in the
World Series is a lost man. One would not
want as a reader a man who did not appreciate the finesse of a double play."

—"In Praise of Readers," 1980

"To be an American and unable to play baseball is comparable to being a Polynesian and
unable to swim."

—The baseball-phobic protagonist of "The
National Pastime," a Cheever short story,
which appeared in *The New Yorker*, September
28, 1953, about a son's struggle to mature in
the face of baseball disasters. His first job, for
example, comes to an abrupt end when at the
annual baseball game he is forced to play and
runs the wrong way, knocking down a runner
coming in to score. He had assumed that a
"baseball diamond, like most things, must
operate on a clockwise principle."

CHISHOLM, SHIRLEY

"It is not heroin or cocaine that makes one an
addict, it is the need to escape from a harsh
reality. There are more television addicts, more
baseball and football addicts, more movie
addicts, and certainly more alcohol addicts in
this country than there are narcotics addicts."

—As a congresswoman, testimony, September 17,
1969, to House Select Committee on Crime

CHYLAK, NESTOR

"Ball players will cheat under any circumstances
if they think they can get away with it. That's
why we're out there. Our job is to prevent it.

"Only the best guys can cheat. Bang, bang
they're gone. Those slow clods can't cheat.
You can spot them dashing for the base from
the stands."

—*Sport,* January 1965

"This must be the only job in America that
everybody knows how to do better than the
guy who's doing it. Sometimes I have this
fantasy: The manager's been popping off all
day and his team's just blown a big lead. I call
time and walk over to the dugout and say very
politely, 'Excuse me, sir. Your second-base-
man just booted one with the bases loaded.'"

—*Los Angeles Times,* April 22, 1978

CICOTTE, EDDIE

"I done it for the wife and kiddies."

—On his career-ending consort with gamblers

"I have played a crooked game and I have
lost."

—As one of the defamed "Black Sox," 1920

CLARK, AL

"I refuse to call a fifty-two-year-old man
Sparky."

—The American League umpire when asked why
he called the Tiger manager "George Anderson,"
1986. In 1981, Clark was quoted saying, "I refuse
to call a forty-seven-year-old man Sparky."

CLARK, JACK

"Being booed in New York or St. Louis is not like getting it here. The fans here just go, "Boo, Dude!"

> —On playing for San Diego; quoted in *The Sporting News Chronicle of 20th Century Sport*

"I feel like I'm on top of the mental aspect, I'm throwing to the right places, running the bases better, I know how many outs there are."

> —As a five-year veteran of the San Francisco Giants; quoted in the *San Francisco Chronicle,* May 1980

CLARK, WILL

"I knew something was wrong when the ground was moving faster than I was."

> —On the 1989 World Series earthquake; widely attributed

"When it first happened, I thought it was fans rocking the stadium. I didn't immediately catch the magnitude of it. It really put baseball in perspective. We're not as worried as much about baseball as about people's health and their property. We'll worry about baseball in time."

> —On the 1989 Loma Prieta earthquake, which took place during the World Series

CLARY, ELLIS

"Baseball isn't keeping up with science. Satellites are sending accurate signals from outer space to earth, but coaches still have trouble transmitting signals from third base to home."

> —As former Washington Senators third-base coach, *Baseball Digest,* February 1961

CLEAVER, ELDRIDGE

"In Soledad state prison, I fell in with a group of young blacks, who, like myself, were in vociferous rebellion against what we perceived as a continuation of slavery on a higher plane.

"We cursed everything American—including baseball and hotdogs."

> —*Soul on Ice*

CLEMENS, ROGER

"I think the only thing I look back on with regret is that I didn't pitch in the seventh game. I was ready to pitch."

> —On the fabled game 6 of the 1986 World Series; quoted by Peter Gammons in *Rocket Man*

Roger Clemens (*Boston Red Sox*)

CLEMENT, AMANDA

"If women were umpiring none of this [row-dyism] would happen. Do you suppose any ball player in the country would step up to a good-looking girl and say to her, 'You color-blind, pickle-brained, cross-eyed idiot, if you don't stop throwing the soup into me I'll distribute your features all over your countenance!' Of course he wouldn't."

> —Said in 1907; quoted in *Women in Baseball* by Gai Ingham Berlage (1994). Clement, the "first official woman umpire in men's baseball," worked for semiprofessional teams "from about 1905 through 1911."

CLEMENTE, ROBERTO

"I want to be remembered as a ballplayer who gave all he had to give."

> —The line became the Pirate outfielder's epitaph after he was killed in a plane crash in a disaster-relief effort in 1973

"If you have an opportunity to make things better, and you don't do that, you are wasting your time on this earth."

> —Spoken at a banquet in Houston in 1971; quoted in Steve Wulf, "Roberto Clemente," *Sports Illustrated*, September 19, 1994

CLEVELAND, GROVER

"How's my old friend, Jimmy Galvin? You know, he and I were good friends when I was a sheriff and mayor of Buffalo."

> —On meeting Cap Anson at the White House; quoted by Lee Allen in *Cooperstown Corner*

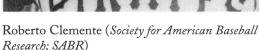

Roberto Clemente (*Society for American Baseball Research; SABR*)

"What do you imagine the American people would think of me if I wasted my time going to the ballgame."

> —On being asked to an 1886 game by Anson and Washington manager Mike Scanlon

CLINTON, HILLARY RODHAM

"Being a Cubs fan prepares you for life—and Washington."

> —*Newsweek*, April 18, 1994

CLINTON, WILLIAM J.

"I identify with Babe Ruth. He was a little overweight and he struck out a lot. But he hit a lot of home runs because he went to bat."

> —Expressing hope that a baseball strike could be ended by the hundredth anniversary of Babe Ruth's birth, *US News & World Report*, February 6, 1995

COBB, IRVIN S.

"As I understand it, sport is hard work for which you do not get paid."

> — "Sports and Pastimes," *Saturday Evening Post*, 1912

COBB, TY

"A ball bat is a wondrous weapon."

> —Widely attributed

"Baseball was one hundred per cent of my life."

> —*The Tumult and the Shouting* by Grantland Rice

"Every great batter works on the theory that the pitcher is more afraid of him than he is of the pitcher."

> —*The Tiger Wore Spikes* by John McCallum, 1956

"Golf is older than baseball and changes have made it a better game. The same is true of football, basketball and other sports. Why should baseball be sacred and untouchable?"

> —On improving baseball. Among other reforms, he favored widening home plate by a couple of inches to give pitchers a better chance. He believed it would make the game more interesting, faster, and more exciting; quoted in the August 7, 1961, *Sporting News*

"I am now 68 years old. I still resent the charge of brutal and intentional spiking. This incident, remember, happened in 1909. This is 1955, and to this day, in meeting some young boy interested in baseball and whose father I might have met, I have been told: 'Oh, you're the man who spiked Baker.'"

> —*Sporting News*, 1955, on the supposed spiking of Home Run Baker

"I fell back on Polonius, when in *Hamlet* he advises Laertes: 'Beware of entrance to a quarrel; but being in, bear't, that the opposed may beware of thee.' No better guide for a ballplayer ever was written."

> —Ty Cobb, with Al Stump, *My Life in Baseball: The True Record* (Garden City, N.Y.: Doubleday, 1961)

"I had to fight all my life to survive. They were all against me . . . but I beat the bastards and left them in the ditch."

> —Quoted in *Baseball: The Early Years* by Harold Seymour

"I have often wished that when I was at the peak of my playing skill in my late twenties or early thirties, I had had another crack at a World Series. I'm sure I would have done better. But that chance never came to me."

> —Quoted in *Baseball As I Have Known It* by Fred Lieb

"I may have been fierce, but never low or underhand."

> —*Baseball: An Informal History* by Douglas Wallop

"I never have slept under the same roof with a nigger, and I'm not going to start here in my own native state of Georgia."

> —On sleeping in the same hunting lodge with Babe Ruth, whom he and some others believed to be part black; quoted in *Baseball As I Have Known It* by Fred Lieb

"I only recall intentionally spiking one man in twenty-four years. He was Frank Baker, who was squarely in the path in a Philadelphia game. . . . There was no other way to reach the base. From the start, I concentrated on a new form of sliding. This was to send my toe for the bag. I only gave them my toe to tag! It was exactly the opposite of crashing in hurling spikes or body at the baseman. I don't know how many hours I worked on my type of sliding—a slide that avoided the tagger. Why, I couldn't have been a rough base runner under my system even if I'd wanted to."

> —Quoted in *The Tumult and the Shouting* by Grantland Rice

"I regret to this day that I never went to college. I feel I should have been a doctor."

> —Widely attributed

"I think if I had my life to live over again, I would do things a little different. I was aggressive, perhaps too aggressive, maybe I went too far. I always had to be right in any argument I was in, and wanted to be first in everything."

> —To comic Joe E. Brown, as reported in *Baseball As I Have Known It* by Fred Lieb. Cobb, near the end of his life, returned to Brown a few days later and said, "Joe, I do indeed think I would have done some things different. And if I had, I would have had more friends."

"I'm coming down on the next pitch, Krauthead."

> —Shouted to shortstop Honus Wagner in the 1909 World Series between the Tigers and Pirates. He did, and Wagner hit him in the mouth, cutting his lip and knocking out two teeth.

"Learn the fundamentals.
Study and work at the game as if it were a science.
Keep in top physical condition.
Make yourself as effective as possible.
Get the desire to win.
Keeping in the best physical condition and having an intense spirit to succeed is the combination for winning games."

> —His "Six Keys to Baseball Success"; quoted in the *Sporting News*, February 20, 1957

"'Many players are thrown out by a split second. When you hit the ball, run it out with all the speed you have, not matter where or how you hit it,' Cobb advised young players. 'This, I claim, will earn you many hits during the season that you would not get otherwise.'"

—Quoted in the *Sporting News,* June 28, 1950

"Somebody will hit .400 again. Somebody will get smart and swing naturally."

—In 1960; quoted in *Heavy Hitters: Lynn, Parker, Carew, Rose* by Bill Gutman

"Speed is a great asset; but it's greater when it's combined with quickness—and there's a big difference."

—Quoted in *The Tumult and the Shouting* by Grantland Rice

"The great American game should be an unrelenting war of nerves."

—Widely quoted Cobb credo, appearing in such places as Bill Gutman's *Giants of Baseball*

"The great trouble with baseball today is that most of the players are in the game for the money that's in it—not for the love of it, the excitement of it and the thrill of it."

—SABR Colletion, 1925

"The longer I live, the longer I realize that batting is more a mental matter than it is physical. The ability to grasp the bat, swing at the proper time, take a proper stance, all these are elemental. Batting rather is a study in psychology, a sizing up of pitcher and catcher, and observing little details that are of immense importance. It's like the study of crime, the work of a detective as he picks up clues."

—*Sporting News,* June 28, 1950

"The present-day boys lack the fighting dedication to the game that was entirely commonplace in my day.

"The men I jousted with in the early years were a strange breed that the United States of America never will see again—as long gone from the scene as the sodbuster, the hide-skinner, the riverboat gambler, and the map makers of the Old West. To them, baseball was a whole way of life, their reason for existence—not a means to another monetary end. They were poor boys from farms and villages, burning with ambition, who studied, practiced, threw themselves into games without thought of injury and who suffered rigors without complaint that would send a modern pro crying to the Players Association for relief."

—Ty Cobb, with Al Stump, *My Life in Baseball: The True Record* (Garden City N.Y.: Doubleday, 1961)

"The screwball will ruin your arm. You'd better forget it."

—What he said to a young pitcher named Carl Hubbell when he was managing the Tigers. In 1950, John Lardner wrote in the *New Yorker* that this bit of wrongheaded advice appeared in so many books on baseball that the experienced reader only had to see the names Cobb and Hubbell on the same page and "you know what comes next without even looking." Lardner added, "In a variation favored by some writers and nearly all radio sports announcers, the name of the young pitcher is withheld until the end of the anecdote—'and that man was Carl Hubbell, who became the greatest screwball pitcher in the world.'"

"The way those clubs shift against Ted Williams, I can't understand how he can be so stupid not to accept the challenge to him and hit to left field."

>—On the "Williams shift of 1948," as the *Sporting News* reported later that year. "The criticism was printed, and someone sent a clipping to Williams. Ted burned. It was pride, and not stupidity, that had urged him to keep swinging naturally into the massed defense in right field. Cobb's remarks, however, may have influenced Ted to swallow his pride and start hitting to left, with successful results."

"When I began playing the game, baseball was about as gentlemanly as a kick in the crotch."

>—Quoted in *The Giants of the Polo Grounds* by Noel Hynd

"When I came up to Detroit I was just a mild-mannered Sunday-school boy."

>—Quoted in *Great Sports Reporting*, edited by Allen Kirschner

"When I played ball, I didn't play for fun. To me it wasn't Parcheesi played under Parcheesi rules. Baseball is a red-blooded sport for red-blooded men. It's no pink tea, and molly-coddles had better stay out. It's a contest and everything that implies, a struggle for supremacy, a survival of the fittest. Every man in the game, from the minors on up, is not only fighting against the other side, but he's trying to hold onto his own job against those on his own bench who'd love to take it away. Why deny this? Why minimize it? Why not boldly admit it?"

>—*My Life in Baseball: The True Record*

"You still can run and you still can hit. Drink a little wine before dinner and you'll play for years."

>—To Stan Musial; quoted by Bob Broeg in *The National Pastime*, fall 1982

"You've got to remember—I'm 83."

>—On why he thought he would hit only .300 against modern-day pitching, SABR Collection

COBBLEDICK, GORDON

"If the other clubs in the American League are going to let one club have a monopoly on all the players of one race of mankind, they are going to give Cleveland a tremendous advantage."

>—Statement made by the *Cleveland Plain Dealer* writer after watching African-American Harry Simpson of the Indians defeat the Red Sox; quoted in the *Sporting News,* February 6, 1952

COCHRANE, GORDON S. "MICKEY"

"The fundamentals that go to make a successful ball player are the same that go to make a sound athlete in any sport—knowledge of the rudiments of the game, an ability to execute plays instinctively, and a positive belief in your ability to do the latter."

—*Baseball: The Fans' Game* (New York: Funk & Wagnalls, 1939)

"One of the freaks of baseball is that the fielder who boots a chance, or makes a costly wild throw, will find himself in a position to win the ball game before it is over. It is another of those percentage things which cannot be explained any more than the fact that the outfielder who makes a circus catch for the last out of the inning is more times than not the lead-off hitter in the next inning."

—*Baseball: The Fans' Game* (New York: Funk & Wagnalls, 1939)

COFFIN, TRISTRAM POTTER

"A large part of the hold that organized baseball has on the American imagination derives from the concept of loyalty to the franchise rather than to the individuals. In a world fast reeling from the rural to the urban, in a country where one does not live where he grew up, in the ever-changing megalopolis, loyalty to a baseball franchise offers the same assurance and stability that 'home for the holidays' does."

—The University of Pennsylvania professor in *The Old Ball Game: Baseball in Folklore and Fiction*

"Baseball has proved itself to be an unusually stable game, needing few major rule changes, satisfying though played day after day, sufficiently complex to fascinate the poet, sufficiently obvious to please the peasant. It offers a more sensitive balance of physical skill, problem solving, and chance than any game I know. It is hard to play well, yet easy to learn. It is fun to watch, yet challenging to study."

—*The Old Ball Game: Baseball in Folklore and Fiction*

"No other sport and few other occupations have introduced so many phrases, so many words, so many twists into our language as has baseball. The true test comes in the fact that old ladies who have never been to the ballpark, coquettes who don't know or care who's on first, men who think athletics begin and end with a pair of goalposts, still know and use a great deal of baseball-derived terminology. Perhaps other sports in their efforts to replace baseball as 'our national pastime,' have two strikes on them before they come to bat."

—*The Old Ball Game: Baseball in Folklore and Fiction*

"Paradoxically, I believe that the more criticism chanted against baseball the more evidence that it is, after all, our national game, immigrating with us in the 18th century, becoming American during the 19th century, vilified by us as we regret the 20th."

—*The Old Ball Game: Baseball in Folklore and Fiction*

COHANE, TIM

AN ODE

"The youthful Granville
Is no Maranville."

> —Note by the sports editor of *Look* that was passed around the press box during the third game of the 1950 World Series when an eighth-inning bobble by Granville Hamner, kid shortstop of the Phils, permitted the Yankees to tie the game

COHEN, JAMES

THE RULES OF LIFE

1. Love your wife and kids.
2. Never break your word.
3. Don't be a jerk.
4. Always stop at a red light.
5. Never extinct anything.
6. Don't argue when you're wrong.
7. Count properly.
8. If you deserve shit, take it.
9. Know your left from your right.
10. Never argue with the umpire.
11. Don't bunt with two strikes.
12. Catch a ball with two hands.

> —Special code of rules lived by Mafia hit man Frank Brady (called Ump) in novel *Ump: A Dark Comedy* (New York: Walker, 1961)

COHEN, MARVIN

"Dream into the open spaces of the baseball turf, even if you're not there at the park. You're there anyway."

> —*The Village Voice*, February 5, 1970

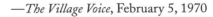

"Man is the measure of all things. The Major League ballplayer is the measure of the distances on his field of trade. Given these, he must do or die, win or lose. It's the majesty that dignity imparts. Proportions and measurements are the poet's tool, the sculptor's trade. And they rule in baseball."

> —*The Village Voice*, February 5, 1970

COHN, LOWELL

"Whenever the Giants call to talk about trades, I bet more than one general manager has had to hold a pillow over his face to keep from laughing into the phone."

> —Writing in the *San Francisco Chronicle*, 1982; quoted by Bob Chieger in *Voices of Baseball*

COLANDER, PAT

"In Chicago, we may not think the Picasso presiding over the Richard J. Daley Center plaza is art, but we know it's a big Picasso and it's the city's Picasso, and when the Cubs made the play-offs, the sculpture wore a baseball cap just like everything else."

> —"A Metropolis of No Little Plans," *New York Times*, May 5, 1985

COLAVITO, ROCKY

"You can't tell how much spirit a team has until it starts losing."

> —As a Tiger outfielder; widely attributed

COLE, NAT "KING"

"If you do nothing else in your life, don't ever sing the National Anthem at a ballgame."

> —After having a difficult time singing it; recalled by Kevin Cowherd in the *Baltimore Sun* in an article on anthem singing, July 9, 2001

COLEMAN, CHOO CHOO

"Mrs. Coleman, and she likes me, Bub."

> —On being asked by broadcaster Ralph Kiner, "What's your wife's name and what's she like?" From Warren Corbett's profile of Kiner on the SABR Biography column at sabr.com.

COLEMANISMS—JERRY COLEMAN

Jerry Coleman, the former Yankee infielder and Padres announcer, has become known for his wonderful twists on straight reporting. Here, from a variety of sources, are some of the best Colemanisms on record.

"And Kansas City is at Chicago tonight, or is that Chicago at Kansas City? Well, no matter, Kansas City leads in the eighth, four to four."

"Benedict may not be hurt as much as he really is."

"Bob Davis is wearing his hair differently this year, short and with curls like Randy Jones wears. I think you call it a Frisbee."

"DiMaggio seldom showed emotion. One day, after striking out, he came into the dugout and kicked the ball bag. We all went, 'Ooh.' It hurt. He sat down and the sweat popped out on his forehead and he clenched his fists without ever saying a word. Everybody wanted to howl. But he was the god. You don't laugh at gods."

"Enos Cabell started out here with the Astros. And before that he was with the Orioles."

"Gaylord Perry and Willie McCovey should know each other like a book. They've been ex-teammates for years now."

"George Hendrick simply lost that sun-blown pop-up."

"Grubb goes back, back. He's under the warning track."

"He can be lethal death."

"He slides into second with a stand-up double."

Jerry Coleman (*San Diego Padres*)

"Hrabosky looks fierce in that Fu Manchu haircut."

"I don't know about Willie Davis. He's not as young as he used to be."

"If Pete Rose brings the Reds in first, they ought to bronze him and put him in cement."

"If Rose's streak was still intact, with that single to left, the fans would be throwing babies out of the upper deck."

"It's a cold night out tonight. The Padres better warm up real good because it's stiff out there."

"I've made a couple mistakes I'd like to do over."

"Larry Lintz steals second standing up. He slid, but he didn't have to."

"McCovey swings and misses, and it's fouled back."

"Montreal leads Atlanta by three, 5–1."

"On the mound is Randy Jones, the left-hander with the Karl Marx hairdo."

"Pete Rose has 3,000 hits and 3,014 overall."

"Rich Folkers is throwing up in the bullpen."

"The big ballpark can do it all."

"There's a hard shot to LeMaster—and he throws Madlock into the dugout."

"There's someone warming up in the bullpen, but he's obscured by his number."

"There's two heads to every coin."

"They throw Winfield out at second, and he's safe."

"Those amateur umpires are certainly flexing their fangs tonight."

"Tony Gwynn, the fat batter behind Finley, is waiting."

"Turner turns into second with a sun-blown double."

"We're all sad to see Glenn Beckert leave. Before he goes, though, I hope he stops by so we can kiss him good-bye. He's that kind of guy."

"Whenever you get an inflamed tendon, you've got a problem. Okay, here's the next pitch to Gene Tendon."

"Winfield goes back to the wall. He hits his head on the wall, and it rolls off! It's rolling all the way back to second base! This is a terrible thing for the Padres!"

> —As Padres radio announcer describing a fly ball off the wall, in "Legends of the Err Waves" by William Taaffe, *Sports Illustrated*, May 20, 1985. This most famous of all Colemanisms sometimes appears in such variant form as this: "There's a fly ball deep to center field. Winfield is going back, back. . . . He hits his head against the wall. It's rolling toward second base."

"With one out here in the first, Dave Roberts looks a lot better than the last time he pitched against the Padres."

"You might want to put this in the back of your craw and think about it."

"Young Frank Pastore may have just pitched the biggest victory of 1979, maybe the biggest victory of the year."

COLEMAN, LEN

"Use of the video replay is not an acceptable practice, part of the beauty of baseball is that it is imperfect. Players make errors. Managers are constantly second-guessed. But the game is played and determined by two teams between the white lines.

"Traditionally, baseball has relied on the eyes of the umpires as opposed to any artificial devices for its judgments. I fully support this policy. Occasionally, however, the umpires, too, will make mistakes; that is also part of the game."

> —National League president, commenting on Frank Pulli's decision to view a replay and change a home run to a double in Florida's 5–2 loss to St. Louis, May 31, 1999; comment made June 1, 1999; quoted in *Baltimore Sun,* June 2, 1999

COLEMAN, VINCE

"I don't know nothing' 'bout no Jackie Robinson."

> —Presumably said in response to a writer who asked him what Jackie Robinson meant to him; see also similar quote by Ken Griffey Jr.

COLETTI, NED

"I learned a long time ago the most predictable aspect of this game is its unpredictability. That's why it is the greatest game."

> —As Dodgers GM, *Washington Post,* August 18, 2006

COLLINS, EDDIE

"If he'd just tip his cap once, he could be elected Mayor of Boston in five minutes."

> —On Ted Williams; quoted in the 50th Anniversary Hall of Fame *Yearbook,* 1989

COLLINS, JAMES A. "RIP"

"What I really was in the majors was the All-American louse. I broke up four no hit games and each time I felt like a heel."

> —Quoted in Collins's *Sporting News* obituary; the first baseman died on April 16, 1970, at age sixty-five

COLLINS, TOM

"Denny used to be barrel-chested, but the staves have slipped."

> —As Milwaukee radio announcer, on Denny McLain's adding a few pounds; quoted in the *Sporting News,* September 5, 1970

CONAN DOYLE, ARTHUR

"It means the largest purse has the best team and there is no necessary relation between the player and the place he plays for."

> —Expressing reservations about professional sports during a 1914 tour of the United States and taking in a game between the New York Yankees and the Philadelphia Athletics; quoted in Daniel Stashower, *Teller of Tales: The Life of Arthur Conan Doyle* (New York: Henry Holt, 1999)

"What is essential is that here is a splendid game which calls for a fine eye, activity, body fitness and judgment in the highest degree. . . . If it were taken up by our different Association teams as a summer pastime, I believe it would sweep this country as it has done in America."

> — "Merits of Baseball," letter to the *Times of London*, October 24, 1924. The Association teams alluded to were cricket teams. One letter responding to Doyle worried that baseball would displace cricket, with disastrous results. "Does Sir Arthur Conan Doyle wish to go to Lord's to see professional baseball players 'sliding to bases' on their chests and stomachs in the mud? I doubt it."

CONCEPCION, DAVE

"I think being able to play the infield, especially shortstop, is something you're born with. You can't learn it."

> —As a former Reds shortstop; *USA Today*, February 19, 1988

CONE, DAVID

"I could make an appearance every day. They think I'm Jewish. I've done six Bar Mitzvahs already. Just think if I had an H in my name."

> —The Met pitcher; quoted in the *Boston Globe*, July 17, 1988

CONIFF, FRANK

"What a town. They boo Willie Mays and cheer Khrushchev."

> —The New York writer on San Francisco, SABR Collection

CONLAN, JOCKO

"I demand respect on the field from managers and players. To me, that's 75 percent of umpiring. The real test of a big league umpire is whether he can take control and runt he ball game."

> —Quoted in the 50th Anniversary Hall of Fame *Yearbook*, 1989

"I know a lot of players complain about night games, long flights and that stuff. I grant you that it's not easy, but it's not too hard either. There is no flight that takes longer than five hours. I wonder what some of those guys would say if they traveled by train like the old days. I can still feel those cinders and smell the smoke that came pouring in the open windows of those old Pullman cars."

> —As a retired umpire; widely attributed

CONLON, CHARLES M.

"The game which seems to breathe the restless spirit of American life, that calls for quick action and quicker thinking, that seems characteristic of a great nation itself, is baseball."

> —"The Base Ball Photographer," *Photographic Times*, 1913

CONNOLLY, TOMMY

"Maybe I called it wrong, but its official."

> —American League umpire; quoted in Mike Sowell, *The Pitch That Killed* (New York: Macmillan, 1989)

CONNORS, BILLY

"The thing you love about Steve Trout is that he's the same whether he's pitching great or pitching bad. The bad thing is he doesn't know the difference."

> —The Seattle pitching coach on his new pitcher; quoted in the *Washington Post*, March 6, 1988

CONNORS, KEVIN "CHUCK"

"I'm the only former major league ball player who crashed the movies whole hog. Accordingly, I'd act like a ball player, not an actor, in the baseball scenes, and in the rest of the film I'd act like an actor, not a ball player."

> —On why he should play the role of Ted Williams in the movies; quoted in *Baseball Digest*, June 1961

"It was easy to figure out Mr. Rickey's thinking about contracts. He had both players and money—and just didn't like to see the two of them mix."

> —On Branch Rickey; quoted in *Baseball Is a Funny Game* by Joe Garagiola

"Kevin [Chuck] Connors, affiliate Brooklyn Dodgers Baseball Club. Recitations, After-Dinner Speaker, Home Recordings for any Occasion, Free Lance Writing."

> —Business card, a baseball rarity in 1949, used before Connors established himself as an actor in TV's *The Rifleman*. He was said to have given the card to Branch Rickey on signing his first contract with the major-league Dodgers.

"You want my blood, please send contract with more money as you can see I . . . am running . . . out of . . . blo . . ."

> —In a note to Buzzie Bavasi, written in red ink; quoted in *Baseball Is a Funny Game* by Joe Garagiola

CONTE, REPRESENTATIVE SILVIO

"And then there was baseball, the glue that could hold the most politically polarized together. The longest-running battles of all surround the annual Congressional Baseball Game. I was the Republican coach, manager, and equipment coordinator, and it was not an event to be missed.

"Over the years I played with the greats: Ford, Bush, and Michel."

> —On his thirty years in Congress; quoted in *Roll Call*, June 18, 1990. He is referring to George H. W. Bush, Gerard Ford, and Bob Michel, who served in the House Republican leadership after Ford.

COOK, BEANO

"Haven't they suffered enough?"

> —On Commissioner Bowie Kuhn's decision to award all of the Iranian hostages lifetime passes to major-league baseball on their return to America in early 1981. The sports commentator (who has been described as "a first-rate football handicapper, but hardly a friend of baseball") made the comment on the radio the day after Kuhn's announcement.

COOKE, ALISTAIR

"I find baseball fascinating. It strikes me as a native American ballet—a totally different dance form. Nearly every move in baseball—the windup, the pitch, the motion of the infielders—is different from other games. Next to a triple play, baseball's double play is the most exciting and graceful thing in sports."

—Widely attributed

COOKE, BOB

"Rex Barney would be the league's best pitcher if the plate were high and outside."

—On the hard-throwing but wild Dodger pitcher of the 1940s who never lived up to the brilliance predicted for him. Says Joe McBride in *High and Inside,* Cooke "perfectly summarized his problem." Quoted in *Baseball,* January 10, 1950.

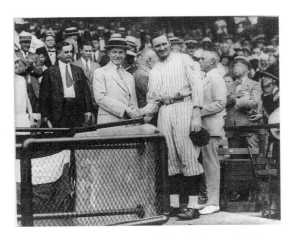
President Coolidge with Walter Johnson, 1925
(*Library of Congress Prints and Photographs Division*)

COOLIDGE, CALVIN

"Baseball is our national game."

—Widely quoted blessing

"It would be difficult to conceive a finer example of true sport."

—Statement to the press after watching three games of the 1924 World Series

"They are great band, these armored knights of the bat and ball. They are held up to a high standard of honor on the field, which they have seldom betrayed. While baseball remains our national game our national testes will be on a higher level and our national ideals on a finer foundation."

—Addressing the Washington Senators outside the White House on October 1, 1924, after they clinched the American League pennant

COOPER, ALICE

"If somebody had told me that you have a choice of being a rock star or playing left field for the Tigers, there would not have been a choice at all. I would have said, 'Where's my locker?'"

—Quoted in *The Final Season* by Tom Stanton, 2000

COOPER, WALKER

"Guglielmo, Passarella, Pinelli, Dascoli, Donatelli, Paparella!"

—As Cardinal catcher when Augie Guglielmo made his first appearance as an umpire. In another version of the same statement Cooper said, "Every guy that gets off the boat has an indicator in his hands."

119

COOPER, WALKER (CONTINUED)

"No one is a pull hitter in the first year of marriage."

> —1945; quoted in Bob Buege's *The Milwaukee Braves: A Baseball Eulogy*

"The fly balls are too high to handle."

> —On a windy day; quoted in *Baseball Is a Funny Game* by Joe Garagiola

"When you get to be my age, you don't hold out—you hold on."

> —On his quick acceptance of terms with the Milwaukee Braves, spring 1953

"Yeah, he's got pretty good stuff. The only trouble is that he drinks it all himself."

> —On a pitcher said to have "good stuff", quoted by Joe Garagiola in *Baseball Is a Funny Game*

COOVER, ROBERT

"I felt like I was part of something there, you know, like in church, except it was more real than any church, and I joined in the score-keeping, hollering, the eating of hot dogs and drinking of Cokes and beer, and for a while I even had the idea that ball stadiums, and not European churches, were the real American holy places."

> —Quoted in John Thorn, *The Game for All America* (St. Louis: Sporting News Publishing, 1988)

CORBETT, BRAD

"Baseball is a tremendous business for men with big egos. But ego can only take you so far. After that, it has to be a good business proposition."

> —Former Texas Rangers owner on why he sold the team; widely attributed

CORDOVA, MARTY

"Go ask them what they're eating besides pitchers."

> —After the Mariners hit 23 home runs against the Twins in six games, *Sporting News*, June 7, 1999

COSTAS, BOB

"Elvis has a better chance of coming back than the Jays."

> —From Game 1 of the 1989 American League Championship Series. The comment did not sit well with Toronto fans, but Costas defended it in an Associated Press story of October 7, 1989: "I said it with Toronto down by four runs, in the ninth inning, against Dennis Eckersley. It's one of my better lines. I'm glad it's immortalized."

"He was our guy. When he was hot, we felt great, when he slumped or got hurt, we sagged a bit, too."

> —Eulogizing Mickey Mantle, *Newsweek,* August 28, 1995

"If someone my age said to me, 'I can't get interested in the game, other than Ripken's night, and I don't know how much of the

World Series I'll watch,' I don't know how much of that argument I can contradict. If you're interested, great; if you're not, I can't tell you that you're wrong. So many fans are not just hurt; they're disinterested. Baseball is no longer worth their time."

—*New York Times,* October 8, 1995, after the 1994–95 baseball strike

"If you could guarantee me that he would run the federal government with that level of insight, I'd call off all the recounts right now."

—During the 2000 election recount in Florida, joking about George W. Bush, who as part-owner of the Rangers in 1993 was the only dissenter in a 27–1 owners' vote for baseball's wild-card playoff system. *Chicago Sun Times,* November 20, 2000.

"On the one hand, they sell history whenever it suits them, and on the other hand, they disrespect it."

—On Major League Baseball's deal to have *Spider-Man 2* bases and pitching rubbers, *Chicago Sun Times,* May 6, 2004

"This guy is so old that the first time he had athlete's foot, he used Absorbine Sr."

—As an NBC sportscaster on the forty-five-year-old Yankee pitcher Tommy John; quoted in the *Sporting News,* September 12, 1988

"You know, I've got so much gas that a bunch of Arabs are following me."

—On consuming bratwurst and other edibles at County Stadium in Milwaukee; quoted in the *Sporting News,* September 9, 1985

COUSINS, NORMAN

"At a Dodger baseball game in Los Angeles, I asked Will Durant if he was ninety-four or ninety-five. 'Ninety-four,' he said. 'You don't think I'd be doing anything as foolish as this if I were ninety-five, do you?'"

—*Human Opinions* by Norman Cousins, 1981

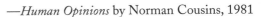

"He was supposed to be as fast as Walter Johnson, and though he couldn't curve them and mix them up like the great Matty [Christy Mathewson], his assortment was better than most. You were attracted by the graceful rhythm of his pitching motion; the long majestic sweep of his arm as he let the ball fly; the poised alertness after the pitch. That was what counted, and you knew it when batter after batter swung ineptly at pitches they couldn't even see."

—On Dizzy Dean; quoted as editor of the *Saturday Review* in Dean's *New York Times* obituary, July 18, 1974

COVELESKI, STANLEY

"It's tomorrow that counts. So you worry all the time. It never ends. Lord, baseball is a worrying thing."

—From "Diamond Quotes" in *Nine,* 2004 edition. This common quotation has been extracted from a longer one which appeared in George Will's *Men at Work*: "The pressure never lets up. Don't matter what you did yesterday. That's history. It's tomorrow that counts. So you worry all the time. It never ends. Lord, baseball is a worrying thing."

CRAFT, REVEREND FREDERICK H.

"First base is enlightenment; second base is repentance; third base, faith, and the home plate the heavenly goal! . . . Don't fail to touch second base, for it leads you onward to third. All of us finally reach the home plate, though some may be called out when they slide Home."

—Officiating at the funeral service for Chris Von der Ahe, former owner of the St. Louis Browns of the American Association, in St. Louis, June 9, 1913; quoted in *Sporting Life*, June 14, 1913; reprinted in *Nineteenth Century Notes* (newsletter of SABR Nineteenth Century Committee), June 1998

Roger Craig (*Detroit Tigers*)

CRAIG, ROGER

"Choo-Choo Coleman would . . . give you the sign and then look down to see what it was."

—Quoted in "Bad Beyond Belief," by Steve Rushin, *Sports Illustrated*, May 25, 1992

"Great pitchers demonstrate composure, pride, and competitive instincts. They don't allow trivial things to upset them . . . Most pitchers deliberately alter their pattern of pitching when a game is not on the line. Why show a hitter your best stuff when the game is out of reach? . . . Players who commit errors need reassurance from the pitcher, who must harbor no grudges . . . A pitcher can't ask for much more than thirteen runs and six double plays."

—Tenets of pitching, gathered from his book *Inside Pitch*

"I think it's odd that everyone expects the players to show emotion. The fans may be near hysteria, but baseball is still our job. We aren't just 'kids' romping in double knits to pass the time."

—*Inside Pitch*

"I personally think it's too bad if a batter gets hit crowding the plate. I know that Don Drysdale, Larry Sherry, and Stan Williams felt the same way when they pitched for the Dodgers in the late 1950s and early '60s. That was the formula I was raised on. Come to think of it, I've never seen a batter apologize for smashing a line drive off some part of a pitcher's torso."

—*Inside Pitch*

"I thought it was from a funeral home."

> —On getting a good-luck telegram from the rock group the Grateful Dead on the eve of the 1989 National League Championship Series; quoted in *Baseball Digest*, April 1990

"I was a pitcher for the World Champion Brooklyn Dodgers my first season in the major leagues in 1955 and now serve as pitching coach of the World Champion Tigers in what probably will be my final season in 1984. What more can a man ask for?"

> —*Inside Pitch*

"It's just a shame, that 50,000 people come out and see an umpire be the deciding point in a ballgame. It's a shame that two clubs battle like that and then the umpire calls a balk, which wasn't a balk."

> —Associated Press Quote of the Week, July 31, 1988, after the game-winning run was scored on an eleventh-inning balk to give the Dodgers a 6–5 victory over his Giants

"Latins seem to have a capacity to pitch frequently. The Latins play winter ball and aren't accustomed to resting their arms. I rested my arm every winter during my professional career. This is a mistake. If I were twenty years old, I'd live in California or Florida so I could throw during the off-season."

> —*Inside Pitch*

"Pitching is essentially a sequential process that requires thinking like a hitter."

> —*Inside Pitch*

"Pitching is the cornerstone of most championship teams."

> —*Inside Pitch*

"The split-finger is a good off-speed pitch that can be thrown at virtually every level of play. Junior high school or even little league isn't too early because this pitch doesn't put strain on the arm and requires only an average-size hand. The key to an effective split-finger is to think fastball."

> —*Inside Pitch*

"There are Opening Day pitchers, and pitchers who start on Opening Day."

> —*Inside Pitch*

"Today, players receive pats on the back. There's really no other way to handle people armed with long-term, guaranteed contracts."

> —*Inside Pitch*

"We want pitchers who aren't happy to leave the game. I'd rather have a pitcher come in and kick the water cooler than someone who is resigned to failure."

> —*Inside Pitch*

CRANE, STEPHEN

"[I] attempted to study literature but found base-ball . . . much more to my taste."

> —Star shortstop of the 1891 Syracuse University baseball team, who left college without a degree but who went on to write *The Red Badge of Courage;* quotation found by John Thorn and presented in *The National Pastime*, winter, 1987

CRAWFORD, CINDY

"Models are like baseball players. We make a lot of money quickly, but all of a sudden we're thirty years old, we don't have a college education, we're qualified for nothing, and we're used to a very nice lifestyle. The best thing is to marry a movie star."

—Quoted in *New Woman*, December 1992

CRAWFORD, SAM

"Believe me, he had a real spitter. He'd try to talk and bubbles would fly all over the place."

—On a pitcher who used soap and saliva to make the ball do tricks; quoted in *Sport*, September 1988

"We'd play a whole game with one ball, if it stayed in the park, lopsided, and black, and full of tobacco juice and licorice stains. The pitchers used to have it all their own way then. Spitballs and emery balls and whatnot."

—Quoted in the 50th Anniversary Hall of Fame *Yearbook,* 1989

CREAMER, ROBERT W.

"After you got a little better at throwing and catching and hitting you badgered older kids into letting you play in their pickup games....

"If you were picked, you'd run to the outfield (you were always sent to the outfield), pound your fist into your glove (or, more often, into a glove a kid on the other team had left on the field when his team went in to bat), jump up and down a little, and yell, 'Hit

it to me, hit it to me,' although you rather hoped they wouldn't."

—"Pop Watts, a Newspaper, and a Day at the Polo Grounds," in Ron Fimrite, ed., *Birth of a Fan* (New York: Macmillan, 1993)

CREPEAU, RICHARD C.

"In its urban setting baseball tended to stress its rural origins and attachments. In doing so, baseball tied itself to one of the most historically enduring and powerful myths in American culture."

—On early-twentieth-century baseball; from "Urban and Rural Images in Baseball," *Journal of Popular Culture*, fall 1975

CRONIN, JOE

"I cannot agree with critics who claim there is too much stress put on the little leagues. To me, that is so much hokum. Boys must have the spirit of competition in some way and there is none better than baseball."

—As American League president; widely attributed

CRYSTAL, BILLY

"I hosted a television special before the [1985] All-Star Game, and Mickey was a guest. In the opening, I told the audience that all I wanted as a kid was to have Mickey Mantle throw me a ball and say, 'You've got a good arm, kid.' For the close, the script (which I selfishly wrote) called for Mickey to do just that. He threw me the ball and said, 'You've got a good arm, kid.'

And I started to cry. I said, 'Stop the tape; I've got something in my eye.'"

> —In a bylined article, "Glove Story: When Billy Crystal Discovered Show Business, Baseball's Loss Was Comedy's Gain," *Los Angeles Times*, June 29, 1986

"I've been all over the world, and the sight of Yankee Stadium for the first time on May 30, 1956, is still the most vivid in my memory. I love Dodger Stadium, but it doesn't smell like there's going to be a game that day. You walk into Yankee Stadium, and you just know, the hot dogs have been there for awhile, and even though the ball park looks different, you know there's going to be a game."

> —"On Bernstein and Picasso, Magic and Michael," *New York Times*, June 2 1991

CULKIN, JOHN M.

"I don't think baseball could survive without all the statistical appurtenances involved in calculating pitching, hitting and fielding percentages. Some people could do without the games as long as they got the box scores."

> —*New York Times*, July 13, 1976

CUMMINGS, CANDY

"A surge of joy flooded over me that I shall never forget. I felt like shouting out that I had made a ball curve; I wanted to tell everybody; it was too good to keep to myself."

> —On finding that he was the first to develop and throw the curveball

CUNNINGHAM, BILL

"I don't like the way he stands at the plate. He bends his front knee inward and moves his foot just before he takes a swing. That's exactly what I do before I drive a golf ball and knowing what happens to the golf balls I drive, I don't believe this kid will ever hit half a midget's weight in a bathing suit."

> —The Boston writer in 1938 on first seeing Ted Williams in spring training, a year before Williams came up with the Red Sox. This quote appears in John Updike's "Hub Fans Bid Kid Adieu," which appears in his *Assorted Prose* and in Williams's *My Turn at Bat*.

CUOMO, MARIO

"There is so much about the game that appeals to the intellect and the psyche. The symmetry of it, the orderliness of it, the fact that it throws off other controls.

"It's greater than time strictures. You know in the other sports . . . you play against the clock and when the clock runs out your chance is over. No clock in baseball. You play until you lose, and if you can keep that rally alive, if you can keep going, if you can keep getting hits, you can play until a week from now. Nothing stops you. There is no parameter that makes it impossible for you to perform still more excellently."

> —As New York governor in the first PBS *Baseball* installment; quoted in the *Toronto Star*, October 15, 1994

CUOMO, MARIO (CONTINUED)

"You will not be able to tell they are capable of greatness *until* you provide them with a packed house, a 3-and-2 count and the game is on the line. You can't tell until the true season starts."

> —As a baseball fan during the 1988 presidential campaign, discussing the candidatses Michael Dukakis, Al Gore, Jesse Jackson, and George H. W. Bush; *Newsweek*, April 4, 1988

CURLEY, TOM

"When the Giants moved to San Francisco I gravitated with them. There was no way I would have rooted against Willie Mays. Ultimately, I think baseball often comes down to one individual player's grip on your psyche. I read every article on Willie Mays over the years."

> —"A Giant Passion," in Karen Mullarkey, ed. dir., *Baseball in America* (San Francisco: Collins, 1991). Curley is president and chief operating officer, *USA Today*.

CURRY, RICHARD L.

"The scheme which has major-league baseball trashing a residential community and tinkering with the quality-of-life aspirations of countless households so that television royalties might more easily flow into the coffers of 25 distant sports moguls is not consonant with present-day concepts of right and justice."

> —Judge, Cook County Circuit Court, Chicago, supporting citizens' protest against night baseball at Chicago's Wrigley Field, March 25, 1985

CURTIS, JOHN

"Between owners and players, a manager today has become a wishbone."

> —*Sports Illustrated*, July 18, 1977

"The first big-league game I ever saw was at the Polo Grounds. My father took me. I remember it so well—the green grass and the green stands. It was like seeing Oz."

> —As a Giants pitcher, 1978

CUSIC, DON

"What baseball and country music have most in common is the ability to provide entertainment for their fans. They touch the lives of the many who sing only in the shower or watch baseball only from an armchair but nonetheless find in country music artists and baseball players something that transcends the ordinary and takes those born without wealth, privilege, or social status and turns them into heroes by virtue of their natural talents, dedication, and hard work. In other words, both baseball and country music are tickets to the American Dream."

> —*Baseball and Country Music*, 2003

D

DAHL, STEVE

"Hey, it was the Sox. They would have lost anyway."

—The Chicago deejay on the tenth anniversary of "Disco Demolition Night," July 12, 1979, in which a promotional stunt turned into a riot and a forfeit for the Sox; quoted in *USA Today,* July 14, 1989

DALEY, ARTHUR

"A baseball fan has the digestive apparatus of a Billy goat. He can, and does, devour any set of diamond statistics with insatiable appetite and then nuzzles hungrily for more."

—Widely attributed

"It rained that day. Even the heavens wept at the passing of Babe Ruth."

—Reporting on Ruth's funeral

"Ottie had charisma long before that over-worked word emerged from the dictionary for everyday use."

—On Mel Ott, *New York Times,* February 13, 1970

"Huckleberry Finn in a baseball uniform."

—On Ralph Kiner

DALEY, BUD

"Well, that's his nickname."

—When in 1964 as a Yankee pitcher, he was asked why fellow pitcher Marshall Bridges was called "Sheriff"; quoted in *Sport,* February 1965

DALEY, JOHN FRANCIS (1887–1988)

"You can't hit what you can't see."

> —Said after pinch-hitting against Walter Johnson in 1912. At 100, Daley was recognized as the major-league baseball player who had lived the longest. He died during the summer of 1988 at 101. He played only in one year in seventeen major league games, and his most famous moment was marked with a comment. Toward the end of his life, he recalled, "There were two outs. I came to bat and hit two foul balls off him. On the next pitch, I saw him wind up and make his delivery—but then I heard the catcher's glove pop and the umpire call me out. I swear to heaven I never saw that pitch! I guess I looked a little dazed on my way back to the dugout. The manager asked me what was the matter, and I turned to him and said, 'You can't hit what you can't see.'"

DANIEL, DAN

"The boy-and-dog sequence in the movie is very tough to take. Ruth almost kills a pooch on the playing field with a batted ball. The boy owner of the dog is disconsolate. Ruth rushes dog and boy down to a hospital and induces a surgeon to work on the canine.

"Of course, the dog recovers. But Ruth misses the game, and for that, we are told, he is fined $5,000 by Huggins."

> —On *The Babe Ruth Story*, which debuted on July 26, 1948; quoted in the *Sporting News*

"You have to watch this man, day in and day out, to appreciate him to the full. You have to see the Yankees when he is not in the line-up to know how much he means to them. You have to live in Pullmans with William, you have to see him in hotel lobbies, you have to analyze him in the harness, before you are able to realize how completely he dominates his field."

> —On Bill Dickey; writing in the *New York World Telegram*, April 27, 1939

DARK, ALVIN

"A manager doesn't hear the cheers. The writers want to know where you made your mistake, not how well your curve is breaking."

> —*The Baseball Card Engagement Book*, 1990

"A trade tells you exactly which side of the hill you're on. The terms, the numbers are like billboards. You don't have to guess."

> —*The Baseball Card Engagement Book*, 1990

"Any pitcher who throws at a batter and deliberately tries to hit him is a Communist."

> —From Joseph R. Conlin, *The Morrow Book of Quotations in American History* (New York: William Morrow, 1984)

"Every player should be accorded the privilege of at least one season with the Chicago Cubs. That's baseball as it should be played—in God's own sunshine. And that's really living."

> —As a Cubs infielder; widely attributed

"Friendships are forgotten when the game begins."

> —As Kansas City A's manager; widely attributed

Alvin Dark (*Author's Collection*)

"Slow thinkers are part of the game, too. Some of these slow thinkers can hit a ball a long way."

> —As Indians manager; quoted in *Baseball Digest,* January 1968

"There'll be a man on the moon before he hits a home run."

> —On Gaylord Perry, as Giants manager in 1968 to sportswriter Harry Jupiter. Perry is quoted in Ron Luciano's *Strike Two:* "So a year later I was pitching against the Dodgers when we got the news that Neil Armstrong had stepped on to the surface the moon. I came to bat about twenty minutes after that, against Claude Osteen—and hit my first major league home run. When Armstrong stepped out on the moon he said, 'That's one small step for a man, one giant leap for all mankind,' and I thought, 'and one home run for Gaylord Perry.'"

DARROW, CLARENCE

"The only perfect pleasure we ever knew."

> —Recalling his youth; quoted in Harold Seymour's *Baseball: The People's Game*

DARWIN, DANNY

"Once you sign a contract, you're little more than cattle. If they don't want you, they can sell you or trade you, and you just moo and move along."

> —"Diamond Quotes," in *Nine,* 2006

"In this game of baseball, you live by the sword and die by it. You hit and get hit. Remember that."

> —As Cleveland Indians manager, on why the knock-down pitch will never leave; widely attributed

"My impression of him is that he pitches as well as he has to. He doesn't worry about his earned run average. He pitches to win. He's businesslike. He reacts to the score so he doesn't mind giving up a run or two. When it's close, he's tougher."

> —On then-Detroit ace Denny McLain, in *Baseball Digest*, February 1961

DAVIS, MARVIN

"As men get older, their toys get more expensive."

—After bidding $12 million for the Oakland A's

DAVIS, MICHAEL

"After the well-documented near-death incident on Mount Moriah, Abraham had a thought. He untied his son and went in search of a five-ounce rock. 'Let's have a nice catch, Isaac,' he suggested, apologetically. 'Soft tosses, only. I brought split wood and a donkey up the mountain, but forgot my mitt.' Isaac said, 'OK, Pop.' As they threw the rock, father and son found a way to talk things over and, generally, had some important moments of bonding, guy-style. And so it has been through the centuries."

—"Bats About the Game: The Jewish Love Affair with Baseball," *Baltimore Jewish Times,* October 8, 1993

DAVIS, RON

"I know winning isn't everything, but with Calvin Griffith winning isn't anything."

—On being traded from the Yankees to the Twins; quoted in Raymond Mungo's *Confessions from Left Field*

DAVIS, TOMMY

"They used to call me lazy or lackadaisical, but the lazier I felt the better I'd hit."

—Quoted by Roger Angell in *Late Innings*

"When there are men on base and I'm at bat, all I can see is dollar signs."

—Quoted by Arnold Hano in *Sport,* December 1963, in an article entitled "I'm for Me"

DAVIS, WILLIE

"Guys in baseball are crazy. They don't understand the consequences of hitting a man with a ball. They don't know the pain and discomfort and downright danger to his life."

—Widely attributed

"I consider myself better adjusted than anyone else in this game. That's because nothing can make me unhappy. If we win, I am happy for myself. If we lose, I am happy because of the happiness it has brought the other guy. There is no way that baseball can upset me."

—As a Texas Ranger; quoted in the *Los Angeles Herald-Examiner,* March 6, 1975

DAY, LARAINE

"I prepared a first big dinner as a celebration for our new position with the Giants. This brought me another dazzling insight into Leo and baseball players in general.

"'What's this?' he asked with distaste, and as if he didn't know.

"'Salad.'

"'Never eat the stuff. Makes your bones soft.'"

—Opinion attributed to Leo Durocher by his wife in her *Day with the Giants*

Deanism has become the term for any one of scores of words, phrases, and statements made by the late Dizzy Dean. Many were technically errors, but often that did not make them any less descriptive. In his own vernacular, for instance, players always "slud into base."

In 1948, Dean got his own radio show, on which he first aired his illuminating colloquialisms to a national audience and got a predictable response from the self-appointed guardians of the mother tongue.

In his book of baseball terms, Jerry Howarth insists that Dizzy put the live television *Game of the Week* on the map when, on the air, he referred to an act of courage as "testicle fortitude." Even with a national television audience, he was able to hold on to what it was that got him there. "The charm of Dizzy Dean," wrote Milton Gross in the *New York Post* (March 11, 1963), "is that he tries to make you believe he's still picking boll weevils out of his ears when he's picking up $100,000 a year broadcasting the game of the week."

"A lot of folks that ain't saying 'ain't' ain't eatin'."

—In response to his critics who thought he was setting a bad example by using the word "ain't" in broadcasts

"Ah won 28 games in '35, and ah couldn't believe my eyes when the Cards sent me a contract with a cut in salary. . . .

"Mr. Rickey said ah deserved a cut because I didn't win 30 games!"

—Quoted by writer Al Abrams from a 1966 interview

"All ballplayers want to wind up their careers with the Cubs, Giants or Yankees . . . they just can't help it."

—Quoted by John P. Carmichael in *My Greatest Day in Baseball*

"But who packs 'em into the park. Mr. Rickey? No, me and Paul."

—In protesting his $18,500 salary in contrast to Branch Rickey's $50,000, *Sporting News*, March 5, 1936

"Folks write in, and out of 150 letters maybe two will call me down."

—On critics of his use of language; quoted by Dan Daniel in the *New York World Telegram and Sun*, 1951

Dizzy Dean (*Author's Collection*)

"Frankie Frisch laid down the law about us Cardinals bein' sure to be in bed by midnight during one series in New York, an' that same night I can't sleep an' I drop into a club on 52nd Street about 2 o'clock in the mornin'. . . . The m.c. he introduces me, like a sap, an' when I get up to bow who do I see across the room but Frisch an' the club secretary. . . . So I grabs the mike an' says, 'An', folks, I wanna introduce to you another great ball player . . . and a grand guy to play for . . . Frankie Frisch!' . . . Yeah, we went home in a cab together, finally."

—Quoted by Jerry Mitchell of the *New York Post* in *Baseball Digest,* January 1943

"Good morning, president. So the old boy is prowling around himself tonight, eh? Well, sir, I'm not one to squawk. Us stars and presidents must have our fun."

—While in the Texas League, Dizzy was out cavorting at 3 a.m. in Wichita Falls when he bumped into the league president, whom he greeted in this manner. From an Associated Press collection of Dean quotes entitled "Dizzy Tales," which ran in July 16, 1974, following his death

"He must think I went to the Massachusetts Constitution of Technology."

—On Branch Rickey's highfalutin' language; quoted in the *Sporting News,* March 26, 1936.

"He once hit a ball between my laigs so hard that my center fielder caught it on the fly backing up against the wall."

—On Bill Terry

"He runs too long in one place. He's gotta lot of up 'n' down, but not much forward."

—On a fellow Cardinal; widely attributed

"He slud into third!"

—As an announcer

"Heck, if anybody told me I was settin' a record I'd of got me some more strike-outs."

—On July 30, 1933, after establishing a modern National League record by striking out 17 batters; quoted by Mel Allen in *It Takes Heart* by Mel Allen and Frank Graha, Jr.

"Hold it folks, here comes a feller up to hit with his legs coming out of his shirtsleeves."

—Describing Ted Kluszewski, a Reds first baseman with enormous, powerful arms; quoted in *Tales from the Dodger Dugout*

"I always just went out there and struck out all the fellas I could," he remembered. "I didn't worry about winnin' this number of games or that number—and I ain't a-woofin' when I say that, either."

—Postcareer recollection which appeared in his *New York Times* obituary, July 18, 1974

"I can't tell you why this game is held up, but you'll find out fast enough iffen you stick your head outta the window."

—Line, oft-quoted, demonstrating his disdain for wartime regulations against revealing weather conditions

"I don't know of any. Nobody ain't bothered to give me any. I have to do this job my own way. I can't be hampered. Sure, sometimes I get too frank. But it ain't venomous. It's just Dizzy Dean."

—Asked what rules and regulations he was given as a broadcaster; quoted by Dan Daniel in the *New York World Telegram and Sun,* 1951

"If them guys are thinking, they're as good as licked right now."

—On hearing on the eve of the '34 Series that Detroit manager Mickey Cochrane was holding team meetings. The Cards won in seven; quoted by George Will in *Men at Work*

"If you had I'd have heard somethin' rattle."

—When umpire George Barr insisted that he had shaken his head answering a question. *It Takes Heart*

"I've just been informed that the fat lady is the queen of Holland."

—While announcing a St. Louis Browns game, he noticed a commotion in the stands and reported to his listeners that "it has something to do with a fat lady." A startled station executive who happened to be in the booth pulled Dean away from the mike and told him the woman happened to be the queen of the Netherlands. After inquiring as to the whereabouts of the Netherlands, Dean returned to the microphone and made the announcement; quoted in Lee Green's *Sportswit*

"I'll tell you how it was, Mr. President. For the first 20 years of my life, I never had enough to eat—and I ain't caught up yet."

—To President Dwight D. Eisenhower, who looked at his golfing partner one day and wondered how 'Ol Diz had let himself balloon to three hundred pounds. From an Associated Press collection of Dean quotes entitled "Dizzy Tales" which ran on July 18, 1974, following his death.

"I'm through talking about things folks ain't seeing."

—As a television sportscaster

"It ain't bragging if you can do it."

—Widely attributed

"I was helpin' the writers out. Them ain't lies, them's scoops."

—On constantly giving sportswriters different places of birth including Lucas, Arkansas; Holdenville, Oklahoma; and Bond, Mississippi; from an Associated Press collection of Dean quotes entitled "Dizzy Tales" which ran on July 18, 1974, following his death

"I'd get me a buncha bats and balls and learn them kids behind the Iron Curtain how to play baseball instead of totin' rifles and swallerin' lies. And if Joe Stallion ever learnt how much dough there was in the concessions at a ball park, he'd quit commanism and get into a honest business."

—Quoted by Bennett Cerf in his *Good for a Laugh*

"If I had known what Paul was gonna do, I would have pitched one, too."

> —On September 21, 1934, Dizzy pitched a three-hitter against Brooklyn in the first game of a doubleheader. Brother Paul pitched a no-hitter in the second game.

"If I have only a fair year, I should win 20 games, but, of course, I expect to have a good season. I am sorry you bush league sports writers are not going to the big parade with me. . . . You know Dean, always good even when I am having an off day."

> —Writing to a sportswriter friend before his first major-league season; quoted in an Associated Press collection of Dean quotes entitled "Dizzy Tales," which ran on July 18, 1974, following his death

"If Satch and I were pitching on the same team, we'd cinch the pennant by July 4 and go fishing until World Series time."

> —On Satchel Paige

"Jeez, they're gonna give me 50,000 smackers just for living."

> —On selling the movie rights to his life story in 1951, Hall of Fame Collection

"Joe, you just gotta get this broken glass away from here. It's cuttin' up the ball!"

> —When he was pitching for an Arkansas hillbilly nine in his salad days, a rival outfit, determined to undo him, sprinkled broken glass around the mound. Diz, barefoot, hurled

six shutout innings without a squawk, but then he stalked over to the rival manager to issue the complaint; quoted by Bennett Cerf in his *The Laugh's on Me.*

"Let the teachers teach English, and I will teach baseball. There is a lot of people in the United States who say isn't, and they ain't eating."

> —Addressing the schoolteachers who criticized his use of improper English as a broadcaster; quoted by Dan Daniel in the *New York World-Telegram and Sun*

"Maybe it's just a coincidence but it was after getting hit in the head in Detroit that I begin to hear rumors about bein' offered a manager's job."

> —"Baseball Managers Ain't Necessary," *This Week,* May 31, 1953

"Me and my father was in the first car and Paul and my uncle was supposed to be followin' real close in the second car. Well, we come to this railroad crossing and we just gets over it before this big, slow freight train comes by. There just didn't seem to be no end to it. Anyway, Paul and my uncle had to wait while the train went by and it was just about two years before they caught up with us again."

> —As a storyteller; quoted by Phil Elderkin in the *Christian Science Monitor,* August 19, 1974

"Me and Paul'll win two games apiece."

—When asked how the St. Louis Cardinal pitching staff could expect to defeat Detroit in the World Series of 1934. Dizzy and Paul Dean won the first, second, sixth, and seventh games of the Series, thus won by the Cardinals, four games to three.

"Mr. Rickey, I'll put more people in the park than anybody since Babe Ruth!"

—To an incredulous Branch Rickey, from a $3,000 rookie. As Red Smith later observed, within three years the busher was putting more people in the park than anybody else, including Ruth, who had never helped the Cardinals draw a dollar.

"My arm is made of rubber, I'll be ready in two days."

—To the press at the beginning of the 1934 season after holding out during most of spring training. He went on to post a 30–7 record for the season; quoted by Leo Durocher in *Nice Guys Finish Last*

"Old Diz knows the King's English. And not only that. I also know the Queen is English."

—On his radio show in response to a letter from a listener which said that he did not know "the King's English"

"Right away, sir. You are number two on my manure list."

—At age 16 at Fort Sam Houston, where he was assigned to shovel manure from the post horse corral, when an officer demanded to know when Dizzy was going to deliver

manure for his flower garden; quoted in *Everything You Always Wanted to Know About Sports and Didn't Know Where to Ask* by Mickey Herskowitz and Steve Perkins

"Say, this is Dizzy Dean. Yep, back in town and I can hear you gnashing your teeth, brother. Just thought I would call and tell you that I am gonna pitch against your ball club this afternoon and hold them to two or three hits."

—After he was given a brief tryout in 1930 in the major leagues, he was sent back to the minors for more seasoning. He went immediately to the ballpark and telephoned the rival manager with this message. He allowed two. From an Associated Press collection of Dean quotes entitled "Dizzy Tales," which ran on July 18, 1974, following his death

"Sin tax? What will those fellers in Washington think of next?"

—Perhaps apocryphal response to charge that his use of language was ruining students' syntax

"Son, what kind of a pitch would you like to miss?"

—Dizzy the baiter. What he supposedly asked a hitter he'd struck out all day

"Spart is pretty much the same as fight or pep or gumption. Like the Spart of St. Louis, that plane Lindbergh flowed to Europe in."

—When pressed for an explanation of the term "spart." which he had broadcast in the sentence "The trouble with them boys is they ain't got enough spart." From Allen Churchill in the *New York Times Magazine;* quoted in *The Reader's Digest Treasury of Wit and Humor*

"Stick your head out of the window and find out why the game was halted."

—Advice to listeners during a World War II broadcast during which he was not supposed to make any mention of the weather "for fear it might affect military operations." Retold on his radio show, July 3, 1948

"That was because they seen me killing squirrels with stones th'owing left-handed. If I'd of th'owed right-handed I would have squashed them."

—On why the men who scouted him reported that he was a left-hander; quoted by Jim Murray (*Los Angeles Times,* July 19, 1974) who said the quote was often-repeated by the late Detroit columnist Doc Green

"The best pitcher I ever seen is ol' Satchel Paige. My fastball looks like a change of pace alongside that little pistol bullet Satch shoots up the plate."

—*Washington Post* at the time of Paige's death

"The Cards had one pitcher who won fourteen straight games in a period of twenty-four days. Then when he lost his fifteenth game, 1–0, his manager fined him fifty bucks!"

—Statement made to underscore the softness of the modern pitcher; quoted by Bennett Cerf in *The Laugh's on Me*

"The doctors x-rayed my head and found nothing."

—After being hit in the head by a thrown ball in the '34 World Series

"The dumber a pitcher is, the better. When he gets smart and begins to experiment with a lot of different pitches, he's in trouble. All I ever had was a fast ball, a curve and a changeup. And I did pretty good."

—*Baseball Digest,* August 1961

"The game was closer than the score indicated."

—After a 1–0 game; quoted by George Will in *Men at Work*

"The only thing I got right was a kickoff."

—On his ill-advised one-game attempt to broadcast football in 1947. According to his obituary in the *St. Louis Post-Dispatch,* Dean referred to the officials as "umpires" and "those guys"; the head linesman was "a guy with a gun who must be low on ammunition or a poor shot, because I ain't seen him hit nobody."

"The players returned to their respectable bases."

—As a radio announcer

"The tying and winning runts are on second and third."

—Line from a game allegedly broadcast by Ol' Diz. One is tempted to call this apocryphal, but considering the fact that it is attributed to Dean, one must withhold such labels.

"There'll never be another like me."

—Oft-quoted line which served as Dean's epitaph. Among others, it was featured in an Associated Press collection of Dean quotes entitled "Dizzy Tales" which ran on July 18, 1974, following his death.

"Well now, a fiddle hitcher is usually a pitcher who's been up there [in the major leagues] a long time and lost his stuff so he takes to fiddle hitchin' to get them batters out. He's a guy what fiddles around—hitchin' his trousers, fixin' his cap, kickin' around the dirt so's the opposing batter will get riled and blown up."

—When asked what he meant when he referred to pitcher Howard Ehmke as a "fiddle hitcher"; quoted in *Baseball Digest,* July 1973

"Well, Pee Wee, I've been watching him for four innings and I believe that's a baseball he's throwin'."

—Quoted in the *Sporting News,* June 13, 1970. Dean was commenting on how present-day baseball announcers tend to be too statistic-minded, too colorless and too dull, and recalled a conversation with Pee Wee Reese when the two of them were on the air. Reese prompted him with this question: "Diz, you've watched this pitcher out there for four innings, and he's doing a great job. What would you say he's been throwin' out there?"

"'What baseball needs,' Diz told reporter John Lardner, 'is wild men like we used to have on the old St. Louis Cards—the gas-house gang—such as me, Rip Collins, Pepper Martin, Frank Frisch, and them.'

"'What was the salary scale in those days?' asked Lardner. 'That,' explained Dizzy Dean, 'is what drove us wild.'"

—Quoted by Bennett Cerf in *The Laugh's on Me*

"Why, they shot the wrong McKinley."

—As a Cardinals announcer, 1950, on umpire William McKinley. At the time it was said that Dean was the only sportscaster who could get away with such a line. It was Dean's way of protesting a bad call, but McKinley thought it so funny that he stopped Dean the next day to tell him so.

"You know how I say, 'Rizzuto slud into second.' I keep saying ain't.

"Well, what's wrong with ain't? And as for saying 'Rizzuto slid into second,' it just ain't natural. Sounds silly to me. Slud is something more than slid. It means sliding with great effort."

—On the use of the word "slud," which brought howls from the linguistic purists; quoted by Dan Daniel in the *New York World-Telegram and Sun,* 1951

DEAN, PAUL

"I don't claim to be the best educated fellow in the world, but then I don't think I'm the most ignorant, either. The same goes for Diz.

"Yes, I know that Diz butchers the English language sometimes during his broadcasts, but I think he does that just because he knows he doesn't need to pay much attention to the words he uses—since the listeners get a big kick out of hearing him make mistakes."

—*Sporting News,* August 1, 1951

DEAN, PAUL (CONTINUED)

"I think all the other players on this club ought to volunteer to take a cut so's Diz can get the salary he wants."

> —On his brother's salary squabbles with the Cardinals, uttered with tongue firmly in cheek; quoted in Mel Allen and Frank Graham's *It Takes Heart*

DEANE, BILL

"Most locals [Cooperstown, N.Y.] hate baseball, and I would venture to guess that fewer than half of Cooperstown's residents have been inside the Hall of Fame. If you want to see a World Series game in a Cooperstown tavern, you have to ask the bartender to change the channel."

—SABR-L, January 26, 2000

DeCINCES, DOUG

"Good defense in baseball is like good umpiring: It's there, you expect it, but you don't really appreciate it. But when it isn't there, then you notice it."

—Quoted in the *Chicago Tribune*, September 9, 1982

"In the back of every player's mind is the hope not to be the goat."

> —As a Baltimore Orioles infielder, on playing in the World Series; widely attributed

DEFORD, FRANK

"Ike was a good baseball fan, but shortly before his first Opening Day [1953] he announced that he would have to pass it up for a golfing vacation. All hell broke loose. The country club over the national pastime! Mercifully, old Jupiter Pluvius saved Ike, Opening Day was rained out, and he made it back from the links in time for the rain date. After that, Ike didn't mess around, boy, he made all Openers until 1959."

> —"The Year in Sports," *Sports Illustrated*, February 15, 1979

"[Baseball's] about lineups, and should the new commissioner [A. Bartlett Giamatti] issue any such papal bull as he did during his tenure at Yale, it ought to be in the form of a lineup card, to be posted in hearts and dugouts everywhere. It should read:

HOME TEAM
Green, CF
History, 1B
Park, RF
Civility, 3B
Individual, 2B
Group, SS
Law, LF
Offense, C
Defense, P

There would be no designated hitter."

> —"A Gentleman and a Scholar," *Sports Illustrated*, April 17, 1989

"Baseball is like the train going by in the night and the whistle blowing, and the little boy is lying in bed and he thinks of how the train is going to all sorts of wonderful, mysterious places in the world. And you would see the standings, every day, and they would read:

New York, Detroit, Boston, Cleveland, Philadelphia, Chicago, Washington, St. Louis, and it was the most evocative train schedule ever printed."

> —"Coming to Baseball . . . but Not Necessarily Being Loved Back," in Ron Fimrite, ed., *Birth of a Fan*

"Surely it is no mere happenstance that the last two words of 'The Star-Spangled Banner' are 'Play Ball!' There must be some psychic connection between the anthem and the games Americans play. Why is that? Almost never is the Banner sung at public events of a nonsporting nature. The anthem never serves as a prelude to a movie or opera or ballet or *Wheel of Fortune*."

> —"Playing It the American Way," *Sports Illustrated*, June 30, 1986

DEMPSEY, RICK

"Mr. President, you go tell the Russians we're having an awful good time over here playing baseball."

> —Baltimore Oriole catcher to President Ronald Reagan, via phone from the Oriole clubhouse in Philadelphia after Baltimore defeated the Phillies to win 1983 World Series, October 16

DENT, BUCKY

"Billy was a true Yankee—one of the truest ever. He always said he wanted to die a Yankee. He was his own man. He was fiery and could be charming. He was a great manager."

> —On Billy Martin after his death in December 1981

DEPEW, SENATOR CHAUNCEY

"All men who have ever lived and achieved success in this world had lived in vain if they knew not baseball."

> —Speech given at Delmonico's restaurant on April 8, 1889, welcoming the Spalding tour back from its World Tour

"When the American baseball team circled the globe, the effete monarchs of the east and the mighty powers of the west bowed their heads in humility and rose in acclaim."

> —Delmonico's speech, April 8, 1889

DEVINE, BING

"In 1977 almost every club will have people playing out their options. So in one year you'll have this great mass of free agents. And after that, you'll have a whole new game. It's been coming since the war. You had thousands of guys who came home from the war wanting to play baseball, and all those towns wanting to have minor-league teams. Then television came along and the trend got reversed. You soon had fewer minor leagues. Then you had the amateur draft and you no longer could go out and sign anybody you wanted. Finally, there were fewer players at the minor-league level, there were more college men in a hurry, there was more money at the top, basketball and golf and football were flooded with money. All sports became professionalized. In baseball, we should have seen it coming and prepared for the transition. Instead, we had dramatic scenes."

> —As Cardinals GM; quoted in the *New York Times*, November 7, 1976

DeWitt, Bill

"The greatest change that has come to base-ball in my time has been its growth. When we won the pennant at St. Louis in 1926, there were exactly five of us in the office: Rickey and Sam Breadon, Clarence Lloyd, who handled business arrangements on the road, a girl stenographer and me."

> —Quoted by Lee Allen when DeWitt was sixty-seven, from *Cooperstown Corner*

Dickey, Bill

"He hits a ball harder and further than any man I ever saw."

> —On Babe Ruth, early in 1951. Dickey had been a teammate of Ruth and had roomed with Gehrig.

"He just went out and did his job every day."

> —On Lou Gehrig; quoted in Raymond Mungo's *Confessions from Left Field*

"I don't recall the name, but you shore were a sucker for a high curve inside!"

> —To a former player who came up to him and asked if he recalled him; quoted by Bennett Cerf in *Try and Stop Me*

"It shore is purty. Much obliged."

> —On receiving a plaque from the Baseball Writers; quoted by Bennett Cerf in *Try and Stop Me*

"You guys got to see this kid we have in camp. Out of Class C ball, hits both ways, 500 feet both ways. You got to see him."

> —At the start of spring training, 1951, to a group of unbelieving reporters on Mickey

Mantle; reported later by Jack Orr in the *Sporting News*

Dickey, Glenn

"The guy with the biggest stomach will be the first to take off his shirt at a baseball game."

> —*San Francisco Chronicle*, 1981

Dillard, Annie

"A baseball weighted your hand just so, and fit it. Its red stitches, its good leather and hardness like skin over bone, seemed to call forth a skill both easy and precise. On the catch—the grounder, the fly, the line drive—you could snag a baseball in your mitt, where it stayed, snap, like a mouse locked in its trap, not like some pumpkin of a softball you merely halted, with a terrible sound like a splat. You could curl your fingers around a baseball, and throw it in a straight line. When you hit it with a bat it cracked—and your heart cracked, too, at the sound. It took a grass stain nicely, stayed round, smelled good, and lived lashed in your mitt all winter, hibernating."

> —On the baseball versus the "dumb softball" she was required to play with in school. From *An American Childhood*

Dilweg, Representative La Vern

"What does baseball do for America? It provides an opportunity for hundreds of thousands of war workers to relax in the fresh air and sunshine—and to continue to enjoy something that has been a significant part of American life for almost 100 years. But more important than that, it provides refreshing newspaper reading for millions of war workers who buy the late afternoon papers at the end of a day's work to get the latest sports results, and who buy the morning paper on the way to work for more recreational reading.

"Baseball news is a refreshing balance against the worrisome news that we are fighting a war. War news is "must reading—it is work. Sports news is refreshment—it is fun.

"These, I believe, are sound, logical arguments for the maintenance of spectator sports on the American scene, but the strongest argument of all, perhaps, is that men in our fighting forces—men in the fox holes, men who have achieved glorious victory in Africa, men who are battling the Japs to a standstill in the Pacific, awaiting only the day when they will launch the victory offensive, and men who are poised for the victorious invasion of Europe—want spectator sports to continue on the home front and hungrily await news of sports results.

"Where can you get a better example of a community rallying around a spectator sport than in Brooklyn, where the exploits of the 'Beloved Bums' on the baseball diamond are the personal concern of every fan in the most rabid baseball community in America?"

—Speech delivered by the Wisconsin congressman in the House of Representatives, 1943

DiMaggio, Dom

"If expansion baseball has so watered down the talent, why aren't the good hitters—Aaron, Clemente, Yastrzemski, Allen, Cedeño—hitting .400."

—*Los Angeles Times*, September 9, 1972

Joe DiMaggio (*New York Yankees*)

DiMaggio, Joe

"A ball player's got to be kept hungry to become a big-leaguer. That's why no boy from a rich family ever made the big leagues."

—Quoted in the *New York Times*, April 30, 1961

"All pitchers are born pitchers."

—Quoted in *Out of My League* by George Plimpton

"'I'd like to be down there enjoying the game with the fans, but it wouldn't work out. You don't get to see the game. And the people around [me] are distracted.' Baseball immortal Joe DiMaggio, watching a game from the press box."

—Quoted in *Life, the Year in Pictures*, 1994

"If anyone wants to know why three kids in one family made it to the big leagues they just had to know how we helped each other and how much we practiced back them. We did it every minute we could."

> —On himself and brothers Vince and Dom; quoted in *Giants of Baseball* by Bill Gutman

"I never saw a young ball player who had so much equipment. This is his fifth year, isn't it? Well, if he doesn't come big this year, I'm afraid he never will. Five years is time enough for anybody."

> —On Mickey Mantle, the *Sporting News*, April 6, 1955

"I no longer have it."

> —On himself, December 1951, turning down a contract renewal offer that carried a salary of $100,000. "When baseball is no longer fun, it's no longer a game. And so I've played my last game of ball"(*Time,* December 24, 1951).

"I think the greatest change [in baseball] has come with the disappearing of the minor leagues. Expansion, of course, has caused this, but too many kids today are playing major league ball and don't belong there."

> —*Dallas Times-Herald*

"I think there are some players who are born to play ball."

> —Widely attributed. *Born to Play Ball* was the title of Charles Einstein's early biography of Willie Mays. It was an extract of this quote.

"I told you fellows last spring I thought this would be my last year. I only wish I could have had a better year. But even if I had hit .350, this would have been the last year for me.

"You all know I have had more than my share of physical injuries and setbacks during my career. In recent years these have been much too frequent to laugh off. When baseball is no longer fun it's no longer a game.

"And so, I've played my last game of ball."

> —From an interview he gave to three reporters in Phoenix in February, 1951; quoted in the *Sporting News,* December 19, 1951

"I'd like to thank the Good Lord for making me a Yankee."

> —Comment made on Joe DiMaggio Day, October 1, 1949, at Yankee Stadium. Joseph P. Val of the *New York World-Telegram* pointed out, "You may not call it the outstanding event, but you must call it sports' outstanding moment of 1949."

"If I were sitting down with George Steinbrenner and based on what Dave Winfield got for his statistics, I'd have to say, 'George, you and I are about to become partners.'"

> —On what his salary would have been in the free-agent market of the 1980s; quoted in *Sports Illustrated,* May 18, 1981

"I'm a ballplayer, not an actor."

> —On why he always maintained a serious look even after hitting a home run.

"I'm just a ball player with one ambition, and that is to give all I've got to help my ball club win. I've never played any other way."

—Quoted in Joseph Durso, *Casey*, 1967

"It's got to be better than rooming with Joe Page."

—Response to being asked whether his marriage to Marilyn Monroe was going to be good for him

"Mr. Barrow, there is only one answer to that—Mr. Gehrig is terribly underpaid."

—When as a young Yankee he was reminded that at $43,000 he was making only a thousand a year less than sixteen-year veteran Lou Gehrig. Recalled in *Sports Illustrated*, April 26, 1976

"No outfielder is a real workman unless he can turn his back on the ball, run his legs off and take the catch over his shoulder. Back-pedaling outfielders get nowhere."

—"How to Play the Outfield" from his *Baseball for Everyone*

"Now I've had everything except the thrill of watching Babe Ruth play."

—On being inducted into the Hall of Fame in 1955. Shirley Povich of the *Washington Post* followed this through and reported: "DiMag said he had come close to seeing Ruth play when the Babe came to San Francisco on a barnstorming tour in 1927. 'I was a kid of 13 when the papers said Babe would be on the team that was coming to Frisco. There was going to be a special price of twenty-five cents for San Francisco kids.'

"Then what did DiMag mean, he'd never seen Ruth play ball?

"'I couldn't raise the twenty-five cents,' said the fellow who later got $100,000 a year from the Yankees."

"She's a plain kid. She'd give up the business if I asked her. She'd quit the movies in a minute."

—On his new bride, Marilyn Monroe, who instead quit the marriage; quoted by William B. Mead in *The Official Yankee Hater's Handbook*

"The phrase 'off with the crack of the bat,' while romantic, is really meaningless, since the outfielder should be in motion long before he hears the sound of the ball meeting the bat."

—*The Second Fireside Book of Baseball*, edited by Charles Einstein

"There is always some kid who may be seeing me for the first or last time. I owe him my best."

—When asked why he put such a high value on excellence; quoted by George Will in *Men at Work*

"There is no trick to catching a ball in the open field, no matter how far it is hit, as long as it stays in the air long enough. The test of an outfielder's skill comes when he has to go against the fence to make a catch."

—Quoted in *Mostly Baseball* by Tom Meany

"There's always some youngster coming up— they'll find somebody."

—Comment made in 1951 when asked who would replace him in 1952. It turns out to be Mickey Mantle; quoted in the *Sporting News*, April 4, 1951

DiMaggio, Joe (CONTINUED)

"Yes I have."

—His response to his wife Marilyn Monroe when she returned after having appeared on ten occasions before one hundred thousand servicemen and said: "It was so wonderful, Joe. You never heard such cheering." As reported by Gay Talese in a 1966 profile for *Esquire* magazine.

"You always get a special kick on opening day, no matter how many you go through. You look forward to it like a birthday party when you're a kid. You think something wonderful is going to happen."

—Widely attributed

DiMaggio, Joseph Peter

"Too many shoes, too many pants."

—Joe DiMaggio's father describing his son's sandlot days; quoted in his *Sporting News* obituary (d. May 3, 1949)

Dinhofer, Shelly Mehlman

"Organized baseball has flourished as the country's major spectator sport. Indeed, the lusty cry 'Play ball' is second only to the national anthem in patriotic fervor. And it has continued so, despite all the vicissitudes of major conflicts, illegitimate schemes, and historic scandals, despite big-business machinations and bad decisions. Under the artificial lights of night-time play and airless domed stadiums, baseball continues because it remains the best and most exciting playground of the American imagination."

—*The Art of Baseball* (New York: Harmony Books, 1990)

Dishman, Glenn

"I'd like to take back a couple of pitches—and maybe put another fielder out there somewhere."

—The Padres pitcher assessing a 12–8 loss to the Phillies, *St Louis Post-Dispatch* October 4, 1995

Ditmar, Art

"First guy who drives in a run we're going to stop the game and give him the ball."

—After a Yankee losing streak (three shutouts) in August 1960; quoted in *Sport*, December, 1960

Dobson, Pat

"Pain is nature's way of telling you the arm doesn't want to throw anymore."

—Quoted in *Mustache Gang* by Ron Bergman

Doby, Larry

"If you're black and you're working in a white man's world and you survive that long, you are strong. The disappointment in the 30 years is in the percentage of black ballplayers—a lot—and you're talking about no black managers now that Frank Robinson is gone, you're talking about one or two blacks in the front offices. It's heartbreaking not to have that representation."

—As a White Sox coach on his thirty years in organized baseball; quoted in the *Los Angeles Times*, July 6, 1977

DOCTOROW, E. L.

"The Giants were dressed in their baggy white uniforms with black pinstripes. The manager, McGraw, wore a heavy black cardigan over his barrel trunk with the letters 'NY' emblazoned on the left sleeve. He was short and pugnacious. Like his team he wore socks with thick horizontal stripes and the small flat cap with a peak and a button on the crown. . . . [He] stood at third base unleashing the most constant and creative string of vile epithets of anyone. His strident caw could be heard throughout the park."

—*The Giants of the Polo Grounds* by Noel Hynd

DODGE, H. C.

"Oh, don't you remember the game of base-
    ball we saw twenty years ago played.
When contests were true, and the sight free to
    all, and home-runs in plenty were made?
When we lay on the grass, and with thrills of
    de-light, watched the ball squarely pitched
    at the bat,
And easily hit, and then mount out of sight
    along with our cheers and our hat?
And then, while the fielders raced after the
    ball, the men on the bases flew round,
And came in together—four batters in all. Ah!
    That was the old game renowned.
Now salaried pitchers, who throw the ball
    curved at padded and masked catchers lame
And gate-money music and seats all reserved
    is all that is left of the game.
Oh, give us the glorious matches of old, when
    love of true sport made them great,

And not this new-fashioned affair always sold
    for the boodle they take at the gate."

—1886; quoted in: John Thorn, *The Game for All America* (St. Louis: Sporting News Publishing, 1988)

DOERR, BOBBY

"It's not so much being knocked down, but it's the idea of knocking me down for something somebody else did. That's what gets me."

—After being low-bridged by Joe Page on May 2, 1948, after back-to-back home runs by Ted Williams and Vern Stephens

DOGGETT, JERRY

"Well, the weatherman said 50 percent chance of rain and he might be right."

—As a Dodgers announcer; quoted by Jay Johnstone in *Temporary Insanity*

DONNELLY, RICH

"I managed a team that was so bad we considered a 2-and-0 count on the batter a rally."

—Recalling hard times in the minors; quoted in the *Sporting News*, May 24, 1989

"We have a shoe contract with Buster Brown."

—As a Pirates coach on the small players on the team; quoted in *Sports Illustrated*, December 28, 1987

DONOVAN, DICK

"Imagine playing baseball at the cocktail hour."

> —On the Senators' plan to begin games at 6:00 p.m. to increase attendance; quoted in *Sports*, December 1963

DOS PASSOS, JOHN

"The judge could hand out twenty year sentences as lightheartedly as he'd fine some Joe five bucks for speeding. It didn't seem to occur to him that he was destroying the lives of decent men. Landis's cracker barrel manner had even taken in some of the defense lawyers. Underneath he was a butcher. The punishment was all out of proportion.

"The crime our boys committed was to take the unpopular side in the struggle to keep America out of war. . . . How could a man live with himself after doing what Kenesaw Mountain Landis did to men's lives for just saying a few illegal words? He throve on it. His recompense was to be handed $25,000 a year as czar of organized baseball."

> —Narrator Blackie Bowman, in *Midcentury* (Cambridge, Mass.: Riverside Press, 1961)

DOUBLEDAY, GENERAL ABNER

"I have the honor to apply for permission to purchase for the Regimental Library a few portraits of distinguished generals, Battle pictures, and some of Rogers groups of Statuary particularly those relative to the actions of the Colored population of the south. This being a colored regiment ornaments of this kind seem very appropriate. I would also like to purchase baseball implements for the amusement of the men and a Magic Lantern for the same purpose. The fund is ample and I think these expenditures would add to the happiness of the men."

> —Former Civil War general, now a colonel in command of the 24th U.S. Infantry's "Colored Regiment," Fort McKavett, Texas, addressing a request to General E.D. Townsend, Adjutant General, U.S. Army, Washington, D.C., June 17, 1871. Despite the claim, long ago disputed, that he invented baseball, this is the only connection that has surfaced tying his name to baseball.

DOWNEY, MIKE

"Billy Martin makes the game lean a little more toward professional wrestling. He might as well wear a hood and come to the park as the Masked Manager."

> —Columnist tiring of Martin's run-ins with umpires; quoted in the *San Francisco Examiner*, May 5, 1983

DOYLE, LARRY

"I'll never forget the day Merkle failed to touch second. I was injured at the time and didn't play that day. I think Buck Herzog was at second. Anyway, Merkle and I went back to our boarding house and he never did have dinner that night, but just stayed in the room."

> —The Giant who roomed with Fred Merkle; from *Cooperstown Corner: Columns from the Sporting News, 1962–1969*, by Lee Allen.

DRAVECKY, DAVE

"All you have to do is pick up a baseball. It begs to you: Throw me. If you took a year to design an object to hurl, you'd end up with that little spheroid small enough to nestle in your fingers but big enough to have some heft, lighter than a rock but heavier than a hunk of wood. Its even, neat stitching, laced into the leather's slippery white surface, gives your fingers a purchase. A baseball was made to throw. It's almost irresistible."

—*Comeback* by Dave Dravecky and Tom Stafford (Zondervan Books)

"Here's how to tell whether I'm pitching at my best: Watch how many bats I break. When my slider is perfectly placed, it comes in at a right-handed batter as though it were off the outside corner of the plate. Then at the last second, when he's decided not to swing, the pitch breaks down and in, onto the outside corner. That's called a backdoor slider.

"It sets up my fastball inside. The batter who's seen that slider on the outside corner is leaning out over the plate. A fastball on the inside corner catches him leaning too far. He swings, but he's hitting on the thin part of the bat, and it shatters.

"That day I broke five bats."

—*Comeback*. The day in question was the second game of the 1987 National League Championship Series in St. Louis—the game during which he ran his postseason record to 19 $^2/_3$ scoreless innings.

"I can often tell whether the baseball is too big as I watch it fly from the umpire's hand to my mitt."

—On a pitcher's ability to tell the difference in individual balls, despite their supposed standardization; from *Comeback*

DREBINGER, JOHN

"He was the most uninhibited human being I have ever known. He just did things."

—On Babe Ruth; quoted by Robert W. Creamer in *Babe: The Legend Comes to Life*

"Roger Maris yesterday became the first major league player in history to hit more than sixty home runs in a season."

—On Roger Maris's 61st home run, *New York Times*, October 2, 1961

"When the One Great Scorer comes to
    write against your name—
He marks—not that you won or lost
    —but how did that last man go out?"

—After missing a play as official scorer

DRESSEN, CHUCK

"It was a good play, but I gotta see him do it again."

—Brooklyn Dodgers manager, after Willie Mays made a running catch, turned 360 degrees and threw out a runner at the plate; widely attributed.

DRESSEN, CHUCK (CONTINUED)

"Just hold them for a few innings, fellas. I'll think of something."

> —Quoted in *You Can't Beat the Hours* by Mel Allen and Ed Fitzgerald

"The announcer says, 'Will the lady who lost her nine children at the ballpark please pick them up immediately. They are beating the Cubs, 10–0, in the seventh.'"

> —In 1981; quoted in Bob Chieger's *The Cubbies*

"The coldest winter I ever spent was a summer in San Francisco."

> —As a Giants manager; widely attributed

"The Giants is dead."

> —One of baseball's most requoted quotes, uttered in the summer of 1951, when the Giants were hopelessly behind Dressen's league-leading Dodgers. The line was rendered classic when the Giants won the pennant from the Dodgers in the ninth inning of the third game of a three-game playoff.
>
> In his column "From the Ruhl Book," Oscar Ruhl wrote in the September 2, 1953, *Sporting News,* that "the Chuck Dressen crusher 'The Giants Is Dead' was posted in the Polo Grounds' clubhouse by Leo Durocher to arouse the Harlemites to a fury.... The Giants, however, promptly proved the correctness of one of Chuck's statements by dropping three straight to the boys from Flatbush.... Incidentally, the *Brooklyn Eagle,* backed by the New York Board of Education, says that Manager Charley Dressen was grammatically correct when he stated that the 'Giants is dead.' A spokesman for the Board of Education told the *Eagle* that the term Giants refers to an entity, a single body. The spokesman explained, 'You would say the United States is, not are, the greatest nation in the world.' Added the spokesman, 'Of course, if one member of the Giants were alive you couldn't say the Giants is dead. But,' he concluded, 'every member of this entity is dead, hence the Giants is, too.'"

"The umpires call Hodges out on bad balls now and then. No doubt they are bad calls. Hodges comes back and tells me how bad they are. But he doesn't tell them. He just walks away from there. I keep telling him, 'You let them know it is a bad call, don't argue or battle about it, but just don't let them think they are right.' He's such a nice guy he wouldn't even do that. The umps think he is the nicest guy in the league. But you don't have to be that nice."

> —On Gil Hodges. As Dodger manager; quoted in the *Sporting News,* 1951

DRUMMOND, CALVIN T. "CAL"

"The worst thing that can happen to a man is to be born without guts and be an umpire. No umpire likes criticism, but you don't expect to be patted on the back. Nobody comes to see you. The managers are going to challenge you because that's their job. The writers and the announcers are going to criticize you. That's their job. What it amounts to is you've got your job and they've got theirs."

> —Quote which appeared in his the *Sporting News* obituary (he died on May 3, 1970 just a day

before the fifty-two-year-old was scheduled to return to the majors after seemingly overcoming a serious injury. Drummond, an American League umpire from 1960–1969, saw his career put on hold in 1969 when a foul ball struck him in the head. The injury was serious and Drummond required brain surgery that would leave him unconscious for two weeks.

DRYDEN, CHARLES

"Of such pleasing incidents is the pastime made up."

> —This was one of eight "Famous Baseball Sayings" collected by Ernest J. Lanigan of the Hall of Fame when he identified himself as "Historian and authority on the game for 65 years"

"The American League consists of Ban Johnson, the 'spit ball' and the Wabash Railroad."

> —Quoted in Alfred H. Spink, *The National Game,* 2nd ed. (St. Louis: National Game Publishing, 1911)

"Washington—first in war, first in peace, last in the American League."

> —Dryden's quote gave rise to an equally unflattering line describing St. Louis: "First in shoes, first in booze, last in the American League."

DRYSDALE, DON

"A torn rotator cuff is a cancer for a pitcher. And if a pitcher gets a badly torn one, he has to face the facts: It's all over, baby."

> —Widely attributed

"My own little rule was two for one—if one of my teammates got knocked down, then I knocked down two on the other team."

> —Quoted in the 1981 Hall of Fame *Yearbook*

"It's driving me crazy. I can't find where he keeps it. Me? I didn't throw the spitter. I was blessed with a long middle finger."

> —On Gaylord Perry, from the jacket of Perry's autobiographical confessional *Me and the Spitter*

"My mother told me never to put my dirty fingers in my mouth."

> —In denying he threw the spitter; widely quoted, including in Whitey Ford's *Slick* and Phil Pepe's *No Hitter*

"Nuts to history. Tell me who won the game."

> —Yelling at a radio in 1965 as he came into a hotel room and listened to Sandy Koufax being described as an immortal because he had just pitched his third no-hitter. Drysdale, who had left the team for one night, knew that the '65 Dodgers often had to get shutouts to win; from George Vecsey's *Baseball Life of Sandy Koufax*

DRYSDALE, DON (CONTINUED)

"Sooner or later, you have to say it's my ball and half the plate is mine. Only I never let on which half of the plate I wanted."

—On pitching, *New York Times*, July 5, 1993

"The pitcher has to find out if the hitter is timid. And if the hitter is timid, he has to remind the hitter he's timid."

—On intimidation; quoted in the *New York Times*, July 9, 1979

"When the ball is over the middle of the plate, the batter is hitting it with the sweet part of the bat. When it's inside, he's hitting it with the part of the bat from the handle to the trademark, when it's outside, he's hitting it with the end of the bat. You've got to keep the ball away from the sweet part of the bat. To do that the pitcher has to move the hitter off the plate."

—Quoted by William Safire and Leonard Safir in *Words of Wisdom*

"When we played, World Series checks meant something. Now all they do is screw up your taxes."

—As an announcer; widely quoted

DUGAN, JOE

"Born? Hell, Babe Ruth wasn't born. He fell from a tree."

—*The Giants of the Polo Grounds* by Noel Hynd

"It's always the same. Combs walks, Koenig singles. Ruth hits one out of the park. Gehrig doubles. Lazzeri triples. Then Dugan goes in the dirt on his can."

—Quoted in the 50th Anniversary Hall of Fame *Yearbook*

"My father looked at the money, then glanced at my seven brothers and sisters. He couldn't contain himself. He said, 'For five hundred dollars you can take the whole family.'"

—As a Philadelphia Athletics bonus baby, SABR Collection 1917

"To understand him you had to understand this: He wasn't human."

—On teammate Babe Ruth

DUNNE, FINLEY PETER

"In me younger days 'twas not considered ray-spectable f'r to be an athlete. An athlete was always a man that was not sthrong enough f'r wurruk. Fractions dhruv him fr'm school an' th' vagrancy laws dhruv him to baseball."

—*Mr. Dooley's Opinions*, 1901

DUQUETTE, TIM

"New England has three great things that everyone agrees on from birth: sitting in the bleachers at Fenway, vacationing at Cape Cod and I've forgotten the third."

—Former Springfield College catcher; quoted in Thomas Boswell, *Why Time Begins on Opening Day* (New York: Doubleday, 1984)

DURBIN, RICHARD H. (D-ILL.)

"Mr. Speaker, I rise to condemn the desecration of a great American symbol. No, I am not referring to flag burning, I am referring to the baseball bat.

"Several experts tell us that the wooden baseball bat is doomed to extinction, that major league baseball players will soon be standing at home place with aluminum bats in their hands.

"Baseball fans have been forced to endure countless indignities by those who just cannot leave well enough alone. Designated hitters, plastic grass, uniforms that look like pajamas, chicken clowns dancing on the baselines, and of course the most heinous sacrilege, lights in Wrigley Field.

"Are we willing to hear the crack of a bat replaced by the dinky ping? Are we ready to see the Louisville Slugger replaced by the aluminum ping dinger? Is nothing sacred?

"Please, do not tell me that wooden bats are too expensive, when players who cannot hit their weight are being paid more money than the president of the United States.

"Please, do not try to sell me on the notion that these metal clubs will make better hitters.

"What is next? Teflon baseballs? Radar-enhanced gloves? I ask you.

"I do not want to hear about saving trees. Any tree in America would gladly give its life for the glory of a day at home plate.

"I do not know if it will take a constitutional amendment to keep the baseball traditions alive, but if we forsake the great Americana of broken-bat singles and pine tar, we will have certainly lost our way as a nation."

—Speech given in the U.S. House of Representatives on July 26, 1989. It was occasioned by a *Sports Illustrated* article on the increasing use of aluminum bats. The speech attracted much media attention, to the surprise of the congressman.

DUROCHER, LEO

"A buffoon is a drunk on a hitting spree. A drunk is a pitcher who's lost his fast ball. A confirmed drunk is a pitcher with a sore arm. An incurable drunk is a pitcher who hasn't won a game all season."

—From *Nice Guys Finish Last*

"As long as I've got one chance to beat you I'm going to take it."

—From *Nice Guys Finish Last*

Leo Durocher (*Houston Astros*)

Durocher, Leo (continued)

"Do you think you could hit half that for me?"

—On calling up Willie Mays from the minors. Mays was reluctant to face major-league pitching. Leo asked him what he was batting in Minneapolis and Mays said .477; from *Willie Mays* by Arnold Hano

"Field, throw, run, hit for distance and hit for average."

—The five things that Willie Mays could do in concert better than anyone else in the history of the game; widely attributed. He refined the sentiment and as Astros manager in 1973 was quoted as saying, "There are only five things you can do in baseball—run, throw, catch, hit, and hit with power."

"Give me some scratching, diving, hungry ballplayers who come to kill you."

—*Nice Guys Finish Last*

"He had everything but luck. If he'd been lucky, he'd have been in the Hall of Fame long ago."

—On the accident-prone Dodgers star Pete Reiser

"He was the best I ever had, with the possible exception of Mays. At that he was even faster than Willie."

—As former New York Giants manager, on outfielder Pete Reiser; widely attributed

"How you play the game is for college boys. When you're playing for money, winning is the only thing that matters. Show me a good loser in professional sports, and I'll show you an idiot."

—*Nice Guys Finish Last*

"I come to win."

—Durocher's personal motto; quoted by Roger Kahn in *How the Weather Was*

"I don't table-hop, I don't eat with drunken bums and as far as I'm concerned you should be eating out of a trough."

—When the president of NBC, which Durocher was working for, called him to his table in a restaurant; from *Nice Guys Finish Last*

"I never did anything I didn't try to beat you at. If I pitch pennies I want to beat you. If I'm spitting at a crack in the sidewalk I want to beat you."

—*Nice Guys Finish Last*

"I never questioned the integrity of an umpire. Their eyesight, yes."

—*Nice Guys Finish Last*

"I'm not one of those old-timers who says everything was better in my day. I think ballplayers today are better than the players were when I played. But whatever happened to 'sit down, shut up and listen'? God forbid you talk to a player that way today. And if players in my day talked to managers the way players today do, well, they were gone in a hurry. In the old days, you never talked to the manager. You heard from the traveling secretary. And if you didn't like it, well son, you could just go home."

—*Los Angeles Herald-Examiner* as a former manager, June 1, 1975

"If a man knows he's played bad ball and won't admit it, he shouldn't be out there."

—As Giants manager

"If any of my players don't take a drink now and then they'll be gone. You don't play this game on gingersnaps."

—As Cubs manager. Widely quoted.

"If I were playing third base and my mother were rounding third with the run that was going to beat us, I'd trip her. Oh, I'd pick her up and brush her off and say, 'Sorry, Mom, but nobody beats me.'"

—Widely quoted

"If somebody came up and hit .450, stole 100 bases and performed a miracle in the field every day I'd still look you in the eye and say Willie[Mays] was better. He could do the five things you have to do to be a superstar—hit, hit with power, run, throw and field. And he had that other magic ingredient that turns a super-star into a super superstar. He lit up the room when he came in. He was a joy to be around."

—Quoted in *Grand Slams and Fumbles* by Peter Beilenson

"I'm wearing the same socks, shirt and under-wear, too!"

—During a winning streak

"In order to become a big-league manager you have to be in the right place at the right time. That's Rule #1."

—From *Nice Guys Finish Last*

"It kills you. You spend your life looking for the great talent that comes along about one a decade, and you have to sit there and see it being thrown away."

—On Cesar Cedeño, whom he managed at Houston; from *Nice Guys Finish Last*

"It's possible to spend money anywhere in the world if you put your mind to it, something I proved conclusively by running up huge debts in Cincinnati."

—Quoted by Burt Randolph Sugar in *The Book of Sports Quotes*

"Joe Louis, Jascha Heifetz, Sammy Davis, and Nashua rolled into one."

—Describing Willie Mays; quoted in *Out of My League* by George Plimpton

"Managing a ball club is the most vulnerable job in the world. From the moment you take the job you're vulnerable. If you don't win, you're going to be fired. If you do win, you've only put off the day you're going to be fired. And no matter what you do, you're going to be second-guessed. The manager is the only person in the ball park who has to call it right now. Everybody else can call it after it's over."

—*Nice Guys Finish Last*

"Nice guys finish last."

—From an interview by Frank Graham. When asked "Why don't you be a nice guy and admit you're wrong?" Durocher answered in an arm-waving tirade, "I don't want to be a nice guy. No nice guys around here . . . Who ever saw a nicer guy in baseball than Mel Ott?" pointing to the opposing dugout, "and where is he?"

According to Paul F. Boller Jr. and John George in their *They Never Said It,* Durocher never put it exactly the way the quote has him saying it. They insist that he actually said of the Giants as a team: "Take a look at them. All nice guys. They'll finish last. Nice guys. Finish last." They add, "But the last two sentences were later 'run together,' giving a new meaning to what the Brooklyn manager was saying." They go on to insist that it was Jimmy Cannon, not Graham, who picked up the phrase as a way of encapsulating Durocher's view of life. Durocher himself, however, used the "run together" version in the retelling and as the title of his 1975 autobiography.

"Nobody ever won a pennant without a star shortstop."

— Quoted by Ken Smith in the 1976 Street and Smith *Baseball Yearbook*

"People are always telling me that the biggest thrill in my life must have been watching Bobby Thomson's home run go into the bleachers. They are wrong on only two counts: (1) I didn't see it. (2) I wasn't thrilled, because I went into complete shock. The mind, I learned that day, can be a very strange and frightening thing."

— *Nice Guys Finish Last*

"Some guys are admired for coming to play, as the saying goes. I prefer those who come to kill."

— Quoted in the *Sporting News,* February 1961

"Something went out of baseball when the Dodgers left Brooklyn, and not all the king's horses or all the king's men can ever put it back."

— *Nice Guys Finish Last*

"The Cubs are not an eighth-place ball club."

— On taking over the Cubs after their eighth-place 1965 finish. Or as Durocher put it later: "The Cubs thereupon sank like a stone into the cellar, giving every card-carrying member of the Baseball Writers Association of America the chance to write, 'Durocher said it wasn't an eighth-place team, and he was right. It's a tenth-place team.'"

"The guy's got a fault? Dandruff, maybe."

— His assessment of Red Sox third baseman Frank Malzone; quoted in *Out of My League* by George Plimpton

"The philosophy on the field was totally different than it is today. Baseball was a form of warfare played under a set of rules that were not necessarily drawn up by the league officials and certainly not by the Marquis of Queensberry."

— On his days as a player, from *Nice Guys Finish Last*

"There are only five things you can do in baseball—run, throw, catch, hit, and hit with power."

— *Time,* July 16, 1973

"There's no question about it, Babe Ruth was the greatest instinctive baseball player who ever lived. He was a great hitter, and he had been a great pitcher. The only thing he couldn't really do was run, but when he went from first to third—or stole a base for you—he invariably made it because he instinctively did the right thing.

"All of which proves, in case you have ever wondered, that you don't have to be a mental giant to be a great baseball player. In anything that took any intelligence, like remembering a sign, the Babe was dumb. Which is why Mr. Huggins never bothered to give him a sign. If not being able to remember the names of teammates he had been playing with for years is a sign of dumbness, then the Babe has to be the dumbest man I have ever known."

—*Nice Guys Finish Last*

"Van Mungo liked to drink a bit. Anything. Even hair tonic."

—Quoted in Raymond Mungo's *Confessions from Left Field*.

"We're in first place, they got to worry. We pick up ground when we get rained out. We're in first place, why worry? Let them worry."

—As Giants manager in 1954 to his team; quoted in Joe Garagiola's *Baseball Is a Funny Game*

"When I was managing Brooklyn I'd have to stop at this light each day on the way home. On the corner was a bar, and the guys would always yell, 'Hey, Leo, who won?' If I said, 'us,' they'd say, 'great going.' If I said, 'Them,' they'd call me a dumb sonofabitch."

—As former Dodgers manager; widely attributed

"You don't save a pitcher for tomorrow. Tomorrow it may rain."

—His second most-quoted remark

"You know what you can do with that petition. You can wipe your ass with it. Mr. Rickey is on his way down here, and all you have to do is tell him about it. I'll play an elephant if he can do the job. This fellow is a real, great ballplayer. He's going to win a pennant for us. From everything I hear, he's only the first. Only the first, boys!"

—Said to would-be signers of a petition drawn up by several veteran Brooklyn Dodger players demanding the removal of Jackie Robinson from the team's first exhibition game during the team's 1947 spring training. Quoted in John J. Monteleone, ed., *Branch Rickey's Little Blue Book* (New York: Macmillan, 1995)

"You think I liked it when I had to go to see Mr. Stengel and say, 'Congratulations, Casey, you played great'? I'd have liked to stick a knife in his chest and twist it inside him.

"I come to play! I come to beat you! I come to kill you! That's the way Miller Huggins, my first manager, brought me up, and that's the way it has always been with me."

—*Nice Guys Finish Last*

DURSO, JOSEPH

"Oriole baseball, as it flourished in 1894, was a combination of hostility, imagination, speed, and piracy."

—*The Giants of the Polo Grounds* by Noel Hynd

DUTIEL, H. J.

"A game which consists of tapping a ball with a piece of wood, then running like a lunatic."

—*Webster's New World Dictionary of Quotable Definitions*

DWYER, JIM

"I love DH'ing. I think it's the greatest job in the world. It's like pinch hitting, except you get a second, third and fourth chance."

—On being a DH; quoted in *The Major League Baseball Newsletter*, May 1989

"The Hall of Fame is for baseball people. Heaven is for good people."

—As a Twin on Pete Rose's chance to enter the Hall of Fame, *Sporting News*, September 11, 1989

DYKES, JIMMY

"I couldn't. I carry my cigars in my back pocket and I was afraid I'd break them."

—Philadelphia Athletics infielder, when asked why he didn't slide

Jimmy Dykes (*Cleveland Indians*)

"Just as I thought, only one 'i.'"

—On being peeved at being called out on strikes, he asked plate umpire George Moriarty how he spelled his last name; quoted in Joseph McBride's *High and Inside*

"The only thing Larsen fears is sleep."

—On Don Larsen as his manager in Baltimore; quoted in *It Takes Heart* by Mel Allen and Frank Graham Jr.

"When you're winning, beer tastes better."

—As Tigers manager; widely atrributed

"Without Ernie Banks, the Cubs would finish in Albuquerque."

—Quoted by Burt Randolph Sugar in *The Book of Sports Quotes*

DYKSTRA, LENNY

"The last time I hit a home run in the bottom of the ninth to win the game was in Strat-O-Matic."

> —On homering to beat the Astros in the bottom of the ninth to give the Mets a come-from-behind win in Game 3 of the 1986 NLCS; widely attributed

"The world will end before there is another .400 hitter. . . . I think that it was mentioned in the Bible."

> —*Baltimore Sun,* December 30, 1990

DYLAN, BOB

"In the Fifties, every red-blooded American boy either wanted to play baseball or be Elvis Presley."

> —*Rolling Stone,* September 7, 2006

E

EAGLETON, SENATOR THOMAS

"With respect to my home city of St. Louis, we once proudly had the title 'First in booze, first in shoes, and last in the American League.' We lost our American League team. Our shoes went to Taiwan and Korea. God, do not take from us our beer."

—On a proposal to add an extra tax on beer; quoted in *Sports Illustrated,* August 9, 1982

EAKINS, THOMAS

"Ball players are very fine in their build. They are the same stuff as bull fighters only bull fighters are older and a trifle stronger perhaps. I think I will try to make a base ball picture some day in oil. It will admit of fine figure painting."

—Artist, in letter to Philadelphia painter and teacher Earl Shinn, 1875; quoted in Shelly Mehlman Dinhofer, *The Art of Baseball* (New York: Harmony Books, 1990)

EARLY, GERALD

"Every team gets 27 outs . . . no matter what the score. In a sense, liberals should love this game because it provides an absolutely level playing field. Three strikes and you're out. Four balls and you walk. Three outs and your side is retired. Everyone is granted the same exact set of opportunities to succeed. But baseball does not promise, simply because each side gets 27 outs, that your chances of winning are truly equal. If the fielding team plays poorly, the batting team is assured of more than 27 outs. Baseball does not equalize team talent or how a team will exploit its opportunities. Conservatives should love baseball: a game of equal opportunity that says clearly that there is no such thing as equal outcomes."

—Explaining baseball to his wife, whose response was "No wonder all our presidents go to ball games." *American Poetry Review,* July–August 1996

"I think there are only three things that America will be known for 2,000 years from now when they study this civilization: the Constitution, jazz music and baseball."

—The writer appearing on Ken Burns's PBS series *Baseball;* quoted in *Life, The Year in Pictures,* 1994

"The real reason black Americans don't play baseball is that they don't want to. They are not attracted to the game. Baseball has little hold on the black imagination, even though it existed as an institution in black life for many tears. Among blacks, baseball is not passed down from father to son or father to daughter ... Even the integration of baseball, symbolized by [Jackie] Robinson, reminds blacks that their institutions were weak and eventually had to be abandoned. As the controversies over reparations for slavery and the Confederate flag have shown, it is difficult to sell African Americans the American past as most Americans have come to know it."

—From his *Time* essay "Where Have We Gone Mr. Robinson?" April 12, 2007, on the decline of African-Americans in baseball

EASLER, MIKE

"I think, you know, the guys are, you know, we're playing hard, you know, we're playing, you know, we're going out there giving everything we've got—I know I am, and I know the other guys are, you know. It's just sometimes, you know, you get guys that's hot like Matthews, he's swinging the bat real good this series, you know, and these guys been throwing good ball games. You get a guy like Niekro, I mean, you know, they can pitch, you know, and these guys come against us, you know, they just love to knock off a pennant contender like us, you know, and, you know, they're just loosey-goosey, you know, they just go out there and just, you know, just try to just bury us, you know, but the thing is, we're playing our type of baseball, you know, and the breaks been going their way."

—In answering the question, "The Braves have beaten you two straight, Mike . . . you guys in a slump?" *Sports Illustrated,* September 15, 1980

EASTER, LUKE

"I just hit 'em and forget 'em."

—As a Buffalo Bison questioned on a colossal home-run ball; quoted in the 1984 *Baseball Research Journal*

EBBETS, CHARLES

"Baseball is still in its infancy."

—In a speech that he gave before the first game of the 1912 season. In 1960, on the occasion of the cornerstone from Ebbets Field being moved to Cooperstown, an article in the *New York Herald Tribune* noted, "Even Ebbets had no idea of how right he was. It was years before the advent of radio, television, night baseball, air transportation, rabbit ball, player representation, pension plan, all-star games, minimum salaries, the negro in baseball and two-platoons." Ebbet's line was one of eight "Famous Baseball Sayings" collected by Ernest J. Lanigan of the Hall of Fame when he identified himself as "Historian and authority on the game for 65 years."

ECHEVARRÍA, ROBERTO GONZÁLEZ

"The gestural code of baseball, in its movements and cadence, is as universal as that of Roman Catholicism. Has anyone noticed the sudden silence before a pitcher delivers the ball, uncannily like the one just before the priest raises the Host? They are the same silence and motion today, when Frank Viola throws, as when Warren Spahn was pitching 30 years ago."

> —"The Altar Boys of Summer," book review of *Baseball and Lesser Sports* by Wilfrid Sheed, in *New York Times Book Review*, June 2, 1991

ECKERSLEY, DENNIS

"It's like the Kennedy assassination. Everyone I see comes up and tells me where they were and what they were doing when Gibson hit that home run."

> —On the pitch he delivered to Kirk Gibson in the ninth inning of Game 1 of the 1988 World Series; quoted in the *Washington Post*, December 24, 1989

EDISON, THOMAS ALVA

"Baseball is the greatest of American games. Some say football, but it is my firm belief, and it shall always be, that baseball has no superior. . . . I have not attended very many big games, but I don't believe you can find a more ardent follower of baseball than myself, as a day seldom passes when I do not read the sporting pages of the newspaper. In this way I keep a close tab on the two major leagues and

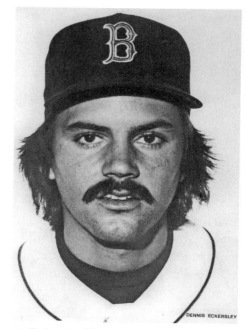

Dennis Eckersley (*Boston Red Sox*)

Ty Cobb with Thomas Edison (*Museum of Modern Art Film Still Archives*)

there was one time when I could name the players of every club in both leagues."

> —Quoted when he was at his Fort Myers, Florida, laboratory, *St. Petersburg Times*, February 25, 1927

"Is that so? I thought you were a batter."

> —To Al Simmons, who had identified himself as an outfielder when the two met at an exhibition game in Fort Myers. As Bob Broeg later wrote of the meeting, "Al beamed. The old boy might not have known a shortstop from a short circuit, but he'd heard about the great Sim, a swaggering, confident slugger, and that was good enough for Bucketfoot Al and made it even. Sim had heard about Edison, too." (Both quotes from the *Sporting News,* June 26, 1971.)

EDITORIALS AND HEADLINES

BALTIMORE SUN

"We do not like to say one word against the rational and healthful amusement of the boys, but they may go in their amusements, and do go, a little further than ought to be allowable. Almost every boy, who can raise a ball, appears to be about this time using it—they are thrown against the sides of houses, regardless of the effect which may be upon window glass or any thing else."

> —February 17, 1847

BASEBALL MAGAZINE

"THOMAS JEFFERSON, when he wrote the Declaration of Independence, made proper provision for baseball when he declared that all men are free and equal. That's why they are at the ballgame, banker and bricklayer, lawyer and common laborer."

> —1901

BOSTON GLOBE

"'There is a man in the government hospital for the insane,' said an ex-governor of Maryland to a Washington letter writer, 'who is perfectly sane on every subject except baseball. He knows more about baseball than any other man in America. The authorities have humored him so that he has been able to cover the walls of his large room with intricate schedules of the games played of every important club, and the individual record of every important player. He takes an astrological view of the game. He explains every defeat and every success on astrological principles. It is because a man was born in this month or under this star or that. He has figured it all out. His sense has gone with it. He is the typical base ball crank.'"

> —April 20, 1884

CHICAGO HERALD AND EXAMINER

"As Jackson departed from the Grand Jury room, a small boy clutched at his sleeve and tagged along after him.

"'Say it ain't so, Joe,' he pleaded. 'Say it ain't so.'

"'Yes, kid, I'm afraid it is,' Jackson replied.

"'Well, I never would've thought it,' the boy said."

> —September 30, 1920; quoted in Eliot Asinof, *Eight Men Out* (New York: Holt, Rinehart and Winston, 1963)

CINCINNATI ENQUIRER

"Whenever a ball looks like this:

0

0

0

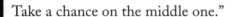

Take a chance on the middle one."

> —Advice offered to players who drank too much, 1903; quoted in Lee Allen's *The Hot Stove League* (1955)

CINCINNATI GAZETTE

"The baseball mania has run its course. It has no future as a professional endeavor."

> — Editorial, 1879

KANSAS CITY JOURNAL

"The absolute poverty of written language to express human emotions was probably first exemplified when the Paleozoic sporting writer with his stylus and his papyrus-pad tried to describe the first cocoanut twirling game between the 'Megatherium Mud Haters' and the 'Megalosaurus Giants.' From that time to this the language of sport has always been in advance of the ages. The baseball writer, with his sleeves rolled up and his trusty typewriter eating on a roll of paper, is a maker of language. His is Nature's own method. He gets close to his readers because he is sublimely free from hampering grammatical forms, and his vocabulary is evolved as he goes along. It weaves itself from the woof of encircling smoke from his malodorous pipe, and as he gaily sails out into the boundless realm of his red and green imagination he coyly picks the choicest idioms and flits from flower to flower in the glorious garden of budding synonym and blooming metaphor.

"The baseball writer writes for those who understand his linguistic vagaries, and revel in the seeming confusion of his complex phraseology. He is the journalistic free lance, who denies the right of precedent and rides roughshod over the stickler for literary finish. He knows his readers and they know him. When he says, 'Tinker led off for the Cubs and ozoned,' every legitimate, thirty-third degree 'fan' grasps immediately the graphic picture thus painted.

"Let the baseball writer alone. In his very frenzied philology he contributes a vivid and refreshing contrast to the wearying precision of the nice, round editorial sentence. And we who also write for a living must confess to a sneaking admiration for his boldness, his originality, and the easy familiarity of his style."

> —From *Kansas City Journal;* reprinted in *Washington Post* (May 3, 1905) and *Sporting Life* (May 20, 1905)

THE NATION

"We do not trust cashiers half so much, or diplomats, or policemen, or physicians, as we trust an outfielder or shortstop."

> —1920

New York Times

"There is really reason to believe that baseball is gradually dying out in this country. It has been openly announced by an athletic authority that what was once called the national game is being steadily superseded by cricket. . . .

. . .

"Our experience with the national game of baseball has been sufficiently thorough to convince us that it was in the beginning a sport unworthy of men and that it is now, in its fully developed state, unworthy of gentlemen."

—Editorial, 1881; quoted in H. Allen Smith, *Low and Inside* (Garden City, N.Y.: Doubleday, 1949)

"Sometimes an idea comes along that is so stupid, all you can do is stand back, give it some room, and stare:

THE LOS ANGELES ANGELS OF ANAHEIM

That is the new official name of a major league baseball team in Southern California that (1) does not play in Los Angeles, (2) is not moving to Los Angeles and (3) has no plans to put Los Angeles on its uniforms."

—January 6, 2005

Saturday Evening Post

"It is important to remember, in an imperfect and fretful world, that we have one institution which is practically above reproach and above criticism. Nobody worth mentioning wants to change its constitution or limit its powers. The government is not asked to inspect, regulate, suppress, guarantee, or own it.

"There is no movement afoot that we know of to uplift it, like the stage, or to abolish it, like marriage. No one complains that it is vulgar, like the newspapers, or that it assassinates genius, like the magazines. It rouses no class passions and, while it has magnates, they go unhung, with our approval.

"This one comparatively perfect flower of our sadly defective civilization is—of course—baseball, the only important institution, so far as we can remember, which the United States regards with a practically universal approval."

—Editorial, 1909; quoted in Ira L. Smith and H. Allen Smith, *Low and Inside* (Garden City, N.Y.: Doubleday, 1949)

Spirit of the Times

"Of all out-door sports, base-ball is that in which the greatest number of our people participate either as players or as spectators. . . . It is a pastime that best suits the temperament of our people. The accessories being less costly than those of the turf, the acquatic course, or the cricket-field, it is an economic game, and within the easy reach of the masses."

—1867; quoted in John R. Betts, *America's Sporting Heritage* (Reading, Mass.: Addison-Wesley, 1974)

THE SPORTING LIFE

"In one respect Chicago is unquestionably the greatest ball town in the world. It will support a losing club more generously than any other city on the map."

—May 22, 1897

THE SPORTING NEWS

IMMINENT DANGER PROFESSIONAL BASEBALL IN A BAD WAY

—Headline in the *Sporting News,* October 13, 1900

THE TIMES (LONDON)

"It may be that the next few years we shall have absorbed all the traditions of baseball [now being played by the British troops], will rise in a body to stretch ourselves at the 'sleepy seventh' and write of the game in language as palpably spirited as it is incomprehensible."

—May 15, 1944

WALL STREET JOURNAL

"FAT LADY SINGS"

—Wall Street Journal headline about the demise of the baseball season, 1994

WASHINGTON POST

"A pitcher and a catcher and Mr. Hoy constitute the Washington base ball club. The other six men who accompany them are put in the field for the purpose of making errors."

—On Dummy Hoy, 1888

EDWARDS, DOC

"Molitor didn't walk across the lake to get here, and he didn't change his clothes in the phone booth. He's just another tough hitter."

—The Cleveland manager after Brewer Paul Molitor extended his hitting streak to 31 games. *USA Today,* August 27, 1987

EGAN, ARTHUR "BEN"

"Babe knew how to pitch the first day I saw him. I didn't have to tell him anything. He knew how to hold runners on base, and he knew how to work on the hitters, so I'd say he was a pretty good pitcher—on his own."

—As Ruth's catcher on the 1914 Orioles; quoted by Lee Allen in his column in *Sporting News,* July 28, 1962

EINHORN, EDDIE

"At Yankee Stadium the fans throw bottles from the outfield. At Comiskey Park, they throw them from the box seats."

—As White Sox owner, 1982; Hall of Fame Collection

EINSTEIN, ALBERT

"Mr. Berg, you teach me baseball, and I'll teach you mathematics. But let's forget it. I'm sure you'd learn mathematics faster than I'd learn baseball."

> —Said, after a brief recital on his violin, to Morris "Moe" Berg shortly after World War II; quoted in Nicholas Dawidoff, "Scholar, Lawyer, Catcher, Spy," *Sports Illustrated*, March 23, 1992

EISENBERG, JOHN

"One of the first baseball commandments, right up there with Thou Shalt Chew Chaw, is Thou Shalt Not Embarrass Anyone Under Any Circumstances (Because Thou Shalt Get It Flung Back In Thou's Face)."

> —"Mike and Cito Show Is an Affair to Forget," *Baltimore Sun*, July 27, 1993

"Ordinarily, ballplayers and other athletes make us feel younger. They entertain and exhilarate us with their grace under pressure, their feats, their highs and lows. They make our days more exciting and remind us of our youth, the games we played, the more careless and carefree days.

"But when a ballplayer makes news because he has cancer, or because he has died, we don't feel younger at all. We feel older.

"Sadder and older.

"A ballplayer's death is a reminder of our own mortality and vulnerability, a reminder of the reality that we're getting older, too.

"We're the same as our childhood heroes in the end, real people susceptible to real troubles. And in that way, their sadness becomes our sadness, too."

> —"Cancer News Shakes O's Family to Core," *Baltimore Sun*, October 7, 1998

EISENHARDT, ROY

"Baseball is a terrific radio sport . . . because radio feeds our imagination. I was a Tiger fan all the time I was growing up, and I have a perfect memory of George Kell and Hoot Evers making certain plays that I heard but never saw. I remember them to this day. I'd be lying out on the grass at home listening to the game, but I was really there in the ballpark. I think baseball has survived all this time because of its place in our imagination—because we've chosen to make the players and the games, something larger than they really are. But television has just the opposite of feet. The players are shown so closely and under such a bright light that we lose all illusion."

> —Oakland A's owner; quoted in Roger Angell, "Being Green," *New Yorker*, (August 15, 1983)

"The easiest thing in sport is to win when you're good. The next easiest is to lose when you're not any good. The hardest—way hardest—is to lose when you're good. That's the test of character."

> —Oakland A's owner; quoted in Roger Angell "Being Green," *New Yorker*, (August 15, 1983)

EISENHOWER, DWIGHT D.

"Dear Mr. Larsen:

It is a noteworthy event when anybody achieves perfection in anything. It has been so long since anyone pitched a perfect big league game that I have to go back to my generation of ballplayers to recall such a thing—and that is truly a long time ago.

This note brings you my very sincere congratulations on a memorable feat, one that will inspire pitchers for a long time to come. With best wishes.

> Sincerely,
> Dwight D. Eisenhower
> President of the United States"

— Quoted in *Baseball: The President's Game* by William B. Mead and Paul Dickson

"Calvin, the wife is away. How about me coming to the ball game?"

— Call received by Calvin Griffith during the 1957 season; quoted in *All-Sports News*, January 1, 1958

"Not making the baseball team at West Point was one of the greatest disappointments of my life, maybe the greatest."

— Quoted by Harold Seymour in *Baseball: The People's Game*

"When I was a small boy in Kansas, a friend of mine and I went fishing and as we sat there in the warmth of the summer afternoon on a river bank, we talked about what we wanted to do when we grew up. I told him that I wanted to be a real major league baseball player, a genuine professional like Honus Wagner. My friend said that he'd like to be president of the United States. Neither of us got our wish."

— Widely repeated statement which has shown up in periodicals ranging from the *Sporting News* to *Reader's Digest*

"You cannot hit a home run by bunting. You have to step up there and take a cut at the ball. Never be more scared of the enemy than you think he is of you."

— SABR Collection

ELDERKIN, PHIL

"To season-ticket holders who still keep score, baseball remains a kind of pseudo-religion that rocks its own cradle. To them the national pastime, when viewed in a ballpark, is not the slow, dreary game the media keeps telling us it is. Instead it is the ultimate game, where threads of the ballet and gymnastics mesh beautifully with speed and power."

— "Baseball's Opening Day Retains Its Rituals," *Christian Science Monitor*, April 5, 1993

ELIA, LEE

"He's not a high-ball pitcher. He's a highball drinker."

— On Bill Caudill; quoted in Jay Johnstone's *Temporary Insanity*

"They can play all the music they want. They can run dancing elephants out there. But don't play between pitches. There's got to be some professionalism."

—On taking his minor-league Clearwater Phillies off the field for ten minutes to protest the playing of polka music between pitches; quoted in the *Washington Post*, July 27, 1990

ELIOT, CHARLES WILLIAM (1834–1926)

"I think [baseball] is a wretched game; but as an object of ambition for youth to go to college for, really it is a little weak. There are only nine men who can play the game, and there are nine hundred and fifty men in college; and out of those nine there are only two desirable positions, I understand—pitcher and catcher—so there is but little chance for the youth to gratify his ambition. I call it one of the worst games, although I know it is called the American national game."

—As Harvard University president *St. Louis Globe-Democrat*, September 12, 1884

"Well, this year I'm told the team did well because one pitcher had a fine curve ball. I understand that a curve ball is thrown with a deliberate attempt to deceive. Surely that is not an ability we should want to foster at Harvard."

—As president of Harvard (1861–1909) responding when asked why he wished to drop baseball as a college sport

ELLARD, GEORGE

"We used no mattress on our hands,
No cage upon our face;
We stood right up and caught the ball,
With courage and with grace."

—1880s, protesting the use of protective gear for catchers

ELLIS, DOCK

"Every time we make trouble, ol' George flies out here from another part of the country and gets in our way. Maybe we should make a lot of trouble, so he'll keep flying out here. Sooner or later, his plane's gonna crash."

—On George Steinbrenner during spring training 1978; quoted by Danielle Gagnon Torrez in *High Inside: Memoirs of a Baseball Wife*, by Sparky Lyle in *The Bronx Zoo*, and in several dozen other works which discuss the Principle Owner

Dock Ellis (*Author's Collection*)

EMERSON, RALPH WALDO

"Bat and Ball.—Toys, no doubt, have their philosophy, and who knows how deep is the origin of a boy's delight in a spinning top? In playing with bat-balls, perhaps he is charmed with some recognition of the movement of the heavenly bodies, and a game of base or cricket is a course of experimental astronomy, and my young master tingles with a faint sense of being a tyrannical Jupiter driving spheres madly from their orbit."

> —From his journal of June 1, 1840. Discovered by Wendy Knickerbocker

ENBERG, DICK

"I suppose they'll start mooing the umpires."

> —The sportscaster on the newly introduced cowhide baseballs; quoted in the *Los Angeles Times,* May 19, 1973

ENDERS, ERIC

"Baseball is virtually the only aspect of U.S. culture embraced by the Cuban Revolution, an enterprise based largely on resisting American imperialism."

> —"Through the Looking Glass: The Forgotten World of Cuban Baseball," *Nine,* 2003

ERSKINE, CARL

"I regret this decision, but I am no longer able to help the team because I cannot give 100 per cent any more."

> —On retiring in June 1959, twenty-eight days short of his tenth year in the majors; quoted by Phil Pepe in *No-Hitter*

ESKOW, JOHN

"More than any other games, baseball gives its players space—both physical and emotional—in which to define themselves."

> —SABR Collection

ESTRADA, CHUCK

"We had a very scientific system of bringing in relief pitchers. We used the first one who answered the phone."

> —On bringing in relief pitchers, as Texas Rangers pitching coach; quoted in *Baseball Digest,* November 1974

EVANS, ANGUS

"The Americans have a genius for taking a thing, examining its every part, and developing each part to its utmost. This they have done with the game of rounders, and, from a clumsy, primitive pastime, have so tightened its joints and put such a fine finish on its points that it stands forth a complicated machine of infinite exactitude."

> —English commentator, on baseball in the early 1900s; quoted in *Why Time Begins on Opening Day*

EVANS, BILLY

"Well, I guess I'm just a big dope. That Series looked all right to me."

> —On his umpiring of the 1919 Black Sox scandal; quoted in the *Sporting News,* July 11, 1951

"The most satisfying thing about staying up here so many years has been being able to outthink opposing scouts and pitchers from time to time. There are never ending changes in the battle between pitchers and hitters. If you're getting hits off a pitcher, he adjusts, if he's getting you out, you adjust."

> —After thirteen seasons in the majors; quoted in *Sports Illustrated*, September 12, 1983

EVANS, DARRELL

"I'm not old. I was just born before a lot of other people."

> —At forty, baseball's oldest player, *New York Times*, September 30, 1987

EVERS, JOHNNY

"My favorite umpire is a dead one."

> —Quoted in *The Empire State of Baseball*. This was in keeping with Evers's character.

EWING, GEORGE

"Exercised in the afternoon in the intervals played at base."

> —Revolutionary War soldier at Valley Forge, April 7, 1778; may be the first record of an actual game of baseball played in America. *The Military Journal of George Ewing (1754-1824), a Soldier of Valley Forge* (Yonkers, N.Y., 1928); quoted in Robert W. Henderson, *Ball, Bat and Bishop* (New York: Rockport Press, 1947).

EWING, WILLIAM

"It wastes time to straighten up."

> —Believed to be the first catcher to throw to second from a crouch, explaining his actions; quoted in *Baseball's Hall of Fame* by Robert Smith

F

FACE, ELROY

"Everyone asks me the same question. They want to know if I'm tired. I always say 'No.' I've pitched so many times, once more doesn't matter."

— During the 1960 World Series, after sixty-eight; appearances in the regular season; quoted in *Baseball Digest,* November 1974

FAIRBANKS, DOUGLAS

"One is always sure to meet people there whom he knows and need never lack for company or a jolly time, even if things do go against his favorites."

— On going to see the Giants at the Polo Grounds; quoted in *Baseball: An Informal History* by Douglass Wallop

FAIRLY CLEAR—RON FAIRLY

As a broadcaster for the Angels, Giants, and Mariners, this man has developed to a fine art the ability to toss off the odd quotation and malapropism.

"Bruce Sutter has been around for a while, and he's pretty old. He's thirty-five years old. That will give you some idea of how old he is."

— As a San Francisco broadcaster

"If I had to name the number one asset you could have for any sport, I'd say speed. In baseball, all a guy with speed has to do is make contact."

— As a Dodger infielder; widely collected

On the air:

"He fakes a bluff."

"Last night I neglected to mention something that bears repeating."

"The Giants are looking for a trade, but I don't think Atlanta wants to depart with a quality player."

"The wind at Candlestick tonight is blowing with great propensity."

"What's to get tired from? This isn't like football or basketball. Even if you play 100 games in the outfield, you handle only six or eight balls a game. What can wear you out? It's hard to get physically tired in baseball, unless you pitch or catch. You only get mentally tired. . . . Many of us couldn't run when we were 21. So guys like us pinch-hit and get on base—and they send in a rabbit to run for us."

> —On playing into one's late forties; quoted in *TV Guide*, May 27, 1978

Ron Fairly (*California Angels*)

FALLS, JOE

"My office lets me write obits and I've never died."

> —As sports editor of the *Detroit Free Press* when asked by a fan how he could write about Denny McLain: "What sport did you every play?"; quoted in the *Sporting News,* April 4, 1970

"Of all our sports, baseball seems to have produced more characters than any other. That's because none of them can hide. What they do, they do out in the open. Even when they do it in private, it somehow becomes public property."

> —On characters in baseball, in *Baseball Digest*, September 1966

FARMER, ED

"If he's Junior Felix, I'd love to see Senior Felix."

> —The Orioles scout on the strength of the rookie outfield; quoted the *Sporting News*, July 17, 1989

"What did he lead the league in? He led the league in manhood, that's what."

> —The Yankee publicist on Mickey Mantle becoming MVP in 1962 with a .321 batting average, 30 homers, and 81 RBIs—none of which led the league

FARRELL, JAMES T.

"My grandmother . . . wanted to see a baseball game because I was so full of baseball in my boyhood, and she most likely wondered what it was which interested her grandson, her son, Tom, and so many of the men. . . . Baseball to her was a part of the new world of America, but she saw it with the wonder of an unlettered peasant woman who had run the fields of Ireland as a girl in bare feet."

— *My Baseball Diary*

"The comprehensibility of baseball is in sharp contrast with so much of the serious-news of the day. . . . It is a self enclosed world of competition and action in which the emotions can have free play without the consequences being dangerous."

— *My Baseball Diary*

"The old-time great ballplayers were stars. Today's great players (as well as .250 hitters) are superstars, thanks to a widespread disrespect for the once respected English language."

— April 1977

"Well, it's a great game, for men as well as kids. You know, I was thinking, if those Europeans that are at each other's throats now in this war had a national sport like baseball, they wouldn't be having this war. You got to have something that lets the steam off, and baseball does that. Yes, sir, if they had baseball, the French would be playing a series in Berlin now, and the Ger-

mans would be yelling kill the ump instead of trying to kill the Frog-eaters."

— Comment by character Guy in *No Star is Lost* (Vanguard Press, 1938); quoted in *My Baseball Diary*

FARRELL, TURK

"Nobody bests Farrell after midnight."

— Boast after beating the Phillies in an extra-inning game that lasted until 1:00 a.m; quoted by Bob Uecker in *Catcher in the Wry*

FEATHER, WILLIAM

"A baseball game is twice as much fun if you're seeing it on the company's time."

— *The Business of Life*

FEENEY, CHUB

"We'll continue to play by baseball rules."

— As National League President on his League's refusal to adopt the designated hitter rule in 1973; widely collected

FEHR, DON

"I don't think American culture would collapse if baseball collapsed."

— The players' union chief; quoted by George Will in his column of March 13, 1990. Will noted at the time: "That flippancy is trivially true and utterly foolish. Symphony orchestras, steel mills—American culture could survive without lots of things. But baseball, unlike, say, the textile industry, depends for its health on a perishable hold on the public's imagination."

FELLER, BOB

"A ball player doesn't spend ten years on the same team without developing an affection for the uniform, the city, the park and certain teammates."

—*Strikeout Story*

"Baseball in the Navy always was much more fun than it had been in the major leagues."

—*Strikeout Story*

He couldn't hit a curveball with an ironing board."

—On Michael Jordan's bid to play for the Chicago White Sox, *Newsweek*, February 21, 1994

"I didn't know much. I just reared back and let them go. Where the ball went was up to heaven. Sometimes I threw the ball clean up into the stands."

—On his abilities in 1937 and 1938; quoted in *Look*, 1951

"I don't think baseball owes colored people anything, I don't think colored people owe baseball anything, either."

—Statement made during a press conference in honor of baseball's 100th-anniversary celebration in 1969. It set off a feud between Feller and Jackie Robinson, whose immediate retort was "I don't think Bob has grown any more from 1947. He has had his head in the sand" (*Sporting News*, August 9, 1969).

"I would rather beat the Yankees regularly than pitch a no-hit game."

—*Strikeout Story*

"Some of my records are not here. Many of them are in jeopardy. But there is one here that is in no danger—most walks in a career and most walks in a season.

"I might have had a shot at some others but for the war and the three-year 'vacation' in the Navy. But you can't saw dust."

—On his Hall of Fame induction, July 23, 1962; quoted in the *New York Times*, July 24, 1962

"Sympathy is something that shouldn't be bestowed on the Yankees. Apparently it angers them."

—*Strikeout Story*

"The starting times are different all over. Twilight games . . . night games . . . day games . . . night doubleheaders . . . day doubleheaders. It ruins your diet. Sometimes you play a day doubleheader . . . and a night game the next day. You have your meals at all different times. It's bound to affect you."

—Complaining to Jimmy Cannon on the 1947 season when there were many doubleheaders created by rainouts

"When I pick up the ball and it feels nice and light and small I know I'm going to have a good day. But if I pick it up and it's big and heavy, I know I'm liable to get into a little trouble."

—Quoted by Jimmy Cannon in the *New York Post*. Feller made the statement during the winter of 1948.

"When I was a tree, with my brothers and sisters, there were many of us there but there is not many of us now. Many of us have been cut down and made into lumber and it came my turn and they cut me down and made me into a big board. And Mister Stucke's manual training boys got me and made me into a home plate for the baseball diamond. And that's the end."

> —School composition, "My Life," written as a seven-year-old in Van Meter, Iowa; quoted in Bob Feller with Bill Gilbert, *Now Pitching, Bob Feller* (New York: Carol Publishing Group, 1990).

FERBER, EDNA

"Any man who can look handsome in a dirty baseball suit is an Adonis. There is something about the baggy pants, and the Micawber-shaped collar, and the skull-fitting cap, and the foot or so of tan, or blue, or pink undershirt sleeve sticking out at the arms, that just naturally kills a man's best points."

> —"A Bush League Hero," in *Buttered Side Down* (New York: Frederick A. Stokes, 1912)

"'Want some peanuts?' inquired her father.

"'Does one eat peanuts at a ball game?'

"'It ain't hardly legal if you don't,' Pa Keller assured her.

"'Two sacks,' said Ivy. 'Papa, why do they call it a diamond, and what are those brown bags at the corners, and what does it count if you hit the ball, and why do they rub their hands in the dust and then—er—spit on them, and what salary does a pitcher get, and why does the red-haired man on the other side dance around like that between the sec-

ond and third brown bag, and doesn't a pitcher do anything but pitch, and wh—?'

"'You're on,' said papa."

> — "A Bush League Hero"

FERGUSON, ANDREW

"Mark McGwire, who is obviously a manly person, is also a product of today's therapeutic culture. He was boasting of the years he spent in therapy, and he has a vocabulary centered on the words beautiful and incredible. I'm sure that Lou Gehrig and DiMaggio and certainly Roger Maris were not the most articulate people in the world, but it is inconceivable that Roger Maris ever would have talked about his therapist."

> —Senior editor at the *Weekly Standard* and a former Bush administration speechwriter, from "The Year of the Goat," *American Enterprise*, January 1999

FERGUSON, ROBERT

"I'm only one man to your thousand, but if you don't think I can protect myself just pitch in and give it a trial."

> —National League umpire, surrounded by an angry mob who threatened to kill him, shouting upon seizing a baseball bat; quoted in Alfred H. Spink's *The National Game*.

FETZER, JOHN E.

"A baseball owner has to live the life of a riverboat gambler, because he can either make a lot of [money] or lose a lot of money in one year. You have to learn to live with that. You have to look at baseball as a love of accomplishment more than just a monetary reward."

—As Tigers owner, *San Francisco Examiner and Chronicle*, May 18, 1975

FIDRYCH, MARK

"Sometimes I get lazy and let the dishes stack up. But they don't stack too high, I've only got four dishes."

—Hall of Fame Collection, 1976

"Well the ball had a hit in it, so I want it to get back in the ball bag and goof around with the other balls there. Maybe it'll learn some sense and come out as a pop-up next time."

—As a rookie in 1976, on why he always threw the ball back to the plate umpire after surrendering a base hit; quoted in *High and Inside: The Complete Guide to Baseball Slang* by Joseph McBride.

Mark Fidrych (*Cleveland Indians*)

FIMRITE, RON

"The romance of baseball . . . is in its capacity for stirring fantasy. We are never too old or too bothered to see ourselves wrapping up a World Series victory with a homer in the final inning of the seventh game."

—In his 1971 book *Way to Go*

"The Yankees, too, are a family. A family like the Macbeths, the Borgias, and the Bordens of Fall River, Massachusetts."

—Comparing the Yankees and the Dodgers; quoted by William B. Mead in *The Official Yankee Hater's Handbook*

"There was but one position to which the clods, the kids with glasses, the little guys, the sissies, the ones that got good grades, the kids who played with girls, were exiled. That would be right field, the Siberia of my youth. Right field was the back of the bus, the slow-learners class, the children's department, a sideshow. . . . Anyone directed to play right field would have given anything to 'be out in left field.'"

—*San Francisco Chronicle*, April 28, 1969

FINLEY, CHARLIE

"He didn't make the games exciting enough when nothing was going on."

—On the firing of radio announcer Jim Woods, *Baseball Digest*, December 1993

"I always wanted to be a player, but I never had the talent to make the big leagues. So I did the next best thing: I bought a team."

—*Time*, August 18, 1975

"I don't want my players counting people in the stands when they should be thinking of the game."

　　—On bonus clauses based on attendance; quoted in *Vida: His Own Story* by Bill Libby and Vida Blue

"If a manager of mine ever said someone was indispensable, I'd fire him."

　　—Widely collected

"I've never seen so many damned idiots as the owners in sport. Baseball's headed for extinction if we don't do something. Defense dominates everything. Pitching is 75 percent of the game, and that why it's so dull. How many times have you seen a fan napping in the middle of a football or basketball game? Hell, in baseball people nap all the time. Only one word explains why baseball hasn't changed: *stupidity*! The owners don't want to rock the boat."

　　—*Time*, August 18, 1975

"Make a walk three balls instead of four. The excitement in baseball comes when men are on base, so let's get more men on base."

　　—Quoted by Art Rosenbaum in the *San Francisco Chronicle*, February 22, 1971

"Prospects are a dime a dozen."

　　—As Oakland A's owner; widely collected

"So you won twenty games? Why didn't you win thirty?"

　　—To Vida Blue during 1972 contract negotiations; quoted in *High Inside: Memoirs of a Baseball Wife* by Danielle Gagnon Torrez

"Sweat Plus Sacrifice Equals Success."

　　—His philosophy of life, sometimes embellished, as in this version from *Vida: His Own Story*: "Sweat plus sacrifice equals success. The three S's. Life is that simple. But everyone isn't willing. I've put a lot of sweat and sacrifice into success in business and I've put a lot of sweat and sacrifice into success in sports, and I'll succeed in sports as I succeeded in business." *Time*, August 18, 1975

"Thank God our fans show more interest than some of our players. If they showed as little interest, they'd all leave before the game was over."

　　—On players leaving the dugout after being taken out of the game at Oakland; quoted in Ron Bergman's *Mustache Gang*.

"The day Custer lost at the Little Big Horn, the Chicago White Sox beat the Cincinnati Red Legs, 3–2. Both teams wore knickers. And they're still wearin' 'em today."

　　—Quoted by Tom Boswell in the *Washington Post*, September 5, 1982; Boswell said that Finley made the point "when hawking his novel notions, such as the orange baseball or double-knit uniforms . . ."

"There's an old saying that pigs get fat and hogs go to market. Well, some of the players these days aren't even pigs or hogs—they're gluttons. We have to keep salaries within reason. If we just rolled over and gave them what they wanted, we'd price ourselves out of business."

> —On the White Sox paying Richie Allen $250,000 a year; quoted in the *New York Times*, February 16, 1975

"The man is literally driving me out of baseball financially. I've been in it for 18 years and I'd love to stay in the game. But by not allowing me to sell Vida Blue, he's depriving me of keeping my ship afloat. I'd stand on top of the Sears Tower—the largest building in the world—waving a sign: 'Fire Bowie!'"

> —On Bowie Kuhn; quoted in the *Washington Post*, February 23, 1978

"We run our club like a pawn shop—we buy, we trade, we sell."

> —On how he operated the Athletics, *Los Angeles Times*, June 23, 1977

FISHEL, ROBERT O.

"Several extensive surveys have been conducted to determine whether or not any of Ruth's 60 home runs in 1927 bounced into the stands. According to all reports, all would have been legitimate homers today—none bounced over the fence."

> —From a May 26, 1961, letter to the Haskin newspaper service, which was questioning a possible cheap homer by Ruth

FISK, CARLTON

"I feel like I'm turning my back on an old friend."

> —On playing in front of the Green Monster as a member of the White Sox after ten years with the Red Sox, *Sporting News*, May 5, 1986

"I forgot to put in one clause I don't have to play when the temperature is lower than my age."

> —On his new White Sox contract at age forty-two. *Sports Illustrated*, February 12, 1990

"If the human body recognized agony and frustration, people would never run marathons, have babies or play baseball."

> —*Sports Illustrated*, July 30, 1979

FITZGERALD, F. SCOTT

"Baseball is a game played by idiots for morons."

> —Quoted by Raymond Mungo in *Confessions from Left Field*

"Ring moved in the company of a few dozen illiterates playing a boy's game. A boy's game with no more possibilities than a boy could master, a game bounded by walls which kept out danger, change or adventure."

> —On the death of Ring Lardner and what Fitzgerald saw as his unfulfilled promise; quoted in the *New York Times Book Review*, June 1, 1986. This quotation and the one before it have given rise to a number of hybrid antibaseball quotations attributed to Fitzgerald along the lines of, "Baseball is a child's game played by a few dozen illiterates."
>
> A fuller version of this quotation as it

appeared in the essay "Ring" in *The Crack-Up*: "Whatever Ring's achievement was, it fell far short of the achievement he was capable of, and this because of a cynical attitude toward his work. How far back did that attitude go?—back to his youth in a Michigan village? Certainly back to his days with the Cubs. During those years, when most men of promise achieve an adult education, if only in the school of war, Ring moved in the company of a few dozen illiterates playing a boy's game. A boy's game, with no more possibilities than a boy would master, a game bounded by walls which kept out novelty or danger, change or adventure."

FITZGERALD, RAY

"A critic once characterized baseball as six minutes of action crammed into two-and-one-half hours."

> —The writer in the *Boston Globe,* 1970

FLANAGAN, MIKE

"I could never play in New York. The first time I ever came into a game there, I got into the bull-pen car and they told me to lock the doors."

> —As a Baltimore Orioles pitcher; quoted in *Sports Illustrated,* October 22, 1979

"None, really. But I never pitch well on days they play the national anthem."

> —When asked if he had any superstitions; quoted in the *Washington Post,* April 2, 1989

F. Scott Fitzgerald (*Library of Congress Prints and Photographs Division*)

"We forgot about the Canadian exchange rate, so it's really only 82 mph."

> —As an Oriole on fellow Oriole Mike Boddicker throwing at a high speed of 88 mph in Toronto; quoted in *Sports Illustrated,* August 26, 1986

"We tried looking for the record-breaking ball out beyond the fence in right, but there were too many of them all bunched up there."

> —Baltimore pitcher, about the Toronto Blue Jays' record-setting 10 home runs in one game against the Orioles. SABR Collection

"You know you're having a bad day when the fifth inning rolls around and they drag the warning track."

> —The Baltimore Orioles pitcher on his craft, *Newsweek,* April 27, 1992

FLANNERY, TIM

"I'm superstitious, and every night after I got a hit, I ate Chinese food and drank tequila. I had to stop hitting or die."

> —As a Padres second baseman on a 14-game hitting streak, *Sports Illustrated*, September 14, 1987

FLETCHER, ART

"Gomez, you must be crazy. It took you 133 years to get to third base and now you want to ruin it."

> —As third-base coach, on Lefty Gomez's request to steal home

FLOOD, CURT

"A well-paid slave is nonetheless a slave."

> —From his book, *The Way It Is*, 1971

"After twelve years in the Major Leagues, I do not feel that I am a piece of property to be bought and sold irrespective of my wishes. I believe that any system which produces that result violates my basic rights as a citizen and is inconsistent with the laws of the United States and of the several States."

> —Letter to commissioner of baseball Bowie Kuhn, December 25, 1969, after Flood had been traded by the St. Louis Cardinals to the Philadelphia Phillies

"Everybody thinks of baseball as a sacred cow. When you have the nerve to challenge it, people look down their noses at you. There are a lot of things wrong with a lot of industries. . . . Baseball is one of them."

> —As St. Louis Cardinal outfielder; widely collected

"I am pleased that God made my skin black but I wish He had made it thicker."

> —*The Way It Is*, 1971

"The funny thing about these uniforms is that you hang them in the closet and they get smaller and smaller."

> —Before a 1981 old-timers' game; quoted in the *Major League Baseball Newsletter*, June 1981

"What about freedom makes us march and picket and sometimes die? It is the right to choose. To me, freedom means simply I belong to me."

> —*The Way It Is*, 1971

Curt Flood (*Author's Collection*)

FOLSOM, LOWELL EDWIN

"No writer since has exceeded these extravagant and fervent claims for the game. Whitman's baseball credo could only have been spoken by a man who grew up with the sport; saw it develop from its slower, more sedate forms into a demanding game of hardball with 'snap and go,' saw the democratic demands of skill force gentlemen to give way to the young roughs; saw the baseball team itself become an image of America, accepting and absorbing men from all walks of life, immigrants from all over the world, molding them into one body, a union committed to a common purpose; saw the sport, starting from Manhattan, spread westward and eventually be played from coast to coast, affirming America's secure occupation of the continent; saw baseball, finally, become an athletic image of his soul, accomplishing the rondure of the world, spreading 'America's game' and 'the American atmosphere' to Australia, Asia, Africa, and Europe, then returning home in triumph and comradeship."

—"America's 'Hurrah Game': Baseball and Walt Whitman," *Iowa Review,* Spring–Summer 1980

FORD, GERALD R.

"I watch a lot of baseball on radio."

—From ABC-TV's *Monday Night Baseball,* 1978; quoted by Bob Chieger in *Voices of Baseball*

"I've had a lifelong ambition to be a professional baseball player, but nobody would sign me."

—To reporters, December 4, 1976

Congressman Gerald Ford (*left*), 1949 (*Gerald R. Ford Library*)

FORD, RICHARD

"It's just a game—baseball—an amusement, a marginal thing, not an art, not a consequential metaphor for life, not a public trust. It may have broken Bart Giamatti's sentimental heart, but it will never break mine. . . . In its behind-the-scenes machinations as sport, baseball has developed unexpected ties to big-time professional wrestling, with that strange spectacle's buffoonish, self-important, overstuffed Steinbrennerish management types spouting gibberish about the best interests of this and such and the need for moral direction, all in counterpoise to sullenly big-muscled, bad-boy superstars nattering and snuffling about not getting any respect and not being in it for the dough, and being in it for the dough."

—"Stop Blaming Baseball," *New York Times Magazine,* April 4, 1993

FORD, WHITEY

"Army life was rough. Would you believe it, they actually wanted me to pitch three times a week."

—*Slick*

"I didn't begin cheating until late in my career, when I needed something to help me survive. I didn't cheat when I won the twenty-five games in 1961. I don't want anybody to get any ideas and take my Cy Young Award away. And I didn't cheat in 1963 when I won twenty-four games. Well, maybe just a little."

—*Slick*

"If we were back to sixteen, the teams would be every bit as good as they were in my day."

—On expansion and the dilution of talent, in *Slick*

Whitey Ford (*New York Yankees*)

"I know Koufax's weakness. He can't hit."

—During the 1963 World Series

"Nowadays, with organized Little Leagues, you might play two games a week and a kid is lucky if he gets to bat six times a week. That's the difference. There's no comparison. We learned how to play by playing."

—*Slick*

"Sooner or later the arm goes bad. It has to. The arm wasn't meant to stand the strain pitching imposes on it. It's unnatural. Sooner or later you have to start pitching in pain."

—Quoted in *Vida: His Own Story* by Bill Libby and Vida Blue

"The way to make coaches think you're in shape in the spring is to get a tan."

—Quoted by Jim Bouton in *Ball Four*

"There's no easier pitch to hit than a spitter that doesn't do anything."

—*Slick*

"You kind of took it for granted around the Yankees that there was always going to be baseball in October."

—*Slick*

"You would be amazed how many important outs you can get by working the count down to where the hitter is sure you're going to throw to his weakness, and then throw to his power instead."

—*The Second Fireside Book of Baseball*, edited by Charles Einstein

FOREMAN, FRANK

"A faint heart is one of the big causes of sore arms."

> —As a Baltimore Orioles pitcher; widely collected

FORMAN, AL

"I occasionally get birthday cards from fans. But it's often the same message: they hope it's my last."

> —National League umpire, *Time*, August 25, 1961

FOSSE, RAY

"Well, that's football."

> —After colliding with Pete Rose in the 1970 All-Star Game; widely collected

FOSTER, GEORGE

"I don't know why people like the home run so much. A home run is over as soon as it starts. . . . The triple is the most exciting play of the game. A triple is like meeting a woman who excites you, spending the evening talking and getting more excited, then taking her home. It drags on and on. You're never sure how it's going to turn out."

> —1978

"The idea isn't to swing for the home run, but to hit the ball hard every time up and hope it goes where nobody can catch it. I'm a .300 hitter because I'm consistent and a home-run hitter because I have power. That's the difference between me and other long-ball hitters. They don't make good contact every time up the way I do, and it kills their over-all average. That's what I mean by being consistent."

> —Quoted in the *Christian Science Monitor*, August 12, 1977

"The more the challenge, the more mental and spiritual strength you can come up with, and the stronger you're going to be in some other situation, away from the ballpark. Baseball is part of life, maybe only a small part, but the important thing is what you overcome inside yourself."

> —Quoted in *Late Innings* by Roger Angell

FOWLER, SENATOR WYCHE

"The confirmation process on Sen. [John] Tower was positively tame compared to the Mets' training camp."

> —The Georgia Democrat comparing Senate hearings for secretary of defense with the New York Mets in spring training; quoted in *USA Today*, March 13, 1989

FOWLES, JOHN

"Though I like the various forms of football in the world, I don't think they begin to compare with these two great Anglo-Saxon ballgames for sophisticated elegance and symbolism. Baseball and cricket are beautiful and highly stylized medieval war substitutes, chess made flesh, a mixture of proud chivalry and base—in both senses—greed. With football we are back to the monotonous clashing armor of the brontosaurus."

> —Comment in *Book-of-the-Month Club News*, October 1977

FOX, CHARLIE

"Dammit, I wish you guys would quit living in the past. Most of my kids have never heard of . . . don't even know what month it is."

> —When writers suggested that his Giants were ready for their traditional June Swoon, *Sporting News,* June 26, 1971

"I don't have any figures to prove it, but there's no doubt in my mind that the average age of big-league [baseball] players [is] now the lowest in history. We've often talked about the age of youth and now we have it, more than ever before. Of course, we should say three cheers, because where would the game be without these kids? Youth has rejuvenated the whole big-league picture. . . . Nobody wins these days unless one or two youngsters come through for them."

> —As Giants manager; quoted in the *Christian Science Monitor,* November 20, 1971

"Our earned-run average looks like the national debt."

> —As Giants manager; quoted by Roger Angell in *Five Seasons*

FOX, NELLIE

"It's a small thing, really, but in the American League the home team takes infield practice last. In the National League the home team takes infield practice first and then goes to the clubhouse to change. In the past couple of weeks I've found myself working out with the visiting team."

> —On the difference in the two major leagues; quoted in *Sport,* July 1964

Nellie Fox (*Author's Collection*)

"On two legs, Mickey Mantle would have been the greatest ball player who ever lived."

> —At the time of Mantle's retirement

FOXX, JIMMIE

"Baseball was mighty good to me, but I was born ten years too soon."

> —After turning up broke in 1958. He hit fifty-eight home runs in '32, but when he slumped to forty-eight in 1933 Connie Mack tried to cut his salary from $16,670 to $12,000.

FOXX, JIMMIE (CONTINUED)

"It's easy. Just be sure your foot is on the bag before you go to catch a thrown ball."

> —To Red Sox skipper Joe Cronin in answer to the question "How do you play first base." Cronin was in the process of selling Foxx to the Cubs and worried that he would have to play first himself; quoted in *Baseball Digest*, October 1942.

"Let me get a good grip on the bat, as if I wanted to leave my finger-prints on the wood: let me swing with a quick snap which comes from a powerful wrist, and, if I've gotten back of the ball it sure will travel."

> —*Famous American Athletes of Today*, 4th series, by Charles H. L. Johnston

FOYTACK, PAUL

"And when that little something extra is missing, generally a lot of baseballs are too."

> —The pitcher on the fact that his fastball lacked a little something extra, collected in *Baseball Laughs* by Herman L. Masin

FRANÇOIS, COMTE DE BARBÉ-MARBOIS

"To-day he sometimes throws and catches a ball for whole hours with his aides-de-camp."

> —Newly arrived secretary to the French legation, observing George Washington at camp at Fishkill, New York, in September 1779. Eugene Parker Chase, ed., *Our Revolutionary Forefathers The Letters of Francois, Marquis de Barbé during His Residence in the United States as Secretary of the French Legation 1779–1785* (New York: Duffield, 1929).

FRANK, LAWRENCE

"Consider the distinction that has arisen among the terms 'bullshit,' 'horseshit,' and 'chickenshit.' Though these words seem to possess a variety of meanings in the folk speech of other folk groups, they have become well defined in the realm of baseball folk speech. The basic distinctions are that 'bullshit' means 'not true,' 'horseshit' means 'bad' or 'low class,' and 'chickenshit' means 'gutless' (i.e., afraid). Further, 'bullshit' is often used as a retort, or as an immediate reaction to an event. It is of a slightly stronger sense than the other two and thus often said in a harsher tone. 'Horseshit' is of a lesser degree accusative and often simply descriptive. Hence it is applicable in many more circumstances than 'bullshit.' 'Chickenshit' is the most specific of the three terms and is thus applicable in fewer situations."

> —*Playing Hardball: The Dynamics of Baseball Folk Speech* (New York: Peter Lang, 1983)

FRANK, STANLEY

"He is easily the slowest ballplayer since Ernie Lombardi was thrown out at first base trying to stretch a double into a single."

> —On Lou Boudreau

"Once an asylum for amiable eccentrics, it has become a lifeless charade by actors who look as impersonal as motorcycle cops."

> —On baseball; quoted in *Sports Illustrated*, August 27, 1962

FRANKFURTER, JUSTICE FELIX

"It would baffle the subtlest ingenuity to find a single differentiating factor between other sporting exhibitions . . . and baseball."

> —When boxing was being denied an antitrust exemption similar to baseball's in 1955. This justice took the minority opinion that baseball deserved no special treatment; quoted with considerable glee, by Bill Veeck in *The Hustler's Handbook*.

FRAWLEY, WILLIAM

"It's a game for the whole family so let's all forget our worries and have fun at the ball game whenever we can get to one. What do you say? Let's go."

> —Commercial (to encourage people to attend baseball games) made for movie theaters in early 1950s by the actor known for his role as Fred Mertz in the *I Love Lucy* television show. See also the entry for Humphrey Bogart, who made commercials of the same sort when organized baseball feared television would keep people out of ballparks.

FRAZIER, GEORGE

"Style was Joe DiMaggio drifting back after a fly ball, but *duende* was DiMaggio banning Peter Lawford from Marilyn Monroe's funeral."

> —The Boston Globe columnist; widely attributed

FREEHAN, BILL

1. Freehan's Law: Never beat yourself.
2. Freehan's Second Law—Always play an expansion club, or a very weak team, toward the end of July and through August, if possible."

> —*Behind the Mask*

"If you've got virgin ears, you better stay off a baseball team's bus."

> —*Behind the Mask*

"The real name of this game is pack and repack."

> —*Behind the Mask*

"There's no time to think about the right way to make a play and then make the play. You just have to do it."

> —*Behind the Mask*

"This game is beautiful. I don't think there's anything in the world that can produce so many emotional highs and lows day in and day out."

> —*Behind the Mask*

FREGOSI, JIM

"Me and my owners think exactly alike. Whatever they're thinking, that's what I'm thinking."

> —As the California Angels manager; widely collected

FREGOSI, JIM (CONTINUED)

"Mitch doesn't have ulcers. He's a carrier."

> —On Mitch Williams, alluding to his storied wildness, *Lexington* [KY] *Herald-Leader*, May 23, 1993

"Some baseball jobs last longer than marriages."

> —After two years as White Sox manager, *Sports Illustrated*, July 4, 1988

FREY, JIM

"I tell him, 'Attaway to hit, George.'"

> —As Royals manager when asked what advice he gave to George Brett about hitting, *Sports Illustrated*, August 25, 1980

"I'm only interested in winning ball games and I can't be worrying about whether the sun's out or the moon's out."

> —As Chicago Cubs manager on controversy over night baseball, *New York Times* June 17, 1988

"If we went by tradition, we'd still be playing without gloves."

> —On the installation of lights at Wrigley Field, *Sports Illustrated*, April 18, 1988

FRICK, FORD

"Here stands baseball's happy warrior, here stands baseball's perfect knight."

> —On Stan Musial during his final day as a player, September 29, 1963

"I can take it if we lose, but I strongly object to our league making a burlesque out of the All-Star Game. I never want to see such an exhibition again."

> —As National League president on the use of the high-arching "eephus" or blooper pitch by the Pirates' Rip Sewell in the 1946 All-Star Game; quoted by Frederick G. Lieb in the July 18, 1970, *Sporting News*.

"I do not care if half the league strikes. Those who do will encounter quick retribution. All will be suspended, and I don't care if it wrecks the National League for five years. This is the United States of America and one citizen has as much right to play as another.

"The National League will go down the line with Robinson whatever the consequences."

> —1947 statement to the St. Louis Cardinals, who were rumored to be planning to strike when Jackie Robinson and his fellow Dodgers came to St. Louis to play. From Stanley Woodward, *New York Herald Tribune*, and quoted by Roger Kahn, *The Boys of Summer*

"I hate this to get out but I really like opera."

> —Widely reported, 1954

"In these wild days of inflation, any workman—common laborer or baseball personality—is entitled to all he can get. Nor do I imply that club owners are by nature so generous or philanthropic that they offer huge contracts as a sympathetic gesture with no thoughts of financial return. I do point out that the reserve clause . . . has given baseball a continuity of action that has developed better competition . . . than would have otherwise been possible."

> —Defending the reserve clause in his 1973 book, *Games, Asterisks and People*.

The Ten Commandments of Umpiring

1. Keep your eye on the ball.
2. Keep all personalities out of your work. Forget and forgive.
3. Avoid sarcasm. Don't insist on the last word.
4. Never charge a player and, above all, no pointing your finger or yelling.
5. Hear only the things you should hear—be deaf to others.
6. Keep your temper. A decision made in anger is never sound.
7. Watch your language.
8. Take pride in your work at all times. Remember respect for an umpire is created off the field as well as on.
9. Review your work. You will find, if you are honest, that 90 per cent of the trouble is traceable to loafing.
10. No matter what your opinion of another umpire, never make an adverse comment regarding him. To do so is despicable and ungentlemanly.

—As National League president; quoted in *Baseball Digest*, June 1949. In publishing the rules, the magazine added: "In fact, many of us other than umpires might accept and put into practice some of Frick's suggestions."

"We wanted to elect them while they are still around to smell the roses."

—On the February 2, 1961, election of Waite Hoyt and Stan Coveleski to the Hall of Fame.

FRISCH, FRANK

"Baseball is like this. Have one good year and you can fool them for five more, because for five more years they expect you to have another good one."

—Quoted in *Baseball Wit and Wisdom* by Frank Graham and Dick Hyman

"It's a beautiful day for a night game."

—As a sportscaster

"Stay away from firearms and don't room higher than the second floor."

—When asked for advice he would give young managers; quoted in *Baseball Digest*, September 1971

"There is no room for likes and dislikes in baseball, and he [John McGraw] had none except a burning desire to win. You don't like your players or dislike them. You can't go far with a friendship team. There's no room for sentiment in baseball if you want to win."

—As told to J. Roy Stockton reprinted in J. Roy Stockton's *The Gashouse Gang and a Couple of Other Guys*, 1936

"Trying to lift Carl Hubbell's screwball was like a guy trying to hit fungos out of a well."

—*Baseball Digest*, July, 1947

Frankie Frisch (*Library of Congress Prints and Photographs, Bain Collection*)

187

FROST, ROBERT

"As I say, I never feel more at home in America than at a ball game, be it in park or in sandlot. Beyond this I know not. And dare not."

—"A Perfect Day—a Day of Prowess," *Sports Illustrated,* July 23, 1956

"Nothing flatters me more than to have it assumed that I could write prose—unless it be to have it assumed that I once pitched baseball with distinction."

—SABR Collection

"Poets are like baseball pitchers. Both have their moments. The intervals are the tough things."

—*Writer's Quotation Book* by James Charlton

"Some baseball is the fate of all of us."

—Quoted in *Diamonds in the Rough—the Untold History of Baseball* by Joel Zoss and John Bowman

FUCHS, JUDGE EMIL

"I won't hear of it. Tell the manager we'll win honorably or not at all."

—Braves owner (1925–1935) who knew little of the game, on being informed that his team had won a game on a squeeze play

FUENTES, TITO

"They shouldn't throw at me. I'm the father of five or six kids."

—On being brushed back, as a Giant; quoted in *Sports Illustrated,* September 9, 1974

FULLER, MARK

"When I went to my first baseball game my father dropped the pencil he was keeping score with. He asked me to climb down to get it and while I was under the seat I missed Frank Torre hit a grand-slam home run."

—In Mike Schacht, *Mudville Diaries: A Book of Baseball Memories* (New York: Avon Books, 1996)

FULLERTON, HUGH S.

"Baseball is the greatest single force working for Americanization. No other game appeals so much to the foreign-born youngsters and nothing, not even the schools, teaches the American spirit so quickly, or inculcates the idea of sportsmanship or fair play as thoroughly."

—Sportswriter; quoted in Steven A. Riess, *Touching Base: Professional Baseball and American Culture in the Progressive Era* (Westport Conn: Greenwood Press, 1980)

"Baseball needs a *Webster* and a standing-Revision Board to keep the dictionary of the game up to date. The sport is building its own language so steadily that, unless some step soon is taken to check the inventive young men who coin the words that attach themselves to the pastime, interpreters will have to be maintained in every grand stand to translate for the benefit of those who merely love the game and do not care to master it thoroughly."

—"The Baseball Primer," *American Magazine,* June, 1912

G

GABLER, NEAL

"It was always the game with the longest bloodlines, the one by which an individual could measure his life just as the country could measure its life: by teams and dynasties and legendary plays."

—"More Than a Game," *Los Angeles Times,* September 13, 1998

GABOR, EVA

"When the man with the stick hits the ball into the audience, is that good?"

—Asked of Jon Miller at an Orioles game, June 8, 1990. Gabor was in the booth with Merv Griffin.

GAETTI, GARY

"I know where they are. Those balls were fouled off. I know what we should do . . . we should put an ad in the newspapers. . . .

Whoever got the first foul ball of the fifth inning and whoever got the first foul ball of the ninth inning. . . . Aw, we'll never get them. Maybe we should just take a ball and say, 'This is it.'"

—On the fact that no one remembered to collect the balls involved in the two triple plays executed by the Minnesota Twins on July 17, 1990; quoted in the following morning's *Boston Globe*. On the lost balls, the *Globe*'s Michael Madden added: "Cooperstown is calling, but nobody can answer."

"It's right up there with lobster."

—Third baseman of the Minnesota Twins, asked to rate the thrill of playing in his first All-Star Game, *Sporting News*, August 1, 1988

GALAN, AUGIE

"Charlie Graham offered Joe to the Cubs before he talked to the Yankees. . . . The Cubs didn't want to take a chance on Joe's knee.

GALAN, AUGIE (CONTINUED)

Can you imagine Joe DiMaggio in Wrigley Field? He would have broken Babe Ruth's home run records."

—From an interview which appeared in the San Francisco *Sunday Examiner & Chronicle*, July 1, 1990

GALBRAITH, JOHN KENNETH

"I last attended a major league baseball game in Washington in the summer of 1934. It was the only one I ever got to; it wasn't very interesting so I didn't go back."

—In a letter to Jim Bouton on the book *Ball Four*; quoted in Bouton's *I'm Glad You Didn't Take It Personally*

GALBREATH, JOHN W.

"There's one thing nicer about winning a Kentucky Derby than rooting your ball team to a world championship. You don't have to feed the horse that won any more the day after the race than you fed him the day before. And you don't have to sign him up for the next year."

—As chairman of the board of the Pittsburgh Pirates and owner of assorted racehorses; quoted in *Sport*, April 1971

GALLAGHER, DAVE

"That's a high chopper over the mound."

—The White Sox outfielder as a helicopter circled Tiger Stadium in Detroit; quoted in the October 1989, *Major League Baseball Newsletter*

GALLICO, PAUL

"Baseball has always chosen the longest way around and never been administered with real intelligence."

—On baseball's self-governing; widely quoted

"God dressed in a camel's hair polo coat and flat camel's hair cap, God with a flat nose and little piggy eyes, a big grin, and a fat black cigar sticking out of the side of it."

—Quoted in *Dictionary of American Biography*. It was written to describe Ruth's visit to a New Jersey hospital to visit the ailing Johnny Sylvester. He opened the description by saying: "It was God himself who walked into the room, straight from his glittering throne."

"It was impossible to watch him at bat without experiencing an emotion. I have seen hundreds of ballplayers at the plate, and none of them managed to convey the message of impending doom to a pitcher that Babe Ruth did with the cock of his head, the position of his legs and the little gentle waving of the bat, feathered in his two big paws."

—*New York Daily News*

"No game in the world is as tidy and dramatically neat as baseball, with cause and effect, crime and punishment, motive and result, so cleanly defined."

— *The Baseball Reader*, edited by Ralph S. Graber

"Once he had that 59, that number 60 was as sure as the setting sun. A more determined athlete than George Herman Ruth never lived. He is one of the few utterly dependable news stories in sports."

—On Ruth's record-setting drive; widely quoted

"The clangy, iron echo of the Yankee Stadium picked up the sentence that poured from the loud speakers and hurled it forth into the world. . . . 'The luckiest man on the face of the earth . . . luckiest man on the face of the earth . . . luckiest man . . . '"

—*Lou Gehrig: Pride of the Yankees* (New York: Grosset & Dunlap, 1942)

"The crowd as a whole plays the role of Greek chorus to the actors on the field below. It reflects every action, every movement, every changing phase of the game. It keens. It rejoices. It moans. It jeers. It applauds and gives great swelling murmurs of surprise and appreciation, or finds relief in huge, Gargantuan laughs. I can stand outside of a ball park and listen to the crowd and come close to telling exactly what is happening on the diamond inside. That quick, sharp explosive roar that rises in crescendo and is suddenly shut off sharply as though someone had laid a collective thumb on the windpipe of the crowd, followed by a gentle pattering of applause, tells its own story, of a briskly hit ball, a fielder racing for it, a runner dashing for the base. The throw nips the runner and the noise too. That steady 'Clap-clap-clap-clap-clap . . .' Tight spot. Men on base, crowd trying to rattle the pitcher. A great roar turning into a groan that dies away to nothing—a potential home run, with too much slice on it, that just went foul. The crowd lives the actions of the players more than in any other game. It is a release and something of a purge. It is the next best thing to participation."

—*Farewell to Sport*, 1938

GAMBLE, OSCAR

"Most of the San Diego fans didn't even know my name. They just called me 2.85. It was a long, long year."

—As a Ranger on his 1978 season with the Padres, who had given him a six-year, $2.85 million contract; quoted in *Sports Illustrated*, April 30, 1979.

GAMMONS, PETE

"Baseball is the best sport to cover because it's *daily*. It's ongoing. You have to fill the need, write the daily soap opera."

—As a sportswriter for the *Boston Globe;* Hall of Fame Collection

"If Bowie Kuhn were alive today, this strike never would have occurred."

—On the 1981 players strike, as a *Boston Globe* reporter. Kuhn was commissioned in 1984. He died on March 15, 2007.

GANZ, LOWELL, AND BABALOO MANDEL

"There's no crying in baseball."

—Hollered by manager Jimmy Dugan (played by Tom Hanks) to player Evelyn Gardner (played by Bitty Schram) in the 1992 film *A League of Their Own*. Ganz and Mandel wrote the screenplay.

"A clubhouse lawyer is a .210 hitter who isn't playing. He gripes about everything. His locker is too near the dryer. His shoes aren't ever shined right. His undershirt isn't dry. His bats don't have the good knots in them that the stars' bats have. He's not playing because the manager is dumb. When he does play he says, 'Well, what could you expect? I ain't played in two weeks.' And he's a perpetual second guesser."

—*Sport*, April, 1962

"Baseball gives you every chance to be great. Then it puts every pressure on you to prove that you haven't got what it takes. It never takes away the chance, and it never eases up on the pressure."

—*Baseball Is a Funny Game*

"Baseball is drama with an endless run and an ever-changing cast."

—*Baseball Is a Funny Game*

"He's even tempered. He comes to the ball-park mad and stays that way."

—On Rick Burleson, SABR Collection

"I believe in telling the people. In fact, I'll try to build up the audience by saying, 'If you've got any friends not listening, call them up. We might have a no-hitter here tonight.'"

—On mentioning no-hitters as a broadcaster; quoted in *No-Hitter* by Phil Pepe

"I see the Mets' bats have arrived!"

—At a banquet as long loaves of bread were brought into the room. This was when the New York team was rich in pitchers but poor offensively; often told.

"I went through life as a player to be named later."

—Epitaphic line, often-quoted by Garagiola and others

"If he held out his right arm, he'd be a railroad crossing."

—On Boog Powell; widely quoted

"It's pitching, hitting and defense that wins. Any two can win. All three make you unbeatable."

—*Baseball Is a Funny Game*

"It's the same as any other ball game you'll remember as long as you live."

—On playing in the World Series

"Maybe one day [attorney] F. Lee Bailey will be the most valuable player in the American League. And the things players are asking—guaranteed playing time, so many starts for pitchers . . . Where will it end? Eventually you'll have a batter file a grievance if he gets a curveball on a 3-and-2 count."

—On the state of the game; as quoted in the *New York Times*, March 27, 1977.

"One thing you can be sure of, you'll never hear anyone say I knew someone exactly like Bart Giamatti."

—At Carnegie Hall, 1989

"One thing you learn as a Cubs fan: When you bought your ticket, you could bank on seeing the bottom of the ninth."

—*Christian Science Monitor*, October 10, 1978

"Players have hurts and fears and anxieties. As an announcer, I'm strictly for the underdog."

—Quoted by Lee Allen in *Cooperstown Corner*

"Stan comes sauntering up to the plate and asks me how my family's making out. Before I can answer him, he's on third base."

—On Stan Musial; quoted in Bennett Cerf's *Life of the Party*

"The Chicago Cubs are like Rush Street—a lot of singles, but no action."

—SABR Collection

"There won't be a hair dryer within 20 miles of the booth."

—On being teamed with another thin-haired broadcaster, Joe Torre, on California Angels' telecasts, 1990 season, *Major League Baseball Newsletter*, April 1990

"This is not a painting."

—As a sportscaster in Cincinnati describing a stunned crowd as the Reds fell behind

"You can plant two thousand rows of corn with the fertilizer Lasorda spreads around."

—On Tommy Lasorda, during an NBC telecast

"You know how particular the players are about the model bats they select every year. Well,

whenever I asked for mine, the clubhouse boy would never ask what kind. He'd ask what for."

—Quoted by Herman L. Masin in *Baseball Laughs*

GARBER, ANGUS G., III

"Baseball is forever, of course, which is why little boys have been trading baseball cards since the turn of the century. The faces change but the game remains the same: vibrant and at once intellectual and visceral. It is why some little boys never grow up.

"Fair or foul. There isn't much of a gray area there. And might does not necessarily make right in this poetic game. No, baseball is fanfare for the common man of uncommon abilities. It isn't hard to relate to a 5-foot-9 shortstop who wears a cap, as opposed to a hulking 290-pound defensive tackle who grunts behind a menacing helmet.

"Baseball endures."

—*Baseball Legends: The Greatest Players, Best Games, and Magical Moments—Then and Now* (New York: Gallery Books, 1989)

GARCIA, DAVE

"Well, sir, I watched and kept score and when the game was over I counted up and there were twenty-eight clear errors on my piece of paper. . . . And that doesn't even count all the errors they made there in the line, where you can't see what's happening."

—As Cleveland Indian manager, intimating that football is much sloppier than the artistic game of baseball

GARCIA, DAVE (CONTINUED)

"Whenever I see a batter digging a hole with his back foot I want to come off the mound and tell him not to bother. He's only gonna have to dig himself a new hole after my next pitch."

—Quoted in *Sport*, January 1956

GARDNER, BILLY

"I hear he's so rich he bought his dog a boy."

—As Twins manager on the club's new owner, Carl Pohlad

"The last time I was here, Howard Johnson's sold only vanilla."

—As new manager of the Kansas City Royals, upon arriving in Fort Myers, Florida, for the first time in twenty-five years. *Sports Illustrated*, March 23, 1987.

GARDNER, ED

"'This guy, Athos and Porthos McGinnes, may be your dish,' says Dugan, the shortstop, to the disconsolate Duffy. 'They call him Two-Top Gruskin for short, I guess, on account of him having two heads.'

"'A pitcher with two heads?' says Duffy dubiously. 'You think it'd be a novelty?'

"'What if it ain't?' points out Dugan. 'Who else could watch first and third base at the same time? Besides, he's a great guy to pitch double-headers.'

"So Two-Top is summoned from his home (Walla Walla, of course) and arrives to sign his contract in a dress suit. 'What are all you guys staring at?' he asks sourly. 'Ain't none of you seen a tuxedo before?'

"'Two-Top,' says Duffy, 'I'm a man of few words. Report tomorrow. There's a uniform and two caps waiting for you. Waiter, bring my new pitcher two beers.'

"Two-Top wins a masquerade that very night by disguising himself as a pair of bookends with a copy of *My Son, My Son* between the two heads. The next afternoon Duffy introduces him to his catcher, Gorilla Hogan, who measures 6 foot 14 inches and squats standing up. 'Most people,' says Duffy proudly, 'calls Gorilla a monstrosity, and I agree with them—a swell guy.' Gorilla soon gets into trouble with Two-Top, however. He signals for a high fast one. Two-Top nods 'yes' with one head, but shakes the other one 'no.' Confused and mortified, Gorilla hurls off his mask and yells to Duffy, 'Duffy, you such-and-such, I am sick and tired of two-headed pitchers around this place.'

"'Take it easy,' soothes Duffy. 'Talk it over with the guy. After all, three heads is better than one.'"

—Part of Two-Top saga by the man who played Archie on the *Duffy's Tavern* radio show; quoted in *Try and Stop Me* by Bennett Cerf 1944

GARDNER, MARTIN

"The story of Casey has become an American myth because Casey is the incomparable, towering symbol of the great and glorious poop-out."

—*The Annotated Casey at the Bat* (New York: Bramhall House, 1967)

GARDNER, PAUL

"Baseball lives at the center of a never-flagging whirl of irreconcilable opinions."

—*Nice Guys Finish Last: Sport and American Life*

GARELIK, SANFORD D.

"A soufflé of nostalgia."

—As New York City Council president on his city's 1972 agreement to buy Yankee Stadium and improve it—whatever the cost—in return for the team's promise to call New York home for thirty years; quoted in the *New York Times*, March 27, 1972

GARNER, JAMES

"I felt like my bubble-gum card collection had come to life."

—The actor, describing what it was like to attend a sports-celebrity awards dinner, as quoted in *Sports Illustrated*, March 11, 1968

GARVEY, CYNDY

"Steve has to take advantage of his peak earning years, but God, sometimes I just wish I had someone to cuddle with. Baseball wives are told how lucky we are, and we're not ungrateful. But I have to have someone to talk to at night. Steve is gone ninety-two days a year. In the off-season, he's busy with business affairs. Sometimes you just crave conversation."

—On her then-husband Steve; quoted by Danielle Gagnon Torrez in *High Inside: Memoirs of a Baseball Wife*

GARVEY, ED

"When you talk about civil liberties in professional sports, it's like talking about virtue in a whorehouse."

—*Village Voice*, December 8, 1975

GARVEY, STEVE

"Lasorda's standard reply when some new kid would ask directions to the whirlpool was to tell him to stick his foot in the toilet and flush it."

—*Garvey*

"Mostly it's the smells that take you back. The smell of fresh-cut grass when you first walk out onto the field. The smell of baseballs and the smell of powdery resin."

—*Baseball Card Engagement Book*, 1988

Steve Garvey (*San Diego Padres*)

"Spring training is like a cat with nine lives. A baseball player has X number of lives and each spring is the birth of a new life."

> —*Baseball Card Engagement Book,* 1988

"The only trouble with Tommy was he had a one-track mind in which the traffic seldom moved."

> —On his former L.A. Dodgers manager, Tom Lasorda; quoted in *Coach and Athletic Director,* February 2003

"We are not surgeons, or even plumbers. Society cannot do without those skills; it can certainly do without ballplayers."

> —*Garvey*

GEHRIG, ELEANOR

"A huge man and a small child combined in one runaway personality."

> —On Babe Ruth in her book *My Luke and I*

GEHRIG, LOU

GEHRIG'S FAREWELL ADDRESS

"Fans, for the past two weeks you have been reading about the bad break I got. Yet today I consider myself the luckiest man on the face of the earth. I have been in ballparks for seventeen years, and have never received anything but kindness and encouragement from you fans. Look at these grand men. Which of you wouldn't consider it the highlight of his career just to associate with them for

Lou Gehrig (*Society for American Baseball Research; SABR* Collection)

even one day? Sure I'm lucky. Who wouldn't consider it an honor to have known Jacob Rupert? Also, the builder of baseball's greatest empire, Ed Barrow? To have spent six years with that wonderful little fellow, Miller Huggins? Then to have spent the next nine years with that outstanding leader, that smart student of psychology, the best manager in baseball today, Joe McCarthy? Sure I'm lucky. When the New York Giants, a team you would give your right arm to beat, and vice versa, sends you a gift—that's something. When everybody down to the groundskeepers and those boys in white coats remember you with trophies—that's something. When you have a wonderful mother-in-law who takes sides with you in squabbles with her own daughter—that's something. When you have a father and a mother who work all their lives so you can have an education and build your body—it's a blessing. When you have a wife who has been a tower of strength and shown more courage than you dreamed existed—that's the finest I know. So I close in saying that I may have had a tough break, but I have an awful lot to live for."

—The farewell speech delivered by Gehrig at Yankee Stadium on July 4, 1939. Gehrig was suffering from amyotrophic lateral sclerosis, which soon became known as Lou Gehrig's disease. He died from it on June 2, 1941.

Almost fifty years later, this is what was said of the speech in an article by Ray Robinson in *Columbia*, the magazine of Gehrig's alma mater, Columbia University: "Gehrig's words have been acclaimed, without sarcasm, as baseball's Gettysburg Address. The event itself must be accorded sport's most agonizing spectacle."

A different version of the address is uttered by Gary Cooper in the film *Pride of the Yankees*. To give it a Hollywood finale, the second sentence of the speech is moved to the end and the movie version concludes with these words:

"People all say that I've had a bad break. But today, today I consider myself the luckiest man on the face of the earth." In his book *High and Inside,* Joseph McBride reports: "His famous speech, by the way, has often been misquoted as the 'lucky guy' speech, even the *New York Times* of July 5, 1939, reported it incorrectly."

"In 1921 McGraw was a sophisticated, experienced baseball man, and I was a dumb, innocent kid. Yet he was willing to let me throw away a scholarship as though it was a bundle of trash."

—On John McGraw; quoted by Fred Lieb in *Baseball As I Have Known It*

"In the beginning, I used to make one terrible play a game. Then I got so I'd make one a week, and finally I'd pull a bad one about once a month. Now, I'm trying to keep it down to one a season."

—To Quentin Reynolds, 1935; quoted in *Sport Magazine's All-Time All Stars* edited by Tom Murray

"It's a pretty big shadow. It gives me lots of room to spread myself."

—On living in Babe Ruth's shadow; in *Baseball As I Have Known It* by Fred Lieb

"One step."

—When asked by Eleanor Gehrig, "What's the difference between a baseball player in the high minor leagues and a man in the major leagues?"; from her book *My Luke and I*

"The ballplayer who loses his head, who can't keep his cool, is worse than no ballplayer at all."

—Widely quoted

"There is no room in baseball for discrimination. It is our national pastime and a game for all.

—His response to the issue of segregated baseball, widely attributed

GEHRIG, LOU (CONTINUED)

"You have to get knocked down to realize how people really feel about you. I've realized that more than ever lately. The other day, I was on my way to the car. I was hailing, the streets were slippery and I was having a tough time of it. I came to a corner and started to slip. But before I could fall, four people jumped out of nowhere to help me. When I thanked them, they all said they knew about my illness and had been keeping an eye on me."

—To Jack Sher shortly before his death; quoted in *Sport*, October 1948

"You have to [take the blame]. What are you going to do—admit to yourself that the pitchers have you on the point of surrender? You can't do that. You must make yourself think that the pitches are just as good as they always have been—or just as bad. So, if you are not hitting, the fault is yours. Having admitted that, what do you do? You ask everybody on the ball club:

"'What am I doing up there that I shouldn't do?'

"You'd be surprised at the answers. One fellow tells you this . . . another tells you that . . . somebody else tells you something else. You've changed your stance. Your feet are too close together . . . or too far apart. You're swinging too soon . . . or too late. You take all the advice you hear . . . and what happens? You're lucky you don't get hit in the head. Then, one day, you start to hit and you know that all the time it was your fault and the pitchers had nothing to do with it."

—His analysis of slumps, originally quoted by Frank Graham in the *New York Journal-American*

GEHRINGER, CHARLIE

"Us ball players do things backward. First we play, then we retire and go to work."

—The Hall of Fame second baseman; quoted in *Grand Slams and Fumbles*

GEISELMAN, GENE

"There are now three different major leagues—the AL, NL and DL."

—Cardinals trainer; quoted in the *Boston Globe*, April 19, 1992

GEIST, WILLIAM

"There are few who could say with certainty that *Orlando Furioso* is the Renaissance epic poem and 'Zeke' Zarilla the right fielder of the 1952 Boston Red Sox, and not the other way around."

—"The Outspoken President of Yale"; quoted in Anthony Valerio, *Bart: A Life of A. Bartlett Giamatti by Him and About Him* (New York: Harcourt Brace Jovanovich, 1991)

GENEVIEVE

GARAGIOLA: Don't you understand baseball?

GENEVIEVE: No, I don't. When my husband took me to a game, he told me to look and try to understand it. I look at a man who was number seven. He has a big number on his back.

GARAGIOLA: Mickey Mantle.

GENEVIEVE: Yes. Mickey has a stick. He drops his stick and runs all over the place. Then he come back to where he was. Everybody shake hands with him and take him away, hide him. He's hiding for a long time. Then he come back and seem very mad.

BISHOP: That's because he lost the ball.

GENEVIEVE: When he come back, he pick up that stick again and they throw balls at him again.

BISHOP: "Well, they're not crazy about him, you see. You have to understand the beginning of it. Mickey Mantle wears number seven, and number seven is the most disliked number in baseball."

GENEVIEVE: Poor man. Why do they put that number on him?

BISHOP: Because he's always the last guy in the locker room. He lives furthest from the ball park. It is just his luck to get there a little late. So they leave the number seven for him. After he puts it on, he comes out on the field.

GENEVIEVE: But why does everybody come to shake hands with Mickey before they hide him?

BISHOP: Because he tells them that tomorrow he is going to wear a different number. So they come over and say "congratulations." The next day, though, he comes out with the same number again, and everybody hollers, "Liar, you said you'd change your number. You're a hypocrite."

GENEVIEVE: But why do Mickey, that poor guy, come back?

GARAGIOLA: The money is good. For Mickey the money is very good.

GENEVIEVE: Oh, he is paid every time he come back from hiding?

GARAGIOLA: Yes, it's piece work. As many times as you go to bat, that's how you get paid. Like with my career. I batted so little that I owe my teams money.

GENEVIEVE: And why do they holler when he rubs his hands in the dirt before he picks up the stick?

BISHOP: Because he makes the bat dirty, and they like the guy on the team who cleans the bats. He is very popular.

GENEVIEVE: Why?

BISHOP: Why? Because baseball is a psychological game. That's the most important thing for you to understand. Now excuse me. We have a message from our sponsor.

—The French TV personality discussing baseball with Joe Garagiola and Joey Bishop on the old Jack Paar *Tonight* show in 1961. This discussion was widely circulated and appears in the May 1961 issue of *Sport* magazine, among other places.

GENT, PETER

"Baseball players are the weirdest of all. I think it's all that organ music."

—From the *Texas Celebrity Turkey Trot*, 1978

GENTILE, JIM

"I can't say for sure, but a couple of times after hitting against him I noticed my bat was warped."

—As an Orioles outfielder on whether or not a certain pitcher was throwing a spitter; widely quoted

GENTRY, GARY

"I make some dumb pitches. If I cut out the dumb pitches, I'll be Tom Seaver."

—The Mets pitcher; quoted in *The Incredible Mets* by Maury Allen

GERLACH, LARRY

"An umpire is a special breed—a natural leader in any endeavor. He is a powerful man, imposing in bearing and forceful in the manifestation of strongly held convictions. He is an extrovert who relishes both the publicity (albeit mostly negative) and the responsibility of his pressure-packed position. Dedicated, determined, egotistical, confident, authoritarian, honest, fair—these are the kinds of adjectives that describe an umpire. And he is a split personality—simultaneously a raging emotional volcano liable to erupt with awesome fury at the slightest provocation and a warm, sensitive, good-natured soul brimming with humanity. They are imposing, appealing, unforgettable men."

—*The Men in Blue* (New York: Viking Press, 1980)

GERONIMO, CESAR

"I was just in the right place at the right time."

—On becoming Nolan Ryan's 3000th strikeout victim; quoted in *Sports Illustrated*, August 4, 1980, as a Cincinnati Red. Geronimo had also been Bob Gibson's 3,000th in 1974.

GERSTLE, PHILLIP

"Football may be the 'disco beat' of modern sports, but baseball is Chopin or the mystique of Mozart. Every baseball game is new with the pristine beauty of the notes of Beethoven's Ninth."

—SABR Collection

GIAMATTI, A. BARTLETT

"All I ever wanted to be president of was the American League."

—As president-designate of Yale University

"Baseball has the largest library of law and love and custom and ritual, and therefore, in a nation that fundamentally believes it is a nation under law, well, baseball is America's most privileged version of the level field."

—Conversations; quoted in *Sports Illustrated*, April 17, 1989

"[Baseball is] intimately wrapped up with one's youth. Baseball is very much about being young again in a harmless way. That's why we call it a baseball park. You can call it a stadium if you want, but they were parks originally. 'Park' is a Persian word and it means 'paradise.' . . . You fly over a major city at night in the summer and suddenly you'll see that green oasis that reminds everybody of baseball's basic mythology: We come from a rural, simpler America. What's home? Home is longing for when you were happy because you were younger. At least you thought you were happier. It's not a game about overpowering somebody else. Home, that's what you call that thing! It's the one baseball fact that I cannot track down in all the histories that I have read. When did that pentagram where you start and to where you aspire to return, when did that get called 'home'? Why isn't it fourth base? What genius so defined the essence of what we're after by calling it home plate?"

—"Front-Office Fan," *Life*, April 1988 (interview)

"Baseball should be ahead of the country in the things that mean the most in terms of the country's best positive, fundamental values. On matters of race, on matters of decency, baseball should lead the way."

—To Claire Smith of the *Hartford Courant*; quoted by Fay Vincent in a December 4, 1989 (speech)

"Call it what you will, the strike is utter foolishness. It is an act of defiance against the American people, and the only summer God made for 1981, and I appeal for it to cease. I do so as a citizen.

"The people of America care about baseball, not about your squalid little squabbles. Reassume your dignity and remember that you are the temporary custodians of an enduring public trust."

—On the strike of 1981, during the strike; recalled by Tray Ringolsby in his memorial column on Giamatti, *Baseball America*, October 10, 1989.

"Dante would have been delighted."

—On accepting the commissionership; quoted by Tom Boswell, September 2, 1989, the day after Giamatti's death

"Home plate also has a peculiar significance for it is the goal of both teams, the single place that in territorially based games—games about conquering—must be symbolized by two goals or goal lines or nets or baskets. In baseball, everyone wants to arrive at the same place, which is where they start."

—*Take Time for Paradise: Americans and Their Games* (New York: Summit Books, 1989)

"I think Dante would have been delighted [about Giamatti's new job as president of the National League]. I think Dante knew very well what the nature of paradise was and what preceded it. He would have approved of any sport whose first game in 1845 was played on something called the Elysian Fields in Hoboken, New Jersey."

—Quoted in Nick Johnson, "Dante to Doerr," *Holyoke* [Mass.] *Transcript-Telegram*

"In no game of ours is failure so omnipresent as it is for the batter who would be the runner."

—*Take Time for Paradise: Americans and Their Games*

"It breaks your heart. It is designed to break your heart. The game begins in the spring, when everything else begins again, and it blossoms in the summer, filling the afternoons and evenings, and then as soon as the chill rains come, it stops and leaves you to face the fall alone. You count on it, rely on it to buffer the passage of time, to keep the memory of sunshine and high skies alive, and then just when the days are all twilight, when you need it most, it stops. Today, October 2, a Sunday of rain and broken branches and leaf-clogged drains and slick streets, it stopped, and summer was gone."

—"The Green Fields of the Mind," *Yale Alumni Magazine*, November 1977

"It is a game that is exciting and stimulating and beautiful and fun, in part because it puts a tremendous premium on individual achievement in the context of a team. . . . I think Americans respond to that check and balance between the premium on the individual's talent and the overall team effort. I think that's part of the game's basic appeal: It is about boundary and rule and law, which we love in all phases of our life. Baseball is part of the fiber of American life, and it must, by nature, appeal to and reflect the accessibility that is one of this society's great virtues. Classes and institutions are not closed off in a democracy and thus baseball must not be either."

> —"Front-Office Fan," *Life,* April 1988
> (interview)

"Luis Tiant, on the one hand, knowing full well the ravages of time—as, of course, we all as human beings come to know them—but on the other hand, ever mindful of the need to advance the human spirit, played the part of a traitor and left Boston for the asphalt pastures of New York."

> —Comment about Tiant leaving the Boston Red Sox and signing with the New York Yankees; quoted in Edward B. Fiske, "Yale's MVP Learns New Signals—and Sends Some," copyright 1979 by the New York Times Company

"O, Sovereign Owners and Princely Players, masters of amortization, tax shelters, bonuses and deferred compensation, go back to work.

You have been trusted with the serious work of play, and your season of responsibility has come."

> —On the 1981 strike, as Yale president, *New York Times,* June 16, 1981

"People will say I'm an idealist. I hope so."

> —At the news conference at which Pete Rose was banished from the game

"The banishment for life of Pete Rose from baseball is the sad end of a sorry episode. One of the game's greatest players has engaged in a variety of acts which have stained the game, and he must now live with the consequences of those acts. . . . There is absolutely no deal for reinstatement. That is exactly what we did not agree to in terms of fixed number of years."

> —On the matter of Pete Rose, August 24, 1989

"[The geometry of the game is] constantly working against action, containing it and releasing it. There's a tremendous counterpoint between energy and order. Nothing is more orderly and geometrically precise than baseball."

> —Quoted in Frank Deford, "A Gentleman and a Scholar," *Sports Illustrated*, April 17, 1989

"The largest thing I've learned [as a baseball executive] is the enormous grip that this game has on people, the extent to which it really is very important. It goes way down deep. It really does bind together. It's a cliché and sounds sentimental, but I have now seen it from the inside. . . . I think I underestimated the depth of this historical enterprise. . . . [Baseball] is an unalloyed good. Of course, there are passions [involved]. But passion is good if it is directed toward a noble end.

"... The number of people on the Faculty of Arts and Sciences at Yale and the number of ballplayers in the major leagues are almost the same—somewhere around six hundred and thirty. And if we're making analogies, the umpires would be the deans. And tenure? Well, I guess even Mike Schmidt doesn't have tenure. Put the two bodies together, and what you have is one vast, unstable company of prima donnas. Skilled, yes, but oh, brother!"

—"Celebration" (1988), in Roger Angell, *Once More Around the Park: A Baseball Reader* (New York: Ballantine Books, 1991)

"There's nothing bad that accrues from baseball. [Realizing] that has been the most rewarding part of all this."

—Quoted by Tom Boswell in his farewell column to Giamatti, September 2, 1989

"There are a lot of people who know me who can't understand for the life of them why I would go to work on something as unserious as baseball. If they only knew."

—During his tenure as National League president

"Not rooting is a deprivation.... It's like loving the theater all your life and then becoming a producer."

—As National League president

GIAMATTI, MARCUS

"This is the last pure place where Americans dream. This is the last great arena, the last green arena, where everybody can learn the lessons of life."

—Quoting his father, Bart, in the *Houston Post*, April 9, 1990

GIAMBI, JASON

"The guy's going to freeze to death. Check him out. He's got no body fat."

—On Athletics second baseman Randy Velarde, who had 7 percent body fat, *New Orleans Times-Picayune*, August 29, 1999

GIANNOULAS, TED

"If you can't stand the heat, stay out of The Chicken."

—The man portraying the San Diego Chicken when asked if he was uncomfortable during a 1980 heat wave. *Sports Illustrated*, July 28, 1980. This may be the best baseball chicken line; the runner-up occurred when Giannoulas was introduced to Skip Carey, who asked, "Why did you cross the road?"

"Who knows? I mean, they have a broadcasters wing. They have a players wing. Maybe one day they'll have a chicken wing."

—Comment by baseball's famous chicken mascot on his prospect of making the Baseball Hall of Fame; quoted in the *Baltimore Sun*, July 3, 1993

GIBSON, BOB

"A curve ball is not something you can pick up overnight. It took me years to perfect mine."

—*From Ghetto to Glory*

"A great catch is like watching girls go by—the last one you see is always the prettiest."

> —Reaction to an excellent catch by his center fielder, *Sports Illustrated*, June 1, 1964

"A wise man once said a baseball takes funny bounces."

> —*From Ghetto to Glory*

"Believe me, I would much rather get three outs on three pitches than three outs on nine pitches, because that's going to make me that much stronger at the end of the game.

"My pitching philosophy is simple. I believe in getting the ball over the plate and not walking a lot of men."

> —*From Ghetto to Glory*

"Hitters aren't stupid, but sometimes I think they believe they are smarter than they really are."

> —*From Ghetto to Glory*

"I don't like all this personal contact with the press. The press expects everyone to be congenial. Everyone's *not* congenial! They want to put every athlete in the same category as every other athlete. It's as if they thought they owned you."

> —Quoted in *Late Innings* by Roger Angell

"I guess I was never much in awe of anybody. I think you have to have that attitude if you're going to go far in this game."

> —Quoted in *Late Innings* by Roger Angell

Bob Gibson (*St. Louis Cardinals*)

"I think it's the life I miss—all the activity that's around baseball. I don't miss playing baseball but I miss . . . baseball. *Baseball*. Does that sound like a crazy man?"

> —In Roger Angell's *Late Innings*

"It is not something I earned or acquired or bought. It is a gift. It is something that was given to me—just like the color of my skin."

> —On his ability to throw a baseball, in *From Ghetto to Glory*

"I've always thought that you only really enjoy baseball when you're good at it. For someone who isn't at the top of the game—who's just hanging on somewhere on down the totem pole—it's a real tough job, every day. But when I was playing I never wished I was doing anything else. I think being a professional athlete is the finest thing a man can do."

—Quoted in *Late Innings* by Roger Angell

"Rules or no rules, pitchers are going to throw spitters. It's a matter of survival."

—*From Ghetto to Glory*

"Why do I have to be an example for your kid? *You* be an example for your own kid."

—On role models, 1970; widely attributed, although some versions have it end with the words "your kid" and others say "your own kid." A longer version begins this way; "Too many people think an athlete's life can be an open book. You're supposed to be an example. . . ."

"Who wants to talk to fans? They always know so much, to hear them tell it, and they always think baseball is so easy."

—Quoted in *Late Innings* by Roger Angell

GIBSON, GEORGE

"I'll quit the game before I put myself into armor."

—The Pittsburgh catcher on the introduction of shin guards in 1907; quoted in *Professional Baseball: The First 100 Years.*

GIBSON, J. J.

"We perceive not only the motion of objects but also the movements of ourselves; the performance of fielding a baseball illustrates both."

—Quoted by G. J. K. Aldersen in "Perceptual Studies: Variables Affecting the Perception of Velocity in Sports Situations," in H. T. A. Whiting, ed., *Readings in Sports Psychology,* 1972

GIBSON, JOSH

"A homer a day will boost my pay."

—*Grand Slams and Fumbles,* 1930

GILBERT, BILL, AND LISA TWYMAN

"Small, fairly tame acts of violence on a baseball field may appear to be much worse than they really are because the game generally lacks physical contact. Also at the heart of baseball is one of the most explicitly warlike charades in all sport: the repeated and possibly fatal confrontation between pitcher and batter."

—"Violence: Out of Hand in the Stands," *Sports Illustrated,* January 31, 1983

GILES, WARREN

"Charlie Finley wouldn't think God would make a good commissioner."

—Widely attributed

"The game has changed since World War Two. . . . Bill Klem was a great umpire, but he could no longer get away with his favorite stunt of drawing a line in the dust and daring a player to cross it and be fined. On the other hand, players can't be permitted to incite riotous scenes as Ducky Medwick did during the 1934 World Series when he disagreed with an umpire's decision. This doesn't mean that umpires should act like robots, or players, display Sunday-go-to-meeting manners. Tempers are bound to explode in the heat of play.

And umpires can't always be right, as Klem insisted he was."

> —As National League president; quoted in *Sport*, March 1962. He made this statement after forty-three years in baseball.

"There is no such thing as a corrupt umpire . . . and there never will be!"

> —*Sporting News*, April 30, 1952

"Who needs New York?"

> —The National League president at the end of 1957, when it became known that both the Dodgers and Giants were moving. This was his answer to the question of whether his league would have a team in the nation's largest city; quoted in *The Incredible Mets* by Maury Allen

"There are some great ballplayers, but there aren't any superstars. Superstars you find on the moon."

> —*Los Angeles Times*, August 3, 1974

GILLIAM, JIM

"You might say I was born on a ball field. There was one on the block where I lived in Nashville, and another right beside the school I went to. I was playing softball at seven and hardball on a sand-lot semipro team, the Crawfords, when I was fourteen. I never did anything but play ball, except one time I worked as a porter in a five-and-ten."

> —Quoted in *Baseball Has Done It* by Jackie Robinson

Jim Gilliam (*Society for American Baseball Research; SABR* Collection)

GILMAN, RICHARD

"Baseball is a game dominated by vital ghosts; it's a fraternity, like no other we have, of the active and the no longer so, the living and the dead."

> —SABR Collection

GIOVANNI, NIKKI

"Baseball is . . . the world's most tranquil sport. It is probably the only active sport where you are not seriously required to be alive to play."

> —"A Patriotic Plea for Poetry Justice," *Sacred Cows . . . and Other Edibles*, 1988

GLANVILLE, DOUG

"To be mentioned in the same breath as Solly Hemus, Boots Day and Chick Fewster is quite an honor. But I'm upset that I didn't make this an incentive clause in my current contract."

> —On finding that he would be the first player to bat at Houston's new Enron Field, joining others who had christened a ballpark. On the list were Hemus (County Stadium), Day (Veterans Stadium), and Fewster (Yankee Stadium); quoted in the *Chicago Sun Times*, March 28, 2000

GLASER, LULU

"Anyone with any real blood in his or her . . . veins cannot help being a fan. Being a true American and being a fan are synonymous."

> —U.S. comic opera performer; first quoted in *Baseball Magazine*

GLASSER, IRA

"You will be pleased to know I stand obediently for the national anthem, though of course I would defend your right to remain seated should you so decide."

> —The head of the American Civil Liberties Union, attending a baseball game with conservative William F. Buckley Jr.; quoted in *Life: The Year in Pictures*, 1994

GLEICK, JAMES

"A properly hurled knuckleball seems to make up its own rules on its way to the plate. It floats, flutters, twitches, lurches, and dives."

> —*New York Times*; quoted in the *New Yorker*, October 26, 1987

GLENN, JOE C.

"It was the closing day of 1933, and I had just returned to the club [from the minors]. We were in Boston. Washington had already clinched the pennant under Joe Cronin. The Red Sox were trying to get people to the park, and since Babe had established his reputation there, first as a pitcher, he was advertised as a special attraction.

"Ruth hadn't pitched in some time, yet he went all the way and won, 6–5. His personal magnetism brought out 30,000, and everyone enjoyed the game."

> —Recalling Babe Ruth's last pitching assignment, which he caught. The recollection appeared in Glenn's obituary in the *Sporting News* on May 6, 1985.

GOETZ, LARRY

"It isn't enough for an umpire merely to know what he's doing. He has to *look* as though he knows what he's doing, too."

> —The National League umpire; quoted in *The Mutual Baseball Almanac* edited by Roger Kahn and Al Helfer

GOETZ, LARRY (CONTINUED)

"The long, drawn-out games are a peeve with the fans, sportswriters and umpires. Do not forget we have to stand out there all the time. We don't go into a dugout and sit every half inning, like the players."

> —The National League umpire; quoted by Arch Ward in the *Sporting News*, May 25, 1955

"People come to see the players. Nobody ever bought a ticket to see a manager."

> —The umpire on why managers should be thrown out before players; quoted in Joe Garagiola's *Baseball Is a Funny Game*

GOLD, TEDDY

"I don't think I'll be a true revolutionary until Willie Mays retires."

> —One of the 1960s urban revolutionaries killed in the explosion of a Greenwich Village, New York, town house; quotation attributed to Gold in Dan Okrent's preface to John Krich's book on baseball in Latin America, *El Béisbol: Travels Through the Pan-American Pastime.*

GOLDEN, HARRY

"As far as teams were concerned, of course, I was always a New York Giants' man. . . . The Giants represented the New York of the brass cuspidor—that old New York which was still a man's world before the advent of the League of Women Voters; the days of swinging doors, of sawdust on the barroom floor, and of rushing the growler."

> —From *For 2 Cents Plain*, appears in *The Giants of the Polo Grounds* by Noel Hynd

GOLDSTEIN, WARREN

"Baseball death is not like other death. Ballplayers die at least twice: once when they retire and then again, usually much later, when their bodies give out. The second death always surprises baseball fans. 'Was he still alive?' we muse, because for us, for all practical purposes—which is to say baseball purposes—he'd been dead for decades."

> —*Newsday*

GOMEZ, JUNE O'DEA

"In the hospital, about a week before he died, the doctor leaned over his bed and said, 'Lefty, picture yourself on the mound and rate the pain from 1 to 10.'

"And Lefty looked at him and said, 'Who's hitting, Doc?'"

> —On Lefty Gomez. *Washington Times*, February 28, 1989

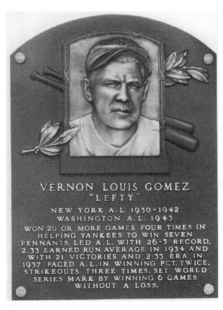

Lefty Gomez (*National Baseball Library*)

They called him "El Goofy," but Vernon "Lefty" Gomez was a crafty Hall of Fame pictcher who had four seasons in which he won twenty games or more. His wit and personality came through in the quotes he left behind.

"Bob Considine, the writer, gave me the 'Goofy' nickname. We were on our way to Washington when he asked me if I'd ever invented anything.

"I said, 'Yes, I've invented a revolving fish bowl that will add ten years to the life of a goldfish. It turns, the fish rest on glass, don't have to expend any energy in swimming and as a result their lives are prolonged.'"

—Quoted by Sec. Taylor of the *Des Moines Register* in the February 1961, *Baseball Digest*

"Charlie Gehringer is in a rut. He hits .350 on opening day and stays there all season."

—SABR Collection

"Clean living, a fast outfield and Johnny Murphy."

—When asked to explain his success. Johnny Murphy saved many games for Gomez. Recalled by Jack Lane in the *Sporting News,* February 12, 1972, on his being elected to the Baseball Hall of Fame

"Don't ask me what the pitch was. It could have been a fast ball down the pipe. With a bat in my hands, I couldn't tell a curve from a Cuban palm ball. I do recall that only one of my eyes was closed when I swung."

—On getting the first hit in the first All-Star Game, 1933; quoted in the *Sporting News* by Wells Twombly, 1973.

"He has muscles in his hair."

—Describing Jimmie Foxx

"Hell, Lou, it took 15 years to get you out of the game. Sometimes I'm out in 15 minutes."

—To Lou Gehrig after he took himself out of the lineup, ending his consecutive games streak; recalled by the *Washington Post* on September 6, 1995, at the time of Cal Ripken's breaking Gehrig's consecutive game record

"He's in a rut. Gehringer goes two for five on Opening Day and stays that way all season."

—On Charlie Gehringer; quoted by Lee Allen in *Cooperstown Corner*

"He's temperamental all right. But it's ninety-eight per cent temper and two per cent mental."

—On a fellow Cleveland pitcher feigning rage after being given the hook; quoted in *Baseball Laughs* by Herman L. Masin.

"He's the first player brought back by Frank Buck."

—On Charlie Keller, the hairy, muscular Yankee pitcher. Buck was a famous hunter. The line was recalled in the "Jupiter" column in the May 27, 1990, *San Francisco Examiner.*

"I don't want to throw him nothin'. Maybe he'll just get tired of waitin' and leave."

> —Preparing to pitch to Jimmie Foxx, answering Bill Dickey's question: "What do you want to throw him?"; quoted in *Grand Slams and Fumbles*

"I know they're hanging up new baseball records every season but they don't seem able to break my record for the longest home run every hit in the Stadium. Jimmie Foxx hit it off me!"

> —Quoted by Bennett Cerf in his *The Laugh's on Me*

"I know they're loaded. Did you think I thought they gave me an extra infield?"

> —On being told by shortstop Frank Crosetti that the bases were loaded; quoted in Joe Garagiola's *Baseball Is a Funny Game*

"I never broke any records. But, now wait a minute! Yes I did. My son had a record I broke once—I think it was Rudolph the Red-Nosed Reindeer."

> —Quoted by Lee Allen in the essay "Goofy Was Six and 0," in *Cooperstown Corner*

"I never had a bad night in my life, but I've had a few bad mornings."

> —Quoted in *Baseball Digest*, March 1961

"I remember walking out here just before that game and looking around, and there were so many people in the stands that—well, there weren't just more people here than in my home town but in my home *county*!"

> —On his first game in the majors, in May 1930; to Roger Angell (quoted in *Five Seasons*), who watched him pitch that day

"I talk 'em out of hits."

> —Widely quoted

"I was so bad I never even broke a bat until last year. Then I was backing out of the garage."

> —Reflecting on inabilities as a batter; widely attributed

"I'll never forget one of my earliest experiences with the Yankees. I was in the bullpen. Herb Pennock was leading, 2–1, in the eighth and a hard liner comes tearing right at him and knocks him down. So they called me. A lot of things run through your mind when you're going up there to relieve in a tough situation. One of them was, 'Should I spike myself?'

"When I got up there Joe McCarthy was waiting. 'O.K., boss,' I told him, 'I know what the situation is. This is the way I'll pitch to Foxx.' McCarthy looked at me and said, 'What's the matter with you, Gomez? That line drive broke the webbing in Pennock's glove. Give him yours and get the hell out of here.'"

> —Quoted by Sid Ziff of the *Los Angeles Mirror-News* during a Gomez luncheon address; quoted in *Baseball Digest* August 1961

"I'm liable to make them forget Gomez."

> —When told that if he would put on fifteen pounds, he would make the Yankee fans forget Jack Chesbro

"I'm throwing twice as hard but the ball is getting there half as fast."

> —On aging; widely quoted

"I've been reading in the papers that you were a smart guy, and I wanted to see what you'd do with that one."

> —When Tony Lazzeri asked him to explain a sudden and mysterious throw to Lazzeri, the second baseman

"Let's wait a while. Maybe he'll get a phone call."

> —After shaking off the catcher's fifth sign

"Maybe the name 'Vernon' that my folks gave me caused me to go off on tangents. I never liked that name. And it wasn't my father's choice either. When I was born, back in 1910, my Irish mother asked my Spanish father what I should be called. My father bent over the cradle, took one look at me, and then said to my mother, 'Let's call it quits.' Ma liked Vernon better."

> —Quoted by Jack Cuddy of United Press International in a 1943 *Sporting News*

"No other left-hander gave me so much trouble. When I think about how many points in Earl Averill's lifetime batting average [.318] came off Gomez deliveries, I thank the good Lord he wasn't twins. One more like him would probably have kept me out of the Hall of Fame."

> —On the Hall of Famer; quoted in the 1989 *Yearbook*

"Nobody can fatten up a greyhound."

> —On the Yankees' attempt to fatten him up during the winter of 1930–1931; quoted in *The Babe Ruth Story*, by Babe Ruth as told to Bob Considine

"One rule I had was make your best pitch and back up third base. That relay might get away and you've got another shot at him."

> —Quoted at a 1961 luncheon address by Sid Ziff of the *Los Angeles Mirror-News*

"The ball came down in Utica. I know. I was managing there at the time."

> —On Willie Mays's first homer hit off the great Warren Spahn

"The secret of my success was clean living and a fast-moving outfield."

> —Quoted by Edward F. Murphy in the *New York Times*, April 25, 1976

"Tomorrow! Who do you think you're marrying, Iron Man Joe McGinnity?"

> —Quoted by Arnold Hano in a 1969 profile of McGinnity in *Sport*. The setup as put by Hano: "In 1932, Vernon Gomez, the very left-handed New York Yankee pitcher, invited his showgirl fiancée, June O'Dea, to Yankee Stadium to see her first big-league game.
> "Gomez pitches well that long hot afternoon, but as luck would have it, lost in the tenth inning, 1–0.
> "Seeing her man disconsolate after the game, the lovely Miss O'Dea stroked his head and said softly: 'Don't let it worry you, honey. You'll go out there and beat them tomorrow.'"

"'Well,' I was just reading in the paper the other day what a smart fellow you were and I was curious to see what you would do in a spot like that.'"

—Explaining why when, with a man on first base, a ball was hit back to Gomez and he threw to Tony Lazzeri, who was at least ten feet off second base, instead of to Frank Crosetti, who was covering the bag. Later manager Joe McCarthy asked Gomez about the throw. "I was a little confused," Gomez said. "When I looked around there were two Dagoes near the bag and I didn't know which one to throw it to.

"McCarthy snorted.

"'There was another one in center field,' he said. 'Why didn't you throw it to him?'"

"When I first signed with the Yankees, the regulars wouldn't talk to you until you were with the team three or four years. Nowadays the rookies get $100,000 to sign and they don't talk to the regulars."

—Quoted in the *Sporting News*, July 25, 1970

"When Neil Armstrong first set foot on the moon, he and all the space scientists were puzzled by an unidentifiable white object. I knew immediately what it was. That was a home run ball hit off me in 1937 by Jimmie Foxx."

—Quoted in the 1989 *Yearbook* of the National Baseball Hall of Fame as a testimony to Foxx. He is also quoted as saying of the same man: "Jimmie Foxx wasn't scouted, he was trapped."

"You keep the salary, I'll take the cut."

—After his bad season in 1935, when Colonel Jacob Rupert proposed cutting his pay from $20,000 to $7,500

"You know, Yankee Stadium's center field is real deep. They didn't know Joe could go back that far on a high fly ball until I pitched. The only time I saw his face was in the clubhouse."

—On why Joe DiMaggio got into the Hall of Fame; quoted in a *USA Today* report on Gomez's funeral, February 24, 1989

"You used to say when I threw it from behind my ear nobody could hit it. So I'm flattered and I throw from behind my ear—and you belt it. I didn't realize till later that you were suckering me into giving away my curve."

—To Hank Greenberg, *Sporting News*, 1948

"You wind him up in the spring, turn him loose, he hits .330 or .340, and you shut him off at the end of the season."

—On Charlie Gehringer; quoted in the 1989 50th Anniversary Hall of Fame *Yearbook*

"You're right, though, about me being a good hitter. Remember the time I knocked myself out of the box? I stepped out of the batter's box and was knocking dirt out of my spikes the way those big hitters do before diggin' in. Crosetti, who was waiting on deck, said, 'Hey Gomez.' I looked around, and hit myself right here on this ankle bone, and had to leave the game."

—Quoted in the Hall of Fame *Yearbook*, 1989

GOMEZ, PRESTON

"You never unpack your suitcases in this business."

— After being fired as a manager

GOMME, ALICE BERTHA

"An elaborate form of this game has become the national game of the United States."

— At the conclusion of a description of rounders in volume two of *Traditional Games of England, Scotland, and Ireland*

GONZALEZ, MIKE

"Good field, no hit."

— Contents of a 1924 telegram that he sent as a scout to a club that was interested in Moe Berg, who generally fit the description. The description has been used ever since to describe a variety of infielders and ranks as one of the most-heard-of all baseball quotations. There are many versions of why the telegram was sent—in one he was asked to scout a man in his native Havana, and in another he was scouting a man for John McGraw of the Giants—but the Berg version is the one heard most often. There are several references which say that it was actually first said by a scout named Adolph Luque.

"I hope to live long enough to spend the rest of my life here."

— At a dinner in St. Louis; quoted in the November 1942 *Baseball Digest*

GOODEN, DWIGHT

"I don't care how much money he makes. He can have my locker, I'll take him to all the best restaurants and show him New York. He can even have my wife. But he can't have my number, no way."

— No. 16 on the arrival of Frank Viola to the Mets, *Sporting News*, August 7, 1989

"I figured that pitchers had a better chance of getting drafted than fielders, so I decided I should be a pitcher. But I never expected to be picked in the first round. I wasn't even sure I'd get picked at all."

— As an eighteen-year-old pitching for Class A Lynchburg, *Baseball America*, August 1, 1983

Dwight Gooden (*New York Mets*)

GOODEN, DWIGHT (CONTINUED)

"I'm glad I don't have to face that guy [Mattingly] every day. He has that look that few hitters have. I don't know if it's his stance, his eyes or what. But you can tell he means business."

—On facing Don Mattingly in a spring-training game against the Yankees; quoted in the *Tampa Tribune*, March 11, 1989

GOODMAN, DANNY

"No individual player is that important; it's the name 'Dodger' that sells."

—Head of advertising and novelties for the Dodgers until his death in 1983; quoted in *Garvey* by Steve Garvey

GOODWIN, DORIS KEARNS

"Except for Eddie Rust and Steve Bartha, who lived on our block and occasionally joined us girls in punchball, Johnny was the first boy my age that I ever really talked to. On the playground at school, the girls would play on one side, the boys on the other. The boys came over to our side to tug our braids and ponytails, then, cackling, retreated. Being able to talk at length to a boy was something special. And it was my passion for baseball that made it possible."

—*Wait Till Next Year: A Memoir* (New York: Simon & Schuster, 1997)

"The game of baseball has always been linked in my mind with the mystic texture of childhood, with the sounds and smells of summer nights and with the memories of my father."

—"From Father, with Love," *Boston Globe*, October 6, 1986.

"The Yankees were the 'Bronx Bombers,' whose pinstriped uniforms signified their elite status, supported by the rich and successful, by Wall Street brokers and haughty businessmen. The Dodgers were 'dem Bums,' the 'daffiness boys,' the unpretentious clowns, whose fans were seen as scruffy blue-collar workers who spoke with bad diction. The Giants, owned since 1919 by the same family, the Stonehams, were the conservative team whose followers consisted of small businessmen who watched calmly from the stands dressed in shirts and ties, their identity somewhat blurred, caught, as they were, between the Yankee 'haves' and the Dodger 'have-nots.'"

—*Wait Till Next Year: A Memoir* (New York: Simon & Schuster, 1997)

GORDON, ALISON

"I once stood outside Fenway Park in Boston, a place where the ghosts never go away, and watched a vigorous man of middle years helping, with infinite care, a frail and elderly gentleman through the milling crowds to the entry gate. Through the tears that came unexpectedly to my eyes, I saw the old man strong and important forty years before, holding the hand of a confused and excited five-year-old, showing him the way. Baseball's best moments don't always happen on the field."

—*Foul Ball! Five Years in the American League* (Toronto: McClelland & Stewart, 1984)

"The game proceeds at just the right pace: the one detractors call boring. It is gentle and relaxed, full of spaces for reflection or conversation, quiet moments in which to relish a play just made or a confrontation about to occur. What's the rush? The longer the game, the more there is to enjoy.

"To find baseball boring is to have missed drama and nuance, the laughter and the tears that come from joy or sorrow. It's a shame."

—*Foul Ball! Five Years in the American League*

GORE, AL

"In this country there have been three baseball players who transcended their sport to become part of American legend. Where Babe Ruth was known for his power and Jackie Robinson was known for his courage, Joe DiMaggio was known for dignity and grace."

—On the passing of Joe DiMaggio, *Boston Globe*, March 1, 1999

GORMAN, LOU

"Wade Boggs could fall out of bed and get a base hit."

—The Red Sox executive doing a guest spot as a broadcaster, *San Diego Union-Tribune*, December 29, 1989

"Where would we play him?"

—When the Boston Red Sox, on August 19, 1990, refused a trade for Willie McGee

GORMAN, TOM

"Anytime I got those 'bang-bang' plays at first base, I called 'em out. It made the game shorter."

—As a retired umpire; widely attributed

"Nobody ever says anything nice about an umpire, unless it's when he dies and then somebody writes in the paper, 'he was a good umpire.' Oh, once in a while a player will tell you that you worked a good game behind the plate, but when that happens, it's always the winning pitcher who says it."

—Quoted in *Catcher in the Wry* by Bob Uecker

"The bigger the guy, the less he argues. You never heard a word out of Stan Musial or Willie Mays or Roberto Clemente. They never tried to make you look bad."

—As an umpire on umpire-baiters, *Sporting News*, August 2, 1975

"To see if you were dying."

—When asked by Leo Durocher why he had come to visit him in the hospital; quoted by David Voight in the fall 1982 *National Pastime*

GOSSAGE, RICH "GOOSE"

"Don't you forget that you play the game from here [pointing to his heart], not here [pointing to his head] and not here [pointing to his wallet]. And the minute you forget that, get the hell out of my game."

—Oakland A's pitcher, during spring training 1992, said to two Chicago Cub minor-league pitchers (Lance Dickson and Turk Wendell) in a bar; quoted in: Tom Verducci, "Making Hay," *Sports Illustrated*, September 12, 1994

"I want out. I'm sick of everything that goes on around her. I'm sick of all the negative stuff and you can take that upstairs to the fat man and tell him I said it."

—His manifesto of August 16, 1982; Steinbrenner responded that he wasn't so fat; quoted by William B. Mead in *The Official Yankee Hater's Handbook.*

GOULD, STEPHEN JAY

"I finally came to understand the unique nature of Red Sox pain—not like Cubs pain (never to get there at all), or Phillies pain (lousy teams, though they did win the Series in 1980), but the deepest possible anguish of running a long and hard course, again and again, to the very end, and then self-destructing one inch from the finish line."

—From "Confessions of a New York Yankee Fan," *Boston Globe*, April 9, 1990

"I first saw DiMaggio play near the end of his career in 1950, when I was 8 and Joe was having his last great season, batting .301 with 32 homers and 122 RBIs. He became my hero, my model, and my mentor, all rolled up into one remarkable man. (I longed to be his replacement in center field, but a guy named Mickey Mantle came along and beat me out of the job.) DiMaggio remained my primary hero to the day of his death, and through all the vicissitudes of Ms. Monroe, Mr. Coffee, and Mrs. Robinson."

—March 9, 1999, obituary which he wrote for the Associated Press

"I love the .400 hitting example because it just makes so much sense once you get it. Everyone is always talking about .400 hitting. And there's an enormous variety of explanations, but they're all based on the same assumption, which seems commonsensical, namely, that .400 hitting once existed and went away, so something bad has affected hitting. Maybe it's that pitching's gotten better, faster, but something bad has happened, either absolutely or relatively. And yet everybody knows that doesn't make sense because everything gets better in sports.

"The whole thing is based on a misperception—misconstruing the number .400 as an entity, as a measure of excellence. People have always assumed that hitting must have gotten worse, either absolutely or relatively, because [.400] disappeared. I argue that if you study things in terms of spread, decreasing spread, you will understand that the decline of .400 hitting is, ironically, measuring the increasing excellence of play. And I've never had any of the major baseball statisticians reject this idea, once they see what I'm saying."

—Gould used baseball to explain the tendency for the disappearance of extreme variation in a species by referring to the fact that nobody had hit .400 since Ted Williams in 1941. Salon.com interview contained in his obituary from the Harrisburg (PA) *Patriot-News,* May 24, 2002.

"I'm a Yankee fan, but I can't help it, so please don't be mad. Serious rooting—of the genre literally rooted in origins and personal histories—is a happenstance of birth and a consequence of genealogy. I grew up in the greatest intersection of time and place that baseball has ever known—New York City, with its three great teams of the late '40s to the debacle of 1958, when the Dodgers and Giants ripped out the soul of my birthplace and relocated at maximal West Coast distances. In my formative years, from 1949 to 1956, six of eight World Series were "subway" clashes between two New York teams; both remaining contests were won by a New York club against an infidel (Yanks over Phils in 1950, and Giants over Indians in 1954)."

—"Confessions of a New York Yankees Fan"

"When the world's tall ships graced our bicentennial in 1976, many of us lamented their lost beauty and cited Masefield's sorrow that we would never 'see such ships as those again.' I harbor opposite feelings about the disappearance of .400 hitting. Giants have not ceded to mere mortals. I'll bet anything that Carew could match Keeler. Rather, the boundaries of baseball have been drawn in and its edges smoothed. The game has achieved a grace and precision of execution that has, as one effect, eliminated the extreme achievements of early years. A game unmatched for style and detail has simply become more balanced and beautiful."

—"The Extinction of the .400 Hitter," *Vanity Fair,* 1983

GOULD, THOMAS

"The pitcher-father tries to complete a throw into the mitt of his mate crouched over home plate. A series of sons step up and each in turn tries to intercept the throw. If any of them is successful, he can win 'home' and defeat the pitcher—if he is able first to complete a hazardous journey out of the adult world of the father's allies."

—A Freudian interpretation of the game from "The Ancient Quarrel Between Poetry and Philosophy"; quoted in the *New York Times Magazine,* September 11, 1983

GRABARKEWITZ, BILLY

"I was X-rayed so often I glowed in the dark."

—As Dodgers third baseman, recalling the successions of injuries—broken finger, wrist, and ankle—he suffered in 1968 in the minors; quoted in the *Sporting News,* June 27, 1970

GRACE, MARK

"It's great stuff. We're not into the electronic age yet. To figure out what the score of the Cubs game is you've got to be able to add. You can't add, you don't know what the score of the game is."

> —On Wrigley Field, *New Orleans Times–Picayune,* July 15, 1999

"You have to give him credit. Most guys don't start cheating until later in their careers."

> —On Arizona Diamondbacks rookie pitcher Byung-Hyun Kim, who was caught with a bandage reeking of a foreign substance while pitching. *New Orleans Times–Picayune,* June 15, 1999

GRAHAM, BILLY

"That was my greatest thrill since I was converted to Christ."

> —On meeting Babe Ruth and shaking his hand; quoted in the *Sporting News,* September 23, 1978

GRAHAM, FRANK

"He's learning to say hello when it's time to say good-bye."

> —On the mellowing of formerly unfriendly Yankee outfielder Bob Meusel; widely attributed

GRANT, M. DONALD

"Everybody recognizes that nobody won."

> —The New York Mets chairman on the 1972 players' strike

GRANT, MUDCAT

"Those fans say things about your mother that makes you want to get up in the stands and punch a few of them."

> —*Joy in Mudville* by George Vecsey

GRAVES, ABNER

"The American game of 'Base Ball' was invented by Abner Doubleday of Cooperstown, New York, either the spring prior [1840], or following [1841] the 'Log Cabin & Hard Cider' campaign of General Harrison for President, said Abner Doubleday being then a boy pupil of 'Green's Select School' in Cooperstown, and the same, who as General Doubleday won honor at the Battle of Gettysburg in the Civil war. . . .

"'Baseball' is undoubtedly a pure American game, and its birthplace Cooperstown, New York, and Abner Doubleday entitled to first honor of its invention."

> —Letter to editor of the *Akron [Ohio] Beacon-Journal,* April 3, 1905; published in the newspaper, April 4, 1905

GREEN, DALLAS

"Isn't that something? The egos are such that they can accept the accolades, but they'd beat you over the head for writing what they did wrong. And all you're looking at is facts."

> —As Yankee manager on players hiding in the trainer's room to avoid reporters. *Sporting News*, May 8, 1989

"I don't mind catching your fastball at all. Naturally, I'd want to have a glove on in case you might be having an especially good day."

> —To pitcher Jim Brosnan, SABR Collection

Dallas Green (*Philadelphia Phillies*)

GREEN, JERRY

"Historically, the Red Sox choke at the most critical of times. It has been the trademark of the franchise—through the eras of Williams, Yastrzemski and Boggs. No manager has been immune from this dreadful habit of late-season collapse."

> —The *Detroit Free Press* writer quoted in the August 7, 1988, *Boston Globe* under the title "What They're Saying About Your Red Sox"

GREENBERG, ERIC ROLFE

"Baseball isn't anything like life. . . . In truth, nothing in the game appealed to me as much as its unreality. Baseball is all clean lines and clear decisions. Wouldn't life be far easier if it consisted of a series of definitive calls: safe or out, fair or foul, strike or ball. Oh, for a life like that, where every day produces a clear winner and an equally clear loser, and back to it the next day with the slate wiped clean and the teams starting out equal. Yes, a line score is a very stark statement, isn't it? The numbers tell the essential story. All the rest is mere detail."

> —Spoken by Christy Mathewson, in *The Celebrant* (Lincoln: University of Nebraska Press, 1983)

"How civilized is baseball . . . how subtle, how refined! . . . It is the most intellectual of the physical sports. It is totally artificial, creating its own time, existing within its own space. There is nothing real about it.

—Spoken by Mister Sonnheim, in *The Celebrant*

"To be a pitcher! I thought. A pitcher, standing at the axis of event, or a catcher with the God-view of the play all before him; to be a shortstop, lord of the infield, or a center fielder with unchallenged claim to all the territory one's speed and skill could command; to perform the spontaneous acrobatics of the third baseman or the practiced ballet of the man at second, or to run and throw with the absolute commitment of the outfielder! And to live in a world without grays, where all decisions were final: ball or strike, safe or out, the game won or lost beyond question or appeal."

—Thoughts of narrator Jackie Kapinski, in *The Celebrant*

GREENBERG, HANK

"The only way you can get along with newspapermen is to say something one minute and something different the next."

—Widely attributed

"When you're playing, awards don't seem like much. Then you get older and all of it becomes more precious. It is nice to be remembered."

—*The 1988 Baseball Card Engagement Book*

GREENE, BOB

"The package was long and narrow. I opened it. Inside was something that brought tears to my eyes and a funny feeling to my throat:

"A Louisville Slugger baseball bat—a Bob Greene autographed model.

"For five minutes I sat there looking at it and caressing it and speaking softly to it . . .

"When I started to show my new bat to people, the response I got was interesting. Women seemed not to care too much; generally they said something like, 'Oh, a baseball bat.' They would inspect it a little more closely, and then say, 'What's your name doing on it?'

"But men—men were a different story. First they would see the bat. They'd say something like, 'A real Louisville Slugger. That's great.' Invariably they would lift it up and go into a batting stance—perhaps for the first time in twenty or thirty years. Then they would roll the bat around in their hands—and finally they would see the signature.

"That's when they'd get faint in the head. They would look as if they were about to swoon. Their eyes would start to resemble pinwheels. And in reverential whispers, they would say: 'That is the most wonderful thing I have ever seen. Your own name on a Louisville Slugger. You are so lucky.' . . .

"As I sit here typing this, a colleague—a male—has just walked up next to my computer terminal, lifted my Louisville Slugger to his shoulder, and gone into a batter's crouch. In a moment, if I'm right, he'll start examining the bat—and in another moment he'll see the autograph.

"I can't wait."

—"Louisville Slugger," from *Cheeseburgers: The Best of Bob Greene* (New York: Atheneum Publishers, 1985)

GREENWALD, HANK

Broadcasting gems:

"Dusty Baker will lead off the ninth, and by the sound of the music, William Tell Overture, he'll be followed by the Lone Ranger and Tonto."

"If you have a batting slump or a cold, you'll get plenty of advice. Chicken soup certainly isn't going to cure a batting slump."

"Tom Griffin will be facing the heart of the order . . . well, maybe not the heart, the kidneys."

—Quoted in the *Giants* magazine, by Art Spander

"I don't mind turning 50. It's just that at the beginning of the season, I was 43."

—On his fiftieth birthday, during a dismal season; quoted in the *Sporting News* August 5, 1985

"If Houston and Montreal stay on top, it'll be the first time the National League playoffs take place entirely outside the United States."

—*Sports Illustrated,* August 6, 1979

"It's great to see Yogi Berra back in uniform, and maybe one of these days we will."

—On seeing Yogi Berra in the multicolored Astros uniform

GREGG, ERIC

"An umpire doesn't eject a manager or player, they eject themselves. They know exactly what they can say and who they can say it to. So when somebody is thrown out, he has either completely lost control, or he intended to be run."

—Quoted by Ron Luciano in *Strike Two*

"My colleagues are not usually thought of as the last of the liberal Democrats. By and large, the umpires are conservative, salt-of-the-earth guys, traditional in American values, flag-waving patriots. . . . None of that is intended as criticism. . . . I'm just making the point that I wasn't exactly umpiring the annual softball game at the NAACP picnic."

—The black umpire in Eric Gregg with Marty Appel, *Working the Plate: The Eric Gregg Story* (New York: William Morrow, 1990)

"Tony Pena, who catches on one knee all the time, has a style all his own, but that's not what makes him famous among National League umpires. It seems he has this problem with, uh, passing wind. I mean, he could just destroy you if you unfortunately were calling pitches behind him. Watch umpires behind Tony Pena sometimes—you'll see time-out called a lot, and the umps walking away just

221

GREGG, ERIC (CONTINUED)

to clear the air. You'd walk away, shake your head, and the fans would never know what was happening."

—Eric Gregg and Marty Appel, *Working the Plate* (New York: William Morrow, 1990)

GREGORY, DICK

"Baseball is very big with my people. It figures. It's the only time we can get to shake a bat at a white man without starting a riot."

—*From the Back of the Bus* by Dick Gregory, 1962

GRELLA, GEORGE

"The group . . . sang . . . 'Take Me Out to the Ball Game.' For the first time, what had always sounded like a carefree, exuberant invitation became something of a hymn, even something of a dirge, a sad song not only for Harold Seymour but for all the fans and players of all the games gone by, with perhaps the hint of hope that baseball really is forever, that they really do play the game in Heaven. If there's no baseball in Heaven, then what's a heaven for?"

—Regarding the spreading of the ashes of Seymour, baseball historian, at Doubleday Field, Cooperstown, New York, June 1995; "Harold Seymour (1910–1992)," *The National Pastime: A Review of Baseball History*, 1997

"Because its long season extends into the Fall, baseball not only introduces the fine weather but also holds off the forces of death, darkness, and sterility until its World Series is over. It guarantees, then, both the sowing and the reaping, the planting and the harvest; it begins in seedtime and ends with the golden haze of Autumn. When it ends its season we must prepare for the long nights of winter darkness, the death of the year, the maimed and maiming rite of football, the death-centered game."

—"Baseball and the American Dream," *Massachusetts Review*, summer 1975

GREY, ZANE

"Every boy likes base-ball, and if he doesn't he's not a boy."

—*Baseball: The Early Years* by Harold Seymour (New York: Oxford University Press, 1960)

GRIFFEY, KEN SR.

"On those last three or four, you were swinging like your mother."

—To his son Ken Jr. regarding a 1999 batting slump, *New Orleans Times-Picayune*, June 7, 1999

GRIFFITH, CALVIN

"The fans like to see home runs, and we have assembled a pitching staff for their enjoyment."

—About the original Washington Senators; quoted by Thom Loverro in the *Washington Times* of January 2, 2000, on the best and funniest quotes that had appeared in sports pages over the course of the previous century

Clark Griffith (*Author's Collection*)

GRIFFITH, CLARK

"The baseball fan who comes into our parks should always be sure that he's watching the same game he played as a boy. He shouldn't be baffled by any confounded new rules. There is no need for any."

> —On attempts to tinker with game; quoted in the *Sporting News,* April 6, 1955

"There is no chance night baseball ever will become popular in the major leagues. The game was meant to be played in the Lord's own sunshine."

> —In 1935; quoted in the *Sporting News*, March 29, 1975

"When I found you had only 15,000 blacks here."

> —On the moment the Twins president decided to move the Washington Senators to Minneapolis, at a Lion's Club meeting in Waseca, Minnesota, September 28, 1978; quoted in the *Sporting News,* October 14, 1978. This remark and others like it ("I moved the team to Minneapolis because you have good, hard-working white people here") caused many problems for the team.

GRIMES, BURLEIGH

"I saw a lot of good hitters but I never saw a better one than Paul Waner. I mean I once threw a side-arm spitter right into his belly and he hit it into the upper deck. I may have got Waner out but I never fooled him."

> —As an Athletics coach, *Sporting News*, April 20, 1955

"Paint him and ship him to Elmira."

> —When he was managing in the majors, he shipped a young rookie pitcher to a Southern Association club. This was his response when the Southern club tried the rookie for a few days, then wired Burleigh: "Your pitcher too green."

"The older pitcher acquires confidence in his ballclub; he doesn't try to do it all himself."

> —*The 1989 Baseball Card Engagement Book*

"Why is it there are so many nice guys interested in baseball? Not me. I was a real bastard when I played."

> —Traditional Grimes-ism

GRIMES, BURLEIGH (CONTINUED)

"Why, they even let the hitters take toe holts!"

—On modern pitching; quoted by Frank Graham, ca. 1950

GRIMM, CHARLIE

"Willie Mays can help a team just by riding on the bus with them."

—As Cubs manager, recalled in an article on Mays turning sixty, in the *Tampa Tribune,* May 6, 1991

GROSS, GREG

"He's a legend in his own mind."

—The Phillies outfielder on shortstop Larry Bowa

GROSSINGER, RICHARD

"Baseball is truly an obscurity. Beside it, dreams and ethnoastronomy are explicit and open books."

—Preface to the baseball issue of *IO Magazine,* 1976

"Never, never will I forget Norman O. Brown attacking me for reading a piece on the Mets to a small group in a private home at Wesleyan; the real mythology of the piece was totally ignored."

—Editor, publisher, and educator on the reception baseball talk often receives; preface to the baseball issue of *IO Magazine,* 1976

GROVE, LEFTY

GROVE'S SUCCESS RULES

Lefty Grove had his own rules for success on the diamond. Here they are:

1. Attend to business.
2. Eat regularly, get at least eight hours' sleep—especially from 10 p.m. to 2 a.m., when sleep is soundest—and observe moderate habits.
3. Don't "know it all"—give the other fellow credit for a little knowledge.

"Kid, when you kick a water bucket never kick it with your toes. Always use the side of your foot."

—On watching a rookie pitcher hurting his foot kicking a water bucket after a loss; quoted by Robert Creamer in *Sports Illustrated*

GRZENDA, JOE

"I'd like to stay in baseball long enough to buy a bus—then set fire to it."

—As a Washington Senators reliever after eleven years in the minors; quoted in the *Sporting News,* July 31, 1971

GUERRERO, PEDRO

"Sometimes they write what I say and not what I mean."

—Criticizing sportswriters; SABR Collection

GUILLEN, OZZIE

"A lot of managers try to control everything in the game. I don't try to do that. What I control is my team. I don't care who you are, I control your [rear end]."

> —*Washington Post*, October 21, 2005, from a larger collection of Guillenisms, "White Sox Manager Has the Gift of Gab"

"A lot of people think I'm crazy and stupid and ignorant, but I think before I talk."

> —*Washington Post*, October 21, 2005

"I don't know if I'm a leader, but I have the biggest mouth."

> —"White Sox Manager Has the Gift of Gab"

"I don't use computers. Yeah, I have e-mail. But what's so hard about e-mail? It's just 'delete, delete, delete.'"

> —"White Sox Manager Has the Gift of Gab"

"I don't want superstars. I want good players. To be a good player, you will play to win, not for your numbers or your stats or to be the best in the game."

> —"White Sox Manager Has the Gift of Gab"

"If I said what I wanted to say, I would get suspended for 20 years. They would maybe fine me $100 million."

> —The Chicago White Sox manager after he was ejected in the second inning for arguing balls and strikes in a 4–0 loss at Detroit; quoted in the *Fort Wayne Journal-Gazette*, August 29, 2006

"I'm smarter than a lot of guys who go to Harvard. When you come to this country and you can't speak any English at 16 years old, and you have to survive, you have to have something smart in your body. If you take one of those Harvard guys and drop them in the middle of Caracas, they won't survive. But if you drop me in the middle of Harvard, I'll survive."

> —"White Sox Manager Has the Gift of Gab"

"We've got five, six guys who should be in. Before I got an opportunity to manage the All-Star game, I would criticize the managers like, 'I couldn't believe he didn't take this guy.' Now I'm put in their shoes, and it's not easy."

> —As White Sox manager, on picking the All-Star team, *Fort Wayne Journal-Gazette*, July 4, 2006

"When you get guys out, you're big. When you don't get guys out, you're fat."

> —On his 270-pound pitcher, Bobby Jenks; quoted in the *Vancouver Sun*, December 26, 2006

"You cannot buy a World Series ring on the streets. Ask Alex Rodriguez. He's got millions of dollars and no rings. That's why I say, 'God bless Derek Jeter.' He's got a lot of money and a lot of rings."

> —"White Sox Manager Has the Gift of Gab"

GULLICKSON, BILL

"It was strange. The only English words I saw were Sony and Mitsubishi."

—Former major-league pitcher, on returning from a trip to Japan, where he signed to play baseball in 1988; quoted in *Sports Illustrated*, February 22, 1988

GUMBEL, BRYANT

"The game of baseball is as American as apple pie. Unfortunately, in many corners, so is racism."

—On the controversy over Cincinnati Reds owner Marge Schott, on *Today* TV show, December 1, 1992

"The other sports are just sports. Baseball is a love."

—As a sportscaster, 1981

GURLAND, ROBERT

"My students think that Leo Durocher was the real philosopher [when he said,] 'Nice Guys Finish Last.' Well, I tell them that Durocher finished last, too."

—NYU professor of philosophy; quoted in the *New York Times*, October 27, 1982

GUTTMANN, ALLEN

"Baseball requires not *literacy*, which might have limited its appeal; rather, it demands . . . *numeracy*, i.e., the ability to work with numbers. Half the drama of the game (the invisible half, which European spectators cannot perceive) lies in the calculations of the fan who understands the significance of a 3–2 count and *knows* that a player batting .347 can bring in the tying run from second base. What other game, with the possible exception of cricket, has complexities of quantification as abstruse and arcane as the rules governing the foul ball (which counts as a strike for the first two strikes but not for the third)?"

—*A Whole New Ball Game: An Interpretation of American Sports* (Chapel Hill: University of North Carolina Press, 1988)

"We have speculated that baseball's primitive traits can be traced back to the fertility rites of the ancient vegetation myths. Despite the sacrificial aspects of the myth, the significance of the fertility ceremonies is affirmative. The earth struggles successfully to free itself from winter's

Tony Gwynn (*San Diego Padres*)

deadly grip, the cycle of the seasons begins anew."

> —*Ritual to Record: The Nature of Modern Sports*
> (New York: Columbia University Press, 1978)

GWYNN, TONY

"He gave me that Nuschler look. His middle name's Nuschler. Will Nuschler Clark. You know that stare he gives sometimes at pitchers? He just looked at me."

> —On how intimidating Will Clark could be;
> quoted in the *Fresno Bee,* August 8, 1993

"One plane went right under us. Another plane went right over us. And one was on our tail like a Russian MIG. I thought we were in *Top Gun.*"

> —On a flight to New York; quoted in the
> *Washington Post,* August 20, 1989

"We know we're better than this, but we can't prove it."

> —On a Padres losing streak; quoted in *USA Today,* July 26, 1989

H

HAAK, HOWIE

"The people won't come out if you have too many blacks on a team, not if you have nine. We're going to have to trade for some whites. I'd say you'd have to have about four whites starting. . . . To me personally, nine blacks would be acceptable. I'd go to a game if there were all blacks out on the field. But I've been hearing people talk and I don't think you can in Pittsburgh."

—Chief Pirates scout; quoted in the *Los Angeles Times,* May 5, 1982

HAAS, BILL

"I got here a couple of days early, but I'm anxious for the workouts to begin. I need the meal money."

—On his early arrival at the Mets training camp in 1964, *Sport,* May 1964

HABEIN, HAROLD C.

"TO WHOM IT MAY CONCERN:

"This is to certify that Mr. Lou Gehrig has been under examination at the Mayo Clinic from June 13 to June 19, 1939, inclusive.

"After a careful and complete examination, it was found that he is suffering from amyotrophic lateral sclerosis. This type of illness involves the motor pathways and cells of the central nervous system and in lay terms is known as a form of chronic polio myelitis [infantile paralysis].

"The nature of this trouble makes it such that Mr. Gehrig will be unable to continue his active participation as a baseball player inasmuch as it is advisable that he conserve his muscular energy. He could, however, continue in some executive capacity."

—Letter released by Habein, a physician at the Mayo Clinic, Rochester, Minnesota, June 19, 1939

HACK, STAN

"That Mays is fantastic. Watch him. Everything he does has the mark of the perfect ball player. Even when he's just catching balls thrown in from the field. He's the best center fielder I ever saw, barring none. He's a great retriever. The minute his glove touches the ball, it's out of his hands and on the way either to the infield or the plate. I've never seen a man get the ball back into play so fast."

—As manager of the Cubs, *Sporting News,* April 13, 1955

HADDIX, HARVEY

"All I know is that we lost the game. What's so historic about that? Didn't anyone ever lose a thirteen-inning shutout before?"

—On losing the game in which he had pitched twelve perfect innings—retiring thirty-six in row—in the thirteenth inning. As Phil Pepe pointed out in *No-Hitter:* "One of the reporters told Haddix what was so historic about his game. Never in the history of baseball had a pitcher worked more than ten perfect innings. One had to go all the way back to 1884 to find Edward Kimber of Brooklyn, who pitched ten perfect innings against Toledo. Neither team had scored when darkness ended the game after ten innings."

HALBERSTAM, DAVID

"By and large it is the sport that a foreigner is least likely to take to. You have to grow up playing it, you have to accept the lore of the bubble gum card, and believe that if the answer to the Mays-Snider-Mantle question is found, then the universe will be a simpler and more ordered place."

—Quoted in Raymond Mungo's *Confessions from Left Field*

"I think walking up to Fenway is thrilling. The approach to it. The smells. You go to Fenway and you think, 'Something wonderful going to happen today.'"

—Quoted by Dan Shaughnessy in the *Boston Globe,* December 25, 1998

"Things as critical as this, the selection of a favored baseball team, are not, as some suspect, a matter of choice; one does not choose a team as one does not select his own genes. They are confirmed upon you, more than we know an act of heredity."

—"The Fan Divided," *Boston Globe Special Supplement,* "Literati on the Red Sox," October 6, 1986

HALL, DONALD

"As we fly over Southern California we see below the ten thousand patterns of base-paths-and-grass. High over Maine forests, over deserts of Arizona, even over Rocky wastes, we spy from our easy chair, elevated to the height of five miles, the small landscape and geometry of baseball. Even over Italy and Japan, even over China, we see beneath us the footprints of the game. World enough we have, from five miles up, as the airplane contributes eternity's viewpoint to the human imagination. From our vertical perch at least we confirm the horizontal game."

—"Shapes of the Game Forever," in Peter H. Gordon with Sydney Waller and Paul Weinman, eds., *Diamonds are Forever; Artists and Writers on Baseball* (San Francisco: Chronicle Books, 1987)

HALL, DONALD (CONTINUED)

"Baseball is continuous, like nothing else among American things, an endless game of repeated summers, joining the long generations of all the fathers and all the sons."

—*Fathers Playing Catch with Sons* (New York: Dell, 1986)

"Baseball is fathers and sons. Football is brothers beating each other up in the backyard."

—*Fathers Playing Catch with Sons*

"For most baseball fans, maybe oldest is always best. We love baseball because it seizes and retains the past, like the snowy village inside a glass paperweight."

—"Fenway Park: Age Cannot Wither Her," *Ford Times*, April 1977; reprinted in Donald Hall, *Fathers Playing Catch with Sons*

"In the country of baseball, time is the air we breathe, and the wind swirls us backward and forward, until we seem so reckoned in time and seasons that all time and all seasons become the same."

—*Dock Ellis in the Country of Baseball*

"The old first baseman, making the final out of the inning, in the last year he will play, underhands the ball casually toward the mound, as he has done ten thousand times. The ball bounces over the lip of the grass, climbs the crushed red brick of the mound for a foot or two, and then rolls back until it catches in the green verge. The ball has done this ten thousand times."

— "The Country of Baseball," in *Dock Ellis in the Country of Baseball,* by Donald Hall and Dock Ellis (New York: Coward, McCann & Geoghegan, 1976); reprinted in *Fathers Playing Catch with Sons.*

"We pretend to forgive failure; really we celebrate it. Bonehead Merkle lives forever and Bill Mazeroski's home run fades."

—*The Baseball Card Engagement Book,* 1990

HAMILL, PETE

"Don't talk to me today about Biafra or Nixon or Vietnam or John Lindsay. The Mets are leading the league. Get out of the way and sing us no more sad songs. I'm going drinking. It's September and the Mets are leading the league."

—On the Mets first taking first place, in the *New York Post;* quoted in *The Incredible Mets* by Maury Allen

"Don't tell me about the world. Not today. It's springtime and they're knocking baseball around fields where the grass is damp and green in the morning and the kids are trying to hit the curve ball."

—Hall of Fame Collection

"When I was a kid, there was nothing else. . . . We had Robinson, Reese and Furillo. We had Stanky and Hodges and Billy Cox. They came to us in the Spring, as certain as rain and birds. They came on the radio, with Red Barber telling their tale, and there was nothing else we wanted."

—As a *New York Daily News* writer; quoted in the 50th Anniversary Hall of Fame *Yearbook,* 1989

HAMILTON, MILO

"Now here is Henry Aaron. This crowd is up all around. The pitch to him . . . bounced it up there, ball one. [Loud round of boos.] Henry Aaron in the second inning walked and scored. He's sitting on 714. Here's the pitch by Downing . . . Swinging . . . There's a drive into left-center field. That ball is gonna beee . . . OUTA HERE! IT'S GONE! IT'S 715! There's a new home run champion of all time! And it's Henry Aaron! The fireworks are going! Henry Aaron is coming around third! His teammates are at home plate. Listen to this crowd."

—Broadcasting on April 8, 1974

HAMMAN, ED

"Once folks got the idea their town could get a major league club, their own local brand of ball wasn't good enough for them anymore. People want the best. Only there ain't enough of the best to go around."

—The Indianapolis Clowns general manager, 1973, on the trend that began when the Braves left Boston for Milwaukee; quoted in *Some Are Called Clowns* by Bill Heward

HAMPTON, MIKE

"I'd say 75 percent would rather see a 10–8 game. The other 25 percent, which are prob-ably the pitchers' parents, would rather see a 1–0 or 2–1 game."

—As a New York Met, on baseball fans, *Chicago Sun Times,* July 13, 2000

HANKS, TOM

"I turned 50 10 days ago. This is the dream you have all the way back."

—Summer 2006 birthday trip to seven ballparks for Hanks staged by director Ron Howard and comedian Dennis Miller. "Tom is so influential that he's arranged a St. Louis Browns game," Miller joked, referring to the defunct team, *Houston Chronicle,* July 21, 2006.

HANLON, NED

"Ballplayers are not school children, nor are umpires schoolmasters. It is impossible to prevent expressions of impatience or actions indicating dissent with the umpire's decision when a player, in the heat of the game thinks he has been unjustly treated. . . . Patrons like to see a little scrappiness in the game, and would be very dissatisfied, I believe, to see the players slinking away like whipped school-boys to their benches, afraid to turn their heads for fear of a heavy fine from some swelled umpire."

—The Orioles manager; quoted the May 25, 1895, *New York Clipper*

HANO, ARNOLD

"I like going to games with my wife. It is an interesting experience. I also like not going with my wife."

—*A Day in the Bleachers* (New York: Thomas Y. Crowell, 1955)

HANO, ARNOLD (CONTINUED)

"This game of baseball has again become a tool of the club owner. Not a gambling tool, as it once was, but a tax-break tool. Stories about baseball might as easily slip onto the financial pages as the sports pages. And they do. The biggest story of the baseball year is the amount of money television people will give baseball for the privilege of presenting a distorted image of the sport to millions of lethargic, uncaring spectators. You measure your sports today by their respective Nielsen ratings. Even the playing fields reflect this new standard. A man flicks his fingers over a bank of computerized buttons, and neon lights flash on a scoreboard showing the figure of a man playing a bugle. In response, 20,000 people mechanically cry: 'Charge!' Fans cheer when they are ordered to."

—"Memo to the New Commissioner," *Sport*, March 1966

"Mays simply slowed down to avoid running into the wall, put his hands up in cuplike fashion over his left shoulder, and caught the ball much like a football player catching leading passes in the end zone.

"He had turned so quickly, and run so fast and truly that he made this impossible catch look—to us in the bleachers—quite ordinary. To those reporters in the press box, nearly six hundred feet from the bleacher wall, it must have appeared far more astonishing, watching Mays run and run until he had become the size of a pigmy and then he had run some more, while the ball diminished to a mote of white dust and finally disappeared in the dark blob that was Mays' mitt."

—Describing the catch made by Willie Mays of a drive hit by Vic Wertz during the 1954

World Series in the Polo Grounds, New York City. *A Day in the Bleachers* (New York: Thomas Y. Crowell, 1955)

HANSON, ERIK

"I was throwing up volleyballs today and they were spiking them for kills."

—The Mariners pitcher on back-to-back White Sox home runs; quoted in the *St. Petersburg Times*, June 14, 1990

HARRELSON, KEN

"Baseball is the only sport I know that when you're on offense, the other team controls the ball."

—*Sports Illustrated*, September 6, 1976

"When you're doing it, when you're hitting home runs, you can get away with anything. But when you're not delivering, it won't work. They don't buy your act."

—As a former Red Sox outfielder

HARRIDGE, WILL

"Arch called me one day and asked me to have dinner with him. I didn't know he had anything in mind other than a sociable dinner until he sprang the All-Star Game idea on me, and I was flabbergasted at first. The idea was sound enough since that was the year of the World's Fair in Chicago and Arch wanted to make an All-Star game one of the highlights. His sales pitch was that it would be a wonderful thing for baseball.

"I told Arch I would submit the proposition

to the owners. The American League owners finally agreed after considerable discussion that it would join strictly as an attraction for the 1933 Fair. At first, the National League opposed it, but finally agreed to play the game for only one year. The game turned out to be so wonderful and so well accepted by the fans that the owners quickly agreed to continue the game and it became a solid fixture."

—On being approached by sportswriter Arch Ward with the idea of an all-star game; quoted in *Professional Baseball: The First 100 Years.* There was an interesting p.s. to the story when Harridge added, "There was one time in the late '30s when some people in the NL felt the game was costly to the prestige of their league because the AL had won four of the first five games. The AL owners undoubtedly would have felt the same way had they been on the losing end."

"To say 'Babe Ruth' is to say 'Baseball.'"

—The American League president on Babe Ruth Day, Yankee Stadium, 1947

HARRIS, ART

"Where else can you play before 50,000 empty seats?"

—Venice, California, high school baseball coach on the prospect of playing in Dodger Stadium, *Los Angeles Times*, May 31, 1972

HARRIS, BUCKY

"Believe what you like; no manager ever resigns."

—As Tigers manager

HARRIS, LENNY

"Hey, I'm not all-time for nothing."

—Florida Marlins infielder and the all-time leader in pinch-hits, after a three-run double off Eric Gagne, August 18, 2004; from the *Orange County Register*

HARRIS, MARK

"Baseball was urgent. Its urgency addicted me. We needed to win every game. The urgency of baseball made me a fan. Every game was crucial. One might be casual about many other things in life, such as love, learning, literature, morals, ethics, politics, religion, and college entrance examinations, but baseball mattered."

—"The Bonding," in Ron Fimrite, ed., *Birth of a Fan*

"Butterflies flutter in my stomach. It was always true of me that I approached a baseball field, whether as a player or as spectator, with a feeling of rising excitement, eager to be there early, fearful of something happening without me."

—"The Bonding," in Ron Fimrite, ed., *Birth of a Fan*

"He was not a bad fellow, no worse than most and probably better than some, and not a bad ballplayer neither when they give him a chance, when they laid off him long enough. From here on in I rag nobody."

—Henry Wiggen on the death of Bruce Pearson, *Bang the Drum Slowly*

HARRISON, BARBARA GRIZZUTI

"I've always thought a baseball field—a small baseball field, Ebbets Field, Wrigley Field—resembled a cloister: a safe, enclosed space, a protected space of leisured ritual, in the world but not part of it. A place of exaltation and resolution."

—From "Red Barber," 1991; quoted in Elinor Nauen, ed., *Diamonds Are a Girl's Best Friend: Women Writers on Baseball*

"When Cookie Lavagetto spoiled Bill Bevens' bid for a no-hitter, Red Barber, after calmly reporting the latter-day miracle, said: 'Well I'll be a suck-egg mule.' It's funny: a red-clay Southerner whose vocal rhythms were derived from *The Book of Common Prayer* and who liked to talk about magnolias spoke to hearts of the stoop-ball, stickball-playing kids of immigrants who barely spoke English."

—Quoted in Elinor Nauen, ed., *Diamonds Are a Girl's Best Friend: Women Writers on Baseball*

HARSHMAN, JACK

"If you don't succeed at first, try pitching."

—Who came up as a first baseman and went to the mound; quoted in *Baseball Laughs* by Herman L. Masin.

HARTNETT, GABBY

"We gotta look at that all season!"

—The National League All-Star Game catcher of the Cubs, yelling to players in the American

League dugout after Carl Hubbell struck out five future Fall of Farmers in succession at the Polo Grounds on July 10, 1934; quoted in Hubbell's *Sporting News* obituary, December 5, 1988

HARTSFIELD, ROY

"Anyone who tells himself he can win a pennant with an expansion team is just spitting into a gale."

—As Blue Jays manager, *Sporting News*, May 13, 1978

HARVEY, DOUG

"That's what it means to be an umpire. You have to be honest even when it hurts."

—After a member of his umpiring crew admitted an error

HARWELL, ERNIE

"Baseball is a ballet without music. Drama without words. A carnival without kewpie dolls."

—From his famous and often-quoted 1955 Opening Day *Sporting News* essay "The Game for All America"

"Baseball is continuity. Pitch to pitch. Inning to inning. Game to game. Series to series. Season to season."

—Quoted in John Thorn, *The Game for All America* (St. Louis: Sporting News Publishing, 1988)

"Baseball? It's just a game—as simple as a ball and a bat. Yet, as complex as the American spirit it symbolizes. It's a sport, business—and sometimes even religion."

> —*The Game for All America*. This appears to be the most often repeated section of the essay.

"God has given him great health and a great work ethic and he has been lucky enough to avoid the kinds of problems that could have very easily ended the streak. Will this record ever be broken again? Well, I know I sure won't be around to see it if it ever is."

> —On Cal Ripken's streak; quoted in the *Washington Post*, September 6, 1995

"In baseball, democracy shines its clearest. Here the only race that matters is the race to the bag. The creed is the rule book. Color is something to distinguish one team's uniforms from another."

> —"The Game for All America"

"Radio was the most important piece of furniture in the house. That was when families stayed together and they felt a loyalty not just to teams but to players.

"Now we're listening to it in cars, on headsets. Radio has a niche because of its portability to the beach, the workplace, the kitchen. Radio is with us all the time. It's background that TV can't match."

> —Retiring in 2002, after fifty-six years as a broadcaster; quoted in the *St. Petersburg Times*, May 17, 2002

HAWKINS, ANDY

"That's baseball."

> —After losing a 1990 no-hitter as a Yankee rookie pitcher after his left fielder dropped a routine fly ball. After the error he walked five and lost 4–0 but was still credited with a no-hitter. In his next start, Hawkins tossed eleven shutout innings and lost again.

HEALY, FRAN

"Crowd? This isn't a crowd. It's a focus group."

> —As New York Mets broadcaster on the sparse attendance at a game in Montreal; quoted in the *San Francisco Chronicle*, December 25, 2002

HEBNER, RICHIE

"I played hockey at Norwood High School in Boston. We'd have 15,000 for some games in the Boston Arena. I was hit on the mouth three times. I was hit by a puck. That cost me a tooth and a half. The half-tooth had the nerve exposed. That's the worst pain I ever felt. But I had them broken twice more. I was hit in a head-on collision and again with a stick in the same place. Then I was hit with a puck on the chin. Twenty stitches. You're better off in baseball."

> —On picking baseball over hockey; quoted as a Pirate by James K. McGee of the *San Francisco Examiner* in the August 1969 *Baseball Digest*

Richie Hebner (*Author's Collection*)

"I stand at the plate in Philadelphia and I honestly don't know whether I'm in Pittsburgh, Cincinnati, St. Louis or Philly."

—Commenting on the cookie-cutter stadiums in the National League in the 1970s

HECHT, HENRY

"What we will remember about Hunter's Yankee years is the way he handled adversity—with humor, with grace, with stoicism. A sort of Hemingway hero, exhibiting grace under pressure and not crying out bitterly because the fates were rolling twos and twelves, not sevens and elevens."

—On Catfish Hunter in the *New York Post*, March 16, 1979

HEGAN, MIKE

"Explaining to your wife why she needs a penicillin shot for your kidney infection."

—Answering the question "What's the most difficult thing about playing major-league baseball?"; quoted in *Ball Four* by Jim Bouton

"The right fielder has to be very careful when a fight breaks out and the benches empty. He's always got his back to the enemy bullpen."

—As a Seattle rightfielder quoted by Vic Ziegel in the *New York Post* and requoted in *Baseball Digest*, August 1969

HELD, WOODIE

"Don't forget to swing hard in case you hit the ball."

—This choice bit of advice is quoted in Joseph McBride's *High and Inside* as the line which will cause people to recall Held long after his .240 lifetime batting average is forgotten.

HEMINGWAY, ERNEST

"A damned good poet and a fair critic; but he can kiss my ass as a man and he never hit a ball out of the infield in his life."

—On T. S. Eliot from a 1950 letter; quoted in Edwin McDowell, "The Literati's Appreciation for Baseball," *New York Times*, April 8, 1981

"Do you believe the great DiMaggio would stay with a fish as long as I will stay with this one? he thought. I am sure he would and more since he is young and strong. Also his father was a fisherman."

—*The Old Man and the Sea*

"Have faith in the Yankees my son."

—*The Old Man and the Sea*

"'I would like to take the great DiMaggio fishing,' the old man said. 'They say his father was a fisherman. Maybe he was as poor as we are and would understand.'"

—*The Old Man and the Sea*

"They can't yank a novelist like they can a pitcher. A novelist has to go the full nine, even if it kills him."

—Quoted in James Charlton's *Writer's Quotation Book*

"Sliding actually is a threat to cut the man at the bag so he will be out of the game. It also raises dust and if you can really come in, you can avoid the tag as far as possible."

—To Lillian Ross, 1948, on why she was right to run rather than slide in softball; quoted by Edwin McDowell in "The Pastime and the Literati," *New York Times*, April 8, 1981

HEMOND, ROLAND

"Veeck knows everything there is to know about running a baseball team. He can count a big stack of tickets just by riffling through them with his thumb. He can tell you what kind of grass you ought to have in the out-field. He can tell you what pitch a pitcher is having trouble with. I've never worked as hard in my life trying to keep up with him, and I've never enjoyed myself more."

—As White Sox GM, on White Sox owner Bill Veeck; quoted in *People*, April 19, 1976

HENDERSON, DAVE

"I don't see any Stanford guys running around here. Look at [Terry] Steinbach. He thinks hockey is a sport."

—On the intelligence of the Oakland team; quoted in the *Philadelphia Inquirer*, April 11, 1989

"I wasn't in a slump. I just wasn't getting any hits."

—After ending an 0-for-20 drought in April 1990; quoted in *USA Today*, April 23, 1990

"'We can't do anything to bring people back and we can't dig people out of the freeway,' he said. 'What we can do is alter people's thought patterns for three hours—get their thoughts on something other than gloom and doom and show signs of resuming life.'"

—As an Oakland A on playing after the 1989 Series earthquake; quoted by Steve Berkowitz in the *Washington Post*, October 20, 1989

HENDERSON, RICKEY

"I don't want to be one of those great players who never made the Series."

—On his 1989 trade from the New York Yankees to Oakland; widely cited at the time

HENDERSON, RICKEY (CONTINUED)

"It gave me no chance. He just blew it by me. But it's an honor. I'll have another paragraph in all the baseball books. I'm already in the books three or four times."

> —On the fastball that made him Nolan Ryan's 5,000th strikeout victim, *Sporting News,* September 4, 1989

HENDRICKS, ELROD

"You know Earl. He's not happy unless he's not happy."

> —On Earl Weaver; quoted in *The Umpire Strikes Back* by Ron Luciano

HENRICH, TOMMY

"Bobby Doerr is one of the very few who played the game hard and retired with no enemies."

> —Quoted in the National Baseball Hall of Fame *Yearbook,* 1989

"Catching a fly ball is pleasure, but knowing what to do with it after you catch it is a business."

> —From Mel Allen's *You Can't Beat the Hours*

"He does everything better than anyone else."

> —On Joe DiMaggio in *Sportsweek,* July 31, 1968

"Landis cleaned it up, and Babe Ruth glorified it."

> —On the contributions of Judge Landis and Babe Ruth to baseball

Tommy Henrich (*New York Yankees*)

"No matter how long a man remains in baseball he always hankers and looks forward to opening days, and believe you me, it takes a young player a long, long time to get over those opening day butterflies and discover finally that he really in an old pro."

> —Said in the spring of 1959 and quoted in Jim Brosnan's *The Long Season*

HERMAN, BABE

"Frankly, I'd prefer someplace else."

> —His oft-reported reply to Dodger owner Charles Ebbets's offer to send him on a trip around the world

Babe Herman (*left*) with Hack Wilson (*National Baseball Library*)

"I don't do it for the money. The longer I stay away from training camp, the less chance I have of being hit by a fly ball."

> —On reporting late, in *The Baseball Card Engagement Book*, 1989

"Please stop writing those awful stories 'bout me being crazy."

> —Line supposedly uttered to reporters before pulling a lit cigar from his pocket and walking away. Herman denied this, but the line and reports of the incident persisted for years.

"The next time he comes in, take him out in the back yard and knock a few flies his way. If he catches any, you'll know it isn't me."

> —On being informed by a downtown Brooklyn bank one day that an impostor was signing his name to worthless checks and cashing them several times a week

HERMAN, BILLY

"A lot of good infielders who can play first, shortstop and third can't play second, and that's because it's an awkward position. Half your throws are behind you. You have to throw sideways and backhanded instead of overhand. You have to throw with runners coming at you from behind. You have to be a little unorthodox."

> —As a Hall of Fame second baseman; quoted in the *Los Angeles Times,* June 20, 1978

"Freddie Fitzsimmons has my name. He once hit me in the on-deck circle."

> —As Red Sox manager on who was the game's best brushback pitcher

HERN, GERALD V.

"Spahn and Sain and two days of rain."

> —From a poem written by *Boston Post* sports editor that appeared in the newspaper September 14, 1948, as Warren Spahn and Johnny Sain led the Braves to the NL pennant. It was entitled "Braves Boast Two-Man Staff; Pitch Spahn and Sain, Then Pray for Rain—but Every Day Is a Dark Day for Tribe." Before his death, Warren Spahn remarked: "Guys who were kids forty years ago learned it as a nursery rhyme. Now they meet me and say, 'Oh, you're *that* Spahn.'" *Wall Street Journal,* August 2, 1985

HERNANDEZ, KEITH

"Good hitting can offset good pitching (an opposite-field double off a perfect pitch on the outside corner at the knees), and bad hitting can offset bad pitching (a comatose batter takes a hanging curve over the heart of the plate on a 3–1 count). For me, this battle of wits and balance of talent between the pitcher and the hitter is baseball. Everything else is secondary."

> —Keith Hernandez and Mike Bryan, *Pure Baseball: Pitch by Pitch for the Advanced Fan* (New York: HarperCollins, 1994)

"Left-handed batters are almost always low-ball hitters. Maybe it has something to do with the left brain/right brain business, I don't know, but it's a fact that many more right-handed batters than left-handed batters can handle the high pitch."

> —*Pure Baseball: Pitch by Pitch for the Advanced Fan*

"If everyone threw like that, I don't think this game would make it. It would be too damned boring."

> —On Astro pitcher Mike Scott, who'd tormented the Mets in 1986 with his split-finger curve

HERNANDEZ, WILLIE

"I have a sore throat, a headache, and a fever, but my arm feels good. I'll try to go out there and do my job."

> —*Inside Pitch* by Roger Craig

HERVEY, LADY MARY LEPELL

"All this last summer they [family of Frederick, Prince of Wales] played abroad; and now, in the winter, in a large room, they divert themselves at base-ball, a play all who are, or have been, schoolboys, are well acquainted with. The ladies, as well as the gentlemen, join in this amusement, and the latter return the compliment, in the evening, by playing for an hour at the old and innocent game of pushpin."

> —Letter, dated November 14, 1748, in *Letters,* London, 1821; quoted in Robert W. Henderson, *Ball, Bat and Bishop* (New York: Rockport Press, 1947)

HERZOG, WHITEY

"Baseball has been good to me since I quit trying to play it."

> —Part of his regularly stated confessions that he was an "awful ballplayer"

"Be on time. Bust your butt. Play smart. And have some laughs while you're at it."

> —His four baseball rules; widely quoted at the time of his resignation as Cardinals manager in July 1990

"Down there, we've got more taverns than grocery stores. I walked in, threw down a bill, and said, 'Give everybody a drink.' Nice gesture, I thought, but down the bar somebody yelled, 'Hey, big shot, your brother is still a better ballplayer than you are.'"

> —On returning to New Athens, Illinois, after reaching the bigs, from "The Whitey Herzog

Whitey Herzog (*Kansas City Royals*)

keys to the bus and say, 'Drive the boys into town tonight. I've got a social engagement.'"

> —On his greatest baseball disappointment, which took place in the early fifties when he played Class D ball in Oklahoma; quoted in the *Sporting News,* March 13, 1989

"One time in spring training, we had the hit-and-run on, and Carl Erskine threw me a curve and I struck out into a double play. I came back to the bench and Casey said, 'Next time, tra-la-la.' I didn't know what tra-la-la meant, but next time up, I hit a line drive, right into a double play. When I sat down, Casey came over and said, 'Like I told you, tra-la-la.'"

> —On playing for Casey Stengel, from "The Whitey Herzog Quote Machine," in the *St. Louis Post-Dispatch* at the time of his 1990 resignation

Quote Machine," in the *St. Louis Post-Dispatch* at the time of his 1990 resignation

"For being book smart, I thought he had a lot of street smarts, which is tough to find sometimes."

> —On A. Bartlett Giamatti at the time of his death; quoted in the *Washington Post,* September 3, 1989

"I had just had six doubles in a doubleheader, and I was hitting .446. I had been in Class D for two years, and I wanted to go up [to Class C]: Vern Hoscheit was the manager, and he told me to come see him in his room after I got cleaned up. I figured I was going up. I had paid my dues. But all he did was flip me the

"You need two things to be a good one—a sense of humor and a bullpen."

> —"The Whitey Herzog Quote Machine"

"If you don't have outstanding relief pitching, you might as well piss on the fire and call in the dogs."

> —*White Rat*

"I'm not buddy-buddy with the players. If they need a buddy, let them buy a dog."

> —*White Rat*

"The only thing bad about winning the pennant is that you have to manage the All-Star Game the next year. I'd rather go fishing for three days."

—*The Baseball Card Engagement Book,* 1989

"The rules are changed now. There's not any way to build a team today. It's just how much money you want to spend. You could be the world champions, and somebody else makes a key acquisition or two and you're through."

—As Royals manager

"Why would I want to do that? Look at Sparky—he's 55, and he already looks 80."

—When asked if he shared Sparky Anderson's desire to manage until he was 80, *Sports Illustrated,* May 22, 1989

"Yeah, and we're missing a little geography and arithmetic around here, too."

—On poor "chemistry" in St. Louis in 1980; from "The Whitey Herzog Quote Machine" in the *St. Louis Post-Dispatch*

"You sweat out the free-agent thing in November. Then you make the trades in December. Then you struggle to sign the guys left in January. And in February I get down to sewing all the new numbers on the uniforms."

—*The Baseball Card Engagement Book,* 1988

"Baseball, like sex and religion, is a complicated game to play, but not hard to understand."

—Quoted in Steve Fiffer, *How to Watch Baseball,* (New York: Facts on File Publications, 1987)

"One of the reasons that so many writers love the Red Sox is that a team without a World Series triumph since 1918 validates the writer's constant sense of insecurity, and thus proves he is sane.

"Writers too, like ballplayers, know what it's like to have their miscues lovingly detailed in the morning papers by people who couldn't carry their hats. Writers know how hard it is to get it exactly right, even 30 percent of the time—which is what a premier batter accomplishes when he hits .300. Writers, if they are realistic, know how unlikely it is that they will realize their ambitions 60 per cent of the time, which is what a team of 24 players has to do to win 97 out of 162 regular-season games and have a good shot at a division title. . . . It is impossible to perform either trade even close to complete perfection."

—*The Progress of the Seasons*

"The Red Sox are a religion. Every year we re-enact the agony and the temptation in the Garden. Baseball child's play? Hell, up here in Boston it's a passion play."

—SABR Collection

"The seductiveness of baseball is that almost everyone with an abiding interest in it knows exactly how it should be played. And secretly believes that he could do it, if only God had seen fit to make him just a little bit less clumsy."

—*The Progress of the Seasons*

HIGGINS, MIKE

"The first thing a manager learns is to stay on the bench."

—As Red Sox manager

HILL, ALBERT G.

"There's a lot of very good physics in baseball. But the use of the word momentum is not one of them. We physicists invent a good word of our own and the sportscasters wreak havoc with it. We mean mass times velocity. They mean hot streak. It's tragic and it gets on my nerves."

—As a retired professor of physics at Massachusetts Institute of Technology; quoted by James P. Sterba in "Science Times," *New York Times*, April 6, 1982

HILL, ART

"The dreams of fame, riches and Paulette Goddard all came to naught. But DiMaggio's *56* goes on forever—or at least until some distant time when I won't give a damn."

—*"Don't Let Baseball Die," I Came to Watch* (Au Train, Mich.: Avery Color Studios, 1978)

"The words, 'Dahlgren, first base,' stunned the crowd into a moment of unplanned silence, which was followed by the unprecedented sound of several thousand people sighing in unison. Then Gehrig trudged painfully up to the plate, carrying the lineup card without his name on it. It was one of the most moving moments in sports history, high drama of the sort you cannot make up."

—From his classic, *I Don't Care If I Never Come Back*

"I wish I could explain *my* lifelong obsession with baseball. But it is like trying to explain sex to a precocious six-year-old. Not that I have ever done this, but I assume the child would say something like: 'Okay, I understand the procedure. But why?' There is no answer for that. You have to be there.

"With baseball, too, you have to be there. But once you have been there, and bought it, you are likely to remain hooked for the rest of your life."

—*"Don't Let Baseball Die," I Came to Watch*

HILL, CALVIN

"Baseball is sitting on the front porch, drinking lemonade, listening to your father talk to his father or his brothers about the game and things that happened that day. Part of the appeal of baseball now is that it's a reminder of the ways things used to be before we became so transient, so mobile, so much in a hurry. Baseball is stopping by the fence to visit; football is honking the horn.

"Before batting practice, baseball players are kidding around, maybe talking to the

Hill, Calvin (continued)

fans, while in a football locker room it's like getting ready to jump out of an airplane, or going into battle. Everybody's in his own world, trying to blot out what's about to happen. Baseball players are intense at getting themselves ready, but by comparison with football players they're a bunch of guys getting ready to go fishing or hunting."

> —A former professional football player, and vice president for personnel of the Baltimore Orioles. "The Joys of Summer," in Karen Mullarkey, ed. dir., *Baseball in America* (San Francisco; Collins Publishers, 1991).

Hill, David

"If anybody talks about any dead guys during a broadcast, I'll sack 'em. I'm sick of dead guys! Whenever I turn on baseball, all I hear about is dead guys. If I hear a name, I'm gonna ask, 'Is he dead?' And if he is, you're fired."

> —Fox Sports president; quoted in the *New York Times Magazine*, May 5, 1996, in a message to executives

Hitchcock, Billy

"So you want to know what's been my most uncomfortable experience in a baseball game. Well, all I can say to that, mister, is that striking out with the bases loaded can put any man in a melancholy mood."

> —*Baseball Magazine,* June 1948

Hoagland, E.

"Baseball has stood for loyalty to the verities, memories of innocence, patience with ritual; surely no one who cared about baseball could be an opportunist at heart."

> —"A Fan's Notes," 1977

Hoagland, Jim

"Understand baseball at its best (a series of individual confrontations disguised as a team sport) and you understand much about the uniqueness of the American spirit."

> —"Baseball and Bordeaux," *Washington Post,* October 3, 1989

Hoak, Don

"I have a great many friends in baseball, but the day I hung up my uniform, I never saw so many doors close so quickly. My phone stopped ringing and I didn't hear from anybody."

> —Comment made after he had left baseball—and just before he got a job as a Pirate announcer. Hoak's name is invoked in a memorable moment in the film *City Slickers.* On a fantasy cattle drive in the 1991 movie, Billy Crystal and his baby-boomer pals are listening to a woman complain about baseball. "My ex-boyfriend was a sports nut," the woman says with some disgust. "I mean, who cares who played third base for the Pittsburgh Pirates in 1960?" Before she can utter another word, Crystal and his two pals blurt out the name in perfect harmony.

HOBSON, BUTCH

"Smell that. That's the best smell in the world, ain't it? When I'm talking to kids, I pass that around, and I say, 'Smell that.' My son and I sit around, watching a game on TV, and take turns smelling it. I want to pass that on. That's the love of the game. I grew up loving baseball. I wanted to go to the ballpark every single day. I'm glad to be here today. Some of the things I did in my life as a player that I try to warn young people about, today—well, I'm lucky to be alive. When I'm teaching baseball to kids, I'm also going to make mention of life and where I was."

> —During a *Boston Globe* interview during which he smells a baseball and passes it to the interviewer, July 9, 2000

HODAPP, JOHNNY

"I remember Tony Lazzeri looking at me after I slid into second base. 'I hope to God you rot here,' he said. 'I'm tired of seeing you down here.'"

> —On his ability to connect for doubles; quoted in 1970

HODGES, GIL

"There are only two kinds of managers. Winning managers and ex-managers."

> —On becoming Mets manager; quoted by Maury Allen in *The Incredible Mets*

HODGES, RUSS

"Branca pitches and Bobby Thomson takes a strike called on the inside corner.

"Bobby's hitting at .292. He's had a single

Gil Hodges (*New York Mets*)

and a double and he drove in the Giants' first run with a long drive to center.

"Brooklyn leads, 4–2. Hartung down the line at third, not taking any chances. Lockman without too big a lead at second, but he'll be running like the wind if Thomson hits one.

"Branca throws. There's a long fly. It's gonna be . . . I believe. . . .

"The Giants win the pennant! The Giants win the pennant! The Giants win the pennant!

"Bobby Thomson hit into the lower deck of the left field stands.

"The Giants win the pennant! And they're going crazy, they're going crazy. Oooh, boy! I don't believe it, I don't believe it, I will not believe it!"

> —His description of Bobby Thomson's historic homer, one of the most thrilling moments of sports broadcasting ever recorded, October 3, 1951; on WMCA tape provided by Dodgers fan Lawrence Goldberg

HODGES, RUSS (CONTINUED)

"If Ben Franklin played shortstop here and made an error, they'd probably boo him for a week, too."

—On the irascibility of the Philadelphia Phillies fans

HOFFMAN, ABBIE

"He showed them it was a game, so they locked him up."

—On Jimmy Piersall, SABR Collection

HOLMES, TOMMY

"A strange and sometimes deceptive racket—baseball."

—In the *Brooklyn Eagle*; quoted in *Baseball Digest*, October 1943. He was commenting on the fact that the fastest man on the '43 Cardinals was the thirty-five-year old Debs Garms.

"Some twenty years ago, I stopped talking about the Babe for the simple reason that I realized that those who had never seen him didn't believe me."

—Hall of Fame Collection

HOME RUN CALLS

"A Ballantine Blast."

—Product call employed by Mel Allen

"Bye-Bye Baby."

—Russ Hodges

"A Case of Wheaties."

—Product call

"A Case of Lucky Strikes."

—Product call before cigarette advertising was banned from the airways

"It might be. It could be. It is! A home run!"

—Harry Caray

"Forget it."

—Vin Scully

"Goodbye, baseball!"

—Dick Risenhoover

"Goodbye, Dolly Grey."

—Leo Durocher

"Hey, Hey."

—Jack Brickhouse

"It's going, going, gone."

—in *The Baseball Catalog* by Mel Allen. Dan Schlossberg insists that while Allen made it famous, it was first used by Cincinnati's Harry Hartman in 1929. It, of course, predates all of this as an auctioneer's call for an object that has been sold.

"Kiss It Goodbye."

—Bob Prince

"An Old Goldie."

—A Red Barber homer at Ebbets Field when the sponsor was Old Gold cigarettes. When there was an "Old Goldie" a carton of said weed would tumble down the protective netting behind the plate as a gift to the slugger and greet him as he crossed the plate.

"Open the Window, Aunt Minnie" or "Open the Window, Aunt Minnie, here it comes."

—Rosey Rowswell, who was referring to an imaginary woman who lived across the street from the park in Pittsburgh. He often embellished this with the sound of breaking glass, a sound obtained by breaking a light bulb.

"Tell it Goodbye!"

—Jon Miller

"That ball is history."

—Eric Nagel

"That ball is out of here."

—Common generic call

"They usually show movies on a flight like that."

—A posthomer call, first attributed to Red Sox broadcaster Ken Coleman, *Sports Illustrated*, August 27, 1979

"This Bud's for you."

—Product call, ca. 1980

"A White Owl Wallop."

—Product call, ca. 1950, used by Mel Allen, among others

"Whoo, boy! Next time around, bring me back my stomach."

—Jack Brickhouse, actually a call used when an opponent's long ball was just foul

See also Hamilton, Milo; Hodges, Russ; and Rizzuto, Phil for calls made on historic home runs (Hank Aaron's 715th, Bobby Thomson's pennant winner, and Roger Maris's 61st).

HOMER

"O'er the green mead the sporting virgins play,
Their shining veils unbound; along the skies,
Tost and retost, the ball incessant flies."

—Quoted by John Montgomery Ward in *Base-Ball: How to Become a Player* (Philadelphia: Athletic Publishing; 1888)

HOOD, THOMAS

"What he hit is history,
What he missed is mystery."

—Impromptu. In reference to a guest's hunting stories, but occasionally applied to baseball, to which it is equally appropriate

HOOPER, HARRY

"You know, I saw it all happen, from beginning to end. But sometimes I still can't believe what I saw: this nineteen-year-old kid, crude, poorly educated, only lightly brushed by the social veneer we call civilization, gradually transformed into the idol of American youth and the symbol of Baseball the world over—a man loved by more people and with an intensity of feeling that perhaps has never been equaled before or since."

> —On the Babe; quoted in the Hall of Fame *Yearbook,* 1989

HOOVER, HERBERT

"I pride myself on being one of the oldest fans. I can certainly count up about seventy years of devotion."

> —Former President Hoover in 1963, at age eighty-eight

"Next to religion, baseball has furnished a greater impact on American life than any other institution."

> —Quoted in Bob Chieger's *Voices of Baseball*

"Somebody has inquired as to whether I will be going to the opening baseball game. I hope to have that pleasure."

> —On April 5, 1932; on April 11, Opening Day, he did

"The rigid voluntary rules of right and wrong, as applied in American sports, are second only to religion in strengthening the morals

Herbert Hoover, 1922 (*Library of Congress Prints and Photographs Division*)

of the American people . . . and baseball is the greatest of all team sports."

> —Widely attributed

"Through sports we 'channel' boys' desire for exercise and let off their explosive violence without letting them get into the police court."

> —Quoted by Harold Seymour in *Baseball: The People's Game*

HOPE, BOB

"That's a lot of money to pay for comedy material."

> —On his failed attempt to buy the Washington Senators for $10 million in the late 1960s; quoted in the February 1969 *Baseball Digest.*

HORLEY, STEVE

"To a pitcher a base hit is the perfect example of negative feedback."

> —Quoted by Jim Bouton in *Ball Four*

HORNSBY, ROGERS

"Any ballplayer that don't sign autographs for little kids ain't an American. He's a Communist."

— *Saturday Evening Post*, June 15, 1963.

"Baseball is my life, the only thing I know and can talk about. It's my only interest. . . . I'm not a good mixer. I get bored at parties and I bore other people. I don't like to get dressed up and go out."

— Quoted in Robert Lipsyte's column, *New York Times*, June 16, 1969

"By trying to hit the ball back at the pitcher. In fact, I always tried to hit the ball back through the box, because that is the largest unprotected area."

— When asked by Frankie Frisch how he used to break a slump. Frisch's reaction: "I played against him for years and now he tells me that." Originally reported by *Seattle Post-Intelligencer,* and carried in the October 1953 *Baseball Digest*

"Cobb is all wet. He talks about a game which had no night play, a game in which the pitcher had everything his own way. He could apply saliva, tobacco juice, mud, talcum powder or a file to the ball. He could load it with phonograph needles, raise the seams and do anything else he wished with it. And a ball remained in play until it was ready to break apart. Now the advantage is all with the hitters."

— On Ty Cobb's criticism of modern (1950s) baseball, in the *Sporting News,* May 7, 1952.

"Eighty percent of big-league ballplayers go out to the race track today. Sneak around in sunglasses. Other 20 percent ain't that holy. Just can't find anybody who'll give 'em free tickets."

— Quoted in the *Saturday Evening Post,* June 15, 1963, demonstrating why he was known as the "Mr. Blunt" of baseball. It recalls another example. When Kenisaw Landis was commissioner he hauled Raj on the carpet. "Do you play the horses?" growled the judge. "Sure," grunted Hornsby, "got any tips?"

"Get a good ball to hit."

— His cardinal rule, which became Ted Williams's, according to the Splendid Splinter's account of things in *My Turn at Bat*

"I don't want to play golf. When I hit a ball, I want someone else to go chase it."

— From a collection of favorite baseball phrases on www.fastball.com, June 1, 2001

"He Couldn't Carry My Bat."

— On Roger Maris on March 22, 1962, in spring training, when Maris would not pose with Hornsby for a UPI photographer. What Hornsby said in full was: "I've posed with some real major leaguers, not bush leaguers like he is. He couldn't carry my bat. He didn't hit in two years what I hit in one."

Writing in the April 4 *Sporting News,* Harold Rosenthal of the *New York Herald-Tribune* gave the line a context: As a result of the episode, Hornsby, who wrote major-league history with his bat, made a major contribution to the game's collection of famous sayings with his disdainful: "He couldn't carry my bat."

His remark ranks with Bill Terry's "Is Brooklyn still in the league?," Chuck Dressen's "The Giants is dead," Charley Ebbets's "Baseball is in its infancy," and Harry Pulliam's "Take nothing for granted in baseball."

"I don't like to sound egotistical, but every time I stepped up to the plate with a bat in my hands, I couldn't help but feel sorry for the pitcher."

—Widely quoted

"I wore a big-league uniform and I had the best equipment and I traveled in style and could play ball every day. What else is there?"

—*Sporting News,* January 19, 1963

"I'd run 'em ragged. They're a gang of lazy loafers. No guts."

—When asked in 1938, as manager of the Browns, what he would do if asked to manage the Red Sox. Writing about it later, Austen Lake of the *Boston American,* who had asked the question, noted: "Did he add, 'But don't print that?' Not he! He invited me to 'put it in ink.'"

"It don't make no difference where I go or what happens, so long as I can play the full nine."

—Quoted by Jack Sher in *Sport Magazine's All-Time All Stars,* edited by Tom Murray

"I've cheated, or someone on my team has cheated, in almost every game I've been in."

—His oft-stated line on the game

"Mostly bums."

—As manager of the Boston Braves in 1928 when asked by owner Judge Emil Fuchs what kind of team he had

"Not with Farrell playing shortstop."

—When asked by a reporter if the Giants could win the pennant in 1927. The question was asked as Hornsby dined with shortstop Eddie "Doc" Farrell.

"People ask me what I do in winter when there's no baseball. I'll tell you what I do. I stare out the window and wait for spring."

—*The Baseball Card Engagement Book,* 1990

"Players who stand flat-footed and swing with their arms are golfers not hitters."

—On why Hank Aaron, a wrist hitter and therefore a good hitter, was destined for greatness. Said when Hornsby was a batting coach for the Cubs in the early 1950s and quoted in Dan Schlossberg's *Hammerin' Hank*

"The big trouble is not really who isn't in the Hall of Fame, but who is. It was established for a select few."

—On certain players not being selected for the Hall of Fame

"The home run became glorified with Babe Ruth. Starting with him, batters have been thinking in terms of how far they could hit the ball, not how often."

—Ca. 1950

HOUGH, CHARLIE

"They look like Hawaiian softball uniforms."

—As a Dodger pitcher on the Astros' new multicolored 1975 uniforms, the *Sporting News,* June 7, 1975

HOUK, RALPH

"Get 30 games over .500 and you can break even the rest of the way."

—As Tigers manager on how to win a pennant

"The mental approach to pinch-hitting—to walk up there cold—is so different from playing regularly that it takes a special talent. Some of the game's greatest haven't been able to handle it. Yet, men with .220 batting averages have been murder when sent up off the bench. I'll tell you this much: It's one of the toughest pressure jobs in baseball, because most of the time it means the ball game."

—As New York Yankees manager

"What do you want in life, a bonus or a limp?"

—The former major-league skipper, on how he persuaded Kirk Gibson to pick baseball over football, from *Coach and Athletic Director*, August 2003

HOUSE, TOM

"A big-league ball club consists of twenty-four adult children, and they hit the video arcade with a vengeance. . . . ballplayers will conservatively spend $50 to$100 in an afternoon before a ball game trying to maximize their scores, and competing with each other to become Masters of the Universe."

—*The Jock's Itch* (Chicago: Contemporary Books, 1989)

HOWARD, ELSTON

"I just won the Nobel Prize of baseball."

—On winning the American League MVP in 1963. Howard was, according to the *Sporting News*, "unprepared for a deluge of hate mail with racial overtones which followed his selection. The hate mail was surprising since the color barrier affecting the MVP award had been broken much earlier in the National League [Jackie Robinson, Ernie Banks, Frank Robinson]."

HOWARD, FRANK

"It's nothing that I don't think you don't really feel or realize isn't going to happen."

—Said by New York Mets manager, June 1983, on the syndicated TV show *This Week in Baseball*, speaking about ballplayers being traded; quoted in *Sports Illustrated*, June 20, 1983

"Mentally, I'm not that disciplined. My concentration breaks down too easily. I just can't stay in a groove long enough."

—On the possibility of hitting sixty home runs; quoted in the *Sporting News*, May 9, 1970

HOYT, WAITE

"A Yankee pitcher never should hold out, because he might be traded, and then he would have to pitch against them."

—Quoted by Frank Graham and Dick Hyman in *Baseball Wit and Wisdom*. Hoyt was traded to the Tigers in 1931 and was shelled by the Yankees the first time he faced them.

"Every big leaguer and his wife should teach their children to pray: 'God bless Mommy, God bless Daddy and God bless Babe Ruth.'"

—Recalled by Fred Lieb in *Baseball As I Have Known It*

"I am almost convinced that you will never learn the truth on Ruth. I roomed with Joe Dugan. He was a good friend of Babe's. But he will see Ruth in a different light than I did. Dugan's own opinion will be one in which Dugan revels in Ruth's crudities, and so on. While I can easily recognize all of this and admit it freely, yet there was buried in Ruth humanitarianism beyond belief, an intelligence he was never given credit for, a childish desire to be over-virile, living up to credits given his home-run power—and yet a need for intimate affection and respect, and a feverish desire to play baseball, perform, act and live a life he didn't and couldn't take time to understand."

—To Robert W. Creamer; quoted in his *Babe: The Legend Comes to Life*

"I want you to watch the crowd come into the stands tonight. Notice how many young couples there are. It continues to amaze me: the number of young people, women especially, who attend games today. Never heard of young men taking their dates to a ball game in my day. Why, they've doubled attendance right there."

—As a Reds broadcaster; quoted by Jim Brosnan in an October 2, 1960, *New York Times* article

"In our day you could have gotten a live catcher and his family for $975."

—On being told that you could buy a bronze limited-edition sculpture of Johnny Bench for $975. *Sports Illustrated,* August 18, 1980

"It's great to be young and a Yankee."

—Popular line attributed to Hoyt

"Joe, so would the Babe."

—To Joe Dugan at Babe Ruth's funeral after Dugan said, "Lord, I'd give my right arm for an ice-cold beer"; widely attributed.

"Listen, punk. Ruth has meant more to ball-players than any man who ever lived. You ought to get down on your knees and thank God that a man like Babe existed. Where do you think you'd be if it hadn't been for the big fellow? Or where would I be? Or any of us? Or where would baseball be if it hadn't been for Babe?"

—Clubhouse speech just after Babe Ruth died and, as the story goes, a brash young rookie said, "The big fellow dead? I suppose we'll have to chip in for flowers."

"The secret of success as a pitcher lies in getting a job with the Yankees."

—Saying in 1927 what was often axiomatic over the next eighty years

HRABOSKY, AL

"A lot of guys even question my sanity. But that's good. I want them to know I'll do anything it takes to win. I want them to think I'm crazy."

—On his game face and demeanor as a Cardinals pitcher; quoted in *Newsweek,* September 15, 1975

"Like all players, I enjoy recognition. And, I'm realistic. I know that the minute I quit playing, no one will care. I'm going to live it up while I can. A year after I have quit, I'll be forgotten."

—As Cards' ace reliever, August 23, 1975

"When I'm on the road, my greatest ambition is to get a standing boo."

—Widely attributed

HRBEK, KENT

"I can run. The hard part is stopping this body."

—The 240-pound first baseman on his base-running style; quoted in the *Sporting News*, April 3, 1989

HUBBARD, CAL P.

"Boys, I'm one of those umpires that misses 'em every once in a while. So if it's close, you'd better hit it."

—*The Baseball Card Engagement Book*, 1989

"But being an umpire wasn't such a tough job. You really have to understand only two things and that's maintaining discipline and knowing the rule book."
"I always hated to throw a guy out of a game, but sometimes it was necessary to keep order. When it was time for a player to go, he went."

—Comments made after being elected the Hall of Fame and recalled in his *Sporting News* obituary

"The call that always seemed the toughest to me was the slide and tag play at second. You can see it coming, but you don't know which way the runner is going to slide, where the throw is going to be and how the fielder is going to take the throw."

—This quotation appeared in the 1989 *Yearbook* of the National Baseball Hall of Fame

HUBBARD, ELBERT

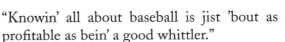

"The new definition of a heathen is a man who has never played baseball."

—*The Roycroft Dictionary and Book of Epigrams*, 1923

HUBBARD, KIN

"Knowin' all about baseball is jist 'bout as profitable as bein' a good whittler."

—From his book *Short Furrows*, 1911

HUBBELL, BILL

"Well, fellers, I found a way to get that dude out."

—As a pitcher for the Phillies, after Rogers Hornsby hit a line drive that caromed high off Hubbell's forehead and was caught by third baseman Russ Wrightstone. Hornsby was 3 for 4 that August 1921 day, and hit .397 for the season.

HUBBELL, CARL

"Hitters always have one thing in mind—they have to protect themselves against the fastball. If they're not ready for the fastball, a pitcher will throw it right by them. If they're ready for the fastball and don't get it, they can adjust to the breaking ball. But with a screwball, it isn't the break that fools the hitter, it's the change of speed. They don't time it."

> —The man who invented the screwball, commenting on Fernando Valenzuela, who threw it, *New York Times,* March 9, 1982

"The screwball's an unnatural pitch. Nature never intended a man to turn his hand like that throwing rocks at a bear."

> —As a former pitcher, 1982

HUGGINS, MILLER

"A good catcher is the quarterback, the carburetor, the lead dog, the pulse taker, the traffic cop and sometimes a lot of unprintable things, but no team gets very far without one."

> —Quoted by Walter Alston in his *Complete Baseball Handbook*

"A manager has his cards dealt to him, and he must play them."

> —As Yankee manager

"A string of good alibis."

> —Asked what a player needs most in a slump; quoted in *High and Inside: The Complete Guide to Baseball Slang* by Joseph McBride.

"Any ballplayers that played for me on either the Cardinals or Yankees could come to me if he were in need and I would give him a helping hand. I made only two exceptions, Carl Mays and Joe Bush. If they were in the gutter, I'd kick them."

> —Quoted by Fred Lieb in *Baseball As I Have Known It*

HUGHES, LANGSTON

"I did not mean to holler so loud when he stole them two bases yesterday, but I could not help myself. I were so proud he were black. . . . I want my race to hit home all the time."

> —On Jackie Robinson

HULBERT, WILLIAM AMBROSE

"I'd rather be a lamppost in Chicago than a millionaire in any other city."

> —The force behind the formation of the National League to A. G. Spalding; quoted widely including in a Steve Wulf profile of Hulbert in the February 26, 1990, *Sports Illustrated*

HUMPHREY, HUBERT

"I take a national view of the American Language and an American view of the National League."

> —When asked as vice president which league would win the World Series 1967, "Scorecard," *Sports Illustrated,* September 11, 1967

"This is the finest opening day I've ever experienced."

> —At the twice-postponed 1968 opener in Washington after rioting prompted by the

Martin Luther King assassination and as the 82nd Airborne still patrolled the city; quoted in the *Sporting News*, April 27, 1968

HUMPHRIES, ROLFE

"Time is of the essence. The crowd and the
    players
Are the same age always, but the man in the
    crowd
Is older every season."

—*Polo Grounds*

HUNT, RON

"Everything worthwhile in life is worth a price. Some people give their bodies to science, I give mine to baseball."

—After setting hit-by-pitch record, 1971. Hunt was hit by pitches 243 times during his career—50 times in the 1971 season.

"I'm glad Baylor broke the record. I was hoping to find someone dumber than me."

—After Don Baylor beat his record of being hit by 243 pitched balls, *Newsweek*, July 13, 1987

HUNTER, JIM "CATFISH"

"He'd give you the shirt off his back. Of course, he'd call a press conference to announce it."

—On Reggie Jackson, SABR Collection

"I had some friends here from North Carolina who'd never seen a homer, so I gave them a couple."

—To the press after giving up homers to Bill Buckner and Willie Crawford of the Dodgers in the 1974 World Series

Jim "Catfish" Hunter (*Author's Collection*)

"If I had done everything I was supposed to, I'd be leading the league in homers, have the highest batting average, have given $100,000 to the Cancer Fund and be married to Marie Osmond."

—SABR Collection

"The sun don't shine on the same dog's ass all the time."

—Standard reaction to the adversity of losing a game, getting injured, etc.

"Thank you, God, for giving me strength, and making me a ballplayer."

—During Catfish Hunter Day at Yankee Stadium, late 1979

HUNTER, JIM "CATFISH" (CONTINUED)

"The thing about Reggie is that you know he's going to produce. And if he doesn't, he's going to talk enough to make people think he's going to produce."

—On Reggie Jackson

HURLEY, ED

"He plays the bag like he came down from a higher league."

—American League umpire commenting on Brooks Robinson, 1958

HURST, BRUCE

"Oh, go wash your car!"

—The San Diego pitcher, who did not use profanity, to an abusive spectator; *Major League Baseball Newsletter*, August 1989.

HURST, TIM

"The pay is good, it keeps you out in the fresh air and sunshine, and you can't beat the hours."

—The umpire's famous line on the salubrious nature of the game. Writing many years later, Jim Brosnan reflected on the line in an article for the *New York Herald Tribune* magazine (April 7, 1966) and wrote, "That probably wasn't Hurst's worst call in a lifetime of arbitrating, but it stands today as a fact-mocking taradiddle."

HUTCHENS, JOHN K.

"No baseball fan has to explain his mania to any other baseball fan. They are a fraternity. It is less easy, often it is hopeless, to try to explain it to anyone else. You grow technical, and you do not make sense. You grow sentimental, and you are deemed soft in the head. How, the benighted outsider asks you with no little condescension, can you grow sentimental about a cold-blooded professional sport?"

—"Confessions of a Baseball Fan," *New York Times Magazine*, July 14, 1946.

"So, for an afternoon, I sit in pleasant surroundings, including the sun, and enjoy myself and my associates in the fraternity of fandom. As the game goes on I not only like it for what it is but I get to thinking of other games and other players, and I like that, too. Bobby Doerr goes back of second to rob Charlie Keller of a single to center, and I remember other great keystone sackers I have seen, Eddie Collins and Gehringer and Hornsby, and so on around the diamond and through the day. I like the sudden, sharp yell of the crowd when a batter catches hold of one with the tying run at first, and the electric tension that goes through a park when a runner and an outfielder's throw are staging a race for the plate. I like the peanut butcher's yapping chant up and down the aisles. I like being for a brief while in a good-natured place that is a self-sufficient little world of its own. This can probably be called escapism. All right, then, it is escapism.

"If memory serves, seeing a ball game was not always so pastoral. In the stands, as on the field, things are more orderly than I seem to remember they were at that old West Side park in Chicago. And that is all right with me, now. I do not find Mr. Williams, of Boston, a villain when he busts one into the right-field stand. I find him a great ball player, and I suspect I enjoy the sight the more for the detachment with which I view it.

"I suspect also, however, that no one ever recovers absolutely from the kind of early conditioning I had. Picking up the sports page in the morning, I can still feel something like a pang if the Cubs or the White Sox lost a ball game the day before. And if they both lost, I can even feel slightly depressed until about 10 A.M."

—*New York Times,* July 14, 1946

HUTCHINSON, FRED

"For five innings, it's the pitcher's game. After that it's mine."

> —As manager of the Tigers in 1953; quoted by Bob Chieger in *Voice of Baseball*

"Never borrow money from your ballclub and never try to fool your manager."

> —His rules for rookies, SABR Collection

Fred Hutchinson (*Author's Collection*)

HUTTON, TOMMY

"He's not the fielder that he was 10 or 15 years ago."

> —The sportscaster on the forty-five-year-old Tommy John, *Sporting News,* May 1, 1989

I

ICHIRO

"Baseball is just baseball."

> —When asked if he would have trouble making adjustments to the American major leagues, *Seattle Post-Intelligencer*, March 30, 2001

"Here they cheer both teams, not just the home team. I like that."

> —Discussing the differences between American and Japanese fans, *Seattle Post-Intelligencer*, March 30, 2001

"I haven't done anything yet."

> —On refusing a *Sports Illustrated* cover story a month into his first season with the Mariners; quoted in the *Japan Economic Newswire*, May 10, 2001

"I hope he arouses the fire that's dormant in the innermost recesses of my soul."

> —On first facing fellow Japanese player Daisuke Matsuzaka, pitcher for the Boston Red Sox, *Time*, April 19, 2007

"I'm eating a lot more pizza for lunch than I'm used to."

> —Asked about his biggest adjustment to American life, *Asahi Shimbun*, May 8, 2001

ILLUZZI, JOE

"The New York Mets proved this season it takes more than talent."

> —The UPI writer after the 1969 Mets finished first in front of the Cubs

INCAVIGLIA, PETE

"People think we make $3 million and $4 million a year. They don't realize that most of us only make $500,000."

> —Texas Rangers outfielder, *Life: The Year in Pictures*, 1991

INSCRIPTIONS

The author has been fascinated with baseball inscriptions since he was a kid and could exit the old Yankee Stadium by way of the outfield and had a chance to examine the graves of Huggins, Ruth, and Gehrig. They claim that these are monuments, but to anybody who saw them firsthand on his way to the subway, they will always be thought of as the graves. Here are a few choice words from that outfield and elsewhere:

A man, a gentleman and a great ballplayer whose amazing record of 2,130 consecutive games should stand for all time. This memorial is a tribute from the Yankee players to their beloved captain and teammate.

> —Inscription on the monument to Lou Gehrig on the outfield monument in Yankee Stadium

. . . and unlikely.

> —Written on a notice at Ebbets Field that said "Capacity of More than 33,000 is unlawful," 1948

A Yankee forever. A man who knew only one way to play—to win.

> —Passage from Billy Martin's plaque at Yankee Stadium

BABE RUTH

Hit his first home run
in professional baseball,
March, 1914. 135 yds. N.W.
In this town George

Herman Ruth acquired
the nickname "Babe."

> —Landmark on Gillespie Street in Fayetteville, North Carolina

Erected in 1955 by the fans of America in honor of a baseball immortal, a champion among champions, whose record on and off the playing field of the National Game will ever stand as a monument to his own greatness and as an example and inspiration to the youth of our country.

> —Inscription on the back of the pedestal of statue of Honus Wagner in Pittsburgh undraped on April 30, 1955

George Herman "Babe" Ruth
1895–1948
A Great Ball Player
A Great Man
A Great American
Erected by
The Yankees
and
The New York Baseball Writers

April 19, 1949

> —The "Babe Ruth Monument" erected by the Yankees and the New York Baseball Writers, at Yankee Stadium, and unveiled by Mrs. Ruth on the opening day of baseball season, 1949

Give me a bastard with talent.

> —Inscription on a pillow on the couch in George Steinbrenner's office in Yankee Stadium according to the *New York Daily News*, April 12, 1982

Matty Was Master of Them All.

> —On a bust of Christy Mathewson, Cooperstown, New York

Our captain and leader has not left us today, tomorrow, this year, next . . . our endeavors will reflect our love and admiration for him.

> —On Thurman Munson's monument in the Yankee Stadium outfield

To Mickey, the greatest of them all. Best Always, Roger Maris.

> —Signed baseball owned by Mickey Mantle, described in *USA Today*, May 25, 1990

To: Red Barber
Pioneer Television Sports Announcer

in grateful appreciation
National Broadcasting Company
August 26, 1939

> —Inscribed on a cigarette box given to Red Barber at his request as a memento of the first televised major-league baseball game. The box contained a bill from NBC for $35.00.

Tyrus Raymond Cobb
1886–1961
Greatest Tiger of All
a Genius in Spikes.

> —Tiger Stadium, unveiled July 17, 1963

You can't interview me here.

> —What Braves owner Ted Turner insists that he wants written on his tombstone

IRVIN, MONTE

"Baseball has done more to move America in the right direction than all the professional patriots with all their cheap words."

> —Widely attributed

"It was his solemn duty to catch a ball that wasn't in the stands."

> —On Willie Mays, May 6, 1981

IRWIN, WILL

"'Playing catch' is the parent of almost all ball games. And it must have flourished for ages before some shrewd genius of a priest saw the opportunity to increase attendance at services by injecting into them a touch of muscular paganism. What the hierarchies of heathendom contributed was team work."

> —Introduction to Robert W. Henderson, *Ball, Bat and Bishop: The Origin of Ball Games* (New York: Rockport Press, 1947)

ISAACS, STAN

"I don't love baseball. I don't love most of today's players. I don't love the owners. I do love, however, the baseball that is in the heads of baseball fans. I love the dreams of glory of 10-year-olds, the reminiscences of 70-year-olds.

"The greatest baseball arena is in our heads, what we bring to the games, to the telecasts, to reading newspaper reports."

—In his column "Diamond Studded Memories," *Newsday*, April 9, 1990

ISTOMIN, EUGENE

"I was studying with Pablo Casals in the Pyrenees Mountains, in France, where he had gone into self-exile from Spain. I listened to the game on the Armed Forces Network.

When Thomson hit the home run I jumped out of my chair and began to yell. I was a Dodger fan but I knew it was the most dramatic moment in sports history. The teams involved, the personalities, the pennant race. I was out of my mind. Everybody in the room was stunned by my behavior. I tried to explain it but they never understood."

—The concert pianist describing his reaction to Bobby Thomson's 1951 homer. The quote was solicited by the Mets, who staged a promotion for the 20th anniversary of the "shot heard 'round the world."

IZENBERG, JERRY

"Watching a spring training game is as exciting as watching a tree form its annual ring."

—Sportswriter, 1981

261

J

JACKSON, BO

"Baseball was fun when I was in college. It's my job now. But I like my 3–11 shift."

> —Comparing Royals' baseball to Auburn baseball; quoted in *The Sporting News,* July 3, 1989

"I really don't know about playing pro baseball. I'm not saying no, and I'm not ruling out the possibility of being drafted. But really, I'm playing baseball this spring to have something to occupy my time."

> —As an Auburn University junior; quoted in the March 25, 1985, *Baseball America.*

"When people tell me I could be the best athlete there is, I just let it go in one ear and out the other. There is always somebody out there who is better than you are. Go ask Mike Tyson."

> —When told he could be one of the best players in history; quoted in *Major League Baseball Newsletter,* May 1990

Bo Jackson (*Kansas City Royals*)

Reggie Jackson (*California Angels*)

"A baseball swing is a very finely tuned instrument. It is repetition and more repetition, then a little more after that."

—*Reggie* by Reggie Jackson

"After Jackie Robinson, the most important black in baseball history is Reggie Jackson. I really mean that."

—*Life*, January 1988

"All the fans in those sections are black, under 10 and don't read the papers."

—On why one section at Yankee Stadium did not boo him after his return from a five-game suspension; quoted in *Sports Illustrated*, August 7, 1978

"Anything that changes your regular swing is going to mess up your natural feeling at the plate, and if you're not natural you're nothing: you're in a slump."

—*Late Innings* by Roger Angell

"Blind people come to the park just to listen to him pitch."

—Commenting on Tom Seaver; quoted in the *All Time Greatest Sports Quotes*

"Every hitter likes fastballs, just like everybody likes ice cream. But you don't like it when someone's stuffing it into you by the gallon. That's how you feel when Ryan's throwing balls by you. You just hope to mix in a walk so you can have a good night and only go 0-for-3."

—On Nolan Ryan, then of the Angels, in *Newsweek*, June 16, 1975

"Fans don't boo nobodies."

—*Baseball Illustrated*, 1975

"For a certain amount of money, you'll eat Alpo."

—On the possibility of playing in Japan in 1989; from a list of "Memorable Quotes of 1988" from the *Tampa Tribune*, December 25, 1988

"Guys who play there say it gets awfully lonely. Hell, for the money they're talking, I can buy some friends and take them with me."

—On his $1-million-plus offer to play in Japan for the '89 season; quoted in *Sports Illustrated*, January 25, 1988

"He should be glad he'll be able to tell his grandchildren he once pitched to Reggie Jackson."

—On pitcher Bruce Hurst, as a .207 hitter; quoted in the May 30, 1983, *Sports Illustrated*

"He's a little older than me, but we have just about the same lifetime figures, if you look them up. So how come Lee gets paid maybe one-eighty or two hundred thousand, and I'm the best damned paid player in the game? Why is that? I'll tell you why. It's because I put the asses in the seats!"

—On Lee May, to a knot of reporters in Baltimore; quoted by Roger Angell in *Late Innings*

"Hitting is better than sex."

—*Esquire*, March 1, 1978

"I am the best in baseball. This may sound conceited, but I want to be honest about how I feel. . . . There is no one who does as many things as well as I do. . . . I can do it all and I create an excitement in a ballpark when I walk on the field."

—From the first of two books titled *Reggie*, this one from 1975 and written with Bill Libby

"I didn't come to New York to be a star. I brought my star with me."

—Widely quoted at the time of his arrival in New York

"I don't mind getting beaten, but I hate to lose."

—*Sepia*, March 1977

"I go to pieces in turmoil, but I thrive on pressure."

—Widely attributed, but apparently not his. To quote from *Reggie:* "There's a quote from 1977 that has followed me around a little bit. It's not up in lights like the one about the straw and the drink, but people seem to remember it. It goes like this: 'I go to pieces in turmoil, but I thrive on pressure.' Didn't say it."

"I have a hard time believing athletes are over-priced. If an owner is losing money, give it up. It's business. I have trouble figuring out why owners would stay in if they're losing money."

—*Los Angeles Times*, March 9, 1976

"I represent both the overdog and the under-dog in society."

—*Rolling Stone*, September 6, 1989

"I think he likes me."

—On California Angels owner Gene Autry signing him to a $700,000-a-year contract; widely attributed, but it made an early showing in the February 8, 1982, *Sports Illustrated*

"It's become a business with us. I used to dream how good it would be to be Willie Mays or Mickey Mantle. My dreams have died. Even the rotten [World Series] rings aren't what they're supposed to be. I'll buy my own diamonds. I can afford it now. No one gives you anything, you've got to get it for yourself."

—On signing with the Yankees at the end of the 1976 season; quoted in *High and Inside: the Complete Guide to Baseball Slang* by Joseph McBride

"I understand people think you [Bo Jackson] can hit .300, get 50 homers and have 50 to 75 stolen bases. That means you can be the best baseball player there has ever been. It's your choice. You can be the next Jim Brown in football or the next Reggie Jackson in baseball."

—Quoted in Douglas S. Looney, "Bo's Not One to Go with the Flow," *Sports Illustrated*, July 14, 1986

"I was reminded that when we lose and I strike out, a billion people in China don't care."

—This line was also attributed to Jim Bouton

"I'd rather hit than have sex. To hit is to show strength. It's two against one at the plate, the pitcher and the catcher versus you. When I'm up there, I'm thinking, 'Try everything you want. Rub up the ball. Move the fielders around. Throw me hard stuff, soft stuff. Try anything. I'm still going to hit that ball.' God, do I love to hit that little round sum-bitch out of the park and make 'em say 'Wow!'"

—As an Oakland Athletic; quoted in *Time*, June 3, 1974

"If I played there, they'd name a candy bar after me."

—As an Oakland A facing free agency, on his fascination with playing in New York. The Reggie Bar was created while he wore the Yankee uniform. It was discontinued after his playing days were over.

"I'm projected as something that's horrible, and it's very, very uncomfortable. I try to give of myself and do things for people, and to be spit at and thrown at and cursed at is a very uncomfortable thing. . . . it's hard to play when somebody says you're no good or somebody says you can't do this or you can't do that or you're a lousy person or you're greedy or egotistical. Those things are tough and unfair. I'm human. I've played my butt off for 10 years. I'm not a loafer. I'm not a jerk. I'm a baseball player. That's what I want to do. I don't want to get famous. If I deserve it with my bat, give me credit. If I don't, leave me be."

—On playing in the East as a Yankee; quoted in the *Dallas Times-Herald*, August 27, 1978

"In June of '67, I got called up to the Kansas City A's for a cup of coffee, but I didn't even have time for cream or sugar."

—*Reggie*

"It's a fickle town, a tough town. They getcha, boy. They don't let you escape with minor scratches and bruises. They put scars on you here."

—On New York in his last Yankee season; quoted by Tom Boswell in the *Washington Post*, April 23, 1988

"My father didn't and still doesn't know what color is. I grew up with white kids [near Philadelphia], played ball with them, went home with them. I didn't know what prejudice was until I got to Arizona State and the football coach told me to stop dating white girls."

—*Everything You Always Wanted to Know About Sports and Didn't Know Where to Ask* by Mickey Herskowitz and Steve Perkins

"My memory of his last game is a touching one, because for the first time since Thurman and I had been teammates, he had to take himself out of a game. His knees had become assassins after all the years of squatting behind the plate, all the games when he'd taken his squat body and hurled it at the game of baseball. There is no tougher possition than catcher. Knee bends are lousy for you to begin with, and Thurman had done about a million of them across his career. Get up. Get down. Get up again. Get down. Come up throwing. Take the chest protector off. Take the shin guards off. Hit. Put them back on. Go back behind the plate and repeat the process. Catching just breaks a man down, inning by inning, game by game, year by year."

—On watching Thurman Munson play his last game; from *Reggie*

"October. That's when they pay off for playing ball."

—As a New York Yankees outfielder, 1980

"People think I hate Billy Martin. I don't. I hate some of the things he did. And I will say I don't understand him. . . .

"Billy Martin is not an intellectual, but there is a cunningness to him that is something to behold."

—*Reggie*

"So many ideas come to you and you want to try them all, but you can't. You're like a mosquito in a nudist camp. You don't know where to start."

—On the slump, in *Sporting News,* June 20, 1970

"Somebody definitely is guilty of taking steroids. You can't be breaking records hitting 200 home runs in three or four seasons. The greatest hitters in the history of the game didn't do that. Bonds hit 73 in 2001, and he would have hit 100 if they would have pitched to him. I mean, come on, now. There is no way you can outperform Aaron and Ruth and Mays at that level."

—Quoted in AP collection of quotes of the year, January 1, 2005

"The balls aren't the same balls, the bats aren't the same length and it's further between bases."

—On playoff pressure, as an Oakland A

"The clubhouse is one of the seductions of baseball, it is a place where you don't have to grow up."

—*Reggie*

"The only difference between me and those other great Yankees is my skin color."

—On Ruth, Gehrig, DiMaggio, et al.; quoted in *High Inside: Memoirs of a Baseball Wife* by Danielle Gagnon Torrez.

"The only reason I don't like playing in the World Series is I can't watch myself play."

—One of his most notorious Reggie-isms.

"The only way I'm going to win a Gold Glove is with a can of spray paint."

—On his fielding ability; widely quoted

"The owners don't like ballplayers who talk a lot. Some other people don't like black people who talk a lot. That's distasteful, but it doesn't surprise me, I think most of the flak about too much money has been aimed at the black players."

—Quoted in *Late Innings* by Roger Angell

"The will to win is worthless if you don't get paid for it."

—*Grand Slams and Fumbles*

"There were very few face-to-face confrontations with Steinbrenner; he'd always use intermediaries whenever he could, or leak a story to the press. Charlie only leaked when he went to the men's room."

—Comparing George Steinbrenner and Charles O. Finley, in *Reggie*

"There will never be another Babe Ruth. He was the greatest home run hitter who ever lived. They named a candy bar after him."

—In 1969 when asked to compare himself to Ruth to a crowd of reporters; quoted in *The Mustache Gang* by Ron Bergman

"There's no way I'll ever sign here. Not enough reporters around."

—Said to Ken Singleton during his season in Baltimore; quoted by Danielle Gagnon Torrez in *High Inside: Memoirs of a Baseball Wife*

"Tiant is the Fred Astair of baseball."

—On Luis Tiant; quoted in *Five Seasons* by Roger Angell

"When you've played this game for 10 years, gone to bat 7,000 times and gotten 2,000 hits, do you know what that really means? It means you've gone zero for 5,000!"

—Quoted in the *Christian Science Monitor*, September 20, 1974

"You don't face Ryan without your rest. He's the only guy I go against that makes me go to bed before midnight."

—*Reggie*

"You know, this team . . . it all flows from me. I've got to keep it going. I'm the straw that stirs the drink . . . Munson thinks he can be the straw that stirs the drink, but he can only stir it bad. . . . The rest of the guys should know that I don't feel that far above them. . . . I mean, nobody can turn people on like I can, or do for a club the thing I can do, but we are still athletes, we're all still ballplayers."

—The famous June 1977 *Sport* magazine quote that so endeared him to his Yankee teammates. Jackson denied the story and the quotes. In *Reggie* (1984) he says of the article by Robert

Ward: "I could have lived with 'the straw that stirs the drink' quote. Ward had obviously taken a thought that took me a paragraph to articulate and compressed it into a sentence. But at least I'd said something like it.

"I have no idea where he got the quote about Munson because I never said anything like that. Not anything even close to it, mostly because I hadn't been around Thurman enough to get any kind of reading on him. But those quotes about him hurt me more than anything, and follow me around to this day."

JACKSON, SHOELESS JOE

"Hey, big mouth, how do you spell triple?"

—Supposed response to a heckling Cleveland fan who kept asking the illiterate Jackson if he could spell "illiterate." After hitting a triple, this was his response. "I ain't afraid to tell the world that it don't take school stuff to help a fella play ball." This is a common version of this story. In another the fan asks Jackson if he can spell "cat" and he leans over and asks him if he can spell "shit."

"No such word 'Say it ain't so' was ever said. The fellow who wrote that just wanted something to say. When I came out of the courthouse that day, nobody said anything to me. The only one who spoke was a guy who yelled at his friend 'I told you the big son of a bitch

wore shoes.' I walked right out of there and stepped into my car and drove off."

—Quoted in Harvey Frommer, *Shoeless Joe and Ragtime Baseball* (Dallas: Taylor Publishing, 1992)

"What a hell of a league this is. Ah hit .387, .408, and .395 the last three years and Ah ain't won nothin' yet!"

—To Ty Cobb; quoted in *Baseball: An Informal History* by Douglass Wallop

JACKSON, TRAVIS

"My greatest thrill? In 1921 I played for Little Rock in the Southern League and the first time I stepped on the field I was in awe. It held 4,500 people and I never saw a park that big. And there I was holding up my pants with a cotton rope."

—The Hall of Famer quoted in the National Baseball Hall of Fame *Yearbook*, 1981

JACOBS, JOE

"I should of stood in bed."

>—The boxing manager after leaving his sickbed to go to the 1935 World Series between Detroit and Chicago. He bet on Chicago; Detroit won. He made this comment on his return to New York. The quote was soon in wide circulation for any exercise in frustration.
>
>As Joseph McBride points out in *High and Inside,* "Jacobs's other famous quotation came on June 21, 1932, when his boxer, Max Schmeling, lost to Jack Sharkey. Grabbing the radio mike, he told a nationwide audience, "We was robbed!"

JAKUCKI, SIG

"Tie your own goddammed shoes, you one-armed son of a bitch."

>—The St. Louis Browns pitcher to one-armed teammate Pete Gray, who asked Jakucki to help him tie his shoes in the clubhouse one day. Gray, an outfielder, played for the Browns in the wartime season of 1945. He was not popular among his teammates.

JAMES, BILL

"Baseball is a wonderful form of education. The ways we have of learning about baseball are better than our ways of learning about anything else. A young child can acquire knowledge about baseball from television, radio, newspapers, books. The game is open to you if you're a poet or an accountant, if you're a left-brain or a right-brain person. Nothing else in this country does so good a job of teaching the public about itself, I go to games, I listen to games on the radio, I watch some on TV, I check the box scores every morning. I have fantasy teams, I read books. The game is everywhere. Following another sport like that is possible, but it's a lot of work. That's one reason people are into baseball. But the green grass and the blue skies are wonderful, too. An athlete can love basketball as much as he loves baseball—but can a poet?"

>—"Phantoms of the Ballyard," in Karen Mullarkey, ed. dir., *Baseball in America* (San Francisco: Collins Publishers, 1991)

"By far, the most important discovery I've ever made is the fact that you can predict a player's major league batting performance based on his minor league record. . . . by far, the most important thing would be that minor league batting stats do predict major league batting stats.

"The second most important thing is that the stability of performance for power pitchers is vastly greater than the stability of performance for finesse pitchers."

>—In Mike Shannon, *Baseball—The Writers' Game* (South Bend, Ind.: Diamond Communications, 1992)

"Sabermetrics is to baseball as psychology is to human nature."

>—Quoted in Joe Klein, "The Media Guide," *Sport,* October 1984

JAMES, BILL (CONTINUED)

"Some years ago, it occurred to me that there must be dozens of ballplayers in each generation who leave a mark on the game in one way or another, and that when you go to a game you can therefore see the tracks of hundreds of players. . . .

"When you see the first baseman playing in front of the base runner, in his line of sight rather than behind him, who are you seeing? Willie Stargell.

"When a hitter stands at the plate in a pigeon-toed crouch, who are you seeing? Rod Carew, of course; nobody did that before Carew. . . .

"I've become convinced that every player who plays the game at the major-league level for any length of time leaves an image lingering behind him, that if you really understood the history of baseball, that if one could see baseball, so to speak, with the eyes of God, one could see in each and every baseball game the image of every good and great player who has ever played."

—*Baseball Book*, 1990

"The best game managers, generally speaking, are those who have the courage to keep their hands in their pockets, let their players play and take the inevitable flak from the fans. A strategic move or two a game is OK, but those guys who are out there pulling levers and pushing buttons like they were playing some super-advanced version of Donkey Kong are probably giving away more on balance than they are getting back."

—*Sport*, July 1984

"The common theory is that it is all right to study baseball as long as you don't become intelligent about it. Once you become serious about it, people think you are wasting your time."

—*University Daily Kansan,* December 5, 1984

"Three days without box scores, Jeez, that's tough."

—On the All-Star break; quoted in Joe Klein, "The Media Guide," *Sport,* October 1984

JEFFCOAT, HAL

"When you first sign that contract as a kid, they tell you your whole future is ahead of you. But they forget to tell you that your future stops at 35."

—As a Cardinals pitcher

JEFFERSON, THOMAS

"Games played with the ball, and others of that nature, are too violent for the body and stamp no character on the mind."

—In a letter to Peter Carr dated August 19, 1785. Jefferson's opinion was shared by many in the ruling class. Princeton College banned "baste ball," a popular game among students, on grounds that it "is in itself low and unbecoming gentlemen Students and . . . is an exercise attended with great danger."

JENKINS, BRUCE

"Weight training is great for endurance, and blocking linebackers, and profiling in hotel bars, but it won't help you on the baseball field. You're either a player or you're not."

—*Life After Saberhagen: Bruce Jenkins' 1986 Guide to Baseball* (Berkeley, Calif.: North Atlantic Books, 1986)

JENNINGS, HUGHIE

"Eeyah-eeyah."

—Call made when Jennings went to the coacher's box

"Hit or get hit."

—His way of saying that if he didn't get one to hit, he would get in the way of the ball; quoted in Robert Smith's *Baseball's Hall of Fame.*

"I owe baseball more than the game owes me. Keep it clean and honest."

—Whispered on his deathbed; quoted by Patrick A. McGuire, "That Winning Season," *Sun Magazine,* April 3, 1994

"I played in Baltimore off and on until 1907, when Detroit drafted me. I was glad to get away from the Maryland burg. It's about the worst baseball town on the map."

—Quoted in Alfred H. Spink, *The National Game,* 2nd ed. (St. Louis: National Game Publishing, 1911)

"I used to say, 'That's the way!' Then I found that it was too dull and tiresome. I wanted something with snap and go to it. So I changed it to 'That's the way-ah!' From this I changed it to just 'The way-ah!' Finally I found I was just yelling 'Ee-yaah!'"

—On his ear-splitting scream from the third-base coaching box; quoted in Neal McCabe and Constance McCabe, *Baseball's Golden Age: The Photographs of Charles M. Conlon* (New York: Harry N. Abrams, 1993)

JENSEN, JACK "JACKIE"

"I like the game, but I don't like the life."

—Quoted in the *Sporting News* obituary after his death on July 14, 1982

JESSEL, GEORGE

"It's possible at this rate that even Willie Mays will be forgotten in 2,000 years."

—Quoted in Arnold Hano's *Willie Mays*

"Sandy Koufax is the greatest Jewish athlete since Samson."

—"Diamond Quotes," *Nine,* 2006

JETER, DEREK

"Some of my teammates have kids, so I know it can be done."

—The Yankees shortstop who, though still a bachelor, holds out hope for one day getting wed and siring children. The *Vancouver Sun,* December 26, 2006, which gave it a "Yogi" for one of the best Yogi Berra–like quotes of the year.

"You fans should enjoy watching this team because you're not going to see many like it."

—2000 World Series MVP when his team was honored with a ticker-tape celebration, *Chicago Sun Times,* October 31, 2000

JOHN PAUL, POPE

"I'm told there was much excitement in St. Louis during the recent baseball season. Well, two great players, Mark McGwire and Sammy Sosa, were competing to break the home-run record. You can feel the same enthusiasm as you train for different goals."

—During his visit to St. Louis in early 1999; quoted in the *Chicago Sun-Times,* January 29, 1999

JOHN, TOMMY

"All winter long, I can't wait for baseball. It gets you back to doing the stuff you love and makes you wish the youthfulness of life could stay with you forever."

—SABR Collection

"It was after he hit it."

—Asked if a pitch smacked four hundred feet for a home run off him by Toronto's George Bell had been out of the strike zone, *Sports Illustrated,* July 6, 1987.

"It's a rule. It's like the 55 mph speed limit. You may not want to drive it. If it's a law you got to abide by it or pay the price. It was a big adjustment for me to exaggerate my stop. But I've got a couple of gimmicks to remind myself."

—On the balk rule, from the compilation "Memorable Quotes of 1988," *Tampa Tribune,* December 25, 1988

"When they operated, I told them to put in a Koufax fastball. They did—but it was Mrs. Koufax's."

—The New York Yankees pitcher, recalling his 1974 arm surgery

Tommy John (*California Angels*)

JOHNSON, BAN

"A good umpire is the umpire you don't even notice. He's there all afternoon but when the game is over, you don't remember his name."

—The pioneer American League president; quoted in Joe Garagiola's *Baseball Is a Funny Game*

"That's the yelp of a beaten cur."

—After Game 2 of the 1911 World Series, White Sox owner Charlie Comiskey went to NL president Heydler to say something wasn't right with the Series play. Heydler related Comiskey's concern to Ban Johnson, who uttered this reply.

JOHNSON, DARRELL

"You just listen to the ball and bat come together. They make an awful noise."

—Seattle Mariner manager, on when to change pitchers, SABR Collection

JOHNSON, DAVEY

"Earl is a master of psychology. He can get the most out of anybody. He used to be a used-car salesman and he can sell anybody, anything, I believe."

—On Earl Weaver; quoted in the *Sporting News*, July 24, 1971

"When you're going good it doesn't get any better than being in New York. But when you're going bad, it doesn't get any worse."

—As Mets manager after the 1980 season

Davey Johnson (*New York Mets*)

JOHNSON, ERNIE

"Henry Aaron is simply smarter than all the pitchers. He deceives pitchers. One of his secrets is his slow manner. He puts pitchers to sleep."

—The Atlanta announcer on Hank Aaron, 1973

"The two best pitchers in the National League don't speak English—Fernando Valenzuela and Steve Carlton."

—As Braves announcer, 1981

JOHNSON, GARY

"Before you draft a kid, you got to know how bad he wants to play. So you don't tell him

he's going to Hollywood. You tell him about the 3 a.m. bus rides, the greasy-spoon food and locker rooms so filthy you suit up at the hotel. If he understands that and still wants to play, he's a prospect."

—As a White Sox scout

JOHNSON, HOWARD

"Maybe they should see if his body is corked."

—On slugger Bo Jackson; quoted in *Sports Illustrated*, August 7, 1989

JOHNSON, HOWARD (CONTINUED)

"The Red Sox are built for Fenway, a home run hitter's park for right-handers. They lack speed. Here you need a combination of everything. If you hit the ball well, it goes out but pitchers know they have some room too.

"And you need speed in the outfield because there is room in the gaps for taking the extra base. We have that."

> —As a Met on Shea Stadium; quoted in the *New York Times,* October 19, 1986

JOHNSON, LYNDON B.

"They booed Ted Williams too, remember? They'll say about me I knocked the ball over the fence—but they don't like the way he stands at the plate."

> —*Baseball: The President's Game* by William B. Mead and Paul Dickson

"We cheer for the Senators, we pray for the Senators, and we hope that the Supreme Court doesn't declare that unconstitutional."

> —On the Washington Senators, from a speech at a luncheon given in connection with the 1962 All-Star baseball game in Washington, D.C., July 10, 1962

JOHNSON, WALTER

"Can I throw harder than Joe Wood? Listen, Mister, no man alive can throw any harder than Smokey Joe Wood."

> —An overly modest encomium from the fastballer nonpareil on the occasion of Wood's spectacular 1912 season

"Feller isn't quite as fast as I was."

> —After seeing Bob Feller in 1946 (shortly before Johnson died) and pressed by friends to compare himself to Feller; quoted by Lee Allen in *Cooperstown Corner*

"I was the greenest rookie that ever was. One evening I was standing out on the sidewalk when a stranger approached and said, 'You're famous already, kid. See, they've named a hotel for you.' I looked across the street and, sure enough, there was a big illuminated sign that read, 'Johnson Hotel.' Well, do you know that I was so green that I actually believe the man?"

> —Quoted in the 50th Anniversary Hall of Fame *Yearbook,* 1989

President Lyndon Johnson Opening Day, 1964 (*Cleveland Public Library*)

Walter Johnson presented with a car (*Library of Congress Prints and Photographs, Bain Collection*)

"Nobody saw it. He hit it and it disappeared."

—On a 1911 home-run hit off him by Rogers Hornsby that went through a hole in the center-field fence; quoted in *Sport Magazine's All-Time All Stars*

"The Swedes are mighty fine people and I don't want to do anything that might offend them."

—On why he never bothered to correct the widespread belief that he was of Swedish decent. He was even called Swede by some; quoted in *It Takes Heart* by Mel Allen with Frank Graham Jr.

"The balls Ruth hit got smaller quicker than anyone's."

—Quoted by Shirley Povich in Gordon Beard, "Shirley Povich Has Been Fighting Deadlines for 70 Years," *Orioles Gazette,* August 13, 1993

"You can't hit what you can't see."

—On his fastball

Walter Johnson (*Society for American Baseball Research; SABR Collection*)

JOHNSTONE, JAY

"Flake? Who's a flake? Have you ever heard of Jackie Brandt? He gets credit for the term. When he was a rookie outfielder for the St. Louis Browns in 1956, a teammate noticed that 'things seem to flake off his mind and disappear.' Jackie once played 27 holes of golf in 101-degree heat before a doubleheader."

—*Temporary Insanity*

"I don't know why ball players like to moon. Maybe it's the only way some of them can figure out how to express themselves."

—On mooning TV talk-show host Merv Griffin, in *Temporary Insanity*

"I went through Cleveland one day and it was closed."

—As a New York Yankee; widely attributed

"Its difficult to gain the respect of a player when you're spraying him with Red Man."

—On Lefty Phillips, in *Temporary Insanity*

"Ted Williams is the man who always said that hitting a baseball was the toughest thing in sports. And I'm a disciple who says that hitting a baseball when you're coming off the bench, bottom of the ninth, against somebody throwing heat or split-fingered magic, is the toughest part of the toughest thing.

"But it's still better than lifting things."

—From *Temporary Insanity*. This—and the original Williams quote—are among a

number of "toughest things" quotes in baseball. For example, Bill Freehan says in *Behind the Mask*: "Catching a knuckleball pitcher is probably the hardest thing in the world."

"The first time I met Moe Drabowsky was at one of Larry McTague's restaurants in New York, and Larry said, 'Jay, I'd like you to meet Moe Drabowsky.' With that, Moe dropped his cocktail glass and reached out to shake my hand. I mean, it shattered all over the floor and he didn't blink an eye. I knew right away that this was my kind of guy."

—Quoted on the inside jacket of *Temporary Insanity*

JOKES

Without further ado:

A baseball manager who had an ulcer was in his physician's office for a checkup. "Remember," the doctor said, "don't get excited, don't get mad, and forget about baseball when you're off the field." Then he added, "By the way, how come you let the pitcher bat yesterday with the tying run on second and two out in the ninth?"

A British visitor to Yankee Stadium, unable to understand the game, left as the scoreboard read:

1 0 0 0 0 0 0 0 0

1 0 0 0 0 0 0 0 0

When asked by a kid outside the gate, "What's the score?" the Briton shrugged, "Oh, it's up in the millions."

A couple of Yogi Berra's waggish teammates on the New York Yankee Ball Club swear that one night the stocky catcher was horrified to see a baby toppling off the roof of a cottage across the way from him. He dashed over and made a miraculous catch—but then force of habit proved too much for him. He straightened up and threw the baby to second base.

—1950s

A man walks into a bar with a dog. The bartender says, "You can't bring that dog in here."

"You don't understand," says the man. "This is no regular dog. He can talk."

"Listen, pal," says the bartender. "If that dog can talk, I'll give you a hundred bucks."

The man puts the dog on a stool, and asks him, "What's on top of a house?"

"Roof!"

"Right. And what's on the outside of a tree?"

"Bark!"

"And who's the greatest baseball player of all time?"

"Ruth!"

"I guess you've heard enough," says the man. "I'll take the hundred in twenties."

The bartender is furious. "Listen, pal," he says, "get out of here before I belt you."

As soon as they're on the street, the dog turns to the man and says, "Do you think I should have said 'DiMaggio'?"

A baseball umpire had such terrible headaches that he went to a doctor to be examined. Finally the doctor said, "I think you need glasses." With that, the umpire jumped to his feet, jerked his thumb, and yelled, "That'll cost you a hundred bucks . . . and, what's more, you're out of the game."

A Spaniard named José came to America and wanted to attend a big-league baseball game. To his dismay, he found all the seats were sold out. However, the management gave him a high flagpole seat. When he returned to his country, his friends asked him: "What kind of people are the Americans?"

He said, "Fine people. They gave me a special seat at the ballgame, and just before the game started, they all stood up and sang, 'José, can you see?'"

A well-tanned man sat down for his supper at one of the more exclusive dining places in New York. He took out his handkerchief and was engaged in some peculiar activity when the head waiter came up.

In a tone that suggested indignation the waiter said, "Sir, when you eat in this place there is no need for you to dust off the plates."

"Sorry," replied the man, "force of habit, I guess. You see, I'm an umpire."

A young man who was much more interested in athletics than in the theater, accompanied his sweetheart to the presentation of a Shakespearean play, just to please her. All through the play he sat with a bored look on his face.

Finally, trying to arouse her companion's interest, the young lady said, "What is the best play that you ever saw?"

Instantly the fellow's face lighted up and he replied, "Tinker touching a man out between second and third and then whipping the ball over to Chance in time to nab the runner going to first!"

—1920s

An elementary-school teacher tells her class to jot down the names of the nine men who, in their opinion, were the greatest in American history. Everybody completes the list but ten-year-old Bill, who sits with his brow furrowed, chewing on his pencil. "What's the trouble, Bill?" inquires the teacher. "Can't you think of nine outstanding Americans?" "I've got eight, all right," answers Bill, "but what I still need is a second baseman."

—1950s

Any baseball team could use a man who plays every position superbly, never strikes out, and never makes an error, but there is no way to make him lay down his hot dog and come out of the grandstand.

"At the end of every season, I quit regularly once a year. Then, soon as it starts to get warm, I come back."

—The minor leaguer when asked by Vida Blue why he hung on; quoted in *Vida* by Richard Deming

At the game:

ENGLISHMAN: What's the man running for?

AMERICAN: He hit the ball.

ENGLISHMAN: I know. But does he have to chase it, too?

"BASEBALL PITCHERS, LEFTIES OR RIGHTIES. Excellent career opportunities are now available for both experienced or inexperienced individuals with local American League team. Requirements entail ability to throw 'strikes.' Salary commensurate with experience. Mail your resume in confidence to: Shaker Advertising, MSA 344 TRIBUNE 60611. Equal Opportunity Employer."

—Ad which ran in the *Chicago Tribune* in May 1978. It was placed by an unknown White Sox fan and received national attention.

Before the existence of the association of clubs (1857), and when the game was to be learned only from witnessing the practice and match games at Hoboken, the prejudice which existed against the game could scarcely be imagined. The favor with which it was regarded may be judged from the observation used by an accidental witness of a game who, after looking for a while, with unfeigned astonishment exclaimed: "I can't see what fun such great, big men can find in hitting a little ball with a big stick and run away like mad, and kick at a sand bag."

—From the first *De Witt Base-Ball Guide*, 1868, and perhaps the first published baseball joke

Dave and Sam played softball together for forty years, when suddenly Dave was killed in a car accident.

Two months later, Sam receives a call from his old pal. "Sam, I've got good news and bad news."

"What's the good news?"

"They've got softball up here in heaven. There's a beautiful playing field, it never rains, and there's a regular game every week."

"That's wonderful, but what's the bad news?"

"You're pitching Friday."

Did you hear about the new Cubs soup?

Two sips and then you choke.

Did you hear that the government of the Philippines is buying the Boston Red Sox?

They're going to rename them the Manila Folders.

Did you hear that (name of any poor fielder) tried to commit suicide?

He stood in the middle of the Interstate and a bus ran through his legs.

Or,

He tried to slash his wrists but the razor took a bad hop.

"Doc," said the obviously disturbed young man to his psychiatrist, "my problem is that I always dream about baseball. Nothing but baseball."

"Don't you ever dream about women?" asked the headshrinker.

"I don't dare," said the young man. "I'm afraid I'd lose my turn at bat."

"Don't try to palm any of this poison off on me," the aging star said. "Every one of these guys who recommended it is dead."

> —On bringing back a bottle of Scotch that bore an unfamiliar label but listed thereon six old kings of England who had declared this to be their favorite brand

GRACE: I don't understand baseball at all, do you?

SALLY: You don't have to understand it. Everything is decided by a man they call a vampire.

—*Baseball Digest,* August 1942

During a recent golf tournament, a player teed off at the first hole. He swung and missed. The crowd magnified the player's embarrassment as he promptly swung again and missed. Outraged, he threw his club as far as he could. And as luck—or lack of it— might have it, he missed several trees and a few people. He started to walk away, when a heckler from the crowd announced, "Why are you leaving now? . . . You've got a no-hitter going."

Gravity is a force. If it were not for gravity or gravitation you could throw a ball into the air and it would stay there. Under such conditions, the World Series could not take place.

How to Diaper a Baby

First, place the diaper in the position of a baseball diamond, with you at bat. Fold second base over home plate. Place baby on pitcher's mound. Then pin first base and third base to home plate.

—This set of instructions has been attributed to many players ("Yogi, I'm here alone and am trying to diaper the baby"), but is really an old comic routine.

"If you don't understand the game you won't enjoy it. I'll explain it to you. The first guy gets up to take his cut. Maybe he whiffs, maybe he gets on. Let's say he gets on. So then there is a guy on first. Then the second guy comes up to take his cut. Maybe he whiffs, maybe he gets on. Let's say . . ."

—Cabdriver explaining the game in a Nunnally Johnson story retold in Fred Schwed's *How to Watch a Baseball Game*

In an attempt to stimulate the interest of the boys in her classroom, an English teacher suggested they write an account of a baseball game as their assignment in English composition. The boys threw themselves into the task with enthusiasm. Within a few minutes, the first paper was handed to the teacher. When she opened it, the story read in its entirety: "Rain—no game today."

It takes longer to go from second to third base than from first to second because there's a shortstop between second and third.

Mickey Mantle, the great Yankee star, was walking in civilian clothes outside the Stadium and was obviously favoring his bad leg. A woman passing by asked a friend, "What's wrong with him?"

"He got hurt playing baseball."

"Won't they ever grow up?" the woman replied.

—1950s

MINISTER: Ah, good morning, Tip! Are you on your way to church?

SLUGGER: No, Reverend. We have a doubleheader with Louisville, and it's my big day.

MINISTER: Well, it's my big day too, but I'm in the right field.

SLUGGER: Is that so? Ain't that sun fierce?

Mrs. Green believed in sharing her husband's pleasures. Right now he was listening to the World Series broadcast, so she listened, too.

"The next batter is Joe DiMaggio," panted the announcer. "He let the first one go by for a called strike. Here comes the second pitch. Joe swings and lifts a long one to right field. There he goes around first, touches second and is on his way to third. The ball is returned to the infield and Joe pulls up at third. Ladies and gentlemen, Joe DiMaggio has just tripled."

Mrs. Green gasped. "Goodness," she said to her husband. "Did he hurt himself?"

Once during spring training, (fill in the name of any player who wears glasses) is stopped by the Florida State Police for speeding. The officer inspects the players license and says, "It says here that you are supposed to wear glasses. Where are your glasses?"

"I don't need glasses, I have contacts," replies the player.

"I don't care who you know," says the cop, "it says on your license you gotta have glasses."

> —This is an old *Mad* magazine joke which is sometimes told as true. It is, for instance, told about Phil Linz in one of the accounts of the late 1960s.

SHE: Oh, look, we have a man on every base.
HE: That's nothing, so has the other side.

> —1930s

The baseball game was tied, 3–3. It was the last half of the tenth inning, the bases were loaded, and the batter had a count of three balls and two strikes on him. Dusk was rapidly turning to darkness. The nervous pitcher called time and walked halfway to the batter's box to confer with the catcher.

"Look, Tom," he said, "it's getting so dark now that nobody can see the ball. I'll wind up and whip my arm down but I won't let go of the ball. You smack your fist into your glove and

make believe you've caught a strike. Maybe the umpire will call it that. It's worth a gamble."

The catcher agreed. But in the meantime the opposing team's coach had called the batter and had given him some instructions and sent him back to the plate.

The stage was set for the deciding pitch. The pitcher went through his motions and brought his arm down with a sharp snap of the wrist. The batter swung, there was the sound of ball against bat (the coach's sound effect), and the batter raced around the bases for a "home run."

The pitcher didn't say a word because he couldn't. If he had admitted that he still had the ball, the man on third would have scored on a balk.

> —From Frederick Meier's *Joke Tellers Joke Book*, 1944

The conceited new rookie was pitching his first game. He walked the first five men he faced and the manager took him out of the game. The rookie slammed his glove on the ground as he walked off and yelled, "Damn it, the jerk takes me out when I have a no-hitter going."

The first historical reference to baseball is in the Bible where, in Genesis 1:1, it says, "In the big inning."

> —This is often told in the context of a real person, for instance, in Kevin Nelson's *Baseball's Greatest Quotes*, the following is said by publicist Wilbur Evans about Texas baseball coach Bibb Falk: "Bibb is so dedicated to baseball that he thought the first verse in the Bible said, 'In the big inning, God created heaven and earth.'"

The neighbor of a rabid baseball fan met him on the streetcar one morning soon after the death of the pope. By way of conversation he started, "Well, I see they're going to select a new pope from the cardinals."

"That so?" answered the fan. "It's too bad then that Dizzy Dean isn't with them anymore."

> —Early version; other Cardinals appear in later examples

The symphony was playing Beethoven's Ninth. The two men who manned the bass horns were bored. Their only part was a couple of deep toots right at the end. They decided to sneak out to a tavern for a beer. They thought in all decency, though, they should give the director notice.

So they wrote a note which said, "Have gone across the street for a beer." They attached it by a paper clip to the last page, but made a mistake and clipped two pages together.

The director waved the baton expertly. Then he came to the next-to-the-last page, turned the sheet, and to his consternation found the note.

He stopped the music and announced in dismay, "It's the end of the Ninth, the score is tied, and the basses are loaded."

Wade Boggs, Steve Garvey, and Pete Rose are in a bar. A pretty woman walks by. "I'm going to ask her out," says Boggs. "You can't do that," says Garvey. "She's carrying my baby." To which Rose adds, "Wanna bet?"

> —1989

"What a day!" exclaimed the businessman as he boarded the evening elevated for his ride home. "One of the boys at the office asked for the afternoon off so that he might attend his grandmother's funeral. I was rather suspicious so I told him I'd accompany him."

The other businessman chuckled and replied, "That was a great idea. Was the game a good one?"

"That's where I made my mistake," sadly admitted the first businessman. "It was his grandmother's funeral."

> —This from a day when bogus funerals were a common excuse for going to a day game

When the New York Yankees visited Puerto Rico in the course of spring training, the Don Q Rum Company staged a great banquet for the ballplayers, newspaper correspondents, and local bigwigs. With every toast, the party grew more convivial. The remarks of Red Smith, *Tribune* sportswriter, were broadcast. He did nobly, but kept referring to his hosts as the "makers of that wonderful Bacardi Run." Every time he said "Bacardi," a mortified Don Q official would jump up and correct him with, "Don Q, señor, Don Q." And every time Red Smith would answer graciously, "You're welcome."

Worst Tag of 1963—The guy who suggested the Phils make a movie of their second-base combination called *Days Wine and Rojas*.

JONES, CLEON

"Some people still might not believe in us, but then some people still think the world is flat."

> —As a Met after winning the 1969 World Series, *The Sporting News Chronicle of 20th Century Sport*

JONES, TODD

"I only pitch one inning. So by the time they realize I don't have anything, the inning's over."

> —On himself; quoted on Motowntigers.com, a Web site for Tigers fans, under the heading "Todd Jones said what?" 2006.

"It may not be pretty, but, most of the time, I get the job done. If the fans can't stand to watch me pitch, just go up and get a hot dog, or go in the kitchen for a sandwich. And, in 15, 20 pitches, it'll be over."

> —As a Tiger, advice to fans on the eve of the 2006 playoffs, in Jack Curry, "Way with Words Helps Jones in His Second Job," *New York Times,* October 27, 2006

"The man has been amazing all year. He's the only guy I know who can wave his hand and make your sandwich taste better."

> —On manager Jim Leyland; quoted on Motowntigers.com, a Web site for Tigers fans, under the heading, "Todd Jones said what?" 2006.

JORDAN, MICHAEL

"I'm not out there sweating for three hours every day just to find out what it feels like to sweat."

> —As a basketball superstar and baseball rookie, *Newsweek,* January 24, 1994

JORDAN, PAT

"My brother [George] and I left no detail unperfected. We discussed the proper way for a pitcher to wear his uniform, and we decided that a fastball pitcher, like myself, should let his pants' legs fall well below his knee before fastening them. Only infielders and pitchers without 'stuff' wore their pant legs fastened at the knees. 'Besides,' my brother said, 'it'll make you look taller in the eyes of the scouts.'"

> —*A False Spring* (New York: Dodd, Mead)

"Success in baseball requires the synthesis of a great many virtues, many of which have nothing to do with sheer talent. Self-discipline, single-mindedness, perseverance, ambition—these were all virtues I was positive I possessed in 1960, but which I've discovered over the years I did not."

> —*A False Spring*

JOSS, NORMAN

"There have been so few perfect games. So very few. And John Lee Richmond, who pitched the first one, ended up as a mathematics teacher at Scott High School in Toledo. I was in his plane geometry class and a nice old man he was. But on the first day of school, he said to me, 'Now look. Your father pitched a perfect game.' Well, so did I. And it doesn't mean anything here. The fact that your father did the same thing isn't going to help you with plane geometry.'"

—The son of Addie Joss, who had in 1908 pitched the fourth perfect game in history. Norman Joss made the statement to Lee Allen in 1963; quoted in *Cooperstown Corner*

JUST, WARD

"Watching a baseball game on television is like chasing the great white whale in a goldfish bowl. It trivializes everything: men two inches high, a ball the size of a bee. It is like looking at the heavens through a dime-store telescope."

—From "Your Ear on the Ball," *New York Times,* April 17, 1984

K

KAAT, JIM

"Every ball park used to be unique. Now it's like women's breasts—if you've seen one, you've seen both."

— His irreverence at work; widely quoted

"I'll never be considered one of the all-time greats, maybe not even one of the all-time goods. But I'm one of the all-time survivors."

— As a Cardinal pitcher

"There's the Hall of Fame and there's the Hall of Achievement and there's also the Hall of Enjoyment. I just hope to be enshrined in the Hall of Enjoyment for a bit longer."

— On his baseball longevity as a Cardinal

"You make a choice on how you want to leave this game. You can go out on your terms or on baseball's terms. If you go out on your terms, you do it like Stargell did, or Bench. But if you say, 'I want to play this game as long as I can,' then you understand you're not going to leave on your own terms."

— Quoted by Paul Domowitz, Knight-Ridder, at the time of Steve Carlton's retirement, 1988

Jim Kaat (*St. Louis Cardinals*)

KAEGEL, DICK

"There are times when the most verbose player will choose not to speak. There are times when a reporter deserves to have a question spit back in his face. But when silence becomes policy, it is not golden."

—As a *Sporting News* alumnus; quoted in the *Sporting News*, July 22, 1978

KAELIN, E. F.

"In all but a very few instances baseball fails to generate any kind of dramatic unity."

—"The Well-Played Game: Notes Toward an Aesthetics of Sport," in Ellen W. Gerber, ed., *Sport and the Body: A Philosophical Symposium*, 1974

KAHAN, OSCAR

"April 1, 1972, will go down as a black date in sports to mark the first general strike."

—The assistant managing editor of the *Sporting News*, in the newspaper, on baseball's first strike

KAHN, ROGER

"A major league baseball team is a collection of 25 youngish men who have made the major leagues and discovered that in spite of it, life remains distressingly short of ideal. A bad knee still throbs before a rainstorm. Too much beer still makes for an unpleasant fullness. Girls still insist on tiresome preliminaries. And now there is a wife who gets headaches or a baby who has colic."

—From "Intellectuals and Ballplayers," *American Scholar*, November 3, 1957

"Football is violence and cold weather and sex and college rye. Horse racing is animated roulette. Boxing is smoky halls and kidneys battered until they bleed. Tennis and golf are best played, not watched. Basketball, hockey and track meets are action heaped upon action, climax upon climax, until the onlooker's responses become deadened. Baseball is for the leisurely afternoons of summer and for the unchanging dreams."

—"Intellectuals and Ballplayers"

"For the Washington Senators, the worst time of the year is the baseball season."

—His often-quoted killer line for the team that left town twice

"It is something to cry about, being an athlete who does not die young."

—Quoted by Jim Bouton in *I'm Glad You Didn't Take It Personally*

"Losing after great striving is the story of man, who was born to sorrow, whose sweetest songs tell of saddest thought, and who, if he is a hero, does nothing in life as becomingly as leaving it. A whole country was stirred by the high deeds and thwarted longings of The Duke, Preacher, Pee Wee, Skoonj and the rest. The team was awesomely good and yet defeated. Their skills lifted everyman's spirit and their defeat joined them with everyman's existence, a national team, with a country in thrall, irresistible and unable to beat the Yankees."

—*The Boys of Summer*

"The romance between intellectuals and the game of baseball is, for the most part, one-sided to the point of absurdity. A large percentage of intelligent Americans evaluate the four hundred men who play major league baseball as awesomely gifted demigods. A large percentage of the muscular four hundred rate intellectuals several notches below umpires."

—*The Second Fireside Book of Baseball,* edited by Charles Einstein

"Yes, I thought, this was how it was to go to a ball game once. This was what it was like to sit in the cheap seats and follow a ball game as a knowledgeable fan. This was how it was when William Mays was young and all the grass was real and the bleachers were a haven, rather than a place of menace where strange young people throw golf balls at the heads of visiting outfielders.

"I have not simply sentimentalized the past, I thought. There really was a 1954."

—From the introduction to the 1982 edition of Arnold Hano's *A Day in the Bleachers*

"You learn to leave some mysteries alone. At 28, I was susceptible to suggestions that I explain—not describe but explain—baseball in America. I published in small quarterlies. I addressed a Columbia seminar, and I developed a showy proficiency at responding to editors who asked me to equate the game in terms of Americana.

"Such phrases now bang against my brain like toothaches. I never look at the old pieces anymore, but I remember some generalizations I drew.

"Baseball is not played against a clock. (But neither is tennis, golf or four-handed gin rummy.)

"Baseball rules have barely changed across generations. (Neither have the rules of water polo.)

"The ball field is a mystic creation, the Stonehenge of America. That is, the bases are a magic 90 feet apart. Think how often a batter is thrown out by half a step, compared to instances when he outruns a hit to shortstop. But artificial surfaces have lately changed the nature, if not the dimensions, of the diamond. A ground ball at Riverfront Stadium moves much faster than the same grounder bouncing on the honest grass of Wrigley Field. Yet at last look, baseball in Cincinnati seemed to be surviving. Batters there are also thrown out by half a step.

"Suppose the bases had been set 80 to 86 feet apart. The fielders simply would have positioned themselves differently, and a ground ball to short would still be a ground ball to short, 6–3 in everybody's scorebook.

"I do believe this: baseball's inherent rhythm, minutes and minutes of passivity erupting into seconds of frenzied action, matches an attribute of the American character. But no existential proclamation, or any tortured neo-Freudianism, or any outburst of popular sociology, not even—or least of all—my own, explains baseball's lock on the American heart.

"You learn to let some mysteries alone, and when you do, you find they sing themselves."

—"Still a Grand Old Game," *Sports Illustrated,* August 16, 1976

"You may glory in a team triumphant, but you fall in love with a team in defeat."

—Widely attributed

KALINE, AL

"I don't deserve such a salary. I didn't have a good enough season last year. This ball club has been so fair and decent to me that I'd prefer to have you give it to me when I rate it."

—To Tiger GM Jim Campbell in 1971 when offered the club's first $100,000 contract; quoted by Arthur Daley in the *New York Times,* January 28, 1973

KANEHL, ROD

"Baseball is a lot like life. The line drives are caught, the squibbers go for base hits. It's an unfair game."

—The New York Mets infielder in 1963; quoted in *The Jocks* by Leonard Shecter

"There isn't anything to the pivot, if you have guts enough to stand there."

—Quoted by Leonard Shecter in *The Jocks*

"You saw it, write it."

—Pat response to writers who asked him about a play; quoted in *The Incredible Mets* by Maury Allen

KASKO, EDDIE

"I'll turn the game over to the players. I'll let them run on their own, hit their pitch, call their game. I'll never call a pitch from the dugout. Never have and never will."

—As freshman manager of the Red Sox; quoted in the *Sporting News,* April 4, 1970

KAUFFMAN, EWING

"Baseball has 24 teams and the owners have inherited wealth, or become wealthy themselves. They are self-confident, egotistical, even egocentric, and need a broad, strong hand in order to keep baseball running smoothly."

—The Royals' owner in federal court January 7, 1977; quoted in the next day's *Washington Post*

KAUFMAN, REVEREND THOMAS H.

"The Babe died a beautiful death. He said his prayers and lapsed into a sleep. He died in his sleep."

—Announcing the death of Babe Ruth, Memorial Hospital, New York, August 16, 1948

KEATING, SENATOR KENNETH

"Baseball needs no defenders or justification. It is part of the very fabric of our society—just as much as if it were written into our constitution.

"[The game] has been part of the growth of America. This was never more apparent than during the days of the war when the entire nation found in baseball a great and certain tranquilizer that was as vital to our security as the sword and shield of our armed might."

—In a speech to the National Association of Professional baseball Leagues convention, November 28, 1962. Keating was a long supporter of organized baseball. He helped defend organized baseball during the congressional investigations of the 1950s.

"'German troops tried to get behind our lines as spy cover, but baseball proved to be the chink in their well-planned armor,' he related. 'Our forces would halt the jeeps at road blocks and ask such questions as: "For which team does Bob Feller pitch? What position does Joe DiMaggio play? What's the nickname of the team in Brooklyn?"

"'No screening process ever proved more successful. Baseball was used as a weapon of war to save lives.'"

> —On how U.S. military personnel made use of baseball during World War II to break up infiltration of spies dressed in the khaki of captured American forces, November 28, 1962

"'I'm still not sure what he said,' related the Senator, 'but he did say it well.'

"'I'd like to have Yogi Berra testify, too. The sight of him taking the fifth amendment would be worth all the trouble.'"

> —On Casey Stengel during the congressional baseball investigations of the 1950s; quoted in the *Sporting News*, November 28, 1962

KEELER, WEE WILLIE

"Hit 'em where they ain't."

> —As the greatest place hitter in baseball, he summarized his batting tactics this way. Bill Stern called him "the most wonderful hitter that ever lived."

KEEN, S. A.

"Any city that champions Base Ball as a means of material prosperity will come to learn that substantial growth must be built on something broader than a base ball bat, and have a boom of more fiber than the huzzas of a past-time Park. A Radical Godliness repudiates Base Ball as a way of sinners. . . .

"Base Ball stands chargeable with:

"First—Nourishing loaferism, it manufactures bummers. It is growing a crop of hoodlums. It literally breeds idleness and good-for-nothing-ness.

"Second—It stimulates spendthrift, reckless, cruel, dishonest spendthrift.

"Third—It fosters gambling. Its very spirit of competition is the taproot of gambling. . . . It is the most stupendous gambling hell extant.

"Fourth—It depreciates personal character. The whole performance of base ball is physical. It is an exhibition of muscle. It doesn't take brains to be a professional on that arena. The whole air of the institution is coarse. Taking all its environments, who can really witness a game of base ball that has any fine sentiment does not feel it lowered, and does not come from it depreciated in tone by the very spectacle.

"Fifth—It impairs business habits. It ungirds the mind for accuracy, fidelity and enthusiasm in business and professional life."

> —From sermon by Dr. S. A. Keen at Roberts Park Methodist Episcopal Church, Indianapolis; quoted originally in *Indiana Phalanx*, May 17, 1888. Requoted by Lindley H. Clark Jr., "Baseball Is Sinful—Especially If You Lose," *Wall Street Journal*, October 14, 1986

KEILLOR, GARRISON

"I am so sorry about all them lying dead on the hill, the trooper from the First Minnesota and all the old women and the farmers . . . and I wish my speech had been great, just as I wish I could bring them all back to life, but it's over and now summer can begin. School can let out. Baseball gets going and the sweet corn begins to get serious."

> —From the essay "How I Came to Give the Memorial Day Address at the Lake Wobegon Cemetery This Year," *We Are Still Married* (1989). It is the only baseball quotation to appear in Catherine Frank's *Quotations for All Occasions* (2000).

"Spit frequently. Spit at all crucial moments. Spit correctly. Spit should be *blown*, not ptu-ied weakly with the lips, which often results in dribble. Spitting should convey forceful-ness of purpose, concentration, pride. Spit down, not in the direction of others. Spit in the glove and on the fingers, especially after making a real knucklehead play; it's a way of saying, 'I dropped the ball because my glove was dry.'"

> —*Happy to Be Here*

"The Babe was a legend then, much like God is today. He didn't give interviews, in other words."

> —On the visit by Babe Ruth in November 1946 to Lake Wobegon, from "Lake Wobegon Games," *Sports Illustrated*, December 22, 1986

KELLEY, STEVE

"Before Gibson, the Dodgers were a team of wimps. Gibson put some growl back into the team. He is a gamer, an overgrown Pete Rose. He is Stallone without a script, Kirkbo. He is Mike Tyson without a driving record. He is the Boz and Butkus of baseball. As a mat-ter of fact, baseball seems almost too tame a game for him. He needs a sport with more hitting. Jungle warfare maybe."

> —The *Seattle Times* columnist on Kirk Gibson; quoted in the *Sporting News*, October 3, 1988

KELLY, MIKE "KING"

"I thinks, me lads, this is me last slide."

> —The record base-stealer, on his deathbed in 1894. He died of pneumonia.

"It depends on the length of the game."

> —Attributed to him as the answer to the question, "Do you drink while playing baseball?"

"We always wore the best uniforms that money could get, Spalding saw to that. We had big wide trousers, tight-fitting jerseys, with the arms cut out clear to the shoulder, and every man had on a different cap. We wore silk stockings. When we marched on a field with our big six-footers out in front it used to be a case of 'eat 'em up, Jake.' We had most of 'em whipped before we threw a ball. They were scared to death."

> —On the Chicago White Stockings of 1882, from an interview with the *New York Sun*

KEMP, STEVE

"It's not easy to hit .215. You have to be going terrible and have bad luck, too."

> —On a batting slump; quoted in the *Sporting News*, July 22, 1985

KENDALL, JASON

"Yesterday some guy told me he came all the way out here from Pittsburgh so his kids could meet me. They were twins. A boy and a girl, named Jason and Kendall. Can you believe that? I mean, what do you say to that? Thanks?"

> —The A's catcher on a strange incident at spring training (MLB.com; cited by John Erhardt in *Baseball Prospectus in the Year in Quotes*, 2006)

Steve Kemp (*Detroit Tigers*)

John F. Kennedy Opening Day, 1961 (*John Fitzgerald Kennedy Library*)

KENNEDY, JOHN F.

"A couple of years ago they told me I was too young to be President and you were too old to be playing baseball. But we fooled them."

> —To Stan Musial of the St. Louis Cardinals at the 1962 All-Star Game in Washington, D.C. Kennedy was forty-five at the time, and Musial was three years younger; quoted in A. K. Adams, *Home Book of Humorous Quotations*

"Last year, more Americans went to symphonies than went to baseball games. This may be viewed as an alarming statistic, but I think that both baseball and the country will endure."

> —*The Kennedy Wit*, edited by Bill Adler

KENNEDY, TERRY

"'I didn't hit like that in the Pony League,' Giants catcher Terry Kennedy said. 'I don't even hit like that in my fantasies. . . . I'm sure that when [Willie] Mays and Mantle were hitting 50 home runs, this is what they looked like.'"

—On Giant Kevin Mitchell, *USA Today*, June 16, 1989

"We play like King Kong one day and like Fay Wray the next."

—As a Padre, *Sports Illustrated*, May 9, 1983

KENNEDY, WILLIAM

"No ball player anywhere moved his body any better than Franny Phalen, a damn fieldin' machine, fastest ever was.

"Francis remembered the color and shape of his glove, its odor of oil and sweat and leather, and he wondered if Annie had kept it. Apart from his memory and a couple of clippings, it would be all that remained of a spent career that had blossomed and then peaked in the big leaguers; far too long after the best years were gone, but which brought with the peaking the promise that some belated and over-due glory was possible, that somewhere there was a hosannah to be cried in the name of Francis Phelan, one of the best sonsabitches ever to kick a toe into third base."

—*Ironweed*, 1984

KENT, JEFF

"I wanted to be Albert Pujols or David Ortiz for one day. Sometimes that's a hell of a lot better than being Jeff Kent."

—As Astros second baseman, after winning Game 5 of the NLCS with a ninth-inning home run, October 18, 2004; quoted from the *Orange County Register*

KERFELD, CHARLIE

"People in New York have black teeth, and their breath smells of beer. And the men are even worse."

—Astros reliever; quoted by Thom Loverro in the *Washington Times*, January 2, 2000

KERN, JIM

"I told him I wasn't tired. He told me, 'No, but the outfielders sure are.'"

—As a Rangers pitcher, recalling a moment when he was removed for a reliever, *Sports Illustrated*, April 9, 1979

KEROUAC, JACK

"To while away the time I play my solitaire card baseball game Lionel and I invented in 1942 when we visited Lowell and the pipes froze for Christmas—the game is between the Pittsburgh Plymouths (my oldest team, and now barely on top of the 2nd division) and the New York Chevvies rising from the cellar ignominiously since they were world champions last year—I shuffle my deck, write out the lineups, and lay out the teams—For hundreds of miles around, black night, the lamps of Desolation are lit, to a childish sport, but the Void is a child too—"

—*Desolation Angels*

"When I grew to the grave maturity of 11 or 12, I saw, one crisp October morning, in the back Textile field, a great pitching performance by a husky strangely old-looking 14-year-older, or 13—a very heroic-looking boy in the morning. . . . his name was Boldieu, it immediately stuck in my mind with Beaulieu—street where I learned to cry and be scared of the dark and of my brother for many years (till almost 10)—this proved to me that all my life wasn't black."

—*Dr. Sax*; quoted by Raymond Mungo in *Confessions from Left Field*

KERRANE, KEVIN

"Scouts don't scout in order to get rich. They scout because they know baseball—from direct experience, not tests—and because they're opinionated men. You could fire them all tomorrow and hire scientists and buy machines, and you'd wind up with lots of numbers and not too many clear recommendations, where a guy is ready to put his own individual ass on the line. It's a unique job. Sometimes I think scouts are like the last real Americans."

—*The Dollar $ign on the Muscle*

KIERAN, JOHN

"Heigh-ho! What a life!"

—On spring training, from his *The American Sporting Scene*, 1941

Idol of cheering millions
Records are yours by the sheaves.
Iron of frame they hailed you
And decked you with laurel leaves.

—On Lou Gehrig; quoted by Raymond Mungo in *Confessions from Left Field*.

With vim and verve he walloped the curve
From Texas to Duluth.
Which is no small task,
And I rise to ask:
Was there ever a guy like Ruth?

—On Babe Ruth, "Baseball," in *The American Sporting Scene*, 1941

KIERNAN, THOMAS

"Indeed, thereafter, and until the time of the assassination of a president twelve years later, the flight of a baseball—that tiny, stitched sphere which streaked with the suddenness of lightning through the gathering dusk below Coogan's Bluff on October 3, 1951, and upon whose trajectory the miracle stunningly unfurled like a banner from heaven—was the single most commonly recalled event in the American experience since the death of yet an earlier president in 1945."

—*The Miracle at Coogan's Bluff* (New York: Thomas Y. Crowell, 1975)

KILLEFER, BILL

"Speed is the basis of successful baseball. It's the watchword of the winning club. It's the most worthwhile talent a club can possess. The proper way to build up a club is to depend upon youth and speed."

—The player and manager; quoted in his obituary in the *Sporting News*. He was a prime advocate of speed as key to a winning team.

KINER, RALPH

"All of his saves have come during relief appearances."

> —On relief pitcher Steve Bedrosian, who was recently traded from the Philadelphia Phillies to the San Francisco Giants; quoted in *Sports Illustrated*, July 5, 1989. Before the month was out, the magazine was able to report this Kinerism: "All of the Mets' road wins against Los Angeles this year have been at Dodger Stadium."

"Cadillacs are down at the end of the bat."

> —In response to being asked why he didn't choke up. In his *Book of Sports Quotes*, Bert Randolph Sugar notes this is often misquoted as: "Home-run hitters drive Cadillacs."

"He's going to be out of action the rest of his career."

> —On Bruce Sutter's career-ending injury; quoted in the *Sporting News*, July 10, 1989

"I don't think we had the pressures then that ballplayers have now, because there was no television."

> —As an announcer on television

"It's like watching Mario Andretti park a car."

> —Describing Phil Niekro's knuckleball, as an announcer

"Two-thirds of the earth is covered by water, the other one- third is covered by Garry Maddox."

> —As a sportscaster, one of his most requoted lines

KING, ADMIRAL ERNEST F.

"Baseball has a rightful place in America at war. All work and no play seven days a week would soon take its toll on national morale."

> —As commander in chief of the U.S. Fleet; quoted in the January 1943 *Baseball Digest*

KING, MARTIN LUTHER JR.

"Jackie Robinson made it possible for me in the first place. Without him, I would never have been able to do what I did."

> —From David Faulkner's *Great Time Coming: The Life of Jackie Robinson from Baseball to Birmingham*. Faulkner's footnote on the quotation states that King made the statement to Wyatt Tee Walker, one of King's oldest aides.

KING, STEPHEN

"The first time anyone suggested to these boys that they must come to love each other while they were on the field, they laughed uneasily at the idea. Now they don't laugh. After enduring the Hampden Horns together, they seem to understand—at least, a little."

> —In the April 16, 1990, *New Yorker*, reporting on his son's Little League baseball team

KINNAMON, BILL

"If you're not an extrovert and you're not at least 5-feet 10-inches tall, you probably won't make it. Most ballplayers figure they can intimidate any small man and they act that way. If he doesn't put them down early and gain their respect right away, he's gone. That's the personal side of it. Mechanically, an umpire must have agility, stamina and be able to run. He's also got to be willing to umpire with pain, because men working the plate often get hit with four tips going 100 miles per hour. That's the physical side of it. An umpire is constantly being tested by managers, coaches and players, so he can't have rabbit ears. Quick decisions aren't that hard if the man is in position. What's hard is making sure they are based on reason. When an umpire throws someone out of the game, 99 percent of the time it's for abusive language and is specifically covered in the rule book. But a player, coach or manager can also be sent to the showers for fighting, throwing a bat or deliberately bumping an umpire. That's the mental side of it."

> —As a former umpire on being an umpire; quoted in the *Christian Science Monitor,* March 3, 1975

"I sincerely believe that you cannot be introverted and be a great official. You must be extroverted to the nth degree. You must have the feeling that you are more than capable of going out there and handling the job. If there is any doubt in your mind, you are never going to make it. You have got to be able to meet people on any level of life and walk up to them as an equal. A major league umpire can walk up to anybody and not be cowed one bit."

> —American League umpire; quoted in Larry R. Gerlach, *The Men in Blue* (New York: Viking Press, 1980)

KINSELLA, W. P.

"A ballpark at night is more like a church than a church. . . . An empty ballpark at night must be like the inside of a pyramid."

> —*Shoeless Joe*

"For some reason, I recall the question at the bottom of the form sent by the Baseball Hall of Fame to everyone who has ever played organized baseball: 'If you had it to do over again, would you play professional baseball?'

"The historian at Cooperstown, Clifford S. Kachline, said he couldn't recall even one ex-player answering 'no' to the question. I wonder if any other profession can say the same?"

> —*Shoeless Joe*

"Annie and I were in Cooperstown once. We looked at Shoeless Joe Jackson's shoes reposing under glass. 'How come a guy named Shoeless Joe had shoes?' Annie wanted to know."

> —*Shoeless Joe*

"'I loved the game,' Shoeless Joe went on. 'I'd have played for food money. I'd have played free and worked for food. It was the game, the parks, the smells, the sounds. Have you ever held a bat or a baseball to your face? The varnish, the leather. And it was the crowd, the excitement of them rising as one when the ball was hit deep. The sound was like a chorus. Then there was the chug-a-lug of the tin lizzies in the parking lots, and the hotels with their brass spittoons in the lobbies and brass beds in the rooms. It makes me tingle all over like a kid on his way to his first double-header, just to talk about it.'"

> —*Shoeless Joe*

KINSELLA, W. P. (CONTINUED)

"It is the same game that Moonlight Graham played in 1905. It is a living part of history, like calico dresses, stone crockery, and threshing crews eating at outdoor tables. It continually reminds us of what was, like an Indian-head penny in a handful of new coins."

—Shoeless Joe

"The play reaffirms what I already know—that baseball is the most perfect of games, solid, true, pure and precious as diamonds. If only life were so simple. I have often thought, If only there was a framework to life, rules to live by. But suddenly I see, like a silver flash of lightning on the horizon, a meaning I have never grasped before.

"I feel as if I've escaped from my skin, as if I left a dry shell of myself back in Iowa. My skin is so new and pink it feels raw to my touch; it's as if I've peeled off a blister that covered my whole body. Within the baselines anything can happen. Tides can reverse, oceans can open. That's why they say, 'The game is never over until the last man is out.' Colors can change, lives can alter, anything is possible in this gentle, flawless, loving game."

—Shoeless Joe

"Three years ago at dusk on a spring evening, when the sky was a robin's-egg blue and the wind as soft as a day-old chick, I was sitting on the verandah of my farm home in eastern Iowa when a voice very clearly said to me, 'If you build it, he will come.'"

—Shoeless Joe

KIRKE, BILL

Matty! Matty!
Drives Cincy batty!

—As a writer for the *New York Journal* on Christy Mathewson, who never seemed to lose to Cincinnati (at one point he had won 30 straight from the Reds).

KIRSHENBAUM, JERRY

"McWhirter has committed most of his *Guinness Book of World Records* 15,000 entries to memory, a feat he explains by saying, 'It's the same as a boy memorizing information about baseball. It's a matter of being interested.'"

—On Norris McWhirter in *Sports Illustrated,* July 30, 1979

KISSINGER, HENRY

"Baseball is the most intellectual game because most of the action goes on in your head."

—Widely attributed

"He could lift baseball above itself. There were better players probably, but there was only one Joe DiMaggio."

—Former secretary of state; quoted in the April 26, 1999, *Chicago Sun Times* at the time of DiMaggio's death

KLEM, BILL

"Baseball is more than a game to me—it's a religion."

—He said this in 1941 at "Bill Klem Day" at the Polo Grounds when he was given a commemorative plague by a group of sportswriters.

"Don't cross the Rio Grande!"

—His way of warning players not to cross a line—sometimes called "Klem's Line"—that he had drawn in the dirt; quoted by Robert Smith in *Baseball's Hall of Fame*.

"Fix your eye on the ball from the moment the pitcher holds it in his glove. Follow it as he throws to the plate and stay with it until the play is completed. Action takes place only where the ball goes."

—Quoted by Frank Frisch in *Sports*, October 1954

Bill Klem (*Library of Congress Prints and Photographs, Bain Collection*)

"For thirty years, Judge, and I always paid off one hundred cents on the dollar."

—What he said to Judge Landis when asked if he had ever bet on horse races

"Gentlemen, he was out . . . because I said he was out."

—After being shown photographic evidence that he had blown a call

"It ain't nothin' till I call it."

—Quoted in *You Can't Beat the Hours* by Mel Allen and Ed Fitzgerald

"I told the umpires to walk back at least 35 feet from home plate. That reduced the arguments. An angry player can't argue with the back of an umpire who is walking away."

—On reacting to a called third strike; quoted in the *Sporting News* by Jimmy Burns, 1948

"Maybe, but I wouldn't have if I had a bat."

—To Hack Wilson, who claimed that Klem missed a pitch

"Mr. Klem, to you, and don't you ever forget it!"

—To any player or manager who called him Bill during a game

"Son, when you pitch a strike Mr. Hornsby will let you know it."

—To a rookie pitcher who complained that the pitches Rogers Hornsby did not swing at were always called balls by umpire Klem

KLEM, BILL (CONTINUED)

"That guy in a twenty-five-cent bleacher seat is as much entitled to know a call as the guy in the boxes. He can see my arm signal even if he can't hear my voice."

—On his pioneering use of hand signals; quoted in *Games, Asterisks, and People* by Ford C. Frick

"The best umpired game is the game in which the fans cannot recall the umpires who worked it. If they don't recognize you, you can enjoy your dinner knowing you did a perfect job."

—Quoted in *Games, Asterisks, and People* by Ford C. Frick

"The most cowardly thing in the world is blaming mistakes upon the umpires. Too many managers strut around on the field trying to manage the umpires instead of their teams."

—Quoted by Jimmy Burns, the *Sporting News,* 1948

"They realized that I umpired the ball. They knew that I was fair, and that I wouldn't take any foolishness."

—On his career; quoted by Jimmy Burns, 1948, in the *Sporting News*

"There are 154 games in a season and you can find 154 reasons why your team should have won every one of them."

—Widely attributed

"Young man, if that bat comes down . . . you're out of the game."

—To Jake Powell, who had just thrown his bat in the air. This may be true, but it has also been attributed to a number of other umpires ejecting disgruntled sluggers.

"Your job is to umpire for the ball and not the player."

—One of his most famous credos

KNEPPER, BOB

"This is not an occupation a woman should be in. In God's society, woman was created in a role of submission to the husband. It's not that woman is inferior, but I don't believe women should be in a leadership role."

—Remarks from Knepper, Houston Astros pitcher and a fundamentalist Christian, regarding Pam Postema, a woman umpire, spring 1988. Needless to say, the quotation—and the sentiment behind it—became an immediate source of controversy.

These are the basic rules of the game which evolved into the modern game of baseball. They were the twenty rules first adopted by Alexander J. Cartwright and a band of New Yorkers on September 23, 1845, the same day on which they gave themselves the name Knickerbockers.

1st. Members must strictly observe the time agreed upon for exercise, and be punctual in their attendance.

2nd. When assembled for exercise, the President, or in his absence, the Vice-President, shall appoint an Umpire, who shall keep the game in a book provided for that purpose, and note all violations of the By-Laws and Rules during the time of exercise.

3rd. The presiding officer shall designate two members as Captains, who shall retire and make the match to be played, observing at the same time that the players put opposite to each other should be as nearly equal as possible, the choice of sides to be then tossed for, and the *first in hand* to be decided in like manner.

4th. The bases shall be from "home to second base, forty-two paces, from first to third base, forty-two paces, equidistant.

5th. No stump match shall be played on a regular day of exercise.

6th. If there should not be a sufficient number of members of the Club present at the time agreed upon to commence exercise, gentlemen not members may be chosen in to make up the match, which *shall not be broken up* to take in members that may afterwards appear, but, in all cases, members shall have the preference, when present, at the making of a match.

7th. If members appear after the game is commenced they may be chosen in if mutually agreed upon.

8th. The game to consist of twenty-one counts, or aces, but at the conclusion an equal number of hands must be played.

9th. The ball must be pitched, and not thrown, for the bat.

10th. A ball knocked out of the field, or outside the range of the first and third base, is foul.

11th. Three balls being struck at and missed and the last one caught, is a hand out, if not caught is considered fair, and the striker bound to run.

12th. If a ball be struck, or tipped, and caught, either flying or on the first bound, it is a hand out.

13th. A player running the bases shall be out, if the ball is in the hands of an adversary on the base, or the runner is touched with it before he makes his base, it being understood, however, that in no instance is a ball to be thrown at him.

14th. A player running who shall prevent an adversary from catching or getting the ball before making his base, is a hand out.

15th. Three hands out, all out.

16th. Players must take their strike in regular turn.

17th. All disputes and differences relative to the game, to be decided by the Umpire, from which there is no appeal.

18th. No ace or base can be made on a foul strike.

19th. A runner cannot be put out in making one base, when a balk is made by the pitcher.

20th. But one base allowed when a ball bounds out of the field when struck.

An additional rule was adopted at the club's fourth annual meeting (April 1, 1848) which stated that the player running to first base is out without being touched with the ball if the fielder on first is holding the ball.

The rules were amended and expanded in 1854.

KNOWLES, DAROLD

"There isn't enough mustard in the whole world to cover that hot dog."

—On Reggie Jackson, 1974

KOOSMAN, JERRY

"I figured I'd better sign before I owed them money."

—On signing for $1,200 with the Mets; he had originally been offered $1,600. The figure kept dropping until Koosman finally gave in and signed.

"I used to be so bad my bat would close its eyes when I came up."

—Quoted by Maury Allen in the *New York Post* and requoted in *Baseball Digest*, August 1971

Jerry Koosman (*New York Mets*)

KOPPETT, LEONARD

"Baseball owners are capitalists, pure and simple, in an age when pure and simple capitalists are harder to find every day."

—*All About Baseball*

"Fear.

"Fear is the fundamental factor in hitting, and hitting the ball with the bat is the fundamental act of baseball.

"The fear is simple and instinctive. If a baseball, thrown hard, hits any part of your body, it hurts. If it hits certain vulnerable areas, like elbows, wrist or face, it can cause broken bones and other serious injuries. If it hits a particular area of an unprotected head, it can kill.

"A thrown baseball, in short, is a missile, and an approaching missile generates a reflexive action: get out of the way.

"This fact—and it is an unyielding fact that the reflex always exists in all humans—is the starting point for the game of baseball, and yet it is that least often mentioned by those who write about baseball."

—*A Thinking Man's Guide to Baseball* by Leonard Koppett

KOUFAX, SANDY

"A guy who throws what he intends to throw—that's the definition of a good pitcher."

—Widely quoted, but it probably first appeared in a *Los Angeles Times* interview of March 31, 1971

"Belonging to a baseball club is like being a member of a social club, Rotary or the Knights of Columbus. Only more so. Instead of dropping in every Wednesday night to listen to the minutes of the last meeting and shoot some pool, you are out with the boys every night.

"In other ways, however, a ball club is nothing at all like a social club. Players are from widely differing backgrounds and have widely differing outside interests. If not for this one common bond, an ability to play baseball better than almost anybody else in the country, it is rather unlikely that any two of us would ever have met. But the differences mean nothing. There is, among us, a far closer relationship than the purely social one of a fraternal organization because we are bound together not only by a single interest but by a common goal. To win. Nothing else matters, and nothing else will do."

—Sandy Koufax with Ed Linn, "What Baseball Means to Me," *Look*, July 26, 1966

"I became a good pitcher when I stopped trying to make them miss the ball and started trying to make them hit it."

—*A Thinking Man's Guide to Baseball*

"I can't believe that Babe Ruth was a better player than Willie Mays. Ruth is probably to baseball what Arnold Palmer is to golf. He got the game moving. But I can't believe he could run as well as Mays, and I can't believe he was any better an outfielder."

—From a *Los Angeles Times* clipping

"I think it's incredible because there were guys like Mays and Mantle and Henry Aaron who were great players for 10 years. . . . I only had four or five good years."

—Quoted in *Hammerin' Hank* by Dan Schlossberg

Koufax, Sandy (continued)

"If I could straighten it out, I'd be pitching at Dodger Stadium tonight."

—The former Los Angeles Dodgers pitcher, when told to keep his arm straight while golfing

"If there was any magic formula, it was getting to pitch every fourth day."

—Explaining early successes; widely attributed

"It's surprising that baseball hasn't had to update anything since Ty Cobb. On a ground ball in the hole, a fast man's still out by a step and a slow man by two steps."

—Quoted in Thomas Boswell, "Koufax: Passing the Art Along," in *How Life Imitates the World Series* (Garden City, N.Y.: Doubleday, 1982)

"I've got a lot of years to live after baseball. And I would like to live them with the complete use of my body."

—Announcing his retirement, November 18, 1966. According to Phil Pepe in *No-Hitter*, he was blunter with his friends, whom he told, "I don't want to spend the rest of my life a cripple."

"People who write about spring training not being necessary have never tried to throw a baseball."

—Commonly quoted

"Pitching is . . . the art of instilling fear."

—Quoted by Robert E. Hold, *The Gashouse Gang*, 1976

"Show me a guy who can't pitch inside and I'll show you a loser."

—Quoted in *Late Innings* by Roger Angell

"The only time I really try for a strikeout is when I'm in a jam. If the bases are loaded with none out, for example, then I'll go for the strikeout. But most of the time I try to throw to spots. I try to get them to pop up or ground out. On a strikeout I might have to throw five or six pitches, sometimes more if there are foul-offs. That tires me. So I just try to get outs. That's what counts: outs. You win with outs, not strikeouts."

—Quoted by Jack Orr in *My Greatest Day in Baseball*

"There are a lot more things in life I want to do, I don't want to do them as a sore-armed person."

—On ending his career; quoted in *Bo: Pitching and Wooing* by Maury Allen

Kramer, Mark

"Baseball is a harbor, a seclusion from failure that really matters, a playful utopia in which virtuosity can be savored to the third decimal place of a batting average."

—SABR Collection

Kranepool, Ed

"He's too good for this league, he should only be pitching in his own league."

—On Sandy Koufax at a point in the 1965 season when he was 18–0 against Kranepool's Mets; quoted in *The Incredible Mets* by Maury Allen

"I don't know what I will do in October. I've never hit in this month before. I'm usually playing basketball in October."

—On the '69 season; quoted in *The Incredible Mets* by Maury Allen

KRAUSE, JERRY

"I'm sure if Willie Mays had started playing basketball at age 9 or 10 and kept at it, he might have been Michael Jordan. Could Michael Jordan have been Willie Mays? Maybe, if he started playing baseball at 9 or 10 and kept at it."

—As general manager of the Chicago Bulls; quoted in the *Chicago Sun-Times*, December 23, 1993

KRAUTHAMMER, CHARLES

"Baseball is so modestly Republican. The World Series is a continuation of the season by other means. Played in real towns, it is awarded, democratically, to the city with the most wins, not the best caterers. And the players are built to human, yeoman scale. Footballers wear uniforms designed to make them mammoth and interchangeable, like the products of an oversized assembly line. Baseball outfits are meant to betray the real body underneath. In baseball's perfectly American balance of anarchy and order, uniforms are worn. But Republican flannels, for God's sake, not the pads and helmets of a Nixonian Swiss guard."

—*Washington Post*, January 25, 1985

"The situation is getting serious. We're running out of enemies. The only people left to hate are the New York Mets and they finished third."

—On the end of the cold war on TV, November 11, 1989

KROC, ROY

"Baseball has prostituted itself. Pretty soon we'll be starting games at midnight so the people in outer space can watch on prime-time television. We're making a mistake by always going for more money."

—On television's control over baseball; quoted in the *New York Times*, February 6, 1977

"I believe a commissioner should be a dictator. If he's a darn good dictator, you give him a gold watch now and then. If he's a lousy dictator, you fire him. Bowie Kuhn is not a good dictator. Authority only goes to those who have the guts to use it and he doesn't use it. How can he allow the American League to play one kind of baseball with the designated hitter and the National League play another type of baseball?"

—As Padres owner; quoted in the *Sporting News*, May 13, 1978

"Ladies and gentlemen, I suffer with you. I've never seen such stupid baseball playing in my life."

—As owner of the San Diego Padres, over the stadium public address system, during the Padres' home-opener loss to Houston, 9–1, on April 9, 1974

KROC, ROY (CONTINUED)

"They can shove it. I've been disillusioned by everyone I've met. There's a lot more future in hamburgers than baseball."

> —On baseball after being fined $100,000 by Commissioner Bowie Kuhn for "tampering" in the free-agent market, by saying he would go after certain players, namely Joe Morgan and Craig Nettles, if they became available

KRUK, JOHN

"If you don't play, I'm taking my ball and going home."

> —Words on a T-shirt the Phillies player commissioned on returning to the team after the removal of a cancerous testicle *Newsweek,* April 25, 1994.

KUBEK, TONY

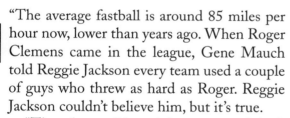

"The average fastball is around 85 miles per hour now, lower than years ago. When Roger Clemens came in the league, Gene Mauch told Reggie Jackson every team used a couple of guys who threw as hard as Roger. Reggie Jackson couldn't believe him, but it's true.

"The players lift weights now and look better in the uniform, but they're not stronger in a baseball sense.

"It is a game of ability and mobility, not a game of strength."

> —*Boston Globe,* 1989

"The greatest teacher is visualization—seeing others do it and aspiring to their level."

> —On learning the game; quoted by George Will in *Men at Work: The Craft of Baseball*

"It's been going on a long, long time. But it's like the Iran-Contra hearings. It's easy to say a guy's doing something, but how do you prove it?"

> —As an NBC baseball analyst and former player, on baseball cheating; quoted in *USA Today* August 14, 1987

KUBEK, TONY SR.

"When the action is at its peak, you should shut up and let the scene tell the story. But some people, like [Howard] Cosell, feel a need to be a part of the moment and can't stay quiet. Jerkocracy, if you will."

> —As an NBC announcer describing the "Cosell syndrome," *Sporting News,* October 21, 1985

"No matter how many errors you make, no matter how many times you strike out, keep hustling. That way you'll at least look like a ballplayer."

> —To his son, Yankee rookie Tony Kubek Jr., 1957

KUENN, HARVEY

"I don't want to hear another [bleeping] question from you. Milwaukee, don't print that. I don't want the people back there to think I swear."

> —On the Metrodome, *The Baseball Card Engagement Book,* 1989

KUHN, BOWIE

"A woman asked me the other day if there's any truth to the rumor that Charlie Finley is out to get me. I said, 'Honey, that ain't no rumor.'"

> —As commissioner; quoted in the *Sporting News,* June 24, 1976

Harvey Kuenn (*Milwaukee Brewers*)

"Baseball is beautiful . . . the supreme performing art. It combines in perfect harmony the magnificent features of ballet, drama, art, and ingenuity."

—As commissioner, 1976

"He had about him a touch of royalty."

—On Roberto Clemente, who died in a plane crash flying relief supplies to Nicaraguan earthquake victims

"I am not very happy when I see stars like Luis Tiant and Tommy John signed by the world champion New York Yankees. The Yankees are fully within their legal rights, but this trend fulfills a prophecy some of us made that the star free agents would tend to sign with the best teams. It's inevitable that this process will lead to a group of elite teams controlling the sport. Already, five teams have signed 53 per cent of the free agents during the first three years of the new system."

—At the 1978 winter meetings, December 4, in Orlando, Florida

"I do not think I exaggerate one bit when I say that legalization could jeopardize the very existence of professional baseball and other professional team sports. It is our position that any form of gambling on professional baseball games, legal or illegal, poses a threat to the integrity of our game, exposes it to grave economic danger and threatens a disservice to the public interest."

—Testifying before the National Gambling Commission February, 1975

"I don't like comparisons with football. Baseball is an entirely different game. You can watch a tight, well-played football game, but it isn't exciting if half the stadium is empty. The violence on the field must bounce off a lot of people. But you can go to the ball park on a quiet Tuesday afternoon with only a few thousand people in the place and thoroughly enjoy a one-sided game. Baseball has an aesthetic, intellectual appeal found in no other team sport."

—From Stanley Frank, "Bowie Kuhn Charts Baseball's Future," *TV Guide*, October 10, 1970

"I don't think that baseball should be exceptionally proud of this day. It's been long overdue."

—On Frank Robinson becoming the first black manager in the majors; quoted in *Five Seasons* by Roger Angell

"I had two reactions, one as a fan and another as commissioner. I was disappointed as a fan, because I like to see worthy candidates honored. But as commissioner, I felt that in the failure there was a vote for the integrity of the system. Nobody should get to Cooperstown with ease."

> —On the fact that no new members were elected to the Hall of Fame in 1971; quoted in the *Christian Science Monitor,* February 2

"Most of us will be here to see major-league baseball on an international basis. Mexico, Venezuela, Cuba, Canada, Japan, Puerto Rico and Panama are among the countries not only eager for it but ready for it. Further away, time-wise, in baseball's global plans is Europe, with Holland and Italy the most advanced in interest, knowledge and facilities. Any new federal sport structures in those places, as well as many others, must include a baseball field."

> —Quoted in the *Los Angeles Herald-Examiner,* January 4, 1974

"Obviously the losers in the strike action taken tonight are the sports fans of America."

> —On the 1972 players strike

"Overall the star of the offense was stolen bases which were up 9.8% and at 3,291 represented the highest total since the record year of 1911. We had three players who stole more than 90 bases for the first time in history. So eye-catching was the gain that one lady wrote to the attorney general of the United States complaining that baseball was a national conspiracy in violation of the antitrust laws engaged in fostering theft. You may think I'm kidding but I'm not. I would give a lot to know how the attorney general answered that particular letter."

> —State of the game report, Dallas, December 8, 1980

"The premium on sound judgment is enormous in a climate of soaring costs."

> —Widely quoted

"The strong identity of the American League, strong identity of the National League, is what makes the World Series the greatest sports event in the country. The Super Bowl is a nice event. But the World Series, I think, is the champ, and the only reason is the sharp competition between the two leagues."

> —In a *Washington Post* interview, November 18, 1975

"We are unable to schedule exhibition baseball in Cuba in March. Our principal incentive has long been that of facilitating the availability of star Cuban players to American baseball audiences, a subject on which you have been unable to provide any encouragement."

> —From the cable to Cuba's subdirector of sports, Fabio Ruiz, thus tabling, perhaps permanently, any quick resumption of baseball with Fidel Castro's Cuba; quoted in the *New York Times,* March 19, 1978

KUPCINET, IRV

"Somebody in baseball has no sense of humor. Marvin Miller should have been invited to throw out the first ball on opening day. After all, he helped throw out the first 86 games of the season."

> —The *Chicago Sun-Times* writer on the strike; quoted in the July 1972 *Baseball Digest.*

L

LaGuardia, Fiorello H.

"You must consider that the one great tie with home for men in Africa, Australia, the Pacific or Europe, aside from family letters, is baseball scores."

—As New York mayor during World War II; quoted in *Baseball: The President's Game* by William B. Mead and Paul Dickson

Lahoud, Joe

"It's easy to stay in the majors for 7 and a half years when you hit .300. But when you hit .216, like me, it's really an accomplishment."

—As an Angels outfielder

LaMar, Chuck

"The only thing that keeps this organization from being recognized as one of the finest is wins and losses at the major-league level."

—On the Devil Rays, *St. Petersburg Times,* March 23, 2005

Lamont, Gene

"I never heard of anyone getting a job they applied for."

—As a Pirates coach on why he would not apply for the job as Seattle manager; quoted in *Sports Illustrated,* June 20, 1988

Lamp, Dennis

"I guess they'll be sending my fingers to Cooperstown."

—After his pitching hand was badly bruised trying to catch the ball that became Lou Brock's 3,000th hit. Lamp served up the pitch in the uniform of the Chicago Cubs, *Sports Illustrated,* August 27, 1989

LANCASTER, DALE

"'Until I saw Mantle peel down for his shower in the clubhouse at Comiskey Park one afternoon, I never knew how he developed his brutal power,' recalls sports columnist Dale Lancaster of the *Aurora, Illinois, Beacon-News.* 'But his bare back looked like a barrelful of snakes.'"

> —The Illinois sports columnist; quoted in *Baseball Stars of 1963*

LANDIS, JUDGE KENESAW MOUNTAIN

"Baseball is something more than a game to an American boy; it is his training field for life work. Destroy his faith in it squareness and honesty and you have destroyed something more; you have planted suspicion of all things in his heart."

> —As Commissioner (1920–1944), on signing high school players; quoted by Harold Seymour in *Baseball, the People's Game*

"Casey Stengel just can't keep from being Casey Stengel."

> —On Stengel's thumbing his nose at Colonel Jacob Rupert during a World Series game. Stengel was in a Giants uniform and was responsible for both of the Giants' wins in the Series. The nose thumbing came after an inside-the-park home run, and Rupert insisted that he be punished. Landis fined him $50; recalled in Fred Lieb's *Baseball As I Have Known It*

"Freddy, what we are looking at now—could this be the highest point of what we affec-

Kenesaw Mountain Landis (*Library of Congress Prints and Photographs Division*)

tionately call our national sport? Greece had its sports and its Olympics; they must have reached a zenith and then waned. The same for the sports of ancient Rome; there must have been a year at which they were at their peak. I repeat, Freddy, are we looking at the zenith of baseball?"

> —To Fred Lieb at the end of the 1924 World Series; quoted in Lieb's *Baseball As I Have Known It*

"I have repeatedly stated on behalf of everybody connected with professional baseball that we ask no preferential treatment—that we would be disgraced if we got it and that we desire that all laws and regulations having to do with the war shall operate upon our personnel precisely as upon the other 130,000,000 of our population."

—On baseball and the Second World War. This was often quoted as Landis's credo.

"It will be the ruination of the individual minor league club owners."

—On Branch Rickey's development of "farms" of minor-league teams for the St. Louis Cardinals; quoted in *Baseball As I Have Known It* by Fred Lieb

"Regardless of the verdict of juries, no player that throws a ball game, no player that entertains proposals or promises to throw a game, no player that sits in a conference with a bunch of crooked players and gamblers where the ways and means of throwing games are discussed, and does not promptly tell his club about it, will ever again play professional baseball."

—Announcement made in August 1921, after a Cook County jury found eight members of the Chicago White Sox not guilty of fixing the 1919 World Series

"They can't come back. The doors are closed to them for good. The most scandalous chapter in the game's history is closed."

—On the "Black Sox" participants

"The only thing in anybody's mind now is to make baseball what the millions of fans throughout the United States want it to be."

—On taking over as commissioner

"There will be no more acts of God."

—In reacting to the fact that the lights had gone out in Milwaukee's Borchert Field just as the home team was about to lose its lead, and Bill Veeck explained it was "an act of God."

"We do not want to be exempt from the liabilities of common life in America. We want the same rules applied and enforced on us as on anyone else. When I give thought to the statutes ruling our lives in war, I think of those fellows in New Guinea crawling in trenches and those fellows in Africa. They have complied with those statutes. This is baseball's position, and I take full responsibility for it."

—In January 1943, after it had been suggested that he go to Washington and have baseball declared an "essential industry," freeing players from the draft. He rejected any such notion and ended the speech on this note: "And about the question of whether baseball is going to die or is going to live, I've formed the habit of living."

LANDREAUX, KEN

"Winning isn't as important as doing well individually. You can't take teamwork up to the front office to negotiate."

—The Los Angeles Dodger outfielder; quoted in *Sports Illustrated*, January 9, 1984

LANE, FRANK

"All you have to do is sit Molotov down between Branch Rickey and Casey Stengel, and in four years Russia will have nothing left but Siberia and a couple of left-handed pitchers."

—As Chicago White Sox general manager on dealing with the Soviets, 1955

LANE, FRANK (CONTINUED)

"I'd rather have two good scouts than two minor league farm clubs. Good scouts can dig up talent; ball clubs are not hard to find."

—Quoted in Joe Garagiola's *Baseball Is a Funny Game*

"If a runner throws out his hand or his arm—even accidentally—and interferes with the pivot man's throw to first base on an attempted double play, both runners are out. But let him crash into some little shortstop or second baseman and deliberately break up the play, and he's just doing his job. It doesn't make sense."

—As Cleveland Indians general manager

"Monday got about $125,000 from the Cubs last season and struck out 125 times. He got paid $1,000 a strikeout. This year he'll probably get $250,000 from the Dodgers, which means he's gotten a raise to $2,000 a strikeout."

—On Rick Monday, *Sports Illustrated*, March 14, 1977

LANE, JACK

"How could he be expected to remember where the bases were? He gets on so infrequently."

—On Marv Throneberry's being called out on a triple because he failed to touch first base

LANSBURGH, SIDNEY JR.

"There's no column on the scorecard headed 'remarks.'"

—Quoted in Julius M. Westheimer's column in the *Baltimore Evening Sun*, March 22, 1979.

It has been widely quoted as "Lansburgh's Observation" and has been applied mostly outside of baseball.

LANSFORD, CARNEY

"Contentment stinks. Stay focused."

—T-shirt worn as a member of the defending world champion Oakland Athletics; quoted in the May 1990 *Major League Baseball Newsletter*.

LAPOINT, DAVE

"I really like your beer."

—Pittsburgh Pirates left-handed pitcher talking to vice president and presidential candidate George Bush, who visited the Pirates' clubhouse in September 1988

LARDNER, JOHN

"Babe Hermann did not triple into a triple-play, but he did double into a double-play, which is the next best thing."

—Widely attributed and quoted. In another version, he says of Herman: "He did not always catch balls on the top of his head, but he could do it in a pinch. He never tripled into a triple play, which os the next best thing."

Babe Ruth and Old Jack Dempsey
Both Sultans of the Swat,
One hits where other people are—
The other where they're not.

—John Lardner quoted by Franklin P. Adams, *The Diary of Our Own Samuel Pepys,* 1935; it appeared earlier in the *Chicago Tribune*

"Dickey, of the St. Louis Yankees, ran home with two on base making three runs over the plate. The Yankees beat St. Louis."

> —Australian newspaper description of an American baseball game of the early 1940s; related in his book *Southwest Passage*

"He can talk all day and all night, on any kind of track wet or dry."

> —On Casey Stengel

"It's significant that the team with the highest income is the team that makes café society news more often. By the same token, the Washington club should be cold sober."

> —On the Washington Senators; widely quoted

"Many critics were surprised to know that the Browns could be bought, because they didn't know that the Browns were owned."

> —On hearing of Bill Veeck's purchase of the St. Louis Browns

LARDNER, REX

"Satchelfoot. Satchel. Satch. Long, lean, canny. Threw the ball from any of three directions. Had four different windups. Had more pitches that a catcher has fingers—among them the hesitation pitch, the blooper, the trouble ball, and the be-ball (it be where I want it to be)."

> —*Sport*, January 1969

Joe E. Brown in film version of Ring Lardner's *Alibi Ike* (*Museum of Modern Art Film Still Archives*)

LARDNER, RING

"Although he is a bad fielder he is also a very poor hitter."

> —Quoted by Clifton Fadiman in *The American Treasury, 1455–1955*

"Be home real soon, Mom, they're beginning to throw the curve."

> —Character in the 1935 film *Alibi Ike*

I'm forever blowing ball games,
Pretty ball games in the air.
I come from Chi
I hardly try
Just go to bat and fade and die;
Fortune's coming my way,
That's why I don't care.
I'm forever blowing ball games,
And the gamblers treat us fair.

> —Parody of "I'm Forever Blowing Bubbles," which he sung in the private railroad cars of the notorious Black Sox of 1919. Lardner knew something was wrong and this was his way of letting all know it; quoted in *Eight Men Out* by Eliot Asinof

"I'm not boastin' about my first experience with [Walter] Johnson, though. They can't never tell me he throws them balls with his arm. He's got a gun concealed about his person and he shoots 'em up there. I was leadin' off in Murphy's place and the game was a little delayed in startin', because I'd watched the big guy warm up and wasn't in no hurry to get to that plate. Before I left the bench Connie says:

"'Don't try to take no healthy swing. Just meet 'em and you'll get along better.'

"So I tried to just meet the first one he threwed; but when I stuck out my bat Henry was throwin' the pill back to Johnson. Then I thought: Maybe if I start swingin' now at the second one I'll hit the third one. So I let the second one come over and the umps guessed it was another strike, though I'll bet a thousand bucks he couldn't see it no more'n I could.

"While Johnson was still windin' up to pitch again I started to swing—and the big cuss crosses me with a slow one. I lunged at it twice and missed it both times, and the force o' my wallop throwed me clean back on the bench. The Ath-a-letics was all laughin' at me and I laughed too, because I was glad that much of it was over."

—*Horseshoes*, 1926

"It all would have been different if Cobb would have stayed in Georgia."

— On Ty Cobb's devastating effect on Cub pitching

"Just keep talking. When you're with a newspaper guy don't try and feed him a story because you don't really know what makes a story he can use. Just keep talking, and he'll get his story."

— To his friend Casey Stengel; quoted by Red Smith, *New York Times*, October 7, 1975

My eyes are very misty
As I pen these lines to Christy
Oh, my heart is full of heaviness today.
May the flowers ne'er wither, Matty
On your grave at Cincinnati
Which you've chosen for your final fadeaway.

— On Christy Mathewson going to Cincinnati as player-manager, 1916. This has been quoted as a poem to the dying Mathewson, but it was actually an allusion to Cincinnati, which was then regarded as a graveyard for major-league talent.

"Nothing on earth is more depressing than an old baseball writer.

— Cited by Roger Kahn in *Into My Own: The Remarkable People and Events That Shaped a Life.* It is often alluded to by aging baseball writers.

"The only real happiness a ballplayer has is when he is playing a ball game and accomplishes something he didn't think he could do."

— Widely quoted

"The Washington Senators and the New York Giants must have played a doubleheader this afternoon—the game I saw and the game Graham McNamee announced."

— After listening to the first World Series broadcast, 1924

"The writer wishes to acknowledge his indebtedness to the Mayo brothers, Ringling Brothers, Smith brothers, Rath brothers, the Dolly sisters, and former President Buchanan for their aid in instructing him in the technical terms of baseball, such as 'bat,' 'ball,' 'pitcher,' 'foul,' 'sleeping car,' and 'sore arm.'"

—Preface to *You Know Me Al*

"When you were sucking rubber nipples, I saw Bill Lange belt out his triples."

—On the player they called "Little Eva"

LARSEN, DON

"No, why should I?"

—When asked if he ever got tired of speaking about his perfect game

"Sometimes a week might go by when I don't think about that game, but I don't remember when it happened last."

—Some years after his 1956 masterpiece

"When it was over, I was so happy, I felt like crying. I wanted to win this one for Casey. After what I did in Brooklyn, he could have forgotten about me and who would blame him? But he gave me another chance and I'm grateful."

—On his perfect World Series game; to reporters in the Yankee locker room

LA RUSSA, TONY

"I'd rather ride the buses managing in Triple A than be a lawyer."

—The attorney-manager in *Sports Illustrated,* July 21, 1986

"The toughest thing for me as a young manager is that a lot of my players saw me play. They know how bad I was."

—As the thirty-year-old manager of the Chicago White Sox, *Sports Illustrated,* June 20, 1983

"When I first became a manager, I asked Chuck for advice. He told me, 'Always rent.'"

—On the baseball wisdom imparted to him by major-league manager Chuck Tanner; quoted in *Life,* January, 1985

LASORDA, TOMMY

"About the only problem with success is that it does not teach you how to deal with failure."

—*The Artful Dodger*

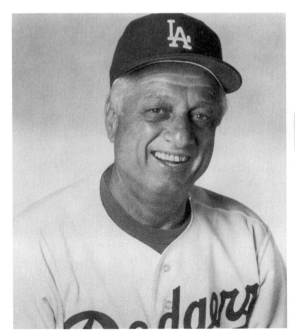

Tommy Lasorda (*Los Angeles Dodgers*)

"*Always* give an autograph when somebody asks you. You never can tell. In baseball anything can happen."

> —Advice given by him to the new Dodgers each year in spring training, according to Roger Angell in *Five Opinions*

"Did you ever hear of a batting-practice pitcher dropping dead? You hear about men dropping dead shoveling snow or mowing the lawn. But not pitching batting practice."

> —On why he pitched batting practice

"He wants Texas back."

> —On Fernando Valenzuela's contract demands

"I believe managing is like holding a dove in your hand. If you hold it too tightly, you kill it, but if you hold it too loosely, you lose it."

> —*The Artful Dodger*

"I bleed Dodger blue, and when I die, I'm going to the Big Dodger in the Sky."

> —His widely quoted loyalty oath

"I found out that it's not good to talk about my troubles. Eighty percent of the people who hear them don't care and the other twenty percent are glad you're having trouble."

> —As Los Angeles Dodger manager

"I know the fans will be back eventually. They can't get this kind of entertainment for the price anywhere. It's like a guy who goes to a smorgasbord and gets a big plate of food for $2 and gets insulted. But still he goes back again because he knows he can't get that kind of food anywhere else for that kind of money."

> —On the 1981 strike; quoted in the *Washington Star*, July 31, 1981

"I motivate players through communication, being honest with them, having them respect and appreciate your ability and your help. I started in the minor leagues. I used to hug my players when they did something well. That's my enthusiasm. That's my personality. I jump with joy when we win. I try to be on a close basis with my players. People say you can't go out and eat with your players. I say, why not?"

> —*New York Times*, May 17, 1982

"I walk into the clubhouse, and it's like walking into the Mayo Clinic. We have four doctors, three therapists and five trainers. Back when I broke in, we had one trainer, who carried a bottle of rubbing alcohol—and by the seventh inning he had drunk it all."

> —On the treatment of injuries, *Sports Illustrated*, May 29, 1989

"I was so elated that we had finally won the world championship that I spent the entire winter eating. Of course, had we lost, I would have been so unhappy I would have spent the entire winter eating."

> —On the 1981 World Series, in *The Artful Dodger*

"My theory of hitting was just to watch the ball as it came in and hit it. As I realized years later, that is still the finest theory of hitting yet devised."

> —*The Artful Dodger*

"No. We don't cheat. And even if we did, I'd never tell you. It's not that I don't trust you—it's all your readers I don't trust."

> —To a reporter before Game 1 of the 1988 NLCS Dodger-Met matchup; appears in *Parade* magazine as the best baseball quote of the year (January 1, 1989)

"Statistics can be misleading. When Drysdale or Gibson pitched, for example, the other team never scored any runs, but when I pitched, they always scored runs!"

> —On his 0–4 major-league pitching record, in *The Artful Dodger*

"The Big Dodger in the Sky has seen fit to bestow upon me and mine a multitude of great moments during my years as leader of the flock."

> —Lasorda invokes the Big Dodger often. At the start of the 1977 season he said, "We'll win if the Big Dodger in the sky wills it." *The Artful Dodger*

LAU, CHARLIE

"Nobody should hit .200. Anybody should hit .250."

> —As Royals batting instructor

"There are two theories on hitting the knuckleball. Unfortunately, neither one of them works."

> —*Baseball Card Engagement Book*, 1989

LAVAGETTO, COOKIE

"The boy [Martin] has everything to become a major league player. He's a natural. He makes little mistakes, but he's only a boy starting out. If he will make a habit of doing the job correctly, he will last a long time in the big leagues."

> —On Billy Martin, May, 1948, the *Sporting News*.

"There is no way you'll get me to knock good base running. But if God were to say to me, 'Tom, you can have your choice of power or speed,' I'd take power. The reason is simple. If a guy beats out a hit and steals second, you've got no assurance he's going to score. But when a man hits one out of the park, you've got a guaranteed run."

> —From an April 3, 1982, *TV Guide* interview

"Think about each pitch like you think about your women, then select one which is particularly appealing."

> —As Spokane manager; quoted in the *Sporting News*, March 28, 1970

Charlie Lau (*Kansas City Royals*)

"You can't make the club in a tub."

> —Standard line to players in the whirlpool;
> quoted by Jay Johnstone in *Temporary Insanity*

"When Billy Martin reaches for a bar tab, his arm shrinks 6 inches."

> —Hall of Fame Collection, 1981

LAW, VERNON

1. If you don't play to win, why keep score?
2. You will never reach second base if you keep one foot on first base.

> —Tenets, from a SABR collection

Vernon Law (*Author's Collection*)

LEE, BILL "SPACEMAN"

"Everything is so specialized now. Once, baseball was a sport where you were supposed to do a lot of things and be able to put it all together. Now we've got the designated hitter, just prolonging the careers of a lot of guys who can't play any more. Maybe we ought to adopt Little League rules where everybody has to play at least three innings a week."

> —*New York Times,* July 30, 1974

"I think there are going to be a lot of Reggies born in this town."

> —After witnessing the last game of the '77
> World Series

"[I would] change policy, bring back natural grass and nickel beer. Baseball is the belly-button of our society. Straighten our baseball, and you straighten out the rest of the world."

> —From an interview, *Los Angeles Times,*
> February 3, 1977

"If it had been me out there, I'd had bitten [his] ear off. I'd have Van Goghed him!"

> —On an important call about an umpire;
> quoted in *Five Seasons* by Roger Angell

"I'm mad at Hank for deciding to play one more season. I threw him his last home run and thought I'd be remembered forever. Now I'll have to throw him another."

> —On Hank Aaron

"In baseball, you're supposed to sit on your ass, spit tobacco, and nod at stupid things."

> —SABR Collection

Bill Lee (*Montreal Expos*)

"It looks like the same thing George Scott wore around his waist when he was trying to lose weight."

　　—On the then-new orange roof on Montreal's Olympic Stadium, *Sports Illustrated*, July 20, 1987

"People are too hung up on winning. I can get off on a really good helmet throw."

　　—*The Baseball Card Engagement Book*, 1990

"The more self-centered and egotistical a guy is, the better ballplayer he's going to be. You take a team with twenty-five assholes and I'll show you a pennant. I'll show you the New York Yankees."

　　—SABR Collection

"The only rule I got is if you slide, get up."

　　—The former Boston Red Sox pitcher on who would manage the Winter Haven, Florida, Super Sox of the Senior Professional Baseball Association, *USA Today*, October 25, 1989

"There's nothing in the world like the fatalism of the Red Sox fans, which has been bred into them for generations by that little green ballpark, and by the Wall, and by a team that keeps trying to win by hitting everything out of sight and just out-bombarding everyone else in the league. . . . All this makes the Boston fans a little crazy. I'm sorry for them."

　　—Quoted in *Late Innings* by Roger Angell

"They all changed. Most of them got agents, and I ceased to talk to 'em. 'Like to use this toilet paper?' 'Dunno, I gotta talk to my agent.'"

　　—On the subject of agents

"What do you expect from a northpaw world?"

　　—As a Red Sox pitcher when asked why southpaws are always depicted as flakes, *Sports Illustrated*, May 29, 1979

"You have a left and a right. The left side controls the right half of your body, and the right side controls the left half. Therefore, left-handers are the only people in their right mind."

　　—On the hemispheres of the brain, SABR Collection

LEFEBVRE, JIM

"The real difference is in the farm system. Our club, for example, had only 12 players in the minors."

—As a coach in Japan on the difference between Japanese and U.S. baseball; quoted in the *Los Angeles Times*, January 22, 1977

LEFKOW, MIKE

"Because it was Mike Schmidt, I talked to a few people who had more experience scoring games, and they said you don't change a decision for that reason. I do understand the historical essence, though."

—The sportswriter for the *Contra Costa [Calif.] Times*, on why he didn't change Mike Schmidt's last at-bat from an error to a hit; the *Washington Times*, June 1, 1989

LEGGETT, WILLIAM

"Pete Rose is the type of person who would run to a funeral and if he didn't like it, would boo the deceased."

—From his *Sports Illustrated* profile of Rose, May 27, 1968

LELAND, JOHN

"Hemingway was one of a few thousand Americans and almost no Frenchmen who watched the New York Giants whip the Chicago White Sox 8–0 on November 8, 1924, in an exhibition game here. The then-new Olympic stadium was too small for baseball, and home runs slammed into the stands counted as two-base hits, the *New York Times* reported. The few befuddled French who showed up never figured out the difference between balls and strikes. Unimpressed by baseball's haute couture, a Paris paper compared unfavorably the Giants' uniforms to those of convicts. 'Kill the umpire,' garbled in translation and retranslation, became 'Death to the arbiter.'"

—Discussion of Stade Yves-du-Manior, in *A Guide to Hemingway's Paris* (Chapel Hill, NC: Algonquin Books, 1989)

LEMON, BOB

"Baseball is a kid's game that grown-ups only tend to screw up."

—As New York Yankees manager, 1979

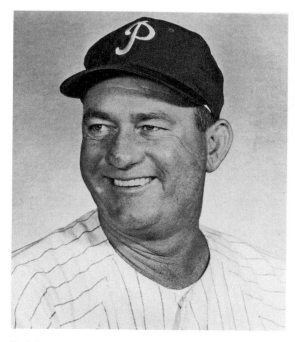

Bob Lemon (*Philadelphia Phillies*)

"I had some bad days in the field. But I didn't take them home with me. I left them in a bar along the way."

> —In his Hall of Fame induction speech at Cooperstown in 1976, Lemon revealed his "secret for success." A variation:

"I never took the game home with me. I always left it in some bar."

> —As a former manager. In *Reggie,* Reggie Jackson calls this "Lem's most famous quote" and then adds that this line came in second: "I drink after wins, I drink after losses, and I drink after rainouts."

"It's like Shakespeare. He writes the plays, and we act them out."

> —On George Steinbrenner during the 1978 season, when he managed the Yankees; recalled in his *New York Times* obituary, January 13, 2000.

"It's not the total job of a manager to motivate the 25 individuals on a big-league roster. Self-motivation is a key to success on any team. . . .

"Too much emphasis is being placed on the word 'motivation.' Each individual should strive to excel himself. If a fellow doesn't want to give 100 per cent, there's nothing a manager can do."

> —As White Sox manager; quoted in the *Washington Post,* May 8, 1977

"I've seen the elephant, heard the owl and flown the screaming eagle."

> —On his being inducted into the Hall of Fame

"This is the way I like it. You guys play, and I sit in the dugout and enjoy."

> —As Yankee manager after winning four in a row; quoted by Reggie Jackson in *Reggie*

"You have a big year and suddenly everybody thinks you're one hell of a speechmaker."

> —Quoted in *Vida: His Own Story* by Bill Libby and Vida Blue

"Well, it's like when I go to a dance. I always go home with the guy who brought me."

> —As a manager on why he started Ed Figueroa in the World Series

LEONARD, BUCK

"I was in Cooperstown the day Satchel Paige was inducted, and I stayed awake almost all that night thinking about it. It's something you never had any dream you'd ever see. Like men walking on the moon. I always wanted to go up there to Cooperstown. You felt like you had a reason, because it's the home of baseball, but you didn't have a special reason. We never thought we'd get in the Hall of Fame. We thought the way we were playing was the way it was going to continue. I never had any dream it would come. But that night I felt like I was part of it at last."

> —*Everything You Always Wanted to Know About Sports and Didn't Know Where to Ask* by Mickey Herskowitz and Steve Perkins

LEONARD, JOHN

"Baseball happens to be a game of cumulative tension. . . . Football, basketball and hockey are played with hand grenades and machine guns."

—*New York Times,* 1975

LETTERMAN, DAVID

"According to the *Sporting News,* over the last four years, Wade Boggs hit .800 with women in scoring position."

—On the Wade Boggs–Margo Adams affair, the *Sporting News,* March 13, 1989

"I heard the doctors revived a man after being dead for four-and-a-half minutes. When they asked what it was like being dead, he said it was like listening to New York Yankees announcer Phil Rizzuto during a rain delay."

—*Late Night with David Letterman,* NBC-TV, 1982

"It was filled with cork, also Styrofoam and ground-up bits of rubber balls. It's the same way they make their hot dogs in Chicago."

—*Late Show* host, joking about Sammy Sosa's corked bat, *Chicago Sun-Times,* June 12, 2003

"T-ball is just like baseball, except there's no pitching—just like the Mets."

—After T-ball was played on the White House lawn, thanks to President George W. Bush, *Chicago Sun-Times,* May 10, 2001

LEWIS, JOE E.

"Rooting for the Yankees is like rooting for U.S. Steel."

—This quote is common and variously attributed, but the wide-mouthed comic appears to have said it first.

LEWIS, LLOYD

"Swarming up from the Texas wheat fields, the Georgia cotton lands, the West Virginia coal mines, the Oklahoma cow ranges and the Ozark farms, the Gas Housers redramatized for the public that old traditional story about the talent of common men. They fit the historic pattern of the American success story, the legend of the country boy who, on native wit and vitality, crashes through, clear up to the top."

—On the 1934 *Gashouse Gang*

LEWIS, SINCLAIR

"A sensational event was changing from the brown suit to the gray the contents of his pockets. He was earnest about these objects. They were of eternal importance, like baseball or the Republican Party."

—*Babbitt,* 1922

"But the game was a custom of his clan and it gave outlet for the homicidal and side-taking instincts which Babbitt called 'patriotism' and 'love of sport.' No sense a man's working his fool head off. I'm going to the game three days a week."

—*Babbitt*

LEYLAND, JIM

"I knew we were in for a long season when we lined up for the national anthem on opening day and one of my players said, 'Every time I hear that song I have a bad game.'"

—As Pirates manager

"It blows my mind. I was in baseball for 18 years before I made $20,000."

—On signing a five-year contract to manage the Marlins for $1.5 million a year; quoted in the *Washington Post*, October 6, 1996

"You are a bunch of losers. All you care about is your own stats. You're worse than a watered-down expansion team. You've given up. You've got no pride, no dignity, no guts."

—The Pittsburgh Pirates manager after one of his team's losses; quoted in *USA Today*, July 21, 1989

LIEB, FRED

"I love baseball. I could watch it every day, every year. And to think I get paid for watching games."

—Cited in his obituary in the *Sporting News;* he had written for the paper for more than fifty years. He died on June 3, 1980.

"Nicknames must be spontaneous, as they rarely can be manufactured. Damon Runyon, well known New York writer, once tried to pin the nickname of High Pockets on George Kelly, the former New York first baseman. While it was taken up by some of his associates, it never became part of the vocabulary of the fans. It was too long and lacked the snap of a nickname like Babe, Rip or Pep.

"What would the writers of the days of Ring Lardner, Damon Runyon, and Charlie Dryden have done with such names?"

—Writing in 1974, after taking a look at the new crop of players—men with names like Bob Apodaca and Al Hrabosky

"Pants had never played ball above the Three-I League and *started life as a bellhop in Dubuque.*"

—On Chisox manager Pants Rowland at the time of the 1917 Series

Sinclair Lewis (*Library of Congress Prints and Photographs Division*)

LINDSTROM, FREDDIE

"Do you know what the cardinal sin was on that ball club? To begin a sentence to McGraw with the words, 'I thought.' . . . 'You thought?' he would yell. 'With what?'"

—Said years after his retirement; quoted in *The Giants of the Polo Grounds* by Noel Hynd

"It was no big deal. Anyone could have done it."

—On his place in history, after two ground balls bounced over his head to cost his Giants the seventh game of the 1933 World Series

LINN, ED

"He was sometimes unbearable, but he was never dull."

—His "epitaph" for Ted Williams, which has been requoted and applied to others. Writing in *Sport,* for instance, Gordon Forbes suggested that it fit Bill Terry.

LINZ, PHIL

"Play me or trade me."

—As a Yankee; this ultimatum has been quoted in many autobiographies. Whitey Ford set up the quotation in *Slick* this way: "Linz was a utility infielder and one of the free spirits on the team. He was a fun-loving guy who liked to crack jokes and most of all liked being a Yankee."

"You can't get rich sitting on a bench—but I'm giving it a try."

—As a Yankee utilityman

LISTS

A FEW TRAINING RULES

1. Always warm up thoroughly before starting to play.
2. Never favor a sore arm. Throw naturally. Most arm trouble comes from a faulty pitching motion, and then from favoring soreness. Only throw as hard as you can naturally and without pressing.
3. Always keep your arm and body well covered until all sweating has stopped. A slow, thorough rub with a dry towel before bathing is better than a massage to keep muscles supple.
4. Never take a bath until you are entirely through sweating. Keep fully clothed and warm until the sweating has stopped.
5. In bathing take plenty of time and finish up with plenty of cold water. This closes the pores, avoids colds, and prevents stiffness.
6. Never prod, jerk, or punch a sore muscle. No painful or extreme treatment is beneficial unless administered correctly by an expert who knows his business thoroughly.

7. Don't drown in liniments.
8. Keep wool on a sore arm or muscle all the time.
9. Don't drink during a game or for two hours afterward. Leave ice water out entirely. It is very dangerous if taken when you are sweating.
10. Don't eat for two hours before a game.
11. Pitchers should do lots of running and daily leg and body calisthenics. It's the legs that make a pitcher, and these exercises are good not only for endurance but for control and steadiness.
12. Here are some home remedies to remember:

    A saturated solution of vinegar and water, equal parts, with salt makes an excellent solution for soaking sprains or strains. Also an Epsom salt pack left on all night.

    Use turpentine on split or bruised finger after first applying ice-pack.

    Zinc ointment always should be used on strawberries or other chafed places.

    Don't neglect little splits, cuts, blisters, skinned spots, or scrapes. Use antiseptics as soon as possible.

—"A Few Training Rules" appears in Babe Ruth, *How to Play Baseball* (New York: Cosmopolitan Books, 1931)

ALL-AMERICAN GIRLS BASEBALL LEAGUE BEAUTY KIT

Should always contain the following:
Cleansing Cream
Lipstick
Rouge—Medium
Cream Deodorant
Mild Astringent
Face Powder for Brunette
Hand Lotion
Hair Remover

You should be the best judge of your own beauty requirements. Keep your own kit replenished with the things you need for your own toilette and your beauty culture and care. Remember the skin, the hair, the teeth and the eyes. It is most desirable in your own interests, that of your teammates and fellow players, as well as from the standpoint of the public relations of the league that each girl be at all times presentable and attractive, whether on the playing field or at leisure. Study your own beauty culture possibilities and without overdoing your beauty treatment at the risk of attaining gaudiness, practise [sic] the little measure that will reflect well on your appearance and personality as a real All American girl.

—"A Guide for All American Girls," given to members of the All-American Girls Baseball League during World War II. The league was the inspiration for the hit movie *A League of Their Own*.

ANCIENT BASEBALL CELEBRITIES

1. The devil was the first coacher—he coached Eve when she stole first; Adam stole second.
2. When Isaac met Rebecca at the well she was walking with a pitcher.
3. Samson struck out when he beat the Philistines.
4. Moses made his first run when he saw the Egyptians.
5. Moses shut out the Egyptians at the Red Sea.
6. Cain made a base hit when he killed Abel.
7. Abraham made a sacrifice.

8. The prodigal son made a home run.
9. David was a long distance thrower.

—From *Baseball Fanthology* by Edward B.
Lyman, 1924

EAGLE SCREAMERS

Pre-Series streamer:
IT'S GONNA BE WE IN '53
First game:
AW, SO WE GAVE THEM ONE
Second game:
!!'?&$-)(-?'&$!
Third game:
ER-SKINS 'EM ALIVE
Fourth game:
LOST WEEK-END? NOT US!
Fifth game:
DO NOT FORSAKE US!
Sixth Game:
XXXXXXXXXXXXXXXXXXXXX
Please omit flowers

—*Brooklyn Eagle* headlines

FDR's BASEBALL IN-BASKET

Some Americans think the president of the United States is the commander in chief of baseball, with sundry powers over the game.

The papers of every president reveal a remarkable array of baseball-related stuff—scores of requests for signed baseballs, sponsorship of teams, testimonials, special favors, and ballpark dedications. In Franklin D. Roosevelt's papers, for example, a few letters in the 1930s addressed significant matters, including requests for his support in sending American teams to Japan. These requests sparked the president's interest and support, but seem to have died from lack of money rather than lack of approval. As late as the fall of 1940, an old United Press reporter named Henry Misslewitz was trying to raise $100,000 to create a Pacific League including Japan and ensuring "peace through baseball."

Some letters are remarkably odd or quaint, ranging from a man who wants Roosevelt to adopt his revolutionary new scoring system to a group of kids who voluntarily include their fingerprints with their request for free uniforms.

Here is a small and select sampling with paraphrases of the White House responses:

A 1934 request for the president to sign a testimonial to Babe Ruth [*OK, but no publicity stunts*]

A 1935 proposal from a group of boys who would be glad to name their team the NRA Eagles in return for White House sponsorship [*Sorry fellas, but no*]

A 1936 request from the Baltimore Elite Giants of the Negro Southern League for the president to throw out the opening ball [*Thanks for the offer, but the president is too busy*]

A 1936 request for use of the president's pass while he is in Canada [*No response*]

A 1936 letter from the Synod of the Reformed Presbyterian Church of North America objecting to his "disregard of the sacredness and rest of the Lord's Day," evidenced by several Sunday press briefings and a baseball game in New York [*OK, but he does go to church*]

A 1937 letter from a distillery asking for permission to decorate the presidential box for opening day [*Outside White House control*]

A request by the *Sporting News* for Roosevelt to award Lou Gehrig a gold watch at the 1937 All-Star Game [*Denied*]

A request to sign a 1938 petition which would change the eligibility rules for students playing in the D.C. high schools [*No*]

A 1939 request that the president send an autographed baseball to a boy who lost his legs in a railroad accident [*Yes*]

A 1939 scheme to create an immense baseball covered with a presidential proclamation concerning the game: it would travel around the nation and be signed by fans [*No*]

A 1941 telegram from the Brooklyn First Committee to the president: "UNLESS YOU ATTEND BROOKLYN DODGERS PARADE THIS MONDAY BROOKLYN WILL SECEDE FROM THE UNION." [*Filed with no answer*]

The volume of letters continued after Pearl Harbor, but requests had a new edge:

A 1942 wire suggesting that the first baseball thrown by the president be labeled "First Offensive Ball" and auctioned to the highest bidder, to benefit Defense Bonds [*File and forget*]

A 1943 postcard telling the president "Don't Let Hitler Kill Baseball" [*Filed*]

A 1943 letter from a Toledo man arguing for a "Black and White All Star Classic" as a step toward "The day when Negro baseball players will be permitted to play beside the White man in the major leagues" [*Ignored*]

A 1943 request from Congressman John McCormack of Massachusetts to get Ted Williams excused from military duty to play in a charity game in Boston [*Denied*]

A 1944 letter nominating Ford Frick of the National League to succeed Judge K. M. Landis on his retirement [*president does not appoint*]

A 1944 note from one Chester Adelberg asking to be made new commissioner on retirement of Judge Landis [*Filed*]

—*Baseball: The President's Game*

FIRST HOME RUNS BY DECADE IN THE TWENTIETH CENTURY

1900: Monte Cross, Philadelphia Phillies, 2nd inning, April 19 at Boston

1910: Tex Erwin, Brooklyn Dodgers, 6th inning, April 15 at Philadelphia

1920: Wally Pipp, New York Yankees, 1st inning, April 14 at Philadelphia

1930: Joe Cronin, Washington Senators, 1st inning, April 15 at Boston

1940: Frank McCormick, Cincinnati Reds, 3rd inning, April 16 at Cincinnati vs. Chicago

1950: Larry Doby, Cleveland Indians, 1st inning, April 12 at Cleveland vs. Detroit

1960: Roy McMillan, Cincinnati Reds, 2nd inning, April 12 at Cincinnati vs. Philadelphia

1970: Lee May, Cincinnati Reds, 4th inning, April 6 at Cincinnati vs. Montreal

1980: George Foster, Cincinnati Reds, 2nd inning, April 9 at Cincinnati vs. Atlanta

1990: Howard Johnson, New York Mets, 1st inning, April 9 at New York vs. Pittsburgh

2000: Shane Andrews, Chicago Cubs, as the Cubs and the Mets play in in the first big league game ever played outside of North America; the Cubs win 5–3

—Source: Society for American Baseball Research

Ford C. Frick's 1973 List of Ten Marks That (He Thought) Would Never Be Broken.

1. Denton (Cy) Young's pitching record of 511 games won during his lifetime career.
2. Charles Radbourne's record of 60 pitching victories in a single season. Set with Providence in 1884.
3. Charles (Kid) Nichols's feat of winning 30 or more games per season through seven consecutive seasons.
4. Walter Johnson's lifetime record of 3,508 strikeouts.
5. Lou Gehrig's record of 2,130 consecutive games.
6. The record of 100 or more RBIs for 13 consecutive seasons, also held by Lou Gehrig.
7. Ty Cobb's record of 4,191 lifetime hits.
8. Joe DiMaggio's record of hitting safely in 56 consecutive games.
9. Babe Ruth's lifetime record of 2,056 bases on balls.

10. Don Larsen's perfect World Series game. This one may be matched some day, but it will never be beaten. You can't beat perfection.

—*Games, Asterisks, and People*

Gifts Presented to DiMag on Joe DiMaggio Day, Yankee Stadium, October 1, 1949

Cadillac automobile, fans of the city of New York; Dodge automobile for his mother, fans of Hoboken, N.J.; Cris-Craft boat, fans of New Haven, Conn.; Baro Thermo calendar watch, fans from Longines Wittenaur Watch Co.; Waltham watch, chain, knife, Knickerbocker Social Club, Westerly, R.I.; wallet with religious gifts, Helen Amen; golf cuff links, Helen Marshall; gold belt buckle, tie pin, cuff links, Crane Social Club, Newark, N.J.; 14-karat gold cuff links and tie pin fashioned from Joe's bat, fans of Swank Jewelry Co.; art work suitable for framing, Charles Flanders, artist; Ray E. Dodge 51-inch loving cup trophy, employees of Dodge, Inc.; television set, employees of A.B. Dumont Co.; television set, employees of Admiral T. V. Corp.; deer rifle, employees of Marlin Firearms Co.; bronze plaque, Grantwood (N.J.) Italian-American Club; $100 fedora hat, MacLachlan Hats, Norwalk, Conn.; golf bag, Delores (Vic) Surmonte Berra-DiMaggio Fan Clubs; electric blanket and radio, General Electric; Thermos water jug set, Billy Pedace, Norwich Conn.; 14-karat gold key chain, autograph in links, Jacques Kreisler Jewelry Co.; silver loving cup, John F. Prince Post, V.F.W.; 25 volumes of Joe DiMaggio records for Yankee Juniors, Capital Records; set of Lionel trains for Joe Jr., Lionel Corporation; driving and sun glasses for Yankee Juniors, W.S. Wilson Corporation; Christmas candy and baseball and bat, Independence (Kan.) Chamber of Commerce; 500 Joe DiMaggio shirts in Joe's name to Yankee Juniors, Allison Mfg. Co. and Saks-34th Street; ship's clock, General Electric; oil painting of Joe DiMaggio, Phillip Patchen, Mamaroneck, N.Y.

Carpeting of his living room, Amsterdam (N.Y.) Rugmakers (Yankee farm club); Westinghouse roaster, Westinghouse Electric Co.; 14-karat gold money clip with open house privileges at Hotels Concourse Plaza and Martinique, from the hotels; four-year college scholarship for a boy of Joe's selection, Il Progresso Newspaper; medal of honor, Il Progresso; 300 quarts of ice cream for any institution designated by Joe, Cardani Ice Cream Co.; statuette, neckerchief and clip, Boy Scouts of America; Air Foam mattress and box spring, Englander Company; cheese, from Fond du Lac (Wis.) farm club; 14-karat gold watch with diamond numerals, Italian Welfare Association, Elizabeth, N.J.; case of shoestring potatoes, Grand Forks (N.D.) farm club; case of Ventura County oranges, sack of walnuts, case of lemonade and case frozen lima beans, from Ventura (Calif.) Chamber of Commerce; hand-painted tie, Christine Wells, Chatham, N.J.; polished wood paper-weight, Twin Falls (Ida.) farm club; leather wallet, Joplin (Mo.) farm club; metal elephant for "good luck," Mrs. Lee Taylor, Hoboken, N.J.; Sterling silver rosary beads for Joe, Jr., St. Joachim's Holy Name Society,

Trenton, N.J.; portrait, Frank Paladino, Brooklyn, N.Y.; *The Sporting News* plaque, *The Sporting News*; dozen golf balls, ash tray and Thermo Tote bag, Newark (O.) baseball club; Columbia bicycle for Joe, Jr., fishing tackle, luggage, Newark (N.J.) committee; a cocker spaniel, American Spaniel Club; plaque, Columbia Civic Club, Newark, N.J.; traveling bag, Mr. Spivicha; certificate of recognition, Italian Historical Society of America; traveling alarm clock, Lux Clock Co. admirers, Waterbury, Conn.; Sterling silver money clip, Lorraine Coville; hand-painted ties for Joe and Joe, Jr., Adele G.; two trophies engraved by children, Mending Heart Foundation, Miami, Fla.; taxi service for 300 fans from Newark—"This ride is on Joe D.," Brown & White Cab Co., Newark, N.J.

—New York Yankee Press Release

Five Favorite Reasons for Delays or Postponements at "the Big O," Olympic Stadium, Montreal

1. Explosion and fire in the stadium tower (which holds up the roof) in 1977
2. Roof up/rain down. The retractable roof was stuck open by rainy, windy conditions last week
3. An 18-wheeler (truck) hit the outfield fence in a pregame parade and destroyed a section of fence in 1987
4. Seals loose on field from a pregame circus in 1985
5. (tie) 500 marching bands take the field and won't leave (actually take too long to file off) in 1987. And squirrel loose on the field and couldn't be caught in 1983

—Expos publicist, Richard Griffin; quoted in *USA Today,* July 28, 1989.

HANK GREENWALD'S OTHER FIVE ALOU BROTHERS

1. Bob
2. Bebop
3. Boog
4. Skip
5. Toot

—The San Francisco Giants broadcaster Tom Gill, from September 16, 1989

PLAYERS' CHOICE

1. Joe Dimaggio's 56-game hitting streak in 1941
2. Hank Aaron's 755 career home runs
3. Pete Rose's 4,256 career hits
4. Orel Hershiser's 59 consecutive shutout innings in 1988
5. Roger Maris's 61 home runs in 1961
6. Nolan Ryan's five no-hitters
7. Jose Canseco's 42-home run, 40-stolen base 1988 season
8. Ted Williams's 406 batting average in 1941 (or anyone who hit .400)
9. Wade Boggs's six consecutive 200-hit seasons
10. Roger Clemens' 20-strikeout game in 1986

—Players' list of most admired baseball milestones, compiled by Joey Johnston of the *Tampa Tribune* during spring training 1989 (from the newspaper, March 26, 1989). Nolan Ryan pitched two more no hitters before he retired.

THE FIVE MOST IMPORTANT EVENTS IN BASEBALL HISTORY 1900–1943

1. Babe Ruth's home-run performances
2. Revelations of 1919 World Series scandal and effect on game
3. Naming of Commissioner Landis
4. Dash of 1914 Boston Braves
5. Fred Merkle play in 1908

—Based on a survey of the Baseball Writers Association of America

LIFE OF THE BALLPLAYER

I. Appreciated Elsewhere
II. Controversial Leader
III. Comeback Kid (!)
IV. Disabled
V. Disappointment (?)
VI. Established Star
VII. Ex-
VIII. Hanger-On
IX. Hero
X. Leader
XI. Phenom
XII. Prospect
XIII. Regular
XIV. Restored (El Comebacko Segundo)
XV. Star
XVI. Superstar cum Celebrity
XVII. Trade Bait
XVIII. Veteran

—Appeared in a *Sports Illustrated* profile of Tom Seaver, July 27, 1981. Seaver at the time was at XVI.

Some Miscellaneous Items Accepted by the Baseball Hall of Fame in 1988

1. 4 x 5 speed graphic press camera used by *Philadelphia Inquirer* photographer, Robert Mooney, 1940s
2. Broadside advertising baseball tournament in Moscow, June 1988
3. Broadside advertising Kansas City Monarchs Negro League game
4. Glove, bats, baseballs, tickets, facsimile World Series ring from movie *Eight Men Out*
5. Henry Chadwick's business card
6. Lee Weyer's collection of umpire paraphernalia
7. Mask worn by White Sox Carlton Fisk during 1988 season when he broke A.L. record form games caught, career
8. Red Murray's sliding pads, circa 1910
9. Souvenir button, Jackie Robinson 1947 Rookie of Year
10. Sports jacket worn by New York Mets' broadcaster Lindsey Nelson
11. Seat from Chicago's Wrigley Field
12. Tudor True-Action Electric Baseball Game, 1960
13. Watch presented to Max Manning, leading Negro League pitcher, 1946

Ten Fast Ones

Here are ten general pitching guides (remembering that no pitching rule is infallible):

1. The guess hitter is that fellow who suddenly looks bad on a pitch that ordinarily doesn't bother him.
2. It takes awhile to spot the first-ball hitter, but once he's spotted, he should never be given a good first pitch.
3. The guess hitter is playing percentages and the more pitches a pitcher can get over the plate the lower the guess hitter's percentage will be.
4. If a pitcher pitches a hitter by an unvarying formula, he'll soon recognize the pattern and set himself for it.
5. The hitter who jumps wildly away from any close pitch is worried about being hit. A pitch which breaks away from him should be effective.
6. A hitter who rocks back on his heels when taking a pitch will probably have trouble with outside pitches.
7. The hitter who chases one pitch outside the strike zone is likely to chase a second.
8. The right-handed batter who's ineffective against a right-hander's curve often gets fat on a left-hander's curve.
9. The lunge hitter (overstrider) will have trouble with a curve or change-up because it's difficult to hit these pitches when the weight is on the front foot.
10. If a hitter looks bad on a pitch (and isn't guessing), that pitch will stick in his mind, the rest of the game; therefore, a hurler's other pitches might increase in effectiveness.

—*Baseball Digest,* April 1958

The Unwritten Samurai Code of Conduct for Baseball Players

Article 1. The player must be a total team member.

Article 2. The player must follow established procedure.

Article 3. The player must undergo hard training.

Article 4. The player must play "For the team."

Article 5. The player must demonstrate fighting spirit.

Article 6. The player must behave like a gentleman on the field.

Article 7. The player must not be materialistic.

Article 8. The player must be careful in his comments to the press.

Article 9. The player must follow the rule of sameness.

Article 10. The player must behave like a good Japanese off the field.

Article 11. The player must recognize the team pecking order.

Article 12. The player must strive for team harmony and unity.

—Robert Whiting, *The Chrysanthemum and the Bat: Baseball Samurai Style*

Three Typical *Sporting News* Headlines, 1962

1. Bargain-Counter Kid Adds Soup at Dish for Crackers
2. ERA King Donovan Buffs Crown for Repeat Reign
3. Hub Hose Peg Kid Mound Comers to Pace '62 Climb

Top Ten of '53

The game's outstanding events during the year were:

1. U.S. Supreme Court decision holding baseball a sport and not a business
2. Transfer of Braves' franchise from Boston to Milwaukee
3. Fifth consecutive World's Series triumph for Yankees
4. Transfer of Browns from St. Louis to Baltimore
5. Dispute between players and club owners on pension plan
6. Acquisition of Cardinals and Sportsman's Park in St. Louis by Anheuser-Busch, Inc
7. No-hitter by Bobo Holloman, Browns' rookie, against Athletics
8. Conference of minor league presidents on remedial legislation at Dallas
9. Tours of Japan by Giants and Eddie Lopat's All-Star team
10. Sale of Yankee Stadium to the Arnold Johnson Corporation

—*Sporting News*, early 1954

Bob Broeg's Ten Most Colorful Players

1) Babe Ruth 2) Casey Stengel 3) Ty Cobb 4) Dizzy Dean 5) Pepper Martin 6) Jackie Robinson 7) Frank Frisch 8) Rabbit Maranville 9) Willie Mays 10) (tie) Satchel Paige and Hack Wilson

—From one of his 1975 *Sporting News* columns

Don Carmen's List of Responses to Reporters—"You saw the game . . . take what you need."

1. I'm just glad to be here. I just want to help the club any way I can.
2. Baseball's a funny game.
3. I'd rather be lucky than good.
4. We're going to take the season one game at a time.
5. You're only as good as your last game (last at-bat).
6. This game has really changed.
7. If we stay healthy we should be right there.
8. It takes 24 (25) players.
9. We need two more players to take us over the top: Babe Ruth and Lou Gehrig.
10. We have a different hero every day.
11. We'll get 'em tomorrow.
12. This team seems ready to get going.
13. With a couple breaks, we win that game.
14. That All-Star voting is a joke.
15. The catcher and I were on the same wavelength.
16. I just went right at 'em.
17. I did my best and that's all I can do.
18. You just can't pitch behind.
19. That's the name of the game.
20. We've got to have fun.
21. I didn't have my good stuff, but I battled 'em.
22. Give the guy some credit; he hit a good pitch.
23. Hey, we were due to catch a break or two.
24. Yes.
25. No.
26. That's why they pay him a million dollars.
27. Even I could have hit that pitch.
28. I know you are but what am I?
29. I was getting my off-speed stuff over so they couldn't sit on the fastball.
30. I had my at 'em ball going today.
31. I had some great plays made behind me tonight.
32. I couldn't have done it without my teammates.
33. You saw it . . . write it.
34. I just wanted to go as hard as I could as long as I could.
35. I'm seeing the ball real good.
36. I hit that ball good.
37. I don't get paid to hit.

—The Philly reliever had these clichés posted on his locker during the 1990 season. The list appeared in an AP item of June 23, 1990.

Walter Johnson's Presidential Record

Walter Johnson, the greatest pitcher of his era and perhaps the greatest of all time, almost always opened the season for the Senators, which meant that he starred at the major leagues' official Opening Day. For the statistically minded, take in the following:

Johnson pitched seven openers with the president of the United States in attendance. He pitched before presidents four times on other than Opening Days. As manager of the Senators, Johnson took part in four presidential Opening Day ceremonies. He managed in two other games that were not openers but at which presidents were present. The Senators played twenty-one games before presidents at which Johnson was neither pitching nor managing but was a member of the team.

As a spectator or journalist (after his career Johnson covered a few games as a broadcaster or writer) he was on hand for six games at which presidents were in attendance.

All told, Walter Johnson and one president or another attended forty-four games together.

The forty-four games broken down by president:

Woodrow Wilson 11 games
Calvin Coolidge 9
Herbert Hoover 8
William Taft 7
Warren Harding 5
Franklin Roosevelt 4

—*Baseball: The President's Game* by William B. Mead and Paul Dickson

"WHO'S ON FIRST"

(Positions)

1st—Who
2nd—What
S.S.—I Don't Care
3rd—I Don't Know
L.F.—Why
C.F.—Because
R.F.—Omitted
P.—Tomorrow
C.—Today

YAZ-ABILIA

Boys' T shirts, sweat shirts and pajamas
Ice cream, frozen confections and milk
Cookies, cakes, muffins and Big Yaz Special Fitness Bread
45 RPM phonograph records and 33⅓ long-playing records
A children's story and picture book on baseball instruction
Baseball caps
Junior baseball sets with plastic ball and bat, baseball strategy board game, baseball target game, bagatelle game, baseball spin-a-game
A baseball action game
Potato chips, mayonnaise, relish
Baseball batting gloves
Frankfurters, scotch ham and cold cuts
Posters (with his blown-up picture)
Boys' jeans and fastback pants
Button and snap warm-up jackets.

—Licenses signed by Carl Yastrzemski at the start of the 1968 season, reported by Ed Linn in *Sport*

LITTLE, GRADY

"Once I manage a game for the Dodgers, people are going to quit asking me about Pedro. They're going to start asking me about what I screwed up in the game that night instead."

> —As the new Los Angeles Dodgers manager, talking in spring training about his decision to keep a tired Pedro Martinez in in the eighth inning of the seventh game of the 2003 American League Championship Series, one in which the Boston Red Sox eventually lost to the New York Yankees. *Baltimore Sun*, July 16, 2006.

LITTLEFIELD, BILL

"A grounds crew made up of about equal parts old men and teenagers scuttles out from somewhere and starts the long process of removing the tarp. As they reveal the soft, dry dirt, you're aware, suddenly and again, of how bright the grass is, how perfect the contrast between the great, green lawn of the outfielders and the arc of the brown infield."

> —Henry Horenstein and Bill Littlefield, *Baseball Days: From the Sandlots to "The Show"* (Boston: Bulfinch Press/Little, Brown, 1993)

"Baseball fields are places of magic and wonder, even those that aren't cut out of Iowa cornfields, because they marry the elegance of geometry with the fascination of history (which is only a fancy name for story-telling) more effectively than any place but a church."

> —*Baseball Days: From the Sandlots to "The Show"*

LITTLEFIELD, DICK

"Trading is rough on a man's family."

> —One of the most traded players of the modern era; quoted in *Baseball Is a Funny Game* by Joe Garagiola

LOCKMAN, WHITEY

"First basemen who tie themselves in knots are not popular with second basemen, third basemen and shortstops."

> —Writing as the 1952 All-Star first baseman for the Giants in the *Mutual Baseball Almanac*

"Power is fine as long as it's consistent. We've had power clubs in the past. But if that power cools, you're in trouble, because you keep waiting for the big inning that never comes. Then, if you can't score with speed or finesse, or have given up too much on defense, there's only one way you can go: You have to lose more often than you win."

> —As Cubs manager in the *Christian Science Monitor*, March 13, 1974

LOES, BILLY

"I have no intention or desire to win 20 games, because they keep expecting it of you."

> —Quoted by Arnold Hano in "I'm for Me," *Sport*, December 1963

"I lost it in the sun."

> —As a Brooklyn pitcher on why he fumbled a ground ball hit to him

LOES, BILLY (CONTINUED)

"When you're president, do something about taxes. They're killing me."

> —On meeting Vice President Richard M. Nixon; quoted in *Sports,* August 1960

LOLICH, MICKEY

"I guess you could say I'm the redemption of the fat man. A guy will be watching me on TV and see that I don't look in any better shape than he is. 'Hey Maude,' he'll holler. 'Get a load of this guy.' And he's a 20-game winner."

> —Apparently Lolich has made this point on more than one occasion, as here is another version: "All the fat guys watch me and say to their wives, 'See, there's a fat guy doing okay. Bring me another beer.' Fat guys need idols too"; quoted in *Sports Illustrated,* June 19, 1972

LONBORG, JIM

"It has to be physical. That's why I'm soaking my arm now. If it was mental, I'd be soaking my head!"

> —When asked if the difficulty in pitching after just two days' rest was physical or mental; quoted in *Baseball Digest,* January 1968

"You can understand the thrill of baseball, but there is something mysterious about skiing."

> —Quoted in *The Summer Game* by Roger Angell

Mickey Lolich (*Detroit Tigers*)

LONG, DALE

"You can shake a dozen glove men out of a tree, but the bat separates the men from the boys."

> —As a Washington Senators first baseman

LONGFELLOW, HENRY WADSWORTH

"[Ball playing] communicated such an impulse to our limbs and joints, that there is nothing now heard of, in our leisure hours, but ball, ball. I cannot prophesy with any degree of accuracy concerning the continuance of this rage for play, but the effect is good, since there has been a thoroughgoing reformation from inactivity and turpitude."

> —As a Bowdoin College student, 1824; quoted by Harold Seymour in *Baseball: The People's Game*

LONGWORTH, ALICE ROOSEVELT

"Father and all of us regarded baseball as a mollycoddle game. Tennis, football, lacrosse, boxing, polo, yes; they are violent, which appealed to us. But baseball? Father wouldn't watch it, not even at Harvard."

> —The quote given to Krock when he called Teddy Roosevelt's daughter to find out why it had been President Taft, and not TR, who established the custom of throwing out the first baseball of the season; quoted by Arthur Krock, *New York Times,* April 5, 1961.

LOPES, DAVE

"My philosophy is to do anything you can to make the other team nervous. A running team puts a lot of pressure on the other side. You pressure the catcher, obviously. But, in addition, you put a lot of heat on the infield. One of those guys in the middle has to be moving, and that opens up another hole to hit through. And very often, the pitcher eases up a little. All this makes the game more exciting for the fans . . . because there's so much action. The most entertaining ball club is one that's aggressive on the base paths. It's a funny thing: Running brings your team together—and also brings the crowd to its feet."

> —The Dodger, from a *Los Angeles Times* interview, February 22, 1976

LOPEZ, AL

"I usually stick out my hand and hope he puts the ball in it. Except the one time I went out to take Early Wynn out. I stuck out my hand and he hit me right in the stomach with the ball."

> —As White Sox manager on making a pitching

Al Lopez (*National Baseball Library*)

change; quoted in the March 1969 *Baseball Digest* by Robert Markus of the *Chicago Tribune*

"It's tough to be pitching and having to worry about what a catcher's gonna call. If a catcher's got a reputation of being a rock head, the pitcher's gonna have to worry that much more."

> —Quoted in *Sox: From Lane and Fain to Zisk and Fisk* by Bob Vanderberg

"The Yankees can be had."

> —From the man who had them twice, as manager of the Cleveland Indians in 1954 and of the Chicago White Sox in 1959; quoted in *The Official Yankee Hater's Handbook* by William B. Mead

"The youngsters coming up now just go through the motions necessary to make the

LOPEZ, AL (CONTINUED)

play. They should bounce around a little, show some life and zip. It adds a little action and gives the fans something to look at—rather than the monotonous routine, no matter how perfectly the play is made."

—As White Sox manager

"They say anything can happen in a short series. I just didn't expect it to be that short."

—Quoted by Donald Honig; 1954, after losing the World Series to the Giants, 0-4

"You make it livelier, and some little guy will hit a homer in June and for the rest of the season he's swinging for the fences and isn't worth a damn."

—On the livelier ball; quoted by Dick Young in the *New York Daily News*; quoted in *Baseball Digest,* February 1969

LOWENSTEIN, JOHN

"Home runs tend to immobilize the outfielders. . . . They should move first base back a step to eliminate all the close play.s . . . World War III would render all baseball statistics meaningless. . . . I don't want to be a star, I just want to twinkle a bit."

—Quoted in Gordon Beard, "'Brother Lo'—He's Still Far Out," *Orioles Gazette,* September 4, 1993

"I flush the john between innings to keep my wrists strong."

—How he remained ready as an Orioles' benchwarmer, *Sports Illustrated,* July 23, 1979

"Sometimes it seems like every other thing you hear is backwards. They tell a hitter that he should 'swing down.' That would be great, if the object of the game were to hit the ball between people's legs. But they've got fences out there and they let you run around the bases for free if you hit it over the wall. So, obviously, you should be swinging slightly up.

"They tell you all your life never to lift weights, then you find out it's just what you should have been doing all along. They tell you always to catch a fly ball with two hands, but, if you think about it, you should almost always catch it one-handed off to the side so your arms don't block your own vision.

"It goes on and on. You see guys stumbling running the bases because they're so determined to 'hit every base with the left foot.' You should question everything."

—Quoted by Tom Boswell in the September 5, 1982, *Washington Post*

"Sure, I screwed up that sacrifice bunt, but look at it this way. I'm a better bunter than a billion Chinese. Those poor suckers can't bunt at all."

—Quoted in *Inside Sports,* July 1981

LUCCHESI, FRANK

"Baseball has been good to me. I'm sick and tired of these punks saying 'play me or trade me.' Let 'em go find a job."

—As Texas Rangers manager; quoted in the *Los Angeles Herald-Examiner,* March 25, 1977

"I'm not making predictions but I think there has been only one man more optimistic than

336

I am. That was General Custer, who told his men, 'Don't take any prisioners.'"

—On becoming manager of the Phillies, 1969

"You cannot serve water with a pitchfork."

—As manager of the Texas Rangers, on the difficulty of winning with a bad team; quoted in *Sports Illustrated,* May 17, 1976

LUCIANO, RON

"A lot of the calls [by an umpire] are guesses. They have to be. How can you really tell, for example, when a ball is trapped [rather than caught] by an outfielder? The gloves today are so big they can cover the side of a building. So you make the call and hope they don't show you up on the instant replay. With balls and strikes, it's impossible to get them right all the time. I mean, every major-league pitch moves some way or other. None go straight, not even the fastballs. And the batters often can't do any better than the umpires."

—Quoted in the *Chicago Tribune,* May 2, 1982

"An umpire either has it or he doesn't, and without it he'll never be a good umpire."

—*Strike Two*

"Any umpire who claims he has never missed a play is . . . well, an umpire."

—*The Umpire Strikes Back*

"Catchers are the most beat-up, bruised, broken, knurled players on the field. They are the only athletes I know who can stick their hands out straight and point behind them."

—*The Umpire Strikes Back*

"Having me come up to the majors so soon after he got there was something like having the dog eat your birthday cake before you got to blow out the candles."

—How Earl Weaver must have felt when Luciano got called up to the majors right after Weaver did, in *The Umpire Strikes Back*

"He's so slow that you could take sequence photos of him with a Polaroid camera."

—On John Mayberry's lack of speed in *The Umpire Strikes Back*

"It would go up, down, inside, up again, down, stop for a sandwich, up, down, then zip across the plate."

—Describing the flight of the knuckleball, in *The Umpire Strikes Back*

"Lou Piniella only argues on days ending with the letter 'y.'"

—*The Umpire Strikes Back* by Ron Luciano

"Managers only know the rules with which they've had problems."

—*The Umpire Strikes Back*

"My face is made for radio."

—*The Umpire Strikes Back*

"My main weakness as an umpire was the fact I could let a molehill become a mountain."

—*The Umpire Strikes Back*

"One reason I never called balks is that I never understood the rule."

—*Strike Two*

"Some umpires tend to pull into a shell and build a fence around themselves. I'd rather get it out. It's like admitting when I make a mistake. There's no way I can keep it in. It helps me relax to admit that I was wrong. People only remember the one mistake, but who the hell is right all the time? I've never met the perfect man and I know I'm going to miss one now and then. You just pray it doesn't happen in a big moment. The umpire who makes a bad call to blow a no-hitter is going to cry himself to sleep for the next 30 nights."

—On fallibility, in a June 27, 1975, *Los Angeles Times* interview

"Sometimes, although many people do not believe this, being screamed at by a manager or player standing inches away, and perhaps spitting tobacco juice on you, is not as much fun as it appears to be from a distance."

—*Strike Two*

"That's like throwing Bambi out of the forest."

—On being the first ump in pro baseball to eject the soft-spoken Mark Belanger from a game, *The Umpire Strikes Back*

"The practical joke is the psychiatry of baseball."

—*Strike Two*

"The umpires have kept this game honest for 100 years. We're the only segment of the game that has never been touched by scandal. We've got to be too dumb to cheat. We must have integrity, because we sure don't have a normal family life. We certainly aren't properly paid.

We have no health care, no job security, no tenure. Our pension plan is a joke. We take more abuse than any living group of humans, and can't give any back. If we're fired without notice, our only recourse is to appeal to the league president. And he's the guy that fires you. If you ask for one day off in the seven-month season, they try to make you feel three inches tall. If you call in sick, you're hounded and ostracized by the brass. Umpires must be the healthiest people on earth because none of us ever gets sick."

—Commonly cited umpire's credo

"Throwing people out of a game is like learning to ride a bicycle—once you get the hang of it, it can be a lot of fun."

—*Strike Two*

"Umpire's heaven is a place where he works third base every game. Home is where the heartache is."

—*Strike Two*

"We got along slightly better than Hugh Hefner and the Moral Majority."

—On Luciano's relationship with Earl Weaver, in *The Umpire Strikes Back*

"What I really hate about umpiring is that we can never win. We don't walk off a field with a grin on our faces."

—*Newsweek,* September 1, 1975

"When I started, it was played by nine tough competitors on grass, in graceful ball parks. By the time I was finished, there were ten men on each side, the game was played indoors, on plastic, and I had to spend half my time watching out for a man dressed in a chicken suit who kept trying to kiss me."

—As former umpire, 1982

"Whenever an umpire settles down to reminisce about his career, he will invariably begin with the six most accurate words in the English language: It wasn't funny at the time."

—*Strike Two*

LURIE, BOB

"A complete ballplayer today is one who can hit, field, run, throw and pick the right agent."

—As San Francisco Giants owner, 1981

LUZINSKI, GREG

"Baseball's a routine. You're doing the same thing day in, day out. You try to reach a certain level and once you're there you try to maintain it. If you don't do it one day there's always the next, and it always comes in a hurry. You can be headlines as a hero one day and a goat the next."

—Quoted in the *Chicago Tribune*, May 2, 1982

LYLE, SPARKY

"Some people say you have to be nuts to be a relief pitcher. But the truth is I was nuts before I ever became one!"

—Quoted in *High Inside: Memoirs of a Baseball Wife* by Danielle Gagnon Torrez

"Why pitch nine innings when you can get just as famous pitching two?"

—SABR Collection

LYNCH, ED

"The bases were drunk, and I painted the black with my best yakker. But blue squeezed me, and I went full. I came back with my heater, but the stick flares one the other way and chalk flies for two bases. Three earnies! Next thing I know, skipper hooks me and I'm sipping suds with the clubby."

—Widely quoted as a Mets pitcher

LYNES, RUSSELL

"The analogy between baseball fans and jazz fans is closer, it seems to me, than that between other audiences. The aficionados are aware of and concerned with the refinements of performance and the particular kinds of poetry in both solo and ensemble performances. (A beautifully executed double steal is as elegant as a Goodman arpeggio.) Like baseball fans, jazz fans know who played where and with whom and to what effect; they talk a rarefied language and drop the names of clarinetists and percussionists as baseball fans do the names of long-forgotten (except by them) shortstops and spitballers. Their retention of detail is prodigious."

—From "Ragtime to Riches," *The Lively Audience: A Social History of the Visual and Performing Arts in America, 1890–1950* (New York: Harper & Row, 1985)

LYONS, TED

"Musial's batting stance looks like a small boy looking around a corner to see if the cops are coming."

—As a White Sox pitcher on Cardinal Stan Musial and his odd crouch at the plate, 1941

M

MacArthur, General Douglas

"It is wonderful to be here, to be able to hear the baseball against the bat, ball against glove, the call of the vendor, and be able to boo the umpire."

> —On his return to the United States from Europe in 1946

"Ty Cobb injected much of his own fighting spirit into that aspect of the American character which has put inspiration and direction behind our progress as a free nation."

> —Foreword to Cobb's *My Life in Baseball: The True Record*

Mack, Connie

"After all my years, there are two things I've never got used to: haggling with a player over his contract, and telling a boy he's got to go back."

> —*From Sandlot to Big League: Connie Mack's Baseball Book*

Connie Mack (*National Baseball Library*)

"Any minute, any day, some players may break a long-standing record. That's one of the fascinations about the game—the unexpected surprises."

> —*My 66 Years in the Big Leagues*

"Baseball was mighty and exciting to me, but there is no blinking at the fact that at the time the game was thought, by solid sensible people, to be only one degree above grand larceny, arson, and mayhem."

—On baseball in the 1880s, in *The Giants of the Polo Grounds* by Noel Hynd

"I remember when Jack [Dunn]—it must have been about 1914—offered me two pitchers, Ruth and Ernie Shore, and told me to take 'em for nothing. I said no.' There was a horrified silence. Then someone said weakly: 'You don't mean Babe Ruth?'

"Connie smiled faintly.

"'Yes. Oh, I didn't turn him down because I didn't think he was good. He was already a star in Baltimore, although I believe Shore's record was even better than Babe's down there.

"'But Jack didn't have any money in those days and we didn't, either. I remember I told him, "No, you keep those fellows, Jack, and sell 'em where you can get some money. You can use it as well as I."

"'Well, sir, he finally sold them to Boston and I think he let the two of 'em go for something like $5,000.'"

—On an offer from the owner of the Baltimore Orioles; quoted by Red Smith in the *Sporting News*, December 23, 1943

"I suppose you know why I took you out. You see, the American League record for striking out is five times in one game, and I didn't want you to tie it in your very first big league game."

—To Jimmy Dykes after he had struck out four times in his first game; quoted in *Good for a Laugh* by Bennett Cerf

I will always play the game to the best of my ability.

I will always play to win, but if I lose, I will not look for an excuse to detract from my opponent's victory.

I will never take an unfair advantage in order to win.

I will always abide by the rules of the game—on the diamond as well as in daily life.

I will always conduct myself as a true sportsman—on and off the playing field.

I will always strive for the good of the entire team rather than for my own glory.

I will never gloat in victory or pity myself in defeat.

I will do my utmost to keep myself clean—physically, mentally and morally.

I will always judge a teammate or an opponent as an individual and never on the basis of his race or religion.

—"Code of Conduct" from *Connie Mack's Baseball Book* (New York: Alfred A. Knopf, 1950)

"Never in a World Series have I seen such awful ketchin."

—On Yogi Berra's performance in the 1947 World Series. Yogi's blunders reached a climax in Game 4, when Al Gionfriddo's steal of second (the fifth off Berra to that point in the Series) encouraged the Yanks to intentionally pass Pete Reiser. Cookie Lavagetto hit next, and Bill Bevens lost a no-hitter, and the game, on one swing.

Mack, Connie (continued)

"One day I had to take him out of a game at Detroit. I was pretty well disgusted when he came into the dugout. I said, 'Pennock, as far as I am concerned, you can sit on the bench and not throw another ball the rest of the season.' He replied: 'If that's the way you feel, either sell me or give me my release.' I traded him—and he later developed into one of the greatest southpaws of all time."

> —On the sale of Herb Pennock, which he regarded as his biggest mistake; quoted by Red Smith in the *Sporting News,* December 30, 1943

"The game has kept faith with the public, maintaining its old admission price for nearly 30 years while other forms of entertainment have doubled and tripled in price. And it will probably never change."

> —In 1931; widely attributed

"No matter what I talk about, I always get back to baseball."

> —At age eighty-eight; quoted in the *Sporting News* March 14, 1951

"There has been only one manager and his name is John McGraw."

> —*The Giants of the Polo Grounds* by Noel Hynd

"We traveled four in a berth and when it came to meal tips, the manager would put down a silver dollar for the whole team."

> —On his first trip to spring training as a player; quoted in the *Sporting News,* April 20, 1955

"Whether a team wins a baseball game or not depends on its pitcher. He is the defensive anchor. He is the one man on the team who comes into active competition with every member of the opposing side. He carries most of the load—some players put it as high as 75 per cent."

> —*Connie Mack's Baseball Book*

"You can't win them all."

> —At the end of the 1916 season when his Athletics lost 116 games

"You're born with two strikes against you, so don't take a third one on your own."

> —Advice to players, including Bing Miller, in whose *Sporting News* obituary it was quoted. Miller died on May 7, 1966.

Mackey, Biz

"A lot of pitchers have a fastball, but a very, very few—Feller, Grove, Johnson, a couple of others besides Satchel—have had that little extra juice that makes the difference between the good and the great man. When it's that fast, it will hop a little at the end of the line. Beyond that, it tends to disappear. I've heard about Satchel throwing pitches that wasn't hit but that never showed up in the catcher's mitt nevertheless. They say the catcher, the umpire, and the bat boys looked all over for that ball, but it was gone. Now how do you account for that?"

> —Mackey is considered by many the greatest catcher in Negro League history. From the papers of John Coates now in the possession of the SABR Collection

MacPhail, Andy

"It does bother me. I'm going to be a household word—like 'toilet.'"

—On not signing Jack Morris with the Twins, *Sports Illustrated*

"It's hard to believe you get a bargain for $1 million, but you do when you consider the way salaries are escalating."

—The Twins GM after signing Kirby Puckett to a three-year contract for a million

MacPhail, Larry

"He'll eat his way out of the major leagues."

—On Boog Powell after he had just come up to the majors. MacPhail later admitted that he "regretted the crack," especially because of Powell's success.

"Keep the customers awake and you'll keep 'em coming."

—On baseball attendance; widely attributed

"So I waited for my first look at the prize package which was worth $50,000. The instant I saw him my heart sank and I wondered why I had been so foolish as to refuse to sell him. In bustled a stocky little guy in a sailor suit. He had no neck and his muscles were virtually busting the buttons off his uniform. He was one of the most unprepossessing fellows I ever set eyes on in my life. And the sailor suit accentuated every defect."

—On first meeting Yogi Berra as Yankees president. Earlier, Mel Ott of the Giants had offered MacPhail $50,000 for Berra. At the time of the offer MacPhail had never heard of Berra but figured he must be good if the Giants would pay $50,000 for him; quoted by Arthur Daley June 1941 in *Baseball Digest*

Maddocks, Melvin

"Watching baseball under the lights is like observing dogs indoors, at a pedigree show. In both instances, the environment is too controlled to suit the species."

—From his "Baseball—The Difference Between Night and Day," *Christian Science Monitor*, April 3, 1985

Maddox, Garry

"As I remember it, the bases were loaded."

—When asked to describe a 1971 grand-slam home run; widely quoted

"With all the glamour attached to hitting the ball out of the park, it takes a lot of discipline to go up there and just try to get a base hit."

—Quoted in the *Christian Science Monitor*, April 25, 1977

Maddux, Greg

"You see it in the drive-through at Wendy's. Some people actually care about what they're doing and some don't. I care. Everybody cares, but it's obvious some care a lot more than others. It just seems like the ones that care the most are the ones that stay around the longest."

—*New York Times*, March 30, 2003

MADLOCK, BILL

"Baseball, hot dogs, apple pie and violent behavior."

> —After a fifteen-day suspension for violent behavior; quoted in the *Washington Post,* June 29, 1980

MAGERKURTH, GEORGE

"Only guys with guts get into jams."

> —Directed at umpire Bill Stewart during the 1946 World Series

MAGLIE, SAL

"The second one lets the hitter know you meant the first one."

> —On a second knockdown pitch

Sal Maglie (*Society for American Baseball Research; SABR*)

"When I'm pitching I figure that plate is mine, and I don't like anybody getting too close to it."

> —*It Takes Heart* by Mel Allen with Frank Graham Jr.

MAHLER, MICKEY

"Every player that has played in three straight years in the majors, I'd send back to the Triple A for a month, just to let them see what it was like so they wouldn't forget how good they have it."

> —From "Diamond Quotes" in *Nine,* 2006

MALAMUD, BERNARD

"It has a mythic quality. You have a confrontation between two forces, the batter, who's a hero, and the pitcher, who's an eternal adversary. It's much like the confrontation between two knights in a tournament, where it can end with a single blow, like the knight cutting off the other knight's head or the ballplayer hitting one into the stands or striking out."

> —On why baseball is celebrated in literature; quoted by Edwin McDowell in "The Pastime and the Literati," *New York Times,* April 8, 1981

"Sometimes when I walk down the street I bet people will say there goes Roy Hobbs, the best there ever was in the game."

> —*The Natural* (film), Roy Hobbs to Harriet Bird on what he hopes to accomplish

"The whole history of baseball has the quality of mythology."

> —Widely attributed

MALONEY, RUSSELL

"Most males who don't care about big-league baseball conceal their indifference as carefully as they would conceal a laughable physical deficiency."

—Quoted by Clifton Fadiman in his *American Treasury 1455–1955*

MANNERS, MISS (JUDITH MARTIN)

"If it's properly done (not aimed at anyone or anyone's shoes) it's part of the charm. It's a terribly basebally thing to do."

—On spitting in baseball; quoted in the *Baltimore Sun*, October 21, 1993

MANTLE, MICKEY

"Al, you don't realize how easy this game is until you get up in that broadcasting booth."

—To Al Kaline after his first World Series game as a sportscaster. From Bill Freehan's *Behind the Mask*

"As far as I'm concerned, Aaron is the best ballplayer of my era. He is to baseball of the last 15 years what Joe DiMaggio was before him.

"He's never received the credit he's due.

"I still think the American League is better but the National has more outstanding stars. The best one is Hank Aaron.

"Ted Williams is the best hitter I ever saw but DiMaggio was the most finished player. DiMag could hit, throw, field and run the bases.

"I put Aaron in the same category. He is loose and agile as a cat. When he hits the ball—man, it's like thunder! And he never makes a mistake.

"If he'd played in New York or on the Pacific Coast, where he could have had the advantage of publicity, he'd be rated with the all-time greatest."

—Quoted in the June 1970, *Baseball Digest*

"Great idea, but I don't remember anything from that year."

—Mantle's answer when a writer asked the Hall of Famer if he would like to coauthor a book about his 1956 Triple Crown season. Recalled when he entered the Betty Ford Center in January 1994 for treatment of his forty-three-year battle with alcohol. *Toronto Star*, January 1, 1995.

"Ever since I retired, I keep having these dreams. The worst one is I go to the ballpark late, jump out of a cab, and I hear 'em calling my name on the public address system. I try and get in and all the gates are locked. Then I see a hole under the fence and I can see Casey looking for me, and Yogi and Billy Martin and Whitey Ford. I try to crawl through the hole and I get stuck at the hips. And that's when I wake up, sweating."

—Quoted by Danielle Gagnon Torres in *High Inside: Memoirs of a Baseball Wife*

"I can't play anymore. I can't hit the ball when I need to. I can't steal second when I need to. I can't go from first to third when I need to. I can't score from second when I need to. I have to quit."

—On why he was retiring, 1968

"I don't care what the situation was, how high the stakes were—the bases could be loaded and the pennant riding on every pitch, it never bothered Whitey. He pitched his game. Cool. Crafty. Nerves of steel."

> —On Whitey Ford

"I have no idea why I liked him so much. We could never figure it out. Me and Whitey Ford and Billy were all so different. That's why we got along so well."

> —On his long friendship with Billy Martin shortly after hearing of Martin's death; quoted in the *Washington Times,* December 29, 1989

"I know men are not supposed to talk about love for other men, especially so-called macho athletes. But I don't mind telling you that I love Whitey Ford. I couldn't love him more if he was my own brother."

> —From the preface to *Slick* by Whitey Ford, signed "Dallas," November 1986

"I never knew how someone dying could say he was the luckiest man in the world. But now I understand."

> —On his own retirement and that of Lou Gehrig; widely attributed.

"My last four or five years with the Yankees, I didn't realize I was ruining myself with all the drinking. I just thought, this is fun. Hell, I used to see guys come into Yankee Stadium from Detroit or Chicago; they'd be out taking batting practice, all of them with hangovers.

But today I can admit that all the drinking shortened my career."

> —Quoted in his *Los Angeles Times* obituary, August 14, 1995

"My views are just about the same as Casey's."

> —Asked by the Senate Anti-Trust Committee what his views were on baseball legislation, July 9, 1958. He followed Casey Stengel, whose views on the matter were puzzling.

"That s.o.b. is so mean he'd fucking knock you down in the dugout."

> —On Early Wynn; Hall of Fame Collection

"They should have come out of the dugout on tippy-toes, holding hands and singing."

> —On seeing the A's new green-and-gold suits, 1963

"When I was 20 years old, I was a better ball player than I am today. I could hit better, run faster and throw better. Yet they farmed me out to the minor leagues. I was too young to take all the pressures of major league ball. When a boy of 20 can handle it, you've got yourself a real special ballplayer—a Williams, a Musial or a Cobb."

> —Quoted in *Baseball Digest,* August 1961

MANUEL, CHARLIE

"I'll tackle that bridge when I get to it."

> —As Cleveland Indians manager; quoted in the *Baltimore Sun,* September 9, 2001

"I'm going to let the chips fall where they lay."

> —Quoted in the *Baltimore Sun,* September 9, 2001

MARANVILLE, WALTER "RABBIT"

"Nobody gets a kick out of baseball anymore, because big salaries and the pension fund have made it a more serious business than running a bank."

—Quoted by Stanley Frank in *Sports Illustrated*, August 27, 1962

"There is much less drinking now than there was before 1927, because I quit drinking on May 24, 1927."

—As Boston Braves manager

MARION, MARTY

"A .220 hitter in the minors will be a .220 hitter all his life."

—As a Cardinal coach; widely attributed

"Give me what I want and I'll take care of myself."

—As a young player Marion balked at signing. Branch Rickey told him: "Accept this, and I'll take care of you."

MARIS, ROGER

"A season's a season."

—As he compiled a 1961 home-run record in a 162-game baseball season, while Ruth did it in 1927 in a 154-game schedule; quoted in *Bo: Pitching and Wooing* by Maury Allen

Walter "Rabbit" Maranville (*Library of Congress Prints and Photographs, Bain Collection*)

"As a ballplayer, I would be delighted to do it again. As an individual, I doubt if I could possibly go through it again."

—Comment made after the '61 season, when he hit sixty-one home runs

"I don't know if I want to go to New York. They'll have to pay me a lot more money because I like it here in Kansas City."

—When told he had been traded to the Yankees; a remark which was apparently facetious but caused him trouble in New York

MARIS, ROGER (CONTINUED)

"I don't think it would be any different. Basically, it's somewhat the same . . . most of it comes off the field, from the press, in restaurants, before and after games. I think the most privacy I had was when the game was going on."

—On the pressure on Hank Aaron as he attempted to break Babe Ruth's mark of 714 career home runs as contrasted with the pressure on him in 1961; quoted by Wayne Minshaw in the *Sporting News* August 4, 1973

"I never wanted all this hoopla. All I wanted is to be a good ball player, hit 25 or 30 homers, drive in around a hundred runs, hit .280 and help my club win pennants. I just wanted to be one of the guys, an average player having a good season."

—After hitting his 50th home run during his 1961 season; quoted by Jack Orr in *My Greatest Day in Baseball.*

"'I probably could have caught the ball,' the veteran major league player said, 'but I would have had to dive for it.'

"'And as long as you were three runs ahead, you decided not to drive,' a reporter suggested.

"'I'm not going to dive into concrete for anybody.'"

—Quoted by Arnold Hano in "I'm for Me" in *Sport,* December 1963

"Maybe I'm not a great man, but I damn well want to break the record."

—On breaking Ruth's record; widely attributed

Roger Maris and Mickey Mantle (*Harry S. Truman Presidential Library*)

MARIS, ROGER, JR.

"To tell you the truth, I've wanted him to hit 62 all along. But I didn't want to just give it to him."

—Roger Maris Jr., after seeing Mark McGwire belt number 61, *St. Louis Post-Dispatch,* October 4, 1998

MARKHAM, CLARENCE M.

"Not even the signing of Jackie Robinson, Larry Doby or Roy Campanella meant as much to Negroes as a whole as the signing of LeRoy Paige, who had been the baseball hero of North America for years.

"They knew he had it and could prove he had it if just given a chance. Don't get me wrong. The Negro race is an appreciative one regardless of what anyone says. No, they have not forgotten that it was Branch Rickey who took the biggest step and made it possible for all that followed. Even when Bill Veeck signed Larry Doby they were grateful. But when it cam to Satchel Paige—well, that was something different. Here was a Negro player who all Negro America knew needed no advance publicity because he had proved his worth down through the years. To Negro America he was no amateur but a star—the biggest they knew—one who knew baseball like an old fox and could play against the finest the white league could find."

—From the October-November 1948 issue of *Negro Traveler;* quoted in *Maybe I'll Pitch Forever* by LeRoy (Satchel) Paige as told to David Lipman

MARQUARD, RUBE

"What a terrific spitball pitcher he was. Bugs drank a lot. He didn't spit on the ball, he blew his breath on it, and the ball would come up drunk."

—On Bugs Raymond, *Sports Illustrated*

MARSHALL, MIKE G.

"I don't know anything about ballet, but I wish people would watch baseball the way ballet fans watch the dance—not to see who wins but to see how well each player performs his part."

—Quoted in the *New York Times,* July 28, 1975

"I really enjoy pitching because, every time I go out there to the mound, I'm facing the top talent in the world. It really becomes an emotional involvement. I'm just tickled to death to be out there. There can be no greater thrill."

—As a Dodger pitcher; quoted in the *Washington Post,* April 16, 1975

"If they worked as hard at their jobs as I do at mine, this country wouldn't have the inflation problem it has now."

—On being booed by the fans in Minneapolis; quoted in *Sports Illustrated,* June 2, 1980

"The anti-intellectualism of baseball has been diminished. People are slowly discovering that there *is* life after baseball."

—Quoted in *Sports Illustrated,* June 10, 1974

MARTIN, BILLY

"Everybody judges players different. I judge a player by what he does for his ball club and not by what he does for himself. I think the name of the game is self-sacrifice."

—As Twins manager; widely attributed

"I don't think so because I've got the reputation for being baseball's bad boy and I don't deserve it. But I think I'd make a good manager. For one thing, I know how to handle men. That's the secret of managing. For another, I know enough about the game, not fundamentals, but executing. I think I could get the most out of players with common sense and psychology. I'm fiery enough and I'd have their respect. Unfortunately I don't think I'll ever get the chance and there's nothing in the world can change that."

—On his chances of ever managing; quoted in *Baseball Digest,* June 1961

"I was afraid of this. The kid looks just like me."

—On being shown Mike and Sharon Hargrove's baby by Sharon; quoted in *High Inside: Memoirs of a Baseball Wife* by Danielle Gagnon Torrez

"I've always said I could manage Adolf Hitler, Benito Mussolini and Hirohito. That doesn't mean I'd like them, but I'd manage them."

—As Yankee manager

"Sometimes I would do just the opposite of what George wanted me to do, because I won't let anyone tell me how to manage. If I'm going down the tube, I'm going to do it my way."

—*Number 1*

"The day I become a good loser, I'm quitting baseball. . . . I always had a temper. I think it's nothing to be ashamed of. If you know how to use it, it can help. Temper is something the good Lord gave me and I can't just throw it out the window."

—At the press conference at which he was announced as the manager of the 1969 Twins; quoted in the *Sporting News,* October 26, 1968

Billy Martin (*Texas Rangers*)

"The idea is to break as soon as the pitcher begins his motion—all you need to see is the guy twitch his wrist, and you take off. Usually, the pitcher will see you and panic. Eight out of 10 times, he'll do something wrong—rush his delivery and put the ball in the wrong place, throw the wrong pitch."

—On the art of stealing home; quoted as Oakland A's manager

"The only real way to know you've been fired is when you arrive at the ballpark and find your name has been scratched from the parking list."

—Widely quoted

"This place stinks. It's a shame a great guy like HHH had to be named after it."

—Manager of the New York Yankees, on his distaste for the Hubert Horatio Humphrey Metrodome in Minneapolis; quoted in the *Sporting News,* August 5, 1985.

"Thurman's death took a lot out of the ball club, took everything out of the club."

—*Number 1*

"What I miss when I'm away is the pride in baseball. Especially the pride of being on a team that wins. I probably was the proudest Yankee of them all. And I don't mean false pride. When it's real on a team, it's a deep love-pride. There's nothing greater in the world than when somebody on the team does something good, and everybody gathers around to pat him on the back. I really love the togetherness in baseball. That's a real true love.

—From by Frank Deford, "Love, Hate and Billy Martin," *Sports Illustrated*, June 2, 1975

"When I get through managing, I'm going to open up a kindergarten."

—Widely quoted

"When you're a professional, you come back, no matter what happened the day before. You don't want 'em to like you. . . . If you're any good, it'll only make you play harder."

—Quoted in *Late Innings* by Roger Angell

MARTIN, PEPPER

"Dizzy, I don't think you're playing this bird Terry deep enough!"

—One afternoon when Bill Terry almost tore Dean's legs off with a wicked liner through the box, scorched Diz's ear with a sizzler that went rocketing into center field, and, on his third hit, almost tore off Dean's glove; quoted by Bennett Cerf in his *Good for a Laugh*

"It's only a small bone."

—Response to reporters' questions about an incident in which he played with a broken finger, but nobody knew it until he threw the ball across the diamond and yards of bandage came following behind

"Well sir, I grew up in Oklahoma and out there, once you start running there ain't nothin' to stop you."

—In answer to a reporter's question: "Mr. Martin, how did you learn to run the way you do? Quoted in *The Baseball Card Engagement Book*, 1988

MARX, GROUCHO

"Yes, and so is everyone else in the league."

—On hearing that Leo Durocher was leading the Giants, *Sports Illustrated*

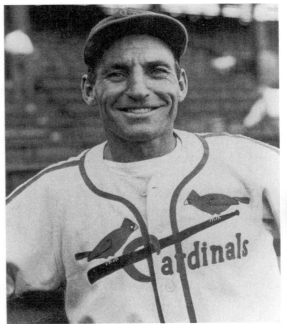

Pepper Martin (*William B. Mead*)

MASON, WALT

"You say your Grandma's dead, my lad, and you, bowed down with woe, to see her laid beneath the mold believe you ought to go and so you ask a half day off. And you may have that same. Alas, that Grannies always die when there's a baseball game. Last year, if I remember right, three grandmas died for you, and you bewailed the passing then of hearts so warm and true, and then another grandma died, a tall and stately dame (the day they buried her there was a fourteen inning game), and when the breezes of the May among the willows sighed, another grandma closed her eyes and crossed the Great Divide. They laid her gently to her rest beside the orchard wall—the day we lammed the stuffing from the reubs from Minniepaul. Go forth my son and mourn your dead, and shed the scalding tear and lay a wreath of flowers upon your eighteenth grandma's bier. While you perform this solemn task I'll to the grandstand go, and watch our pennant winning team make mincemeat of the foe."

> —One of his daily newspaper "Prose Rhymes." Mason (1836–1939) was read by an estimated ten million readers and was called "The Poet Laureate of American Democracy."

MASTERSON, BAT

"Everybody in life gets the same amount of ice. The rich get it in the summer and the poor in the winter."

> —Quote found in typewriter of *New York Telegram* sports editor Bat Masterson after he suffered a fatal heart attack; widely quoted

MATHEWS, EDDIE

"I'm just a beat up old third baseman. I'm just a small part of a wonderful game that is a tremendous part of America today . . . my mother used to pitch to me and my father would shag balls. If I hit one up the middle, close to my mother, I'd have some extra chores to do. My mother was instrumental in making me a pull hitter."

> —On his induction into the Hall of Fame, August 7, 1978

"It's only a hitch when you're in a slump. When you're hittin' the ball, it's called rythym."

> —Quoted by Roger Angell in *Late Innings*

"When you're a kid, what fun the game is! You grab a bat and glove and ball, and that's it. I know what Ted Williams and Stan Musial when they said it got tougher to get in shape every year."

> —Quoted by Lee Allen in his *Sporting News* column of March 30, 1968

MATHEWSON, CHRISTY

"A boy cannot begin playing ball too early. I might almost say that while he is still creeping on all fours he should have a bouncing rubber ball."

> —*Baseball: An Informal History* by Douglass Wallop

"A pitcher is not a ballplayer."

> —One of his most quoted lines, it has been given various interpretations, but most like this by George Plimpton in *Out of My League.* "What he meant was that a pitcher is a specialist, an artist, with all the accompanying

need of consolation and encouragement. Mollycoddling is almost as important to him as the rosin bag."

"A young ballplayer looks on his first spring training trip as a stage-struck young woman regards the theatre. She can think only of the lobster suppers and the applause and the colored lights."

—Widely attributed

"I have seen McGraw go onto ballfields where he is as welcome as a man with the black smallpox. . . . I have seen him take all sorts of personal chances. He doesn't know what fear is."

—Quoted in *The Giants of the Polo Grounds* by Noel Hynd

"In most Big League ball games, there comes an inning on which hangs victory or defeat. Certain intellectual fans call it the crisis; college professors, interested in the sport, have named it the psychological moment, Big League managers mention it as the 'break,' and pitchers speak of the 'pinch.' This is the time when each

Christy Mathewson (*Library of Congress Prints and Photographs, Bain Collection*)

team is straining every nerve either to win or to prevent defeat. The players and spectators realize that the outcome of the inning is of vital importance. And in most of these pinches, the real burden falls on the pitcher."

—*Pitching in a Pinch* by Christy Mathewson

"Many baseball fans look upon an umpire as a sort of necessary evil to the luxury of baseball, like the odor that follows an automobile."

—*Pitching in a Pinch*

"Speaking pretty generally, most managers prefer to use this 'inside' game, though, and there are few vacancies in the Big Leagues right now for the man who is liable to steal second with the bases full."

—*Pitching in a Pinch*

"There is a lot to baseball in the Big Leagues besides playing the game. No man can have a 'yellow streak' and last. He must not pay much attention to his nerves or temperament. He must hide every flaw. It's all part of the psychology of baseball. But the saddest words of all to a pitcher are three—'Take Him Out.'"

—*Pitching in a Pinch*

"They ain't no such animal. Anybody's best pitch is the one the batters ain't hitting that day. And it doesn't take long to find out. If they start hitting my fast ball, they don't see it anymore that afternoon. If they start getting ahold of my curve ball, I just put it away for the day. When they start hitting both of them on the same day, that's when they put me away."

—On being asked what was his best pitch by Jim McCulley; quoted in 1948 in the *Sporting News*

MATHEWSON, CHRISTY (CONTINUED)

"You must have an alibi to show why you lost. If you haven't one, you must fake one. Your self-confidence must be maintained."

—Quoted by Grantland Rice in *The Tumult and the Shouting*

MATTHAU, WALTER

"You couldn't help but be exhilarated by the sight of one of our own guys looking like Colossus. . . . He put to rest the jokes about the only things Jews could wind up doing was working as a presser or cutter or salesman . . . He eliminated all those jokes that started with 'Did you hear the one about the little Jewish gentleman.'"

—On Hank Greenberg, baseball's first major Jewish star; quoted by Richard Greenberg in the program to his play *Take Me Out*

MATTINGLY, DON

"His reputation preceded him before he got here."

—On meeting Dwight Gooden in an exhibition game; quoted in *Sports Illustrated*, April 3, 1989

"Has he ever been here the first day? You have to say Rickey's consistent. That's what you want in a ballplayer, consistency."

—The New York Yankees first baseman, after outfielder Rickey Henderson failed to show up for spring training for the fifth straight year. *Chicago Tribune*, March 9, 1989

"Honestly, at one time I thought Babe Ruth was a cartoon character. I really did, I mean, I wasn't born until 1961, and I grew up in Indiana."

—On his 1985 batting feats putting him into the pantheon of baseball greats, the *Sporting News*

"I like being close to the bats."

—On moving his Yankee Stadium locker in the clubhouse; quoted in the September, 1981 *Major League Baseball Newsletter*

"Playing my entire career in New York I have learned a tremendous amount about the rich history and tradition of baseball. It, in many ways, is embarrassing to me that the owners and players are responsible for shutting down an industry that even the acts of World War I and World War II couldn't do."

—On the 1994 strike and shortened season. From a prepared statement which began, "The shortened 1994 major league baseball season and cancellation of the postseason has been very difficult for me to accept. I share the same disappointment and concerns for the game like the millions of fans and my fellow players do throughout the country. *Bergen Record* [NJ], September 16, 1994.

MAUCH, GENE

"Baseball and malaria keep coming back."

—As California Angels manager in 1982

"He talks very well for a guy who's had two fingers in his mouth all his life."

—As Montreal Expos managers, on suspected spitballer Don Drysdale, new California Angels announcer, 1972

"I'm not the manager because I'm always right, but I'm always right because I'm the manager."

— As Expos manager; widely attributed

"Losing streaks are funny. If you lose at the beginning you got off to a bad start. If you lose in the middle of the season, you're in a slump. If you lose at the end, you're choking.

— As Expos manager; widely attributed

"Most one-run games are lost, not won."

— As Phillies manager; widely attributed

"Play him, fine him, and play him again."

— As Phillies manager, on how to handle Richie Allen

"Sometimes I look on Roy as my nephew, but sometimes only as my sister's son."

— As Twins manager on having Roy Smalley, a blood relative, on his roster, *Sports Illustrated*, May 26, 1980

"The biggest reason that we are where we are is the curtailment of late-inning lead dissipation. But we had to play catch-up baseball, and we did manage to win four games. That is a characteristic the team has displayed all season: resiliency to adversity."

— After his Angels fell behind seven times during an eight-game home stand, the *Sporting News*, September 23, 1985

"The worst thing is the day you realize you want to win more than the players do."

— To a rookie manager as Twins manager; widely attributed

"There should be a new way to record standings in this league: one column for wins, one for losses and one for gifts."

— As Phillies manager; widely attributed

"They took something out of the game when they deleted the assists and putouts from the box scores. On the old box scores, you could generally tell how well a man pitched just by looking at the assists."

— As Phillies manager; quoted in *Baseball Digest* January, 1968

"You have to bear in mind that Mr. Autry's favorite horse was named Champion. He ain't ever had one called Runner-Up."

— As Angels manager on Angels owner Gene Autry's desire to get in the World Series, *Sports Illustrated*, June 1, 1987

MAYBERRY, JOHN

"If I'm breaking them, they're dying in style."

— The Kansas City Royals infielder, on his unusual number of broken bats; widely attributed

MAYE, LEE

"I'm nothing for August."

— On a batting slump; widely quoted

MAYS, CARL

"I intend to keep on and work as well as I can to provide a home and comfortable future for my family. This is what I shall try to do, for that is my lookout. What people may wish to think about me or say about me is their lookout."

—After his fastball had killed Cleveland's Roy Chapman in 1920; quoted in Mike Sowell's *The Pitch That Killed*

MAYS, WILLIE

"Baseball is a fun game. When the game began to be a 'job,' that bothered me. That's why I quit, when it began to be work. In baseball, at a certain age, you have to get out. You can't go back. There is nothing to go back to."

—From an *Atlanta Constitution* interview, October 12, 1974

"Baseball is a game, yes. It is also a business. But what is most truly is disguised combat. For all its gentility, its almost leisurely pace, baseball is violence under wraps."

—From Arnold Han's *Willie Mays*

"Baseball players are no different from other performers. We're all actors, when you come down right to it, so I always though I had to put a little acting into the game—you know, make it more interesting to the fans. So, whenever a ball was hit to the center field, I'd try to time it right and get under the ball just in time to make the catch. It always made the play look a little more spectacular."

—From a June 1974 television interview

"Don't get me wrong, I like to hit. But there's nothing like getting out there in the outfield, running after a ball and throwing somebody out trying to take that extra base. That's real fun."

—Quoted in the *Sporting News*, April 20, 1955

"Every time I look at my pocketbook, I see Jackie Robinson."

—Widely quoted

"I don't compare 'em, I just catch 'em."

—When asked if his most recent miraculous catch was his best

"I like to play happy. Baseball is a fun game, and I love it."

—Quoted in the *Sporting News*, July 25, 1970

"I look at the kids over here, and the way they're playing and the way they ar fighting for themselves, and that says one thing for me: 'Willie, it's time to say good-bye to America.'"

—Gesturing toward the Mets bench, on his farewell day as a Met at Shea Stadium, 1973

"I remember the last season I played. I went home after a ballgame one day, lay down on my bed, and tears came to my eyes. How can you explain that? It's like crying for your mother after she's gone. You cry because you love her. I cried, I guess, because I loved baseball and I knew I had to leave it."

—*Sports Illustrated*

"I think I was the best baseball player I ever saw."

—*Newsweek,* February 5, 1979

"If you can do that—if you run, hit, run the bases, hit with power, field, throw and do all the other things that are part of the game— then you're a good ballplayer."

—Quoted in the *Sporting News,* July 25, 1970

"It's not hard. When I'm not hitting, I don't hit nobody. But when I'm hitting, I hit anybody."

—Quoted by Edward F. Murphy in the *New York Times,* April 25, 1976

"Sure, they were fine, but I think the biggest home run this year was by [Astronaut Alan B.] Shepard."

—Asked for a reaction to his four home runs in a game in Milwaukee; quoted in *Baseball Digest,* July, 1961

"They throw the ball, I hit it; they hit the ball, I catch it."

—His formula for baseball success; quoted, among other places, in the novel *Taxi Dancer* by Joe T. Haywood

"We gave him $47 million. For that, he ought to pick up his [own] award."

—At a dinner in New York in February 1994 to receive Barry Bonds's MVP Award when he criticized his godson for not showing up himself, *Toronto Star,* January 1, 1995.

"When you catch a ball high, head high or higher and have to make a throw afterwards, what do you do? You have to bring the ball down before you can get it away.

"But when you catch the ball as I do you are in position to get rid of it right now without any delay."

—On making his famous "basket" catches; quoted by Sec Taylor of the *Des Moines Register* in the September, 1964 *Baseball Digest.*

MAZEROSKI, BILL

"That is what makes baseball the great game that it is."

—As a Pirate, when asked what he thought about a rookie swearing at him; widely attributed

McCABE, CHARLES

"San Francisco has been saying for decades that it is big league. In its own heart it has never been quite sure. These days it is."

—The sports columnist, on transfer of Giants from New York to San Francisco, *New York Herald Tribune,* May 24, 1958

"A manager who cannot get along with a .400 hitter ought to have his head examined."

> —On managing Ted Williams; quoted by Joe Williams, *Sporting News,* 1948

"I never challenged an umpire except on rules. I never went to the mound to take out a pitcher and I never roamed the dugout. I was there, seated in the middle, the command post. So I eat, drink and sleep baseball 24 hours a day. What's wrong with that? The idea of this game is to win and keep winning."

> —Credos as repeated with small variation throughout his life. These versions appeared in the *Sporting News* obituary

"Lou Gehrig will not be in the lineup today. Babe Dahlgren will take his place. I do not know when Lou will be able to play again."

> —At a press conference, May 2, 1939

"Shucks, what does dropping to sixth place mean at this stage of the race? Or even seventh or eighth. It doesn't mean a thing. But what does mean something is that .500 mark. This morning we were two games under that figure. Had we lost this afternoon we now would be three. But I went all out to keep us from sinking any lower. So we won and now we're only one below. Tomorrow we'll go with Lefty Gomez and if all goes well we should be back at the .500 level by tomorrow night. Never go below .500 if you can help it.

"A club that can hold itself even with that figure when things are going pretty badly, is never wholly out of the running. Let things get straightened out and the club goes on a winning streak and the next thing you know it is right up there with the leaders.

"But let a club sink anywhere from eight to ten games below .500, even in May or early June, and that club's season is pretty well wrecked. Because even if it does eventually get hot and win a bunch in a row it still isn't anywhere when the streak is stopped."

> —On watching the .500 mark in a pennant race. He went into the discourse after a player had suggested that he had pitched Red Ruffing out of order to keep from dropping into sixth place; quoted by John Drebinger of the *New York Times* in the November 1949, *Baseball Digest*

Joe McCarthy (*Library of Congress Prints and Photographs Division*)

Ten Rules for Success in the Major Leagues

1. Nobody can become a ballplayer by walking after a ball.
2. You will never become a .300 hitter unless you take the bat off your shoulder.
3. An outfielder who throws after a runner is locking the barn door after the house is stolen.
4. Keep you head up, and you may not have to keep it down.
5. When you start to slide, slide. He who changes his mind may have to change a good leg for a bad one.
6. Do not alibi on bad hops. Anybody can field the good ones.
7. Always run them out. You can never tell.
8. Do not quit.
9. Do not fight too much with the umpires. You cannot expect them to be as perfect as you.
10. A pitcher who hasn't control, hasn't anything.

—*Baseball Digest,* August 1986

"You don't say anything to a .400 hitter except, 'How do you do sir.'"

> —McCarthy, a stickler for proper dress, such as shirts and neckties, answering a reporter who asked if he was going to require Ted Williams to wear a tie. Williams was notoriously anti-necktie and as the *Sporting News* once put it, he thought they were "ornaments for racks."

"You have to improve your club [even] if it means letting your own brother go."

> —To writer Ed Fitzgerald; quoted in Jim Bouton's *I Managed Good, But Boy Did They Play Bad*

McCARVER, TIM

"A curveball from a left-handed pitcher to a left-handed hitter is the most dangerous pitch there is."

> —Quoted in *USA Today,* April 23, 1990

"Bob Gibson is the luckiest pitcher I ever saw. He always pitches when the other team doesn't score any runs."

> —Widely quoted

"I remember one time going out to the mound to talk with Bob Gibson. He told me to get back behind the batter, that the only thing I knew about pitching was that it was hard to hit."

> —*SABR Collection*

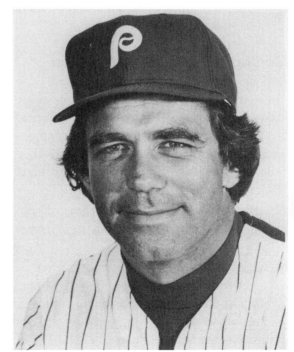

Tim McCarver (*New York Mets*)

McCARVER, TIM (CONTINUED)

"When Steve and I die, we are going to be buried in the same cemetery, 60'6" apart."

—As Phillies catcher, who caught all of Steve Carlton's games in 1977

McCATTY, STEVE

"It took eight hours . . . seven and a half to find the heart."

—On hearing of Charlie Finley's heart surgery; quoted by Jay Johnstone in *Temporary Insanity*.

"Some of our guys would have to pick up the ball and hit it three times to get it that far."

—On Bruce Bochte's 450-foot home run, *Sports Illustrated*

McCAULEY, GERARD F.

"As soon as the American earth softens mackinaws are shed for sweaters and American boys are feeling the sting of balls snapping into gloves, anticipating that in a very short time the trees will bud, the sun will linger, telling them baseball is here."

—"The Million-Dollar Infield," in Donald Hall et al., *Playing Around* (Boston: Little, Brown, 1974)

McCLURE, A. K.

"I bid you Godspeed, for an institution that teaches a boy that nothing but honesty and manliness can succeed must be doing missionary work every day of its existence. It will not only make a high standard of baseball men, but the world better for its presence."

—As editor of the *Philadelphia Times* on the American Baseball Players and their 1881 Tour of the World; quoted in the 1984 *Baseball Research Journal* by Peter Levine

McCOVEY, WILLIE

"The fans sitting up there are helpless. They can't pick up a bat and come down and do something . . . The professional athlete knows there's always another game or another year coming up. If he loses, he swallows the bitter pill and comes back. It's much harder for the fans."

—Quoted in *Late Innings* by Roger Angell

McDOUGALD, GIL

"If it works, it's a great play. If it doesn't, it's a horseshit play."

—Discussing the Williams shift; widely quoted

McDOWELL, CHARLIE

"Baseball has nearly all the qualities and the narrative that the country has. It's competitive, it's got the joshing and the intellectual side—the great students of it—it's also got labor unions and management, gimmicks and promotion and venality, and great public fools and great public heroes, self-serving people and generous people, and it has pride and unity of town and country, and it will do for a figure of the American system."

—Speaking in Ken Burns's PBS series *Baseball;* quoted in the *Toronto Star*, October 15, 1994

McDowell, Sam

"Baseball is both the greatest and worst thing that ever happened to me. Not because people asked too much of me, but because I asked too much of myself. As it turned out, my talent was a curse. The curse was the way I handled it and didn't handle it."

—As a Giants pitcher; widely attributed

"It's no fun throwing fast balls to guys who can't hit them. The real challenge is getting them out on stuff they can hit."

—As a Cleveland Indians pitcher; widely attributed

McGeehan, W. O.

"I am quite sure that statistics will show that the greatest number of successes have been scored by those who have led moderately dirty lives."

—On the habits of ballplayers; widely quoted

McGlothlin, Jim

"When you're 21, you're a prospect. When you're 30, you're a suspect."

—As a White Sox pitcher; widely attributed

McGovern, Arthur

"The Babe is a superman. He can derive more nourishment from a piece of bread than the average man can get from a whole loaf."

—On Babe Ruth; widely quoted

McGraw, John J.

"Curve balls in the dirt."

—His advice on pitching to Babe Ruth, 1921. Another version of this sentiment was "Throw a slow curve at his goddamned feet."

"I name Wagner first on my list, not only because he was a great batting champion and base-runner, and also baseball's foremost shortstop, but because Honus could have been first at any other position, with the possible exception of pitching. In all my career, I never saw such a versatile player."

—Quoted in the *Sporting News*'s obituary of Honus Wagner, who died on December 6, 1955

"I think we can win it—if my brains hold out."

—On the 1921 pennant race; widely quoted

John J. McGraw (*Library of Congress Prints and Photographs, Bain Collection.*)

McGraw, John J. (continued)

"In playing or managing, the game of ball is only fun for me when I'm out in front and winning. I don't give a hill of beans for the rest of the game."

—*The Giants of the Polo Grounds* by Noel Hynd

"No club that wins a pennant once is an outstanding club. One which bunches two pennants is a good club. But a team which can win three in a row really achieves greatness."

—Quoted in *The Babe Ruth Story* by Babe Ruth as told to Bob Considine

"See that? That cement head is thinking more about that girl than today's game. Remember this, son. One percent of ballplayers are leaders of men. The other 99 percent are followers of women."

—To a rookie after spotting a player ogling a woman in the stands; quoted by David Voigt in *The National Pastime,* fall 1982

"Sportsmanship and easygoing methods are all right, but it is the prospect of a hot fight that brings out the crowds."

—Quoted in *The Baseball card Engagement Book,* 1989

"The main idea is to win."

—His motto; widely attributed

"The team that gets off to a good start wins pennants."

—Widely attributed

"There is but one game, and that game is baseball."

—McGraw, in a story under his byline in *Baseball Magazine,* May 1920

"Why shouldn't we pitch to Babe Ruth? We pitch to better hitters in the National League."

—On the eve of the 1921 World Series

"You think the greatest thing in the whole world would be to become a baseball player. If the best thing has already happened, what's next?"

—His widely quoted retirement line

McGraw, Tug

"I don't need them. Just being lefthanded is like taking a greenie a day."

—On taking pills; quoted in *Sport,* May 1971

"I don't know, I never smoked Astroturf."

—When asked whether he favored grass or artificial turf; this quote is also widely ascribed to Bill Lee

"I love the crowd. Whenever I need something extra, I look up and there it is."

—Quoted in *Late Innings* by Roger Angell

"If that was the case I'd be in the trainer's room soaking my head in ice. I've never been paid a dime for my brains."

—When asked if relief pitching was not mostly mental after winning the 1980 World Series opener; quoted in the *New York Times,* October 16, 1980

"Ninety percent I'll spend on good times, women and Irish whiskey. The other 10 percent I'll probably waste."

> —Philly pitcher, on how he intended to use his $275,000 salary, *Sports Illustrated*, April, 1975

"Some days you tame the tiger, and some days the tiger has you for lunch."

> —Widely quoted, 1989

"Ya gotta believe."

> —July 1973 motto and exhortation which was used in the New York Mets' move from sixth place to the National League pennant. The *Sporting News* headline for Game 2 of the '73 World Series read, "Tug's Battle Cry Inspires Mets: You Gotta Believe!" The Mets won 10–7 in 12 innings. McGraw uttered the phrase after a clubhouse speech by M. Donald Grant while the Mets floundered; McGraw yelled: "He's right! He's right! Just believe! You gotta believe!" (Speculation was that the puckish McGraw was mocking Grant. He probably was, but the expression still became the team's rallying cry down the stretch.)

McGRORY, MARY

"Baseball is what we were. Football is what we have become."

> —From John Leo's "Now Don't Interrupt!" (best sayings of 1996, *U.S. News & World Report*, January 13, 1997)

McGWIRE, MARK

"I'm in awe of myself."

> —After hitting his 70th home run at the end of his record-breaking season, recalled at year's end in *Newsweek,* December 28, 1998

"I'm not here to talk about the past."

> —Before a House committee investigating steroid use in baseball on March 17, 2005. Because baseball is so tied to its past, this may have been the line which most hurt the slugger in the eyes of the media and the public; widely reported.

McKECHNIE, BILL

"You can't even celebrate a victory. If you win today, you must start worrying about tomorrow. If you win a pennant, you start worrying about the World Series. As soon as that's over, you start worrying about the next season."

> —Frank Graham and Dick Hyman, *Baseball Wit and Wisdom*, 1962

McLAIN, DENNY

"When you can do it out there between the white lines, you can live any way you want."

> —As a Tigers pitcher; widely attributed

McLUHAN, MARSHALL

"Baseball is doomed. It is the inclusive mesh of the TV image, in particular, that spells . . . the doom of baseball now, but it'll come back. Games go in cycle."

> —Social philosopher in 1969; quoted by Ira Berkow in the *New York Times,* February 20, 1983

McMillan, Roy

"Never saw a curve ball before."

—When asked as a prospect why certain odd
pitches threw him after being brought up
from softball. He was signed nonetheless;
quoted in the *Sporting News,* 1953

McMorris, Jerry

"There is no way to save the season. It would
take an absolute miracle. It's a disgrace that
this group of people can't save the season, as
great as this game has been to all of us."

—Colorado Rockies owner at the beginning
of the 1994 baseball strike, *USA Today,*
September 13, 1994

McNally, Dave

"The only thing Weaver knows about pitching is that he couldn't hit it."

—On Earl Weaver; a quote often repeated by
Jim Palmer and other Oriole pitchers of the
Weaver era

McNamara, John

"This winter is a lot more enjoyable than last.
I haven't stepped on my tongue. My head was
on the floor so much last winter I kept step-
ping on it."

—As manager of the Red Sox, on the winter he
spent trying to explain how his club lost the
1986 Series. *Sporting News,* December 21,
1987

Mead, William B.

"We hate the New York Yankees for many
reasons.

"They're spoiled, rotten.

"They think they're such Hot Stuff.

"Their owner is obnoxious.

"They pout, sulk and whine, no matter
how much they're paid and pampered.

"Their fans are gross and crude.

"I could go on, and I will. So could you. That's
what this book is about. Most all good Americans hate the Yankees. It is a value we cherish
and pass along to our children, like decency
and democracy and the importance of a good
breakfast. Along with the Pledge of Allegiance,
hatred of the Yankees should be part of the nat-
uralization test for new U.S. citizens. If it were,
everybody would pass."

—*The Official New York Yankees Hater's
Handbook*

"The first Yankee haters were New Yorkers.
They were fans of the New York Giants . . ."

—*The Official New York Yankees Hater's
Handbook*

Meany, Tom

"All the king's horses and all the king's men
couldn't put Boston baseball together again."

—On the sale of Babe Ruth and other key
players, including the great 1915 outfield

"Always within Mantle is the knowledge that
any game he plays could be his last—one
throw, one swing, one slide could write the
end of his major league career. Yet Mick plays

every game to the hilt, a tremendous tribute to his courage."

—*Sport,* December 1957

"Why bother to even play the season? He should go straight to Cooperstown."

—On the buildup accorded to rookie Clint Hartung; widely quoted

MEDICH, DOC

"It certainly was a great thrill. And someday he can tell his grandchildren that he hit against me."

—On pitching to Hank Aaron; widely quoted

MEDWICK, DUCKY

"Your holiness, I'm Joseph Medwick. I, too, used to be a Cardinal."

—During World War II the former St. Louis Cardinal visited the Vatican with a group of servicemen who had been granted an audience. As each man approached him, the Pope asked the visitor his vocation in civilian life. When Medwick's turn came he stepped forward and delivered the line which soon appeared in places as diverse as the *Reader's Digest* and *The Holy Name Journal*

"MELVILLE."

"Base ball is getting to be the most predominant institution in this State. Clubs are forming in every country town and village, and a great many matches have been played this season."

—Letter from Boston to *The New York Clipper,* September 11, 1858 signed simply "Melville."

This quotation has appeared in several papers and books on early baseball and has led to speculation as to whether it was a letter from Herman Melville. Herman Melville's great-grandson Paul Metcalf offered this opinion on reading the quotation: "I'm virtually certain the Meville mentioned in *The Clipper* is not the whale man. First, he signs himself 'Melville', not 'Herman Melville'—this was not characteristic. Secondly, during the summer of 1852 he was at his home in Pittsfield, not at all in Boston, and the *Clipper* article mentions baseball in Boston. Thirdly, baseball was simply not his style—Whitman, yes, but not Melville." At another point in the letter Metcalf writes: "Meville's concerns in 1852, were tragic; and populist . . . he was becoming more and more a prisoner of his aristocratic heritage. Baseball, no."

MENCKEN, H. L.

"I hate all sports as rabidly as a person who likes sports hates common sense."

—Quoted by Dr. Laurence J. Peter in *Peter's Quotations*

"I know of no subject, in truth, save perhaps baseball, on which the average American newspaper, even in the larger cities, discourses with unfailing sense and understanding."

—Quoted by Theo Lippman Jr., "Uncensored Commentaries? Yeah, Right," *Baltimore Sun,* August 31, 2003

"I still believe that it is the best game ever invented. No other comes within miles of it. It is clean, swift, and open, and it takes smartness as well as muscle. I am sorry to hear it is

H. L. Mencken (*National Press Club Archives.*)

losing popularity in the schools and colleges. As Americans abandon it, the Japanese take it up. Perhaps that is only one more proof that as Japan rises in the world, the United States goes down."

—On CBS Radio, May 2, 1940, rediscovered by Mencken biographer Marion E. Rodgers

MERCHANT, LARRY

"He gets base hits in the present and lives in the past. He should be dancing the Charleston, drinking sarsaparilla and wearing a big-rimmed fedora."

—On Pete Rose, *Sports Illustrated*

MERCKER, KENT

"The doc [who] looked at the MRI told me I had an old elbow. I told him, 'I could have saved you $750 and 45 minutes and told you that before I got here. I also have an old knee, old feet and an old wife.'"

—As a thirty-eight-year-old lefthander on being placed on the disabled list by the Reds, with a sore elbow, *Philadelphia Inquirer,* May 26, 2006

MERKLE, FRED

"I suppose that when I die, the epitaph on my tombstone will read 'Here lies Bonehead Merkle.' The tough part of it is that I can't do things other fellows do without attracting any attention. Little slips that would be excused in any other players are burned into me by crowds. Of course, I make my mistakes with the rest, but I have to do double duty. If any play I'm concerned in goes wrong, I'm the fellow that gets the blame, no matter where the thing went off the line. I wish folks would forget. But they never will."

—Quoted in Neal McCabe and Constance McCabe, *Baseball's Golden Age: The Photographs of Charles M. Conlon* (New York: Harry N. Abrams, 1993)

MERRILL, STUMP

"Nothing. How about some practice?"

—As Yankees first base coach when asked by his wife, Carole, what a first-base coach did other than "pat guys on the read end when they reached base"; quoted in the *Sporting News,* April 15, 1985

MERULLO, LEN

"A big player has to prove he can't play; a little one has to prove that he can."

—As a Cubs scout; quoted in the June 1961 *Baseball Digest*

MESA, JOSE

"If I face him, I'll hit him, I won't try to hit him in the head, but I'll hit him. And if he charges me, I'll kill him. If I face him 10 more times, I'll hit him 10 times. Every time."

—On former Cleveland teammate Omar Vizquel as a Philadelphia Phillies closer. Vizquel had criticized Mesa in his 2002 autobiography, saying the reliever blew Game 7 of the 1997 World Series. The two were teammates on the Indians from 1992 to 1998. *Cincinnati Post*, March 12, 2003, from *Bucks County* [PA] *Courier Times*. This quotation has been used subsequently to demonstrate the level of hostility players can put into words.

MEYER, BILLY

"You clowns can go on *What's My Line?* in full uniforms and stump the panel."

—As Pittsburgh Pirates manager addressing his team after they had lost another of the 112 games they were to lose during the 1952 season; widely quoted

MEYER, RUSS

"I know that pitchers who refuse to follow knockdown orders are liable to a fine of $50. I was never fined because I always followed orders. If the manager told me to knock down a hitter, I did. But I do know of cases where pitchers were fined that amount because they were reluctant to knock down a batter. Something should be done to stop this. Of the nine managers I pitches for, Eddie Sawyer [Phils] was the only manager who never ordered me to throw at a hitter. Somebody's going to get killed one of these days, watch and see."

—As a former major-league pitcher; quoted in the February 1961 *Baseball Digest*

MEYERHOFF, MICHAEL K.

"When Dad can't get the diaper on straight, we laugh at him as though he were trying to walk around in high-heel shoes. Do we ever assist him by pointing out that all you have to do is lay out the diaper like a baseball diamond, put the kid's butt on the pitcher's mound, bring home plate up, then fasten the tapes at first and third base?"

—From "Of Baseball and Babies: Are You Unconsciously Discouraging Father Involvement in Infant Care?" *Young Children*, May 1994

MICHAEL, GENE

"Building a ball club is an art, not a science. Our first instinct is to be aggressive. Go for what you need first, then worry about consequences, because there are no worse consequences than losing."

—As Yankees GM; widely attributed

MICHAELS, AL

"He's a better interview from the left side than the right side."

> —The ABC-TV announcer, after interviewing switch-hitting Pittsburgh third baseman Bobby Bonilla before the Pirates' nationally televised game with the New York Mets August 1. *Sporting News*, August 15, 1988

MILLER, BING

"I just can't understand why so many players take so many third strikes.... I went to bat more than 6,000 official times and the only time I took a called third strike was in my last year in the majors. I figured it was time to quit then."

> —Quoted in his *Sporting News* obituary. He died May 5, 1965.

MILLER, DENNIS

"Unfortunately he would have bet on whether he made it through or not."

> —On Pete Rose's quote about how he would have run through fire in a gasoline suit to play baseball, *Pittsburgh Post-Gazette*, July 21, 2006

MILLER, JON

"There's just something about the game. It spans seven months. It's good company. It's not once a week. I also think it mirrors life in that it's constant and you have to keep going on days when you're not at your best. You go out and play if your best player is hurting, if you've got to call a kid pitcher up from the minors, if everything seems to be going

wrong. Everyone goes through periods like that in their personal lives."

> —*Washington Post*, April 1, 1994

MILLER, MARVIN

"Money is not the issue. The real issue is the owners' attempt to punish the players for having the audacity not to crawl."

> —From "Diamond Quotes," *Nine*, 2004 edition

MILLER, RAY

"I refuse to ever be negative. If I'm losing ten to nothing in the ninth inning with two outs, I just know that if we get two people on we're going to win."

> —*Spring Training* by William Zinsser (New York: Harper & Row, 1989)

"Like those special afternoons in summer when you go to Yankee Stadium at two o'clock in the afternoon for an eight o'clock game. It's so big, so empty and so silent that you can almost hear the sounds that aren't there."

> —*Sports Illustrated*

"Sutton has set up such a fine example of defiance that someday I expect to see a pitcher walk out to the mound with a utility belt on—you know, file, chisel, screwdriver, glue. He'll throw a ball to the plate with bolts attached to it!"

> —On Don Sutton's illegal pitches; quoted by Danielle Gagnon Torres in *High Inside: Memoirs of a Baseball Wife*. Miller was an Oriole coach when he made the statement.

"There ain't a lefthander in the world who can run a straight line. It's the gravitational pull on the earth's axis that gets 'em."

—As a pitching coach, 1987

"We ask our guys to do three things—work fast, throw strikes and change speeds."

—Quoted in Richard Justice, "Miller's Creed: Work Fast, Pitch Strikes, Alter Speeds," *Baltimore Sun*, March 18, 1984. Variations: "I've always said you work fast, change speeds, throw strikes" (*Baltimore Sun*, May 31, 1999); "Throw strikes, change speeds, work fast" (quoted in *Men at Work* by George F. Will [New York: Macmillan, 1990]).

"When somebody on your team does that, you say, 'What guts. What a gamer.' When a guy on the other team does it, you say, 'What a dummy. There's no percentage in that.' When it's the other guy, you become a cynic."

—As an Orioles coach on seeing a player hit the wall making a catch; widely attributed

"You feel guilty telling the batters to go out there and get a hit. They look at you funny, as if to say, 'You try it.'"

—As a Baltimore Orioles coach, 1980

MITCHELL, GEORGE

"One of the baseball-team owners approached me and said: 'If you become baseball commissioner, you're going to have to deal with 28 big egos,' and I said, 'For me, that's a 72 percent reduction.'"

—U.S. Democratic Senate majority leader, when he was being talked about as the next baseball commissioner, *Washington Post*, May 4, 1994

MITCHELL, KEVIN

"He's not human. Somebody made him."

—On Will Clark after the 1989 NLCS; quoted in *Baseball America*, November 25, 1989

MITCHELL, LIZ

"You've got to time your babies for the off-season and get married in the off-season and get divorced in the off-season. Baseball always comes first."

—As the wife of Paul Mitchell; quoted in *High Inside: Memoirs of a Baseball Wife* by Danielle Gagnon Torrez

MIZE, JOHNNY

"The greatest player I ever saw was a black man. He's in the Hall of Fame, although not a lot of people have heard of him. His name is Martin Dihigo. I played with him in Santo Domingo in winter ball in 1943. He was the manager. He was the only guy I ever saw who could play all nine positions, run and was a switch hitter. I thought I was havin' a pretty good year myself down there and they were walkin' him to get me."

—On Martin Dihigo; quoted in the 1989 50th Anniversary Hall of Fame *Yearbook*

"Rabbit Maranville was working with kids for the *Journal-American* when he died in January of '54. The next summer he was voted into the Hall of Fame. Why did his record get so much better after he died?"

—Widely quoted

MIZE, JOHNNY (CONTINUED)

Johnny Mize (*Andy Moresund Collection*)

"Sure, I would have liked to have made a connection in baseball, but there were never any offers. One owner told me I had a job with his club anytime I wanted it. When 'anytime' came, he said there were no openings. The coaching jobs have gone to the .250 hitters."

—Quoted in the *Sporting News*, August 1970

"The pitcher has to throw the ball in the strike zone sooner or later and the rules allow the hitter to hit only one fair ball each time he bats, so why not hit the pitch you want to hit and not the one he wants you to hit?"

—Tip on hitting which is quoted in Leonard Safir and William Safire's *Good Advice*

MONDAY, RICK

"It actually giggles at you as it goes by."

—On Phil Niekro's knuckleball, *Sports Illustrated*, August 1, 1983

MOONEY, ROGER

"The phrase is actually 'pitchers and catchers report to spring training' but the first three words do the trick. It means another baseball season is beginning."

—*Bradenton Herald*, February 11, 2007

MOORE, MARIANNE

"Ballplayers' uniforms seem to me not so trim as formerly. They should not look like babies' sleepers or snowsuits."

—Quote by the seventy-nine-year-old poet in *Sports Illustrated*, November 13, 1967

"Fanaticism? No. Writing is exciting and baseball is like writing."

—From *Baseball and Writing* by Marianne Moore in the *New Yorker*, December 9, 1961

MORGAN, JOE L.

"A good base stealer should make the whole infield jumpy. Whether you steal or not, you're changing the rhythm of the game. If the pitcher is concerned about you, he isn't concentrating enough on the batter."

—Quoted by Roger Angell in *Five Seasons*

"He can step on your shoes, but he doesn't mess up your shine."

—On Frank Robinson's ability to dispense criticism as a manager; quoted in *Sports Illustrated*, July 13, 1981

"I take my vote as a salute to the little guy, the one who doesn't hit 500 home runs. I was one of the guys that did all they could to win. I'm proud of all my stats, but I don't think I ever got one for Joe Morgan. If I stole a base, it was to help us win a game, and I like to think that's what made me a little special."

> —On being elected to the Hall of Fame, January 10, 1990

"Personally, I'm happy for baseball that I won. What I mean is that kids should strive to be complete players. With the designated-hitter rule in the American League, I hear some kids saying, 'Well, I can hit, so I guess I can be a designated hitter.' But there's more to baseball than just doing one thing."

> —On being a "complete player" when named National League MVP for 1975

"Players are funny. They respect guys who make a lot of money, even if they don't deserve it. The manager is the most important guy on the team and should be treated on a higher level. Coaches should be regarded highly, too, but because of their comparatively low salaries, they're not. I don't think that's fair."

> —As a Philly. *Sports Illustrated*, April 16, 1983

MORRIS, JACK

"Baseball has nothing to do with reality. It has nothing to do with whether children are going to bed hungry. It's just an occupation and a game. It's not going to solve world hunger or world poverty. It's not going to solve federal deficits. Baseball is a fantasy."

> —What he told a reporter after a particularly disgraceful outing against the Minnesota Twins at about the same time that Ken Burns's eighteen-hour PBS show was released; quoted in the *Toronto Star*, October 15, 1994

"Most people believe Babe Ruth was the greatest baseball player ever. I wonder if he could have hit the split-fingered fastball? Ty Cobb? I've seen his swing. I know he could hit it! Maybe they could adjust and be the stars of today. I know there will be teams better than ours. That's the way of the world. Everything gets better."

> —To reporters after a 1983 victory; quoted by Roger Craig in *Inside Pitch*

MORSE, JACOB C.

"The American would not sacrifice a morning for a cricket game. He is quick and active, nervous and energetic, and he wants his sport to answer the requirements of his temperament. Base ball has answered his purpose admirably."

> —*Sphere and Ash: History of Base Ball* (Boston: J. F. Spofford, 1888)

MOXSON, EPHRAIM

"I've been a sports fan since I was a kid, a typical Jewish guy. Ever since I can remember, whenever I came across a Jewish athlete, I felt a sense of pride, not that I didn't feel pride for Einstein and Freud and Marx. But Sandy Koufax? Yeah, that's pretty special."

> —Quoted in Michael Ollove, "Cause for Ethnic Pride," *Baltimore Sun*, December 18, 1999. Moxson is copublisher of *Jewish Sports Review*

MOYED, RALPH

"It's not that I don't like baseball. There's not that much to dislike. It's great for athletes who get winded playing croquet."

— As columnist for the *Wilmington News-Journal*; quoted in *USA Today*, February 19, 1988

MULL, MARTIN

3. Fewer people named Bubba.
4. The players needn't pose as college graduates
11. The game is civilized to the point that the trousers have pockets.
15. You can be missing a thumb and still count the players on two hands.
16. You can wear the hat backwards.
17. Yelling "Grand Slam!" in a crowded bar is less dangerous than squealing 'Oooooooh flea-flicker!'"

— "Why Baseball Is Better Than Football: 20 Reasons," *Philip Morris Magazine*, spring 1988

MULLINIKS, RANCE

"I don't know about bats but they make great fishing poles."

— Asked about graphite and aluminum bats; *USA Today*, July 21, 1989

MUNGO, VAN LINGLE

"Don't anybody ever get into trouble but me?"

— Question he asked after getting into a hotel room brawl during spring training in Havana in 1941. The Brooklyn Dodgers pitcher had a proclivity for getting in trouble.

MUNSON, THURMAN

"I'm a little too belligerent. I cuss and swear at people. I yell at umpires and maybe I'm a little too tough at home sometimes. I don't sign as many autographs as I should and I haven't always been very good with the writers."

— Description which served as Munson's epitaph. It appeared in several of the obituaries that followed his sudden death in an airplane crash.

"Maybe they made me captain because I've been here so long. [But] If I'm supposed to be captain by example, then I'll be a terrible captain."

— 1976 quote recalled in his Associated Press obituary after dying in an August 2, 1979, airplane crash

MURCER, BOBBY

"If they check the upper deck, they might find Patty Hearst hiding out."

— On the sparse crowds at Candlestick Park; quoted in the *Sporting News* July 122, 1975

"Trying to hit him is like trying to eat Jell-O with chopsticks."

— On knuckleballer Phil Niekro; widely quoted

"You decide you'll wait for your pitch. Then as the ball starts toward the plate, you think about your stance. And then you think about your swing. And then you realize that the ball that went past you for a strike was your pitch."

— On slumps; widely quoted

Thurman Munson (*New York Yankees*)

MURFF, RED

"Has the best arm I've ever seen in my life. Could be a real power pitcher some day."

— From a 1965 scouting report on a high school pitcher from Alvin, Texas, named Nolan Ryan

MURNANE, TIM

"There is an array of colored players around the large cities. Their playing is more picturesque to look at than their pale-faced brothers."

— As quoted by David Q. Voight in *America Through Baseball*. Murnane made the quote as sports editor of the *Boston Globe* in 1987.

"We got our language from the English and most of our institutions from the Dagos and the Dutch [sic]. But there are two things I teach the boys that are all American. One's the good old fag and one's baseball."

— Quoted by Voight, it originally appeared in May 8, 1909, *Collier's*

MURPHY, EDWARD T.

"Overconfidence may cost the Dodgers sixth place."

— The writer on the Dodgers of the '30s; widely quoted

MURRAY, JIM

"A business executive is standing in his office looking down over the city. . . . Suddenly, a falling figure shoots past the window. 'Oh, oh,' the man says, glancing at his chronometer. 'It must be June. There go the Giants.'"

— *The Best of Jim Murray*, 1965

"A society or industry built on slavery cannot survive emancipation. Just ask Jefferson Davis."

— On the end of the reserve clause; widely quoted

"Baseball is not precisely a team sport. It is more a series of concerts by the artists."

— *Los Angeles Times*, 1979

"He was a symbol of indestructibility—a Gibraltar in cleats."

— On Lou Gehrig

"His face looks like a closed fist."

— Describing Hank Bauer

"Is baseball a business? If it isn't, General Motors is a sport."

— Widely attributed

"Finley is a self-made man who worships his creator."

— On Charlie Finley, *Sports Illustrated*

"The Baseball Diagnosis is foolproof. The box score is the most reliable X-Ray in the world."

— Widely attributed

"The first thing they teach you in this newspaper game is that the public doesn't give a damn about your adventures in getting the story. As an old editor of mine used to say, 'Just give me the cops and robbers, not the hardships. Save those for your book.' Another said, 'Don't tell me how tough it is to get copy out of a World Series. I was at Salerno.'"

— In a 1975 column

"The last time Willie Mays dropped a pop fly he had a rattle in one hand and a bonnet on his head."

— June 1964

"Well, God is getting an earful today."

— On the death of Casey Stengel, September 29, 1975; from Murray's column, October 1, 1975

"Well, we're all 10 years older today. Dizzy Dean is dead. And 1934 is gone forever. Another part of our youth fled. You look in the mirror and the small boy no longer smiles back at you. Just that sad old man. The Gashouse Gang is now a duet. Dizzy died the other day at the age of 11 or 12. The little boy in all of us died with him. . . . But, for one brief shining afternoon in 1934, he brought a joy to that dreary time when most we needed it. Dizzy Dean. It's impossible to say without a smile. But, then, who wants to try? If I know Diz, he'll be calling God 'podner' someplace today. I hope there's golf courses or a card game or a slugger who's a sucker for a low outside fastball for old Diz. He might have been what baseball's all about."

— *Los Angeles Times*, July 19, 1974. Murray's tribute to Dean, "He Never Gave Up," was inserted into the *Congressional Record* by Senator Barry Goldwater, who termed it the best of all the stories written on Dean during the days after his death.

MURTAUGH, DANNY

"A bad call [in baseball] is one that goes against you."

— *TV Guide*, May 6, 1978

"It's late in a tight game, the other team has a run in scoring position with two out. Your pitcher is leading off your half of the inning. Do you gamble on him getting the side out and giving you a chance to use a hitter for him? Or do you bring in bullpen help, like Roy Face, a pitcher you don't want to hit for? That's a manager's hardest decision."

— As Pirates' manager on the toughest place for a manager to be in; quoted in *Baseball Digest*, June 1961

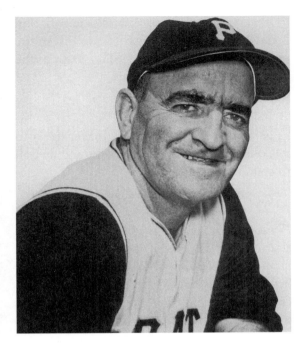

Danny Murtaugh (*Author's Collection*)

"The more patient you are, the better manager you'll be. When I first came up as manager I was too demanding. I had to learn to expect a man to do something that he is not capable of doing. Now I try to analyze and find out their capabilities and then never ask them to exceed them."

　—*New York Times*, March 23, 1975

"The night we won the World Series, I was understandably feeling my oats. I asked my wife how many really great managers she thought there were in baseball. Glaring at me, she said, 'I think there's one less than you do.'"

　—Quoted in *Sport*, May 1961

"Why, certainly I'd like to have that fellow who hits a home run every time at bat, who strikes out every opposing batter when he's pitching, who throws strikes to any base or the plate when he's playing outfield, and who always is thinking about two innings ahead just what he'll do to baffle the other team. Any manager would want a guy like that playing for him. The only trouble is to get him to put down his cup of beer and come down out of the stands and do those things."

　—On the ideal player; quoted as Pirates manager by Fred Russell of the *Nashville Banner*. It appeared in the November 1974, *Baseball Digest*.

MUSBURGER, BRENT

"It's too bad ol' Harry Caray himself didn't get to sing 'Take Me Out to the Ball Game.' Can you just hear the Japanese saying, 'They have an announcer named what?'"

　—Commenting on ESPN Radio about the Chicago Cubs versus New York Mets games in Tokyo to start the 2000 season, *Baltimore Sun*, April 23, 2000 (The Arena: Sports Plus)

MUSER, TONY

"There are only two stats that matter to a team, and that's RBI and runs scored, Everything else is individual stuff, arbitration stuff."

　—As Royals manager, *Baseball Digest*, August 1998

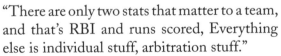

MUSIAL, STAN

"I have a darn good job, but please don't ask me what I do."

> —On his position as senior vice president of The St. Louis Cardinals; quoted in *Sports Illustrated,* June 20, 1988

"I love to play this game of baseball. I love putting on the uniform."

> —Quoted by Arnold Hano as Musial leaves the game in *Sports Magazine's All-Time All Stars*

"I never realized that batting a little ball around could cause so much commotion. I know now how Lindbergh must have felt when he returned to St, Louis."

> —After getting his 3,000th hit a Wrigley Field (May 13, 1958) on his return to St. Louis to address a huge crowd. When he mentioned Lindbergh somebody yelled, "What did he hit?"

"On an all-star team, I vote for players of one kind—those I enjoy watching the most the ball is hit or pitched in their direction."

> —As a Cardinals senior vice president; quoted in the *Los Angeles Times,* March 30, 1971

"The first principle of contract negotiation is don't remind them of what you did in the past; tell them what you're going to do in the future."

> —Widely attributed

"The key to hitting for a high average is to relax, concentrate—and don't hit the fly ball to center field."

> —Quoted in the Hall of Fame *Yearbook,* 1989

"The one unbreakable rule about hitting is this: if a batter hits well with his own particular stance and swing, think twice—or more—before suggesting a change. There is no one correct way to bat, and so of course there is no one correct stance to look for."

> —In *The Mutual Baseball Almanac* edited by Roger Kahn and Al Helfer

MUTRIE, JIM

"My big fellow! My giants! We are the people!"

> —Manager of the New York Gothams, during midseason 1885, after a great victory that moved the Gothams into second place behind the Chicago White Stockings, thereby proclaiming the new nickname for the team. Mike Lessiter, *The Names of the Games* (Chicago: Contemporary Books, 1988)

N

NADER, RALPH

"The arrogance of the owners and their lack of sensitivity toward their fans is accelerating. They never ask the fans what they think of the policies and rules these owners set. And the fans have a right to know the full costs they are paying, as taxpayers, for the municipal stadiums most of them can't get into, even if they could afford a ticket."

—On forming a new consumer group to be called FANS (Fight to Advance the Nation's Sports); quoted in the *New York Times,* September 28, 1977

NARRON, SAM

"Keep those nits and gnats off the base [referring to lower portion of the batting order], 'cause those lions and tigers will get ya."

—On how to win ball games

NEAGLE, DENNY

"The ball hit my bat."

—Notoriously weak-hitting Pittsburgh pitcher, trying to explain how he hit a grand-slam homer; quoted in *Baltimore Sun,* July 7, 1995

NELSON, LINDSEY

"I figure, if anything I say in the broadcasting booth can influence anything going on down on the field, I ought to be getting more money."

—On mentioning an ongoing no-hitter from the broadcast booth; quoted in *No-Hitter* by Phil Pepe

"If the World Series runs until election day, the networks will run the first one-half inning and project the winner."

—SABR Collection

"I have observed that, generally speaking, network sports announcers did not tend to live to a ripe old age. On the other hand, I had noticed that baseball announcers seemed to go right on forever. Bob Elson had been calling balls and strikes since the beginning of time. Harry Caray must have started with Abner Doubleday, and was still going strong."

—On leaving a position as a network announcer to become a Met broadcaster

"If the World Series runs until election day, the networks will run the first one-half inning and project the winner."

—SABR Collection

"[They] looked like the Light Brigade at Balaclava. They bravely took the field each day and were systematically destroyed."

—On the first-year Mets

NETTLES, GRAIG

"I don't think there's any loyalty in baseball at all. It's become such a transient business. If you knew you were going to be with a team 10 years, then you could be loyal to a tradition. But when you know they can get rid of you tomorrow . . ."

—As a Yankee; quoted in the *Los Angeles Times*, March 23, 1978

"If this club wants somebody to play third base, they've got me. If they want somebody to go to luncheons, they should hire George Jessel."

—After being fined $500 for missing a luncheon; quoted in *Sports Illustrated*, May 1, 1978

"The best thing about being a Yankee is getting to watch Reggie Jackson play every day. The worst thing about being a Yankee? Getting to watch Reggie Jackson play every day."

—Quoted in Reggie Jackson's *Reggie*

"What the Yankees need is a second-base coach."

—As a Yankee, 1982

Graig Nettles (*New York Yankees*)

"When I was a little boy, I wanted to be a baseball player and join a circus. With the Yankees I've accomplished both."

> —Quoted by Murray Chass in "The Money Players," in *The Yankees,* by Dave Anderson, Murray Chass, Robert Creamer, and Harold Rosenthal, 1979

"You've gone from Cy Young to Sayonara in one year."

> —To Sparky Lyle; quoted on his dwindling pitching powers, in *The Bronx Zoo* by Sparky Lyle and Peter Golenbock

NEWBERY, JOHN

B is for
Base-ball
The Ball once struck off,
Away flies the Boy
To the next destined Post,
And then Home with Joy.

> —*A Little Pretty Pocket-Book,* published in London, England, by John Newbery in 1744. At least eleven English editions were published between 1744 and 1790 (earliest extant is 1767); republished in the United States several times between 1762 and 1787; quoted in Robert W. Henderson, *Ball, Bat and Bishop* (New York: Rockport Press, 1947).

NEWCOMBE, DON

"Do you know what Jackie's impact was? Well, let Martin Luther King tell You. In 1968, Martin had dinner in my house with my family. This was 28 days before he was assassinated. He said to me, 'Don, I don't know what I would have done without you guys setting up the minds for people for change. You, Jackie, and Roy will never know how easy you made it for me to do my job.' Can you imagine that? How easy we made it for Martin Luther King!"

> —From an oral history, entitled "In the Footsteps of a Legend," on the impact of Jackie Robinson on baseball which appeared in the April 12, 2007 issue of *Time*

Don Newcombe *(Society for American Baseball Research; SABR Collection)*

NEWCOMBE, DON (CONTINUED)

"There is a distinct lack of concern on the part of management. It's paranoia on their part. They want to keep it quiet and out of the newspapers. They want you to believe that nothing this could happen in their organization."

—On organized baseball's attitude toward alcoholism

NEWSOM, BOBO

"All they did was announce the Giants had bought more parking space for the customers next to the Polo Grounds. It's the first time I was ever cut off a roster to make room for a parking lot."

—On being released from the New York Giants the same day that expanded parking was announced; quoted by Shirley Povich in the *Sporting News*, July 7, 1948

"He has a weakness for doubles."

—When asked if he had discovered rookie Joe DiMaggio's weakness

"Those maggots are nuts."

—On the owners; quoted by Stan Baumgartner in the January 21, 1948

"You spend the first six years in baseball learnin' how to pitch and the next six wishin' you'd known it from scratch."

—*The Baseball Card Engagement Book*, 1990

NIEDENFUER, TOM

"The only way that shot would have stayed in the ballpark is If it hit the Goodyear blimp."

—After serving up Jack Clark's three-run, ninth-inning, 450-foot homer that won the final game of the 1985 NLCS for St. Louis; quoted in the 1986 *Official Baseball Guide*.

NIEKRO, JOE

"I sometimes have to file my nails between innings."

—As a suspended Minnesota Twins pitcher; quoted widely (e.g., *USA Today*, August 14, 1987)

NIEKRO, PHIL

"It's like the sun coming up every morning. You just don't know what time."

—On Hank Aaron's ability to hit home runs, uttered just after he had hit Number 700; quoted in the *Detroit Free Press*, July 23, 1973

NIXON, RICHARD M.

"If I had a second chance, and could choose to be a politician or go into sportswriting—not playing but writing—I would have taken writing. . . . I love the game, love the competition."

> —As former president to ESPN's Roy Firestone on July 15, 1992

"If I had my life to live all over again, I'd have ended up as a sportswriter."

> —Uttered on July 22, 1969, when a group of ballplayers visited him at the White House. They were in Washington for the All-Star Game. On hearing the remark, Joe Garagiola, who was with the group, said, "I won't sleep any better tonight knowing Nixon wants to be a sportswriter."

Casey Stengel and Richard Nixon (*Nixon Project National Archives*)

"It's terrific for someone to be able to bust out and do the thing he really wants to do."

> —On his son-in-law David Eisenhower getting a summer job as a statistician for the Washington Senators; quoted in the *Sporting News*, June 6, 1970. Eisenhower's reaction: "I'd have taken this job just for a pass in the bleachers. Nothing beats baseball."

"Were you told how the All-Star Game came out?"

> —One of his first questions to the *Apollo 11* astronauts on their splashdown in the Pacific after their epic moon landing

Phil Niekro (*National Baseball Library*)

Some names were just meant for baseball. Ernie Banks used to list names fit only for sluggers: Babe Ruth, Mickey Mantle, Harmon Killebrew, Frank Howard, and Ron Swoboda—the name, according to columnist George Vecsey, that Banks "most liked to roll around on his tongue . . . worth 500 home runs in itself, or so it seemed at the time."

It would seem then that many players have fine given names and need no nickname beyond their real name or a modification of what appeared on a birth certificate. This is the case with Mel Ott, Reggie Jackson, Rickey Henderson, Maury Wills, Rod Carew, Pete Rose, Lou Brock, Willie McCovey, Darryl Strawberry, Cal Ripken Jr., and too many others to mention.

Others get just the right touch with the addition of a perfect, tidy nickname. This is clearly the case with Catfish Hunter, Boog Powell, Ty Cobb, Cy Young, Rusty Staub, Sparky Lyle (whose real name is Albert), and Tug McGraw (who insists that his nickname is a throwback to his days as a breast feeder). Some have been given great baseball names as Lawrence Peter Berra was turned into "Yogi," Dorrel Norman Elvert Herzog into "Whitey," and the late Alfred Manuel Martin into "Billy."

In fact, some names have such impact that they tend to be recalled long after the player's field performance. This is true of those rich, hot fudge sundae names like Sibby Sisti, Van Lingle Mungo, Debs Garms, and Snuffy Sternweiss. Add to these names of more recent vintage like Blue Moon Odum and Oil Can Boyd.

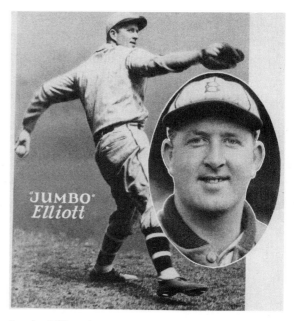

Jumbo Elliott (*Andy Moresund Collection*)

As many baseball columnists have discovered on slow days, the nicknames are a show in themselves—that is, if one is fascinated with monikers on the order of Bow Wow Arft, Biddie McPhee, Turkey Mike Donlin, Swish Nicholson, Inky Strange, Inch Gleich, Coyote Wet, Foghorn Myatt, Easter-Egg Head Shellenback, Bitsy Mott, Pebbles Glasscock, Possum Belly Whitted, Hooks Wiltse, Piano Legs Gore, Piano Legs Hickman, Bunions Zeider, Slewfoot Butler, Orator O'Rourke, Oyster Tommy Burns, Sea Lion Hall, Pinky Hargrave, Fats Fothergill, Stubby Overmire, Bama Rowell, Arky Vaughan, Popeye Mahaffey, Boob McNutt, Moose Drops, Four-Sack Dusak, Buttermilk Tommy Dowd, Trolly Line Butler,

Ding-a-Ling Clay, Buttercup Dickerson, Battleship Gremminger, Boardwalk Brown, Heine Meine, Chicken Wolf, Phenomenal Smith, Jumbo Elliott, Lollypop Killefer, Sweetbreads Bailey, Beartracks Javery, Bullet Joe Bush, Childe Harold Janvrin, Frosty Bill Duggleby, Nemo Munns, Mountain Music Melton, Poll Perritt, Sabu Schuster, Unser Choe, Zorie Rhem, Tarzan Parmelee, True Gun Hart, Ginger Beaumont, Ubbo Ubbo Hornung, Cannonball Titcomb, and Dandelion Pfefier.

Still other names seem to be preordained—or, at least used to be. If your name was Rhodes you were Dusty as naturally as Sad was for Sams and Professor or Specs was for players with glasses. Similarly, Collinses have tended to be called Rip, and Gordons, Flash. Red is a product of hair color, and a host of names are there for the eccentric (Dizzy, Moon Man, Orbit, etc.).

Time was when all players of Teutonic descent named Henry became Heinie, and before World War II it was common to dub

Teddy Ballgame (*Society for American Baseball Research; SABR Collection*)

big left-handed pitchers Rube—Rube Waddell, Rube Marquard, Rube Benton, and Rube Walberg, who was also known as Swede. There were others named Swede, as well as Greeks, Frenchys, and more than a couple Dutches who took their name from the German name for the fatherland, Deutschland. Walkers were called Dixie if they were from the South. Players with M.D.'s or D.D.S.'s got called Doc, as in the cases of Al "Doc" Bushong, Mike "Doc" Powers, and others. Particularly skinny guys tended to get called Blade or Slats, and if your name was Campbell, odds are that they would call you Soup or Soupy.

But beyond all of this the game has a penchant for titling things—people, places and things. The game creates a seemingly endless

The Bambino (*Joe Roberts Photo*)

and mellifluous list of titles, honorifics, and, for the lack of a better term, "noms de press." The players called Walter Johnson Barney, but it was the press that called him Big Train. Any good sportswriter can work a few of these into one great sentence: "Rocket Robert's legal stuff is as formidable as the Great Scott's suspect stuff" (Tom Boswell, *Washington Post*, October 18, 1986). These titles are quotations in themselves and worthy of display and occasional comment:

A

Alex the Great Grover. Cleveland Alexander.

The All-American Out. Leo Durocher, so dubbed by Babe Ruth according to Durocher in *Nice Guys Finish Last*. Later applied to a number of players, including Jerry Koosman.

The Amazing Mays. Willie Mays.

The Amazing Rickey Machine. Rickey Henderson.

The American Peasant. Umpire George Pipgras.

The Ancient Mariner. Gaylord Perry, who got it when he went to the Seattle Mariners late in his career. Red Smith also put the handle on an older Rabbit Maranville "because of the way he hopped around the infield gathering grounders."

The Apache. Howard Nunn.

The Apollo of the Box. Tony Mullane.

The Arkansas Hummingbird. Lon Warneke.

The Arkansas Traveler. Travis Jackson.

Arriba! Roberto Clemente.

A-Rod. Alex Rodriguez.

The Astoria Eagle. Hughie McQuillan.

B

Babe Ruth's Legs. Sammy Byrd, who was a defensive replacement for the Babe.

The Baby Bull. Orlando Cepeda.

Baby Cakes. Jim Palmer, an allusion to his Jockey shorts ads, say many, but it predated the ads and referred to his love of pancakes.

The Bad Boy of the Diamond. Don Black.

Bad Henry. Hank Aaron, from a time when bad meant good, but mainly because he was bad for pitchers. The name was hung on him by Sandy Koufax according to Dan Schlossberg in *The Baseball Catalog*.

Bags. Jeff Bagwell.

The Bambino. Babe Ruth. Italian for "baby," it was one of a number of names used to describe Ruth in print. (Fred Lieb, the great baseball writer, once wrote that Ruth didn't need any name other than Babe: "Babe went as naturally with Ruth as ham goes with eggs. There were several explanations for how Ruth got the name, but Lieb said that

Ruth told him that it started when he was a young lad taken to St. Mary's School in Baltimore. "Some of the older kids picked on him," Lieb reported. "He did considerable crying, so they called him Babe." Yet there is evidence that Ruth was not Babe on the field. As Tristram Potter Coffin points out in his book on the folklore of baseball, *The Old Ball Game*, "Ruth was called 'Jidge' by most of his teammates and 'the Big Monk' or 'Monkey' by most of his opponents."

The Barber. Sal Maglie.

The Barnum of the Bushes. Joe Engel.

The Base Burglar. Lou Brock.

Baseball's Man of the Hour. Ralph Kiner.

Baseball's Quiet Man. Bill Dickey.

Bay's Ball. The 1989 World Series.

The Beast. Jimmy Foxx.

The Beloved Bums. The Brooklyn Dodgers.

Big Ben. Larry Bearnarth.

The Big Bear. Fred Hutchinson.

Big Blue. The Los Angeles Dodgers.

The Big Cat. Johnny Mize because of his grace and fluid movement.

The Big Donkey. Frank Thomas.

Big Ed. Ed Delahanty.

The Big Hurt. Frank Thomas.

Big Mac. The Macmillan *Baseball Encyclopedia*, Mark McGwire.

The Big Mon. Rico Carty.

The Big Moose. Edward Walsh.

The Big O. Bob Oliver.

Big Papi. David Ortiz

Big Poison/Little Poison. Paul Waner along with his brother Lloyd. The lore of the game insists that the brothers got these names as someone with the sound of Brooklyn in their voice referred to them as "big person" and "little person." Although almost identical in size, Paul was three years older, making him Big Poison. Others insist that Big Poison was a simple reference to the fact that Paul batted between .321 and .380 during his first dozen seasons.

The Big Red Machine. The Cincinnati Reds during any year beginning with the numbers 197.

Big Sam. Samuel Thompson.

Big Six. Sobriquet of Christy Mathewson, with several different explanations, including that of a powerful typographical trade union known as the Big Six and a famous horse-drawn fire engine of the era known as the "Big Six." Writer Frank Graham, however, studied the matter and concluded that it came from an exchange something like this:

> FIRST PLAYER: How big do you think that big kid is?
>
> SECOND PLAYER: Six feet.
>
> FIRST PLAYER: He's the biggest six you ever saw—a big six.

The Big Train. Sobriquet of the powerful Walter Johnson, not to be confused with Rufus "Big Train" Johnson. Walter's nickname seems to have been created by Grant-land Rice, who wrote in 1922, "The Big Train comes to town today."

The Big Toe. John Smoltz.

The Big Unit. Randy Johnson.

Bijou of the East. Fenway Park.

Billy Buck. Bill Buckner.

Billy the Kid. Billy Martin.

The Bird. Mark Fidrych because he cut a figure like Big Bird of *Sesame Street* fame.

The Black Babe Ruth. Josh Gibson.

The Black Ty Cobb. Oscar Charleston.

Black Magic. Satchel Paige.

The Black Matty. Satchel Paige, an allusion to Christy Mathewson.

Bleacher Bums. Cubs fans in the cheap seats.

The Blimp. Babe Phelps.

Blue Moon. John Odom. "His boyhood friends nicknamed him 'Moon' because of his moon-shaped faced," says Mike White-ford in *Talking About Baseball*. "Later his professional teammates embellished the nickname to 'Blue Moon' because he often appeared downcast."

Boilin' Boily. Burleigh Grimes.

Boom Boom. Walter Beck, who, according to Lee Allen in *The Hot Stove League*, acquired it "one day at the old Baker Bowl in

Philadelphia when ball after ball boomed off his delivery and hit the tin of the right field fence."

The Boomer. George Scott and David Wells.

The Bones Battery. Catcher Connie Mack and pitcher Frank Gilmore, two tall, skinny guys, who worked together in the 1880s.

Born to Be a Met. Marvin Eugene Throne-berry, whose initials are MET.

The Boston Massacre. The Red Sox' 1978 fade.

The Boy Manager. Lou Boudreau on taking over the Indians.

The Boy Wonder. Bucky Harris for managing the Senators to a pennant at age twenty-seven. Also, Johnny Bench.

The Brat. Eddie Stanky.

The Brew. Harmon Killebrew.

The Broadcaster. Tommy Byrne for his running commentary during games in which he played.

The Bronx Bombers. Traditional sobriquet of the New York Yankees.

The Bronx Zoo. The Yankees since the 1971 book of the same title.

Brother Lo. John Lowenstein.

Bucketfoot Al. Al Simmons.

Buffalo Head. Don Zimmer. See *Loyal Order of the Buffalo Heads*.

The Bull. Greg Luzinski.

Bullet Bob. Bob Feller.

Buy a Vowel. Kent Hrbek.

Bye-Bye. Steve Balboni, who got it when he was hitting homers with great frequency in the minors but soon saw its limitation. Still in the minors, he told the *Sporting News,* "Every time I strike out or fly out you can hear them yelling bye-bye. I can't seem to stop it so I'm going to quit trying."

C

The Capital Punisher/Capital Punishment. Frank Howard, as a Washington Senator slugger.

Captain Carl. Carl Yastrzemski.

Captain Hook. Sparky Anderson, for his reliance on relief pitchers during his years as Reds manager.

Captain Midnight. Lee Walls.

Captain Video. Tony Gwynn.

Casey's Little Bobo. An early Billy Martin.

The Chairman of the Board. Whitey Ford, a name given to him by Elston Howard according to Ford in *Slick.*

The Champ. Harold "Peewee" Reese, who was a marbles champ as a kid.

Charlie Hustle. Pete Rose. According to George Vecsey, the *New York Times,* July 26, 1985, the title was bestowed on a "sultry Sunday afternoon in Tampa, Florida in 1963 when two Yankees watched him run during an exhibition." Vecsey continued, "Ah, but

the reader already knows that the two fat-cat Yankees, guffawing at the intense rookie, were Whitey Ford and Mickey Mantle."

Chef. Gary Sheffield

The Chief. Allie Reynolds, because he was part Creek Indian.

Choke vs. Clutch. The traditional outcome of key series between the Boston Red Sox and the New York Yankees.

Circus Solly. Art Hoffman.

The Clouting Cossack. Lou Novikoff.

The Clown Prince of Baseball. Al Schacht.

The Cobra. Dave Parker, who, according to Mike Whiteford in *Talking About Baseball,* got the name because "his coiled batting stance reminded Pirate announcer Bob Prince of a cobra."

The Colonel. Jim Turner.

Columbia Lou. Lou Gehrig.

The Commerce Comet/The Commerce Kid. Mickey Mantle.

The Count. John Montefusco.

Country. Enos Slaughter. To many older baseball fans this ranks as one of the all-time great baseball names, along with Virgil "Fire" Trucks and Wilmer "Vinegar Bend" Mizell.

Cousin Ed. Ed Barrow.

The Crab. Jesse Burkett and John Evers.

Crazy Horse. Tim Foli.

The Cricket. Bill Rigney.

Crime Dog. Fred McGriff. "Crime Dog" was bestowed on him by ESPN sportscaster Chris Berman noted for his unusual and idiosyncratic player nicknames. The nickname is a play on McGruff, a cartoon dog created for American police to raise children's awareness of crime prevention.

The Cry Baby Indians. The 1940 Cleveland Indians, who had petitioned the front office to remove manager Ossie Vitt, who the players contended had been mean to them. The team became the laughingstock of the American League and attracted other nicknames including "the Bawl Team" and "the Half Vitts."

Cy Old. Jim Palmer after winning the Cy Young Award for the third time.

D

D-Train. Dontrelle Willis.

The Daffiness Boys. The Brooklyn Dodgers ca. 1936, and the Dean Brothers.

Daddy Wags. Leon Wagner.

Dapper Dan. Dan Howley.

The Dazzler. Arthur Charles Vance.

The Dead End Kid. Pepper Martin.

The Dead Sox. The Red Sox when the offense is failing.

The Dean. Chuck Tanner.

Dear Old Roger. Roger Connor.

Death to Flying Things. Jack Chapman and Robert V. Ferguson.

Dem Bums. Sobriquet of the Brooklyn Dodgers.

Designated Gerbil. Don Zimmer.

Dice K. Daisuke Matsuzaka.

Dr. K. Dwight Gooden.

Dr. No. Chuck Hiller.

Dr. Strangeglove. Dick Stuart, whose defensive abilities did not rank with his ability as a hitter.

Donny Baseball. Don Mattingly.

Double X. Jimmie Foxx, supposedly because he was listed in early scorecards with a single X.

Dreamer's Month. March because, as Bob Uecker puts it in *Catcher in the Wry*, "in March, on paper, every team looks stronger than it did a year ago."

The Duke of Flatbush. Duke Snider, who got the name Duke as a kid.

The Duke of Milwaukee. Al Simmons.

The Duke of Tralee. Roger Bresnahan.

The Durable Dutchman. Lou Gehrig.

E

Elmer the Great. Walter Beck.

The Earl of Baltimore. Earl Weaver.

The Earl of Snohomish. Earl Averill born in Snohomish, Washington, May 1, 1902.

The $11,000 Lemon. Rube Marquard because of his poor showing just after being purchased by the Giants for what was a staggering sum in 1908.

El Duque. Orlando Hernandez.

El Espirador. Mario Mendoza. "The vacuum cleaner" in English, and a reference to his ability at shortstop.

El Tiante. Luis Tiant.

F

The Father of Black Baseball. Rube Foster, who organized the first Negro League.

The Father of the Curveball. William "Candy" Cummings.

Fifth Avenue. Lyn Lary.

The First. Jackie Robinson.

The Flying Dutchman. Honus Wagner.

The Fordham Fireman. Johnny Murphy, one of the first great relief pitchers.

The Fordham Flash. Frankie Frisch, a Fordham graduate and one of the rare college graduates of his era in baseball. It was said that Frisch's name sounded like "bacon frying in a skillet."

The Fowlerville Flailer. Charlie Gehringer.

Frankie the Crow. Frank Crosetti for his chatter.

Fred Flintstone. Fred Gladding.

The Freshest Man on Earth. Arlie Latham.

The Friendly Confines. Wrigley Field.

G

G Man. Jason Giambi.

The Gashouse Gang. Sobriquet of the St. Louis Cardinals in the 1930s, especially the 1934 St. Louis Cardinals, an aggregation which also included such well-named gents as Ducky Medwick, Rip Collins, Dizzy Dean, Pepper Martin, Spud Davis, Lippy Leo Durocher, Tex Carlton, and Wild Bill Hallahan. Medwick, by the way, never liked the name "Ducky," but it stuck, and there was nothing he could do about it.

The Gause Ghost. Joe Moore of Gause, Texas.

The Gentle Giant. Ted Kluszewski.

Gentleman Jim. Jim Lonborg.

The Georgia Flash. Ty Cobb.

The Georgia Ghost. Ty Cobb.

The Georgia Peach. Sobriquet of Ty Cobb.

Gettysburg Eddy. Edward Plank.

The Glider. Ed Charles.

The Gliding Panther of Second Base. Napoleon Lajoie.

The Good Humor Man. Roy Campanella.

El Goofy. Vernon "Lefty" Gomez.

Gooney Bird. Don Larsen.

Gorgeous George. George Sisler.

The Grand Old Man of Baseball, or The Grand Old Man. Connie Mack. This was sometimes shortened to GOM.

Le Grand Orange. Rusty Staub.

The Gray Eagle. A prematurely gray Tris Speaker.

The Great. Art Shires.

The Great Agitator. Billy Martin.

The Great Dean. Dizzy Dean.

The Great Gabbo. Frank Gabler. In *High and Inside,* Joseph McBride says that the name was adapted from the name of the novel by F. Scott Fitzgerald.

The Great One. Roberto Clemente.

Great Scott. George Scott.

The Great Wall. See *The Green Monster.*

The Greatest Day in the Baseball Year. Induction Day at Cooperstown.

The Green Monster. The great wall in left field at Fenway Park.

The Griffmen. Clark Griffith's Washington Senators.

The Grounded Blimp. Babe Phelps, who was simply the Blimp, before he refused to fly.

H

Hairs vs. Squares. The 1972 World Series, which pitted the hirsute Oakland A's against the clean-shaven Cincinnati Reds.

Half-Pint. George Rye.

Hammerin' Hank. (a) Hank Bauer, (b) Hank Aaron, (c) Hank Greenberg.

Hankus-Pankus. Hank Greenberg.

Happy Jack. John Chesbro.

Harry the Cat. Harry Brecheen.

Harry the Hat. Harry Walker.

Harry the Horse. Harry Danning.

The Hatchet. Umpire Ken Kaiser.

The Heavenly Twins. Tommy McCarthy and Hugh Duffy.

High Pockets. George Kelly. Damon Runyon pinned this nickname on Kelly, the former New York first baseman, because he had to reach high for his shirt pocket chewing tobacco.

High Rise. J. R. Richard.

Hit 'Em Where They Ain't. Wee Willie Keeler.

The Hitless Wonders. The 1906 White Sox, who won their pennant with few good hitters and only six home runs all season.

The Home of Baseball. Cooperstown, New York.

Home Run Baker. John Franklin Baker, who won the name in the 1911 World Series.

The Home Run King. Babe Ruth.

The Hoosier Comet. Oscar Charleston.

The Hoosier Hammerer. Chuck Klein.

The Hoosier Thunderbolt. Amos Rusie.

Hot Rod. Rod Kanehl.

The Hoover. Brooks Robinson.

The House That Ruth Built. Sobriquet of Yankee Stadium.

The Human Mosquito. Jimmy Slagle.

The Human Rain Delay. Mike Hargrove.

The Human Vacuum Cleaner. Brooks Robinson.

I

The Idol of Baseball Fandom. Ty Cobb.

The Incredible Heap. Kenny Kaiser.

The Invincible One. Warren Spahn.

The I-70 Series. 1985, the all-Missouri Series; the name acknowledged the linking of St. Louis and Kansas City by Interstate 70.

The I-95 Series. 1983, between the Baltimore Orioles and the Philadelphia Phillies, whose cities are linked by Interstate 95.

The Iron Horse. Sobriquet of Lou Gehrig.

The Iron Man. (a) Joseph McGinnity, (b) Umpire Bill McGowan for working 2,541 consecutive games over a period of sixteen and a half years.

J

The Japanese Babe Ruth. Sadaharu Oh.

Joe D. Joe DiMaggio.

John McGraw's Boy. Mel Ott.

Jolly Cholly. Charlie Grimm.

Joltin' Joe. Joe DiMaggio, a title stemming from and aided by a popular song with a refrain "Joltin' Joe DiMaggio."

Jumbo Jim. Jim Nash.

Junior. Ken Griffey.

K

The Ken and Barbie of Baseball. Steve and Cyndy Garvey.

Kentucky Colonel. Earl Combs.

The Kid. Tommy McCarthy, Norman Elberfeld, Charles Nichols, William Gleason, and Ted Williams, among others.

The Killer. Harmon Killebrew as a feared slugger.

The Killer Bees. 1987 Red Sox batting order starting with Burks, Barrett, Boggs, and Baylor, with Buckner batting seventh.

The King. (a) Harmon Killebrew, (b) Alex Kellner.

The King and the Crown Prince. Babe Ruth and Lou Gehrig.

King Carl. Carl Hubbell.

King Kong. Charlie Keller.

King Larry. Napoleon Lajoie.

The King of Clout. Babe Ruth.

L

Lady. Charles Baldwin, who is listed in the *Baseball Encyclopedia* as "Lady." (Some years back the *Sporting News* suggested a chorus line of baseball players to include Baldwin as well as Lena Blackburn, Tillie Shafer, Sadie McMahon, Kittie Bransfield, Dolly Stark, Goldie Holt, Carmen Hill, and the Ryan "sisters" Blondy and Rosie. Then there were Cuddles Cottier, who played for the Washington Senators in the late 1960s, Daisy Davis, Bonnie Hollingsworth, Fay Thomas, and Snooks Dowd.)

Larrupin' Lou. Lou Gehrig.

Larry, but they call him Larry. Larry Cox. It took a May 1980 press release from the Seattle Mariners to explain this one; "They say he looks like Larry Fine of Three Stooges fame, but his name is already Larry, thus the qualification in the nickname."

Leo the Lip. Leo Durocher.

The Lightning Lad. Carlton Fisk.

The Lip. Leo Durocher.

Little Eva. Bill Lange, who was so named because he was so unlike the other Little Eva.

The Little General. Gene Mauch.

The Little Giant. Mel Ott.

The Little Globetrotter. Billy Earle.

The Little Miracle of Coogan's Bluff. The New York Giants of 1951 from the point in mid-August when they were 13 ½ games out of first.

Little Napoleon. John J. McGraw.

Little Poison. Lloyd Waner who, according to his 1982 the *Sporting News* obituary, got the name when "an Eastern fan with a Brooklyn accent called him a 'little person' but it came out as 'little poison.'" See also *Big Poison.*

The Little Round Man. Jimmy Dykes.

The Little Steam Engine. Pud Galvin.

Lord Byron. Umpire Bill Byron.

Lou'siana Lightnin'. Ron Guidry.

The Loyal Order of the Buffalo Heads. Sarcastic name for a group of Red Sox who played for Don Zimmer, who was known as "Buffalo Head" to his men.

The Lumber Company. The 1976 Pirates.

Lusty Lou. Lou Novikoff.

M

The McGrawmen. The New York Giants under John McGraw.

McGraw's Boy. Mel Ott.

McLucky. Dave McNally.

M&M Boys. Mickey Mantle and Roger Maris.

The Mackmen. The Philadelphia A's under Connie Mack.

The Macaroni Pony. Bob Coluccio.

Mad Dog. Greg Maddux and Bill Madlock.

The Mad Hungarian. Al Hrabosky.

The Mad Monk. Russ Meyer.

The Mad Russian. Lou Novikoff.

The Mahatma. Branch Rickey, a name given to him by the press.

The Mail Carrier. Earle Coombs.

The Major. Ralph Houk.

The Man. Stan Musial.

Man o' War. Sam Rice.

The Man with the Golden Arm. Sandy Koufax.

The Margo Embargo. A ban on coverage of the Wade Boggs–Margo Adams affair put into effect in March, 1981, by the Detroit Sports Broadcasters Association.

Marse Joe. Joseph McCarthy.

Marvelous Marv. Marvin Throneberry.

Master Melvin. Mel Ott.

Matty the Great. Christy Mathewson.

The Mechanical Man. Charles Gehringer.

The Meek Man from Meeker. Carl Hubbell.

The Meeker Magician. Carl Hubbell.

Memphis Bill. Bill Terry.

Mick the Quick. Mickey Rivers.

Mickey Mouth. Mickey Rivers.

The Mighty Mite/The Mite Manager. Miller Huggins.

The Million Dollar Baby from the 5&10 Cent Store. Lewis "Hack" Wilson.

The Miracle Man. George Stallings for his stewardship of the 1914 Braves. See *The Miracle Team.*

The Miracle Mets. The 1969 World Champions.

The Miracle Team. The 1914 Braves, who were in last place on July 19 but went on to win the pennant.

Mr. Ballgame. Ted Williams.

Mr. Baseball. (a) Connie Mack, (b) Bob Uecker, who, in his book *Catcher in the Wry* points out that he is known by this title by "a generation that never saw me play."

Mr. Blunt. Rogers Hornsby, about whom Bob Broeg once said he "must have thought that diplomacy was a respiratory disease."

Mr. Bones. Kent Tekulve.

Mr. Brave. Hank Aaron.

Mr. Candy. Reggie Jackson, after the Reggie chocolate bar made its debut in 1978.

Mr. Cub. Ernest Banks.

Mr. Dodger. Vin Scully, an honor bestowed on the announcer by Tommy Lasorda.

Mr. Impossible. Brooks Robinson.

Mr. Milkshake. Bill Virdon.

The Mistake by the Lake. The Cleveland Indians.

Mr. Moist. Gaylord Perry.

Mr. October. Reggie Jackson. In his auto-biography *Reggie,* Jackson says that it was given to him by Thurman Munson at the beginning of the 1977 Series and it was meant sarcastically because Jackson had done so badly during the playoffs against the Royals.

Mr. Shortstop. Marty Marion.

Mr. Sunshine. Ernie Banks.

The Mole. Rod Kanehl, for his fascination with the New York subways during his Mets' years.

The Monsignor. Vada Pinson because players confided in him.

The Monster. Dick Radatz.

The Moon Man. (a) Jay Johnstone. "I'll tell you how [he] got his nickname," Expos manager Bob Rogers explained on more than one occasion. "One day he lost a ball in the sun, but when he came back to the bench he said, 'I lost it in the moon.' After that we called him Moon Man." (b) Steve Hovley, (c) Mike Marshall, (d) Mike Shannon.

Mountain Music. Cliff Melton.

The Mullethead. George Brett.

The Mummy. Joe Coates.

Murderers' Row. (a) The heart of the 1927 New York Yankees batting order—Tony Lazzeri, Lou Gehrig, Babe Ruth, Earle Combs, and Bob Meusel. "Murderers' Row wasn't named for me as so many people think," Babe Ruth recalled later. "I just joined the Row when I joined the Yankees." (b) The heart of the 1919 New York Yankee batting order—Ping Bodie, Roger Pekinpaugh, Duffy Lewis, and Home Run Baker.

The Mustache Gang. The Oakland A's of the early 1970s.

My Favorite Martian. Jay Johnstone.

The Mysterious Dr. Lau. Charlie Lau.

N

Nails. Lenny Dykstra.

The Nashville Narcissus. Red Lucas.

Neon. Deion Sanders.

The New Breed. Early Mets fans, from the 1961–1962 ABC television series of the same name.

The Nickel Series. Series between New York teams when the cost of a subway ride was *5 cents.*

The Noblest Roman. Charles Comiskey.

O

The Octopus of Baseball. Marty Marion.

Oil Can. Dennis Boyd, who got the name, according to a *USA Today* interview of February 28, 1988, "for draining beer cans in his hometown of Meridian, Miss., where beer is called oil." He attempted to shed the name, which sometimes led to unfortunate word-play ("The Can is leaking," said Vin Scully during the 1986 World Series when Boyd got into trouble).

Oil Can Harry. Ray Oyler.

Old Aches and Pains. Luke Appling.

The Old Arbiter/The Old Arbitrator. Bill Klem.

The Old Bear. Fred Hutchinson.

Old Biscuit Pants. Lou Gehrig.

The Old Fox. Clark Calvin Griffith.

The Old Hoss. Charles Radbourn.

Old Man River. Connie Mack.

The Old Master. Bob Gibson.

The Old Meal Ticket. Sobriquet of Carl Hubbell.

The Old Perfessor. Casey Stengel, who, like Babe Ruth, may have had the perfect baseball nickname because not one fan in a dozen knew that his real name was Charles and that Casey stood for the initials of his hometown, Kansas City. Fred Lieb once commented on natural nicknames like Casey: "nicknames must be spontaneous, as they rarely can be manufactured." Early in his career he was called Dutch.

Old Pete. Grover Cleveland Alexander.

Old Reliable. Tommy Henrich.

The Old Roman. Charles Comiskey.

Old Second Inning. Tim McCarver. Bill Lee gave him the name, which he explained

in his autobiography, *The Wrong Stuff,* was "due to his habit of having to take a dump in the john between the first and second inning of each game."

Ol' Shitfuck. Joe Schultz because Jim Bouton quotes him saying "shitfuck" twenty-one times in *Ball Four.*

Old Soupbone. Carl Hubbell.

Old Stubblebeard. Burleigh Grimes.

Old Tennis Ball Head. Steve Hovley.

Old Tomato Face. Nick Cullop, whose face tended to redness.

The Old Warhorse. Enos Slaughter.

The One and Only. Babe Ruth.

The Only Del. Edward Delahanty.

The Only Nolan. Edward Sylvester Nolan.

Orang-Outang. Earl Averill.

Orator Jim. James O'Rourke.

The Other Babe. Babe Herman.

P

The Pale Hose. The White Sox.

The Peerless Dutchman. Honus Wagner.

The Peerless Hal. Hal Chase.

The Peerless Leader. Sobriquet of Frank Chance, from which Red Smith derived his "the Practically Peerless Leader," for Leo Durocher.

The Penguin. Ron Cey.

The People's Cherce. Dixie Walker.

The Perfect Ballplayer. George Sisler.

Pete the Hustler. Pete Rose.

The Phantom. Julian Javiar because, as is explained in Bob Gibson's *From Ghetto to Glory,* "he makes the double play so quickly and gets out of the way of the runner so fast, he's like a phantom."

The Pirates' Second Shortstop. Pie Traynor.

Pistol Pete. Pete Reiser.

Poosh 'Em Up. Tony Lazzeri.

The Pretzel Battery. Ted Breitenstein and Heinie Peitz.

The Pride of the Yankees. Lou Gehrig.

Prince Hal. Hal Schumacher.

The Principle Owner. George Steinbrenner.

Pudge. Carlton Fisk and Ivan Rodriguez.

The Puker. Umpire Paul Pryor because he once threw up on catcher Johnny Roseboro at Dodger Stadium.

Q

The Quakers. The early Philadelphia Phillies.

R

The Rabbi of Swat. Moe Solomon.

Rabbit. Walter James Vincent Maranville, who, depending on your source, got the name from (a) his pep and the way he hopped around the bases, or, (b) his willingness to wiggle his ears for the fans. (According to reporters, when Maranville toured Japan the fans went crazy wiggling their hands against the side of their heads like rabbit ears. He, of course, reciprocated.) Or, (c) as Leo Durocher puts it in *Nice Guys Finish Last,* "The Rabbit was a little fellow, that's how he got his nickname."

The Rajah. Rogers Hornsby.

The Rape of the Red Sox. The period from the championship years of 1915 and 1916 to 1923, when they were in the cellar because the team's owner was allegedly selling off his best players to finance Broadway shows.

Rapid Robert. Bob Feller. Roy Blount Jr., writing in *Inside Sports,* had this to say about the name; "The world will always know Bob Feller as 'Rapid Robert,' but his **fellow Indians called him 'Inky' because he had himself incorporated.**"

The Roadrunner. Ralph Garr.

The Reading Rifle. Carl Furillo.

The Red Rooster. Doug Rader.

Reggie's Regiment. Fans who came to the stadium to see Reggie Jackson hit home runs in Oakland.

The Rock of Snohomish. Earl Averill.

The Rocker or **Rocket Man** or **Roger the Rocket.** Roger Clemens, from his style of delivery.

The Ruppert Rifles. The New York Yankees under the ownership of Jacob Ruppert.

The Ryan Express. Nolan Ryan.

S

The Say Hey Kid. Willie Mays.

Scrap Iron. (a) Ed Beecher. (b) Clint Courtney, (c) Bob Stinson, (d) Phil Garner.

Schoolboy. Lynwood Rowe.

The Scot Heard 'Round the World. Bobby Thomson.

The Screaming Skull. Sal Maglie.

Señor October. David Ortiz

Señor Papi. David Ortiz.

The September Massacre. What happened to the Red Sox in 1978.

The Series by the Bay. 1989.

Sgt. Hank. Hank Bauer.

Shoeless Joe. Joe Jackson.

Shot Heard 'Round the World. Bobby Thomson's 1951 playoff home run.

Shrek. Kevin Mench.

The Shuttle Series. The 1986 World Series, an allusion to the fact that Boston and New York are linked by two air shuttle services.

The Silent Captain of the Red Sox. Bobby Doerr, a title given to him by Ted Williams.

The Silent Pole. Harry Coveleski.

The Silver Fox. Duke Snider.

The Singer Throwing Machine. Bill Singer.

Sir Timothy. Tim Keefe.

Sky King. Denny McLain, given when he took flying lessons.

Sky Young. Denny McLain, given to him when he won the Cy Young Award.

The Skydome Summit. The April 10, 1990, meeting of President George Bush and Prime Minister Brian Mulroney of Canada in the Toronto Skydome. The meeting was followed by a Blue Jays–Texas Rangers game.

Sliding Billy. Bill Hamilton.

The Snake Man. Moe Drabowsky.

The Space Man. Bill Lee.

The Southside Hitmen. The Chicago White Sox when they are hitting.

The Splendid Splinter. Ted Williams, who was given the name before he shattered a jet in Korea in a crash landing.

The Sport of Eggheads. Baseball.

The Squire of Kennet Square. Herb Pennock.

Stan the Man. Stan Musial. In *The Baseball Life of Sandy Koufax*, George Vecsey says: "How Musial used to murder those Bums! Every time he came to bat, the fans used to groan, 'Here comes that man again! Stan the Man!' Now everybody in baseball called him 'Stan the Man.'"

Stan the Man Unusual. Don Stanhouse for his spaceyness. Writing on the topic of names in *Inside Sports*, Roy Blount Jr. said that this one was so good that it deserved its own title, "the Splendid Sobriquet." It was originally created by Mike Flanagan, who Blount dubbed "the Dubber."

The Staten Island Scot. Bobby Thomson.

Steady Eddie. Ed Kranepool.

The Stick. Candlestick Park.

The Straw That Stirs the Drink. Reggie Jackson.

Subway Series. Any World Series in which two New York teams participate. As of this writing the last one took place in 2000 between the Yankees and the Mets, and before that in 1956 between the Yankees and the Dodgers.

Sudden Sam. Sam McDowell, for the fact that when opposing batters were asked how his fastball approached they would say something like, "All of a sudden, man, all of a sudden."

The Suds Series. 1982, which saw two teams, the Brewers and Cardinals, from cities with strong links to beer. The Milwaukee team is named for that city's production of beer, and the St. Louis team was owned by the Busch family of the Anheuser-Busch breweries.

Suitcase Bob. Robert Seeds. Two good explanations for this nickname: that he was an oft-traded player who lived out of his suitcase, and that he had big suitcase-sized feet. Take your pick.

The Sultan of Swat. Babe Ruth.

The Sultan of Swish. Dave Nicholson.

Super Joe. Joe Charboneau.

The Swamp Fox. Al Dark.

Sweet Juice. William "Judy" Johnson.

Sweet Lou. Lou Piniella, who actually hailed from Tampa and is of Spanish descent. Originally "Sweet Lou from Peru."

T

The Tabasco Kid. Norm Elberfeld.

Taj O'Malley. Dodger Stadium.

The Tall Tactician. Connie Mack.

Tanglefoot Lou. Lou Gehrig, early in his career.

The Tater Man. George Scott.

Ted Threads. Ted Williams as manager of the Washington Senators, so named, according to the June 6, 1971, *Washington Star,* "by his charges, who are amazed at his casual wardrobe."

Teddy Ballgame. Ted Williams. In *My Turn at Bat* Williams says that he got this from the son of a friend who met Williams at age two and several years later said he wanted to go back to Fenway Park to see Teddy Ballgame.

Ten to Two. Art Fowler because, as Sparky Lyle points out in *The Bronx Zoo,* "that's the way his feet point."

The Thin Thunderbolt. Ted Williams, so called by Bob Feller in *Strikeout Story* and elsewhere.

Three-Finger. Mordecai Brown.

Thunderpup. Shawn Dunston.

The Time Zone Without a Team. The Rocky Mountain Time Zone, a sobriquet used in selling organized baseball on a team in Denver.

Tobacco John. John Lanning.

Tom Terrific. Tom Seaver.

The Toy Cannon. Jim Wynn.

Toys in the Attic. Frank Bertaina, a name given to him in Baltimore by Moe Drabowsky.

Trader Jack. Jack McKeon.

The Tribe. The Cleveland Indians.

Truthful Jeems. Jim Mutrie.

The $25 Million Dollar Man. Dave Winfield, so called by Reggie Jackson in *Reggie*.

Twinkle Toes. George Selkirk for his distinctive way of walking. He stole only 41 bases in his career despite the name.

Two Head. Babe Ruth. Baseball historian Robert Smith has noted that this name was used by other players and that it drove him wild. It alluded to the fact that his head seemed twice normal size.

The Ty Cobb of the National League. Honus Wagner.

Uncle Robby. Wilbert Robinson, whose team in Brooklyn was known as "the Robins" in his honor.

Uncle Tired. Tommy Davis.

The Unholy Trio. Mickey Mantle, Billy Martin, and Whitey Ford.

The Union Man. Walter Holke.

The Unknown Soldier. Commissioner General William D. Eckert.

Venus de Milo Outfield. Any group that is pretty to look at but has no arms.

Vincent Van Go. Vince Coleman.

Vinegar Bend. Wilmer Mizell. After being elected to the House of Representatives from North Carolina in the 1960s, he explained the name, which was also the name of his hometown. "A railroad was being built in that part of Alabama a long time ago. The diet of the railroad workers included sorghum molasses. A barrel of the molasses soured into vinegar and was poured into Escatawapa River at a place where it makes a bend, and ever since the place has been called Vinegar Bend."

The Wahoo Barber/Wahoo Sam. Sam Crawford.

Wamby. Bill Wambsganss, who had a true nom de press. He was rewarded for the feat of completing the only unassisted triple play in World Series history (1920) by having his name cut to Wamby by typesetters. Modern record book compilers have put his name back together. (Wamby was one of a number of examples where early sportswriters compressed names to fit headlines and box scores. Ping Bodie's real name was Francesco Pezzolo. Another case was that of Rinaldo Angelo Paolinelli, who was trimmed down to Babe Pinelli. Writing in 1974, Fred Lieb took a look at the new crop of players—men with names like Bob Apodaca and Al Hrabosky—and asked, "What would the writers of the days of Ring Lardner, Damon Runyon, and Charlie Dryden have done with such names?").

The Waterbury Wizard. Jimmy Piersall.

The Weatherman. Mickey Rivers for his ability to predict the weather.

Wee Willie. Willie Keeler.

What's the Use. Pearce Chiles.

The Wheeze Kids. The 1983 Philadelphia Phillies, who one preseason observer said were composed of veterans destined to make cameo appearances at old-timers' games.

The Whip. Ewell Blackwell.

The White Gorilla. Goose Gossage.

The White Rat. Whitey Herzog.

The Whiz Kids. The 1950 Phillies.

Why Me? Danny Cater, who asked this question every time he was put out on a great play.

Wiggly Field. Candlestick Park after the 1989 World Series earthquake.

Wild Bill. Bill Donovan.

The Wild Hoss of the Osage. Sobriquet of Pepper Martin.

Wild Thing. Mitch Williams

The Wizard of Gauze. Trainer Jim Dudley.

The Wizard of Oz. Ozzie Smith.

The World Serious. The World Series, a phrase made famous by Ring Lardner, but heard much earlier [first] from the lips of New York Giant Josh Devore in 1911 by Fred Lieb.

X

X-Factor. David Eckstein.

Y

The Yankee Clipper. Long-established sobriquet of Joe DiMaggio, but it was also used derisively for George Steinbrenner, who insisted that his players be clean-shaven.

Ye Childe Harold. Pete Reiser.

The Year of the Asterisk. The strike-interrupted 1981 season, when most records and statistics were marked with an asterisk.

The Year of the Lockout. 1990.

The Year of the Rookie. 1986 (Canseco, Joyner, et al.).

The Year of the Zero. 1968.

Young Cy Young. Irving Young, who pitched for the Boston Nationals while Cy Young pitched for the Boston Americans. Cy Young's real name was Denton True Young, and Cy was short for Cyclone. Over the years there have been a number of Cys up to the "Cy Clone" handle attached to Baltimore Oriole Storm Davis because of his resemblance to Cy Young Award–winning pitcher Jim Palmer, who was once dubbed Cy Old.

NORWORTH, JACK

TAKE ME OUT TO THE BALLGAME

"Katie Casey was baseball mad,
Had the fever and had it bad;
Just to root for the hometown crew,
Ev'ry sou—Katie Blew
On a Saturday her young beau
Called to see if she'd, like to go,
To see a show but Miss Katie said no,
I'll tell you what you can do

Take me out to the ball game,
Take me out with the crowd
Buy me some peanuts and cracker jack,
I don't care if I never get back,
Let me root, root, root for the home team,
If they don't win it's a shame
For it's one, two, three strikes you're out,
At the old ball game.

Katie Casey saw all the games,
Knew the players by their first names;
Told the umpire he was wrong
All a-long—good and strong—
When the score was just two to two,
Katie Casey knew what to do,
Just to cheer up the boys she knew,
She made the gang sing this song:

Take me out to the ball game,
Take me out with the crowd
Buy me some peanuts and cracker jack,
I don't care if I never get back,
Let me root, root, root for the home team,
If they don't win it's a shame
For it's one, two, three strikes you're out,
At the old ball game.

> —1908. First stanza from original draft; second stanza published 1908. Set to music by Albert Von Tilzer.

"Not bad. The peanuts were good too."

> —Author of "Take Me Out to the Ball Game," asked how he liked seeing his first ball game at Ebbets Field in 1942, thirty-four years after writing the song (Vance Garnett, "Our Other Anthem," *Washington Post*, April 25, 1995)

NOTICE

ALL REQUESTS FOR LEAVE OF ABSENCE ON ACCOUNT OF GRANDMOTHER'S FUNERAL, SORE THROAT, HOUSECLEANING, LAME BACK, TURNING OF THE RINGER, HEADACHES, BRAIN STORM, COUSIN'S WEDDING, GENERAL AILMENTS OR OTHER LEGITIMATE EXCUSES MUST BE MADE OUT AND HANDED TO THE BOSS NOT LATER THAN 10 A.M. ON THE MORNING OF THE GAME.

> —Traditional gag notice hung in offices and factories when all games, including the World Series, were played in sunlight

NOVAK, MICHAEL

"Baseball is as close a liturgical enactment of the white Anglo-Saxon Protestant myth as the nation has. It is a cerebral game, designed as geometrically as the city of Washington itself, born out of the Enlightenment and the philosophies so beloved of Jefferson, Madison, and Hamilton. It is to games what the *Federalist Papers* are to books: orderly, reasoned, judiciously balanced, incorporating segments of violence and collision in a larger plan of rationality, absolutely dependent on an interiorization of public rules."

—*The Joy of Sports*

"Baseball is a Lockean game, a kind of contract theory in ritual form, a set of atomic individuals who assent to patterns of limited co-operation in their mutual interest."

—*The Joy of Sports*

"Baseball is unlike football or basketball in not being governed by a clock. Until the last out has been registered, anything can happen. Even in the last of the ninth, with two out, a team can suddenly, surprisingly, score 5 or 7 or 9 or 11 runs. It is part of the brilliant fairness of the game. You must, in the end, defeat yourself, use up in vain your own equal chances."

—*The Joy of Sports*

"It is hard to imagine a democratic republic without baseball for the instruction of its citizens."

—*The Joy of Sports*

"Players in baseball are like the links in a chain, the chain being no stronger than its weakest link. They perform their actions not so much in unison as serially. Basketball and football are considerably more corporate, require a far higher degree of unity, represent a quite different vision of America."

—*The Joy of Sports*

NOVIKOFF, LOU

"I got such a good jump on the pitcher."

—Explaining why he stole third base with the bases loaded; quoted in Richard Cahan and Mark Jacob, *The Game That Was: The George Brace Baseball Photo Collection* (Chicago: Contemporary Books, 1996)

O

ODOM, JIM

"No manager ever thinks he got a break. I call them like I see them, and I don't care what team it is. If I'm right only half the time, I'm batting .500—and I never saw a ball player bat .500."

—On umpiring

ODOM, JOHN "BLUE MOON"

"We liked the idea that we were a family. We could fight each other in the clubhouse and fight together outside the clubhouse. That's what made us so good. You went to the ballpark never knowing what was going to happen."

—On the great Oakland teams of the 1970s; quoted thirty years after the fact in the *San Francisco Chronicle*, October 14, 2001

John "Blue Moon" Odom (*Author's Collection*)

OHLMEYER, DON

"We're looking for four games and out. The faster it's over with, the better it is."

—NBC entertainment executive on the eve of 1997 Indians-Marlins World Series because it was bad for TV ratings, *Cleveland Plain Dealer*, October 22, 1997. He later apologized.

OKRENT, DANIEL

"Baseball means what those of us who hold it in our hearts need it to mean. It can be a game, a pastime, or it can be something by which we measure the seasons of our lives, or it can be something that serves metaphorically for the battles, the wars, the triumphs and the tragedies of any kind of human conflict. And I think, more than anything else, it tells me that there is something in the world that I can count on and that is never going to let me down."

—Quoted in Ken Burns and Lynn Novick, "Why Baseball?" *Baltimore Sun*, September 11, 1994

OKRENT, DAN, AND HARRIS LEWINE

"Perry's agent approached the makers of Vaseline, the product Perry reputedly used for his spitball, for a possible endorsement contract. A company representative replied, 'We soothe babies' asses, not baseballs.'"

—On Gaylord Perry in *The Ultimate Baseball Book* by Daniel Okrent and Harris Lewine

OLBERMANN, KEITH

"When the game's lush past is so easily connected to its present, when the fans of today inherit some intuitive knowledge of the grace of Joe DiMaggio or the passion of Roberto Clemente or the durability of Cy Young, when baseball alone among the sports not only supports but virtually mandates Old-Timers' Days, why doesn't the game do more to preserve, emphasize and even boast of its heritage? That's like asking, How in the heck did Apple ever lose to Microsoft?"

"Of course, we're talking about baseball here, a sport whose defending champion is nothing more than a no-freezes Rotisserie team, a sport willing to sacrifice its identity for the short-term profits of interleague play. The inescapable lesson to fans born with the marvelous ability to travel backward or forward within baseball? Stand still, shut up and buy whatever memorabilia are thrown at you."

—"Eight Degrees of Eckersley," *Sports Illustrated*, April 20, 1998

OLDS, SHARON

"Baseball is reassuring. It makes me feel as if the world is not going to blow up."

—*This Sporting Life* (Milkweed Editions, 1987)

OLERUD, JOHN

"I was told you're nobody until you do, but I still don't like it."

—As a Toronto rookie, on becoming the 1,079th player to be struck out by Nolan Ryan; quoted in the May 1990 *Major League Baseball Newsletter*

OLESKER, MICHAEL

"Forget all that stuff about the romance of baseball, which is just an act of hitting a round object with a piece of wood and then running like crazy. The real romance is inside our heads, put there by the people like Chuck Thompson, nurturing each new generation, spreading the lore of the game between pitches.

"They take the simple fact of grown men acting like children and put poetry around it."

—"Chuck Thompson Put the Audio into Boys' Dreams," *Baltimore Sun,* February 11, 1993

"Baseball, where the public scratching of various body parts is considered quaint pastoral ritual. Hey! Can't you guys do that at home?! . . .

"Baseball's a game in which grown men wear little beanies and knickers in public, even though strangers are watching them. . . .

"The game is played by those whose emotional development was arrested as they reached adulthood, who held on to the values of the schoolyard, to win at all costs, to look for the edge, and to fight ferociously when they think they're being cheated, the way children will."

—"Expect to Rate as an Adult? Don't Expectorate at Umps," *Baltimore Sun,* October 1, 1996

"Baseball is a game for children played by adults who act like children. The catcher yells, 'Way you chuck 'em in, hon,' to the pitcher, who stands on a little hill and scratches himself in public. The batter attempts to hit a ball with a club formerly used in the Cro-Magnon period. The base runner, attempting to break up a double play, slides with spikes high into the second baseman, who pivots and throws sidearm to first, so the ball seems to come at the runner's eyeballs. The debutante ball, this ain't."

—"A Kid's Game, Played by Overgrown Children," *Baltimore Sun,* May 21, 1998

"There are days when you know that God invented baseball to give us all a concept of eternity, when the game moves so slowly that it hangs heavy as a beer-bloated belly."

—In his *Baltimore Sun* column, April 5, 1983

OLIVER, GENE

"We hit the dry side of the ball."

—As a Milwaukee Braves infielder, on how to hit a spitball

O'LOUGHLIN, SILK

"There are no close plays. A man is always out or safe, or it is a ball or a strike, and the umpire, if he is a good man and knows his business, is always right. For instance, I am always right."

—Quoted in Christy Mathewson, *Pitching in a Pinch* (New York: Putnam, 1912)

O'MALLEY, PETER

"I believe salaries are at their peak, not just in baseball, but in all sports. It's quite possible some owners will trade away, or even drop entirely, players who expect $200,000 salaries. There's a superstar born every year. . . . But still there is no way clubs can continue to increase salaries to the level some players are talking about."

—As Los Angeles Dodgers president in 1971

O'MALLEY, PETER (CONTINUED)

"I don't think any man can predict what form sports will take in the next 100 years, and I don't think it matters. I wouldn't object to pink baseballs or orange balls or more innings or fewer, or more balls and strikes or fewer, or designated second-basemen. The details of competitive games aren't really important. What is important is the idea of a competitive pastime. I expect that to survive."

> —As Dodgers president, in the *Los Angeles Times,* January 26, 1975

"To me he was the greatest Dodger of them all."

> —On Roy Campanella at the time of his death, *Washington Post,* June 28, 1993

"When you think of all the cameras you'd need to do a perfect job, the complications are enormous. One complication alone—the delays you'd have while the umpires consulted their TV sets—probably outweighs the problems caused by an umpire's occasional mistake. A ballgame isn't like a horse race, in which one camera can determine who won after they raise the inquiry sign. Baseball's answer is to pay the umpires well and train them well. I believe the integrity of the game is safe in their hands."

> —The Dodger president on the use of television; quoted in the *Los Angeles Times,* February 7, 1977

O'MALLEY, WALTER

"Baseball isn't a business, it's more like a disease."

> —Widely attributed

Walter O'Malley (*Author's Collection*)

"If we televised home games in a spread-out place like Los Angeles, where our patrons drive miles, no one would come except the players' wives. And a lot of them might stay home, too."

> —Interview with the Dodgers chairman, *TV Guide,* April 5, 1975

"We [in baseball] have been hurt by philosophy differences in the two leagues; we have never been quite able to get together. For instance, when the Yankees were the hottest team in baseball, the National League asked for inter-league play. We were turned down. When the Yankees cooled off and good teams developed in the National League, the Americans asked for inter-league play. And the Nationals turned them down. We keep going in different directions."

> —Quoted in the *Los Angeles Herald-Examiner,* February 25, 1971

O'NEIL, BUCK

"Baseball is better than sex. It is better than music, although I do believe jazz comes in a close second. It does fill you up."

> —Quoted in his *New York Times* obituary, October 8, 2006

"Don't feel sorry for us, Joe. We played the game with a group of guys who had a passion for the game. They had a passion for life. And were a very special group. The only reason we wanted to play in the other league was to prove to them we were as good or better than they were. Other than that, don't feel sorry for us."

> —Recalled by Joe Morgan at O'Neil's funeral, AP, October 16, 2006

"I think we are the cause of the changes. Some of the changes that have been made were because of us. We did our duty. We did the groundwork for the Jackie Robinsons, the Willie Mayses, and the guys that are playing now. So why feel sorry for me? We did our part in our generation, and we turned it over to another generation, and it's still changing, which is the way it should be."

> —Quoted in his *Boston Globe* obituary, October 8, 2006

"'I saw baseball was a good way to make a living,' he said. 'So I decided that's what I wanted to do. It was better than working in the celery fields.'"

> —Quoted in his *Boston Globe* obituary, October 8, 2006

"The Negro Leagues Baseball Museum is my pride and joy. That's the top of the line for my life. We're telling the story, the history, of not only Negro league baseball, but of the segregation era. That was the reason we had the Negro leagues, because we couldn't play in the major leagues, so we organized a league of our own, which was outstanding."

> —*Los Angeles Times*, July 25, 2006

"There's nothing greater for a human being than to get his body to react to all the things one does on a ball field. It's as good as sex; it's as good as music; it fills you up. Waste no tears for me. I didn't come along too early. I was right on time."

> —As a Chicago Cub scout and former first baseman for the black Kansas City Monarchs, at the third annual Negro Baseball League Reunion in Ashland, Kentucky, June 1981; quoted by Bruce Anderson in "Time Worth Remembering," *Sports Illustrated*, July 16, 1981

O'NEILL, PAUL

"I'm happy to be part of the Yankee stigma."

> —On being traded by Cincinnati to New York Yankees, in 1992; quoted in the *Washington Post*, February 21, 1993

"It's cool. It's a beautiful stadium, and the crowds are amazing. The fans, the fights, the beer throwing, the noise level. There's so much excitement it makes me wonder what it would be like here if the team becomes a winner."

> —On Yankee Stadium, *St. Louis Post-Dispatch*, April 21, 1993

O'NEILL, TIP

"It was around the early 1970s. He was making around $60,000 a year but he told me he was fed up with baseball and wanted to start a career in politics. I asked him what job he wanted. He said he would like to run for lieutenant governor, and I told him I would try to help him get the nomination from the Democratic party. Then he asked me how much it paid. I told him $12,500. That was the end of his political ambitions."

> —The former Speaker of the House on a conversation he had with Carl Yastrzemski; quoted in the *Boston Globe,* July 25, 1989

"That was the only year [1888] in baseball that a base on balls counted as a base hit. He would get up and foul them off until he got a base on balls. The Irish loved him. Everywhere there's a Tip O'Neill, but he's the original Tip O'Neill."

> —On Edward O'Neill of the Browns and how the Massachusetts representative got his nickname; quoted from a C-SPAN interview in the *New York Times,* September 12, 1986

ONSLOW, JACK

"Hello, Jack Onslow, this is everybody."

> —As White Sox manager; quoted by John P. Carmichael in the *Chicago Daily News*

OPPENHEIMER, JOEL

"It also makes it easy for the generations to talk to one another."

> —*New York Times,* June 17, 1979

O'REILLY, JANE

"The one nice thing about sports is that they prove men do have emotions and are not afraid to show them."

> —From "The Girl I Left Behind" (1980); quoted by André Bernard in *American Scholar,* autumn 2000

OREM, PRESTON D.

"A proposed rule change to provide that in case any club proved to be 'composed of gentlemen of color' their membership should be considered forfeited was unanimously adopted, although with a smile all around."

> —Report on the 1870 meeting of the New York State Association; quoted from his *Baseball (1845–81),* from the newspaper accounts

---

ORGANIZED BASEBALL

Modern professional baseball is based on one central document, which defines its integrity:

"MEMORANDUM OF AGREEMENT between the Sixteen Clubs, constituent members of the National League of Professional Base Ball Clubs and of the American League of Professional Base Ball Clubs, parties of the first part, and Kenesaw M. Landis, party of the second part.

In an earnest effort to insure to the American public high-class and wholesome professional baseball, the Clubs by contract dated January 12, 1921, have agreed to submit themselves to the jurisdiction of a Commissioner with broad powers of decision in case of disputes relating to the conduct of the National Game. They have called upon the party of the second part to accept the office of Commissioner because he, in their judgment, individually possesses the necessary qualifications, and because the principal recreation of the American people should be administered in a way that comports with the dignity of his judicial office. The party of the second part has accepted his election as commissioner and is desirous of rendering additional public service in that capacity."

—Agreement between the National League of Professional Base Ball Clubs and each of its eight constituent clubs, of the one part, and the American League of Professional Base Ball Clubs, and each of its eight constituent clubs, of the other part, in which "the office of Commissioner is hereby created." The agreement appears here with the permission of the presidents of each league and the copy itself was provided by the National Baseball Library.

The importance of these words were put into context by Commissioner Bowie Kuhn in a state-of-the-game report in Nashville on December 5, 1983:

"A little look at history will take you back in terms of the Commissionership to the beginning, to 1921, when a curly-haired old tough-minded federal judge was about to become Commissioner. He did something else very important. He said I want more than a legal document—that's what the Major League Agreement is, it's a legal document, it gives the Commissioner certain powers, they change very little over the years, to the extent they have changed they've changed adversely in terms of the Commissioner's powers—he said something more. He said I want a moral covenant with ownership to steadfastly support the Commissioner. I want a moral covenant by which they say, 'We will stand behind you come thick or thin regardless of what you do, regardless of what our individual personal feelings might be about its rightness or wrongness. We have given you a tough job and we will stand behind you, and we will support you. There will be no knives in your back.' And they wrote a letter to Commissioner Landis, they all put their names on it, and in less fancier language than I have used, it said what I have suggested. And that, I think, is important because beyond the legalities, beyond the words of the agreements, beyond all the interpretations should lie a strong moral commitment on the part of ownership to support their Commissioner, support him in every possible way every day, not to undermine him, not to try to break his power, not to try to break his spirit, but to support him because the game requires it. And if they don't do it, believe me, there is very big trouble ahead. And nobody worth his salt should take the job unless he is given that kind of commitment by ownership."

OROSCO, JESSE

"I haven't had a summer in 25 years. I think it's that time."

> —On his retirement after twenty-four major league seasons, 2004; quoted in AP collection of quotes of the year, January 1, 2005

O'ROURKE, JIM

"There was no paraphernalia in the old days with which one could protect himself. No mitts, no, not even gloves, and masks, why you would have been laughed off the diamond had you worn one behind the bat. In the early days, the pitcher was only 50 feet away from the batsman, and there was no penalizing him if he hit you with the ball."

> —The Hall of Famer on the good old days; quoted on December 4, 1913

OSBORN, DON

"The one thing wrong with our pitchers is they all have to pitch the same night."

> —As a Pirates coach

OSINSKI, DAN

"Better make it six. I can't eat eight."

> —When asked if he wanted his pizza sliced into six or eight pieces. This line has been credited to Yogi Berra as well, and the true originator may never be known.

OSLER, SCOTT

"George Steinbrenner is the salt of the earth, and the Yankee players are the open wounds."

> —"Thoughts on the Business of Life," *Forbes,* October 27, 2003

"The new official slogan: 'Major League Baseball: *!'"

> —*San Francisco Chronicle,* March 13, 2006, suggesting Barry Bonds's chase of Hank Aaron's home-run record could lead to the same type of debate that followed the breaking of Roger Maris's single-season home-run record, now owned by Mark McGwire

OSTEEN, CLAUDE

"Slapping a rattlesnake across the face with the back of your hand is safer than trying to fool Henry Aaron."

> —As a Dodgers pitcher; quoted in *Hank Aaron . . . 714 and Beyond* by Jerry Brondfield

OTIS, AMOS

"I get on base by making good contact with the ball, but whenever I hit a home run I'm as surprised as everybody else."

> —As a Royal; quoted in the *Christian Science Monitor,* October 13, 1978

OTT, MEL

"Every time I sign a ball, and there must have been thousands, I thank my luck that I wasn't born Coveleskie, or Wambsganss, or Peckinpaugh."

—Quoted in *Sport Magazine's All-Time All Stars* by Al Stump

"He seemed to be doing everything wrong, yet everything came out right. He stopped everything behind the plate and hit everything in front of it."

—On Yogi Berra, whom he tried to buy for the Giants before the Yankees fully realized how good he was; quoted in the Hall of Fame *Yearbook,* 1989

OWENS, PAUL

"The toughest thing about managing is standing up for nine innings."

—As manager of the Philadelphia Phillies; quoted in *Sports Illustrated,* October 13, 1973

OZARKISMS—DANNY OZARK

Danny Ozark is a man with a particular ability to fracture the language. Many of these were originally brought to the attention of the world by Bill Conlin of the *Philadelphia Daily News.*

"Contrary to popular belief, I have always had a wonderful repertoire with my players."

—When asked if he had problems with his players

"Don't you know I'm a fascist? You know, a guy who says one thing and means another?"

—When asked why he never gave straight answers; quoted by Jay Johnstone in *Temporary Insanity*

"Even Napoleon had his Watergate."

—Said after a ten-game losing streak had reduced the Phils' 15½ game lead to 3½. Widely quoted, this "Ozarkism" appeared in *Sports Illustrated,* April 30, 1979, among other places.

"Half this game is 90 percent mental."

—Widely quoted

"I don't want to get into a Galphonse-Aston act."

—Widely attributed

"It is beyond my apprehension."

—After being swept three games by Atlanta in 1976

"It's not a question of morality."

—When asked about the morale of the Phillies. Sometimes stated as "This team's morality is not a factor."

"[It] was not intimidating and, furthermore, I will not be cohorsed."

—When his job with the Phillies was in jeopardy and general manager Paul Owens was making trips with the team

411

"Mike Andrews's limits are limitless."

— Widely quoted

"What makes him unusual is that he thinks he's normal and everyone else is nuts."

— On Jay Johnstone

"That's very disturbing."

— Philadelphia Phillies manager, told his team was seven games behind with six to play

"Who knows what evil lurks in the hearts of men except the Shadow?"

— After managing well and outfinessing an opponent, this was the line Danny used to accept press plaudits

Danny Ozark (*Philadelphia Phillies*)

P

PAGE, JOE

"I hate his guts, but there never was a better manager."

>—On Yankee manager Joe McCarthy; quoted in McCarthy's *Sporting News* obituary

PAGNOZZI, TOM

"Hate the city, hate the ballpark, hate the Mets. Other than that, it's great."

>—St. Louis catcher on three-game stopover in New York City, in *The Sporting News Chronicle of 20th Century Sport*

PAIGE'S RULES, ETC.—LEROY ROBERT "SATCHEL" PAIGE

Tutored by life itself, Leroy Robert "Satchel" Paige had an ability with words that rivaled his ability with a baseball.

"Age is a question of mind over matter. If you don't mind, it doesn't matter."

>—Widely attributed, one of his most famous lines and one that he used on a number of occasions

"Ain't no man can avoid being born average, but there ain't no man got to be common."

>—Widely quoted

"All this comin' and goin'. Rookies flyin' up the road and old-timers flyin' down, and nobody in between but me an' old John Mize, standin' pat, watchin' 'em go by.

"And I ain't even sure about ol' John. Maybe he's flyin' on, too. If he is, I can always watch 'em go by myself. Time ain't gonna mess with me!"

>—*Collier's*, June 13, 1953

"Baseball is too much a business to them now. I loved baseball. I ate and slept it. But now the players, instead of picking up the sports page, pick up the *Wall Street Journal*. It's different."

> —On the new breed of players. The comment was made at the time of his induction into the Hall of Fame, August 9, 1971.

"But signing Jackie like they did still hurt me deep down. I'd been the guy who'd started all that big talk about letting us in the big time. I'd been the one who'd opened up the major league parks to the colored teams. I'd been the one who the white boys wanted to barnstorm against. I'd been the one who everybody'd said

Satchel Paige (*National Baseball Library*)

should be in the majors. But Jackie'd been the first one signed by the white boys and he'd probably be the first one in the majors."

> —On Jackie Robinson in *Maybe I'll Pitch Forever*

"Cool Papa Bell was so fast he could get out of bed, turn out the lights across the room and be back in bed under the covers before the lights went out."

> —Widely attributed. Bill Moushy wrote in 1999: "Bell was a guard at the St. Louis City Hall in 1969 before he became 'famous.' I interviewed him. He said that light switch had a short in it, so when Paige turned it in the off position, it did not turn the light off. Bell was in bed when the light actually went off."

"He asked me to throw at a cigarette as a plate and I threw four out of five over it."

> —On Bill Veeck's 1948 test to see if Paige was ready for the majors; quoted by the AP on his election to the Hall of Fame, February 9, 1971

"How old would you be if you didn't know how old you were?"

> —Traditional response to questions about his age

How to Keep Young

1. Avoid fried meats which angry up the blood.
2. If your stomach disputes you, lie down and pacify it with cool thoughts.
3. Keep the juices flowing by jangling around gently as you move.

4. Go very light on the vices, such as carrying on in society. The social ramble ain't restful.
5. Avoid running at all times.
6. Don't look back. Something might be gaining on you.

—*Collier's,* June 13, 1953, is where they first appeared as a sidebar to an article on Paige. It is, of course, one of the most famous set of life rules ever set in print. Despite this they are often mangled in the requoting—"Don't look behind something might be catching up with you" is how it appears in one nonbaseball book (*The Rivals: America and Russia Since World War II* by Adam B. Ulam). For many years after they appeared Paige gave out business cards with his rules on the back.

"I am the proudest man on the face of the earth today."

—On being inducted into the Hall of Fame, August 9, 1971

"I don't generally like running. I believe in training by rising gently up and down from the bench."

—On training; quoted by George Plimpton in *Out of My League*

"I don't know what you're going to do, Mr. Dean, but I'm not going to give up any runs if we have to stay here all night."

—To Dizzy Dean during a barnstorming tour when they were locked in a 0–0 tenth-inning tie. Paige won the game in the thirteenth inning. The incident was recalled in the *Detroit Free Press* on Paige's election to the Hall of Fame, February 10, 1971.

"I never saw a boy with a bat in his hands so confused as that boy was when he bunted. He didn't want to bunt. He wanted to stop himself, but it looked to me like he didn't know what to do with that bat."

—On Mickey Mantle during the 1953 season after he had attempted to bunt on a third strike. The quote was cited for many months to come by those who questioned Mantle's much-lauded role as Joe DiMaggio's replacement.

"I never threw an illegal pitch. The trouble is, once in a while I toss one that ain't never been seen by this generation."

—*Washington Post,* June 10, 1982

"I still say I'm the luckiest man on earth to have pitched for 50 years."

—Quoted at about the time of his seventy-fifth birthday, AP, February 3, 1981

"I want to be the onliest man in the United States that nobody knows nothin' about."

—Quoted by Dave Anderson in the *New York Times,* June 10, 1982

"If a man can beat you, walk him."

—His baseball philosophy; quoted in an AP profile, February 3, 1981

"If Mr. Hornsby'd known as much about hitting as he thought he knew about pitching, Ty Cobb never would have held all those hitting records. Hornsby would have."

—On Rogers Hornsby as his manager on the Browns; quoted from *Maybe I'll Pitch Forever*

"It got so I could nip frosting off a cake with my fastball."

—*Maybe I'll Pitch Forever*

"It's funny what a few no-hitters do for a body."

—*Maybe I'll Pitch Forever*

"I've said it once and I'll say it a thousand times, I'm 44 years old."

—Ritual response to the question of age; quoted widely

"Just take the ball and throw it where you want to. Throw strikes. Home plate don't move."

—Advice to rookie pitchers

"Listen, if I had it to do all over again, I would. I had more fun and seen more places with less money than if I was Rockefeller."

—Widely quoted at the time of his death

"Man, what a pitcher's graveyard."

—On first seeing Fenway Park

"Nobody likes the ball low and away, but that's where you're going to get it from me. I been pitching it there 50 years, away from them. That way they can't hurt you. You keep the ball in the park."

—To Ernie Banks on an Atlanta radio show; quoted in the *Sporting News*, September 7, 1968

"Ol' Satch threw a lot of things, but my natural stuff was always good enough. I didn't need any spit to help out."

—*Maybe I'll Pitch Forever*

"One day, when I was pitchin' to Cool, he drilled one right through my legs and was hit in the back by his own ground ball when he slid into second."

—On Cool Papa Bell; quoted in *The National Pastime*, fall 1982

PAIGISMS

1. Coaches try to change motion and batting stances of young players. They should leave 'em alone.
2. I call this night baseball heaven, playing when it's cool. Guys now don't know how it was. Now it's like falling into a mint of money.
3. Pete Rose is the toughest hitter in the game today. He gets a piece of the ball. I love him, he plays hard, like I did when I pitched.
4. All the young hitters try to hit home runs all the time. There's no more squeeze or drag bunting.
5. Millionaires took over, and changed the game completely.
6. Pitchers today have arm trouble because they sit on the bench and don't work enough.

—Opinions of the state of the game; quoted in an AP story of February 3, 1981

"Skidoodle is a game I invented some years ago to exercise without doin' myself permanent harm. I throw the ball on one bounce to another man, he bounces it back at me. We jangle around. Nobody falls down exhausted."

—On exercise; this seldom-cited advice appeared in *Collier's*, June 13, 1953, with his often-quoted rules for staying young

"The one change is that baseball has turned Paige from a second-class citizen into a second-class immortal."

—On induction into the Hall of Fame

"There never was a man on earth who pitched as much as me. But the more I pitched, the stronger my arm would get."

—Quoted by Joseph Durso in his obituary, *New York Times*, June 9, 1982

"There you is and there you is going to stay."

—After walking a leadoff batter and before striking out the next three; quoted in the October 23, 1978, *Wall Street Journal*

"They said I was the greatest pitcher they ever saw. . . . I couldn't understand why they couldn't give me no justice."

—One of the rare comments made by Paige on the justice in his career. He made the comment late in life, and it was quoted in his *Sporting News* obituary. He died on June 8, 1982.

"They've done a lot of investigating and, to tell the truth, it's got where it puzzles me myself. They couldn't find my record in Mobile because the jail had moved and the judge had died. They did a lot of checking on my family and found I had some relatives 200 years old."

—On his age, at the press conference called to announce his signing as a player-coach of the Atlanta Braves, 1968

"We don't stop playing because we get old. We get old because we stop playing."

—*Chicago Sun Times*, June 5, 2001

"Well, if there ain't been no color line in the game, I might have made more money and got in trouble with Sam [the government]."

—*Sporting News*, December 19, 1964

"You gotta keep the ball off the fat part of the bat."

— Advice to pitchers; widely attributed

PALMEIRO, RAFAEL

"I have never used steroids. Period. I don't know how to say it any more clearly than that."

—The Baltimore Orioles slugger, before a House committee investigating steroid use in baseball on March 17, 2005. On August. 1, 2005, he was suspended for ten days after a positive steroid test. At that time he said in a conference call with reporters: "I hope the fans understand I've worked very hard over a long twenty-year career. I put in a lot of time and a lot of effort into my career. I made a mistake and I'm facing it. I hope people learn from my mistakes. I hope the fans forgive me." Widely reported

PALMER, JIM

"I don't want to win my 300th game while he's still here. He'd take credit for it."

> —On Earl Weaver, Hall of Fame Collection

"I hate the cursed Oriole fundamentals. . . . I've been doing them since 1964. I do them in my sleep. I hate spring training."

> —Quoted by Tom Boswell in the *Washington Post*, it appears in Roger Angell's *Late Innings*.

"Most pitchers are too smart to manage."

> —Widely quoted

"There's only one cure for what's wrong with all of us pitchers, and that's to take a year off. Then, after you've gone a year without throwing, quit altogether."

> —SABR Collection

"Two weeks . . . maybe three. You never know with psychosomatic injuries."

> —Asked how long he'd be on the disabled list

PAPER, HERBERT H.

"It is well to remember that a Martian observing his first baseball game would be quite correct in concluding that the last two words of the National Anthem are: PLAY BALL!"

> —As faculty member at Hebrew Union College, writing in the *Cincinnati Enquirer*, April 2, 1989

PARETSKY, SARA

"The baseball season has started and the Cubs are already in mid-season form, losing their first game in extra innings. So many things these days make me cry, I wish the Cubs weren't one of them."

> —Online Library of Congress chat, April 3, 2001

PARKER, DAN

"Summer or winter or any season, Flatbush fanatics don't need no reason. Leave us root for the Dodgers, Rodgers. That's the team for me."

> —Rallying cry from poem "Leave Us Go Root for the Dodgers, Rodgers"

"The reason the Yankees never lay an egg is because they don't operate on chicken feed."

> —*Sports Illustrated*, April 7, 1958

"The Redhead is so careful of the truth, he uses it very sparingly."

> —On Larry MacPhail, SABR Collection

"Your arm is gone, your legs likewise,
But not your eyes, Mize, not your eyes."

> —His ode to the aging Johnny Mize; widely attributed

PARKER, DAVE

"I do it to get up for the game, get in the clubhouse before a game and really start airing it out, saying things like, 'I'm wall to wall and

Dave Parker (*Society for American Baseball Research; SABR*)

tree-top tall. Two things for sure, the sun's gonna shine and I'm going three for four."

> —On getting ready to play; quoted in *Heavy Hitters: Lynn, Parker, Carew, Rose,* by Bill Gutman

"September is pantyhose month. No nonsense."

> —Not widely quoted, a great line

PARKER, WES

"I don't think we ought to get paid for that one."

> —After Al Downing won a game in ninety minutes for the Dodgers, a new Dodger Stadium record for the speed of a game; quoted by Roger Angell in *Five Seasons*

"I think $200,000 for one year is the limit any star can hope to make. I also think that the player who seeks and gets that much may be pricing himself right out of the game."

> —As a Dodger in the *Los Angeles Times,* March 24, 1971

"What I wonder is, where are the guys who just love to play baseball?"

> —As a former player

"Players believe the mystique about big-league baseball probably more than kids or fans do. It's those two words that are not applied to any other sport—big league."

> —Widely attributed

PARRISH, LARRY

"My advice to them is to DH and play golf."

> —As Rangers DH on the objections voiced by Boston's Jim Rice and Toronto's George Bell in spring training about being assigned DH duties

PARROTT, HAROLD

"Nobody could match his knack for putting a dollar sign on a muscle."

> —Dodger secretary, marveling at team executive Branch Rickey's uncanny ability for evaluating baseball prospects; quoted in *High and Inside: The Complete Guide to Baseball Slang* by Joseph McBride

"When you come right down to it, the baseball owners are really little boys with big wallets."

> —*The Lords of Baseball*

PASCARELLI, PETER

"Given baseball's brave, new world of constantly shifting loyalties and rapidly inflating egos, we will likely never again see the likes of Brooks Robinson."

> —*Philadelphia Inquirer,* January 13, 1983

"He represented a rare meshing of city and personality, the interaction between a sometimes forgotten town tacked amid the flashier worlds of Washington, Philadelphia and New York and an unspoiled star player who led the city into the world's spotlight and never was changed by the glitter. Even today, Robinson remains the symbol of the Orioles."

> —On Brooks Robinson; writing in the *Philadelphia Inquirer,* January 13, 1983

PATEK, FRED

"A heck of a lot better than being the smallest player in the minors."

> —As a Kansas City Royals shortstop, on how it felt to be the smallest player in the majors

"I feel we're all overpaid. Every professional athlete is overpaid. I got a phenomenal contract—much more money than I ever thought I'd make. I wouldn't say I'm embarrassed by it, but deep down I know I'm not worth it. To my shame, though, I have to admit I asked for it."

> —The Kansas City shortstop, in *Late Innings* by Roger Angell

PATRICK, MARK

"Nolan Ryan recorded his 5,000th strikeout on a 96 mph fastball. Its ironic it was against the A's, since that's the same speed Jose Canseco drives his car through a school zone."

> —Host of sports show, WNBE Indianapolis; widely quoted, including in the September 4, 1981, *Sporting News.*

PATTEN, GILBERT (WRITING AS BURT L. STANDISH)

"'Safe home,' rang the voice of the umpire. Then another roar, louder, wilder, full of unbounded joy! The Yale cheer! The band drowned by all the uproar! The sight of sturdy lads in blue, delirious with delight, hugging a dust-covered youth, lifting him to their shoulders, and bearing him away in triumph. Merriwell had won his own game, and his record was made. It was a glorious finish!"

> —From *Frank Merriwell at Yale* (1903) and a typical "Frank Merriwell Finish." In this one, pitcher and Yale freshman Merriwell comes to the plate in the ninth inning with two outs and a man on first to win the game.

PATTERSON, BOB

"It was a cross between a screwball and a changeup—a screw-up."

> —Chicago Cubs reliever, describing the pitch on which he surrendered a game-winning home run to the Cincinnati Reds' Barry Larkin; quoted in *Sports Illustrated,* May 6, 1996

PAUL, GABE

"A clubhouse lawyer is somebody the manager invents to blame for his own deficiencies."

—*Sport,* April 1962

"It will revolutionize baseball; it will open a new area of alibis for the players."

—Comment on the Houston Astrodome

"Our scout reports say Aaron isn't good enough defensively to hang on at second in the majors. Those same reports, however, show no particular batting weaknesses."

—As general manager at Cincinnati to reporters at the 1953 World Series

"Players who create controversy are winning players who can perform under pressure."

—As Yankees general manager

"The great thing about baseball is that there's a crisis every day."

—Widely quoted

"There are things you can do when you have talent that are colorful. If you do them without talent, they're bush."

—As Indians general manager

"You can't outsmart 'em in baseball, but you can outwork 'em."

—As new Cleveland general manager; quoted in *Baseball Digest,* July 1961

PAXON, F. L.

"Baseball succeeded as an organized spectators' sport, but it did also what neither racing nor boxing could do in turning the city lot into a playground and the small boy into an enthusiastic player. The cigarette pictures of leading players that small boys of the eighties collected by scores indicate at once their interests and their naughty habits. Baseball became a game for everyone."

—"The Rise of Sport," *Mississippi Historical Review,* September 1917

PEGLER, WESTBROOK

"He could throw a lamb chop past a wolf."

—On Lefty Grove, in the *Chicago Daily News*

"When you hold the ball between your thumb and forefinger, you can hear a rabbit's pulse beat."

—Commenting on the new "live" ball, 1920

PEÑA, TONY

"I always say that English doesn't go to bat and English doesn't field . . . but language is fundamental for communication. . . . That's why Latin players sometimes take time to develop."

—Quoted in the July 20, 1990 *Boston Globe*

PENN, IRVING

"I feel comfortable in looking at a baseball diamond. It is for me typical of the formalized, unchanging stages on which a variety of chance human and space relationships can occur. I have at times found it satisfying to work in a studio with a fixed set and predetermined lighting. The human relationships being the only day-to-day variant."

—Writing in *Portfolio* magazine, 1950; quoted in *Vanity Fair*, March 1990

PENNOCK, HERB

PENNOCK'S 10 COMMANDMENTS FOR PITCHERS

1. Develop your faculty of observation.
2. Conserve your energy.
3. Make contact with players, especially catchers and infielders, and listen to what they have to say.
4. Work everlastingly for control.
5. When you are on the field always have a baseball in your hand and don't slouch around. Run for a ball.
6. Keep studying the hitters for their weak and strong points. Keep talking with your catchers.
7. Watch your physical condition and your mode of living.
8. Always pitch to the catcher and not the hitter. Keep your eye on that catcher and make him your target before letting the ball go.
9. Find your easiest way to pitch, your most comfortable delivery—and stick to it.
10. Work for what is called a rag arm. A loose arm can pitch overhanded, side-arm, three-quarter, underhanded—any old way—to suit the situation at hand.

—Developed many years ago and originally published in the *Sporting News*. In one requoting (*Sporting News*, April 24, 1971) Pennock added: "I might give you an eleventh commandment and, that is, don't beef at the umpire. Keep pitching with confidence and control of yourself as well as of the ball. Don't get it into your head the umpire is your worst enemy. Fury is as hard on you physically as emotionally."

PEPITONE, JOE

"I love baseball, and I hate to see what it's doing to itself. There's so much dead time in it that it's the most boring sport in the world to watch."

—*Joe, You Coulda Made Us Proud*

PERRY, GAYLORD

"Going back down to the minors is the toughest thing to handle in baseball."

—*Me and the Spitter*

"Greaseball, greaseball, greaseball. That's all I throw him, and he still hits them. He's the only player in baseball who consistently hits my grease. He sees the ball so well, I guess he can pick out the dry side."

—On Rod Carew; quoted in *Newsweek*, July 11, 1977

"I'd always have [grease] in at least two places, in case the umpires would ask me to wipe off one. I never wanted to be caught out there without anything. It wouldn't be professional."

—*Me and the Spitter*

"I reckon I tried everything on the old apple but salt and pepper and chocolate sauce topping."

—After being elected to the Baseball Hall of Fame in 1991, *Los Angeles Times,* August 20, 2006

"Primarily, every rule change over the past 10 years has been against pitchers: lowering the mound, the designated hitter. I've got a kid 6 years old. He likes sports, but I definitely won't let him pitch. There would be too many things against him."

—Quoted in the *Los Angeles Herald-Examiner,* March 10, 1974

"The league will be a little drier now, folks."

—On his retirement at age forty-five; quoted in *Sports Illustrated,* October 3, 1983

Gaylord Perry (*Seattle Mariners*)

"The trouble with baseball is that it is not played the year 'round. In order to make a living, the poor guys like myself have to go back and work on the farm in the wintertime to make ends meet. I mean, all that farming can tire a man."

—As a Padres pitcher; quoted in the *Christian Science Monitor,* September 9, 1978

"Wait until Tommy meets the Lord and finds out that He's wearing pinstripes."

—On hearing of Tommy Lasorda's belief that the Lord wears Dodgers Blue

"You ain't gonna believe this. But I got a plus-16. I passed with flying colors. Four practice runs and two film runs, and I passed every time. I told them what I said that night—I didn't go putting anything on the ball."

—On his appearance on a short-lived TV show called *Lie Detector* after a ten-day suspension for throwing a doctored ball; quoted in the *New York Times,* October 31, 1982

PESKY, JOHNNY

"I think if you're Red Sox, well, it's something you're born with, an affection that you have."

—Quoted in George V. Higgins, *The Progress of the Seasons* (New York: Prentice Hall, 1990)

"It's such a simple game, and it's so hard to play."

—Quoted in George V. Higgins, *The Progress of the Seasons*

"When you win, you eat better, sleep better and your beer tastes better. And your wife looks like Gina Lollobrigida."

—As Boston Red Sox manager, 1962

PETERMAN, CY

"They sing of joy when long lost sons come home. They prate of happiness when wars are done. But did you ever see a homer in the ninth that tied the score? There, ladies and gentlemen, is joy."

> —Writer for the *Philadelphia Evening Bulletin*, on the home run by Mule Haas of the Philadelphia Athletics that tied the fifth game of the 1929 World Series with the Chicago Cubs in the ninth inning, October 14; quoted in *Sports Illustrated*, August 19, 1996

PETERS, HANK

"If I knew than what I know how, I wouldn't have made the trade. But if I knew what I know now, I wouldn't have voted for Richard Nixon."

> —As the Orioles general manager who traded for Reggie Jackson only to see him become a free agent and leave the club

"He did it all despite arthritic knees, a troublesome hip, aching feet and assorted other ailments. He did it in the Candlestick Park cold and despite more intentional walks than any player of his era."

> —On Willie McCovey, writing in the *Oakland Tribune*, January 9, 1986, on McCovey's election to the Hall of Fame

PETERSON, HAROLD

"Abner Doubleday didn't invent baseball. Baseball invented Abner Doubleday."

> —Widely quoted from his book, *Baseball and Mr. Spalding*

PETERSON, ROBERT W.

"One summer day in 1939 a kid squatted on the bank behind home plate at Russell Field in Warren, Pennsylvania, fielding foul balls (which could be redeemed for a nickel each—no small consideration in those days), and saw Josh Gibson hit the longest home run ever struck in Warren County. It was one of many impressive feats performed by touring black players that excited the wonder and admiration of that foul-ball shagger. This book is the belated fruit of his wonder."

> —From the introduction to his book *Only the Ball Was White*, which was the beginning of the belated fascination with the accomplishments of the men who played in the Negro Leagues. Bowie Kuhn recalled in his memoir *Hardball* that when he became baseball commissioner in 1969, a debate had arisen over whether to induct stars of the Negro Leagues into the Hall of Fame. The Peterson book, Kuhn said, "focused greater attention on the accomplishments of Negro League players."

PEVERELLY, CHARLES

"It is a game which is peculiarly suited to the American temperament and disposition; the nine innings are played in the brief space of two and a half hours, or less. From the moment the first striker takes his position, and his bat poises, it has an excitement and *vim* about it, until the last hand is put out in the ninth inning. There is no delay or suspense about it, from beginning to end. in short, the pastime suits the people, and the people suit the pastime. It is also, comparatively, an economical recreation; the uniform is not costly, the playing implements, colors, and furnishing of a neat club room, need not occasion an extravagant outlay when divided, pro rate, by the members of a full club. . . . Baseball does not demand from it votaries too much time, or rather, too great a proportion of the day. In the long sunshiny days of summer, games are frequently commenced at four and even five o'clock in the afternoon, and completed some time before sunset. Consequently the great mass, who are in a subordinate capacity, can participate in this health-giving and noble pastime."

—In his *Book of American Pastimes*, 1866

PHELPS, WILLIAM LYON

"There is more knowledge of human nature displayed in this poem than in many of the works of the psychiatrist. There is nothing so stupid as Destiny. It is a centrifugal tragedy, by which our minds are turned from the fate of Casey to the universal. For this is the curse that hangs over humanity: our ability to accomplish any feat is in inverse ration to the intensity of our desire."

—In admiration of Ernest L. Thayer's "Casey at the Bat;" quoted in *Xaipe* (the magazine of Alpha Delta Phi, Thayer's fraternity), spring 1989

PHILLIPS, HAROLD "LEFTY"

"Every club's the same. You've got two, maybe three guys who do their job and never complain, never say a word. Then you've got about 14 guys who might mumble but they're mild, and easy to handle. It's the other six or seven guys. Every time they're told to do something, the first thing they do is ask, 'Why?' They always want to know, 'Why?'"

—As California Angels manager on the modern ballplayers

"Grading hitters is about like making out report cards. You can rate just about all hitters in baseball on a scale from A to F. There aren't many A's around. And the guys who get A pluses, well, they're just plain rare."

—As Angels manager

"In my opinion a manager who fusses and argues with the umpires about trick pitches disturbs his own batters more than the opposition. They make the hitter believe that the pitcher has some kind of an edge on them and it usually works to the pitcher's advantage."

—On the spitter; quoted in *Baseball Digest*, February 1969

Lefty Phillips (*California Angels*)

PHILLIPS, HAROLD "LEFTY" (CONTINUED)

"Our phenoms ain't phenomenating."

  —As Angels manager on the productiveness of his rookies; quoted in *The Baseball Card Engagement Book*, 1988

PHILLIPS, LOUIS

"If the connection between the 'new' theatre and baseball once seemed tenuous, recent trends in the theatre . . . trends such as Happenings, Action Theatre, Game Theatre, Ray Gun Theatre etc. . . . have now rendered the distinction between sport and theatre, between theatre and baseball obsolete."

  —"The Mets and the New Theatre,'" *Journal of Popular Culture*, fall 1968

PIERSALL, JIMMY

"That way I can see where I've been. I always know where I'm going."

  —On hitting his 100th home run and running the bases backward; widely quoted

"The good right fielder does not ad-lib."

  —As the fielding sensation of the Red Sox; quoted in *The Mutual Baseball Almanac* edited by Roger Kahn and Al Helfer

"Yogi Berra called me one day. His wife had just had a baby and he said, 'Hey, Piersall, you've got nine kids, how about giving a few tips on changing diapers? . . .' So I said, 'Yogi, you take a diaper and put it in the shape of a baseball diamond. Take the baby's bottom and put it on the pitcher's mound. Take first base and pin it to

Jimmy Piersall (*California Angels*)

third. Take home and slide it into second.' He said, 'That's easy, I can do that.' I said, 'Wait a minute, Yogi. One thing about this game, when it starts to rain, there's no postponement.'"

  —*Sports Illustrated*, June 6, 1977

PINIELLA, LOU

"I cussed him out in Spanish, and he threw me out in English.

  —As a Yankee on an argument he had with umpire Armando Rodriguez, *Sports Illustrated*, September 1, 1975

"What Cal has done is incomprehensible to me. I don't think another player will come along and do what he has done. We are seeing the last of a dinosaur."

—As Mariners manager on Cal Ripken Jr.'s consecutive-game record, *Washington Times*, September 6, 1995

PINSON, VADA

"I'm going to get myself a corked bat and blast one out of here. What's the suspension for Old-Timers games, 10 years?"

—Before an old-timers' exhibition

PINTER, DAVID

"That pitch killed him. Baseball killed Donnie Moore."

—Agent on the suicide death of his client, former California Angels pitcher Donnie Moore, who gave up a home run in the '86 ALCS that kept his team out of the World Series; quoted in the *San Diego Union-Tribune*, December 29, 1989

PLIMPTON, GEORGE

"Deprive a ballplayer of his gum, or his chaw, and he's more uncomfortable than if you threw a hat on his bed—which they spoke of as being the most devastating bit of bad luck that could be suffered."

—*Out of My League*

"I have a theory: The larger the ball, the less the writing about the sport. There are superb books about golf, very good books about baseball, not many good books about football, and very few good books about basketball. There are no books about beachballs."

—Widely quoted as "Plimpton's Theory" or "Plimpton's Correlation." It may have first appeared in *Sports Illustrated*, May 10, 1982.

"There's sort of a universal wish among us all to be the great American sports hero. Thurber once said that 95 per cent of the male population put themselves to sleep striking out the lineup of the New York Yankees. It's the great daydream, an idea that you never quite give up. Always, somewhere in the back of your mind, you believe Casey Stengel will give you a call."

—*Dallas Times-Herald*'s "Sportweek" December 15, 1978

"There was no lazier or more pleasant pastime than watching good fungos hit, unless it was catching them."

—*Out of My League*

POVICH, SHIRLEY

"Milwaukee's major league appetites commenced too high on the hog."

—On the Braves, in the *Washington Post*, 1955,

"The million-to-one shot came in. Hell froze over. A month of Sundays hit the calendar. Don Larsen today pitched a no-hit, no-run, no-man-reach-first game in a World Series."

—On the first World Series perfect game, in the *Washington Post*, October 1956

POVICH, SHIRLEY (CONTINUED)

"There's a couple of million dollars' worth of baseball talent on the loose ready for the big leagues, yet unsigned by any major league. There are pitchers who would win twenty games a season . . . and outfielders who could hit .350, infielders who could win recognition as stars, and there's at least one catcher who at this writing is probably superior to Bill Dickey, Josh Gibson. Only one thing is keeping them out of the big leagues, the pigmentation of their skin. They happen to be colored. That's their crime in the eyes of the big league club owners."

> —*Washington Post*, April 7, 1939; quoted in the 1981 Hall of Fame Yearbook

PRESLEY, ELVIS

"I like playin' softball . . . but watchin' baseball? I don't want to knock the national pastime, but, mister, a lot of nothin' happens."

> —*The World According to Elvis* by Jeff Rovin

PRINCE, BOB

"Calling a game with cold dispassion is a cinch. You sit on your can, reporting grounders and two-base hits lackadaisically. You've got no responsibilities. But rooting is tough. It requires creativeness. It also fulfills your function, which is to shill. You are the arm of the home club who is there to make the listener happy."

> —The Pittsburgh sportscaster on being a "homer" for the Pirates; quoted in his *Sporting News* obituary. He died on June 10, 1985.

"It's ridiculous that we are gathered here tonight to honor a man who made more than 7000 outs."

> —The Pirates' announcer at Stan Musial's retirement dinner

PRINCE OF WALES

"I consider Base Ball an excellent game; but Cricket a better one."

> —Response after watching Americans playing a baseball game in England during the winter of 1888–89

PUCKETT, KIRBY

"At the first card show, I felt bad seeing those little kids paying to get my autograph. It didn't hit me right. I felt it in the heart. I made a vow that once the contract is over, I'm done. I'll still sign, but not for money. I wouldn't do it for a million dollars."

> —On accepting money for signing autographs; quoted in the *Montgomery Journal*, December 29, 1989

"The better he gets, the better he's going to be."

> —On the skills of Minnesota Twins center fielder Torii Hunter; quoted in *Sports Illustrated*, April 22, 2002

PULLIAM, HARRY

"Take nothing for granted in baseball."

> —As National League president. This was one of eight "Famous Baseball Sayings" collected by Ernest J. Lanigan of the Hall of Fame when he identified himself as "Historian and authority on the game for 65 years."

Q

QUIGLEY, MARTIN

"Baseball is a hard game for hard men. Played with undivided interest, it is a satisfying outlet for rugged men who like physical effort. Premiums are paid for strenuous effort and for the subordination of self-interest for the good of the team. Played halfheartedly, baseball is a waste of time and energy. Baseball is not a halfway game. Players and managers who take it easy on the field come to grief and failure. To play baseball, you have to get wet all over."

> —From his baseball novel, *Today's Game* (New York: Viking Press, 1965)

"The story of the curveball is the story of the game itself. Some would say of life itself."

> —From his *The Curve Ball in American Baseball History*

QUINDLEN, ANNA

"I've always liked baseball, even as a child, when tradition dictated that I should be pro-hibited from playing, and my three brothers should be egged on. I like the sense of both the camaraderie and the aloneness of it, the idea of nine men working together in a kind of grand pavane—pitcher to catcher, short-stop to second baseman to first baseman—and the idea of one man looking down the loaded barrel of a pitcher's arm and feeling the nice clean solid thunk as he hits a ball that will fly into the bleachers. (I like basketball, too. I do not like football, which I think of as a game in which two tractors approach each other from opposite directions and collide. Besides, I have contempt for a game in which players have to wear so much equipment. Men play basketball in their underwear, which seems just right to me.)"

> —"A Baseball Wimp," *New York Times,* reprinted in *Living Out Loud,* (1988); quoted in Elinor Bauen, ed., *Diamonds Are a Girl's Best Friend: Women Writers on Baseball* (Boston: Faber & Faber, 1994)

The late side-arm pitcher was one of the game's great aphorists.

"A manager uses a relief pitcher like a six-shooter. He fires until it's empty and then takes the gun and throws it at the villain."

—*The Baseball Card Engagement Book,* 1989

"God is concerned with hungry people and justice, not my saves."

—On his refusal to use the phrase "God's will," recalled at the time of his death, *Sports Illustrated,* Oct 12, 1998

"He didn't sound like a baseball player. He said things like 'Nevertheless' and 'If, in fact.'"

—On Milwaukee's Ted Simmons, *Sports Illustrated,* August 10, 1981

"Hitters call my fastball the Peggy Lee. They look at it and ask, 'Is that all there is?'"

—*Baseball Digest,* September 1985

"I don't think baseball is real life. But strikes are real life. It took up seven weeks of real time. That's a fifth of a pregnancy."

—The Kansas City Royals pitcher on the 1981 strike

"I don't think there are any good uses for nuclear weapons, but then, this may be one."

—On first seeing the Minnesota Metrodome before the 1987 World Series; widely quoted

"I found a delivery in my flaw."

—On his pitching problems, *Baseball Digest,* September 1985

"I thought they were in a zone, but they were playing man-to-man."

—On his third career batting appearance, as a St. Louis reliever, which resulted in a ground out to the Giants' Robby Thompson; quoted in the June 1981 *Major League Baseball Newsletter.*

Dan Quisenberry
(*Kansas City Royals*)

"I want to thank all the pitchers who couldn't go nine innings, and Manager Dick Howser, who wouldn't let them."

> —On winning the AL Fireman of the Year Award for 1982; quoted in *Sports Illustrated*, December 6, 1982

"I'm looking forward to putting on my glasses with the fake nose so I can walk around and be a normal person."

> —On being asked by a reporter: "What do you plan to do after the Series is over?"

"It has options through the year 2020—or until the last Rocky movie is made."

> —On the details of his 1990 contract; quoted in the *Major League Baseball Newsletter*, April 1990

"It really helps to be stupid if you're a relief pitcher. You can't be thinking about too many things. You can't be on the mound worrying about a 35-inning streak where you haven't given up a double to a left-handed batter or something. Relief pitchers have to get into a zone of their own. I just hope I'm stupid enough."

> —*Los Angeles Times*, June 26, 1982

"I've had so many good things happen to me. So why not me?"

> —On the cancer that took his life at age forty-five, *Sports Illustrated*, October 12, 1998

"I've seen the future and it's much like the present, only longer."

> —Widely quoted

"Natural grass is a wonderful thing for little bugs and sinkerball pitchers."

> —Widely quoted

"No man is worth more than another, and none is worth more than $12.95."

> —On ballplayers' salaries, *Sports Illustrated*, Oct 12, 1998

"Our fielders have to catch a lot of balls—or at least deflect them to someone who can."

> —On the Royals during a short period of ineptness; quoted in *Sports Illustrated*, May 28, 1984

"Reggie Jackson hit one off me that's still burrowing its way to Los Angeles."

> —Widely attributed, from 1981

"Some people throw to spots, some people throw to zones. Renie throws to continents."

> —On fellow pitcher Renie Martin's control problems; quoted in *Sports Illustrated*, April 13, 1981

"The batter still hits a grounder. But in this case the first bounce is 360 feet away."

> —As a Kansas City Royal on what happened when his sinker wasn't working, *Sports Illustrated*, September 29, 1980

"There is no homework."

> —On being asked what was best thing about baseball, 1981

"When I came over here, I always heard it was a stronger league, with amphetamines all over the clubhouse, but all I found was Michelob Dry."

> —On his switch to the National League Cardinals from the American League Royals; quoted in the *Sporting News*, April 3, 1989

R

RAMIREZ, RAFAEL

"A walk won't get you off the island."

> —On the free-swinging style of Dominican players. This quotation first appeared in several newspapers on June 1, 1986, when as a Braves shortstop he had three walks in the first forty-five games. Later versions of the quotation have been embellished—e.g., "You have to swing like a man. A walk won't get you off the island."

RAPER, JOHN W.

"Hit the ball over the fence and you can take your time going around the bases."

> —*What This World Needs*, 1954

RASCHI, VIC

"Nobody on our team seemed to know anything about Aaron except Eddie Stanky, the manager. He knew that Henry was potentially a fine player and he talked about everything except the way he parted his hair. He could run, field, throw, and, of course, hit. He had such great wrists, like Ernie Banks, it was hard to fool him."

> —From the man who gave us Aaron's first home run; quoted in *Hank Aaron . . . 714 and Beyond* by Jerry Brondfield

RAUCHER, HERMAN

"Hermie had done all that could humanly be done with the small bedroom in the bungalow that had been allotted to him. One wall, the one with the window, he decorated with autographed pictures of Mel Ott, Johnny Rucker, and Hank Danning because he was a Giant fan. All the autographs were forged because the Giants were in New York and Hermie lived in Brooklyn, and to wait till the Giants came to Brooklyn and then to have the audacity to be seen asking the Giants for autographs—it was much too risky."

> —*The Summer of '42*, appears in *The Giants of the Polo Grounds* by Noel Hynd

REAGAN, RONALD

"Nostalgia bubbles within me and I might have to be dragged away."

— On being presented with a room containing a record thirty-two members of the Hall of Fame, March 27, 1981

"This is really more fun than being president. I really do love baseball and I wish we could do this out on the lawn every day. I wouldn't even complain if a stray ball came through the Oval Office window now and then."

— On playing ball with old-timers while celebrating National Baseball Month, 1983. He also declared that baseball was "our national pastime, that is if you discount political campaigning."

REARDON, JOHN "BEANS"

"If the Pope was an umpire he'd still have trouble with the Catholics."

— *Morrow's International Dictionary of Contemporary Quotations*

"I'm very glad to receive the Klem Award, but I'll tell you the truth. Klem hated my guts and I hated his."

— The former umpire, on receiving the Bill Klem Award, 1970

REASONER, HARRY

"Statistics are to baseball what a flakey crust is to Mom's apple pie."

— *60 Minutes*, October 20, 1985

Ronald Reagan with Frank Lovejoy, *The Winning Team* (*Museum of Modern Art Film Still Archives*)

REED, ISHMAEL

"Ethnic life in the United States has become a sort of contest like baseball in which the blacks are always the Chicago Cubs."

— *Writin' Is Fightin'* (Atheneum 1988)

REESE, DICK

"The Babe always thought he was the best home run hitter. He wanted to be the best. If he had known someone [Roger Maris] was going to break his record of 60 in a season, he would have hit 70.

"If he had known that some day someone was going to break 714, he would have hit 800.

"The power wasn't only in Ruth's bat.

"I remember when Joe McCarthy took over as manager. Ruth had been getting about 150 walks a year with Tony Lazzeri hitting behind him most of the time.

"I heard him walk up to McCarthy and say, 'I'll tell you how to make out the lineup. I'm going to

REESE, DICK (CONTINUED)

bat third and I want [Lou] Gehrig behind me. You can fill out the other seven spots.'

"McCarthy said, 'That's fine with me, Babe.'"

—On Babe Ruth; quoted by Dick Miller in the *Sporting News,* August 4, 1973

REESE, HAROLD "PEE WEE"

"I wasn't trying to think of myself as being the Great White Father. It didn't matter to me whether he was black or green, he had a right to be there too."

—On his immediate befriending of Jackie Robinson when he joined the Brooklyn Dodgers in 1947, recalled in his *New York Times* obituary, August 16, 1999

"Thinking about the things that happened, I don't know any other ball player who would have done what he did. To be able to hit with everybody yelling at him. He had to black all that out, black out everything but this ball that is coming in at a hundred miles an hour and he's got a split second to make up his mind if it's in or out or up or down or coming at his head, a split second to swing. To do what he did has got to be the most tremendous thing I've ever seen in sports."

—Interview, ca. 1970; quoted by Roger Kahn in *The Boys of Summer*

REGAN, PHIL

"When I was a little boy, my mother warned me never to stick my dirty fingers in my mouth."

—Accused of throwing the spitball

REICHARDT, RICK

"The key to a player's longevity in this game is his legs. He can hide such shortcomings as bad eyesight or slow reactions and cover them up for a couple years, but he can't hide bad legs."

—As a White Sox infielder

REILLY, RICK

"Rooting for the Yankees takes all the courage, imagination, conviction, and baseball intelligence of Spam. It's like rooting for . . . Bill Gates to hit Scratch 'n' Win.

"Hating the Yankees is an American tradition that has been honored throughout this century. Remember, nobody ever wrote a play called *Damn Diamondbacks!*"

—"The Team I Love to Hate," *Sports Illustrated,* November 1, 1999 ("The Life of Reilly")

REISER, PETE

"Ever watch a high school baseball game? The next time you do, notice that all the pitchers and batters look like models off the cover of an old baseball guide. You can tell by the way they exaggerate their movements that they're self-conscious—that they think everybody's watching them. And, of course, it just about ruins their chances of getting the job done right. To succeed in this game, a player has to concentrate so intently on what he's doing, he doesn't even know there are people watching him. He's got to black everything out of his mind except the job he's doing. Then he has a chance to get it done."

—As a Dodgers coach; quoted in the September 1964 *Baseball Digest*

"No, I don't have any regrets. Not about one damned thing. I've had a lot of good experiences in my life, and they far outnumber the bad. Good memories are the greatest thing in the world, and I've got a lot of those. And one of the sweetest is of the kid standing out on the green grass in center field, with the winning runs on base, saying to himself, 'Hit it to me. Hit it to me.'"

> —Quoted in the *Yearbook* of the Baseball Hall of Fame, 1989

"One night when I was managing Green Bay and we were playing Cedar Rapids. Frank Howard, who got a $108,000 bonus, hit a dinky fly back of shortstop. Dennis Menke, their $115,000 shortstop, Bob Click, their $75,000 center fielder, and Bob Taylor, their $100,000 left fielder, went for it. I can't remember who caught it. I was too busy counting their money."

> —As a Dodgers coach; quoted in *Baseball Digest,* June 1961

"They've got a lot of names for pitches now, but there are only so many ways you can throw a baseball."

> —As a Cubs coach

REUSS, JERRY

"If you think it's an advantage, it is. If the other teams think it is, it's a bigger advantage. Actually, it means nothing."

> —The Los Angeles Dodgers pitcher, on the value of experience in a pennant race

REVERING, DAVE

"If you want to get off this team, you have to take a number."

> —On the Yankees in 1981 just before being traded to Toronto; quoted by William B. Mead in *The Official Yankee Hater's Handbook*

REYNOLDS, ALLIE

"I always felt the pitcher had the advantage. It's like serving in tennis."

> —Widely quoted

"You get smart only when you begin getting old."

> —Widely quoted

Allie Reynolds (*New York Yankees*)

REYNOLDS, QUENTIN

"Men have been known to win boxing titles with lucky punches. Only last September, we saw a ranking player of somewhat dubious talent win the tennis championship at Forest Hills. Souped-up horses have come from nowhere to win the greatest stakes only to retire into the oblivion of mediocrity. But when a ball club wins a major-league pennant, it has gone through a back-breaking 154-game schedule that presents the severest of all tests. No pennant race was ever decided by a lucky fluke; a team has to have championship class to came out on top after 154 games have been played."

—*Sport,* December 1950

"One of baseball's oldest traditions is that all ballplayers are penurious. It is a well known fact that waiters flee when they see ballplayers approaching their tables, and that porters run out for a cup of coffee when a train bearing a ball club steams into a station. Ballplayers have long been regarded as leaders in the 'never-tip-more-than-a-nickel' school, and for a player to order a round of double drinks is to put a knife into the back of this tenderly fastened legend."

—*Sport,* April 1950

RHODEN, RICK

"It was the toughest thing I ever did. But the truth is I never really considered not pitching."

—On pitching the day he learned that his brother had died the previous day in a car wreck. Rhoden pitched a 4–3 win; quoted in *High Inside: Memoirs of a Baseball Wife* by Danielle Gagnon Torrez

RHODES, JAMES LAMAR "DUSTY"

"I even had a nickname. You have to have a nickname to be remembered."

—Hero of the 1954 World Series for the Giants; quoted in *Where Have You Gone, Vince DiMaggio*

RICE, GRANTLAND

"A white streak left Babe Ruth's 52-ounce bludgeon in the third inning of yesterday's opening game at the Yankee Stadium. On a low line it sailed, like a silver flame, through the gray, bleak April shadows, and into the right field bleachers. And as the crash sounded, and the white flash followed, fans arose en masse . . . in the greatest vocal cataclysm baseball has ever known."

—*New York Tribune,* April 19, 1923, describing the first home run in Yankee Stadium's inaugural game, April 18, 1923, as the Yankees defeated Boston, 4-1

"Babe Ruth's record of 60 home runs in one year may be broken, although personally I hope it stands for eternity. It has almost been equaled twice. But it is a sure thing that Cobb's mark of 4,191 base hits will never be approached."

—*The Tumult and the Shouting*

"Christy Mathewson brought something to baseball no one else had ever given the game—not even Babe Ruth or Ty Cobb. He handed the game a certain touch of class, an indefinable lift in culture, brains, personality."

—Quoted in Phil Pepe's *No-Hitter*

"If it isn't, son, you've got one helluva scoop."

> —On being asked by a cub reporter, "Isn't that the sun setting over there in the West?"

"It's not whether you win or lose, it's how you play the game."

> —His most famous line

"McGraw's very walk across the field in a hostile town was a challenge to the multitude."

> —*The Giants of the Polo Grounds* by Noel Hynd

"The Big Guy's left us with the night to face,
And there is no one who can take his place.

> —On the death of Babe Ruth

"The knightliest of all the game's paladins."

> —His description of Christy Mathewson

Grantland Rice (*Library of Congress Prints and Photographs Division*)

"Yet, I'd take my chance with fame,
Calmly let it go at that,
With the right to sign my name
Under 'Casey at the Bat.'"

> —*(The Masterpiece)*

RICHARDS, PAUL

"I don't communicate with players. I tell them what to do. I don't understand the meaning of communication."

> —As Chicago White Sox manager when asked if he planned to initiate a dialogue with one of his players, *New York Daily News,* January 20, 1980

"I want a team that can get somebody out."

> —As a frustrated Orioles manager; widely quoted

"If you can say the morale of your club is good after losing 10 out of 12 games, then your intelligence is a little low."

> —As Orioles manager

"If there was a league in this nation that that team would have won in, it has not been brought to my attention. And that includes the Little League."

> —On the 1976 White Sox to Bob Verdi of the *Chicago Tribune;* quoted in *Sox from Lane and Fain to Zisk and Fisk* by Bob Vanderberg

"If you're a good loser, you keep on losing."

> —Quoted in *Sox from Lane and Fain to Zisk and Fisk* by Bob Vanderberg

RICHARDS, PAUL (CONTINUED)

"The most valuable sign a club can steal is the hit-and-run. Most managers admit that's the only one they try to steal."

> —As Orioles manager, *Sporting News,* May 4, 1955

"This man hit 531 homers and did everything else he did on one leg."

> —On Mickey Mantle

"Today's athletes run faster and make a lot more plays in the field. But the name of the game is still pitching and it ain't going to change. Pitching was 80 percent of baseball when John McGraw managed and it's still 80 percent of baseball."

> —As White Sox manager

"When you have dumb people working for you, don't have them work a whole day. Let them work half days, and then they only screw up half as much."

> —Quoted by Whitey Herzog in his autobiography *White Rat*

"You just don't want a knuckleballer pitching for you. Of course, you don't want one pitching against you either."

> —Quoted by Tommy Lasorda in *The Artful Dodger*

RICHARDSON, BOBBY

"If baseball is a game of inches generally speaking, then it follows that it is specifically a game of split-seconds for second-basemen.

There is no position on a baseball team which places such a high premium on timing."

> —From *Sport,* September 1965

RICHMOND, PETER

"Real grass is the stuff of baseball dreams; no one lays AstroTurf in a cornfield. A field of grass between two crops is the natural place for anyone to play a game of baseball, and our grass diamonds set among buildings are the urban echo of that rural fact."

> —From his 1993 book *Ballpark: Camden Yards and the Building of an American Dream*

RICHTER, FRANCIS

"A great sport, representative and typical of the people who practice it . . . one that stimulates all the faculties of the mind—keenness, invention, perception, agility, celerity of thought and action, adaptability to circumstances—in short all the qualities that go to make the American man the most highly-organized, civilized being on earth."

> —The editor of *Sporting Life* at a turn-of-the-century banquet; quoted by Peter Levine in the *1984 SABR Baseball Research Journal*

"We have always been inclined to consider Ewing in his prime as the greatest player of the game from the standpoint of supreme excellence in all departments—batting, catching, fielding, base running, throwing and Baseball brains—a player without a weakness of any kind, physical, mental or temperamental."

> —On Buck Ewing, in the *1911 Reach Guide*

They called him Mahatma, and although he died in 1965, his influence on the game will probably be discernible as long as the game is played.

"A baseball box score is a democratic thing. It doesn't tell how big you are, what church you attend, what color you are, or how your father voted in the last election. It just tells what kind of baseball player you were on that particular day."

> —Said to Jackie Robinson; quoted in Robinson's *I Never Had It Made* (New York: G. P. Putnam's Sons, 1972)

"A fourth major league is just around the corner. As soon as we get underway, it will be ready to fall into place."

> —President of the Continental League—the third major league—scheduled to begin play in 1961; quoted in the *Sporting News*, January 13, 1960. As noted in *The Experts Speak: The Collection of Misinformed Prediction*, "On August 2, 1960, the Continental League folded without playing a single game. No subsequent third—or fourth—major league has ever been formed."

"A full mind is an empty bat."

> —Widely attributed

"A game of great charm in the adoption of mathematic measurements to the timing of human movement, the exactitude and adjustments of physical ability to hazardous chance. The speed of the legs, the dexterity of the body, the grace of the swing, the elusiveness of the slide—these are the features that make Americans everywhere forget the last syllable of a man's last name or the pigmentation of his skin."

> —Before a congressional committee in May 1960

"A great ballplayer is a player who will take a chance."

> —Widely quoted

"As a matter of fact I do not deserve any recognition from anybody on the Robinson thing. It is a terrible commentary on all of us that a part of us should not concede equal rights to everybody to earn a living."

> —To Frank Stanton, January 18, 1949; quoted by Murray Polner in his biography of Rickey

"Addition by subtraction."

> —One of the most commonly cited Rickeyisms, the Mahatma applied it to trades, releases, etc.

"Baseball has given me a life of joy."

> —Quoted by Roger Angell in *Late Innings*

"Baseball is a game of inches."

> —*Quote*, July 31, 1966

"Baseball people—and that includes myself—are slow to change and accept new ideas. I remember that it took years to persuade them to put numbers on uniforms."

> —Writing in *Life*, August 2, 1954

Branch Rickey (*National Baseball Library*)

"Don't be idle. Idleness is the most damnable thing. And don't be idle in uniform when you're not playing."

—John J. Monteleone, ed., *Branch Rickey's Little Blue Book* (New York: Macmillan, 1995)

"Fill in any figure you want for that boy. Whatever the figure, it's a deal."

—On seeing Mickey Mantle in spring 1951. He took a checkbook out of his pocket, ripped out a check, signed his name, and handed it over to co-owner Dan Topping of the Yanks, who happened to be seated right next to him.

"Fustest with the mostest."

—Motto which he invoked when discussing his invention of the farm system, breaking the color bar, etc.

$$\left[\frac{H+BB+HP}{AB+BB+HP} + \frac{3(TB-H)}{4AB} + \frac{R}{H+BB+HP}\right] -$$

$$\left[\frac{H}{AB} + \frac{BB+HB}{AB+BB+HP} + \frac{ER}{H+BB+HB}\right.$$

$$\left. - \frac{SO}{8(AB+BB+HB)} - F\right] = G$$

—"Goodbye to Some Old Baseball Ideas," *Life,* August 2, 1954. Formula for baseball in which the first set of brackets represents offense and the second set represents defense, and the letter G is games over 500. HP, for example, in the equation represents hit by pitch and HB is hit batsman. The difference between the two equals the efficiency of the team. Rickey revealed this formula in a bylined article in of *Life*. The formula and its detailed explanation were entirely serious and today are regarded as the beginning of intense statistical analysis of baseball such as that employed by Sabrmatricians.

"He can't hit, he can't run, he can't field, he can't throw. He can't do a goddamn thing . . . but beat you."

—On Eddie Stankey. Here is the history of the quote as related by Clay Felker in a profile of

Stankey in a 1951 issue of the *Sporting News*. "Just for the record, it might be interesting to relate how that famous statement used so often in describing Stankey originated and who said it first.

"Branch Rickey, addressing 150 players at his 'school' in Sanford, Fla., in the spring of 1946, said it this way, according to Dodger Historian Harold Parrott: 'He cannot hit, he cannot throw and he cannot outrun his grandmother . . . but, if there is a way to beat the other team, he'll find it.

"Leo Durocher and many writers have repeated this epigram in several variations, until it now ranks with 'Good field—no hit' as a baseball classic."

"He is the kind of boy who makes his scout's job safe for 20 years."

—On Gil Hodges on his arrival in Brooklyn, 1947

"He that will not reason is a bigot.
"He that cannot reason is a fool.
"He that dares not reason is a slave."

—Three lines framed and hung in his offices in St. Louis, Brooklyn, and Pittsburgh and cited in Murray Polner's biography of Rickey

"He's either the greatest rotten third baseman in baseball or the rottenest great third baseman. But he's never in between."

—On Frenchy Bordagaray

"How to use your leisure time is the biggest problem of a ballplayer."

—Widely quoted

"I am alarmed at the subtle invasion of professional football, which is gaining preeminence over baseball. It's unthinkable."

—On the importance of a new league; quoted by Arthur Daley in the *New York Times*, August 20, 1959

"I believe that racial extractions and color hues and forms of worship become secondary to what men can do. The American public is not as concerned with a first baseman's pigmentation as it is with the power of his swing, the dexterity of his slide, and the gracefulness of his fielding or the speed of his legs."

—*Reader's Digest,* February 1949

"I can't tell the difference between dark skin and light skin. I'm interested enough to know the likes and dislikes of men, but it never occurred to me that it was necessary to select a team because of race, creed, or color. I'll go down on that. I'm out to win a pennant. If this fellow can help me more to win the pennant as a team fact, I'm going to employ him. And I did."

—On Jackie Robinson, from the press conference following a *Look* magazine article that accused Rickey of excessive moralizing when the announcement was made that Jackie Robinson would join the Montreal club for the 1946 season; cited in *Branch Rickey's Little Blue Book* by John J. Monteleone

"I did not mind the public criticism. That sort of thing has not changed any program I thought was good."

—Widely quoted

"I don't believe I'm going to be able to speak any longer."

> —Last words, delivered at age eighty-three as he slumped over the dais while being inducted into the Missouri Sports Hall of Fame on November 13, 1965. He went into a coma and died on December 9; quoted in his *New York Times* obituary, December 10, 1965

"I just can't slow down. I'd rather die ten minutes sooner than be doing nothing all the time. But I do hope that on some distant day in the future my funeral cortege will move at a leisurely pace."

> —On retirement; quoted in an AP biographical "sketch" issued November 1, 1964. Found in the Rickey file at the National Baseball Library.

"I have always believed that a little show of force at the right time is necessary when there's a deliberate violation of law. . . . I believe that when a man is involved in an overt act of violence or in destruction of someone's rights, that it's no time to conduct an experiment in education or persuasion."

> —On putting down a revolt among a clique of Dodgers who were objecting to bringing Jackie Robinson onto the team; quoted in Robinson's *I Never Had It Made*

"I want to sign the best ballplayers around. Even 15- and 16-year-olds. We do that right away and we'll have an edge on the other clubs within too or three years. So we're going to beat the bushes

and we'll take whatever comes out . . . and that might include a Negro player or two."

> —Testing his plan to sign a black athlete to Dodger aids and officials, pre-1947; quoted in *Giants of Baseball* by Bill Gutman.

"If I were to write four units on the board as the qualities of a player, I should have to give about two points to the legs and one to the arm and one to power. Because the arm is used only defensively. The power is used only offensively. The legs are so much in evidence—both offensively and defensively."

> —From *Branch Rickey's Little Blue Book* by John J. Monteleone

"Intuition is our subconscious reaction in time of stress."

> —Quoted by Murray Polner in his biography of Branch Rickey.

"It is gripped and thrown the same as a fast ball. The moisture on the upper fingers insulates the ball against normal friction there. The thumb is thus the last point to impart spin, which means that the spin will be forward, the reverse of the action of the fast ball. It baffles the hitters at the plate. It is easy on the arm and on the intelligence. Judas priest, I could teach any strong young man to master the thing in a week."

> —Describing the spitball; quoted by John Lardner in the June 17, 1950, *Saturday Evening Post*

"It was in 1959 that baseball had a bill before the Congress to validate the reserve clause. It really could have established a tremendous monopoly for there could not even be any room for any kind of a third major league.

"As president of the Continental League at the time, I spent three weeks in Washington, and I learned much about lobbying. Senator Johnson of Colorado, who knew his way around and was invaluable, worked with me. I did a lot of leg-running at that time, but Johnson did a lot of mind-running.

"We introduced, we the Continental League, an amendment to baseball's bill, providing that there could be any number of expansions, all cities, how they would come into major-league baseball's structure—a couple of pages. That caused a lot of discussion.

"Baseball had a very able man, a very wise man, handling its affairs in Washington. His name was Paul Porter. He knew everybody. 'Why no,' said Porter to our proposed amendment. 'Why yes,' said Johnson, who knew a few people himself.

"And when the vote came, we lacked abut three or four votes of getting a majority out of it, after the commissioner had been told by Mr. Porter that the most votes the Continental League amendment would get could be 18. Well, we got 42 votes, I think it was, and just a few transferred to the other side could have won for us.

"Well, Ford Frick was terribly upset. He was terribly disappointed by the watchmen. This was the first show of strength by the Continental League, and it shocked the hell out of them!

"Within a week's time . . . within a week of that vote by the Senate of the United States, I am on the phone. Two men are greatly interested. Could I meet, the caller asks, with the American and National League for a conference?"

—On expansion; quoted by Dick Young, *Sport*, July 1964

"It will be highly embarrassing if I die before the culmination of this program."

—On taking over the Pirates for rebuilding at age seventy; quoted by Arthur Daley in the *New York Times*, November 17, 1967

"It's as inevitable as tomorrow, but perhaps not as imminent."

—On winning a World Championship

"It's the most champagne I've had in four years. I'd rather beat the Yankees than any other team."

—In 1964, as consultant to the World Champion Cardinals; quoted in *The Sporting News Chronicle of 20th Century Sport*

"Jackie, we've got no army. There's virtually nobody on our side. No owners, no umpires, very few newspapermen. And I'm afraid that many fans may be hostile. We'll be in a tough position. We can win only if we can convince the world that I'm doing this because you're a great ballplayer, a fine gentlemen."

—To Jackie Robinson on the situation he could face on the Brooklyn Dodgers; quoted in *Giants of Baseball* by Bill Gutman

"Judas Priest."

—His strongest expletive, which also became something of a trademark

"Leisure is the handmaiden of the devil."

—As Cardinals general manager

"Luck is the residue of design."

—The most famous and oft-quoted Rickeyism, it was embedded in a longer sentiment: "Things worthwhile generally just don't happen. Luck is a fact, but should not be a factor. Good luck is what is left over after intelligence and effort have combined at their best. Negligence or indifference or inattention are usually reviewed from an unlucky seat. The law of cause and effect and causality both work the same with inexorable exactitudes. Luck is the residue of design." The words were recorded by Arthur Daley, one of America's greatest sports writers, in the *New York Times* (November 17, 1965).

"Man may penetrate the outer reaches of the universe, he may solve the very secret of eternity itself, but for me, the ultimate human experience is to witness the flawless execution of the hit-and-run."

—Widely quoted

"[Men who] are about to climb down the other side of the hill."

—His view of the Mets' 1962 draft choices

"May I say very seriously that there is nothing in the files or in my writings anywhere worthy of preservation for posterity."

—Letter to David C. Mearns, chief, Manuscript Division, Library of Congress, November 30, 1962. The papers of both Branch Rickey and Jackie Robinson are in the Library of Congress.

"Mr. Robinson was a player of undoubted major league caliber. Brooklyn was looking for good, young players. True, Robinson was black—but he could run, he could hit, he was an excellent glove man, and he had the flaming competitive spirit of a champion. Baseball must face facts. Ethnic prejudice has no place in sports, and baseball must recognize that truth if it is to maintain stature as a national game."

—Looking back on Jackie Robinson's debut; quoted in Ford Frick's *Games, Asterisks and People*

"My father was 86 when he died. As an old man he was still planting peach and apple trees on our farm near Portsmouth, Ohio. When I asked who could take in the fruit he said, 'That's not important. I just want to live every day as if I were going to live forever.'"

—On life and longevity; quoted in his *New York Times* obituary, December 10, 1965, after he died at age eighty-three

"No, this is not Branch Rickey, Senior! This is Branch Rickey!"

> —On being confused with Branch Rickey Jr., his son, at the Dodgers' camp at Vero Beach, Florida; quoted in the *New Yorker*, May 27, 1950.

"One of nature's noblemen."

> —His description of Pepper Martin

"Only in baseball can a team player be a pure individualist first and a team player second, within the rules and the spirit of the game."

> —From *The American Diamond*, 1965

"Our pitching staff is a conspiracy of ifs."

> —As St. Louis Cardinals manager

"Over there is the ocean. You are out in that ocean in a little skiff, a frail little craft, bobbing up and down on a storm-tossed sea. I come along on a big boat, crowded with people. We are sailing along, oblivious to the surging waves.

"Ours is a big luxury liner, capable of riding out the tempest.

"We look over the rail, and down in the murky foam we spot you in your little boat, the waves threatening to capsize you any second. Somebody cries: 'Stop . . . We must rescue him . . . Take him aboard.' So we halt the boat and we take you on and you're one of us, then, and no longer at the mercy of the angry waters.

"Don't you see what I mean. We took you out of Oklahoma, a wanderer at the mercy of the elements, and brought you into our organization, made you one of us, a great name, a great pitcher. Just sign here . . . please. That's right . . . and see you at training."

> —This is Casey Stengel's version of Branch Rickey's signing Dizzy Dean. It appeared in the May 1945 *Baseball Digest*, where it was introduced this way: "They sat across from one another at Rickey's desk. A contract awaiting only Dean's signature lay at the former Cardinal general manager's elbow. The top was off the ink bottle—the pen at hand. Then Branch went to work as only he can."

"Problems are the price you pay for progress."

> —Widely attributed

"Still I do not feel that the farming system we have established is the result of any inventive genius—it is the result of stark necessity. We did it to meet a question of supply and demand of young ball players. We learned long before that partnership operation of minor clubs was not feasible—that there were too many clashing influences. So we now operate these as separate units—technically they are parts of our system, but in reality they are separate clubs, apart from the Cardinals, all basically self-sustaining and operated within the letter and spirit of the code so far as the baseball rules relate to the minors and majors."

> —On his creation of the farm system; quoted in the *Sporting News*, December 1, 1933

"Take that extra base every time. Make them throw after you, make them hurry their throws. You'll get thrown out sure, but for every time they throw you out now, you will make them hurry and throw wild later. You will reap a golden harvest of extra bases."

> —Advice to Jackie Robinson; quoted in the
> *Sporting News,* 1947

"Ted, don't worry about anything. You'll play another five years."

> —To Ted Williams in Korea. Williams was thirty-
> five at the time and played part of the 1953
> season and seven more. Recalled by Tom Weir
> in his May 25, 1990, *USA Today* column.

"That preliminary move Stanley uses at the plate is a fraud. When the ball leaves the pitcher's hand, that is the time you take a picture of a batsman to determine the correctness of his form. Now the ball has been pitched and Stanley takes his true position. He is no longer in a crouch and his bat is fully back and so steady a coin couldn't fall off the end of it. Then the proper stride and the level swing. There is no hitch. He is ideal in form."

> —On Stan Musial on the day of his retirement,
> September 29, 1963; quoted in the *Sporting
> News,* October 12, 1963

"The finest collection of young athletes I have ever assembled on a playing field."

> —His version of "I've got a great bunch of kids
> on this team"; quoted in the *New Yorker,* May
> 27, 1950

"The greatest untapped reservoir of raw material in the history of our game is the black race."

> —On the singing of Jackie Robinson

"The man who has the infinite capacity to take a bad situation and make it immediately worse."

> —On Leo Durocher

"The man with the ball is responsible for what happens to the ball."

> —Answering the question of whether the
> pitcher or catcher is responsible for pitching
> sequences

"The most important single qualification a man should have to marry one of my daughters is infinite kindness. Infinite kindness will sustain a marriage through all its problems, its uncertainties, its illnesses, its disappointments, its storms, its tension, its fear, its separation, its sorrows. Out of infinite kindness grow real love and understanding and tolerance and warmth. Nothing can take the place of such an enduring asset."

> —From Murray Polner's *Branch Rickey*

"There was never a man in the game who could put mind and muscle together quicker and with better judgment than Robinson."

> —As Dodgers president on Jackie Robinson

"They finished last—on merit."

> —On his 1952 Pirates; quoted in his AP
> obituary

"Thinking about the devil is worse than seeing the devil."

— Widely attributed

"This ball—this symbol; is it worth a man's whole life?"

— From a *Sports Illustrated* interview with Gerald Holland

"Thou shalt not steal. I mean defensively. On offense, indeed thou shall steal and thou must."

— SABR Collection

"Time proves all things."

— One of his favorite sayings

"Trade a player a year too early rather than a year too late."

— One of his baseball tenets

"Try to land anyway. I'll take the responsibility."

— To a pilot who had just told him that the field ahead was closed because of fog; quoted by Arthur Daley in the *New York Times*, October 26, 1955

"We would have finished last without you."

— To Ralph Kiner, after Kiner was told he would have to take a 25 percent pay cut despite having hit 37 home runs and leading the league for the seventh straight time

"What I'm telling you is this: there is a Negro ballplayer coming to the Dodgers, not the Brown Dodgers. I don't know who he is and I don't know where he is and I don't know when he's coming. But he is coming. And he is coming just as soon as we can find him. My wife is utterly opposed to my doing it. The family is dead set against it. But I have got to do it. I will do it. I am doing it."

— What he told Red Barber when the rest of the world believed he was forming a new Negro League team; quoted by Arthur Daley in the *New York Times*, April 9, 1968

"What makes you or breaks you is the ability to choose from among the in-betweens those boys who will go on to make good."

— Quoted in his AP obituary

"What's your name? Where are you from? . . . How do you held a curve ball? . . . You married? . . . Why not? You a coward? . . . Got a change of pace? . . . What's your dad do? . . . Let's see your fast ball. . . . Got any brothers and sisters? . . . Now, son, there are three things that govern the behavior of a pitched ball—the speed that it travels forward, the speed that it rotates on its axis, and the direction of the rotation. You control the forward speed with your arm and wrist. You control the speed of rotation with the pressure of your fingers. You control the direction of rotation with the position of your fingers. . . . Got a girl? . . . Good. . . . The most important thing in pitching is the element of surprise—you have to throw every pitch with the same motion. . . .

"What's her name? . . . There are two ways of surprising a batter. One is in the sphere of space. When the ball hops or sinks or curves, the batter can't be sure where it's coming. The other is in the sphere of time. If you throw fast one time and slow another time and medium slow another time, the batter can't be sure when it's coming. I like a young man who does both. . . . Where does she live?"

> —Talking to a new pitcher at the Dodgers' training camp at Vero Beach; quoted by Robert Rice in the *New Yorker*, May 27, 1950. Rice commented, "Any pitcher who has experienced the physical, mental, and emotional strain of working with Rickey for half an hour is likely thereafter to regard pitching a nine-inning game as a peaceful way of spending a summer afternoon."

"You wouldn't disprove his story by the way he smelled."

> —On the return of Cardinal Flint Rhem, who claimed he had been kidnapped by gangsters, locked in a hotel room, and forced to drink great quantities of liquor at gunpoint

RICKEY, BRANCH JR.

"Don't do it. . . . I've seen a sandlot team clobber him. All he'll do is take up space for two years and give the papers more ammunition to throw at you."

> —The Brooklyn Dodgers official advising his father, the team's general manager, not to sign Sandy Koufax, 1955; quoted in *The Experts Speak*

RICKLES, DON

"I would like to be a general manager and have the guys come and get them girls and sit and drink with them and tell them what bad years they had."

> —To Bob Uecker, on becoming a baseball GM, from *Catcher in the Wry*

RIGNEY, BILL

"It's not big if you look at it from the standpoint of the national debt."

> —As new manager of the Twins when asked if the team's earned run average was astronomical, in the *Sporting News*, April 25, 1970

"Of all the things we have in this game—hits and runs and stolen bases and home runs— the thing we have the most of is outs."

> —*The Baseball Card Engagement Book*, 1990

RILEY, JAMES WHITCOMB

Mr. Blue Jay, full o' sass,
In them base-ball clothes of his,
Sporting 'round the orchard jes'
Like he owned the premises.

> —The Hoosier poet's *Knee Deep in June*

Bill Rigney (*California Angels*)

RINCON, JUAN

"No one wants to be in my pants right now."

—Twins reliever, after giving up a game-tying rally to the Yankees in the Division Series, October 9, 2004, from the *Orange County Register*

RIPKEN, CAL JR.

"I want people to think of me as an iron man. I feel as strong physically as I did earlier in the season, but there have been times when it's been tough mentally. You get tired of thinking and tired of concentrating, and then

as you pop up or strike out, you say, 'How did I do that? I wasn't even thinking.'"

—Quoted in *Sports Illustrated,* October 3, 1983

"If I handpicked 12 off days every year, I guarantee you I'd hit 10 or 15 points higher."

—Quoted in the *Washington Post,* April 1, 1994

"The last thing you want to do is to go down in the history of all-star game competition as the only injury sustained during the team picture."

—When he played on 1996 American League team despite breaking his nose on Roberto Hernandez's forearm during a team photo mishap, *Newsweek,* July 22, 1996

"Tonight I stand here, overwhelmed, as my name is linked with the great and courageous Lou Gehrig. I'm truly humbled to have our names spoken in the same breath.

"Some may think our strongest connection is because we both played many consecutive games. Yet I believe in my heart that our true link is a common motivation—a love of the game of baseball, a passion for your team, and a desire to compete on the very highest level.

"I know that if Lou Gehrig is looking down on tonight's activities, he isn't concerned about someone playing one more consecutive game than he did. Instead, he's viewing tonight as just another example of what is good and right about the great American game. Whether your name is Gehrig or Ripken; DiMaggio or Robinson; or that of some youngster who picks up his bat or puts on his glove: You are challenged by the game of

RIPKEN, CAL JR. (CONTINUED)

baseball to do your very best day in and day out. And that's all I've ever tried to do.

"Thank you."

—Conclusion of text delivered at ceremonies following Ripken's 2,131st consecutive game on September 6, 1995, delivered at Oriole Park at Camden Yards early on the morning of September 7; quoted in the *Baltimore Sun,* September 7, 1995

RIPKEN, CAL SR.

"I'm still very mad about the way we embarrassed ourselves. We didn't belong in the league. I don't know what league we belonged in. That was a poor excuse for baseball. It's pretty difficult to do that, watch 10 balls go out.

"Damn difficult. I couldn't even go to sleep last night, and games usually don't affect me. And to think I said in April that we would be contending in the AL East, and we come in here and throw 10 balls out of the park.

"Last week, I was talking about getting back to .500. Then we go out and pick up our 81st loss. When you give up 10 homers and give up 18 runs, then think you can win 19 in a row, you have to be out of your mind."

—After the Baltimore Orioles' loss to the Toronto Blue Jays, 18–2, on September 14, 1987, during which Toronto hit 10 home runs; quoted in "Orioles Out of Their League Monday," *Baltimore Sun,* September 16, 1987

RIPLEY, ROBERT

"John Sturm, New York Yankee *First* baseman, was *First* up in the *First* inning of the *First* game of his *First* World Series and made the *First* hit of the game on the *First* day of October. He also made the *First* out and the *First* put-out and was the *First* man hit by a pitched ball."

—The "Believe It or Not" man citing one of his favorite examples; quoted in *Baseball Magazine,* October 1950

RITTER, LAWRENCE

"Baseball is a team game, but it is played by individuals who do their job singly and alone, in the full glare of the spotlight. They will be praised or blamed, become heroes or goats, depending on their performance under pressure."

—*The Story of Baseball* (New York: William Morrow)

"The most overrated underrated player in baseball."

—On Tommy Henrich. Ritter reports that the remark was "a wiseass remark made at a gathering of sportswriters in 1980 which was first picked up by the *Village Voice.*"

"The best thing about baseball today is its yesterdays."

—This has been attributed to Ritter, who says it first appeared in an advertisement for old World Series programs in the mid-1970s

RIVERS, MICKEY

"To hit .300, score 100 runs and stay injury-prone."

—On his goals for the 1983 season; quoted in the *St. Petersburg Times*, March 30, 1983

"I can't tell you why one man hits better under pressure than another, because I don't think you can reduce hitting to a formula. But I can tell you this: The best hitters do their thinking before they get to the plate. After that, they hit by reacting; and they don't just make contact, they drive the ball."

—As a Yankee; quoted in the *Christian Science Monitor*, July 5, 1978

"Man, it was tough. The wind was blowing about 100 degrees."

—The Rangers DH on game conditions; quoted in *Sports Illustrated*, July 18, 1983

"Me and George and Billy are two of a kind."

—In denying that he'd have troubles with owner George Steinbrenner or manager Billy Martin if he want back to the Yankees in 1983

"Out of what? a thousand?"

—On hearing Reggie Jackson brag about having an IQ of 160

RIXEY, EPPA

"If I had my life to live over again, I would do exactly as I have done. I would welcome an opportunity to play big league baseball. The old game has bestowed upon me a far wider reputation than I would ever have gained by holding test tubes over Bunsen burners in a chemical laboratory."

—On his original plans to be a chemist; quoted in *Cooperstown Corner: Columns from The Sporting News 1962–1969* by Lee Allen

"They're really scraping the bottom of the barrel, aren't they?"

—On being elected to the Hall of Fame, January 27, 1963, by the Veterans' Committee. Rixey died on February 28, 1963. Before his election he had been in Cooperstown and sent postcards to friends which said, "I finally made it to Cooperstown—for one day."

RIZZUTO, PHIL

"Here comes Roger Maris. They're standing up, waiting to see if Roger is going to hit No. 61! Here's the windup . . . the pitch to Roger . . . WAY OUTSIDE, ball one. And the boos get louder. Two balls, no strikes, on Roger MAris. Here's the windup . . . fastball HIT DEEP TO RIGHT, THIS could be IT! WAY BACK THERE, HOLY COW HE DID IT! 61 HOME RUNS!! They're fighting for that ball out there. Holy cow . . . another standing ovation for Roger Maris!"

—Broadcast on October 1, 1961

"Holy cow!"

—As New York Yankees announcer

"I'll never forget September 6, 1950. I got a letter threatening me, Hank Bauer, Yogi Berra and Johnny Mize. It said if I showed up in uniform against the Red Sox I'd be shot. I turned the letter over to the FBI and told my manager Casey Stengel about it. You know what Casey did? He gave me a different uniform and gave mine to Billy Martin. Can you imagine that! Guess Casey thought it'd be better if Billy got shot."

> —Quoted by Barry Stainback in *Sport*, December 1961

"I'll take any way to get into the Hall of Fame. If they want a batboy, I'll go in as a batboy."

> —Statement repeated on more than one occasion

"They've got so many Latin players, we're going to have to get a Latin instructor up here [in the booth]."

> —As a New York Yankees announcer talking about the Montreal Expos, *Sporting News*, April 24, 1989

"Those huckleberries in the National League didn't want to do anything that the American League wants to do."

> —As a Yankee broadcaster on the alternating-designated-hitter rule for World Series play, during a New York–Toronto telecast, September 25, 1977

"Well, that kind of puts the damper on even a Yankee win."

> —As an announcer on hearing the news bulletin that Pope Paul VI had died, August 6, 1978

ROBERTS, ROBIN

"In the long history of organized baseball, I stand unparalleled for putting Christianity into practice. And to prove I was not prejudiced, I served up home run balls to Negroes, Italians, Jews, Catholics alike. Race, creed, nationality made no difference to me."

> —From "Diamond Quotes," in *Nine*, 2006

"There is no doubt that some one who tries to throw a curve or pitch at an early age before he's developed, before his hand is big enough to grip the ball correctly, will damage his arm."

> —As a former Phillies pitcher

"When Mickey Mantle bunted with the wind blowing out in Crosley Field."

> —When asked to describe his greatest All-Star Game thrill; quoted in *Sports Illustrated*, July 24, 1978

"When I was with Houston at the end of my career, Bob Gibson walked up to me one day when I was ruining in the outfield. He asked me why I didn't quit, and said what a shame it was that I was ruining a great career and just trying to hang on. Years later, I saw Gibson trying to do the same thing."

> —Quoted by Paul Domowitz of Knight-Ridder at the time of Steve Carlton's retirement, 1988

ROBINSON, BROOKS

"Fifty years from now I'll be just three inches of type in a record book."

> —Quoted by Al Stump in *Sport*, October 1963

"I'll play out the string and leave baseball without a tear. A man can't play games his whole life."

—Quoted by Al Stump, *Sport*, October 1963

"It's a pretty sure thing that the player's bat is what speaks loudest when it's contact time, but there are moments when the glove has the last word."

—*Third Base Is My Home*

"I've always said when I broke into baseball was an average player. I had an average arm, average speed and definitely an average bat. I am still average in all of those."

—On coming into the game in 1955; quoted in the *Dallas Times-Herald*, May 4, 1975

"I've never been hurt by a ground ball, and yet I've got more false teeth than a Polish fullback. Funny isn't it?"

—On being led off to the dentist after breaking two incisor teeth in a batting cage as he lost control of his bat and it ricocheted off the cage and hit him in the mouth; quoted in *Sport Magazine's All-Time All Stars*

"This is my best time of the year. Heck, once the season starts, I go to work."

—On spring training

ROBINSON, FRANK

"Close don't count in baseball. Close only counts in horseshoes and grenades."

—So widely quoted that few recall that Frank Robinson was the first to say it. It made an early appearance in print in *Time,* July 31, 1973.

"I don't see anyone playing in the major leagues today who combines both the talent and the intensity that I had. I always tried to do the best. I knew I wouldn't always be the best, but I tried to be. I expect that of my players today and of my kids. My wife says I shouldn't expect that of my children but I don't think that's asking too much."

—On his election to the Hall of Fame, January 14, 1982

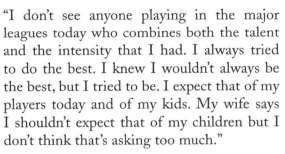
Brooks Robinson (*Baltimore Orioles*)

ROBINSON, FRANK (CONTINUED)

"If I had one wish in the world today, it could be that Jackie Robinson would be here to see this happen."

> —On being made the first black manager, in Cleveland, at a press conference in the fall of 1974

"In 1982 in San Francisco, we finished two games out and they gave me 24 hours to get out of town. Here, we finish two games out and we get a pep rally and a parade."

> —As Baltimore Orioles manager, speaking to Orioles fans who celebrated the team's second-place finish in the AL East in 1980

"It's nice to come into a town and be referred to as the manager of the Cleveland Indians instead of as the first black manager."

> —*Sporting News*, October 25, 1975

"Managers don't have as much leverage as they used to have. We can't really be the boss. If I say to a veteran player, 'If you don't perform, you may be sent back to the minors,' they look at me and say, 'Who are you kidding. I'm not going anyplace. . . . I've already had three years in the major leagues. You can't send me back to the minor leagues without my OK.'"

> —Quoted in the August 1981 *Washingtonian*

"No, I don't think my presence will cause an increase in black attendance at Cleveland. People came out to see the players. When do you see a manager anyway? When he's out on

Frank Robinson (*Baltimore Orioles*)

the field arguing with the umpires, making a fool of himself—you know he can't win—and when he brings out the lineup card."

> —After being named the first black manager, on CBS's *Face the Nation*, October 13, 1974

"Pitchers did me a favor when they knocked me down. It made me more determined. I wouldn't let that pitcher get me out. They say you can't hit if you're on your back. But I didn't hit on my back. I got up."

> —As a retired player

"The fan is the one who suffers. He cheers a guy to a .350 season, then watches that player sign with another team. When you destroy fan loyalties, you destroy everything."

> —As an Orioles coach, on free agents

"There's too much of it, particularly in the American League. There's absolutely no way you can go barreling into second base and dump a guy on a double play, like you should do, when you've been fraternizing with him before a game."

—On fraternization, as a Baltimore Oriole; quoted in *Sports Illustrated,* April 12, 1971

"We're not the O's anymore. We're the 1's."

—On his 1988 Orioles after they beat Chicago 9–0 for their first victory of the season after 21 losses. From the list "Memorable Quotes of 1988" from the *Tampa Tribune,* December 25, 1988

ROBINSON, JACKIE

"Above anything else, I hate to lose."

—Quoted in *Giants of Baseball* by Bill Gutman

"At the beginning of the World Series of 1947, I experienced a completely new emotion, when the National Anthem was played. This time, I thought, it is being played for me, as much as for anyone else. This is organized major league baseball, and I am standing here with all the others and everything that takes place includes me."

—From *This I Believe*

"Baseball is like a poker game. Nobody wants to quit when he's losing; nobody wants you to quit when you're ahead."

—Quoted in *Giants of Baseball* by Bill Gutman

"Baseball, like some other sports, poses as a sacred institution dedicated to the public good, but it is actually a big, selfish business

with a ruthlessness that many big businesses would never think of displaying."

—From *I Never Had It Made*

"Black players have saved baseball, kept baseball on top. But I think football and basketball have moved beyond baseball in race relations; in many instances, they hire a man to do a job regardless of his skin color. Baseball is still wallowing around in the 19th century, saying a black can't manage, a black can't go into the front office . . . I think baseball is very vindictive. I think, very frankly, that a black man who is willing to accept their dictates and do what they want him to do can get along beautifully. But if you're a man and you stand on your own

Jackie Robinson (*Museum of Modern Art Film Still Archives*)

two feet, then look out. I think this is basically the problem today with baseball."

—As a former player; quoted in the *New York Times,* December 5, 1971

"Fear is a two-edged sword that sometimes cuts the wielder."

—From Richard Newman's *African American Quotations* (Phoenix: Oryx Press, 1998)

"How you played in yesterday's game is all that counts."

—Quoted in the *Diamond Angle,* vol. 1, no. 5

"I guess if I would choose one of the most important moments in my life, I would go back to 1947, in the Yankee Stadium in New York City. It was the opening day of the World Series and I was for the first time playing in the series as a member of the Brooklyn Dodgers team. It was a history-making day. It would be the first time that a black man would be allowed to participate in a World Series. I had became the first black player in the major leagues."

—From *I Never Had It Made*

"I realized how much our relationship had deepened after I left baseball. It was that later relationship that made me feel almost as if I had lost my own father, Branch Rickey, especially after I was no longer in the sports spotlight, treated me like a son."

—From *I Never Had It Made*

"I think it's a tragedy that baseball is still wallowing in the nineteenth century saying Negroes can't manage white ballplayers."

—Quoted by Milton Richmond in his UPI column of April 9, 1968

"I'm not concerned with your liking or disliking me. . . . All I ask is that you respect me as a human being."

—Quoted in *Grand Slams and Fumbles*

"I've been riding on Cloud Nine since the election, and I don't think I'll ever come down. Today, everything is complete."

—On being inducted into Baseball's Hall of Fame, July 23, 1962. Robinson was the first black to be elected.

"Most whites, in my opinion, [those that oppose] are afraid of something they need not fear. We have no intention of invading their rights but we feel they also should not invade upon ours."

—1952 letter to a fan which was first published in Tim Kirkjian's *America's Game.* Kirkjian said to a reporter for the *Washington Times,* April 23, 2000: "That letter is pretty cool because we're hearing his voice—and it's the most powerful voice in the book. When you're talking about baseball history, you have to start with Jackie Robinson."

"Pop flies, in a sense, are just a diversion for a second baseman. Grounders are his stock in trade."

—Quoted in *Mutual Baseball Almanac* edited by Roger Kahn and Al Helfer

"Quit praying for me alone, Ma, and pray for the whole team."

> —Letter to his mother during the latter part of his rookie year. Reportd in *Time*, September 22, 1947, in an article on his being named Rookie of the Year

"The way I figured it, I was even with baseball and baseball with me. The game had done much for me, and I had done much for it."

> —From *I Never Had It Made*

"There is no easy place for the old ball player in society."

> —Quoted in Roger Kahn's *How the Weather Was*. Kahn says that Robinson said this a few weeks before he died.

"They voted Casey the greatest living manager. That's a lot of bull—a joke.

"The only thing a manager has to do is relate to the players. Who did Casey ever relate to? Nobody but himself."

> —On Casey Stengel; quoted by Will Grimsley of the AP in the *San Francisco Chronicle*, October 25, 1969

"We live in a materialistic society in which money doesn't only talk—it screams. I would not forget that some of the very ballplayers who swore the most fervently that they wouldn't play with me because I was black were the first to begin helping me, giving me tips and advice, as soon as they became aware that I would be helpful to them in winning the few thousand more dollars players receive as world Series champs. The most prejudiced of the club owners were not as upset about the game being con-

taminated by black players as they were by fearing that integrating would hurt them in their pocketbooks."

> —From *I Never Had It Made*

"Well, I broke in tonight."

> —After being thrown out of his first major-league game, August 24, 1948, at Forbes Field

ROCKER, JOHN

"I would retire first. It's the most hectic, nerve-racking city. Imagine having to take the [Number] 7 train to the ballpark, looking like you're [riding through] Beirut next to some kid with purple hair next to some queer with AIDS right next to some dude who just got out of jail for the fourth time right next to some 20-year-old mom with four kids. It's depressing."

> —Atlanta Braves pitcher, on ever playing for a New York team; quoted in Jeff Pearlman, "At Full Blast," *Sports Illustrated*, December 27, 1999–January 3, 2000

"The biggest thing I don't like about New York [City] are the foreigners. I'm not a very big fan of foreigners. You can walk an entire block in Times Square and not hear anybody speaking English, Asians and Koreans and Vietnamese and Indians and Russians and Spanish people and everything up there. How the hell did they get in this country?"

> —Quoted in Jeff Pearlman, "At Full Blast"

ROCKWELL, NORMAN

"I unconsciously decided that, even if it wasn't an ideal world, it should be and so painted only the ideal aspects of it—pictures in which there are no drunken slatterns or self-centered mothers . . . only foxy grandpas who played baseball with the kids and boys who fished from logs and got up circuses in the backyard."

— *Washington Post,* May 27, 1972

RODRIGUEZ, ALEX

"You kind of get tired of giving the other team credit. At some point you've got to look in the mirror and say, 'I sucked.'"

— As Yankees third baseman, after New York lost to Detroit in the AL Division Series

ROE, PREACHER

"Every pitch, perfect or not, is a potential home run."

— *The Baseball Card Engagement Book,* 1990

"Some days you eat the bear. Some days the bear eats you. Yesterday the bear ate us."

— Pet adage as a Dodger

ROE, ROCKY

"You've had a great night if they're not waiting for you after the game with tar and feathers."

— The umpire; quoted in *Strike Two* by Ron Luciano

ROEDER, BILL

"The Dodgers hit short and run long."

— On the 1947 Brooklyn Dodgers

ROGERS, WILL

"Any man, woman, or child in the United States that don't love Walter Johnson and admire him as a man is not a good American."

— "Everybody Is Pulling for Walter," *New York Times,* September 28, 1924

"Baseball is a skilled game. It's America's game—it, and high taxes."

— Widely quoted

"Baseball needed a touch of class and distinction. So somebody said: 'Get that old boy who sits behind first base all the time. He's out there every day anyhow.' So they offered him a season's pass and he jumped at it. But don't kid yourself that that old judicial bird isn't going to make those baseball birds walk the chalk-line."

— On Judge Kenesaw Mountain Landis; quoted in J.G. Taylor Spink, *Judge Landis and Twenty-five Years of Baseball* (New York: Thomas Y. Crowell, 1947)

"Baseball teams go south every spring to cripple their players. In the old days they only stayed a couple of weeks. . . . nowadays, they stay till they get them all hurt."

— Widely attributed and commonly cited each year when spring training begins

Will Rogers (*Library of Congress Prints and Photographs Division*)

"My idea of the height of conceit would be a political speaker that would go on the air when that World Series is on."

—His column of October 3, 1928

"You hear ten people ask, 'Who is going to pitch for the Yankees tomorrow?' where you don't hear one ask, 'Who is going to be elected?'"

—His column of September 24, 1928

ROJAS, COOKIE

"There's a ballplayer who does two things at the same time. He pitches—and digs for oil."

—On underhanded relief pitcher Ted Abernathy; quoted in *Baseball Digest*, August, 1968

ROONEY, ANDY

"Baseball has been called 'The National Pastime.' It's just the kind of game anyone deserves who has nothing better to do than try to pass his time. My own time is passing plenty fast enough without some national game to help it along. What does 'pastime' mean anyway? And why doesn't it have two t's?"

—From an essay which begins: "I hate baseball. I have always hated baseball. As a matter of fact, I have a hard time liking anyone who does like baseball." From *A Few Minutes with Andy Rooney* (New York: Atheneum, 1981)

"They can make 250 bats from one good tree. How's that for a statistic, baseball fans?"

—Hall of Fame Collection

ROOSEVELT, FRANKLIN D.

"Hello, Joe? It's Frank. Giants three, Dodgers nothing."

—Telephone call to Joseph Stalin, attributed in *The Faber Book of Anecdotes* (where it is said to be "almost surely apocryphal")

"I have no expectation of making a hit every time I came to bat. What I seek is the highest possible batting average, not only for myself, but for my team."

—Radio chat May 1933; quoted in the April 1948, *Baseball Magazine*

ROOSEVELT, FRANKLIN D. (CONTINUED)

"If I didn't have to hobble up those steps in front of all those people, I'd be out at that ball park every day."

—Comment recalled later by Clark Griffith

"The White House
Washington
January 15, 1942

My dear Judge:

Thank you for yours of January fourteenth. As you will, of course, realize the final decision about the baseball season must rest with you and the Baseball club owners—so what I am going to say is solely a personal and not an official point of view.

I honestly feel that it would be best for the country to keep baseball going. There will be fewer people unemployed and everybody will work longer hours and harder than ever before.

And that means that they ought to have a chance for recreation and for taking their minds off their work even more than before.

Baseball provides a recreation which does not last over two hours or two hours and a half, and which can be got for very little cost. And, incidentally, I hope that night games can be extended because it gives an opportunity to the day shift to see a game occasionally.

As to the players themselves, I know you agree with me that the individual players who are active military or naval age should go, without question, into the services. Even if the actual quality to the teams is lowered by the greater use of older players, this will not dampen the popularity of the sport. Of course, if an individual has some particular aptitude in a trade or profession, he ought to serve the Government. That, however, is a matter which I know you can handle with complete justice.

Here is another way of looking at it—if 300 teams use 5,000 or 6,000 players, these players are a definite recreational asset to at least 20,000,000 of their fellow citizens—and that in my judgment is thoroughly worthwhile.

With every best wish,

Very sincerely yours,

Franklin D. Roosevelt
Hon. Kenesaw M. Landis
333 North Michigan Avenue
Chicago, Illinois"

—The so-called Green Light Letter, which kept the game going during World War II

Franklin D. Roosevelt (*Joe Roberts Photo*)

"You know how I really feel? I feel like a baseball team going into the ninth inning with only eight men left to play."

> —To Clark Griffith, president of the
> Washington Senators, eight days before his
> death; quoted in an article by Griffith in *This
> Week*, April 10, 1955

ROOSEVELT, THEODORE

"DEAREST ARCHIE:

Quentin is now taking a great interest in baseball. Yesterday the Force School nine, on which he plays second base, played the P Street nine on the White House grounds where Quentin has marked out a diamond. The Force School nine was victorious by a score of 22 to 5. I told Quentin I was afraid the P Street boys must have felt badly and he answered, "Oh, I guess not; you see I filled them up with lemonade afterward!"

> —From the White House, March 15, 1908,
> to his son Archie, from *Theodore Roosevelt's
> Letters to His Children*

"There is little point in the mere development of strength. The point lies in developing a man who can do something with his strength; who not only has the skill to turn his muscles to advantage, but the heart and the head to direct that skill, and to direct it well and fearlessly. Gymnastics and calisthenics are very well in their way as substitutes when nothing better can be obtained, but the true sports for a manly race are sports like running, rowing, playing football and baseball, boxing and wrestling, shooting, riding, and mountain climbing."

> —*Harper's Weekly*, December 23, 1893

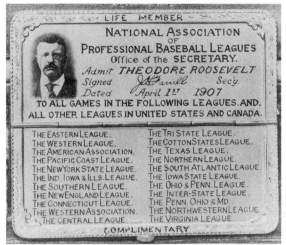

Teddy Roosevelt's Season Pass (*National Baseball Library*)

"When money comes in at the gate, sport flies out at the window."

> —Quoted in *Baseball: The Early Years* by Harold
> Seymour

ROOT, CHARLIE

"Baloney. If he had pointed to the stands, he'd have gone down on his fanny. I'd have loosened him up. Nobody facing me would have gotten away with that."

> —On Babe Ruth's called shot during the 1932
> World Series; quoted in *Baseball's Golden Age:
> The Photographs of Charles M. Conlon*

"Am I still in uniform? Then I ain't retired."

> —During spring training 1989 when asked about formally ending his playing career (he had not had an at bat since August 17, 1986); quoted by Bruce Lowitt in the *St. Petersburg Times,* March 23, 1989

"Bart Giamatti was one of the smartest guys around. But how smart could you be if you're 70 pounds overweight and smoke five packs of cigarettes a day? He was a walking time bomb."

> —Responding to the suggestion that the stress of the investigation of his gambling contributed to the death of the former baseball commissioner, *USA Today,* July 28, 1998

"Believe me, publicity isn't what it's made out to be."

> —On a fellow player Kal Daniels complaining at the time of his trade that he had not been given enough publicity in Cincinnati, *Sports Illustrated,* July 31, 1989

"Brooks Robinson belongs in a higher league."

> —Widely quoted

"Doctors tell me I have the body of a thirty-year-old. I know I have the brain of a fifteen-year-old. If you've got both, you can play baseball."

> —At age forty-four, on longevity

Pete Rose (*Cincinnati Reds*)

"Gullett's the only guy who can throw a baseball through a car wash and not get the ball wet."

> —On the fastball of rookie Don Gullett, *Sporting News,* October 24, 1970

"He's an intellectual from Yale, but he's very intelligent."

> —On A. Bartlett Giamatti, the baseball commissioner–elect, *Life,* January 1989

"How can anyone as slow as you pull a muscle?"

> —To Tony Perez, SABR Collection

"I don't read many truths in the paper. Then again, I haven't read the papers. But I hear about it. It would scare me to read the paper. I didn't know I had enough time to do the things I'm suppose to be doing. I'm tired of seeing my picture on the front page of *USA Today*. That's the only paper I get. But you can't put much stock in papers. They only cost 50 cents."

    —On allegations about his gambling, *Sporting News*, July 17, 1989

"I don't think any player ever gets tired when he's hitting [well]. The ball looks bigger than usual and the fielders seem spaced way out. When you're not hitting, the ball looks smaller and it seems like even the umpires have gloves and you can't find a hole."

    —Quoted in the *Los Angeles Times*, August 11, 1978

"I haven't missed a game in two and a half years. I go to the park sick as a dog and, when I see my uniform hanging there, I get well right now. Then I see some of you guys and I get sick again."

    —On the press, as a Red

"I told him who to watch. I said if you want to be a catcher, watch Johnny Bench. If you want to be a right-handed power hitter, watch Mike Schmidt. If you just want to be a hitter, watch me."

    —On teaching his son Pete Jr. about the game, *USA Today*, April 4, 1989

"I wish there was some way I could have gotten a college education. I'm thinking about buying a college, though."

    —Quoted in *Sports Illustrated*, May 2, 1988

"I'd be willing to bet you, if I was a betting man, that I have never bet on baseball."

    —1989, prior to his banishment from baseball

"I'd walk through hell in a gasoline suit to keep playing baseball."

    —Hall of Fame Collection

"If there was ever a war, I'd fight for the United States."

    —His answer to critics who thought he was making a mistake endorsing Japanese products; quoted in *Sports Illustrated*, June 29, 1981

"If you play an aggressive, hustling game, it forces your opponents into errors. It helps you at every level but is perhaps most important when you get to the majors. The good major-league teams don't make many mistakes, so by playing aggressively you've got a much better chance to make the error happen."

    —Quoted in *Heavy Hitters: Lynn, Parker, Carew, Rose* by Bill Gutman

"I'm just like everybody else. I have two arms, two legs and 4,000 hits."

    —On assuming his duties as playing manager of the Reds; quoted in *The Sporting News*, September 3, 1984

"I'm not bad. I'm no Joe Morgan, but I'm pretty good for a white guy."

    —On his speed; widely attributed, 1979

"I'm trying to figure out what they're doing. I get on a plane in San Diego and they're shooting film. I get off a plane in Cincinnati and they've got another crew from CBS shooting me. After a game, CBS, ABC, NBC are all in here. CBS has been with me something like 68 days. How much footage do they need of a guy?"

— On the media during the investigation of gambling charges against him; quoted in wire service reports, May 2, 1989

"It doesn't take much to get me up for baseball. Once the National Anthem plays, I get chills. I even know the words to it now."

— "La Vie en Rose," *Philadelphia Inquirer,* August 12, 1981

"I've lost my self-respect."

— At his sentencing for income tax evasion, *Life: The Year in Pictures, 1991*

"Playing baseball for a living is like having a license to steal."

— Widely attributed

"Pressure? Well, it ain't hitting in 44 straight games, because I done that and it was fun. The playoffs are pressure."

— His standard answer to a standard question.

"Say, this is some kind of game, isn't it?"

— Coming up to bat for the Cincinnati Reds in the tenth inning of the tied and retied sixth game of the 1975 World Series, to Carlton Fisk, the Red Sox catcher; quoted in Roger Angell, *Five Seasons*

"So what do I do now? How do I rest? Do I sit on the bench? Do I stand? I wish somebody could tell me how to rest."

— On Philly Manager Pat Corrales's decision to rest him by keeping him out of the starting lineup for a game against the Astros; quoted in *Sports Illustrated,* May 16, 1983

"Some of those fans would boo the crack in the Liberty Bell."

— On the fans in Philadelphia, "Quotebook 76," *Los Angeles Times,* January 1, 1977

"Sure I do, and if someone paid you $6,000 a game, you'd have fun as well."

— When asked if he enjoyed playing baseball

"The hardest thing is not making the big leagues. Rather, it is staying in the big leagues."

— Quoted by Walter Alston in his *Complete Baseball Handbook*

"The team that wins two-thirds of its one-run games usually wins the pennant."

— Widely attributed

"You pick up the paper sometimes and read where a player says, 'I can't play for this manager.' Makes me laugh. You don't play for the manager, you play for the team. This is who I play for [the Reds]. I play for 24 other players, the manager and the trainer—everybody on the team."

— Quoted in the *Dallas Times-Herald,* March 13, 1974

"Your Honor, I would like to say that I am very sorry. I am very shameful to be here today in front of you. I think I'm perceived as a very aggressive, arrogant type of individual. But I want people to know that I do have emotion, I do have feelings, and I can be hurt like everybody else. And I hope no one has to go through what I went through the last year and a half. I lost my dignity, I lost my self-respect, I lost a lot of dear fans and almost lost some very dear friends."

—To Judge Arthur Spiegel, on being sentenced on tax evasion charges, July 19, 1990

"When you play this game 20 years, go to bat 10,000 times, and get 3,000 hits, do you know what that means? You've gone 0 for 7,000."

—As quoted by Joe Garagiola in *It's Anybody's Ballgame*

"With the money I'm making, I should be playing two positions."

—From 1977; widely quoted

"You always have to have luck to win, and sometimes the best team is just the luckiest."

—Quoted in *Late Innings* by Roger Angell

ROSEBORO, JOHN

"Some people expected the Yankees to hit him. I don't see how they possibly could when they hadn't seen him. There are guys in our league who see him all the time and still can't hit him."

—On Sandy Koufax in 1963, from *The Sporting News Chronicle of 20th Century Sport*

ROSEN, AL

"The greatest thrill in the world is to end the game with a home run and watch everybody else walk off the field while you're running the bases on air."

—Quoted in Frank Graham and Dick Hyman, *Baseball Wit and Wisdom*, 1962

ROSENBLATT, ROGER

"Taking life 90 feet at a time."

—On *Special Edition*, PBS, April 5, 1979

ROSENTHAL, HAROLD

"Organized baseball is a highly complete field of activity. There is more to it than meets the eye, more than the two or three hours of competition with one team winning, the other losing. For every player that is seen on the field, hitting, running, or throwing, there are perhaps a dozen people backing him up in vital roles."

—*Baseball Is Their Business*, 1952

"The imprint of baseball greatness is upon Mickey Mantle just as surely as the portrait of Thomas Jefferson graces the current three-cent stamp, but it may still take a while before the American sporting public becomes aware of the magnitude of Mickey's talents."

—"Mantle Made It the Hard Way," *Sport*

ROSS, MURRAY

"Baseball is part of a comic tradition which insists that its participants be humans, while football, in the heroic mode, asks that its players be more than that."

—From "Football and Baseball In America in Sport and Society," *Sport and Society* (Boston: Little Brown, 1973)

ROTH, PHILIP

"Baseball—with its lore and legends, its cultural power, its seasonal associations, its native authenticity, its simple rules and transparent strategies, its longeurs and thrills, its spaciousness, its suspensefulness, its heroics, its nuances, its lingo, its 'characters,' its peculiarly hypnotic tedium, its mythic transformation of the immediate—was the literature of my boyhood."

—"My Baseball Years," *New York Times,* Opening Day, April 2, 1973

"My family would have been shocked if I had made the baseball team. Maybe I would have been too. Surely it would have put me on a somewhat different footing with this game that I loved with all my heart, not simply for the fun of playing it (fun was secondary, really), but for the mythic and aesthetic dimension that it gave to an American boy's life—particularly to one whose grandparents could hardly speak English. For someone whose roots in America were strong but only inches deep, and who had no experience, such as a Catholic child might, of an awareness hierarchy that was real and felt, baseball was a kind of secular church that reached into every class and region of the nation and bound mil-

lions upon millions of us together in common concerns, loyalties, rituals, enthusiasms, and antagonisms. Baseball made me understand what patriotism was about, at its best."

—"My Baseball Years"

"Whaling has already been used."

—When asked why he selected baseball as the subject for *The Great American Novel;* quoted by John R. Cashill in "The Life and Death of Myth in *American Baseball Literature,*" a paper delivered to the Popular Culture Convention, May 3, 1974.

ROUSH, EDD

"One of my chores was to milk the cows, which meant getting up before dawn and going out to that cold dark barn. I didn't expect to make it all the way to the big leagues, I just had to get away from them damn cows."

—*The Baseball Card Engagement Book,* 1988

ROVE, KARL

"Anything involving baseball."

—Powerful adviser to President George W. Bush, answering the question of whether there was a domestic issue he did not have a hand in. *Time,* December 27, 2005

ROWE, SCHOOLBOY

"How'm I doing, Edna."

—Radio remark made to his wife just before a 1934 World Series game. Rowe's Tigers were playing the Cardinals, and such bench jockeys as Dizzy Dean and Leo Durocher razzed him unmercifully about the remark.

ROWLAND, CLARENCE "PANTS"

"All umpires ought to tip their hats whenever Ban Johnson's name is mentioned."

—The umpire and executive on the American League president known for his support of his umpires; quoted in *Baseball: The Early Years* by Harold Seymour

ROWSWELL, ROSEY

"Open the window, Aunt Minnie—here it comes."

—Pittsburgh Pirates sportscaster whenever a Pirate hit a home run in Forbes Field, a small baseball park situated near a residential area

ROYKO, MIKE

"Hating the Yankees is as American as pizza pie, unwed mothers, and cheating on your income tax."

—SABR Collection

"I suggest something I call The Cavarretta Response.

"This response should be made part of baseball's official rules; 'If a pitcher throws a ball that forces a batter to fall down to avoid being struck in the head, the batter may, during the course of the game, fling his bat at the pitcher's head.'"

—"Should Rules of Baseball Be Civilized?" *Houston Chronicle*, August 6, 1987

"New York didn't need that 1969 pennant.... all Cub fans wanted was that one measly pennant. It would have kept us happy until the twenty-first century. But New York took that from us and I can never forgive that."

—SABR Collection

"The Cubs striking is about as significant as the buggy-whip manufacturers going on strike. What difference does it make?"

—*Chicago Sun-Times*, 1986

RUDI, JOE

"Let me tell you something about hitting. When you're going good, it doesn't make any difference who the pitcher is, whether it's a night game or a day game, or where the ballpark is located. I don't take a lot of theories up to the plate with me. I look for what I think is a good pitch and then I swing at it. If there is more to hitting than I just told you, I don't know about it."

—As an Angel; quoted in the *Christian Science Monitor*, May 5, 1977

RUEL, MUDDY

"I was closer to Chapman than anyone else on earth, and right now, almost 30 years later, I still believe it was an accident, pure and simple.

"You know, Chapman had a peculiar stance. It is literally true that he would have been hit on the head by a perfect strike. He crowded the plate and hunched over it. His head was in the strike zone.

"That's what happened the day he was killed. I saw the pitch coming. I saw Ray standing there never moving so much as a muscle. He must have been paralyzed, fascinated like the rabbit by the snake.

"Then I heard the crack. I can hear it yet. It sounded exactly like a fastball meeting the bat. I saw the ball roll toward the pitcher's box. I was just a kid then, and pretty fast on my feet. I pounced across the plate, snatched up the ball and fired it toward first base. Only then did I see the look on Carl Mays' face. I turned around, Chappie was half-sitting, half-sprawling in the batter's box. I tried to rush to him, but Speaker and Steve O'Neill and Jack Graney got there ahead of me. I guess I was glued to the ground.

"I knew right then that I had seen a man killed by a baseball."

—Yankee catcher during the fatal incident; quoted by Ed McAuley of the *Cleveland News*, in a 1948 issue of the *Sporting News*

RUFFING, CHARLEY "RED"

"Run, run, run."

—His "three rules" of training to be a great pitcher. As he explained in the March 9, 1949, *Sporting News:*

"You see, some of these guys think they are working out by jogging from left field to right field. They cut corners to boot and then they walk back. By running I mean going around from first base to third, then catching your breath and doing it all over again.

"Some of the young guys on the Yankees used to kid me about going to bed at 7:30 p.m. after running all day long. But as the years went by I noticed I was still up there when they were forgotten.

Red Ruffing (*New York Mets*)

"There are two important things to remember. Keep in shape and know where each pitch is going. It pays off.

"I knew where my pitches were going because I worked on control continuously. I never had a curve ball. If I threw a curve at a batter he'd laugh. But, by being able to pitch the ball hard and where I wanted, I became successful. Ask Hank Greenberg, I struck him out a few times."

—Quoted in the *Sporting News*, March 7, 1951

RUIZ, CHICO

"Bench me or trade me."

—As an Angel; widely attributed

RUNGE, ED

"It's the only occupation where a man has to be perfect the first day on the job and then improve over the years."

—On his profession, as an American League umpire; quoted in *Sports Illustrated*, August 20, 1973

RUNYON, DAMON

"Between things human, it's never 4–1, it's mostly 6–5."

—Widely attributed

"Mathewson pitched against Cincinnati yesterday. Another way of putting it is that Cincinnati lost a game of baseball. The first statement means the same as the second."

—Quoted by Bob Chieger in *Voices of Baseball*

"Pitchers sometimes let their wits go wool gathering."

—Widely quoted

"This is the way old Casey Stengel ran running his home run home to a Giant victory by a score of 5 to 4 in the first game of the World's Series of 1923.

"This is the way old Casey Stengel ran, running his home run home when two were out in the ninth inning and the score was tied and the ball was bounding inside the Yankee yard.

"This is the way—

"His mouth wide open.

"His warped old legs bending beneath him at every stride.

"His arms flying back and forth like those of a man swimming with a crawl stroke.

"His flanks heaving, his breath whistling, his head far back . . .

"The warped old legs, twisted and bent by many a year of baseball campaigning, just barely held out under Casey Stengel until he reached the plate running his home run home."

—In the *New York American*, October 11, 1923

RUPPERT, JACOB

"Close games make me nervous."

—As to why he preferred seeing his team win 10–0 and the line he seems to have been most remembered for

"I found out a long time ago that there is no charity in baseball, and that every club owner must make his own fight for existence."

—On a league profit-sharing plan during the Depression

"Mr. George H. Ruth:
You are hereby notified as follows:
1. That you are unconditionally released.
Jacob Ruppert."

> —Letter supposedly sent to Babe Ruth,
> February 1935; quoted in *Giants of Baseball* by
> Bill Gutman

"There is no charity in baseball. I want to win the pennant every year."

> —As owner, New York Yankees; in *The Giants of the Polo Grounds* by Noel Hynd

"There is no such money in baseball. Ruth is the first ball player to get $80,000, and he will be the last. The trouble with being a club owner is that even if you are a sound businessman in your nonbaseball enterprise—in my case, beer brewing and real estate—you became a fan once you get into baseball. You start doing all sorts of foolish things financially. For me, Ruth's $80,000 contract is 'one of those foolish things.'"

> —Quote unearthed in early 1963 when Mickey
> Mantle and Willie Mays signed for $100,000
> apiece; quoted by Dan Daniel in the March 16,
> 1963, *Sporting News*

"What's the matter with you? Other pitchers win their games 9–3, 10–2. You win yours 2–1, 1–0. Why don't you win your games like the others?"

> —The Yankee owner to pitcher Waite Hoyt

Jacob Ruppert shakes hands with Commissioner Landis, 1923 World Series (*National Baseball Library*)

"When the Yankees score eight runs in the first inning and slowly pull away."

> —The Colonel as owner of the New York
> Yankees (1915–1939), on his idea a of a
> perfect day at the stadium

RUSHIN, STEVE

"I've not yet forgotten the faces of two 10-year-olds straining to peer into an empty Tigers dugout after a game and awed by what they saw: a floor littered with loogies, chaws, Bubble Bubble and snot rockets, prompting one of the boys to whisper, as if seeing the face of God, 'Whoa. *Goobers.*'"

> —"My House," *Sports Illustrated,* August 23,
> 2003

"Take a gander at the wondrous mug of [Don] Zimmer, the Yankees' bench coach: His face looks like a beanbag chair that'd been sat on by a fat guy."

—"October Fest," *Sports Illustrated*, October 13, 1997

RUSKIN, SCOTT

"I don't even pick up a bat. I don't have a bat. I have two batting gloves, but they're only to keep my hands warm."

—As a Pittsburgh rookie reliever on batting; quoted in the June 1990, *Major League Baseball Newsletter*

RUSSELL, LILLIAN

"'Bug' as thus applied I find means a person of peculiar eccentricities, born of frenzy and expressed in wild, incoherent shrieks that develop a monomania called baseballitis."

—"The Rejuventation of a Fan," *Baseball Magazine*, January 1909

"The game is wholesome. Its very vital call is its unquestioned integrity and it gives one the chance to 'smile out loud' under God's clear sky and to take in life-giving breaths of fresh air every time one empties the lungs with a lusty cheer."

—"The Rejuvenation of a Fan"

Lillian Russell (*Library of Congress Prints and Photographs Division*)

RUTH, BABE

"A ballplayer don't have time to read and it isn't good for the eyes. A ballplayer lasts only as long as his legs and eyes . . . if somebody reads a book to me I get more out of it. I memorize nearly all of it; when I read it myself I forget it."

—Ruth, interviewed by Carl Sandberg, whose question was: "At least a million hot ball fans in this country, admirers of yours, believe in the Bible and Shakespeare as the two greatest books ever written, and some of them would like to know if there are any special parts of these books which are favorites of yours?" Reported in *The American Scrapbook* (New York: Wm. H. Wise, 1928)

"A man ought to get all he can earn. A man who knows he's making money for other people ought to get some of the profit he brings in. Don't make any difference if it's baseball or a bank or a vaudeville show. It's business, I tell you. There ain't no sentiment to it. Forget that stuff."

—Quoted in *Babe* by Robert W. Creamer

"A man who has put away his baseball togs after an eventful life in the game must live on his memories, some good, some bad."

—From *The Babe Ruth Story,* by Babe Ruth as told to Bob Considine

"All I can tell them is pick a good one and stick to it. I get back to the dugout and they ask me what it was I hit and I tell them I don't know except it looked good."

—Quoted by Clifton Fadiman in *The American Treasury 1455- 1955*

"As Duke Ellington once said, the Battle of Waterloo was won on the playing fields of Elkton."

—According to Grantland Rice in *The Tumult and the Shouting,* this was the Babe's articulation of the historic remark that the Battle of Waterloo had been won on the playing fields of Eton. Rice added that when pressed, Ruth explained his interpretation this way: "About that Wellington guy I couldn't know. Ellington, yes. As for that Eton business—well, I married my first wife in Elkton [Maryland], and I always hated the goddamn place. It musta stuck."

"As soon as I got out there I felt a strange relationship with the pitcher's mound. It was as if I'd been born out there. Pitching just felt like the most natural thing in the world. Striking out batters was easy."

—On first pitching at age fourteen or fifteen; quoted in *Giants of Baseball,* by Bill Gutman

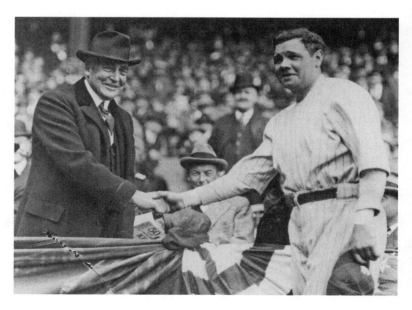

Babe Ruth and Warren G. Harding (*National Baseball Library*)

Babe Ruth with Mascot (*Library of Congress Prints and Photographs, Bain Collection*)

"Aw, everybody knows that game, the day I hit the homer off Charlie Root there in Wrigley Field, the day, October 1, the third game of that 1932 World Series. But right now I want to settle all arguments. I didn't exactly point to any spot, like the flagpole. Anyway, I didn't mean to, I just sorta waved at the whole fence, but that was foolish enough. All I wanted to do was give that thing a ride . . . outa the park . . . anywhere."

> —Quoted by John P. Carmichael in *My Greatest Day in Baseball*

"Ball players should get all they can in the way of salary from their bosses, and there should be no ceiling on salaries."

> —To Jimmy Burns on his way to spring training, 1948, the year he died

"Baseball changes through the years. It gets milder."

> —From *The Babe Ruth Story*, as told to Bob Considine

"Baseball was, is and always will be to me the best game in the world."

> —From *The Babe Ruth Story*

"Cobb is a prick. But he sure can hit. God Almighty, that man can hit."

> —Quoted in William Curran's *Big Sticks*

"Don't quit until every base is uphill."

> —From *The Babe Ruth Story*, as told to Bob Considine

"From now on I intend to organize my own law out there in right field.

"From now on any fan who thinks he has a license to use bad language in the right field bleacher is going to get a fine surprise.

"Anybody who thinks he gets the privilege of calling me all sorts of nasty names when he pays 50 cents to go into the bleachers is in for another thought.

"If any fan in the future uses indecent language, either to me or any other Yankee, I will stop the game, call a policeman, and have the fan thrown out of the park. I am going to be my own law from now on."

> —At a schoolboy baseball rally sponsored by the *New York Telegram*; quoted in the May 30, 1920, *Telegram*

473

"Gee, it's lonesome in the outfield. It's hard to keep awake with nothing to do."

> —On playing the outfield in the majors for the first time; quoted in *Babe: The Legend Comes to Life* by Robert W. Creamer

"He ruined one of the American League's great ball clubs by systematically selling star after star to the rich owners of the Yankees, Col. Jake Ruppert and Col. T. L. Huston."

> —On Harry Frazee, the man who sold him to the Yankees; quoted by Alexander Theroux, in the *Boston Globe*, July 2, 1989

"Hot as hell, ain't it, Prez?"

> —On being introduced to Calvin Coolidge on a particularly hot day at the Washington ball park; quoted by Roger Kahn in *How the Weather Was*, by Robert Creamer in *Babe*, and elsewhere

"How to hit home runs: I swing as hard as I can, and I try to swing right through the ball. In boxing, your fist usually stops when you hit a man, but it's possible to hit so hard that your fist doesn't stop. I try to follow through in the same way. The harder you grip the bat, the more you can swing it through the ball, and the farther the ball will go. I swing big, with everything I've got. I hit big or I miss big. I like to live as big as I can."

> —Quoted by William Safire and Leonard Safir in *Words of Wisdom*

"I bet five thousand dollars on them Harvards. But the Yales win it. I'm off that football business, too."

> —To Grantland Rice, on football betting; quoted in *The Tumult and the Shouting*

"I cried when they took me out of the Polo Grounds."

> —On moving to new Yankee Stadium in 1923; quoted in William Curran's *Big Stick*

"I didn't mean to hit the umpire with the dirt, but I did mean to hit that bastard in the stands. If I make a home run every time I bat, they think I'm all right. If I don't, they think they can call me anything they like."

> —Quoted in *Babe* by Robert W. Creamer

"I don't give a damn about any actors. What good will John Barrymore do you with the bases loaded and two down in a tight ball game. Either I get the money or I don't play!"

> —To Red Sox owner and theatrical producer Harry Frazee, who had said the Babe was asking for more than the great Barrymore; quoted in *Giants of Baseball* by Bill Gutman

"I honestly don't know anybody who wants to live more than I do. It is a driving wish that is always with me these days, a wish that only a person who has been close to death can know and understand."

> —On his illness, from *The Babe Ruth Story*

"I know, but I had a better year than Hoover."

—Reply when a reporter objected that the salary he was demanding was greater than that of President Hoover, 1930. Ruth asked for and got $80,000 a year compared to the president's $75,000. The line appears in many variant forms from the very simple "I had a better year" to this version from the August 10, 1956, *New York Post*: "What the hell has Hoover got to do with it? Besides, I had a better year than he did."

"I suppose you were in the war?"

—On being introduced to Marshal Foch, the great French war hero, while Foch making a tour of the U.S. in the early 1920s

"I thank heaven we have had baseball in this world . . . the kids . . . our national pastime."

—From his words on Babe Ruth Day at Yankee Stadium, 1947

"I wanted to stay in baseball more than I ever wanted anything in my life. But in 1935 there was no job for me, and that embittered me."

—Quoted in Kenneth Richards's *People of Destiny*

"I'd play for half my salary if I would hit in this dump all the time."

—Before the third game of the 1932 World Series, as he and Lou Gehrig put on a slugging show for the folks at Wrigley Field. Gehrig hit seven balls out, Ruth nine. Ruth hollered this line at the Cubs, who were watching.

"If I'd just tried for them dinky singles I would've batted around six hundred."

—Quoted in William Curran's *Big Sticks*

"If it wasn't for baseball, I'd be in either the penitentiary or the cemetery. I have the same violent temper my father and older brother had. Both died of injuries from street fights in Baltimore, fights begun by flare-ups of their tempers."

—Quoted by Fred Lieb in *Baseball As I Have Known It*

"It's hell to get older."

—Comment he began making about 1931

"I've heard people say that the trouble with the world is that we haven't enough great leaders. I think we haven't enough great followers. I have stood side by side with great thinkers—surgeons, engineers, economists, men who deserve a great following—and have heard the crowd cheer me instead. . . .

"I'm proud of my profession. I like to play baseball. I like fans, too. . . . But I think they yelled too loudly and yelled for the wrong man. . . .

"Most of the people who have really counted in my life were not famous. Nobody ever heard of them—except those who knew and loved them. . . . I knew an old priest once. . . . How I envy him. He was not trying to please a crowd. He was merely trying to please his own immortal soul. . . . So fame never came to him.

"I am listed as a famous home-runner, yet beside that obscure priest, who was so good and so wise, I never got to first base."

—Under his byline in the article "Fame—What I Think of It," in the August 1933 *American* magazine

"I've never heard a crowd boo a homer, but I've heard plenty of boos after a strike-out."

—Quoted in *Grand Slams and Fumbles*

"Just one. Whenever I hit a home run, I make certain I touch all four bases."

—When asked if he believed in any superstitions; widely attributed

"Nothing doing on politics."

—On refusing to have his picture taken with Republican presidential nominee Herbert Hoover, 1928

"Paris ain't much of a town."

—On a visit to France with his wife and daughter; quoted by Roger Kahn in *How the Weather Was*

"Scallions are the greatest cure for a batting slump ever invented."

—Comment made while eating his way out of a slump, 1934

"Speaking of my 60 home runs in 1927, they were made before many of the parks had been artificially changed so as to favor the home-run hitter. I hit them into the same parks where, only a decade before, ten or twelve homers were good enough to win the title. They said they livened the ball up for me, and some of the writers called it the jack-rabbit ball. Well, if they put some of the jack in it around the 1927 period, they put the entire rabbit into it in 1947 and at the same time shortened a lot of fences. But my old record has held up."

—From *The Babe Ruth Story* by Babe Ruth

"Thank you very much, ladies and gentlemen. You know how bad my voice sounds. Well, it feels just as bad. . . . There's been so many lively things said about me, I'm glad I had the opportunity to thank everybody. Thank you."

—April 27, 1947, at Yankee Stadium. This is the day that fans observed "Babe Ruth Day" throughout the nation in honor of the seriously ill former "Sultan of Swat." The largest observance was held at the Stadium in New York, where 58,331 persons tendered the Babe the greatest ovation in the history of the national pastime. Barely able to speak, Ruth stood up before a microphone to thank the cheering crowd.

"That last one sounded kind a high to me."

—Questioning the umpire abut three fast pitches that he had not seen

"The Cubs had [censored] my old team-mate Mark Koenig by cutting him for only a measly, [censored] half share of the Series money.

"Well, I'm riding the [censored] out of the Cubs, telling 'em they're the cheapest pack of [censored] crum bums in the world. We've won the first two and now we're in Chicago for the third game. Root is the Cubs' pitcher. I pack one into the stands in the first inning off him, but in the fifth it's tied four to four when I'm up with a man on base. The Chicago fans are giving me hell.

"Root's still in there. He breezes the first two pitches by—both strikes! The mob's tearing down Wrigley Field. I shake my fist after that first strike. After the second, I point my bat at these bellerin' bleachers—right where I aim to park the ball. Root throws it, and I hit that [censored] ball on the nose—right over the [censored] fence for two [censored] runs.

"'How do you like those apples, you [censored, censored, censored],' I yell at Root as I head towards first. By the time I reach home I'm almost falling down I'm laughing so [censored] hard—and that's how it happened."

—At a dinner for Mr. and Mrs. Walter Lippmann in Florida, March 1933, in response to Mrs. Lippmann's question abut his "called homer" in the 1932 Series. This version appears in Grantland Rice's *The Tumult and the Shouting*.

"The only real game, I think, in the world is baseball. As a rule people think that if you give boys a football or a baseball or something like that they naturally became athletes right away.

"But you can't do that in baseball. You've got to start from away down at the bottom, when the boys are six or seven years of age. You can't wait until they're 15 or 16. You've got to let it grow up with you, if you're the boy. And if you try hard enough you're bound to came out on top, just as these boys here have came to the top now."

—From *The Babe Ruth Story* as told to Bob Considine

"The termites have got me."

—To Connie Mack the day before he died of cancer, 1948

"The worst of this is that I no longer can see my penis when I stand up."

—On gaining weight; quoted by Fred Lieb in *Baseball As I Have Known It*

"They'll never build any monuments to Harry Frazee in Boston."

—On the man who sold him to the Yankees

"They're coming out in graves."

—His most famous malapropism

"They were sweet to hit. They were just cousins. Walter Johnson and Grove were just as true as a rifle shot. Johnson was fast, much faster than Grove ever was, but he didn't have a curve and all you had to do was stand up and let him hit your bat. Grove was easy to follow all the way and he supplied the power, too."

—On the greats of his time; quoted by Stan Baumgartner, *Sporting News*, 1948

"What I am, what I have, what I am going to leave behind me—all this I owe to the game of baseball, without which I would have come out of St. Mary's Industrial School in Baltimore a tailor, and a pretty bad one, at that."

—Comment made as he watched the making of *The Babe Ruth Story* in Hollywood; quoted in the *Sporting News* at the time of his death on August 16, 1948

"Yeah, that's why I used to send a taxicab to the Alma Hotel the day you were gonna pitch. I never wanted you to get lost in the subway going to the Stadium."

—To George Earnshaw, who denied being a "cousin" to Babe Ruth, 1948

RUTH, BABE (CONTINUED)

"You know, for me, this is just like an anniversary myself, because, 25 years ago yesterday I pitched my first baseball game in Boston for the Boston Red Sox. [Applause.] So it seems like an anniversary for me, too and I'm surely glad and it's a pleasure for me to come up here and be picked also in the Hall of Fame."

—Speech given on being inducted into the Baseball Hall of Fame, June 12, 1939

"You need a certain number of breaks in baseball and every other calling."

—From *The Babe Ruth Story*

"You've got 10 years ahead of you in the big leagues, Lou. Save your dough. Start one of those trust funds. Every dollar you save will be one more laugh when your home-run days are over."

—To Lou Gehrig; quoted in Jack Sher's October 1948 profile of Gehrig in *Sport*

RUTH, CLAIRE

"Babe would often sit by the phone, waiting for the call that never came. Sometimes, when he couldn't take it any longer, he'd break down, put his head in his hands, and weep."

—Recalling the Babe after his career was over; quoted in *Giants of Baseball* by Bill Gutman

"For a year now the pressure on me has been tremendous. I'm fed up with it."

—Early in the 1974 season as Hank Aaron closed in on Ruth's record of 714 home runs.

RYAN, MIKE

"Last year they had four catchers out hurt and now they're going to bean one."

—As a Phillies catcher on being assigned to catch the first ball of the season from a helicopter

RYAN, NOLAN

"I can't think of anything more humiliating than losing a ballgame to a guy who steals home on you. It happened to me one time against Kansas City. I had a 2-and-2 count on the hitter—and Amos Otis broke from third. The pitch was a ball and he slid in safe. I felt like a nickel."

—As an Angels pitcher; quoted in the *Los Angeles Herald-Examiner*, July 13, 1977

Nolan Ryan (*Texas Rangers*)

S

SAGE, GEORGE H.

"The origins of modern baseball are shrouded in history, but it is a well-established fact that baseball was the first professional sport to appeal to the masses."

—From *Sport and American Society: Selected Readings,* 1970

SAIN, JOHNNY

"You have no idea the pressure a young pitcher is under. I've walked out to the mound in the middle of an inning and the pitcher couldn't tell me his telephone number. By walking out, you calm him down. . . . Yelling at a boy from the bench is confusing and ridiculous."

—As a pitching coach; widely quoted

SALINGER, J. D.

"My brother Allie had this left-handed fielder's mitt. He was left-handed. The thing that was descriptive about it, though, was that he had poems written all over the fingers and the pocket and everywhere. In green ink. He wrote them on it so that he'd have something to read when he was in the field and nobody was up at bat."

—Holden Caulfield, in *The Catcher in the Rye*

SALISBURY, LUKE

"Baseball is more like a novel than like a war. It is like an ongoing hundred-year work of art, peopled with thousands of characters, full of improbable events, anecdotes, folklore and numbers."

—From his *The Answer Is Baseball,* 1989

SAMUELSON, PAUL

"A rule was not made in heaven that the swag was to be divided the way it has been. As the rules change, it will be divided differently, and baseball players will be rewarded in the same fashion as Hollywood stars, hotshot ad copywriters and people who can guess what the future price of soybeans will be. The lucky recipients of these muscular skills will begin receiving some of these economic rents."

—On free agency; quoted in the *New Times,* June 10, 1977

SANCHEZ, ANIBAL

"It's a little crazy. I wasn't sure what he was at first, but it's always nice to see him because it means we usually have a lead. Fans in Venezuela get really excited in the stands, but there is no Mr. Celery. The people there are really loud with noisemakers and signs. They yell the whole game. It's that way in all Latin countries. But no, no Mr. Celery. If they did, it might be a man dressed as a plantain."

—The Red Sox righthander on Class A Wilmington mascot Mr. Celery. John Erhardt, "Year in Quotes," *Baseball Prospectus,* 2005.

SANDERS, DEION

"There is always something you have to work on in baseball. You never have control of the situation. The pitcher does."

—On why the Atlanta Falcons' number one draft pick and a Class AAA baseball player for the New York Yankees thought football was easier than baseball; quoted in *USA Today,* July 28, 1989

SANDERS, SAMUEL

"I'm a fanatic. Baseball is really what I think about all the time. And Itzhak lives on Riverside Drive in the same house where Babe Ruth lived. He thinks maybe in the same apartment. It drives him wild to think he might be taking a shower where Babe Ruth did."

—The classical pianist on Itzhak Perlman, the renowned violinist, at a University of Kansas recital to which Dan Quisenberry showed up with signed baseballs inscribed "My best, to the best." According to the *New York Times,* the dean of the school said they had arranged the appearance by Quisenberry in place of the customary bouquets. They all gathered at a reception nearby, and the talk naturally got down to serious baseball. "We talked mostly about last season," Sanders reported. "Itzhak and I are terrific fans. I grew up in the Bronx, a block from Yankee Stadium. I played stickball in the street in 1961, the year Roger Maris hit the 61 home runs. I always knew when he hit another one. You could tell just from the noise."

SANTO, RON

"Funny, but there is less pressure being three or four games behind in a pennant race than three or four ahead. Last year, we kept looking back over our shoulder."

—As a Cubs infielder; widely quoted

SARANDON, SUSAN

"Never root for a team whose uniforms have elastic stretch waistbands. They are unsightly and without grace. I would as soon see Baryshnikov dance in a leisure suit. It is the reason the Cubs never make it—the problem is in their waistbands, not their starting rotation.

"Always root for a team whose uniforms have belt loops. Good belt loops are critical.

". . . Listen to me—you cannot root for any team that plays on plastic grass or under a roof. The biorhythms get jammed amidst all those petroleum by-products. Domed stadia are a symbol of the violation of the ozone layer."

> —"May Annie Savoy's Red-Hot Rules for Better World Series Viewing," *TV Guide,* October 15–21, 1988

SAROYAN, WILLIAM

"Baseball is caring. Player and fan alike must care, or there is no game. If there's no game, there's no pennant race and no World Series. And for all any of us know there might soon be no nation at all. It is good to care—in any dimension. More Americans put their caring into baseball than into anything else I can think of—and most of them put at least a little of it there. Baseball can be trusted, as great art can, and bad art can't."

> —Quoted from *Sports Illustrated* and used in a mass mailing to *Sports Illustrated* advertisers, June 8, 1959

"Two events are supremely beautiful: the strikeout and the home run. Each is a difficult and unlikely thing flawlessly achieved before your eyes."

> —In a letter to *Life,* August 23, 1954

SASSER, MACKEY

"I called the doctor and he told me the contraptions were an hour apart."

> —As New York Mets catcher on how he knew his wife was in labor, 1988

SCHAAP, DICK

"It was the first time a game has ever been called on account of candy bars."

> —On the occasion of Yankee fans throwing their free Reggie candy bars down on the field after a Jackson home run

SCHACHT, AL

"They have crooked arms. They throw crooked, they walk crooked and they think crooked. They even wear their clothes crooked. You have to figure they're a little crazy."

> —On left-handed pitchers, oft-quoted

SCHAEFER, WILLIAM DONALD

"You look at prestige, you look at jobs, you look at the things it generates in a city. You won't be able to replace them, and once they're gone, they're gone."

> —As governor of Maryland, on the Orioles, *Reason,* May 1990

SCHANBERGER, E. L.

"Reports from this camp indicate that he has some good prospects among his rookies. For one there is a youngster named Frank Ruth, a Baltimore boy, who has been the pitching mainstay of a local industrial school team for years. He has shown Dunn so much that the manager makes the bold statement that he will stick with the team this season, both on account of his hitting and his portside flinging."

> —Report to the *Sporting News* by one of its correspondents on a rookie at spring training for the Baltimore Orioles. The report appeared on March 19, 1914, and was the first time that Babe Ruth's name appeared in the *Sporting News,* albeit as "Frank"; quoted by Lee Allen in *Cooperstown Corner*

SCHEINBLUM, RICHIE

"The only good thing about playing in Cleveland is you don't have to make road trips there."

> —As a Cleveland Indian

SCHILLING, CURT

"Mystique and aura? Those are dancers at a nightclub."

> —As Diamondbacks pitcher, when asked on the eve of the 2001 World Series about the prospect of facing the storied New York Yankees (the D-backs went on to win the Series in seven games); quoted in *Sports Illustrated,* January 26, 2004

"The stress level of pitching in a major league game is 10 times that of pitching in the minor leagues. If you have a kid on a limited pitch count all the way through the minors, and then when he gets to the big leagues you want him to throw 150 pitches a game, it's just not going to work. Pitch counts for the most part are incredibly overrated."

> —*Baseball Digest,* September 1999

SCHMIDT, MIKE

"Anytime you think you have the game conquered, the game will turn around and punch you right in the nose."

> —Hall of Fame Collection

"I could ask the Phillies to keep me on to add to my statistics but my love for the game won't let me do that."

> —On retiring suddenly on May 29, 1989. At the time, Tom Boswell called him "The best all-around baseball player of the last 15 years, and the greatest third baseman of all time."

"I don't think I can get into my deep inner thoughts about hitting. It's like talking about religion."

> —Said to Roger Angell in *Late Innings*

"I go into the book store and see all these baseball books. This one from a guy who has played a year and a half. That one from a guy who has played 4$^{1}/_{2}$ years."

> —On why in his seventeenth year in the game he was still waiting to start his autobiography; quoted in *USA Today,* July 14, 1989

"Pete Rose is the most likable arrogant person I've ever met."

—Widely quoted

"If you're associated with the Philadelphia media or town, you look for negatives. . . . I don't know if there's something in the air or something about their upbringing or they have too many hoagies, too much cream cheese."

—Quoted in *USA Today*, March 9, 1989

"They read their sports pages, know their statistics and either root like hell or boo our butts off. I love it. Give me vocal fans—pro or con—over the tourist-types who show up in Houston or Montreal and just sit there."

—As a Philly on Philadelphia fans; quoted in the *Los Angeles Times*, March 31, 1975

"You're trying your damnedest, you strike out and they boo you. I act like it doesn't bother me, like I don't hear anything the fans say, but the truth is I hear every word of it and it kills me."

—Widely quoted

SCHOENDIENST, RED

"Run everything out and be in by twelve."

—The St. Louis Cardinals manager, to his players, 1968

SCHOENSTEIN, RALPH

"Lori now felt that America was divided into two groups: those who loved baseball and jerks. She was shocked to hear from her sister, who had gone to study art in Oakland, that when Eve-Lynn had mentioned Keith Hernandez at a party one night, the people there did not know if she was talking about a drummer or the president of Mexico."

—*Diamonds for Lori and Me* (New York: Beech Tree Books, William Morrow, 1988)

SCHOTT, MARGE

"I don't believe it. Snow this morning and now this. I feel cheated. This is not supposed to happen to us. Not in Cincinnati. This is our day. Our history. Our tradition. Nobody feels more than me."

—The Reds owner on the death of umpire John McSherry and the postponement of the game after the seventh pitch of Opening Day, April 1, 1996. Schott will later apologize and send flowers. But the *Dayton Daily News* will report on the 28th that the flowers she sends were given to her by a television station covering the Reds.

"They never ask for a raise."

—On why pets are lovable, after death of her Saint Bernard, *Newsweek*, August 10, 1991

"Why do we need so many scouts? All they do is sit around and watch baseball games."

—To former Reds GM Bill Bergesch in 1985; quoted in *USA Today Baseball Weekly*, June 5–11, 1996

SCHUERHOLZ, JOHN

"George Brett could roll out of bed on Christmas morning and hit a line drive."

—As Royals GM; quoted in the *Washington Times*, June 15, 1989

483

SCHULIAN, JOHN

"A mouse studying to become a rat."

—Describing Billy Martin; quoted widely at the time of Martin's death in late 1989

SCHULZ, CHARLES

"Beethoven can't really be great because his picture isn't on a bubble gum card."

—Lucy to Charlie Brown, *Peanuts*

"Hold on to the ball until he goes away."

—Linus's advice to Charlie Brown when confronted with a batter who hits a home run every time he comes to bat, *Peanuts*

"I hit a home run in the ninth inning, and we won! I was the hero!!"

—Charlie Brown hits his first home run after forty-three years as the comics' most hapless athlete, *Peanuts*, March 30, 1993

"I think we'd better change our signals. . . . One finger will mean the high straight ball, and two fingers will mean the low straight ball!"

—Catcher to pitcher, *Saturday Evening Post* cartoon, April 15, 1950

"One thing I do well is hit fly balls. There's nothing quite like being able to hit towering flies. It's not like writing Beethoven's Ninth, but it's definitely in the top two."

—Quoted in "Good ol' Charlie Schultz," *Sports Illustrated*, December 23, 1985

SCHUMACHER, GARY

"The atom bomb secrets have been sold to Spalding."

—On the rabbit ball of the early 1950s

SCHUMAN, WILLIAM

"Baseball was my youth. Had I been a better catcher, I might never have become a musician."

—Schuman, a major U.S. composer, was president of the Juilliard School of Music (1935–1961) and in 1962 became president of Lincoln Center for the Performing Arts, New York City; quoted in Martin Gardner, *The Annotated Casey at the Bat* (New York: Bramhall House, 1967)

SCHWED, FRED, JR.

"'Box scores.' Only the sophisticated will be able to decipher them. The number of people with the special knowledge to do this is limited, on this continent, to a bare forty or fifty million."

—*How to Watch a Baseball Game* (New York: Harper Brothers, 1957)

SCOTT, GEORGE

"When you're hitting the ball, it comes at you looking like a grapefruit. When you're not, it looks like a black-eyed pea."

—Quoted in *Grand Slam and Fumbles*

SCULLY, VIN

"Football is to baseball as blackjack is to bridge. One is the quick jolt, the other the deliberate, slow-paced game of skill. But never was a sport more ideally suited to television than baseball. It's all there in front of you. It's theatre, really. The star is the spotlight on the mound, the supporting cast fanned out around him, the mathematical precision of the game moving with the kind of inevitability of Greek tragedy. With the Greek chorus in the bleachers!"

> —In the *Los Angeles Times*, June 20, 1976

"He pitches as though he's double-parked."

> —On watching fast-working Bob Gibson of the St. Louis Cardinals mow down the Dodgers, 4–0, in a game; quoted in *Baseball Digest*, September 1972

"How good was Stan Musial? He was good enough to take your breath away."

> —Dodger telecast, summer of 1989

"I really love baseball. The guys and the game. And I love the challenge of describing things. The only thing I hate—and I know you have to be realistic and pay the bills in this life—is the loneliness of the road."

> —Widely quoted

"I would think that the mound at Dodger Stadium right now is the loneliest place in the world."

> —As Sandy Koufax stood four strikes away from a perfect game, broadcasting from Dodger Stadium, September 9, 1965

"It's a mere moment in a man's life between an All-Star Game and an old-timers game."

> —Widely quoted

"It's a passing of a great American institution. It is sad. I really and truly feel that. It will leave a vast window, to use a Washington word, where people will not get major league baseball, and I think that's a tragedy."

> —As long-time announcer on NBC's *Game of the Week* telecasts, reflecting on the end of a thirty-two-year weekend tradition as CBS and ESPN take over coverage of major league baseball; quoted in the *Sporting News*, October 9, 1989, from his last Game of the Week broadcast

"It's easier to pick off a fast runner than to pick off a lazy runner."

> —From a collection of favorite baseball phrases on fastball.com (June 1, 2001)

"People will forever say to me, 'I love to hear your voice because it reminds me of when I heard it a long time ago. It reminds me of summer nights in the backyard with my dad,' or fishing or something."

> —Quoted in the *St. Petersburg Times*, May 17, 2002

"[Jackie] Robinson was by far the most exciting player I have ever seen. There is only one guy in baseball who even comes close and that is Willie Mays."

> —*The Sporting News Chronicle of 20th Century Sport*

"The Yankees have done it. They have marched through Georgia and it seems to me history told us about that once before, the last time led by Sherman, tonight by Joe Torre."

> —From CBS Radio; quoted in the *Washington Post*, October 26, 1996. Leonard Shapiro of the *Post* commented: "Sportswriting 101 teaches that any comparison between games and war be avoided. And yet, coming from Scully, doing the Series play-by-play for CBS Radio, it provided the perfect ending to a game exceeded in drama perhaps only by the events of the previous night, when the Yankees won in 10 innings."

"With radio . . . you come into the booth, and there's an empty canvas. And you get all your paint and brushes, and you mix your paints. And then you have a broad swath here and fine line there. And at the end of three hours, you say, 'Well, that's the best I can do today.' On television, you walk in and the picture's already there. So what you're doing is shading, subtle things."

> —*Boston Globe* obituary for Scully, November 25, 2003

SEAVER, TOM

"If the Mets can win the World Series, the United States can get out of Viet Nam."

> —Hall of Fame Collection, 1969

"If you don't think baseball is a big deal, don't do it. But if you do it, do it right."

> —On a player who had dissipated his talent; quoted in *The Suitors of Spring* by Pat Jordan

"In baseball, my theory is to strive for consistency, not to worry about the 'numbers.' If you dwell on statistics, you get shortsighted; if you aim for consistency, the numbers will be there at the end. My job isn't to strike guys out; it's to get them out, sometimes by striking them out."

> —*New York Times* interview, January 11, 1976

"Miracle, my eye."

> —On the Mets' incomparable 1969 season

"My children will be able to take their children to the Hall of Fame and say, 'There's your grandfather. He was pretty good at what he did.' It's something that solidifies a family."

> —*Chicago Tribune*, August 2, 1992

"The good rising fast ball is the best pitch in baseball."

> —Quoted by Walter Alston in his *Complete Baseball Handbook*

"Whenever a player raises the top salary in any sport, it has to help everybody below. The owners might not want to admit it, but it's absurd to think it won't help. The one thing it definitely does is give us a better understanding of our worth. Pitchers with comparable records and ability have a valid point in seeking a comparable salary."

> —Interview in the *Los Angeles Times*, January 12, 1974

SEINFELD, JERRY

"Like anyone in this city waits to be given the right before they start bragging."

> —On hearing that 2000's Subway Series between the Mets and Yankees was about "bragging rights" in New York; quoted in the *Baltimore Sun*, September 9, 2001

SEITZER, KEVIN

"I opened me eyes to see if I was in heaven or if I was in Milwaukee."

> —Milwaukee Brewer infielder, after being hit in the face by a pitch from New York Yankee pitcher Melido Perez; quoted in *Sports Illustrated*, August 16, 1994

SELIG, BUD

"Baseball is in the middle stages of what I absolutely believe will be a very, very strong renaissance by the turn of the century."

> —Quoted in the *Philadelphia Daily News*, August 11, 1998, shortly after taking over as commissioner

"I congratulate Barry Bonds for establishing a new career home run record. Barry's achievement is noteworthy and remarkable. While the issues which have swirled around this record will continue to work themselves toward resolution, today is a day for congratulations on a truly remarkable achievement.

> —In a prepared statement released on August 7, 2007, the night Barry Bonds eclipsed Hank Aaron's home-run record with No. 756

"The problem in sports marketing, particularly in baseball, is you're always walking a very sensitive line. Nobody loves tradition and history as much as I do."

> —On the uproar over the decision, revoked one day later, to advertise the movie *Spider-Man 2* on the base covers at a major league games; reported in *Time*, May 17, 2004

SERVICE, ROBERT W.

I'd rather, I can tell you flat,
When for Parnassus bound,
Have authored "Casey at the Bat"
Than odes of Ezra Pound.

> —The Canadian master rhymer, from the poem "Low Brow"

SEWELL, JOE

"I'm indeed happy I'm among the present today to get this award. . . . I would like to see the greed, selfishness and hate eliminated from our game. These elements shouldn't exist as they do today."

> —On being inducted into the Hall of Fame, August 8, 1977

SEWELL, RIP

"First the players want a hamburger, and the owners gave them a hamburger. Then they wanted a filet mignon, and they gave them a filet mignon. Then they wanted the whole damn cow, and now that they got the cow they want a pasture to put him in. You just can't satisfy them, and I have no sympathy for any of them."

> —The former Pirates pitcher on modern-day players; widely quoted

SEYMOUR, HAROLD

"To ascertain who invented baseball would be the equivalent of trying to locate the discoverer of fire."

> —From *Baseball: The People's Game*

"And have is have, however men do catch."
—*King John*

"And what a pitch . . . !"
—*Henry VI*, Part I

"And when he caught it, he let it go again."
—*Coriolanus*

"And watch'd him how he singled . . ."
—*Henry VI*, Part III

"Foul . . . ?" —*The Tempest*

"He comes the third time home . . ."
—*Coriolanus*

William Shakespeare (*Library of Congress Prints and Photographs Division*)

"Hence! home . . . get you home . . ."
—*Julius Caesar*

"He's safe."—*Measure for Measure*

"I am safe."—*Antony and Cleopatra*

"I'll catch it ere it come to ground."
—*Macbeth*

"I shall catch the fly . . ."—*Henry V*

"I thank you for your good counsel. Come, my coach!—*Hamlet*

"Look to the plate."—*Romeo and Juliet*

"My heels are at your command; I will run."
—*The Merchant of Venice*

"O my offense is rank, it smells to heaven."
—*Hamlet*

"O, 'tis fair . . . " —*Troilus and Cressida*

"Sweet sacrifice."—*Henry VIII*

"That one error fills him with faults."—*The Two Gentlemen of Verona*

"There is three umpires in this matter . . ."
—*The Merry Wives of Windsor*

"They that . . . pitch will be defiled."—*Much Ado About Nothing*

"Thy seat is up . . . high."—*Richard II*

"What wretched errors . . . !"—*Sonnets*

"When time is ripe—which will be suddenly, I'll steal . . . "—*Henry IV,* Part I

"Your play needs no excuse."—*A Midsummer Night's Dream*

> —From several collections, including one distributed by the Folger Shakespeare Library in Washington, compiled by Edward F. Murphy, who teaches corrective mathematics at St. Rose of Lima School, Manhattan. An item from the July 21, 1981, *USA Today*

underscores the role of the Bard in baseball: "San Diego's 17 runs against Pittsburgh Tuesday night set a club record for most runs in a nine-inning game. Afterward, manager Jack McKeon quoted from Shakespeare's *Othello* when talking about his club's resurgence and the sudden spirited play of LF [left fielder] Chris James. 'How poor are they that have not patience,' McKeon said. When asked what play that was from, McKeon responded, 'Pickoff.'"

SHAMSKY, ART

"I don't know anything about baseball. I just close my eyes and swing. Sometimes it hits the bat."

> —The Met; quoted in Maury Allen's *The Incredible Mets.*

SHAUGHNESSY, DAN

"It's not just a ball game, you bum, it's art, religion."

> —Writing in the *Indianapolis Star;* quoted in the literature put out by Peter C. Bjarkman, Ph.D., "The Baseball Professor"

"The Red Sox truly are the boys of summer; it's always been the fall that's given them trouble."

> —In his *The Curse of the Bambino,* 1990

"The red, white and blue bunting is in place— a sure sign that today is special. Bunting is reserved for the Opener and for post season play, and in Boston we haven't seen much of

the stuff in October. In New York City, middle-aged men associate bunting with golden autumn afternoons at Yankee Stadium. Here, a Fenway photo with bunting in the background usually means Opening Day."

> —"Essay on the Red Sox, Opening Day, 1990," *Boston Globe,* April 9, 1990

SHAW, GEORGE BERNARD

"America's tragedy."

> —What he dubbed baseball; quoted by David Q. Voight in *America Through Baseball*

"As far as I can grasp it, it [baseball] combines the best features of that primitive form of cricket (the only tolerable one) known as tip and run, with those of lawn tennis, puss-in-the-corner, and Handel's 'Messiah,' and it surpasses them all (except Handel), in giving scope for the lighter human faculties of rhetoric, irony, and eloquent emotional appeal.

"I do not know how it is in America; but in England the audience always stands up for the Hallelujah Chorus. In America during a game of baseball it stands up for the seventh inning."

—"An American Baseball Game," North American Newspaper Alliance, 1924; reprinted in Karl J. Holzknecht, *A Freshman Miscellany* (New York: Prentice-Hall, 1930)

"As I left the ground one of my courteous hosts expressed a hope that I would come again. When a man asks you to come and see baseball played twice it sets you asking yourself why you want to see it played once. That is a totally unanswerable question. It is a mad world.

"But I will not deny that I enjoyed the afternoon. I may have the makings of a fan in me for all I know."

—"An American Baseball Game"

"Baseball has the great advantage over cricket of being sooner ended."

—"An American Baseball Game"

"I shall never forget that Mister McGraw, in whom I at last discovered the real authentic, MOST REMARKABLE MAN IN AMERICA, shook hands with me. He even shook hands with the Duke [of York], but though he was very nice to us there is no denying that he played us both right off the stage."

—"An American Baseball Game"

George Bernard Shaw (*Library of Congress Prints and Photographs Division*)

"Who is this Baby Ruth? And what does she do?"

—To an American journalist, in Tom Meany, *Babe Ruth*

SHAW, IRWIN

"Gas stations, parking lots, and grocery shops, stood on remembered fields, where you shagged flies and slid home with the winning run."

—On Brooklyn; cited in *Baseball: The People's Game* by Harold Seymour and elsewhere, from *Voices of a Summer Day*

"The sounds were the same through the years—the American sounds of summer, the tap of bat against ball, the cries of the infielders, the wooden plump of the ball into catchers' mitts, the umpires calling 'Strike three and you're out.' The generations circled the bases, the dust rose for forty years as runners slid in from third, dead boys hit doubles, famous men made errors at shortstop, forgotten friends tapped the clay from their spikes with their bats as they stepped into the batter's box, coaches' voices warned, across the decades, 'Tag up, tag up!' on fly balls. The distant, mortal innings of boyhood and youth . . ."

—*Voices of a Summer Day*

SHEA, BILL

"Families go to ballparks and that is why baseball is still our national game."

—As a Mets executive; widely quoted

"Oh, until about five minutes after I'm dead."

—When asked how long Shea Stadium would carry his name; quoted in *Joy in Mudville* by George Vecsey. Shea died in 1991.

SHECTER, LEONARD

"Mantle was never much of a student of baseball. Born with marvelous skills, he played it intuitively, never having to pay much attention to what was going on."

—From *The Jocks*

"The manager was fired twice, but was hired again on the grounds that he's a sound baseball man. A sound baseball man is anybody who has been fired twice."

—From *The Jocks*

SHEED, WILFRID

"Baseball is not a set of isolated explosions like football, but a steady, timeless pleasure that builds as gracefully as it plays—and can only have one climax.

"Do not mess with it, gentlemen."

—From "Sliding for Dollars: The Split Season of 1981," in *Baseball and Lesser Sports* (New York: HarperCollins, 1991). Sheed is lamenting the playoffs.

"Forget what you have seen on TV; nothing in life so far has prepared you for that first squint down the ramp—at the impossibly green grass and the golden patch of infield and the figures in white moving across it. It is your first glimpse of perfection, and from then on even the rank smells of mustard and grade Z beef will be transubstantiated by it, and the hum of the crowd will sound like a choir of angels, every time you enter a ballpark. And perfection only becomes more so as the home team explodes out of the dugout and the play begins."

—From the essay "The Game That Never Ends," in John Weiss, *The Face of Baseball* (Charlottesville, Va.: Thomasson-Grant, 1990)

"It's *baseball*—big-league baseball. Which meant, if all else failed, that you at least got to see the most elegant practice sessions before the game to be found in any sport, including music.

"Offhand, I can't think of any other sport, except maybe billiards, where the practice sessions are worth the price of admission."

> —*My Life as a Fan* (New York: Simon & Schuster, 1993)

"Such is the sweep of baseball history that it picks up for you in your absence and fills you in upon your return like a chatty landlady . . . who is always bursting with news for you."

> —*My Life as a Fan* (New York: Simon & Schuster, 1993)

"The Dodgers clinching the pennant in 1941 filled me with the kind of elation that one allegedly gets just before an epileptic fit: little did I know that I would have to live for such moments for the next fifteen years. For Dodger fans, the pennant race was inevitably the spree and the World Series (or playoff) was the hangover."

> —From *My Life as a Fan;* quoted by André Bernard in *American Scholar,* autumn 2000

SHEFFIELD, GARY

"You look at this organization from the outside and you think first class, first class, first class. But it's not a family-oriented team. In L.A., wives can fly on the plane; with the Yankees, they can't. With other teams, the wives always have functions to bring them together. Not here. You don't know what half the wives look like."

> —On the Yankees, in a *New York* magazine article, August 2005. He also said of the team: "This is the first team I've been on where no one sits at their locker. It's where you build your chemistry, just talking about life. I'm used to having six chairs around me, but here if there are six chairs, then there's going to be 20 reporters. People here are having me sign a dozen balls and two jerseys 10 minutes before the games."

"Why shouldn't I tell the truth? I ain't trying to get no Pepsi commercial."

> —In explaining why he speaks so freely, in a *New York* magazine article, August 2005

SHELLENBACK, FRANK

"They think it was a dangerous pitch. On the contrary, it was one of the safest. That's because you could control it exceptionally well. Look back at the great spitball pitchers—fellows like Burleigh Grimes, Red Faber, Jack Quinn, Clarence Mitchell and Bill Doak. They all had superlative control.

"The spitter was the unfortunate victim of a furor. There was a tremendous hue and cry at the time about freak deliveries of any kind. And there were dangerous ones like the emery ball, the shine ball and the mud ball. Few pitchers knew where they were going and they endangered the lives and livelihood of the hitters. But I'll always say that the spitter was as harmless as a change of pace is today."

> —The once great Pacific Coast League spitballer; quoted in the *Sporting News,* March 25, 1953

SHEPHERD, JEAN

"Being a White Sox fan meant measuring victory in terms of defeat. A 6–5 defeat was a good day. A big rally was Wally Moses doubling down the right-field line."

> —SABR Collection

"Bullfrog Bill Dietrich was a symbol of White Sox frustration. He had a 7–15 record one year and actually held out because it was a good year for him. The fans would watch him shake off two signs from the catcher and break up. They knew he had only two pitches—slow curve and wild fast ball."

> —Commonly quoted

"If I were going to storm a pillbox, going to sheer, utter, certain death, and the colonel said, 'Shepherd, pick six guys,' I'd pick six White Sox fans, because they have known death every day of their lives and it holds no terror for them."

> —This is the original quote from the late comedian. It is often recalled in an abbreviated form: "If I was going to storm a pillbox, I'd pick six White Sox fans, because they have known death every day of their lives and it holds no terror for them." The original appeared in the *Chicago Tribune,* June 26, 1991.

SHERIDAN, PAT

"You can ask your kid, 'Do you want to go to the Skydome or Europe.'"

> —The Detroit outfielder on the $6.50 hot dog and $3.50 beer at Toronto's new Skydome; quoted in Tracy Ringolsby's June 18, 1980 column in the *Dallas Morning News*

SHIBE, BENJAMIN F.

"If money talks it is hard to understand how silence is golden."

> —Philadelphia Athletics owner; quoted in *Sporting Life,* May 20, 1905

SHIELDS, MARK

"Among the luckiest breaks of my life was to be born and raised in a loving family of Boston Red Sox fans. As a Red Sox fan, you learn early that life will not work out, that the Boss's pampered nephew—not the deserving night-school graduate—gets the coveted promotion, that the sweet, freckle-faced girl next door will get passed over for homecoming queen."

> —His column of October 26, 2004

"I once sat next to Hank Aaron on an airplane. He was not huge. His playing weight was 180 pounds and he stood just 6 feet. Unlike professional basketball players and football players, whose size is a dead giveaway, baseball players for the longest time looked like somebody else in the elevator or in your carpool.

"But in the last 15 years, baseball sluggers have looked less and less like the guy next door and more and more like the Incredible Hulk."

> —His syndicated column, March 14, 2006

SHIELDS, MARK (CONTINUED)

"In 2005, for the first time in 33 years, Washington, D.C., will have its own Major League Baseball team. The former Montreal Expos will be reborn as the Washington Nationals. This is good news obviously for the people in and around Washington, but it may be even better news for the people of the nation. Why? The country and its capital city especially have much to learn from baseball, a sport that is the very antithesis of influence-peddling and special privileges. Neither a six-figure soft money contribution nor the best-wired lobbyist on K Street can bend the rules: Three strikes, and you're out."

— His column of December 28, 2004

"Why does the usually excellent ESPN use time and tape each night to show all the home runs hit that day? Home runs almost all look the same. Baseball's most exciting hit is not the home run; it is the triple."

— His column of May 30, 2006

SHIFLETT, DAVE

"Baseball is something of a ballet, the trouble is that the music is substandard (they use pretty much the same score at the hockey rink) and the performers often spit tobacco juice all over the place. It is interesting to watch the coaches send signals to their players, which they do by squinting, twitching their noses and grabbing their body parts."

— Editor, *Rocky Mountain News;* quoted from *Houston Chronicle,* April 29, 1990

"Reading about baseball is a lot more interesting than reading about chess, but you have to wonder: Don't any of these guys ever go fishing?"

— *Houston Chronicle,* April 29, 1990

SHOR, TOOTS

"I don't know if I'm making a mistake, but I'm raising my kid as a Giant fan."

— Widely quoted

"I have a son and I make him watch the Mets. I want him to know life. It's a history lesson. He'll understand the Depression."

— Hall of Fame Collection, 1962

"It shows what you can accomplish if you stay up all night drinking whiskey all the time."

— On the Hall of Fame induction of Whitey Ford and Micky Mantle, Hall of Fame Collection, 1974

"Scuse me, somebody important just came in."

— To Sir Alexander Fleming, discoverer of penicillin, after spying Mel Ott coming through the door of his restaurant; widely quoted

SHORT, ROBERT E.

"Naturally the quality will drop off, but heck, there's a top and bottom to every manure pile."

— The late Washington Senators owner on his belief that there should be forty major league teams

"We need great players and these guys are controversial. With McLain pitching, even if we have a bad team, they'll come to see him because he's a face. Ted Williams is a face. Flood is a face. Frank Howard is a face. Without Frank Howard last season, we wouldn't have drawn flies."

—As Senators owner on acquiring controversial players (Denny McLain and Curt Flood) for the 1971 season; quoted in the *Washington Post*, November 29, 1970

SHRIVER, CHUCK

"The beauty and joy of baseball is not having to explain it."

—Cubs public relations man; widely quoted

SHUBA, GEORGE

"I don't read fiction. I read other stuff, about atomic bombs and 'I Was a Prisoner of the Reds,' stuff like that. You can learn something from them. When I was a kid, I used to read fiction. In the stories, the fellow would always hit a home run in the ninth inning to win the game. Since then, I have found out that things don't happen that way in real life. So I don't read fiction any more."

—As a Dodger, *Sporting News*, April 27, 1955

SIDEY, HUGH

"He may be the most openly avid sports fan ever to occupy the White House. The magical perquisites of the Presidency have opened the floodgates of five decades of stored-up sports yearning, squirreled away by a Mittyish man who right now might trade Air Force One for the honor of having spit in his glove and pitched a no-hitter or having rifled the pass down-field for the winning Rose Bowl score."

—On President Nixon; writing in *Life*

SIGNS, PLAQUES, AND SCOREBOARD NOTATIONS

"And they still stink."

—During the 1920s and '30s, when Philadelphia Phillies inhabited the Baker Bowl, the fence in the right field was adorned by a giant advertisement for soap that read: "The Phillies Use Lifebuoy." This only encouraged fans to add this sour retort, recalled in 2007, when the Phillies prepared to celebrate their 10,000th loss as a ballclub in the summer of 2007.

AVOID 5 O'CLOCK SHADOW

—Gem blade sign which adorned the Green Monster in Fenway Park before it was painted green in 1947

BABY RUTH

—Sign once outside Wrigley Field on the roof of a building outside the right-field fence. Its significance is spelled out by Michael Benson in his *Ballparks of North America:* "It came down during the Durocher years, but till then it was rumored by fans under nine to be a marker commemorating the landing spot of the most mythological of Ruthian homers."

BASEBALL LIKE IT OUGHTA BE

—Sign in Shea Stadium

BILLY MARTIN. ALWAYS NO. 1

—The marquee at Yankee Stadium, December 26, 1989

DOUBLEDAY FIELD
WHERE BASEBALL
WAS INVENTED AND
FIRST PLAYED IN 1839

—New York State Highway sign which long-adorned Doubleday Field in Cooperstown, New York

CLUBHOUSE CREDO

What you see here
What you hear here
What you say here
Let it stay here
When you leave here.

—Universal clubhouse instruction which is termed unwritten but does, in fact, appear in black and white on many clubhouse walls. It was the violation of this credo which was at the basis of the strong criticism that attached itself to Jim Bouton's best-selling *Ball Four.*

EACH 24 HOURS, THE WORLD TURNS OVER ON SOMEONE WHO IS SITTING ON TOP OF IT.

—Sign spotted in Detroit manager Sparky Anderson's office, 1984

EXTRAORDINARY ACHIEVEMENT AWARD TO BILLY MARTIN, FOR HAVING REACHED THE AGE OF 50 WITHOUT BEING MURDERED BY SOMEONE . . . TO THE AMAZEMENT OF ALL WHO KNOW HIM.

—Plaque placed in Billy Martin's office, 1978; quoted by Murray Chass, "The Money Players," in *The Yankees* by Dave Anderson, Murray Chass, Robert Creamer, and Harold Rosenthal, 1979

HE THAT WILL NOT REASON IS A BIGOT
HE THAT CANNOT REASON IS A FOOL, AND
HE THAT DARES NOT REASON IS A SLAVE.

—Sign which appeared over the desk of Branch Rickey

HIT SIGN—WIN SUIT

—Sign placed by Abe Stark, clothier and borough president of Brooklyn and placed at the base of the right-field wall at Ebbets Field (below the screen) and protected/defended by Dixie Walker, Carl Furillo, and a host of visiting-team right fielders. "Trouble was," wrote Dick Young in the *New York Post* in 1983, "in order to hit the narrow painted sign along the base of the scoreboard in right center, one had to bang a line drive past some of the best outfielders known to baseball." A *New Yorker* cartoon of 1938 by the great

George Price gave the sign a certain comic immortality as an outfielder leaps to catch a ball in front of a portly clothier guarding a sign that reads HIT THIS SIGN AND ABE FELDMAN WILL GIVE YOU A SUIT ABSOLUTELY FREE.

KEEP YOUR SOX ON, HOME AND AWAY

—Billboard over Fenway Park (ca. 1975) advertising a radio station that broadcast Red Sox games

LAST YEAR ZACK WHEAT CAUGHT 288 FLIES

TANGLEFOOT CAUGHT 15 BILLION

—Ballpark ad of the 1920s dreamed up by the Tanglefoot Flypaper Company and cited in Joseph McBride's *High and Inside: The Complete Guide to Baseball Slang*

THE RED SOX USE IT

—From a Lifebuoy Soap sign which was on the wall at Fenway Park before it was painted green in 1947

SAY IT AIN'T SO, BART

—Billboard in downtown Cincinnati after Commissioner A. Bartlett Giamatti banned Pete Rose from baseball

SCHAEFER

—Post–World War II scoreboard sign in Ebbets Field which relayed scorer's decisions as either the H for hit or the E for error lit up

WE WANT BEER.

—Chant that went up in 1931 when President Herbert Hoover showed up for a World Series game in Shibe Park. This was the twelfth year of Prohibition.

WELCOME TO ROYSTON HOME OF BASEBALL'S IMMORTAL TY COBB

—Sign at the city limits of Royston, Georgia, at the time of Cobb's death. Cobb posed in front of it with local dignitaries on July 8, 1961, nine days before his death, for the last photos ever taken of him.

WHEN TWO MEN AGREE ON EVERYTHING, ONE IS UNNECESSARY.

—Sign in the office of White Sox owner Philip K. Wrigley, ca. 1943

WHEN WE PLAY AS A TEAM, I'LL FIGHT AS A TEAM.

—Notice posted by Coach Al Bumbry in Red Sox clubhouse in July 1989 as the team seemed to be in a particularly tumultuous period; reported in the *END Globe*, July 18, 1989

WISH—TO END ALL THE KILLING IN THE WORLD HOBBIES—HUNTING AND FISHING

—Items about Angel reliever Bryan Harvey flashed on the scoreboard at Anaheim Stadium; quoted in *Sports Illustrated*, September 1, 1989

SIMMONS, CURT

"Trying to throw a fastball by Hank Aaron is like trying to sneak the sun past a rooster."

> —Widely quoted remark by a man who Dan Schlossberg said had an "uncanny ability to handle Aaron." Aaron himself once said, "Over the years, Curt Simmons was the toughest. Even though I had trouble with Curt, things usually even out in baseball. One year, a pitcher can give you a lot of trouble but the next year you catch up with him. But Simmons gave me the most problems."

SIMMONS, HARRY

"No sweeping improvements, please."

> —This was one of eight "Famous Baseball Sayings" collected by Ernest J. Lanigan of the Hall of Fame when he identified himself as "historian and authority on the game for 65 years"

SIMMONS, LON

"I met him on the space shuttle."

> —As A's announcer, on Bill Lee, 1981

SIMMONS, TED

"I think most ballplayers read the sports pages, but I'm sorry to say that in most cases that's all they read."

> —Widely quoted

"As far as I'm concerned, there is no greater pleasure in the world than walking up to the plate with men on base and knowing that you are feared."

> —Quoted in *Late Innings* by Roger Angell

"I always loved baseball most. I really think I love it more all the time. . . . There is no better game—I don't care if it's bridge or hockey or baseball or backgammon."

> —Quoted in *Late Innings*

"There are things about some professional athletes that I cannot stand—the pretense, the egos, the pomposity, the greed."

> —As a Cardinal catcher; widely quoted

SIMON, NEIL

"How am I ever going to play for the Yankees with a name like Eugene Morris Jerome? You have to be a Joe . . . or a Tony . . . or Frankie . . . If only I was born Italian . . . All the best Yankees are Italian . . . My mother makes spaghetti with ketchup, what chance do I have?"

> —Musings of fifteen-year-old Eugene Jerome, living in Brooklyn in 1937 in *Brighton Beach Memoirs* (New York: Signet, 1986). Play first presented on December 10, 1982 at Ahmanson Theatre in Los Angeles, and on March 21, 1983, at Alvin Theatre in New York City, with Matthew Broderick playing Eugene

SIMON, ROGER

"Putting lights in Wrigley Field is like putting aluminum siding on the Sistine Chapel."

> —The columnist; widely quoted, 1988

SINGLETON, KEN

"A man once told me to walk with the Lord. I'd rather walk with the bases loaded."

—After forcing in a run with a walk in the 1983 World Series, SABR Collection

"My bubble-gum card just came alive."

—Watching Brooks Robinson play in a 1966 uniform at an Orioles old-timers' game

"When a bat feels right, the balance is so perfect it feels weightless. I spent my whole career looking for a bat that felt as good as the broom handles I used to play stickball."

—*The Baseball Card Engagement Book,* 1990

SKOWRON, BILL "MOOSE"

"I don't always swing at strikes. I swing at the ball when it looks big."

—Quoted in the *Sporting News,* March 18, 1960

"If a guy went 0-for-8, and we won a double-header, I'd expect this guy to be happy, right? And say we lost a doubleheader and he goes 7-for-8, and he's joking around the clubhouse—forget those guys. I don't want him to be laughing when we're losing and he gets his hits. To me, that's an individual-type ballplayer."

—Quoted in *Sox: From Lane and Fain to Zisk and Fisk* by Bob Vanderberg

SLAUGHTER, ENOS

"I never felt as bad when my father died as I did when I was released by the Cardinals.

The Cards were all fine people, except one. That was Eddie Stanky."

—Comment attributed to him on the winter banquet trail in *Sport,* February 1956

"I was baseball. Whatever uniform I had on, I gave 110 percent. I'm getting a little bit older now and I'm not as young as I used to be, but my heart and soul is still there."

—At eighty-three, on the occasion of the unveiling of his statue outside Busch Stadium in St. Louis, *Chicago Sun-Times,* July 19, 1999

"One year I hit .291 and had to take a salary cut. If you hit .291 today, you'd own the franchise."

—As a former player; quoted in the *New York Times,* May 15, 1977

"Run? I like to run. I like to hustle too. And anybody who can't hustle every minute of the two hours it takes to play a ball game ought to get out of the game and stay out."

—After the 1946 World Series; quoted in *The Sporting News Chronicle of 20th Century Sport*

SLOCUM, WILLIAM J.

I wonder where my Babe Ruth is tonight?
He grabbed his hat and coat and ducked from
  sight.
He may be at some cozy roadside inn,
Drinking tea—or maybe gin.
He may be at a dance, or may be in a fight.
I know he's with a dame,
I wonder what's her name,
I wonder where my Babe Ruth is tonight?

—Parody sung at the New York Baseball Writers' Dinner, 1926; quoted in *The Dictionary of Bibliographical Quotation*

"As Ruth goes, so go the Yankees."

—Slogan especially true in certain seasons, such as 1923

"Baseball, apple pie and Chevrolet."

—Advertising slogan from Detroit

"Baseball Fever—Catch It!"

—Since 1987, the slogan of Major League Baseball

"Baseball in '87."

—Washington, D.C.; rallying cry, late 1970s and early 1980s

"Break Up the Yankees."

—Rallying cry dating from 1927

"Cub Power!"

—Battle cry of the '61 Cubs

"Enjoy the Game."

—Lackluster official theme/slogan of the lackluster '81 Phillies. In early '81 *USA Today* listed all of the team themes for the year and some made the Phillies theme seem positively exciting, e.g., "Sounds like a great time" (Padres), "You gotta be there" (Orioles), "I feel good" (Giants), and "I believe in baseball" (Mariners).

"George Must Go."

—As described in *USA Today*, August 28, 1989: "Sunday, as the Yankees committed four errors in an 8–5 loss to the Orioles, the 43,791 at Yankee Stadium tossed paper planes on the field, banded together for choruses of "George must go" and booed the Yankees for most of 2½ hours. (See also "Steinbrenner sucks!" below.)

"It's a whole new ballgame."

—Oft-used slogan. It was the official theme of, among others, the 1989 Texas Rangers, the motto of Bob Short's 1969 Washington Senators, and the debut slogan for the 1977 Toronto Blue Jays.

"Kill the Umpire!"

—Traditional threat which dates back deep into the nineteenth century. It appears in "Casey at the Bat" (1888), among other places.

"Last in the East, First in Pantyhose."

—A 1970 *Washington Post* headline that became the slogan that stuck to the '70 Senators after the team handed out 14,960 pair of pantyhose to women who attended three early season Pantyhose Nights

"Let's Do It Again."

—White Sox 1984 slogan after winning the A.L. West championship in 1983

"Let's Make the Axis lose the game: No Huns; No Blitz; No Terrors."

—Prize-winning anti-Nazi slogan, World War II

"Slide, Kelly, slide."

—Refrain of a nineteenth-century song dedicated to King Kelly, but later used to spur others on.

"Spahn and Sain, then pray for rain."

—Motto of the Boston Braves in the late 1940s when the team's success depended on the pitching of Warren Spahn and Johnny Sain, each of whom sometimes pitched on two days' rest

"Stairway to the Majors."

—Slogan of the Cape Cod Baseball League Inc.

"Steinbrenner sucks!"

—Cry of frustrated Yankee fans first heard in unison in April 1982 when Reggie Jackson first returned to the Stadium after being traded away by owner George Steinbrenner. The chant went up after California Angel Jackson hit a home run against his former teammates.

"The Cubs are due in '62."

"The Cubs are going to shine in '69."

—Two of Ernie Banks's own mottoes for the Cubs

"There's no power shortage at Shea."

—Official slogan of the 1982 Mets, which alluded to the fact that the Yankees were losing Reggie Jackson as the Mets were acquiring George Foster

"The Rally Begins."

—Official theme of the 1987 Twins, who went all the way

"The Wonderful World of Baseball."

—Slogan of Major League Baseball during the years of Commissioner Eckert

"Throw strikes! Babe Ruth is dead."

—Slogan used by several major-league pitching coaches, 1990

"To hell with Babe Ruth!"

—The name Babe Ruth was so synonymous with America that during World War II—which began for the U.S. in 1941, six years after Ruth's retirement—Japanese troops goaded American GIs with this refrain. This may have been the magazine and Hollywood film version of much cruder goads in which Ruth's name was used. In *Hammerin' Hank* by Dan Schlossberg, the author alludes to Hank Aaron's pursuit of Ruth's record and says, "Some of Ruth's old fans are now saying 'To hell with Hank Aaron.'"

"Tommy and Joe and pray for snow."

—White Sox variation on an old theme (see *Spahn and Sain, then pray for rain*) used in early 1962, when the only two dependable starters on the team were Tommy John and Joe Horlen

"Wait till next year."

—Perennial slogan of the Brooklyn Dodgers

"We are fam-a-lee!"

—Pittsburgh Pirate rallying cry in 1979, when the team went all the way, led by the man they called "Pops," Willie Stargell

"We don't want your Barbie Dolls, we just play with bats and balls."

—Girls' baseball cheer, Greenbelt, Maryland, 1994; quoted in the *Washington Post*, August 15, 1994

"We're No. One!"

—Often-used slogan which was first popularized by the 1969 Mets. In 1977 it was chanted on Opening Day as the Toronto Blue Jays played and won their very first home game.

"Where have you gone, Joe DiMaggio?"

—Question asked by Simon and Garfunkel in their song, "Mrs. Robinson."

"Who killed baseball?"

—Popular question in the early 1890s; cited in *The Giants of the Polo Grounds* by Noel Hynd

"Why Not?"

—Slogan of the 1981 Baltimore Orioles

"We'll win more in '64."

—Slogan of the 1964 Mets

"Ya gotta believe!"

—Slogan of the Mets as they closed in on their division in 1973; coined by Tug McGraw. (See *McGraw Tug*, for more on the background of the slogan.)

SMITH, H. ALLEN

"In June, 1911, a man sat in the death house of the Nevada State Penitentiary awaiting execution for murder. His name was Pat Casey, and in better days he had been a professional baseball umpire.

"His last request? He had one, all right. He wanted to umpire one more ball game.

"So the game was arranged. It was played the afternoon before Pat Casey marched forth to his death. Casey called balls and strikes for nine innings—and not once did a convict player dispute a decision."

—Retold by Bennett Cerf in *The Laugh's on Me*

SMITH, HAL

"When Red was with the Cardinals the first time, he wore No. 2 and had two children. When he was with the Braves, he wore No. 4 and had four children. When he returned to the Cardinals, he was given No. 16, so—"

—As a Cardinal, explaining why he gave up uniform number 2 to Red Schoendienst; quoted in *Baseball Digest*, July 1961

SMITH, KEN

"For Christ sakes, we're running a business here. Does Macy's play 'The Star-Spangled Banner' before opening its doors every day?"

> —On the playing of the national anthem before each game; widely attributed

SMITH, MAYO

"Open up a ballplayer's head and you know what you'd find? A lot of little broads and a jazz band."

> —Quoted by George Will in *Men at Work: The Craft of Baseball*

"The trouble with some pitchers these days is that they don't know the difference between an ache and a pain. One needs work and the other needs rest."

> —As Detroit Tigers' manager; quoted in the *Sporting News*, August 15, 1970

SMITH, MIKE

"Be sure to put some of them neutrons on it."

> —Telling a waitress what he wanted on his salad

"I'm here to pay my accidentals."

> —Paying his incidental expenses at a hotel checkout counter

"I'm not a home run pitcher. I'm a singles pitcher."

> —On his pitching

Mayo Smith (*Detroit Tigers*)

"I've been healthy my whole career except for nagging injuries the last few years."

> —On his career. All of the above from a collection of his malapropisms in the *Washington Post*, March 9, 1986

SMITH, RED

"A yammer of radio announcers . . . a grouse of ballplayers . . . a conceit of managers . . . a dawdle of magnates . . . a Braille of umpires . . . and a bibulation of sportswriters."

> —A grouping of species; quoted by Bob Broeg in the December 4, 1976, *Sporting News*

"Alphabetical."

> —His nickname for J. G. Taylor Spink of the *Sporting News*

"As a ballplayer, Dean was a natural phenomenon, like the Grand Canyon or the Great Barrier Reef. Nobody ever taught him baseball and he never had to learn. He was just doing what came naturally when a scout named Don Curtis discovered him on a Texas sandlot and gave him his first contract."

> —Quoted in Dean's *New York Times* obituary, July 18, 1974

"Black-jowled, swaggering, snarling, fighting against age and an overwhelming weariness, Old Burleigh Grimes took fame by the throat today and claimed her for his own."

> —From a 1931 story in which the St. Louis Cardinals took the World Championship from the Philadelphia Athletics. It was only after the overwrought piece appeared that Smith realized that he had neglected to give the score of the game; from *Red* by Ira Berkow

"Branch Rickey is a player, manager, executive, lawyer, preacher, horse-trader, spellbinder, innovator, husband and father and grandfather, farmer, logician, obscurantist, reformer, financier, sociologist, crusader, sharper, father confessor, checker shark, friend and fighter. Judas Priest! What a character!"

> —John J. Monteleone, ed., *Branch Rickey's Little Blue Book* (New York: Macmillan, 1995)

"I can think of three managers who weren't fired. John McGraw of the Giants, who was sick and resigned, Miller Huggins of the Yankees, who died on the job, and Connie Mack of the Athletics, who owned the club."

> —In the *New York Times*, September 27, 1979

"It was a month of Sundays."

> —Column lead on the day after Bobby Thomson's home run

"It wasn't just that he hit more home runs than anybody else, he hit them better, higher, farther, with more theatrical timing and a more flamboyant flourish. Nobody could strike out like Babe Ruth. Nobody circled the bases with the same pigeon-toed, mincing majesty."

> —*Grand Slams and Fumbles*

"Ninety feet between home plate and first base may be the closest man has ever come to perfection."

> —Widely quoted

"1961—It was the year when Charles O. Finley, out of the wisdom gleaned from five months' experience in the game, successfully challenged Calvin Griffith for distinction as the Club Owner Most Likely to Louse Up Any Franchise He Gets His Cotton-Pickin' Paws On....

"He is bitter about newspaper criticism and aggrieved to find his welcome wearing thin in the prairie metropolis. In the latter respect, he may have just cause for complaint, for he has, after all, brought a rare distinction to Kansas City. For the city of his adoption he has produced something no other city in the major leagues ever could boast—a tenth-place club."

—Red Smith, "After the Blood, Sweat, and Cheers Are Over," August 1961, in *The Best of Red Smith*, 1963

"No other Irishman excels Walter O'Malley at musical keening, at crying with a loaf of bread under each arm."

—"O'Malley's House of Horrors," December 1955, in *The Best of Red Smith*, 1963

"Now it is done. Now the story ends. And there is no way to tell it. The art of fiction is dead. Reality has strangled invention. Only the utterly impossible, the inexpressibly fantastic, can ever be possible again."

—Describing Bobby Thomson's pennant-winning home run, October 3, 1951, in his column entitled "Miracle of Coogan's Bluff," *New York Herald Tribune*, October 4, 1951

"Of the 43 names printed on the ballot, 14 appear for the first time, and two of these are odds-on to win election without delay. They are Henry Aaron and Frank Robinson. They will not be unanimous selections; there ain't no such animal.

"At least there never has been, not even in January 1936, when the first election was held, with all the greatest players of this century, up to then, eligible.

"Of the 226 voters in that go-round, four left Ty Cobb's name off their ballots, 11 ignored Babe Ruth and Honus Wagner, 21 gave the back of the neck to Christy Mathewson, and 37 passed up Walter Johnson. That was the first class enrolled, and the tabulation always comes to mind when somebody claims a popish infallibility for inmates of the press box."

—On the Hall of Fame electors, *New York Times*, December 1, 1981

"Probably it is the game's subtle and infinite variety that fascinates the intellectual. Its beauty and rhythm makes the music poets hear."

—"Nash, a Discriminating Fan, Chose Baseball as Favorite," *Baltimore Evening Sun*, May 29, 1971

"Sportswriting is the most pleasant way of making a living that man has yet devised."

—Widely quoted

"'The Ancient Mariner' . . . an aging shortstop who now stoppeth one in three."

—On Rabbit Maranville

"The baseball mind is a jewel in the strict sense—that is to say, a stone of special value, rare beauty, and extreme hardness. Cut, polished and fixed in the Tiffany setting of a club owner's skull, it resists change as a diamond resists erosion."

—*New York Herald Tribune*, August 7, 1961. A much tightened version appears in several collections of quotations (e.g. *Say It Again* by Dorothy Uris). That version: "The baseball mind is a jewel—a stone of special beauty, rare value, and extreme hardness. It resists change as a diamond resists erosion."

"The game has been over for half an hour now, and still a knot of worshipers stand clustered, as around a shrine, out in right field adoring the spot on the wall which Cookie Lavagetto's line drive smote."

—On Cookie Lavagetto's game-winning hit in the 1947 World Series

"The human ear is a wonderful instrument, but not so wonderful as the Stengel larynx."

—Quoted in the 1976 New York Mets Scorebook

"The last people who went broke in baseball were Roy and Earl Mack, Connie's sons. And I claim they did it on merit."

—SABR Collection

"The meat-and-potatoes sport—baseball."

—Widely attributed

"The natural habitat of the tongue is the left cheek."

—On covering sports; quoted by Richard Kluger, in *The Paper: The Life and Death of the New York Herald Tribune*

"The Yankees have a guy named DiMaggio. Sometimes a fellow gets a little tired of writing about DiMaggio. A fellow thinks, 'There must be some other ballplayer in the world worth mentioning.' But there isn't really, not worth mentioning in the same breath as DiMaggio."

—*The Giants of the Polo Grounds* by Noel Hynd

"To say that Branch Rickey has the finest mind ever brought to the game of baseball is to damn with the faintest of praise, like describing Isaac Stern as a fiddler. From the day in 1903 when Branch signed as a catcher for LeMars, Iowa, at $150 a month, he was a giant among pygmies. If his goal had been the Supreme Court of the United States instead of the Cincinnati Reds, he would have been a giant on the bench."

—*New York Herald Tribune*; quoted in the 1989 *Yearbook* of the Baseball Hall of Fame

"Tom Seaver has been one of the finest pitchers in the game . . . He is his own man, thoughtful, perceptive and unafraid to speak his mind. Because of this, M. Donald Grant and his sycophants put Seaver away as a troublemaker. They mistake dignity for arrogance."

—On the trade that sent Tom Seaver to the Reds from the Mets

SMITH, REGGIE

"If I'm going to be struck out, that's the way to go. It may sound strange, but I actually enjoyed that. It was like a surgeon's knife—quick and painless."

—After being struck out by Nolan Ryan; quoted in *Sports Illustrated*, August 11, 1980

"When I think of the $100,000 ballplayer, I think in terms of Willie Mays, Mickey Mantle, Sandy Koufax, Bob Gibson and Don Drysdale. I also think of Joe Morgan. These people did it all. They had to work up slowly to that $100,000 figure, the symbol of a very special ballplayer."

—As a Dodger; quoted in the *Los Angeles Herald-Examiner*, March 13, 1978

SMITH, ROBERT

"Cardinal rule for all hitters with two strikes on them: Never trust the umpire!"

—*Words of Wisdom,* William Safire and Leonard Safir

SMITH, SAM

"Let's face it, there are folks down here who just don't want their kids growing up to admire a Negro ballplayer even if he's Willie Mays or Hank Aaron."

—The president of the Southern League; quoted by David Q. Voight in *America Through Baseball,* from J. Anthony Lucas, "Down and Out in the Minor Leagues," *Harper's,* June 1968

SNIDER, DUKE

"In the split second from the time the ball leaves the pitcher's hand until it reaches the plate, you have to think about your stride, your hip action, your wrist action, determine how much, if any, the ball is going to break and then decide whether to swing at it."

—On why batting a ball is not as simple as it looks; the *Sporting News,* November 19, 1952

"Man, if I made $1 million, I would come in at six in the morning, sweep the stands, wash the uniforms, clean out the offices, manage the team and play the games."

—As a new member of the Hall of Fame, on salaries; quoted in *Sport,* April 1980

"The greatest competitor I've ever seen; I've seen him beat a team with his bat, his ball, his glove, his feet and, in a game in Chicago one time, with his mouth."

—On Jackie Robinson; in Snider's induction speech into the Baseball Hall of Fame, August 3, 1980

"We wept, Brooklyn was a lovely place to hit. If you got a ball in the air, you had a chance to get it out. When they tore down Ebbets Field, they tore down a little piece of me."

—On the Dodgers moving from Brooklyn to Los Angeles in 1958; quoted in the *New York Times,* January 10, 1980, on his election to the Hall of Fame.

SNYDER, BRAD

"Robinson and Flood took professional athletes on an incredible journey—from racial desegregation to well-paid slavery to being free and extremely well paid. [Jackie] Robinson started the revolution by putting on a uniform. Flood finished it by taking it off. Robinson fought for racial justice. Flood fought the less-sympathetic fight for economic justice. They never stopped fighting for freedom. Curt Flood dedicated his life to making Jackie Robinson proud."

—From his biography of Curt Flood, *A Well-Paid Slave,* 2006

SNYDER, BRAD (CONTINUED)

"Today's athletes have some control over where they play in part because in 1969 Flood refused to continue being treated like hired help. But while Robinson's jersey has been retired in every major league ballpark, few players today know the name Curt Flood, and even fewer know about the sacrifices he made for them."

—From *A Well-Paid Slave*, 2006

SOUTHWORTH, BILLY

"Gentlemen, swinging the bat is a great exercise. It strengthens the diaphragm and loosens pent-up emotions in the chest. Besides, you may hit the ball."

—From his speech to the Cardinals before the third game of the 1944 World Series; quoted by John P. Carmichael of the *Chicago Tribune* in the *Chicago Daily News*. The quote appears in the June 1949 *Baseball Digest*.

SPAHN, WARREN

"A pitcher needs two pitches, one they're looking for and one to cross them up."

—His *New York Times* obituary, November 26, 2003

"After what I went through overseas, I never thought of anything I was told to do in baseball as hard work. You get over feeling like that when you spend days on end sleeping in frozen tank tracks in enemy-threatened territory. The Army taught me something about challenges and what is important and what isn't."

—From Gary Bedingfield's *Baseball in World War II*

Warren Spahn (*Cleveland Indians*)

"He was something like 0 for 21 the first time I saw him. His first major league hit was a home run off me, and I'll never forgive myself. We might have gotten rid of Willie forever if I'd only struck him out."

—On Willie Mays; quoted in Spahn's *New York Times* obituary, November 26, 2003

"Hitting is timing. Pitching is upsetting timing."

—Hall of Fame Collection

"I felt like, wow, what a great way to make a living. If I goof up, there's going to be a relief pitcher come in there. Nobody's going to shoot me."

—On returning to baseball after World War II; quoted in *USA Today*, May 25, 1990

"I'm probably the only guy who worked for Stengel before and after he was a genius."

> —Alluding to the fact that he had pitched for Stengel on the '42 Braves and the '65 Mets; quoted in *Sports Illustrated*, August 20, 1973

"I'm smarter now than when I had the big fastball. Sometimes I get behind hitters on purpose. That makes them hungry hitters. They start looking for fat pitches. I make my living off hungry hitters."

> —*Time*, 1960

"It will be a great honor if I'm voted in, but it's something a player should never expect will happen."

> —On being voted into the Hall of Fame; widely quoted

"One of the things I dislike about baseball today is we've made nonathletes out of pitchers. They pitch once a week. They count the pitches. They don't hit. They don't run the bases. That's not my kind of baseball."

> —In 1999, at the All-Star Game in Boston's Fenway Park, when Spahn took a dim view of modern-day pitching, particularly in the American League with its designated hitter; *Boston Globe* obituary, November 26, 2003

"The difference between winning 11 games and winning 20 for a pitcher is bigger than anyone out of baseball realizes. It's the same for hitters. Someone who hits .300 looks back on the guy who batted .295 and says 'tough luck buddy.'

"Twenty games is the magic figure for pitchers, .300 is the magic figure for batters. It pays off in salary and reputation.

"And those are the two things that keep a ballplayer in business."

> —*My Greatest Day in Baseball* by Bob Ajemian

"Well, there was the Battle of the Bulge."

> —When asked if he had ever felt more pressure than he had when pitching in a World Series. The response was recalled in his *Washington Post* obituary, November 25, 2003. His World War II Army service had included duty with an engineering unit that worked on the bridge at Remagen.

"Willie Mays seems to be swinging bad."

> —The Milwaukee Braves pitcher, just before a game in which Mays hit four home runs, tying a record that has yet to be broken, April 28, 1961

"You don't just throw the ball, you propel it."

> —*Pitching to Win* by Raymond L. Hicks

SPALDING, A. G.

"Baseball gives . . . a growing boy self-poise and self- reliance. Baseball is a man maker."

> —*America Through Baseball* by David Q. Voight

"Baseball is the exponent of American Courage, Confidence, Combativeness, American Dash, Discipline, Determination, American Energy, Eagerness, Enthusiasm, American Pluck, Persistency, Performance, American Spirit, Sagacity, Success, American Vim, Vigor, Virility."

> —An alphabetical recitation; quoted by Peter Leving in the 1984 *Baseball Research Journal*

SPALDING, A. G. (CONTINUED)

"No other position on a ball team has shown such a change for the better in recent years as first base. But a few years back the sole idea of a first baseman's qualifications was ability to hit the ball hard. Little attention was paid to his fielding."

—1907; quoted in *Kings of the Diamond* by Lee Allen and Tom Meany

"Professional baseball is on the wane. Salaries must come down or the interest of the public must be increased in some way. If one or the other does not happen, bankruptcy stares every team in the face."

—To O. P. Caylor of the *Cincinnati Enquirer,* January 1881

Albert Goodwill Spalding (*Library of Congress Prints and Photographs Division*)

"The genius of our institutions is democratic; Base Ball is a democratic game."

—*Baseball: The Early Years* by Harold Seymour

"Two hours is about as long as an American can wait for the close of a baseball game—or anything else, for that matter."

—Quoted by Edward F. Murphy in the *New York Times,* April 25, 1976

"You cannot keep anything secret in baseball."

—About the effort to keep secret the signing of four Boston players with Chicago in 1875, thus violating the constitution of the National Association of Professional Base Ball Players (the secret lasted ten days); quoted in Alfred H. Spink, *The National Game,* 2nd ed. (St. Louis: National Game Publishing, 1911)

SPEAKER, TRIS

"If you put a baseball and other toys in front of [an American] baby, he'll pick up the baseball in preference to the others. The American boy starts swinging the bat about as soon as he can lift one."

—Quoted by Hank Kilroy in the January 1951 *Baseball Magazine*

"It would be useless for any player to attempt to explain successful batting."

—*Baseball Magazine* interview, ca. 1917

"Luck is the great stabilizer in baseball."

—*Baseball Magazine* interview, ca. 1917

Tris Speaker (*Library of Congress Prints and Photographs, Bain Collection*)

"Ruth made a grave mistake when he gave up pitching. Working once a week, he might have lasted a long time and become a great star."

　　—On Babe Ruth's future, 1921; widely quoted

SPELLMAN, CARDINAL

May
The Divine Spirit
That Animated
Babe Ruth
To Win The Crucial
Game of Life
Inspire The Youth
Of America!

　　—The epitaph on the grave of Babe Ruth
　　(1985–1948) and Claire Ruth (1900–1976),
　　Gate of Heaven Cemetery, Hawthorne, New
　　York

SPIEGEL, JUDGE ARTHUR S.

"Foremost, we must recognize that there are two people here: Peter Rose, the living legend, the all-time hit leader, and the idol of millions; and Pete Rose, the individual, who appears today convicted of two counts of cheating on his taxes. Today, we are not dealing with the legend. . . . After carefully considering all of these factors, I have concluded that Mr. Rose must serve some time in a prison setting for his crime in order to maintain respect for the law. . . . The sentence in total is that Peter E. Rose will be confined at an institution of the Bureau of Prisons for a period of five months. . . . Following the five months of imprisonment, Mr. Rose will be required to serve three months in a community treatment center or halfway house as a condition of his supervised release. The supervised release will last one year under the conditions previously noted. There is a fine of $50,000, to be paid immediately."

　　—On sentencing Pete Rose, July 19, 1990

SPINK, ALFRED H.

"The position of shortstop was not considered important by the early professional teams until Dickey Pearce of the Atlantics commenced playing that position. Then it was that the business in that portion of the field was brought into the limelight for the first time."

　　—1910; quoted in *Kings of the Diamond* by Lee
　　Allen and Tom Meany

SPINK, C. C. JOHNSON

"The higher a man goes up in the economic scale, the less likely he is to have a nickname. . . . It's that way in baseball. . . . now that the players have become big money men."

> —*Sporting News,* 1979. Spink suggested the proper new nickname was "Mister." Another theory which has been bandied about is that they went into decline beginning in 1960 when Bill Veeck first started putting names on the back of uniforms and nicknames weren't needed anymore to help remember players.

SPRINGSTEAD, MARTY

"Every play there [second base] is crucial. They're always close. I don't know how the guy who invented the game knew to put the bases 90 feet apart and make all the calls so close."

> —Quoted in: *Baseball Digest,* November 1983

STALLINGS, GEORGE

"Bases on balls, you fathead, was the cause of it all."

> —Presumably the last words of the 1914 Miracle Braves manager as he emerged from a coma to address his doctor as to the cause of his sickness, while in an ambulance heading for Haddock, Georgia, on May 13, 1929; he expired two minutes later. The source is according to Rabbit Maranville, in John Updike's *Run, Rabbit, Run,* published in 1991 by the Society for American Baseball Research.

STANDISH, BURT L.

(See *Patten, Gilbert.* Standish was Patten's pseudonym.)

STANHOUSE, DON

"What can you tell me I don't know? I know the bases are loaded. I know we are leading by one run. I know I have two balls on the batter. I know I have to throw a strike. I know I have to try."

> —Words delivered to Orioles pitching coach Ray Miller to cut short a 1984 mound conference; quoted in *Sports Illustrated,* April 16, 1979

STANKY, EDDIE

"The ants get on base and the bulls knock 'em in."

> —A favorite saying; quoted in his *Washington Post* obituary, June 8, 1999

STANKY, MRS.

"Dear Son:

Received your letter and am sorry to hear that you are so homesick.

You will notice that I did not forward any money for your passage to Philadelphia. The reason was not that I didn't have it to send to you, but that you were trying to tell me in your letter that you wanted to come home right away.

Edward, I have tears in my eyes while I'm telling you this, but if you do come home, please do not come to 915 East Russell Street. We do not want quitters in this family.

Your Mother."

> —Letter received when, just after breaking into organized baseball, he became homesick and asked his mother for money to come home; quoted in the *Sporting News,* 1951

STANLEY, BOB

"I hope he doesn't yell at me like I used to yell at my managers."

> —The retired Boston Red Sox reliever, on the prospect of coaching son Kyle's Little League team, the *Sporting News,* January 8, 1990

STARGELL, WILLIE

"I love September, especially when we're in it."

> —*Heavy Hitters: Lynn, Parker, Carew, Rose* by Bill Gutman

"I'm always amazed when a pitcher becomes angry at a hitter for hitting a home run off him. When I strike out, I don't get angry at the pitcher, I get angry at myself. I would think that if a pitcher threw up a home-run ball, he should be angry at himself."

> —As a Pirate; *Sporting News,* July 17, 1971

"Trying to hit him was like trying to drink coffee with a fork."

> —On trying to bat against Sandy Koufax;

quoted by Ray Fitzgerald of the *Boston Globe* in the May 1972 *Baseball Digest.* Later Stargell reworked the quote for Steve Carlton: "Sometimes I hit him like I used to hit Koufax, and that's like drinking coffee with a fork. Did you every try that?"

"It's supposed to be fun. The man says 'Play ball,' not 'Work ball,' you know. . . . You only have a few years to play this game, and you can't play it if you're all tied up in knots."

> —Quoted by Roger Angell in *Late Innings*

"They give you a round bat and they throw you a round ball. And they tell you to hit it square."

> —*New York Times,* April 2, 1978. A similar quotation has been attributed to Pete Rose: "Hitting a baseball is the hardest thing to do in all sport. Think about it: You've got a round ball, a round bat, and the object is to hit it square."

"Under pressure, you want to be at peace with yourself. You want your energy to flow, not feel knotted. You don't want to be too sharp. You don't want to be too flat. You just want to be natural."

> —Widely attributed

STAUB, RUSTY

"Sure, I'll miss playing, but I think I'm ready for this. Let's face it, I've already had three 'last' seasons."

> —On becoming a Mets spring training instructor; quoted in the *Washington Post,* March, 3, 1986

STEINBERG, SAUL

"Baseball is an allegorical play about America, a poetic, complex, and subtle play of courage, fear, good luck, mistakes, patience about fate, and sober self-esteem. . . . It is impossible to understand America without a thorough knowledge of baseball."

— *Saul Steinberg* by Harold Rosenberg, 1978

STEINBRENNER, GEORGE

"I don't agree with free agency, but it wasn't my leadership that created it."

—Responding to Commissioner Bowie Kuhn's lament about the Yankees signing free agents; quoted in *Sports Illustrated*, December 18, 1978

"I like my horses better because they can't talk to sportswriters."

—On his Thoroughbreds; quoted in *Sports Illustrated*, April 22, 1985

"I want to sincerely apologize to the people of New York and to fans of the New York Yankees everywhere for the performance of the Yankee team in the World Series. I also want to assure you that we will be at work immediately to prepare for 1982."

—His press release issued after the 1981 season

"I'm like Archie Bunker, I get mad as hell when my team blows one."

—*New York Times*, September 20, 1981

"It was just a big, unanimous thing that grew until it filled the park."

—On the spontaneous "Steinbrenner sucks!" chants at Yankee Stadium; quoted by William B. Mead in *The Official Yankee Hater's Handbook*. Mead also cites Ron Guidry's response to the same chant: "It's about the only fun time I had in the game."

"It's just getting crazy. Shocked? Yes. How can you pay a ballplayer $3 million or $3.5 million a year when the head of the Chiefs of Staff is making just $77,000 a year? Some way, somehow, someone has to say, 'Stop! Can one man make a $3 million difference in a ballclub?' I don't know."

—*Washington Times*, January 29, 1990

"I've always said that if you wait and keep your mouth shut, things will come around right."

—Quoted by William B. Mead in *The Official Yankee Hater's Handbook*.

"I've had a belly full. When I look at some of those construction workers in New York, climbing around 20 stories high, working for their bucks the way they do, as hard as they do, and a cab driver eight or ten hours a day . . . and I see how hard these guys work, and then they come out here [to the ballpark], and they pay their good money to see what happened last night, when we [the Yankees] got wiped out 14–2, in a lackadaisical performance, that gets to me. I'm tired of the complaining. [Baseball players] should be the happiest guys in the world; they're being paid megabucks for playing a kids' game."

—On the *CBS Morning News*, August 5, 1982

"Owning the Yankees is like owning the *Mona Lisa*. That's something you never see."

—As New York Yankees owner, on whether he would sell the team; widely quoted

"Tell Munson to shave his beard off or I'll find him $500. Take Nettles out of the lineup. He's just not doing his job. Piniella's only batting .167 against Cleveland left-handers. Bench him till the Indians leave town."

—Typical instructions called to the Yankee dugout; quoted in *High Inside: Memoirs of a Baseball Wife* by Danielle Gagnon Torrez

"There are only so many ulcers in the world and I make certain that other people get them."

—On the secret of his success; from *Coach and Athletic Director*, August 2003

"They weren't even worth watching!"

—On his Yankees, who played so poorly in a doubleheader against the Chicago White Sox on the night of August 3, 1982, that with this comment he said that all thirty-four thousand fans at the Stadium that night could come to another game free.

"We plan absentee ownership. I'll stick to building ships."

—As president of the American Shipbuilding Company, speculating on his future role

as a member of the syndicate that had just purchased the New York Yankees from CBS; quoted in the *New York Times*, January 3, 1973. This quotation appears in *The Experts Speak, the Definitive Compendium of Misinformation*.

STEINHAGEN, RUTH ANN

"I admire him now more than ever before. He showed so much courage as he lay there on the floor. The way he looked up at me and kept smiling."

—Talking to reporters after she shot Phils first baseman Eddie Waitkus in her Chicago hotel room early on June 15, 1949, as quoted in the *St. Louis Post-Dispatch* of June 16

STELLO, DICK

"Listen, Alex, on a clear day I can see the sun, and that sucker is 93 million miles away!"

—As a Texas League umpire when accused by Fort Worth manager Alex Grammas of not being able to see if a ball was fair or foul 250 feet away; quoted in *Strike Two* by Ron Luciano.

"Umpiring is a profession where you're expected to be perfect from the first day, and then you have to show constant improvement."

—As National League umpire, *Sporting News*, August 16, 1975

Stengelese. Term coined to cover the vocabulary and implausible brand of double-talk spoken by the late Casey Stengel. "By talking in the purest jabberwocky he has learned that he can avoid answering questions," wrote Gayle Talbot of the AP in 1954, "and at the same time leave his audience struggling against a mild form of mental paralysis" (*San Francisco Call-Bulletin,* February 1). In 1975 another Associated Press writer took this stab at it; "He often was difficult to understand because of the rapid-fire, rambling, double-talk manner in which he spoke and his constant use of non-sequiturs, gibberish and broken English." His speech also contained truth and fact which Max Kase of the *New York Journal-American* (October 9, 1960) said made, "unscheduled appearances like a run in a girl's stocking." Kase added, "The charm of Stengelese is in its confusion or am I Stengelese-ing a bit myself."

Writing in *Newsday* the day after Stengel retired from baseball, George Vecsey had this to say about Stengelese: "He could have fun with it. When people from out-of-town gaped at him during the World Series, he turned on the Stengelese. It was what they had come for. When the radio and television poked their microphones in front of him, he turned on the Stengelese. He knew it made them mad. When the entire nation was watching him, he turned on the Stengelese. It was noblesse oblige."

Some drove the point home with stronger force. Wells Twombly of the *San Francisco Examiner* called Stengelese a "flagrant put-on." He added, "He did it on purpose." Twombly insisted that Stengel was totally lucid and straightforward when unguarded but that he put on the act when the press was about."

It is hard to describe—Red Smith once likened it to "picking up quicksilver with boxing gloves"—but here is an example from a 1958 congressional hearing investigating the need for baseball anti-trust legislation. From the *Congressional Record,* July 9, 1958.

SENATOR LANGER: I want to know whether you intend to keep on monopolizing the world's championship in New York City?

Casey Stengel (*New York Yankees*)

MR. STENGEL: Well, I will tell you. I got a little concern yesterday in the first three innings when I saw the three players I had gotten rid of, and I said when I lost nine what am I going to do and when I had a couple of my players I thought so great of that did not do so good up to the sixth inning I was more confused but I finally had to go and call on a young man in Baltimore that we don't own and the Yankees don't own him, and he is doing pretty good, and I would actually have to tell you that I think we are more the Greta Garbo type now from success.

We are being hated, I mean, from the ownership and all, we are being hated. Every sport that gets too great or one individual—but if we made 27 cents and it pays to have a winner at home, why would you have a good winner in your own park if you were an owner?

That is the result of baseball. An owner gets most of the money at home and it is up to him and his staff to do better or they ought to be discharged.

. . . The sixty-eight-year old Perfessor turned the proceedings into what ranks as one of the most impressive performances ever staged before the "world's greatest deliberative body" (as the Senate immodestly calls itself). The kicker came with the appearance of Mickey Mantle:

SENATOR KEFAUVER: Thank you very much, Mr. Stengel. We appreciate your presence here. Mr. Mickey Mantle, will you come around? . . . Mr. Mantle, do you have any observations with reference to the applicability of the antitrust laws to baseball?

MR. MANTLE: My views are just about the same as Casey's

—*Congressional Record,* July 9, 1958

It is also important to know that Stengelese harbored its own vocabulary, which had to be mastered in order to comprehend the whole. Some key terms:

"Butcher boy"—A chopped ground ball, or as a verb, to chop down on the ball, to "butcher boy" it.

"Doubleheaded"—Doubleheader; as George Vecsey once quoted him as saying, "and you notice that they lost a doubleheaded" (*Newsday,* September 3, 1965).

"Embalmed"—Sleeping.

"Fairly amazing"—Good.

"Green pea"—Rookie or player without seasoning.

"He could squeeze your earbrows off."—Said of a particularly strong or tough player.

"He's a remarkable"—A compliment.

"Hold the gun"—I want to change pitchers.

"I shouldn't tell you this but . . . "—Words used to indicate that he was planting a story with a reporter.

"Last night"—The last game he managed even if it was the previous Saturday afternoon.

"My fella/that fella"—Player whose name he did not choose to use, which was often. "To Casey, everyone is a fella, the listener supplies names at his own risk," said *Time*, October 3, 1955. When he was managing the Yankees, Mickey Mantle was "my big fella" and Phil Rizzuto was "my little fella."

"My writers"—Sports reporters.

"Ned in the third reader"—Naîveté.

"Now wait a minute, Doctor, let me tell you something."—Said to writers when the conversation was getting away from him to regain their attention.

"Plumber"—Good fielder, e.g., "that plumber at third base for Baltimore was Brooks Robinson.

"Road apple"—Bum.

"Whiskey slick"—Describing a playboy.

"Worm killers"—Low balls.

"You're full of shit and I'll tell you why."—When he was prepared to clinch an argument.

"The Youth of America"—Rookies.

"About this autograph business. Once, someone in Washington sent up a picture to me and I wrote, 'Do good in school.' I look up, this guy is seventy-eight years old."

> —As New York Yankees manager

"Ain't it funny, Bill, how all of a sudden I got so smart and you got so dumb."

> —In 1949, after he had been named manager of the year and he ran into the 1948 manager of the year, Billy Meyer; quoted in the *New York Journal-American*, October 9, 1960.

"All I ask is that you bust your heiny on that field."

> —Quoted by Billy Martin in *Number 1*

"Amazing strength, amazing power. He can grind the dust out of the bat. He will be great, super, wonderful. Now if he can only learn to catch a fly ball."

> —On Ron Swoboda as a new Met; quoted by Maury Allen in *The Incredible Mets*

"And so you can say this tremendous and amazin' new club is gonna be ready in every way tomorrow when the bell rings and that's the name of my right fielder, Bell."

> —Finale to April press conference introducing the New York Mets in their debut year of 1962. Stengel had introduced all of his players but had been unable to recall the name of right fielder Gus Bell; quoted in Roger Angell's *Five Seasons*

"As great as the other men were on the ball club, there comes a time when you get a weakness and it might be physical."

> —On personnel; quoted by Harold Rosenthal in a February 22, 1964, piece on Stengel and the winter banquet circuit, entitled "Case Hits New Heights as Oral Pearl Pitcher"

"At the end of this season they're gonna tear this place down. The way you're pitchin', that right-field section will be gone already."

> —To pitcher Tracy Stallard at the Polo Grounds, 1963; widely attributed

"[Baseball] has been run cleaner than any business that was ever put out in the 100 years at the present time. . . . If I was a chamber of commerce member and I was in a city, I would not want a baseball team to leave the city as too much money is brought into your city, even if you have a losing team and great if you have a winning ball team."

—Testimony on baseball ethics given to the Senate Antitrust Committee looking into the matter of baseball, July 9, 1958

"Baseball is different today. They got a lot of kids now whose uniforms are so tight, especially the pants, that they cannot bend over to pick up ground balls. And they don't want to bend over in television games because in that way there is no way their face can get on camera."

—Quoted in the *Christian Science Monitor,* October 14, 1971

"Being with a woman all night never hurt no professional baseball player. It's staying up all night looking for a woman that does him in."

—Oft-quoted curfew line; another in the same vein: "You gotta learn that if you don't get it by midnight, chances are you ain't gonna get it, and if you do, it ain't worth it."

"Been in this game a hundred years, but I see new ways to lose 'em I never knew existed before."

—On the Mets when he managed them

"Best thing wrong with Jack Fisher is nothing."

—The New York Mets manager on his best pitcher

"Can't anybody here play this game?"

—His second or third most famous line, first posed as a question about the original New York Mets

"Do you know what finally slowed Cobb down? Well, I'll tell you. Pitchers wore him out by throwing over to first base. They wore down his legs by making him jump back to the bag. There was no rule saying they couldn't keep doing it. And if they did it long enough, Cobb lost the snap and jump he needed to steal second. He told me that himself."

—On Ty Cobb; quoted by Ed Rumill of the *Christian Science Monitor,* in the November, 1961 *Baseball Digest*

"Don't cut my throat, I may want to do that later myself."

—What he was alleged to have said to a barber. This line is one of the most repeated in the lore of the game.

"Don't drink in the hotel bar, because that's where I do my drinking."

—A Stengel rule of the road trip; quoted in *Slick* by Whitey Ford with Phil Pepe

"Everyone is going down there and they got to do it on the ball field and not off the ball field."

—On training camp; quoted by Harold Rosenthal in a February 22, 1964, piece on Stengel and the winter banquet circuit

"Forty years ago you would not have had it around here yourself and you would not have cameras flying around here every five minutes but we have got them here and more of them around here than around a ball field. I will give you that little tip."

> —On pay television during the 1958 antitrust hearings

"Give 'em here. I'll sign anything but veal cutlets. My ball-point pen slips on cutlets."

> —On autographs; quoted by Elston Howard in the October 1967 *Reader's Digest*

"Good pitching will always stop good hitting and vice-versa."

> —Widely quoted

"He calls for the curve ball too much. He don't hit it . . . and he don't think nobody else can."

> —On catcher Chris Cannizzaro

"He fields better on one leg than anybody else I got on two."

> —On an aging, injured Gil Hodges as a Met; quoted in *The Incredible Mets* by Maury Allen

"He has it in his body to be great."

> —On the young Mickey Mantle; quoted by Maury Allen in *You Could Look It Up*

"He has wonderful stuff and wonderful control and throws strikes, which shows he's educated. But then, say you're educated and you can't throw strikes. Then they don't leave you in too long."

> —On Mike Marshall, then with the Los Angeles Dodgers

"He played first base and the outfield, pinch-hit, and did everything but collect tickets."

> —On the versatility of Tommy Byrne

"He should lead the league in everything. With his combination of speed and power he should win the triple batting crown every year. In fact, he should do anything he wants to do."

> —On Mickey Mantle, early in 1951

"He threw the ball as far from the bat and as close to the plate as possible."

> —On Satchel Paige

"He wanted to see poverty, so he came to see my team."

> —On seeing the crowd in front of the Pittsburgh Hilton waiting for presidential candidate Lyndon B. Johnson, April 24, 1964; quoted later by George Vecsey in *Newsday*.

"He was my banty rooster. Whitey used to stick out his chest, like this and walk out to the mound against any of those big pitchers."

> —On Whitey Ford; quoted in the 1989 Hall of Fame *Yearbook*

"He was striking out men with his ambition. He walks on his toes like a girl but he jumps up in the dugout for every out like it was the last out, so you know he's serious about baseball."

> —On Tug McGraw; quoted by Berry Stainback, *Sport,* April 1966

"He was very brave at the plate. You rarely saw him fall away from a pitch. He stayed right in there. No one drove him out."

> —On Babe Ruth; quoted by Robert W. Creamer in *Babe: The Legend Comes to Life*

"He'd fall in a sewer and come up with a gold watch."

> —On Yogi Berra; quoted by Milton Gross in the August 1972, *Baseball Digest*

"He's a good manager. He might be a little selfish about some of the things he does and he may think he knows more about baseball than anybody else, but it wouldn't surprise me if he was right."

> —On Billy Martin in the *Sporting News,* August 23, 1975

"He's a great hitter until I play him."

> —On Met Jerry Lumpe. This comment and others like it came under fire in an article in the July 31, 1965, *Saturday Evening Post,* entitled "The Last Angry Old Man," by Ed Linn, who documented a pattern of criticizing his players in public. "You open the paper in the morning," said Clete Boyer, "and you read how lousy you are." Another case in point cited by Linn was the case of Chris Cannizzaro, who Stengel always called "Canzoneri." The next quotation yielded this comment from Linn: "Everyone laughed heartily except possibly Cannizzaro."

"He's a remarkable catch, that Canzoneri. He's the only defensive catcher in baseball who can't catch."

> —Quoted by George Vecsey, *Newsday,* August 31, 1965

"He's dead at the present time."

> —Quoted by Berry Stainback, *Sport,* April 1966. Stengel was referring to Larry Gilbert.

"He's great but you gotta play him in a cage."

> —On Jimmy Piersall; quoted in *Everything You Always Wanted to Know About Sports and Didn't Know Where to Ask* by Mickey Herskowitz and Steve Perkins. Because of Piersall's problems—described in *Fear Strikes Out*—this line has been cited as evidence of Stengel's cruelty to his own players.

"He's throwing grounders."

> —On a pitcher who was wild and low

"Hey Heffner, take 'em down to that other field and find out if they can play on the road."

> —Directive to coach Don Heffner during spring training at the expansive St. Petersburg facility, 1963

"Hi, I'm Dutch Stengel. I'm a new player on this team. I'd like to take batting practice."

> —When he reported to the Brooklyn Dodgers in 1912, rookies were not permitted to take batting practice. Casey, an avid batsman, had cards printed up with this terse message which he handed to his teammates; quoted in "Memories of Casey—and Stengelese," *San Francisco Examiner,* September 30, 1975

"Hornsby could run like anything but not like this kid. Cobb was the fastest I ever saw for being sensational on the bases but he wasn't a long hitter. They're been a lot of fast men but none as big and strong as Mantle. He's gonna be around a long time, if he can stay well, that fella of mine."

> —Early assessment of Mickey Mantle as the fastest slugger he ever saw, Hall of Fame Collection

"How can a guy who's so big and strong hit the ball so near?"

> —On watching the immense Washington Senator Frank Howard take a mighty swing at a ball that dribbled into the infield; quoted in *Baseball Digest*, March 1965

"How the hell should I know? Most of the people my age are dead."

> —On being asked by a reporter what people "your age" think of modern-day ballplayers or, depending on the source, being asked about his future. It appears to date from the spring of 1965. Later versions of this Stengelism often appeared as part of longer quotations, such as this on the subject of his age: "Just say I'm a man that's been around for a while, a man that's been up and down, a man that's played with the dead ball and the lively ball and lived to tell the difference. Why, most people my age are dead now and you can look it up."

"I ain't gonna comment about a guy which made $100,000 writing how my club lost."

> —When asked to comment on Douglass Wallop's *Damn Yankees*; quoted in Bennett Cerf's *Life of the Party*

"I broke in with four hits and the writers promptly decided they had seen the new Ty Cobb. It took me only a few days to correct that impression."

> —Widely attributed

"I came in here and a fella asked me to have a drink. I said I don't drink. Then another fella said I hear you and Joe DiMaggio aren't speaking and I said I'll take that drink."

> —Before the 1951 All-Star Game; quoted in the *Sporting News*, 1955

"I can make a living telling the truth!"

> —Oft-used line, according to George Vecsey, *New York Times*, September 20, 1981

"I couldna done it without my players."

> —On winning the 1958 World Series as Yankee manager

"I didn't get the job through friendship. The Yankees represent an investment of millions of dollars. They don't hand out jobs like this just because they like your company. I got the job because the people here think I can produce for them. I know I can make people laugh. And some of you think I'm a damn fool."

—At his first press conference as Yankee manager, 1949

"I don't know if he throws a spitball, but he sure spits on the ball."

—On an opposing pitcher, as Yankees manager

"I don't know if you should hand it to him or mail it to him. If you hand it to him he's liable to drop it."

—On Marv Throneberry being awarded a silver tray after being elected Met's Good Guy by sportswriters; quoted in *The Incredible Mets* by Maury Allen

"I don't like them fellas who drive in two runs and let in three."

—As Yankee manager

"I feel greatly honored to have a ballpark named after me, especially since I've been thrown out of so many."

—In 1952 when the municipal ballpark in Glendale, California, his native town, was renamed Stengel Field; from an August 1985 AP story by Martha L. Willman

"I got a kid, Greg Goosen, he's 20 years old and in ten years he's got a chance to be 30."

—The Ole Perfesser was obviously not impressed with the burly catcher. In some versions of this quotation, Casey says, "He's 11 years old, and in ten years he has a chance to be 20."

"I got one that can throw but can't catch, and one that can catch but can't throw, and one who can hit but can't do either."

—On his three Mets catchers

"I got players what got bad watches, they can't tell midnight from noon."

—On curfews; quoted by Red Roley of the *New York Daily News* in the Mets' 1976 *Scorebook*

"I had many years that I was not so successful as a ballplayer as it is a game of skill."

—On his playing career; quoted in the *Baseball Digest,* June 1986

"I have no hobbies. Most of my off-season time is taken up with baseball business. If it isn't, I'd quit and get out of the game.

"Baseball is my very life, my one consuming interest."

—Quoted in the *Sporting News,* September 21, 1955

"I have one, but I'd rather have ballplayers. I'm not down here to start a new race of men. . . . I'm down here to get some ballplayers."

—In answer to the question, "Do you maintain a strict curfew during spring training?" as Mets manager in St. Petersburg; quoted by the AP in an October 1, 1975, article

"I have seen a lot of guff about the spitter, how it was barred in 1920 on account of it was in the same class with the shine, emery, talcum, tobacco juice and phonograph needle balls which produced a grand carnival of cheating.

"Now, they were right to bar all them cheating deliveries. But the spitter wasn't anything like the other pitches. Sure, it meant using an outside agency. But developing the spitter meant honest effort. The umpire saw what the pitcher was doing out in broad daylight. There were no night games.

"Well, the spitter and the cheaters were making the pitchers too strong. So the club owners, which they were after more hitting, barred the spitball along with the other 'foreign agency' deliveries, and gave the spitter a bad name.

"Another thing worked against the spitter. We began to get more women at ball games and some of the owners became fancy, thinking of sanitation.

"They said the spitter was filthy. Well, it wasn't any Little Lord Fauntleroy pitch. Some of the hurlers really slobbered all over the leather. But it deserved a better fate and a better name."

> —Thanksgiving Day 1961 at the Macy's Parade in New York; quoted in the *Sporting News,* December 6, 1961

"I haven't always been this lucky. Back in the Depression days, somebody suggested I invest in a turkey farm. I didn't do it. A little later, President Roosevelt declared two Thanksgivings. Just think—I could have sold twice as many turkeys.

"Then I looked for some other business investment. 'Everybody's got to have widow shades,' I said. So I bought a shade factory. Then some Italian guy invents Venetian blinds, and I go busted."

> —On success; quoted by Will Grimsley in an AP story of October 20, 1973

"I know damn well he didn't miss third, he's standing on it."

> —After being advised that it wouldn't be wise to protest when Marv Throneberry was called out for missing first base after hitting an apparent triple, since he'd missed second as well

"I make out they're a misprint and turn to the financial section."

> —As Mets manager in response to Yankee manager Ralph Houk when asked, "It must be tough when you look at all those .190 and .211 Mets batting averages in the papers. How do you do it?"; quoted in *Sport,* 1963

"I may be able to sell tickets with my face."

> —When he came to New York for the Thanksgiving Day parade in 1961. It was an attempt to get the new team in the public eye. Stengel was no stranger to promotion, and was a familiar figure in New York City baseball circles.

"I now will say this for him, whether he can talk for himself or not, I had 15 pitchers who said they couldn't pitch to him, and it turned out they couldn't pitch to nobody."

> —On Choo Choo Coleman; quoted in *Sport,* April 1966, by Berry Stainback

"I once had a guy who could hit a ball, pop, off a wall, but couldn't field. He stayed in the big league for 8 years."

> —When asked if he was eating only a candy bar for lunch. And when asked what his reply had to do with the candy bar he said, "Do you know where he came from? Hershey, Pennsylvania, that's where"; quoted by Maury Allen in *You Could Look It Up*

"I see where he didn't touch first and I know he's gonna be called out which he is when he gets to third. So I go out there to see what can be done about it and I says to the umpire: 'He did too touch first base.' And the umpire says to me: 'I don't know about first but I called him out because he didn't touch second.' In that case, I got to admit he didn't touch first, either."

> —On Marv Throneberry and the 1962 Mets; originally quoted by Max Kase in the *New York Journal-American*

"I started out to be a dentist. The dean of my school said, 'Why don't you be an orthodontist?' That way I could have got a lot of rich kids and put a black filling in their mouth. The dean said 'Always try to be a little different.' And today I make speeches all over. People ask me 'Casey, how can you speak so much when you don't talk English too good?' Well, I've been invited to Europe, and I say,

'They don't speak English over there too good, either.'"

> —Captured by Ira Berkow in 1975, the year Stengel died at age eighty-five; quoted in the *New York Times,* April 15, 1981

"I told the writers, if you're going to print anything about us, you can say for the bridegroom that it's the best catch he ever made in his career."

> —On his 1924 marriage to actress Edna Lawson

"I was fired. When a club gets to discharging a man on account of age, they can if they want to."

> —At the press conference at which it was announced he would no longer manage the Yankees. This came after the Yankees lost the 1960 World Series and the team "retired" Stengel after twelve years as manager.

"I was pitching batting practice and they told me not to throw hard. I wanted to impress the manager, so I threw as hard as I could. Then hitters commenced hitting balls over buildings. Then I threw harder and they hit the ball harder. Then, I told the manager I was really an outfielder."

> —Recalling his first tryout with Kansas City of the American Association in 1910; quoted in "Memories of Casey—and Stengelese," *San Francisco Examiner,* September 20, 1975.

"I was such a dangerous hitter I even got intentional walks during batting practice."

> —As Yankees manager, reminiscing, Hall of Fame Collection

"I wish the season opened tomorrow because we're going to surprise a lot of people. Everybody tells me I look wonderful and maybe I do—on the outside. But I don't look so good on the inside. Those 120 losses we had last season do something to you. But our organization hasn't been sleeping this winter and I'll guarantee we'll be better next year."

>—On the '63 Mets; quoted in the *Sporting News*, December 15, 1962

"I'd be an astronaut. I love the moon."

>—When asked, at age eighty-five, whether, if he had his life to live over, he would go into baseball again, *Chicago Tribune*, October 1, 1975

"If anyone wants me, tell them I'm being embalmed."

>—Said after lengthy delays on a Milwaukee-to-Houston flight kept him up for twenty-four hours straight

"If everybody on this team commenced breaking up the furniture every time we did bad, there'd be no place to sit."

>—After Ron Swoboda tore up the dugout

"If I I'd wanted a fighter, I'd have hired Rocky Marciano."

>—To Billy Martin after a brawl, *Chicago Tribune*, October 1, 1975

"If I'm looking at you, you're hitting. . . .

If I'm walking away from you and spitting, you're hitting. . . .

If I'm looking at you and spitting, you're NOT hitting. . . .

If I'm walking away and not spitting, you're NOT hitting."

>—Signs as recited by Dodger Frank Skaff just as he had been told by Stengel; quoted in Dick Young's column, *New York Daily News*, February 11, 1972. Skaff added: "Those are exactly what his signs were. I'll never forget them. They give you an idea of why some of those guys were missing them."

"If liking a kid who will never let you down in the clutch is favoritism, then I plead guilty."

>—On Billy Martin; quoted widely at the time of Martin's death

"If they produce as well on the field as they do off the field we'll win the pennant."

>—At the beginning of the 1962 Mets season, when he proposed an outfield of three men—Bell, Ashburn and Thomas—with twenty children between them; quoted in *The Incredible Mets* by Maury Allen

"If this keeps up I'm about to manage until I'm a hundred."

>—After the Mets enjoyed their first four-game winning streak; quoted by Maury Allen in *You Could Look It Up*

"If you watch him, he is called safe a lot."

>—Said of Frank Robinson; quoted in *Sports Illustrated*, April 1991

"If we'd had them when I was playing, John McGraw would have insisted that we go up to the plate and get hit on the head."

—On batting helmets; quoted in the *Sporting News*, 1955

"If we're going to win the pennant, we've got to start thinking we're not as good as we think we are."

—Admonishing his Yankees, spring 1953

"If you're playing baseball and thinking about managing, you're crazy. You'd be better off thinking about being an owner."

—As New York Yankees manager

"If you're so smart, let's see you get out of the Army."

—Reply wired to a soldier who had cabled Stengel to criticize a strategic move; quoted in the *Sporting News*, September 14, 1955

"I'll never make the mistake of being seventy again."

—On announcing his retirement as manager of the New York Yankees in 1960; quoted in Norman MacLean, *Casey Stengel: A Biography*, 1976. Stengel liked the line so much that he repeated it for years to come in this form: "I was 70 years old, and I'll never make the mistake of being 70 years old again."

"I'm pleased to be managing the New York Knickerbockers."

—At the California press conference announcing that he would manage the expansion of the New York Mets

"I'm thankful I had baseball knuckles and couldn't become a dentist."

—Referring to his brief career as a dental student, during his induction speech to the Hall of Fame, July 25, 1966

"In 1950, we discovered Whitey Ford in the school at Phoenix, Arizona. He did not belong to the New York club, but was supposed to move up to Kansas City, and it wasn't a sure thing he would stick there. But he made the Yankees, went to Kansas City, came back in time to take nine in a row, and won the World's Series finale with the Phillies. Remember? All right. Comes 1951, and the rookie camp at Phoenix which preceded the arrival of the Yankees.

"Gil McDougald, Mickey Mantle and Tom Morgan were listed as the property of Kansas City. There was no certainty they could make that club. But they landed on the New York squad. But for them, we never would have taken that third pennant, but for McDougald we might not have beaten the Giants in the World's Series.

"Well, here it is 1952."

—Quoted in the *Sporting News*, February 13, 1952

"In Tokyo, we drew 250,000 in the streets, not on the sidewalks, but in front of automobiles. They are trying to play baseball over there with small fingers and they are going to build a stadium where you don't need a tar-pol-eon. Japan . . . Mexico . . . South America—I'd like to see it played but you got to have weather at the same time or else how could you play?"

—Testimony on international baseball given to the Senate Antitrust Committee looking into the matter of baseball, July 9, 1958

"It just shows you how easy this business is."

—Comment to the press after his fledgling New York Mets beat his former team, the Yankees, 4–3, on March 23, 1962, in exhibition play

"It only helps them if they can play."

—On players who didn't drink; quoted by Maury Allen in *You Could Look It Up*

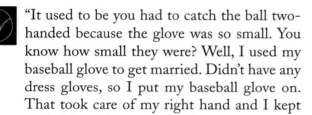

"It used to be you had to catch the ball two-handed because the glove was so small. You know how small they were? Well, I used my baseball glove to get married. Didn't have any dress gloves, so I put my baseball glove on. That took care of my right hand and I kept my left hand in my pocket."

—*Sporting News,* July 29, 1972

"It was a remarkable thing. Cobb would put on the hit-and-run and he'd never stop at first base. He'd go right on to second—an' where's the right fielder gonna throw the ball? There's only one place, he's got to throw it to second base with the shortstop covering.

"So when the right fielder gets over his surprise, he throws to second base an' Cobb slides in on his backside an' wraps his legs around the fella. So how's he gonna throw the ball home now, which is where the other runner is because he didn't stop at third base, either? An' it's a run scored an' it's a great play.

"Tried it once myself. Know what happened? They got me at second base an' got the other fella at the plate an' my manager said maybe I shouldn't try that play anymore."

—On how Ty Cobb was able to score a man from first on a single to right field; quoted in *Sport,* September 1970

"It's wonderful to meet so many friends that I didn't used to like."

—After playing in the 1971 old-timers game at Cincinnati's Riverfront Stadium. Many of the players were old adversaries; quoted in the September 1971 *Baseball Digest*

"I've been married without children many years. You generally know who you're married to. I know my ball club."

—Quoted by Arthur Daley, *New York Times,* July 12, 1970

"Joe DiMaggio is the best ball player I ever managed. Mantle is the best one-legged ball player."

—*Washington Post,* September 1, 1965

"Just when my fellows learn to hit in this ball park, they're gonna tear it down."

—As Mets manager, on the Polo Grounds, 1965, Hall of Fame Collection

"Kid, you're too small. You ought to go out and shine shoes."

—On Phil Rizzuto, as a Brooklyn tryout; widely attributed

"Left-handers have more enthusiasm for life. They sleep on the wrong side of the bed and their head gets more stagnant on that side."

 —Widely attributed

"Let him hit ya; I'll get you a new neck."

 —To a batter coming up with the bases loaded, as Mets manager

"Let me tell you about him. I give him one point for speed. I do this because he can run fast. I give him another point because he can slide fast. Then I give him a point because he can bunt. I also give him a point because he can field, very good around the fences, even on top of the fences. Next, I give him a point because he can throw. A right fielder has to be a thrower or he's not a right fielder. So I add up my points and I've got five for him before I even come to his hitting. I would say this is a good man."

 —On Roger Maris; quoted by Jack Orr in *My Greatest Day in Baseball*

"Look at him. He doesn't drink, he doesn't smoke, he doesn't chew, he doesn't stay out late, and he still can't hit .250."

 —On Bobby Richardson, as Mets manager

"Lopat looks like he is throwing wads of tissue paper. Every time he wins a game, fans come down out of the stands asking for contracts."

 —SABR Collection

"Lucky for you the kid isn't in this league. He couldn't hit .220 with such umpiring."

 —To an umpire who earlier told Stengel that his son was batting .344 in another league.

This quote dates back to his days as manager of the Braves when they were known as the Boston Bees; quoted in the *Sporting News*, February 28, 1939

"Make 'em pay you a thousand dollars. Don't go help those people with their shows for coffee-and-cake money. You're the Yankees—the best. Make 'em pay you high."

 —To his Yankee players on personal appearances; quoted in *Time*, October 3, 1955

"Managing a team back then was a tough business. Whenever I decided to release a guy, I always had his room searched first for a gun. You couldn't take any chances with some of them birds."

 —On managing the Brooklyn Dodgers in the 1930s

"Managing is getting paid for home runs someone else hits."

 —*The Macmillan Dictionary of Quotations*

"Maybe God can do something about such a play; man cannot."

 —On Pittsburgh Pirate Bill Virdon's key eighth-inning hit in the seventh game of the 1960 World Series. (Pittsburgh went on to win 10–9).

"Mr. Berra always knew the pitchers and he liked to talk to the batters, and besides which he got them into the World Series, so you'd have to say he ain't failed yet. Besides, maybe he can still swing the bat for me."

 —On hiring Yogi Berra for the Mets in 1965, after Berra managed the Yankees into the seventh game of the 1964 World Series; quoted by George Vecsey in *Joy in Mudville*

"Mister, that boy couldn't hit the ground if he fell out of an airplane."

> —When he was managing the old Boston Braves and he was asked about the merits of a recruit whom he had sent away to the minors for further seasoning; quoted in *Baseball Digest,* March 1972

"Most ball games are lost, not won."

> —Widely quoted

"Mungo and I get along fine. I just tell him I won't stand for no nonsense—and then I duck."

> —As Dodgers manager on Van Lingle Mungo

"My health is good enough above the shoulders."

> —On assuming the helm of the Mets, when asked about his health; quoted in *The Incredible Mets* by Maury Allen

"Nah, I'm just the fella who plays him on TV."

> —When spotted in a hotel lobby by a man who asked, "Are you Casey Stengel?"; quoted by Maury Allen in *You Could Look It Up*

"No, even my players aren't players."

> —When a cabbie asked Stengel if the writers sharing a cab with him were players, AP article of August 9, 1985

"Nobody ever had too many of them."

> —On pitchers

"Now a truck comes out to help the bat boy with his terrible burdens."

> —On modern methods; quoted by Art Rosenbaum in the *San Francisco Chronicle,* September 26, 1963

"Now, boys, I know you're doing the best you can, and I'm not complaining about losing. But, gee, couldn't you take a little longer doing it?"

> —Comment to the Boston Braves, the worst team he managed before the early Mets; quoted in H. L. Masin's *Baseball Laughs*

"Now you take Ernie Lombardi who's a big man and has a big nose and you take Martin who's a little man and has a bigger nose. How do you figger it?"

> —SABR Collection

"Nowadays when a pitcher gets a ball close to a hitter, the hitter comes back to the bench and says:

'You know, I think he was throwing at me.'

"When I broke in, I knew damned well they were throwing at me. The first month I was in the league, I spent two weeks on my back at the plate."

> —Ca. 1950

"Old-timers weekends and airplane landings are alike. If you can walk away from them, they're successful."

> —As Dodgers manager

"On what they're paying me here, I'm so hollow that I'm liable to explode like a light bulb if I hit the ground too hard."

—What he said when he was rebuked for not sliding into base during his playing days in Pittsburgh

"One day when I was managing Toledo, I pitched Roy Parmalee, a real wild guy, for some scouts to watch, hoping to sell him for $100,000. He began walking everybody, and, with the bases full, a batter hit a liner that struck Permalee on the left hand. He shook the gloved hand. I rushed from the dugout. 'Shake your right hand,' I ordered. 'It's my left hand that's hurt,' he said. 'Make out like it's your pitching hand,' I said. 'I want to get you out of here gracefully.'"

—Quoted in the *Sporting News,* May 4, 1955

"Our ball club has been successful because we have it, and we have the spirit of 1776. We put it into the ball field. . . . if I have been in baseball for 48 years there must be some good in it. . . . I went to work [in baseball], the first year I received $135 a month. I thought that was amazing."

—Testimony on the success of the New York Yankees given to the Senate Antitrust Committee looking into the matter of baseball, July 9, 1958

"Pitchers can't pitch without catchers. When the ball gets lively, now what are you gonna do? I don't want guys in the stands catching that ball. I want my right fielder to get it, not some guy in a bow tie that had to pay his way in."

—Quoted in the *Los Angeles Times,* April 2, 1971

"Right now we're playing bad every place. Not hittin', not pitchin', and not fieldin' too good. And judgin' by what I read in the newspapers, the Yankee writers are in a slump, too."

—After losing a string of nine games in 1953; quoted in an AP biographical sketch, September 1, 1966

"Sain don't say much, but that don't matter much, because when you're out there on the mound, you got nobody to talk to."

—On Johnny Sain, as Yankees manager, 1953

"Say, I've got a tip on the market for you fellows.

"Buy Pennsylvania Railroad, because by tomorrow night about a dozen of you bums will be on it, riding in all directions."

—To his 1921 Toledo Mud Hens after an extraordinarily shameful defeat when he found them in the clubhouse studying the financial pages. The team had many former major leaguers who had invested their money in stock; quoted by David Cataneo in the *Boston Herald,* April 25, 1990

"Say you're educated, and you can't throw strikes, then they don't leave you in too long."

—Cited in President Donald Kennedy's Stanford University farewell in this context: "Education is also no guarantee of anything. For a really full life it is quite possibly necessary, but it is not also sufficient . The best state of this proposition we owe to the noted philosopher Casey Stengel, who said, 'Say you're educated, and you can't throw strikes, then they don't leave you in too long.'"

"Shea Stadium has fifty-four restrooms, and I need one now."

> —Asked to say something about Shea Stadium by a comedian at Chicago's Edgewater Beach Hotel who was trying to save his own act by introducing personalities in the audience

"Slogans that are going all over the world and are spoken at different dinners."

> —On Met banners; quoted by Harold Rosenthal in a February 22, 1964, who wrote a piece on Stengel and the winter banquet circuit

"So what if DiMaggio doesn't talk to me. He's getting paid to play ball, and I'm getting paid to manage. If what I'm doing is wrong, my bosses will fire me. I've been fired lots of places before. He doesn't get paid to talk to me, and I don't either."

> —On Joe DiMaggio's initial trouble accepting him; quoted by Ira Berkow in the *New York Times,* April 15, 1981

"Softball is interesting. The parent . . . is more enthusiastic about [his] boy than some stranger that comes to town and wants to play in a little wooden park. . . . I don't happen to have any children but I wish Mrs. Stengel and I had eight. I would like to put them in on that bonus rule."

> —Testimony on softball given to the Senate Antitrust Committee looking into the matter of baseball, July 9, 1958

"Son, if you want to pitch in the major leagues, you'll have to learn to catch those in your mouth."

> —1960, to Yankee pitcher Mark Freeman, who had just committed a balk because a fly flew in his eye; *New York Post,* July 9, 1970

"Son, we'd like to keep you around this season, but we're going to try to win a pennant."

> —To a Yankee rookie

"Sure holds the heat well."

> —After the 1966 All-Star Game in St. Louis, when the temperature hit 113 degrees on the field and someone asked him how he liked the new St. Louis ball park; quoted by Bill Freehan in *Behind the Mask*

"Sure I played, did you think I was born age 70 sitting in a dugout trying to manage guys like you."

> —At age seventy-two when asked by Mickey Mantle if he had ever played ball, *Simpson's Contemporary Quotations*

"Sure I smoke but not all the time. I stop when I go to bed and you can look it up."

> —Responding to a newspaper survey on famous people who smoked; quoted by Maury Allen in *The Incredible Mets*

"Tell Robinson he's Chock Full of Nuts."

—On Jackie Robinson, 1964, and a reference to Robinson's employer. Robinson was a frequent critic of Stengel; quoted by George Vecsey in *Joy in Mudville*

"That feller runs splendid but he needs help at the plate, which coming from the country chasing rabbits all winter give him strong legs, although he broke one falling out of a tree, which shows you can't tell, and when a curve ball comes he waves at it and if pitchers don't throw curves you have no pitching staff, so how is a manager going to know whether to tell boys to fall out of trees and break legs so he can run fast even if he can't hit a curve ball?"

—Quoted by Joseph Durs, in *Casey*, 1967

"That game was so famous they never used me."

—On the fourteenth inning 1916 World Series game in which Babe Ruth pitched for the Red Sox. Stengel was on the Dodgers' roster but did not get to play; quoted by Leonard Koppett, *New York Times*, October 27, 1973

"That young fella has effeminate appeal, just like me."

—After meeting singer Robert Goulet; quoted in "Memories of Casey—and Stengelese," *The San Francisco Examiner*, September 30, 1975

"That's a lot of bunk about them five-year building plans. Look at us. We build and win at the same time."

—As Yankee skipper; quoted in the *Sporting News*, April 6, 1955

"The altitude bothers my players at the Polo Grounds and that's below sea level."

—When asked before an exhibition game in Mexico City if the altitude bothered his players; quoted in an AP piece, October 1, 1975

"The combined results of all our catchers turned out fairly good and then bad."

—On Mets catching in 1963; quoted by Harold Rosenthal in a February 22, 1964, piece on Stengel and the winter banquet circuit

"The league folded in July and I'm still waiting around for my back pay."

—On his first baseball assignment in 1910, recalled often in later years; quoted in *The Incredible Mets* by Maury Allen

"The man was either out too late or up too early."

—On Don Larsen violating the Yankees' midnight curfew and smashing a car into a tree during spring training, 1956; quoted in *It Takes Heart* by Mel Allen with Frank Graham Jr. much later, on his eighty-fourth birthday, he adapted the quotation: "Right now I remind myself of some of the players I used to manage. I am either out too late or up too early"; quoted in the *Sporting News*, October 12, 1974

"The Mets are gonna be amazin'."

—When he was first hired to manage the Mets, he made an appearance on a float in the Thanksgiving Day parade in New York. On that day in 1961 he delivered this line; quoted in "Memories of Casey—and Stengelese," *San Francisco Examiner*, September 30, 1975

"The Mets have been paying me for the past 10 years and people ask me what I do for them. I don't bother them, that's what."

—As former Mets manager; quoted in the *Washington Post,* January 27, 1974

"The secret of managing is to keep the guys who hate you away from the guys who are undecided."

—Said on numerous occasions; widely quoted

"The trick is growing up without growing old."

—Quoted in *Stengel: His Life and Times* by Robert W. Creamer

"The trouble with women umpires is that I couldn't argue with one. I'd put my arms around her and give her a little kiss."

—*Time,* August 11, 1975

"The way he's going I'd be better off if he was hurt."

—On Moose Skowron, who was in a slump; quoted by Steve Jacob in the Baseball Writers Association of America 1972 *Scorebook*

"The way our luck has been lately, our fellows have been getting hurt on their days off."

—As New York Mets manager, 1962

"The Yankees don't pay me to win every day—just two out of three."

—Widely quoted

"Them are the only ones the other teams ain't hitting."

—On being asked why he kept light-hitting Choo Choo Coleman in the lineup when Coleman's only attribute appeared to be blocking pitches in the dirt

"Then I'd have two languages I couldn't speak, French and English both."

—When Jim Fanning of the Expos asked Casey Stengel why he never visited Montreal; quoted in *Baseball Digest,* March 1971

"There are more men playing and the tough part now is that maybe three or four are playing with dead arms and dead legs because it's too long a season and you've got to stay in shape every day and maybe get stale."

—On baseball in the mid-seventies; quoted in an August 17, 1975, AP dispatch

"There comes a time in every man's life, and I've had plenty of them."

—One of his most quoted lines, these are the words that ultimately marked his grave at Forest Lawn Memorial Park in Glendale, California

"There's never been anyone like this kid which we got from Joplin. He has more speed than any slugger and more slug than any speedster—and nobody has ever had more of both of them together."

—On Mickey Mantle early in Mantle's career; quoted by Bob Deindorfer in *Baseball Stars of 1963*

"There's room for only one clown on this team."

—After Jimmy Piersall rounded the bases backward after hitting his first National League homer (and one hundredth career blast) as a member of the Mets; Piersall was released soon afterward

"These fans are very rabid like they were very collegiate or something because it takes four hours for us to leave our dressing room after a game, which is good because the concessions people sell a lot of hot dogs, which is good for our business and I like that. I expect that very soon they will carry one of my players out on their shoulders like he just caught the winning touchdown for Yale. They are very patient and that's good. These fellows of ours are going to keep right on improving because they are better than most folks think and not as bad as they used to be. Because it would be hard to be as bad as that."

—Describing Mets fans of the early sixties; quoted by Wells Twombly in the *Sporting News,* October 18, 1975

"They brought me up to the Brooklyn Dodgers, which at that time was in Brooklyn."

—As Mets manager, Hall of Fame Collection, 1962

"They say he's funny. Well, he has a lovely wife and family, a beautiful home, money in the bank, and he plays golf with millionaires. What's funny about that?"

—On Yogi Berra; widely attributed

"They say some of my stars drink whiskey, but I have found that the ones who drink milkshakes don't win many ball games."

—As Yankees manager; widely quoted

"They say you can't do it, but sometimes it doesn't always work."

—Quoted by Edward F. Murphy in the *New York Times,* April 25, 1976

"They used to say that in the American League they'd tell the pitchers not to throw over to first too much so there'd be more stealing and more excitement in the new league. I played in the National, and they'd throw over quick and scare you to death and the next nine times you wouldn't try to steal. But in the American, they had Ty Cobb and that president—Ban Johnson, you know—sort of quietly let the world get around, and that was how they are played."

—This secret bit of baseball history; quoted in the *New York Times,* October 27, 1973, by Leonard Koppett

"This baseball is a funny game. Just as I start telling people, 'We're making slow but sure improvements,' bop, we slide back again."

—After his 50–112 1965 season with the Mets; quoted in *Baseball as I Have Known It* by Fred Lieb

"This boy could pick up all the marbles in this circuit—batting, home runs, runs driven in. Nothing is beyond him. Nothing. He could be the No. 1 player of our league."

—On Mickey Mantle, *Sporting News,* March 16, 1955

"This club plays better baseball now. Some of them look fairly alert."

> —In 1969, still a fan, on his Mets

"This Mr. Berra, who ranks only behind Dickey and Cochrane as catchers in the American League but can play the outfield, too, where he did once when I only lost the pennant by two games."

> —To Larry King on his radio show; quoted in *Sport*, July 1959

"Tommy, I don't want you to sit in a draft. Don't slip and fall in the shower. And under no circumstances are you to eat fish, because them bones could be murder. Drive carefully, and stay in the slow lane, and sit quietly in the clubhouse until the game begins. I can't let anything happen to you."

> —To Tommy Henrich

"Up there, people are beginning to talk."

> —Pointing to the stands and responding to a pitcher asking why he had to come out of a game; quoted in the *New York Journal-American* by Max Kase, October 9, 1960

"Vince is the only player I ever saw who could strike out three times in one game and not be embarrassed. He'd walk into the clubhouse whistling. Everybody would be feeling sorry for him, but Vince always thought he was doing good."

> —On Vince DiMaggio; widely quoted

"Wake up, muscles—we're in New York now."

> —To himself in 1921, on entering the Polo Grounds after being traded to the Giants by the Phillies

"We got a lot from Johns Hopkins, but them we thought was from the college turned out to be from the clinic."

> —On trying to sign college men during his early days with the New York Mets; recalled by Lindsey Nelson and quoted in the *Sporting News*, April 11, 1970

"We had to purchase these men from the demon salesmen in baseball to get into business. And sometimes we put these men back up for sale. And those wonderful salesmen, those wonderful people in baseball, would you believe it, they don't want those men back."

> —On the New York Mets, while receiving an award as "baseball's top salesman of 1962" from the Sales Executive Club, New York, May 1, 1962

"We have the most first basemen, the largest and they eat the most, which you should see their hotel bills."

> Quoted in the *Sporting News*, April 13, 1955

"We seemed to have misplaced home plate like when I was 12 years Yankee manager there was two seasons we misplaced the pennant."

> —On the futility of managing the Mets; quoted in the *Chicago Tribune*, October 1, 1975

"We was going to get you a birthday cake, but we figured you'd drop it."

—To Marvelous Marv Throneberry, on Stengel's birthday, when Throneberry asked why he had not gotten a cake on his birthday; quoted by Arthur Daley in the *New York Times*, July 16, 1976

"Well, that's baseball. Rags to riches one day and riches to rags the next. But I've been in it 36 years and I'm used to it. Just stay calm and take things in stride."

—Quoted in the *Sporting News*, November 3, 1948

"Well, we've got this Johnny Lewis in the outfield. They hit a ball to him yesterday, and he turned left, then he turned right, then he went straight back and caught the ball. He made three good plays in one."

—When asked about his team on the *Today* show, and recalled in *Baseball Digest*, August 1969.

"Well, you know my home town in Kansas City, Missouri, so a number of people when I started out in baseball called me Casey for Kansas City, and then there was the old story of Casey at the Bat and I struck out a number of times on my first two years that I played ball, and I received the name from that strike out Casey."

—Asked about his nickname in a February 2, 1944, Armed Forces Radio Service interview

"We've got to learn to stay out of triple plays."

—When asked whether he had any thoughts on next year, after the Mets had ended their 1962 season hitting into a triple play

"What about the shortstop Rizzuto who got nothing but daughters but throws out the left-handed hitters in the double play?"

—At a baseball dinner in early 1954; quoted in Robert W. Creamer's *Stengel: His Life and Times*

"What do ya think, I was born old?"

—Stengel when he astounded Mickey Mantle by showing him how to play the right-field wall at the old Ebbets Field. This is what he said to the young Mantle; quoted in "Memories of Casey—and Stengelese," *San Francisco Examiner*, September 30, 1975

"When a fielder gets the pitcher into trouble, the pitcher has to pitch himself out of a slump he isn't in."

—*The Gospel According to Casey* by Ira Berkow and Jim Kaplan

"When I first played the game they couldn't play on the Sabbath because that was the preachers' day to collect. I still remember my first game against Babe Ruth and that day he hit two over my head and then I knew who Babe Ruth was."

—During his twenty-minute acceptance speech on induction into the baseball Hall of Fame, July 25, 1966. He concluded that speech by saying: "We appreciate every boys' group, girls' group, poem, and song. And keep goin' to see the Mets play."

"When I played in Brooklyn, I could go to the ball park for a nickel carfare. But now I live in Pasadena, and it costs me $15 or $16 to take a cab to Glendale. If I was a young man, I'd study to become a cab driver."

—Widely quoted

"When we are getting some hits we aren't getting them when we have somebody on the bases. It's very aggravating. But maybe it's better to see them left there than not getting them on at all. If they keep getting on you got to figure one of these days they'll be getting home. Or it could be one of these years, you know."

—Quoted in *Casey Stengel* by Frank Graham Jr.

"Whenever he came into a game people would stop eating their popcorn."

—On Ryne Duren; widely quoted

"Why has our pitching been so great? Our catcher, that's why. He looks cumbersome, but he's quick as a cat. He springs on a bunt like it was another dollar. And nobody's ever gonna have to throw a benefit for him neither. Money is the last thing he thinks about at night before he goes to sleep. . . . To me, he is a great man."

—On Yogi Berra; quoted in an article by Ira Berkow on Stengel, *New York Times*, April 15, 1981

"Yes, well, doctor, you want to know about my pitching and the answer is, what town are we in and do they play at night and what about that new building next to the hotel? I was having my breakfast and eggs cost too much and I broke in with Kankakee in 1910 but the league folded. If you was a pitcher then and there were no relief pitchers and you was expected . . ."

—On being asked who his pitcher would be the next day; quoted by George Vecsey in "The Best of Casey," *Newsday*, August 31, 1965

"You can get into the greatest business in the world because you can manufacture money by yourself on the field."

—On opportunities for young men in the game; quoted by Harold Rosenthal in a February 22, 1964, piece on Stengel and the winter banquet circuit

"You can/could look it up."

—Tagline to many of his stories, statistics, and claims. This is how the *New York Times* regarded the line in an October 19, 1960, "Man in the News" profile: "So remarkable is his memory that he has virtually total recollection of each encounter. 'You can look it up,' he'll say to doubters. They do and doubt no longer." James Thurber used the phrase as the title for a short story about a midget who once played in the big leagues, but on all accounts Stengel said it most often, if not first. Researcher Charles D. Poe has put together a small file of others who have used it in the Stengelian manner, including Leo Durocher, Jim Bouton, Rollie Fingers, and Jay Johnstone.

"You can't go out to the mound hobbling and take a pitcher out with a cane."

> —On announcing the end to his active life in baseball; quoted in "Memories of Casey— and Stengelese," *San Francisco Examiner*, September 30, 1975

"You commence gettin' tired 2 days later from staying up all night which it wasn't cause you're going West and you can't even get a sandwich in the whole town."

> —On arriving in Los Angeles after a long trip; quoted by Maury Allen in *You Could Look It Up*

"You couldn't play on the Amazin' Mets without having held some kind of record, like one fella held the world's international all-time record for a catcher getting hit on the ankles."

> —As former Mets manager, 1967

"You have to draft a catcher, because if you don't have one, the pitch will roll all the way back to the screen."

> —On why his first draft choice as New York Mets manager was an unknown catcher

"You have to go broke 3 times to learn how to make a living."

> —While discussing the Depression; quoted by Maury Allen in *You Could Look It Up*

"You done splendid."

> —Accolade reserved for best players; quoted in *Casey Stengel His Half-Century in Baseball*, by Frank Graham Jr.

"You fellers should do real good here now that I've added my fellers to your fellers. And the one who should help you most is a feller I shouldn't have given you. He's old but he still glues his meat together after he gets hurt."

> —Describing Enos Slaughter. He is quoted by Ben Epstein of the *New York Mirror* (in the September 14, 1955, *Sporting News*) to underscore the point that: one of the more intriguing phases of Casey's dugout dissertations is his analyzing the opposition without mentioning a single name.

"You got to get twenty-seven outs to win."

> —When with the Yankees

"You look there into the Cincinnati dugout and what do you see? All mahogany. Then you look at our bench and all you see is driftwood."

> —On his Mets, on a day they played the Reds

"You make your own luck. Some people have bad luck all their lives."

> —To his Mets on making excuses; quoted by George Vecsey in *Newsday*, August 31, 1965

"You put the whommy on him but when he's pitchin', the whommy tends to go on vacation."

> —After his team was shut out by Sandy Koufax; quoted by Maury Allen in *You Could Look It Up*

"You say, here is the opportunity and the Youth of America says, 'How much are you going to pay me?' It's like going to the university—they want the biggest, the best, the most. If necessary, we'll pay the bonuses. But they should earn it."

> —On the rookies; quoted by George Vecsey in *Newsday*, August 31, 1965

STENGEL, EDNA

"Dear, I think one of your players is dead!"

—Uttered by Mrs. Stengel to Casey when she noticed Jim Coates, who always slept with his eyes open, asleep; quoted in the 1981 *SABR Review of Books*

STEVENS, BOB

"The only man who could have caught it hit it."

—The *San Francisco Chronicle* writer's line on a Willie Mays hit; quoted by Tom Callahan in the *Washington Post*, October 22, 1989

STEWART, JON

"Baseball experts claim that without [Mike] Mussina, the Baltimore Orioles' sole attraction will be the Apply Arthritis Cream to Cal Ripken Day."

—On *Comedy Central*; quoted in *Chicago Sun Times*, December 18, 2000

STONE, HARVEY

"He was always something special, a natural born hitter, has the greatest baseball instinct and greatest pair of wrists I ever saw."

—The trainer during Hank Aaron's break-in at Jacksonville, 1953; quoted in *Hank Aaron . . . 714 and Beyond* by Jerry Brondfield

STONE, STEVE

"In '77 I led the White Sox with 15 wins despite the fact that we had Alan Bannister committing 40 errors at short, Jorge Orta, the only second baseman with a Teflon glove, Eric Sodeholm, who had limited range, at third, and Ralph Garr in left, who could have played an entire game without his glove and nobody would have known the difference."

—Quoted in the *New York Daily News*, March 7, 1982

"It must be about an elbow specialist."

—After seeing Jim Palmer read *Doctor Zhivago; The Baseball Card Engagement Book*, 1988

"Pitching is really just an internal struggle between the pitcher and his stuff. If my curve ball is breaking and I'm throwing it where I want, then the batter is irrelevant."

—As a Baltimore pitcher

"This is one of the few times you get to see your own last rites."

—Announcing his retirement

"Why should I throw at him for getting a few hits off me? When I strike him out three times a game, does he try to throw his bat at me?"

—As an Orioles pitcher, on throwing at batters; widely attributed

STONEHAM, HORACE

"The kids? I feel sorry for the kids. But I haven't seen many of their fathers recently."

—Explaining the move of the Giants to San Francisco; quoted in *The Giants of the Polo Grounds* by Noel Hynd

STOPPARD, TOM

"I don't think I can be expected to take seriously any game which takes less than three days to reach its conclusion."

— British playwright and cricket enthusiast; quoted in the *Guardian* (London), December 24, 1984

STOTZ, CARL E.

"How did Little League get started? Well, one Sunday afternoon, after I was married and had a baby daughter, I was snoozing on the glider out on the back porch, when my two young nephews, 'Major' and Jimmy Gehron, six and eight years old, woke me up and wanted me to play catch with them.

"After a lively session of baseball I asked the boys, 'How would you fellows like to play on a regular team, with uniforms, a brand new ball for every game, and bats that you could really swing?'

"Then the questions started. Uncle Tuck, who would we play? . . . Do you think people would come to see us play? . . . And would there ever be a band playing?

"Before I knew it, I had promised those kids just what I had dreamed of when I was their age. That started things going. Looking back now, I'd say it was really because I found a group of young men in my community who joined right in when I put the problem up to them. Their help and enthusiasm made it possible to start what developed into the Little League movement you know today."

— The founder of Little League, from his book *At Bat with Little League.*

STUART, DICK

"I had such a good year. I didn't want to forget it."

— The Boston Red Sox slugger, explaining to a cop why his car still had 1963 plates, 1964

"I know I'm the world's worst fielder, but who gets paid for fielding? There isn't a great fielder in baseball getting the kind of dough I get for hitting."

— Quoted by Carl Yastrzemski in *Yaz*

"I want to walk down the street and hear them say, 'Jesus, there goes Dick Stuart!' I crave publicity."

— Quoted by Arnold Hano in *Sport*, December 1963, in an article titled "I'm for Me."

"No more than usual."

— Asked if he was dizzy after being hit by a pitch

"One night in Pittsburgh, 30,000 fans gave me a standing ovation when I caught a hot dog wrapper on the fly."

— Hall of Fame Collection

"You gotta have the park."

— Explaining his success at Fenway Park; widely attributed

SUKEFORTH, CLYDE

"Jackie Robinson is one of the best ball players I ever saw. He can beat you so many ways. We always had a saying in Brooklyn, if the game went into the late innings, Jackie would find a way to win it. I believe he has the most amazing reflexes I ever saw on an athlete."

—As a Pirate coach; quoted in the *Sporting News,* May 25, 1955

SULLIVAN, FRANK

"Spread out, guys, so they can't get all of us with one shot."

—As a Phillies pitcher seeing a crowd during a team losing streak

SULLIVAN, TED

"They are making 'lawn tennis home runs' nowadays. Home run hitting has degenerated into a burlesque. . . . Modern baseball has become a game of home runs."

—Manager and organizer of the St. Louis Browns in the American Association of the 1880s; quoted in the *New York Sun,* May 18, 1927

SUNDAY, BILLY

"He works as noiselessly as a Corliss engine, makes hard plays easy, is great in a pinch and never gets cold feet."

—On Nap Lajoie, uttered when the evangelist wore the uniform of the White Sox

Billy Sunday (*Library of Congress Prints and Photographs Division*)

"I heard the Lord ask me to play ball for Him, so I signed up! Boys, I'm finished with baseball and this wild life, for I've seen the Light! I'm going into the service of God!"

—On getting religion after sauntering out of a saloon and into a rescue mission during his ninth season in baseball; quoted in *Baseball's Unforgettables* by Mac Davis

"Lord save us from off-handed, flabby cheeked, brittle boned, weak-kneed, thin-skinned, pliable, plastic, spineless, effeminate, ossified three-karat Christianity."

—Quoted in William G. McLoughlin, *Billy Sunday Was His Real Name* (Chicago: Univ of Chicago Press 1955)

SUSCE, GEORGE

"You'll soon be down to .280 where you belong."

> —To Tiger Marvin James Owens during a 1934 pennant drive when he was batting .365. The nine candid words uttered the day after Susce was called up by the club. He was sent back to the minors the next day by manager Mickey Cochrane, who had heard the remark. He thus cut himself out of the World Series; quoted in *Baseball Digest,* August 1943

SUTTON, DON

"Whenever I pitch during the regular season, it's work. To me it's a routine thing, like going to the office or walking into a factory. You have a job to do and you go out and try to do it. But the playoffs, the World Series and things like the All-Star game are just plain fun."

> —As a Dodger; quoted in the *Los Angeles Times,* October 6, 1978

SUTTON, LARRY

"Good hands, good power, runs exceptionally well, nice glove, left-handed line drive hitter. Good throwing arm. May be too damn aggressive, bad temper."

> —His scouting report on Casey Stengel, 1911; quoted in Kevin Kerrane's *Dollar Sign on the Muscle*

SUZUKI, ICHIRO, *SEE* ICHIRO

SWOBODA, RON

"If we lost, I'd be eating my heart out. But since we won, I'll only eat one ventricle."

> —On the '69 Mets; quoted by George Vecsey in *Joy in Mudville*

"The way we're going, it's hard to keep your feet on the ground. You feel inebriated, high. If they could package us I don't think we'd be legal."

> —As his '69 Mets were closing in on the National League pennant; quoted by Larry Merchant in the January 1970 *Baseball Digest*

T

Taft, William Howard

"The game of baseball is a clean straight game, and it summons to its presence everybody who enjoys clean, straight athletics. It furnishes amusement to the thousands and thousands. And I like it for two reasons—first, because I enjoy it myself and second, because if by the presence of the temporary chief magistrate such a healthy amusement can be encouraged, I want to encourage it."

> —May 4, 1910, in a speech in St. Louis. This is how Taft's role as first fan was described in the 1911 *Spalding's Official Base Ball Guide*: "President Taft believes in Base Ball. . . . He tells his friends that it is a pastime worth every man's while and advises them to banish the blues by going to a ball game and waking up with the enthusiasts of the bleachers who permit no man to be grouchy among them."

"That's it. That's the last time I'll ever pitch. If that team hit me as well as they did, I must be through. I'll never pitch again."

President William Howard Taft (*Library of Congress Prints and Photographs Division*)

> —As a semipro pitcher after being yanked from a game in 1882. He did not pitch again until he threw out the first ball as president twenty-eight years later.

"To Walter Johnson with the hope that he will be as formidable as in yesterday's game."

> —Inscribed ball April 14, 1910, the day after he had thrown the first presidential opening ball to Johnson

TALESE, GAY

"Wall Street bankers supposedly back the Yankees; Smith College girls approve of them. God, Brooks Brothers and United States Steel are believed to be solidly in the Yankees' corner. . . . The efficiently triumphant Yankee machine is a great institution, but, as they say, who can fall in love with U.S. Steel?"

> —"There Are Fans—and Yankee Fans," *New York Times,* June 29, 1958

TAMMEUS, BILL

"He accomplished something endearingly American. He found a small measure of fame in his very obscurity. So long, Dutch. We'll try to keep your memory alive, such as it was."

> —The *Kansas City Star* on the death of Emil Verban (June 26, 1989), who George Will once called "the patron saint of Cub fans because he symbolizes mediocrity under pressure." (In Verban's career, he slugged only one homer in 2,911 at bats.)

"The worst part about moving the clocks back is that it delays the start of spring training by an hour."

> —Columnist for the *Kansas City Star;* quoted in the *Baltimore Sun,* November 2, 1993

TAMONY, PETER

"That baseball . . . is played only in the United States, and that the game is not international is of little moment in the excitement attending the outcome of the [World] Series. Whichever team wins holds the Championship of the World, and is thus, in our scheme of things, entitled to a place just to the right of that of the gods."

> —Quoted in *News Letter and Wasp,* October 13, 1939

TANANA, FRANK

"It requires a lot of skill and a lot of effort to throw a baseball to a certain location with something on it. That's the damn good thing about baseball: There's so much effort and skill involved. The hardest thing to do, they say, is to hit a baseball. The reason it's so hard is the people who throw it."

> —Pitcher, California Angels, on pitching, in the *Los Angeles Times,* October 7, 1977

TANNER, CHUCK

"Having Willie Stargell on your ball club is like having a diamond ring on your finger."

> —*Time,* October 29, 1979

"If you don't like the way the Atlanta Braves are playing, then you don't like baseball."

> —The Braves manager after his team had grounded into fifteen double plays in a four-game series; quoted in the *Baltimore Sun,* April 26, 1987

"It's hard to win a pennant, but it's harder losing one."

> —As Pirates manager; widely quoted

TANNER, CHUCK (CONTINUED)

"The greatest feeling in the world is to win a major league game. The second-greatest feeling is to lose a major league game."

> —As Pirates manager; quoted in the *Sporting News*, July 15, 1985

"People never look at it that way, but a 162-game season is actually made up of three parts, consisting of 54 games each. While it's nice to get away well during those first 54 games, it isn't absolutely necessary. Mostly it's what a team does during that second 54-game stretch that determines where it is going to finish at the end of the season. If a manager has his pitching and his defense set by then and he's also getting consistency from his hitters, then he can generally count on being a pennant contender for the rest of the year. What you have to remember is that baseball isn't a week or a month but a season—and a season is a long time."

> —As Pirates manager; quoted in the *Christian Science Monitor*, June 3, 1982

"You can have money piled to the ceiling, but the size of your funeral is still going to depend on the weather."

> —As Pirates manager on the importance of happiness and satisfaction in playing the game; quoted in the *Sporting News* May 20, 1979

TANTON, BILL

"Will we ever see another Babe? Certainly we will, in time, and maybe we have one in our midst now. Does anyone doubt that Jackie Joyner-Kersee might be a big-league prospect if she had concentrated on baseball? And with ballplayers having broken the $3 million-a-year salary barrier, won't the extraordinary woman athlete be tempted to go for it . . . ?

"We will see a woman in the majors before we see one in the NBA or NFL, and when it happens—not *if* it happens—it will excite the masses like nothing we have ever seen in sports. If you can remember the furor over Billie Jean King and Bobby Riggs' tennis battle of the sexes in [1973] . . . , you can imagine how big this one will be."

> —Writing in the *Baltimore Evening Sun*, 1989

TARBELL, IDA

"It is a poor management indeed, these days, and a thoroughly soured [work] force which does not support departmental nines . . . What the game is doing for health and sociability in American industries cannot be estimated."

> —The social reformer writing in 1915; quoted in *Baseball: The People's Game* by Harold Seymour.

TAYLOR, ZACK

"We've got to realize the world has changed. The dollar is worth 40 cents, and players must get the salaries they are worth. I don't think there are as many top-grade, or colorful, players as in my day. So, those who do stand out also stand out in the payrolls. My top as a player was $11,000 with the 1929 championship Cubs, and for a Florida Cracker that was a lot of money."

— Quoted in the *Sporting News*, February 12, 1958. Taylor was a major-league catcher, 1920–35, and manager of the St. Louis Browns.

TEBBETTS, BIRDIE

"Ballplayers keep books. They mark it down if they owe you something. They mark it down in the back of their minds. Then, they wait to repay it. Sometimes it takes so long that when a guy finally gets even, you have trouble remembering what the original grievance was. But the player involved remembers. Every man one day walks back across the shadow he has cast."

— As a manager of the Reds; quoted in *Sport*, December 1957

"I once said to Joe McCarthy, 'If Ted Williams played regularly in Yankee Stadium, he'd surely break Babe Ruth's record.' All McCarthy said was, 'Lou Gehrig didn't,' and it was a good answer."

— Quoted in the *Sporting News*, April 13, 1955

"If I owned Casey Stengel's oil wells, I wouldn't finish my sentences either."

— As Reds manager, April 20, 1955

"Really, I have nothing new to introduce to managing. Whatever success you have as a manager belongs to the players. The only thing I bring with me to this new job is a great desire to win."

— Quoted in the *Sporting News*, October 14, 1953, after being selected to manage the Cincinnati Reds

"The Hall of Fame, let them have it. Let them put all the great players in it. But I'd like to put a wing on it for fellows like Phil Rizzuto and myself—not that I'm putting myself in a class with Rizzuto. I'm speaking of a type now. Fellows like Rizzuto and Billy Martin."

— Quoted by Frank Graham in the August 1950, *Baseball Digest*

"The myth is that you put a Yankee uniform on a player and he becomes great."

— The former major-league player and manager; quoted by William B. Mead in *The Official Yankee Hater's Handbook*

"When Bobby Doerr and I were with the Red Sox, we pleaded with Ted Williams to tip his cap when the fans applauded his home runs. We pointed out that as great a slugger as Babe Ruth was, he used to do it and we finally convinced him. Next time up, Ted hit one a country mile into the right-field bleachers. I was anxious to see what he was going to do. He dropped his bat, lowered his head in the funny way of his and as he began loping toward first base, we could hear him muttering: 'I won't do it, I won't do it, I won't do it,' and he didn't."

— As Reds manager; quoted in the *Sporting News*, April 6, 1955

TEBEAU, PATSY

"A milk-and-water, goody-goody player can't wear a Cleveland uniform."

— The Cleveland manager, 1892; quoted by Raymond Mungo in *Confessions from Left Field*

TEMPLETON, GARRY

"I'm not up on counts and taking pitches. I swing the bat. If you can concentrate, hitting is easy."

— Quoted in *Late Innings* by Roger Angell

TENACE, GENE

"That isn't an arm, that's a rifle."

— On seeing Johnny Bench throw to second; quoted in *Mustache Gang* by Ron Bergman

TENER, JOHN K.

"This is a war of democracy against bureaucracy. And I tell you that baseball is the very watchword of democracy. There is no other sport or business or anything under heaven which exerts the leveling influence that baseball does. Neither the public school nor the church can approach it. Baseball is unique. England is a democratic country, but it lacks the finishing touch of baseball."

— National League president and former governor of Pennsylvania; quoted in *Baseball: The Early Years* by Harold Seymour

TERRY, BILL

"Are the Dodgers still in the league?"

— 1934, often-stated alternative version of Terry's "Is Brooklyn still in the league?"

"Baseball must be a great game to survive the fools who run it."

— Dick Kaegel, editor of the *Sporting News*, used this quote in writing about labor

Garry Templeton (*San Diego Padres*)

problems in the game and wrote of the quotation: "Bill Terry, the old New York Giant, is supposed to have made that comment upon some occasion of disgust with the game's poobahs" (May 30, 1981). His observation has been treasured through the years.

"He was the type of fellow who would call all the pitches until you got in a spot, then he'd leave you on your own."

— On John McGraw, who he followed as New York Giants manager

"I don't know what kept me out, newspapermen or just that you don't want me up here. But I finally made it and I want to thank God for it. It is a distinct honor to be here and a part of the Hall of Fame."

—On being inducted into the Hall of Fame,
August 10, 1954

"I had great control, I never missed hitting the other fellow's bat."

—Quoted by Quentin Reynolds, *Collier's*,
March 31, 1934, on his futile attempts to
pitch

"I played baseball because I could make more money doing that than I could doing anything else."

—Often-stated by Terry, a determined realist;
quoted widely

"Is Brooklyn still in the league?"

—One of the most famous—and infamous—
quotations in the history of the game.
Writing in *Sport*, Gordon Forbes said of the
question: "No war ever began with a more
infuriating declaration. The Dodgers and
their fans stewed all summer waiting for
revenge." In an interview with Fred Russell of
the *Nashville Banner*, which is quoted in the
May 1969 issue of *Baseball Digest*, Terry said:
   "I'll tell you the truth about it, exactly
what happened. You recall that we won the
pennant in 1933 and beat Washington in
the World Series. Naturally I was proud of
such an accomplishment, but not so cocky

or foolish that I went around making ugly remarks about other terms.

   "In January of 1934 I went up to New York from Memphis to talk over the coming season with Giant officials. A little press conference was set up. We were discussing other National League clubs and Roscoe McGowen of the *Times*, one of the veteran writers, asked: "What about Brooklyn, Bill?'

   "'I haven't heard from them in a couple of weeks,' I joked. 'Are they still in the league?'

   "The rest is history. That night every paper in New York headlined the story: 'Terry Asks If Brooklyn's Still in the League.'

   "When the season opened and we played Brooklyn at Ebbets Field, they showered me with tomatoes. But the worst came as the season ended. We were playing the Dodgers in Brooklyn again, needing a win to tie St. Louis for the pennant. There must have been 35,000 people there. As the game ended and they had whipped us, it seemed to me that every fan there threw either a cat or a dog at me. These animals were falling all over me. It was a circus. All because they figured I had insulted Brooklyn."

"I've got to get out of the lineup pretty soon. I'm not going to wait for the fans to yell, 'Why don't you drop dead, you bum?' I've got too much pride for that."

—At thirty-six, early in the season of 1935;
quoted by Gordon Forbes in *Sport*, May 1965

"No business in the world has ever made more money with poorer management."

—After resigning as manger of the New York Giants in late 1941; quoted in *The Imperfect Diamond* by Lee Lowenfish and Tony Lupien (Stein & Day, 1980). A longer version of his farewell to baseball: "I intend to devote myself to my cotton business and watch baseball from the outside. I'm not worried about the game. No business in the world has ever made more money with poorer management. It can survive anything."

"To hit .400 you need a great start and you can't have a slump. The year I did it, I was around .410, .412 all season, and I was really hitting the ball on the nose. Hitting is a business. With two strikes, you really protect that plate."

—Quoted by Bill Gutman in *Heavy Hitters*

"You've bought yourself a cripple."

—Bill Terry as manager of the New York Giants, ridiculing New York Yankee farm-system director George Weiss for purchasing the contract of rookie prospect Joe DiMaggio, who had injured his left knee in a nonbaseball accident earlier; uttered in the spring of 1935 and quoted in *The Experts Speak*.

TERWILLIGER, WAYNE

"There's just so much inside here. It's like a shopping center."

—As a Twins coach on the Toronto Sky Dome; quoted in the *Sporting News*, September 18, 1989

THAYER, ERNEST L.

The outlook wasn't brilliant for the Mudville
    nine that day;
The score stood four to two with but one
    inning more to play.
And then when Cooney died at first, and Bar-
    rows did the same,
A sickly silence fell upon the patrons of the
    game.
A straggling few got up to go in deep despair.
    The rest

Clung to that hope which springs eternal in
    the human breast;
They thought if only Casey could but get a
    whack at that—
We'd put up even money now with Casey at
    the bat.

But Flynn preceded Casey, as did also Jimmy
    Blake,
And the former was a lulu and the latter was a
    cake;
So upon that stricken multitude grim melan-
    choly sat,
For three seemed but little chance of Casey's
    getting to the bat.

But Flynn let drive a single, to the wonder-
    ment of all,
And Blake, the much despised, tore the cover
    off the ball;
And when the dust had lifted, and the men
    saw what had occurred,
There was Jimmy safe at second and Flynn
    a-hugging third.

Then from 5,000 throats and more there rose
    a lusty yell;
It rumbled through the valley, it rattled in the dell;
It knocked upon the mountain and recoiled
    upon the flat,
For Casey, mighty Casey, was advancing to the
    bat.

There was ease in Casey's manner as he
    stepped into his place;
There was pride in Casey's bearing and a smile
    on Casey's face.
And when, responding to the cheers, he lightly
    doffed his hat,
No stranger in the crowd could doubt 'twas
    Casey at the bat.

Ten thousand eyes were on him as he rubbed
    his hands with dirt;
Five thousand tongues applauded when he
    wiped them on his shirt.
Then while the writhing pitcher ground the
    ball into his hip,
Defiance gleamed in Casey's eye, a sneer
    curled Casey's lip.

And now the leather-covered sphere came
    hurtling through the air,
And Casey stood a-watching it in haughty
    grandeur there.
Close by the sturdy batsman the ball unheeded
    sped—
"That ain't my style," said Casey. "Strike one,"
    the umpire said.

From the benches, black with people, there
    went up a muffled roar,

Like the beating of the storm-waves on a stern
    and distant shore.
"Kill him! Kill him!" shouted some one in the
    stand;
And it's likely they'd have killed him had not
    Casey raised his hand.

With a smile of Christian charity great Casey's
    visage shone;
He stilled the rising tumult, he bade the game
    go on!
He signaled to the pitcher, and once more the
    spheroid flew;
But Casey still ignored it, and the umpire said,
    "Strike two."

"Fraud!" cried the maddened thousands, and
    echo answered fraud;
But one scornful look from Casey and the
    audience was awed.
They saw his face grow stern and cold, they
    saw his muscles strain,
And they knew that Casey wouldn't let that
    ball go by again.

The sneer is gone from Casey's lip, his teeth
    are clenched in hate;
He pounds with cruel violence his bat upon
    the plate.
And now the pitcher holds the ball, and now
    he lets it go,
And now the air is shattered by the force of
    Casey's blow.

Oh, somewhere in this favored land the sun is
    shining bright;
The band is playing somewhere, and some-
    where hearts are light,

THAYER, ERNEST L. (CONTINUED)

And somewhere men are laughing, and somewhere children shout;
But there is no joy in Mudville—mighty Casey
has struck out.

> —What is probably the most popular poem ever
> written by an American. It is almost certainly the
> most recited, most parodied, and most sequeled.
> It first appeared on page four of the *San Francisco
> Examiner,* June 3, 1888, under the byline "Phin."

THEROUX, ALEXANDER

"Many have been the great legendary oppo-
nents. Greek and Trojan. Roman and Hun.
Huron and Algonquin. Aztec and conquista-
dor. Arab and Jew. Boer and Xhosa. Tacitus and
Domitian. Mozart and Salieri. Tchaikovsky and
Brahms. And it's been no different in nature.
Digger wasp and spider. Mongoose and cobra.
The sailfish is the archenemy of the shark.

"Then there are the heterosporous combi-
nations of cherry and choke tree, cedar and
ash. Natural enemies. Vine and bay, burr and
lintle. Threatening entities. Hostile camps.
It's not an exaggeration to say that on this
long list should be entered one of the fiercest
rivalries in the history of baseball: the Boston
Red Sox and the New York Yankees."

> —Writing in the *Boston Globe* magazine, July 2,
> 1989

THOMAS, DAN

"They ought to make a rule that if a guy gets
hit and is able to get up, they should tie the
pitcher's hands behind his back and let the
hitter smack him in the face."

> —The Brewer on batters being hit by pitched balls;
> quoted in the *New York Times*, May 15, 1977

THOMAS, FRANK

"Don't try to tell me you still have a fastball.
Know how much I think of your fastball? The
first time you throw it to me today, I'm gonna
embarrass you. I'm gonna reach right over the
plate and catch it barehanded."

> —To former teammate Warren Spahn before a
> spring 1963 game, *Sport*, July 1963

THOMAS, GORMAN

"There's no telling what that ball was worth
before I signed it."

> —When asked to sign an old baseball that had
> already been signed by Babe Ruth, Hank
> Aaron, Mickey Mantle, and Joe DiMaggio

"They know when to cheer and they know
when to boo. And they know when to drink
beer. They do it all the time."

> —As a former Brewer on the Milwaukee fans,
> *Baltimore Sun*, April 26, 1987

THOMPSON, FRESCO

"He wore a glove for one reason: it was a
league custom. The glove would last him a
minimum of six years because it rarely made
contact with the ball."

> —On Babe Herman

"What do you want, a bonus or a limp?"

> —On trying to persuade a prospect to choose
> baseball over football; widely attributed

"When I broke into baseball, each club had two scouts—one west of the Mississippi and the other east of the Mississippi. Now the Dodgers have a scout who works the west side of Wilshire Boulevard and another who works the east side."

> —The Dodgers vice president; quoted in the March 1965, *Baseball Digest*

"When I went to the winter meetings, I'd see sixty managers who'd just been fired hanging around looking for jobs. There were only two or three unemployed front-office men. The odds looked good."

> —On why he had gone to work in the Dodger front office

"Where triples go to die."

> —Describing Willie Mays's glove; recalled in an article on Mays turning sixty in the *Tampa Tribune*, May 6, 1991

THOMPSON, MORTON

"He reached puberty, but forgot to touch second."

> —On a managing editor he once worked for. Charles Einstein, writing in the *San Francisco Chronicle* (September 13, 1969), called it "one of the fine lines in American writing for sheer description."

THOMSON, BOBBY

"Cloud nine. How else can I describe the feeling? We beat the Dodgers. We won the pennant. I hit a home run. Everybody went nuts. Storybook stuff, the whole thing. I still don't know why I was hyperventilating as I ran around the bases. It must have been the excitement, the pure joy, all those amazing feelings just coming together."

> —Describing his feelings on hitting the three-run home run in the bottom of the ninth inning to win the 1951 National League pennant for the New York Giants versus the Brooklyn Dodgers, on October 3. Bobby Thomson with Lee Heiman and Bill Gutman, *The Giants Win the Pennant! The Giants Win the Pennant!* (New York: Kensington Publishing, 1991)

"I didn't run around the bases—I rode around 'em on a cloud. Wow, I still don't know what time it is or where I am. Frankly, I don't care."

> —On his pennant-winning home run, in *the Sporting News Chronicle of 20th Century Sport*

THORN, JOHN

"Baseball has been very, very good to us. It has given America rest and recreation, myths and memories, heroes and history. It has mirrored our society and sometimes propelled it, offering models for democracy, community, commerce and common humanity. And as our national game, baseball in no small measure defines us as Americans, enriching our language and imagery and connecting us with our countrymen in a grand tradition that crosses all barriers of generation, class, race and creed."

> —*The Game for All America* (St. Louis: Sporting News Publishing, 1988)

THORN, JOHN (CONTINUED)

"There are those who complain that baseball is too slow, too dull, too old-fashioned. Too much standing around, too much time-wasting. Let's speed it up, they say—make it more like football or basketball or hockey. They see inactivity and they think nothing's going on. How sad! They look but they do not see."

—*The Game for All America* (St. Louis: Sporting News Publishing, 1988)

THORPE, JIM

"Sure! I played baseball in 1909 and 1910 in the Carolina League but I had no idea I was a pro. I got $60 a month for expenses and that's all. I wouldn't even have tried for the Olympic team had I thought I was a pro."

—*New York Telegram*, July 21, 1948. During the 1912 Olympics held in Stockholm, Thorpe won medals in pentathlon and decathlon events. He was stripped of them, however, when it was reported that he had been paid for playing professional baseball during two summers, causing him to lose his amateur status. In 1982, nearly thirty years after his death, the International Olympic Committee reversed its original ruling, and Jim Thorpe was officially recognized as the winner of the events he had won in 1912.

THRIFT, SYD

"I got a sore throat and a cough just from spending two weeks on the phone talking to those clowns [other general managers]. I think when it comes to trading, the Ameri-

Jim Thorpe (*Library of Congress Prints and Photographs, Bain Collection*)

can League is 98 percent air and about two percent balloon."

—As Yankees general manager; quoted in the *Washington Times*, April 24, 1989

THRONEBERRY, MARV

"I am a sweet hitter. Not really a great hitter. Just a sweet hitter."

—On himself; often-quoted, this statement appears in *Joy in Mudville* by George Vecsey

"I still don't know why they asked me to do this commercial."

—One of his signature lines in the Miller Lite TV ads

"My town is halfway between Memphis and some good bird dog hunting."

—On Collierville, Tennessee; quoted by Maury Allen in *The Incredible Mets*

THURBER, JAMES

"He [Milt Kline] gets Rube Waddell mixed up with Rube Marquard, for one thing, and anybody does that oughta be put away where he won't bother nobody. So I can't tell you the exact margin we win the pennant by. Maybe it was two and a half games, or maybe it was three and a half. But it'll all be there in the newspapers and record books of thirty, thirty-one years ago and, like I was sayin', you could look it up."

—"You Could Look It Up," *Saturday Evening Post*, 1941; reprinted in *My World—and Welcome To It*, published 1942 by Harcourt, Brace

"The majority of American males put themselves to sleep by striking out the batting order of the New York Yankees."

—Widely attributed

Marv Throneberry (*Author's Collection*)

THYLIN, HERB

"Al Gore got the most hits, but George W. Bush scored the most runs. This baseball analogy explains why Bush won and Gore lost. Al Gore got the most votes and lost; but George W. Bush scored more electoral votes and won. This is the way the baseball is played and this is the way presidential elections are held."

—Letter to the Editor of the *Seattle Times*, December 4, 2000

TORBORG, JEFF

"I don't think it will affect his mobility. Electrical storms might be a problem."

—The Chicago White Sox manager, when asked about the metal plate inserted in catcher Carlton Fisk's broken right hand, *Sports Illustrated*, May 8, 1989

"There must be some reason why we're the only ones facing the other way."

—On being a catcher

"When you talk velocity, Nolan threw the hardest. Nolan threw it down in the strike zone harder than any human being I ever saw.

"In 1973 against the Boston Red Sox, Nolan threw a pitch a little up and over my left shoulder. I reached up for it and Nolan's pitch tore a hole in the webbing of my glove and hit the backstop at Fenway Park."

—As White Sox manager, on catching Nolan Ryan and Sandy Koufax; quoted in *USA Today*, August 22, 1989

TORGESON, EARL

"Because I want to be able to see."

—The bespectacled White Sox first baseman on being asked by veteran broadcaster Jack Brickhouse, "Earl, why do you wear glasses when you play ball?" *Chicago Tribune*, April 8, 1994

TORRE, JOE

"Unless you understand what sport is all about and how important winning is to you, I don't think you understand the insult part of this thing."

—Rejecting an incentive-based contract from the Yankees after 12 years of post-season play. October 24, 2007

"When we lose I can't sleep at night. When we win I can't sleep at night. But when you win you wake up feeling better."

—As New York Mets manager

TORREZ, DANIELLE GAGNON

"But that was what opening day was all about, and it was only one of the many unwritten 'rules' I'd soon learn: as a baseball wife, your entire life focused on this day and the 161 other days like it throughout the year. Unless hospitalized or blocked by some other tragedy, you always came out to cheer. You went to every home game and followed, by radio or TV, every game on the road. Since your man's performance was continually measured and reported in the minutest detail by con-sumers (fans), employers (owners and managers), and outside analysts (the press), you were expected to counter this pressure with visible and enthusiastic support. Attending that initial game when all the heat began was a must."

—On the rules of being a baseball wife from her *High Inside: Memoirs of a Baseball Wife*. Her second rule: "Support your husband's superstitions, whether you believe them or not." Because of the second rule, she says, "I joined players' wives who ate ice cream in the sixth inning or tacos in the fifth, or who attended games in a pink sweater, a tan scarf, or a floppy hat."

"The Yankee uniforms did not have commanding dark blue pinstripes for nothing. If your husband dropped a fly ball or allowed too many hits or struck out at a crucial moment, you might suddenly have a hard time making simple conversation."

—Quoted in *High Inside: Memoirs of a Baseball Wife*

"When you marry a baseball player, you marry the man, you marry baseball, you marry its rules."

—As the former wife of pitcher Mike Torrez in her *High Inside: Memoirs of a Baseball Wife*

TORREZ, MIKE

"No pitcher *ever* wants to leave."

—Quoted by Danielle Gagnon Torrez in *High Inside: Memoirs of a Baseball Wife*

TREBELHORN, TOM

"[Phil] Niekro cheated for 40 years and they're trying to make it up in one year."

—The Milwaukee Brewers manager complaining about the unusually high number of balks being called against pitchers during the 1988 season, *USA Today*, April 12, 1988

"Running a ball club is like raising kids who fall out of trees."

—As Brewers manager; quoted in the *Sporting News*, May 15, 1989.

TRESH, TOM

"Superstition. Those guys aren't superstitious. They're just too cheap to send out their laundry."

—On players who don't change their clothes during a winning streak; quoted in *Sport*, July 1963

TREVINO, LEE

"If a baseball player strikes out, he still gets paid. He just goes back to the dugout. . . . If a baseball player strikes out, it should cost him. He should get so much for a single, a double and a home run. And if he makes an error, that costs him $1,000."

—The golfer on why baseball players should be paid like golfers; quoted in the *Los Angeles Times*, June 9, 1982

TRIANDOS, GUS

"I don't need a chest protector. I need a bra."

—The former Oriole at an old-timers game

TRILLO, MANNY

"The best thing about baseball is that you can do something about yesterday tomorrow."

—As a Phillies infielder; widely quoted

TRIMBLE, JOE

"The imperfect man pitched a perfect game yesterday."

—On Don Larsen's perfect World Series game, in the *New York Daily News*, October 9, 1956.

TROUT, PAUL "DIZZY"

"I figured if that guy [Dean] can get 30 or 40 thousand a year for being a screwball, that's for me. From now on, call me Diz."

—On letting himself be called "Dizzy." Quoted in his *Sporting News* obituary. He died on February 28, 1972, at age fifty-six. He once explained the origin of the nickname: "I was pitching in the minors and all of a sudden it started to pour. I saw this awning in center field and started to run under it. The only trouble was the awning was painted on the wall. From then on I was Dizzy."

"My pitching secret? It's simple. Nobody likes to hit a man who wears glasses."

—*The Sporting News Chronicle of 20th Century Sport*

TROUT, PAUL "DIZZY" (CONTINUED)

"One day I was pitching against Washington and the catcher called for a fast ball. When it got to the plate, it was so slow that two pigeons were roosting on it. I decided to quit."

—Quoted in his *Sporting News* obituary

"See that right arm? It's strong from milkin' cows. I milked so many in my day that even now when I meet anybody, I reach for one finger instead of the whole hand."

—Opening remark from his banquet circuit speech; quoted in *Baseball Digest*, May 1945

TRUDEAU, G. B.

"I wonder why they cover sports other than baseball.... To each his own, I guess."

—Thoughts of Rick Redfern in a *Doonesbury* cartoon, October 6, 1985

TRUDEAU, PIERRE

"Canada is a country whose main exports are hockey players and cold fronts. Our main imports are baseball players and acid rain."

—As Canadian prime minister; quoted in *Sports Illustrated*, July 26, 1982

TRUMAN, HARRY

"And may the sun never set on American baseball."

—From his seventy-fifth-birthday message to the National League in 1951 and used for years to come by opponents of night baseball

President Harry Truman (*Martin Luther King Library, Washington, D.C.*)

"I couldn't see well enough to play when I was a boy, so they gave me a special job—they made me the umpire."

—Often-quoted line on his childhood approach to the game

"You don't have to weigh 250 pounds to make good in baseball, and you don't have to be 6'7", either. I like that. I was a little fellow myself."

—Widely attributed

TUDOR, JOHN

"If [bleeping] Congress was in Wisconsin, would we have to go up there and play? You've got a chance for it to be 30 degrees and drizzling and you've got guys coming off two weeks of spring training. It's just not a good idea."

—On playing a 1990 preseason exhibition game in Washington, D.C.; quoted in Marc Topkin's column in the April 8, 1990, *St. Petersburg Times*

TUNIS, JOHN R.

"Real sport is an antidote to fatalism; the deep objective of games is really to train one's reflex of purpose, to develop a habit of keeping steadily at something you want to do until it is done. The rules of the game and the opposition of other players are devices to put obstacles in your way. The winner must keep everlastingly after his objective with intensity and continuity of purpose."

—*Reader's Digest*, February 1942

TURAN, KENNETH

"Baseball endures at least in part because it is a contemplative sport that delights in nuances. Not a brazen game, eager to sell its thrills cheaply, but rather an understated affair that must be courted if it's to be loved."

—*It's a Grand Old Game*, 1979

TURLEY, BOB

"The most important thing our little league had was equipment. We were so tickled with our uniforms that we should show up for a six thirty twilight game at about noon."

—*The Baseball Card Engagement Book*, 1989

TURNER, TED

"If you ever get a chance to buy a baseball team, do so. It's very fun."

—A speech to the McCallie School in Chattanooga

"One of my goals in life was to be surrounded by unpretentious, rich young men. Then I bought the Braves and I was surrounded by twenty-five of them."

—Widely attributed

"They're a shelter all right. A bomb shelter."

—On his Braves as a tax shelter; quoted in *Sports Illustrated*, June 4, 1979

TWAIN, MARK

"A certain ancient game, played with a ball, hath come up again, yet already are all mouths filled with the phrases that describe its parts and movement; insomuch, indeed, that the ears of the sober and such as would busy themselves with weightier matter are racked with the clack of the same till they do ache with anguish."

—An Extract from *Methuselah's Diary*

"Baseball is the very symbol, the outward and visible expression of the drive and push and rush and struggle of the raging, tearing, booming nineteenth century."

> —April 8, 1889, at a banquet at Delmonico's restaurant in New York City, honoring baseball players returning from the 1888– 1889 Spalding round-the-world-tour. Twain ended the speech with the toast: ". . . and so I drink long life to the boys who ploughed a new equator round the globe stealing bases on their bellie."

Mark Twain (*Library of Congress Prints and Photographs, Bain Collection*)

"It was a project of mine to replace the tournament with something which might furnish an escape for the extra steam of the chivalry, keep those bucks entertained and out of mischief, and at the same time preserve the best thing in them, which was their hardy spirit of emulation. I had had a choice band of them in private training for some time, and the date was now arriving for their first public effort.

"This experiment was baseball. In order to give the thing vogue from the start, and place it out of the reach of criticism, I chose my nines by rank, not capacity. There wasn't a knight in either team who wasn't a sceptered sovereign. As for material of this sort, there was a glut of it always Arthur. You couldn't get those people to leave off their armor; they wouldn't do that when they bathed. They consented to differentiate the armor so that a body could tell one team from the other, but that was the most they would do. So, one of the teams wore chain-mail ulsters, and the other wore plate-armor made of my new Bessemer steel. Their practice in the field was the most fantastic thing I ever saw. Being ball-proof, they never skipped out of the way, but stood still and took the result; when Bessemer was at the bat and a ball hit him, it would bound a hundred and fifty yards sometimes. And when a man running, and threw himself on his stomach to slide to his base, it was like an iron-clad coming to port. At first I appointed men of no rank to act as umpires, but I had to discontinue that. These people were no easier to please than other nines. The umpire's first decision was usually his last; they broke him in two with a bat, and his friends toted him home on a shutter. When it was noticed that no umpire ever survived a game, umpiring got to be unpopular. So I was obliged to appoint somebody whose rank and lofty position under the government would protect him. . . . The first public game would certainly draw fifty thousand people; and for solid fun would be worth going around the world to see. Everything would be favorable; it was balmy and beautiful spring weather now, and Nature was all tailored out in her new clothes."

—On the dangers of umpiring a game when knighthood was in flower; from *A Connecticut Yankee in King Arthur's Court*

"TWO HUNDRED & FIVE HUNDRED DOLLARS REWARD—At the great baseball match on Tuesday, while I was engaged in hurrahing, a small boy walked off with an English-made brown silk UMBRELLA belonging to me, & forgot to bring it back. I will pay $5 for the return of that umbrella in good condition to my house on Farmington avenue. I do not want the boy (in an active state) but will pay two hundred dollars for his remains. Samuel L. Clemens"

—Classified ad placed in the May 20, 1875 *Hartford Courant*

TYLER, ANNE

"Baseball was the only sport that made sense, she said; clear as Parcheesi, clever as chess."

—Ezra Tull takes his mother, Pearl, to a Baltimore Orioles game; from *Dinner at the Homesick Restaurant.*

U

Ueberroth, Peter

"A cloud hangs over baseball. It's a cloud called drugs and it's permeated our game."

> —*New York Times,* September 25, 1985

"A lot of substance and not much style."

> —Characterizing his five years as baseball commissioner, which he summed them up this way: "The game is profitable, ticket prices have risen by an average of only 60 cents, stadiums have nonalcohol sections, his marketing, licensing and corporate sponsorship departments have a framework for profits in place that should serve the game for years."—Quoted by Richard Justice, *Washington Post,* March 10, 1989

"Baseball is a public trust. Players turn over, owners turn over and certain commissioners turn over. But baseball goes on."

> —*New York Times,* May 12, 1985

"Baseball will not ever, as long as I am around, consider it in any way, shape, or form."

> —As commissioner, on the instant replay; quoted in *USA Today,* October 6, 1986

"Catfish Hunter had the distinction of playing for both Charlie Finley and George Steinbrenner, which is enough in itself to put a player in the Hall of Fame."

> —Widely quoted

"The best words—most fun words—in our language are 'play ball.' Those words conjure up home runs and strikeouts, extra innings and double plays. 'Play ball' is what baseball is all about—its call to arms—and there isn't a baseball fan in the USA and Canada who isn't a little excited over the beginning of a new season."

> —"Baseball Is Better, It's Time to Play Ball!" *USA Today,* April 4, 1986

"The integrity of the game is everything."

> —Urging players to submit to drug tests, *New York Times,* May 12, 1985

"There are enough players on a team that will take a bat in their hand and take you in a room if they think you're using drugs. There's enormous peer pressure."

> —As commissioner; quoted in *USA Today*, February 19, 1988

"What sets baseball apart? What do you love about it?

"I love the tradition, and I love the drama. Every baseball game has drama. It's not just an end-of-the-season thing. I love the pace. I mean, it just works. All the way through."

> —From Frank DeFord, "The Boss Takes His Cuts," in *Sports Illustrated*, April 15, 1985

"When Pee Wee Reese wrapped an arm around the shoulders of Jackie Robinson in a show of support and respect for a friend and teammate. Robinson was being harassed by the opposing team. That moment to me is a perfect illustration of what baseball is all about."

> —The former commissioner in answer to the question of what event he would have liked to have seen in baseball; quoted in the 50th Anniversary Hall of Fame *Yearbook*, 1989

UECKER, BOB

"Anybody with ability can play in the big leagues. To last as long as I did with the skills I had, with the numbers I produced, was a triumph of the human spirit."

> —From *Catcher in the Wry*. The lifetime .200 hitter has made the point many times, paraphrasing himself, e.g., "Anyone with talent can play in the Major Leagues; for

someone like me to stay around as long as I did, I think that's a much greater achievement."

"But they had a Bob Uecker Day Off for me once in Philly."

> —On his lack of recognition, *Los Angeles Times*, March 28, 1983

"Career highlights? I had two. I got an intentional walk from Sandy Koufax, and I got out of a rundown against the Mets."

> —On his playing days, when named to the broadcasters wing of baseball's Hall of Fame, *Chicago Sun-Times*, March 18, 2003

"He struck out three times and lost the game for his team when a ball went through his legs at third base. Parents were throwing things at our car and swearing at us as we left the parking lot. Gosh, I was proud. A chip off the old block."

> —On a Little League game in which his then-fourteen-year-old son was playing; quoted in *Sports Illustrated*, September 8, 1980

"I made a major contribution to the Cardinals' pennant drive in 1964. I got hepatitis."

> —Widely attributed

"I set records that never will be equaled—in fact, I hope 90 per cent of them don't even get printed. When I looked to the third base coach for a sign, he turned his back on me. I was offered a job as a coach—a second base coach. When I went to bat with three men on and two out in the ninth, I looked over in the other team's dugout, and they were in street clothes. The manager told me to go to the plate without a bat—and hope for a walk.

"They said I was such a great prospect that they were sending me to a winter league to sharpen up. When I stepped off the plane, I was in Greenland. At all those banquets, stars get up and give credit to their coaches and parents. I give credit to no one. I made myself what I am today.

"Joe Torre's brother Frank sells Adirondack bats and he sent me a dozen with handles on both ends. Philadelphia is such a bad city that when a plane lands there, nobody gets off, everybody gets on. Even if you win a rowing race in Philly, they boo you unless you go over the rapids. Instead of having the word 'Powerized' on my bats, they say, 'For Display Only.'"

—Recalling his career for Neal Russo, in the *St. Louis Post-Dispatch* and quoted in *Baseball Digest*, June 1972

"It is dangerous for an athlete to believe his own publicity, good or bad."

—*Catcher in the Wry*

"It was great. I got to meet a lot of important people. They all sit behind home plate."

—On catching Phil Niekro's knuckleball, 1981; widely attributed

"It's great to be out here again. I tell you, if I'm going to blow out someday, I want it to be at the ballpark. Really, it'd be great. I'd blow out, they'd cart me around the field a couple of times, the fans would cheer and then, poof, out the main gate. Gone."

—At fifty-four, after a mild heart attack; quoted in the *Washington Times*, March 6, 1989

"Philly fans are so mean that one Easter Sunday, when the players staged an Easter egg hunt for their kids, the fans booed the kids who didn't find any eggs. They even boo the National Anthem."

—As a former Phillies catcher, *Los Angeles Times*, April 1, 1971

"The average age in Sun City, Arizona, is deceased."

—Widely quoted

"The cops picked me up on the street at 3 a.m. and fined me $500 for being drunk and $100 for being with the Phillies."

—Recalling his time with the Phillies (1966–67); quoted in the *Sporting News*, September 26, 1988

"The highlight of my baseball career came in Philadelphia's Connie Mack Stadium when I saw a fan fall out of the upper deck. When he got up and walked away the crowd booed."

—Quoted in *Grand Slams and Fumbles*

"The players are at home, hanging around with their wives. The big thing about that, it's going to produce a bigger father/son/daughter game next year."

—As a broadcaster on the 1981 players' strike

"The way to catch a knuckleball is to wait until the ball stops rolling and then to pick it up."

— Widely attributed

"Winning and losing is nothing. Going out and prowling the streets after the game is what I liked. You'd get half in the bag and wake up the next morning with a bird in your room—that's what baseball is all about."

— Comment made on the *Tonight Show* and quoted in *Catcher in the Wry*

"You know, I signed with the Milwaukee Braves for $3,000. That bothered my dad at the time, because he didn't have that kind of dough to pay out. But eventually he scraped it up."

— Quoted in the *San Francisco Examiner*, March 29, 1984

"When I played, they didn't use fancy words like that. They just said I couldn't hit."

— On players claiming to suffer from emotional distress

UPDIKE, JOHN

"All baseball fans believe in miracles, the question is, how *many* do you believe in?"

— From "Hub Fans Bid Kid Adieu," *New Yorker*, October 22, 1960

"Fenway Park, in Boston, is a lyric little band-box of a ballpark. Everything is painted green and seems in curiously sharp focus, like the inside of an old-fashioned peeping-type Easter egg."

— "Hub Fans Bid Kid Adieu"

"Gods don't answer letters."

— On Ted Williams's failure to acknowledge fans' cheers after his last home run, in "Hub Fans Bid Kid Adieu."

V

VALENTINE, BILL

"Dark charged out on the field and I was shocked at the language he used. He suggested there had not been a marriage in my family for three generations."

— On why the umpire threw Cleveland manager Alvin Dark out of a game; quoted in *Sport*, September 1968

VALENTINE, BOBBY

"You're not dealing with real professionals in the clubhouse. You're not dealing with real intelligent guys for the most part. A lot can swim, but most of them just float along, looking for something to hold on to."

— New York Mets manager, concerning ballplayers on his team; quoted in S.L. Price, "Valentine's Day," *Sports Illustrated*, October 11, 1999

Bobby Valentine (*Texas Rangers*)

Fernando Valenzuela (*Los Angeles Dodgers*)

VALENZUELA, FERNANDO

"How could I be tired? It's only the sixth inning."

> —After being asked by Tommy Lasorda if he was tired; quoted in Raymond Mungo's *Confessions from Left Field*

VAN LOON, CHARLES E.

"In the corner groceries and cigar stands from Maine to California you can meet fellows who know more about baseball strategy than the men who get twenty thousand a year for handling a pennant winning club."

> —*New York Times*, April 26, 1953

VAN SLYKE, ANDY

"I have an Alka-Seltzer bat. You know, 'Plop, plop, fizz, fizz.' When the pitchers see me walking up there they say, 'Oh, what a relief it is.'"

> —On his batting troubles during the first half of the 1989 season; quoted in the July 10, 1989, *Sporting News*

"If everyone were like him, I wouldn't play. I'd find a safer way to make a living."

> —After Mitch Williams narrowly missed his head twice in the process of striking him out; quoted in the *Sporting News* July 17, 1989

"It seems like Satan has thrown the DH into our game."

> —*Sporting News*, October 3, 1988

Andy Van Slyke (*St. Louis Cardinals*)

Van Slyke, Andy (continued)

"I've never even hit batting practice before a crowd that small at Busch."

> —The former St. Louis Cardinal, referring to the crowd of 1,511—smallest in Busch Stadium history—that watched the Pirates' 4–3 victory, September 14, 1989; quoted in *USA Today* September 15

"Last year, we had so many people coming in and out they didn't bother to sew their names on the backs of the uniforms. They just put them there with Velcro."

> —On the 1987 Pirates; quoted in the *Sporting News,* April 1, 1988

"Only calling Nancy Reagan."

> —Asked if he had any special pregame superstition; quoted in the *Sporting News,* May 23, 1988

"The only thing that would remind me of Three Rivers is if I stood at home plate—and looked straight down."

> —Spoken at 1993 All-Star Game, marveling at the baseball atmosphere at Oriole Park at Camden Yards, as opposed to dreary Three Rivers Stadium in Pittsburgh; quoted in Ken Rosenthal, "Resisting Stand-ins, Angelos Attracts the Standouts," *Baltimore Sun,* January 21, 1995

"With the Cardinals, everybody would be reading the business section to see what their stocks were doing. You get to this locker room in the morning, and everybody is looking at the sports page to see if Hulk Hogan won."

> —Comparing the Pirates to his former teammates on the Cardinals; *Sporting News,* October 10, 1988

"They wanted me to play third base like Brooks, so I did play like Brooks—Mel Brooks."

> —On his early days as a Cardinal third baseman; quoted in *Sports Illustrated,* March 13, 1989; the allusion is to Brooks Robinson

Vance, Dazzy

"Pitchers aren't ball players."

> —Often-quoted line, which first appeared in the August 14, 1957, *Sporting News.* It came in response to the question of why pitchers weren't good batters. His full response was, "People have asked me that question many times and I believe I have it figured out. Pitchers aren't going to like the answer I give, but it's true, and it is in four short words. They aren't ball players."

Vance, Sandy

"I put my whole heart and soul into baseball, then, one day, it was all over. When you leave baseball you leave part of your childhood behind."

> —On his arm going dead; quoted in the *New York Daily News,* September 14, 1977

Vanderberg, Bob

"I learned at an early age that no Sox lead—in a ballgame or in a pennant race—was safe."

> —From his book *Sox: From Lane and Fain to Zisk and Fisk*

VAUGHAN, BILL

"As a nation we are dedicated to keeping physically fit—and parking as close to the stadium as possible."

—In the *Kansas City Star*, 1981

"If you dust off old junk sometimes you come up with a gem."

—On the Houston Astrodome, in *Half the Bottle*

"What it adds up to is that it is not baseball's responsibility to fit itself into our frantic society. It is, rather, society's responsibility to make itself worthy of baseball.

"That's why I can never understand why anybody leaves the game early to beat the traffic. The purpose of baseball is to keep you from caring if you beat the traffic."

—From his *Kansas City Star* column; quoted in the *Sporting News*, August 15, 1970

VAUGHN, MO

"Nothing's more exciting than knowing you've got four at bats every day. There's nothing better in life than that. I don't have kids. I don't have hobbies. This is what I do—I hit. I feel like hitting is a war, and you better be a warrior and you've got to be crazy. . . . That's all I do is hit. It's all I think about every day."

—Quoted in Tom Verducci, "Triple Threats," *Sports Illustrated*, July 1, 1996

VEALE, BOB

"Good pitching always stops good hitting and vice versa."

—As a Pirates pitcher; widely attributed

VECSEY, GEORGE

"After retirement, Mantle made a living off being the celebrity drunk golfer, America's guest. Few people worried about his dangerous excesses, his broken family, until Mantle got scared and got sober. And then he was forgiven immediately with a great rush of public sympathy. It's too bad Mantle did not have more time, sober and healthy and mature, to enjoy the affection."

—*New York Times*, August 14, 1995

"Baseball is the best sport of all partly because it is about going home. Luke Appling knew the feeling of rounding the bases at the age of 75. That competitive cuss named Pete Rose would love to match old Luke in the year 2016. (Can't you see him licking his chops and daring 80-year-old Bob Gibson to groove one? For that matter, can't you see Gibson knocking Rose flat on his Steinbrenner?)

"It's up to Rose. He must begin by performing public service in his hometown, and he must seek help for his behavior, to learn why he was out of control. Rose must start a new life with his second family in Florida, and learn to live without the buzz that got him in trouble. Then perhaps there will be room for mercy."

—"Appling, Rose and an Inner Circle," *New York Times*, January 6, 1991

"When the entire nation was watching him, he turned on the Stengelese. It was noblesse oblige."

—Recalled on Stengel's death, September 29, 1975

Son of the owner of the Chicago Cubs, this Veeck was the master of sensational promotion and outrageous opinion.

"A man who is cautious never sleeps with a girl, quite. He's so timid he never savors anything completely. Even an after-dinner speaker should be a little drunk on a tightrope. It keeps everyone's attention. Don't be cautious, Tony. Just don't be injudicious. If you write out your remarks it's an insult to an audience. It shows that your first priority is to protect yourself from them. They sense it. If you just have a few notes on a scrap of paper, you'll walk away with more friends. They'll think, 'Hey, he's honest.'"

> —To Tony La Russa, overheard and quoted by Thomas Boswell in the *Washington Post*, May 31, 1981

"An island of surety in a changing world."

> —His short definition of baseball

"Anything you do to enhance sales is a promotion."

> —Widely quoted

"Baseball doesn't belong to the old guys spinning their tales or to the newspapermen or to the operators. Baseball is where you find it, and you find it on the field. You're never any closer to the game than you are to the players."

> —From *Veeck—as in Wreck* by Bill Veeck with Ed Linn

"Baseball is like our society. It's becoming homogenized, computerized. People identify with the swashbuckling individuals, not polite little men who field their position well. Sir Galahad had a big following—but I'll bet Lancelot had more."

> —Quoted in a *Washington Post* interview, February 11, 1971

"Baseball is the only game left for people. To play basketball now, you have to be 7 ft. 6 in. To play football, you have to be the same width."

> —Widely quoted

"Baseball is the only thing besides the paper clip that hasn't changed."

> —1974

"Baseball's unique possession, the real source of our strength, is the fan's memory of the times his daddy took him to the game to see the great players of his youth. Whether he remembers it or not, the excitement of those hours, the step they represented in his own growth and the part those afternoons—even one afternoon—played in his relationship with his own father is bound up in his feeling toward the local ball club and toward the game. When he takes his own son to the game, as his father once took him, there is a spanning of the generations that is warm and rich and—if I may use the word—lovely."

> —In his 1965 *Hustler's Handbook*

"Building a ball team is like dealing yourself a poker hand. You have all winter to rummage around through the deck for the best possible combination of cards."

> —From *Veeck—as in Wreck*

"But if you are going to have a fight with a visiting club, be sure to insult them the day they come to town, and not the last day of the series. It pays off better."

> —On feuds; quoted in the *Sporting News*, March 10, 1948

"Circumstances alter cases."

> —Responding to Yankee general manager George Weiss's question "Would you have agreed to this when you had the Indians?" Veeck was asking the Yankees for half their radio revenues because his team, the Browns, was half the attraction.

Bill Veeck in "The Kid From Cleveland" (*Museum of Modern Art Film Still Archives*)

"Eddie, how would you like to be a big-league ballplayer? Eddie, you'll be the only midget in the history of the game. You'll be appearing before thousands of people. Your name will go into the record books for all time. You'll be famous, Eddie. You'll be immortal."

> —On Eddie Gaedel's August 19, 1951, appearance, in *Veeck—as in Wreck*

Everybody's going to see the Indians play,
Everybody's going this year they say;
That impulse obey,
Get tickets, don't delay,
Cause everybody's going to see the Indians play.

> —Singing commercial for Bill Veeck's 1947 Cleveland Indians; quoted in the *Sporting News*. If Veeck didn't write it, he certainly had a hand in writing it.

"Gabe has been a good friend through lo these many years, in good times and bad. Too bad he had to get tied up with a bum like Steinbrenner."

> —On Gabe Paul

"Hating the Yankees isn't part of my act, it is one of those exquisite times when life and art are in perfect conjunction."

> —*New York Times*, July 16, 1979

"His background will help him, because he'll have a better appreciation of the clowns he's got playing."

> —On learning that Yankees general manager Michael Burke had once been the general manager of the Ringling Brothers Circus

"I decided to withdraw my name when I didn't get a single vote on the first 11 ballots."

—On why he was not named commissioner; quoted in *Baseball Digest*, April 1969

"I do not think that winning is the most important thing. I think winning is the only thing."

—As president, Chicago White Sox; quoted in *The Management Evolution*, American Management Association, 1963

"I guess I'm just not bright enough to stop."

—Explaining how he kept up his hectic twenty-four-hour-a-day schedule

"I have always maintained that the best remedy for a batting slump is two wads of cotton. One for each ear."

—From *The Hustler's Handbook* by Bill Veeck and Ed Linn

"I have discovered, in twenty years of moving around a ball park, that the knowledge of the game is usually in inverse proportion to the price of the seats."

—As Chicago White Sox owner

"I try not to kid myself. You know, I don't mind romancing someone else, but to fool yourself is pretty devastating and dangerous."

—From *Sox: From Lane and Fain to Zisk and Fisk* by Bob Vanderberg

"I'd like to be devious, but I can't find it in myself."

—*Chicago* magazine, July 1978

"If I could have picked my own place in the game of baseball, I would have been out there on the field, making stunning plays at shortstop like Lou Boudreau, or turning casually at the crack of the bat to make one of those brilliant over-the-shoulder catches of Joe DiMaggio. ('Yay, Veeck!')"

—From *Veeck—as in Wreck*

"If there is any justice in this world, to be a White Sox fan frees a man from any other form of penance."

—Quoted in *Sox: From Lane and Fain to Zisk and Fisk* by Bob Vanderberg, along with an additional line from Vanderberg: "And, it might be added, pennants." The line originally appeared in *Veeck—as in Wreck*.

"If U.S. Grant had been leading an army of baseball players, they'd have second guessed him all the way to the doorknob of the Appomattox Courthouse."

—From *The Hustler's Handbook*

"In fact, I even kept on voting for him after he died, because I'd rather vote for a dead man with class than two live bums."

—On voting for Socialist candidate Norman Thomas; quoted by Thomas Boswell in the *Washington Post*, May 31, 1981

"In modern baseball the winning equation is Power + Pitching = Pennant."

—From *Veeck—as in Wreck*

"In 1951, in a moment of madness, I became owner and operator of a collection of old rags and tags known to baseball historians as the St. Louis Browns."

—Opening line of *Veeck—as in Wreck*

"In the 1960s there was a period of unrest, speed and violence in this country. There was the war in Vietnam. There was mugging, meanness and violence. In this spirit, football and basketball were natural sports. . . . [But then], suddenly, people were tired of violence. They were seeking stability and escape. They were tired of concrete, steel and artificiality. They found baseball again, a sport to be savored. The game is perfect for the time right now and that's one of the reasons attendance is up all over the country."

—Quoted in an interview in the *Dallas Times-Herald*, July 19, 1977

"It is a game to be savored rather than taken in gulps."

—Widely attributed

"It isn't the high price of stars that is expensive, it's the high price of mediocrity."

—As White Sox owner

"It is played by people, real people, not freaks. Basketball is played by giants. Football is played by corn-fed hulks. The normal-sized man plays baseball and the fellow in the stands can relate to that."

—Why baseball is the national pastime, 1975

"It never ceases to amaze me how many of baseball's wounds are self-inflicted."

—From *The Hustler's Handbook*

"Josh Gibson was, at the minimum, two Yogi Berras."

—Hall of Fame Collection

"Look, we play the 'Star-Spangled Banner' before every game. You want us to pay income taxes, too?"

—Quoted in Andrew Zimbalist's *Baseball and Billions*

"My epitaph is inescapable. It will read, 'He sent a midget up to bat.'"

—A number of variations on this Veeckism have appeared, including this one from *Veeck—as in Wreck:* "If I returned to baseball tomorrow, won ten straight pennants and left all the old attendance records moldering in the dust, I would still be remembered, in the end, as the man who sent a midget up to bat."

"Not really. They lean towards cash."

> —When asked whether free agents lean toward playing in big cities; widely attributed

"Now more than ever, we need a change of pace in baseball. Ball parks should be happy places. They should always smell like freshly cut grass."

> —1981

"One of the cardinal rules of baseball is that a manager will dispute a bad call against his team, not because he expects the decision to be changed but as a matter of competitive pride and team spirit."

> —From *Veeck—as in Wreck*

"One of the myths by which we live is that the 'real' baseball fan loves a 1–0 game and abhors a 'sloppy' 8–6 game. Even the most cursory studies show that fans love 8–6 games and are bored to death by classic 1–0 pitchers' battles."

> —From *The Hustler's Handbook*

"Politeness is the end of passion."

> —On the end of his first marriage and other matters; quoted by Thomas Boswell in the *Washington Post*, May 31, 1981

"Progress brings complaints. Years ago, players squawked because numbers were put on their uniforms. Now, they're unhappy because I've put their names on, too."

> —*Sport,* June 1960

"Resign."

> —Asked what he would do if he were made commissioner of baseball, July 10, 1973

"Sometime, somewhere, there will be a club nobody really wants. And then Ole Will will come wandering along to laugh some more. Look for me under the arc lights, boys. I'll be back."

> —Teamless, 1962; widely quoted at the time

"Sooner or later, the lame, the halt, and the blind all seek refuge with us."

> —On the 1977 White Sox, when Veeck, with only one good leg and diminished hearing, signed several "hurt" players; quoted in *Sox: From Lane to Fain to Zisk and Fisk*

"Sports are becoming increasingly more important as our world becomes more disordered, as society seems to be based on such shifting sands. It's the one thing in which there is a clearly defined area of play, rules and penalties that apply to all. Three strikes and you're out—even if [attorney] Edward Bennett Williams defends you."

> —Quoted in the *Washington Post*, August 31, 1975

"Suffering is overrated. It doesn't teach you anything."

> —On his many ailments and operations; quoted by Thomas Boswell in the *Washington Post,* May 31, 1981

"Sure I remember—Al Capone was a great baseball fan. I remember he would come into the ball park and people would cheer him."

> —From an interview with Bob Vanderberg; quoted in *Sox: From Lane and Fain to Zisk and Fisk*

"That's the true harbinger of spring, not crocuses or swallows returning to Capistrano, but the sound of a bat on the ball."

> —As White Sox owner, 1976

"The best trades are the ones you don't make."

> —After the 1948 season, when Veeck had refrained from trading manager-shortstop Lou Boudreau and the Indians had gone on to win the pennant and the World Series. As *Sport* magazine saw it in January 1956: "The statement quickly became a classic among baseball quotations. There have been echoes of the quote ever since—and quite a few even before 1948."

"The Mets achieved total incompetence in a single year, while the Browns worked industriously for almost a decade to gain equal proficiency."

> —*Veeck—as in Wreck*

"The original idea of the bleachers was for the guy who couldn't afford season box seats, but could shell out cash for an outfield seat on a day-to-day basis. . . . Maybe the time has come when they don't need that guy. You can buy those seats the days they're not sold out, but the rest of the time you're not welcome? It does seem that way, doesn't it? I guess that's what happens when marketing experts come in and take over."

> —On the Cubs' 1985 decision to sell bleacher seats in advance

"The sixties was a time for grunts or screams. . . . The sports that fitted the times were football, hockey and mugging."

> —Quoted by George Will in his March 29, 1982, *Washington Post* column

"The year 1961 may not have been much for baseball but it was a vintage year for vocabulary. Frick taught the schoolchildren of the nation the meaning of the work 'asterisk,' and the CIA taught them the meaning of the word 'fiasco.' The comparison is apt."

> —*Veeck—as in Wreck*

"There are reasons why you sometimes think a player will perform better for you than for the club he's with. Usually it has to do with architecture of your park."

> —*Veeck—as in Wreck*

"There is no nicer way to spend an afternoon than to be out there in the sun, without your shirt on, to have a few beers and tell a few lies. Nothing in the country compares to that. It is pure, unadulterated love for baseball. It is the greatest buy in the country. You can't beat the price or the entertainment."

> —Said of Wrigley Field, Chicago; quoted in *Cubs Vine Line,* March 1986

"They had to learn more about the game to maximize their small ability. The star doesn't have to think, he just walks up and hits the ball or rocks back and throws it. The fringe player has to scheme and connive and study just to hold a job, and in the process he learns more about the game and about people than the star ever does."

—On why so many great managers were not great players; quoted in the *New York Times*, July 28, 1974

"They said my scoreboard in Chicago was bush, but there are 11 of them in baseball today. I drew 5,000 extra fans a day to see the scoreboard. I think I'll draw 2,000 to see the tote board."

—On the unveiling of an exploding tote board at his Suffolk Downs racetrack; quoted in the *Sporting News,* July 18, 1970

"This is a game to be savored, not gulped. There's time to discuss everything between pitches or between innings."

—Hall of Fame Collection

"This is an illusionary business. The fan goes away from the ballpark with nothing more to show for it than what's in his mind. When you sell a chair, or a house, or a car, you can develop a contented customer based on the quality of your product. Three years from now he can look at it with a feeling of satisfaction—'Best buy I ever made.' But in baseball, all he ever walks away with is an illusion, an ephemeral feeling of having been enter-

tained. You've got to develop and preserve that illusion. You have to give him more vivid pictures to carry away in his head."

—From a *TV Guide* interview, June 5, 1976

"Though it is a team game by definition, it is actually a series of loosely connected individual efforts."

—*Scholastic Coach,* December 1983

"To compare baseball with other team games is to say the Hope Diamond is a nice chunk of carbon. The endless variety of physical and mental skills demanded by baseball is both uncomparable and incomparable."

—Widely quoted

"We would've given him the land, of course, but you can't tow a piece of land into a ballpark."

—On giving a boat to Nellie Fox on Nellie Fox Night. Fox sold the boat to buy some land; quoted in *Sox: From Lane and Fain to Zisk and Fisk* by Bob Vanderberg

"We're doing this whole think backward. Attorneys should wear numbers on their backs, and box scores should have entries for writs, dispositions and appeals."

—Widely attributed

"What we have are good gray ballplayers, playing a good gray game and reading the good gray *Wall Street Journal.* They have been brainwashed, dry-cleaned and dehydrated! They have been homogenized, orientated and indoctrinated! Their mouths have been washed out, their appetites stunted, their personalities bleached! They say all the right things at all the right times, which means that they say nothing.

"Ruth was not unique. Wake up the echoes at the Hall of Fame and you will find that baseball's immortals were a rowdy and raucous group of men who would climb down off their plaques and go rampaging through Cooperstown, taking spoils, like the Third Army busting through Germany.

"Deplore it if you will, but Grover Cleveland Alexander drunk was a better pitcher than Grover Cleveland Alexander sober."

—From *The Hustler's Handbook*

"When the Supreme Court says baseball isn't run like a business, everybody jumps up and down with joy. When I say the same thing, everybody throws pointy objects at me."

—From *The Hustler's Handbook*

"When you're out there in the big-league pressure cooker, a pitcher's attitude—his utter confidence that he has an advantage of will and luck and guts over the hitter—is almost as important as his stuff."

—From *The Hustler's Handbook*

"You say 'Yogi' at a banquet and everybody automatically laughs, something Joe Garagiola discovered to his profit many years ago."

—From *The Hustler's Handbook*

VERDUCCI, TOM

"The single-season home run record is the most revered mark in sports. It's engraved on Maris's tombstone. No date of birth or death, just 61 and '61. The home run *is* America—appealing to Americans' roots of rugged individualism and their fascination with grand scale. They gape at one of McGwire's blasts the same way they do at Mount Rushmore, Hoover Dam and the Empire State Building."

—"Making His Mark," *Sports Illustrated,* September 14, 1998

VERSALLES, ZOILO

"If you get to one base and you can see the ball on the ground in the outfield, run like hell to the next base."

—On running the bases

VERTLIEB, DICK

"When the end of the world comes, Seattle will still have one more year to go."

—The former Mariner executive; quoted in Raymond Mungo's *Confessions from Left Field*

VIDAL, GENE

"Baseball is the favorite American sport because it's so slow. Any idiot can follow it. And just about any idiot can play it."

—The father of Gore Vidal; quoted in Gore Vidal, "West Point," *New York Review of Books,* October 18, 1973; reprinted in Gore Vidal, *Matters of Fact and of Fiction; Essays 1973–1976* (New York: Random House, 1977)

VIDAL, GORE

"These presidential ninnies should stick to throwing out baseballs, and leave the important matters to serious people."

—About U.S. presidents, "The State of the Union," *Esquire*, May 1975

VINCENT, FAY

"As all of us are aware, and no one more than I, Bart has a singular skill as a public speaker. He spoke well because he thought so well. But I point out to you that the most often quoted remark of Bart's brief tenure as Commissioner is a very simple declarative sentence. That sentence is the cornerstone on which I will build my own administration. Bart said very simply, 'No one is bigger than the game.' I repeat today what Bart said in August, no one—no player, no executive, no owner, no commissioner, no umpire—is bigger than the game."

—On A. Bartlett Giamatti and the office of commissioner, an address given at the winter meetings December 4, 1989

"I was a Yankee fan. I will face up to it. Bart [a lifelong Boston Red Sox fan] would look at me and say, 'Can you believe this man is a Yankee fan?' He made it sound like I was a child molester. I used to say, 'But, Bart, we won, and you lost.'"

—Quoted by Tim Kurkjian in the *Baltimore Sun*, October 27, 1989

"I'm going to go to spring training with a shout and a song, singing merrily as I go along."

—On going to spring training in 1990 after a ten-day delay because of a labor dispute; quoted by Murray Chass in the *New York Times*, April 9, 1990

"It's hard, even at this point in my life, to identify why baseball is so permanently affixed to the American soul. I think I'm wise enough to know that if you don't understand all there is to know, you're careful about tampering with it."

—On taking office as commissioner; quoted in the *Washington Post* by Richard Justice, September 15, 1989

"Our modest little sporting event."

—Putting the World Series into the context of the 1989 earthquake; widely quoted

"One of the lessons I'm learning—and it's a painful one—is how confrontational and litigious all American life is. I see in my own responsibilities how difficult it is to get decisions accepted without litigation, without some ultimate review."

—As commissioner, *Newsweek*, July 20, 1992

"Owners are fighting owners; owners are fighting the players union; the union is fighting everything. And all the while there is no commissioner. Too many of those who steward the game still don't understand that they hold baseball in trust for the public and that baseball deserves better."

—A year after being ousted from the office of commissioner, *New York Times*, October 1, 1993

"The game will survive long past you or I."

—At a press conference following the October 1989 World Series earthquake

"This is not a day for concerns. This is a day for pleasure. There are concerns in baseball but they get dissolved in the bright sunshine. . . . And this is my weather. I want credit."

—On Opening Day at Shea Stadium, 1990

VON DER AHE, CHRIS

"Do you know who iss talking mitt you tonight? Vell, iff you don't, it iss der possman, der president uff der Browns—undt I pay der bills. Now, iff you fellows don't get better, I vill do someding. Undt while I won'd mention names, yet, all I say to you iss [and he pointed his finger straight at one of the alleged culprits] you, Pat Tebeau—you juss bedder vatch oudt!"

—President of the St. Louis Browns during a losing streak. The quote was recalled in the *Sporting News,* October 9, 1957, by police captain Elias Hoaglund, who uncovered key evidence in the Black Sox scandal.

VOZZOLO, STEVE, AND JOE MANNING

"Sometimes you win. Sometimes you lose. Sometimes it rains."

—"Sometimes It Rains," album *I Love Baseball,* L & R Productions/VOZZ-MANN Music (East Hartford, Conn., 1994). Also spoken in the movie *Bull Durham.*

W

WADDELL, RUBE

"You're a liar. There ain't no Hotel Episode in Detroit."

—On being fined $100 by a thoroughly exasperated manager, Waddell, the picture of injured innocence, demanded, "What did I do now?" "The fine," explained the manager, "is for that disgraceful hotel episode in Detroit"; quoted by Bennett Cerf in his *The Laugh's on Me*.

WAGNER, HONUS

"I don't want my picture in any cigarettes, but I also don't want you to lose the ten dollars, so I'm enclosing my check for that sum."

—After Pittsburgh's official scorer took $10 for a picture of Wagner for a tobacco card; quoted by Bennett Cerf in *Try and Stop Me*

Honus Wagner (*Society for American Baseball Research; SABR*)

"I never have been sick. I don't even know what it means to be sick. I hear other players say they have a cold. I just don't know what it would feel like to have a cold—I never had one."

> —As an active player; quoted by Fred Lieb in *Baseball as I Have Known It*. Lieb's comment: "He wasn't bragging. Other players attested to that. I think he was so well put together and his system so well adjusted that his bodily functions were near to perfection. This is especially remarkable because for several years, starting at age twelve, he worked in a mine near his hometown of Mansfield, Pennsylvania, now renamed Carnegie."

"I won't play for a penny less than fifteen hundred dollars."

> —Widely quoted ultimatum

"In all my years of play, I never saw an ump deliberately make an unfair decision. They really called them as they saw 'em."

> —On why he never fought with umpires; quoted by Jack Sher in *Sport Magazine's All-Time All Stars*

"Keeler could bunt any time he chose. If the third baseman came in for a tap, he invariably pushed the ball past the fielder. If he stayed back, he bunted. Also, he had a trick of hitting a high hopper to an infielder. The ball would bounce so high that he was across the bag before he could be stopped."

> —On Willie Keeler; quoted in the Hall of Fame *Yearbook,* 1989

"There ain't much to being a ballplayer, if you're a ballplayer."

> —His most-quoted line

"Things were changing fast by that time. Women were beginning to come to the ball parks. We hadda stop cussin'."

> —On the year 1901; quoted in Jack Sher's "The Flying Dutchman," *Sport,* June 1949

WAGNER, LEON

"I play for the poor man. I try to give a thrill to the lunch bucket fan. I know their plight. I worked in a factory in high school. The poor folk who lay out the hard bread to see a game. That's where my heart lies. The rich don't need heroes."

> —The veteran outfielder; quoted in *Baseball Digest,* August 1968

"It's all right to have a hitch in your swing but when you have a flaw in your hitch you're in trouble."

> —Quoted in *Baseball Digest,* April 1969

WAINWRIGHT, LOUDON

"Baseball, above all sports, has a richness and a kind of broad usefulness far beyond the complex pleasures it offers as a game. For those uncounted millions of Americans (mostly but by no means all male) who've developed their own unbreakable connections with it, baseball is, in fact, a resource with some amazing applications.

"It gives memory a home, for one thing, which leads the average fellow, looking back, to think his past was pretty lively after all. Who ever played the game who doesn't have a mini-gallery of Big Diamond Moments?

"But what the game mostly does for its lovers is somehow to provide a superb mix of men, atmosphere and action for the creation of popular myth and metaphor. Its possibilities for heroics, for humor and—naturally—for disaster have made baseball a tremendously fertile field for imaginative writers either of fiction or of the history of sport.

"'You learn the game as a child,' a friend told me. 'It's like being a Catholic. It's with you forever.' Figuratively speaking, baseball contains the summer, and there is something, too, about its open-ended time scheme that makes the game especially dramatic. It isn't ended by the clock; it's ended by what the players do.

"Perhaps most of all it is a game where every player, sooner or later, is pitilessly exposed. At some gulp of a moment, he is spotlighted by the action, and there he is—there we all are—heroes or goats."

> —"Take Me Out to the Library," *Life*, May 1984 "The View from Here."

WAITKUS, EDDIE

"I don't know what got into that silly honey. Why pick on a nice guy like me?"

> —Talking to reporters at his hospital bedside a day after being shot by Ruth Ann Steinhagen; quoted in the *St. Louis Post-Dispatch*, June 17, 1949

MY BIGGEST THRILL IN BASEBALL

"In 1949 I was shot by a deranged girl. After I was released from the hospital, I was sent to Florida by the Phillies to see if I might recover enough to resume baseball. The schedule laid out for me was a nightmare. I was in a bad nervous condition, and I grew more depressed each day. Then I met a girl

who knew a lot about human nature—who had faith in me. I went on to a good season and the newspapers commended me for the 'Comeback of the Year.' (The girl who helped so much is now my wife.)"

> —Statement which appeared on the back of his 1955 Bowman baseball card. At this point Waitkus played for the Baltimore Orioles.

WAITS, RICK

"The difference is, it used to be you got paid after you did it. Now you get paid before."

> —As a Cleveland Indians pitcher on baseball salaries

WALKER, DIXIE

"That was 35 years ago. I've said all I'm going to say on that subject. There is one more thing I'll add: Jackie Robinson was a great ballplayer."

> —On his view of Jackie Robinson, stated shortly before his death in 1982 and quoted in his AP obituary, which also stated, "When Jackie Robinson, the first black player in the majors, joined the Dodgers in 1947, Mr. Walker asked to be traded and was sent to the Pittsburgh Pirates, where he ended his career in 1949."

WALKER, HARRY

"Nobody pays much attention to inexperience any more. As long as a boy can get the job done, what difference does it make? I'll pull a kid down out of one of those fruit trees if he shows me he can play ball."

> —From Cocoa, Florida, interview; quoted in the *New York Times*, March 20, 1971

"One thing all managers hear that doesn't make any sense at all is for a pitcher to say, 'I ought to have a right to stay in and win or lose my own game.' He doesn't have that right. It isn't just his game. There are 24 other players who have a stake in it, plus the manager and the coaches, and everybody else in the organization. All have worked to field the team and are affected by what happens."

—As Houston manager; quoted in the *Sporting News,* 1970

"The most exciting hit in baseball is the triple. . . . You usually have two or three men handling the ball, and, if everything fits together, the runner is flagged down on a close play. On doubles and triples, several men must contribute. On a home run, one man does it all."

—As Houston Astros manager

"The papers aren't going to win a game for me. And I don't need anybody to tell me I lost."

—As Astros manager on why he never read the papers; quoted in the *Sporting News,* June 13, 1970

"Left hand . . . right hand."

—Ritual chant for Harry "the Hat" Walker, described in 1947 by the *Sporting News.* "First, there is silence as he steps out of the batter's box. Then when he puts his bat between his knees and starts to dust off his hands, the bobby soxers begin to giggle. As he reaches for his hat the throng starts to murmur, then men, women, boys and girls chant, 'Left hand . . . right hand' (as he rubs his forehead with first one elbow and then the other, holding his hat in the unoccupied hand).

Harry Walker (*Houston Astros*)

"Walker then pats his hair carefully with one hand and then the other. Finally, he puts his cap back on his head, rubs his hands again, picks up his bat and steps into the box.

"The fans let out a cheer or heave a sigh of relief . . . and wait patiently for three innings to see him do it again."

"This is still a young club here. This is a profession like learning to be a doctor or lawyer. I mean that seriously. That is, it is a miracle if a man can become a really good ball player in less than six to eight years."

—As Astros manager, the *Sporting News,* July 6, 1968

WALKER, HARRY (CONTINUED)

"When you're winning, they say you have aggressive players when they spout off. When you're losing, they call it dissension."

—In his first press conference as Astros manager; quoted in the *Sporting News,* July 6, 1968

WALKER, RUBE

"They're all the old Giant fans and all the old Dodger fans put together, plus they had a few years without baseball to get even nuttier."

—On the fans flocking to Shea Stadium; quoted in the *Sporting News,* June 13, 1970

"We had a long conference out there on the mound as Ralph Branca was brought in from the bullpen. Branca's first pitch was a called strike. I went out to talk to him again after that pitch. We decided to brush Thomson back with a fast ball. Branca didn't get the ball far enough inside. Thomson seemed to hesitate before swinging, but he whipped the bat real good and I can still see that ball going into the left field stands.

"It was awful enough losing the pennant, but as the fans stormed on the field I got knocked flat and they stepped right over me getting to the Giant players. That's the lowest I've ever been, mentally and physically."

—The Brooklyn catcher recalling Bobby Thomson's pennant-winning 1951 home run; quoted in *Baseball Digest* by Fred Russell of the *Nashville Banner,* June 1970

WALLOP, DOUGLASS

"For the afternoon had proved an axiom long known to baseball men, and known now even to Applegate.

"And this was that not even the devil could force an umpire to change his decision."

—Lesson learned by the devil in the person of Applegate in *The Year the Yankees Lost the Pennant.* It was made famous in the line ". . . not even the devil could force an umpire to change his decision" when the book became *Damn Yankees* on Broadway and in Hollywood.

WALTERS, BUCKY

"Hell, if the game was half as complicated as some of these writers make out it is, a lot of us boys from the farm would never have been able to make a living at it."

—From *You Can't Beat the Hours* by Mel Allen and Ed Fitzgerald

1. There is no mystery to pitching.
2. The object simply is to get the ball over.
3. Each pitcher has to learn to make the most of what he has.
4. Maybe it's time to revise pitching standards, and not expect a man to complete half or three-quarters of the games he starts.
5. I don't think it's necessary to enlarge the strike zone or bring back a lot of mechanical pitches.
6. If they want to do something for the pitchers, then let them raise the seams on the ball.
7. Pitchers will learn or figure out some way

to get even with the hitters and eventually stop them.

—His "Mound Philosophy"; quoted in the *Sporting News,* November 30, 1955

WAMBSGANSS, BILL

"Cleveland was playing Chicago. [White Sox] Runners were on first and third. [The Indians'] Schalk signaled to the moundsman for a curve. Speaker saw the signal flashed and ordered a delayed double steal. Gleason caught that signal, the White Sox switched positions and Schalk signaled for a pitchout.

"The pitchout signal was caught by Uhle, who was coaching, and Speaker signaled for a change. The result was that the runners held their bases and the pitcher wasted a ball. Schalk signaled again, the infield changed and Speaker ordered a delayed steal. Ray was warned and ordered another pitchout, but no sooner had he flashed that signal than Speaker had ordered another wait and Schalk, thinking to outguess Tris, ordered a fast ball. As Schalk changed his signals Speaker, guessing that he would do exactly that, signaled for the hit-and-run, with the result that a hit whipped through the infield, winning the game."

—Describing the greatest play he had ever witnessed; for the *New York Evening Post,* and reprinted in *Collier's,* August 2, 1924, under the heading "Brainwork on the Diamond"

WANER, PAUL

"Be relaxed, don't wave the bat, don't clench it. Be ready to hit down with the barrel of the bat. Just swing it and let the weight drive the ball. Let the pitcher move first. Then, as he draws his arm back, you draw the bat back and you are ready. If a pitcher sees you fiddling with the bat, he'll stall until your arms are tired before you even get a chance to hit."

—Advice to young batters, *Sporting News,* April 27, 1955

WARD, JOHN MONTGOMERY

"Second base is the prettiest position to play of the entire infield. In the number of chances offered it is next to first base, and in the character of the work to be done and the opportunities for brilliant play and the exercise of judgment, it is unsurpassed.

"The qualities of mind and body necessary to constitute a good modern pitcher are rarely combined in a single individual. First-class pitchers are almost as rare as prima donnas, and out of the many thousand professional and amateur ball players of the country not more than a dozen in all are capable of doing the position entire justice.

"The simplest of the three outfield positions is the left field, and one evidence of this is seen by the fact that a left fielder almost invariably leads in the averages."

—1889; quoted in *Kings of the Diamond* by Lee Allen and Tom Meany

WARHOL, ANDY

"Sports figures are to the '70s what movie stars were to the '60s."

—*Time,* November 21, 1977

WARREN, EARL

"I always turn to the sports section first. The sports section records people's accomplishments; the front page nothing but man's failures."

—Quoted in *Sports Illustrated*, July 22, 1968

WASHINGTON, CLAUDELL

"I was just stunned a little and couldn't move for a couple of minutes. Someone offered me a hot dog, but I wouldn't take it. It didn't have mustard."

—After falling into the box seats at Fenway Park trying to make a catch on April 25, 1990; from the *Washington Times*, April 27, 1990

WATERS, PATTY

"We have a group of letters from a local school. I don't know if the teacher was making fun of us, but the kids' letters suggested [the players] chew gum and stick it on the end of their bats to help make contact, or put it in their gloves so they might catch a ball."

—As an administrative assistant in the Orioles' public relations office, on some of the suggestions

she had received to help the Orioles, who lost their first twenty-one games of the season; from a list of "Memorable Quotes of 1989" from the *Tampa Tribune*, December 25, 1988

WATHAN, JOHN

"When I asked, 'How would you like to be married to a major league manager' my wife said, 'What, is Tommy Lasorda getting a divorce?'"

—On being named Kansas City Royals manager; widely quoted

WATSON, BOB

"We're only one player away from being the best team in baseball—Steve Carlton."

—The Atlanta Braves first baseman; quoted in *Sports Illustrated*, April 14, 1983

WAYNE, JOHNNY AND FRANK SHUSTER

"Oh what a rogue and bush league slob am I who has 10 days hitless gone?"

—From the Canadian comics' "Shakespeare on Baseball" sketch; quoted in Wayne's July 19, 1990, obituary in the *Boston Globe*

WEAVERISMS—EARL'S PEARLS

As manager of the Baltimore Orioles, Earl Weaver was cranky and quotable, and his lines on the game will be quoted for many years to come.

"A manager wins games in December; he tries not to lose them in July."

—Widely attributed. Weaver had several versions of this sentiment, for instance, "A

manager's job is simple. For 162 games you try not to screw up all that smart stuff your organization did last December."

"Baseball is pitching, 3-run homers, and fundamentals."

—Quoted by Tom Boswell in *How Life Imitates the World Series*

Earl Weaver (*Baltimore Orioles*)

"Coaches are an integral part of any manager's team. Especially if they're good pinochle players."

— *Winning!* 1972

"Don't worry. The fans don't start booing until July."

— As Orioles manager to a new manager, SABR Collection

"Economics played a role. Raleighs have gone from $6.50 to $9 a carton, but there's a $3/4$-cent coupon on the back. You can get all kinds of things with them—blenders, everything. I saved up enough one time and got Al Bumbry."

— On coming out of retirement to return as Orioles manager; quoted in the *Sporting News*, July 22, 1985

"From what I've observed, owners don't fire managers merely for losing. They fire them if the public is complaining. In some cases, the public will say it wasn't the manager's fault. But when it blames the manager, the owner feels he has to move, and the lovable old skipper gets thrown out on his can. . . . In most cases, the 'public' is the press. If the press writes that the fans feel the manager is doing a bad job, that usually means the press feels he's doing a bad job."

— Quoted in the *Los Angeles Herald-Examiner*, April 22, 1976

"Good ballplayers make good managers, not the other way around. All I can do is help them be as good as they are."

— *Time*, July 23, 1979

"I don't think, in all the years I managed them, I ever spoke more than 30 words to Frank and Brooks Robinson."

— Quoted by Warner Fusselle in *Baseball . . . a Laughing Matter*

"I have more fights with Jim Palmer than with my wife. The Chinese tell time by the 'Year of the Horse' or the 'Year of the Dragon.' I tell time by the 'Year of the Back,' the 'Year of the Elbow.' Every time Palmer reads about a new ailment, he seems to get it. This year it's the 'Year of the Ulnar Nerve.' Someone once asked me if I had any physical incapacities of my own. Know what I answered? 'Sure I do,' I said. 'One big one: Jim Palmer.'"

— On Jim Palmer; quoted in Danielle Gagnon Torrez's *High Inside*

"I never got many questions about my managing. I tried to get 25 guys who didn't ask questions."

> —Quoted by Warner Fusselle in *Baseball . . . a Laughing Matter*

"I think there should be bad blood between all clubs."

> —Following an Orioles-Yankees beanball incident, responding to a reporter's question as to whether he expected such antagonism; quoted in *Sports Illustrated,* July 21, 1982

"I'm 420 games over .500. That's 10 years of 100–60 and then some. So that's gonna stay there. On my tombstone, just write: 'The sorest loser that ever lived.'"

> —On saying good-bye to baseball; October 1986; quoted by Tom Boswell the *Washington Post,* October 6, 1986

"I'd rather have them out at the park booing than at home kicking the television set or complaining that the movie was lousy."

> —On the fans; widely quoted

"If he [umpire Steve Palermo] ever touches me again without that blue uniform on, I'll consider it assault, and his family will have to fly in to see him at Johns Hopkins Hospital."

> —Quoted in Thomas Boswell, "Earl Weaver," *Washington Post Magazine,* March 28, 1982

"If you know how to cheat, start now."

> —On the mound to a struggling Ross Grimsley

"It always looks easy when it's over. But when you're playing each game, it isn't easy. We have a 34–15 record in one-run games. Now, looking back, it would seem we didn't have any trouble at all."

> —Quoted in the *Sporting News,* October 10, 1970

"It's what you learn after you know it all that counts."

> —Title of his book, with Berry Stainback, published 1982 by Simon & Schuster

"I've got nothing against the bunt—in its place. But most of the time, that place is at the bottom of a long-forgotten closet."

> —Quoted by Warner Fusselle in *Baseball . . . a Laughing Matter*

"Nobody likes to hear it, because it's dull. But the reason you win or lose is darn near always the same . . . pitching."

> —Quoted in the *Los Angeles Times,* June 16, 1978

"Smart managing is dumb. The three-run homers you trade for in the winter will always beat brains. The guy who says, 'I love the challenge of managing,' is one step from being out of a job. I don't welcome any challenge. I'd rather have nine guys named Robinson."

> —Quoted in Thomas Boswell, "Earl Weaver," *Washington Post Magazine,* March 28, 1982

"Take your bat with you."

> —When told by slumping Oriole outfielder Al Bumbry that he was about to go to chapel services; quoted in *Sports Illustrated*, May 7, 1979

"The thing that has surprised me most in baseball is the amount of integrity that most umpires have. It actually took me a while to believe what a good game they'd give you the next night after a blowup."

> —Quoted in Thomas Boswell, "Earl Weaver," *Washington Post Magazine*, March 28, 1982

"There is only one legitimate trick to pinch-hitting, and that's knowing the pitcher's best pitch when the count is 3 and 2. All the rest is a crapshoot."

> —Quote in the May 27, 1978, *TV Guide*

"There's no such thing as pressure. It's all in your mind. But if there were such a thing as pressure, it would be the worst in the playoffs. The playoffs are just a mother."

> —Widely attributed

"This ain't a football game. We do this every day."

> —Quoted by George Will in his March 28, 1982, column

"Unless the stock market goes through the floor, this is the last day I ever have to work in my life. Anybody says that isn't nice is lying."

> —Said by Weaver after his first losing Orioles team ended with stretches of 0–4, 2–12, 9–32

"You've got a hundred more young kids than you have a place for on your club. Every one of 'em has had a goin' away party. They been given the shaving kit and the fifty dollars. They kissed everybody and said, 'See you in the majors in two years.' You see these poor kids who shouldn't even be there in the first place. You write on the report card '4–4–4 and out.' That's the lowest rating in everything. Then you call 'em in and say, 'It's the consensus among us that we're going to let you go back home.'

"Some of 'em cry. Some get mad. But none of 'em will leave until you answer 'em one question: 'Skipper, what do you think?' And you gotta look every one of those kids in the eye and kick their dreams in the ass and say no. 'If you say it mean enough, maybe they do themselves a favor and don't waste years learning what you can see in a day. They don't have what it takes to make the majors. Just like I never had it.'"

> —As quoted by Tom Boswell

WEBSTER, MITCH

"It'll be great not to have to listen to two national anthems."

> —The outfielder on being traded to the Cubs after being with the Toronto Blue Jays and Montreal Expos, the *Sporting News*, August 8, 1988

WEEKS, LINTON

"The baseball bat is pure, sleek, sure-balanced and nearly perfectly shaped. It has masculine force, feminine curves. It feels primeval in the hands—mystical/mythical—a club held by opposable thumbs and complex-muscled hands."

> —In the *Washington Post*, August 23, 2005

WEIR, TOM

"OAKLAND—The only local flavor still missing from this Bay Bridge World Series is an earthquake, and the Athletics and Giants just might be capable of rattling one up without Mother Earth's help."

>—From a column entitled "Seriously, Let the Earthquake Begin," in *USA Today*, October 13, 1989. The last line of the column, "So bring on that earthquake, Seriesly." The fifteen-second 7.1-magnitude earthquake hit on October 17, disrupting the Word Series. It has been termed the biggest shakeup in sports history.

WEISS, GEORGE

"There is no such thing as second place. Either you're first or you're nothing."

>—As Yankee GM; widely quoted

"These people . . . these noisy people with their bed sheets . . . Where do they come from? . . . Why don't they keep quiet?"

>—On the Mets' first Banner Day, in 1963; quoted in George Vecsey's *Joy in Mudville*

"To hell with newspapermen. You can buy them with a steak."

>—As a Yankee executive

"You eat like a Yankee, but you don't perform like one on the field."

>—Yankee GM on firing a player who kept running up large room-service bills on the road; quoted in *Baseball Digest*, July 1961

WEISS, MRS. GEORGE

"I married him for better or worse, but not for lunch."

>—On her husband's retirement as a Yankee executive in 1960. This has been quoted often but increasingly without proper attribution.

WEISS, WALT

"I can't even relate to what he's doing. You can say it's awesome and it's incredible and you can use all the superlatives, but you still can't really relate to it. It's 13 years without missing a game. When you say 2,000-and-some games people don't think about how long that is, but when you say 13 years without missing a game, that puts it into better perspective. There's a lot of traffic out there around second base. Just diving for a ball, you can jam your shoulder. Jumping over a runner, you can land and twist your knee. There's so many different ways you can get injured at shortstop."

>—As Colorado Rockies shortstop on Cal Ripken Jr.'s consecutive game-record, *Washington Times*, September 6, 1995

WELLS, DAVID

"I'm fat. You're ugly. I can diet."

>—When asked by HBO's Armen Keteyian about seemingly never-ending references to the left-hander's weight, *Chicago Sun-Times*, June 20, 2001

"There is a new invention called the coat."

>—White Sox pitcher on why there is no excuse for small baseball crowds, even in chilly Chicago, *Chicago Sun-Times*, April 17, 2001

WEST, WOODY

"To be alive is an earnest thing, Thomas Carlyle intoned, and the great British essayist was correct, of course. But a steady diet of earnest is rather like a surfeit of vitamin C: A good thing itself can be toxic in excess. The human head demands surcease, requires at times to lapse into the softer rhythms of existence. Which is why a wise Providence generated the genius that invented baseball."

—"Calling a Foul in the Fairest Game," *Insight*, March 24, 1986. (Editors' Page)

WESTRUM, WES

"I had one foot in the grave and the other on a banana peel."

—As New York Mets manager, on his reason for resigning; widely attributed

"It's like church. Many attend but few understand."

—As a San Francisco Giants coach, on baseball. It is one of the most quoted of all baseball quotations and one used on a several occasions in the baseball writing of George Will.

"Well that was a cliff-dweller."

—After a close game; quoted by George Vecsey in *Joy in Mudville*

WHITE, BILL

"I leave the details to the managers. When I started out I used to work a lot of crossword puzzles. It really infuriated Eddie Stanky. He'd holler, 'Get a rule book, read the rules.' I'd tell him, 'That's what they're paying you for.'"

—On why he avoided rules disputes; quoted in *Sport*, November 1966, as a Philly

"It was the day of integration at a school. The mobs were outside, screaming, cursing, carrying signs. A Negro woman came through the mob with her little girl and brought her into the school. A white woman came through with her little girl and brought her into the school. After the white woman dropped off her little girl, she came outside and joined the mob. Everyone was afraid. What would happen to the white children in integration? It was terrible. They were frightened something awful. Late that afternoon the white girl came home. 'What happened?' her mother asked anxiously. 'What happened with you and the colored girl?' The little white girl looked at her mother. 'We were both so scared,' she said, 'we sat and held hands all day.'"

—White, an African American, was a St. Louis Cardinals first baseman; quoted in Steve Gelman, "Bill White: A Man Must Say What He Thinks Is Right," *Sport*, July 1964

"Umpiring's tough . . . you're always half wrong."

—As a telecaster, WPIX, June 23, 1982

"Very few people at 350 Park Avenue ever played the game."

—On retiring as National League president; the address is that of the commissioner's office; quoted in the *Boston Globe*, April 19, 1992

WHITE, BILL (CONTINUED)

"Winfield robs Armas of at least a home run."

> —As an announcer on a great Dave Winfield catch during the 1981 ALCS; quoted in *Sports Illustrated,* October 26, 1981

WHITE, FRED

"Well, I see in the game in Minnesota that Terry Felton relieved himself on the mound in the second inning."

> —The Royals broadcaster noticing wire-service summary that mistakenly listed the same man as the starter and the relief pitcher for the Minnesota Twins; quoted in the *St. Louis Post-Dispatch,* July 1, 1986

WHITMAN, BURT

"The more I see of Babe, the more he seems a figure out of mythology."

> —The Boston sportswriter, 1918

WHITMAN, WALT

Approaching Manhattan, up by the long-
  stretching island,
Under Niagara, the cataract falling like a veil
  over my countenance,
Upon a door-step . . . upon the horse-block of
  hard wood outside,
Upon the race-course, or enjoying pic-nics or
  jigs or a good game of base-ball . . .

> —*Leaves of Grass,* (Brooklyn, N.Y.: Rome Brothers, 1855)

Walt Whitman (*Library of Congress Prints and Photographs Division*)

"I believe in all that—in baseball, in picnics, in freedom: I believe in the jolly all-around time—with the parsons and the police eliminated."

> —On "Free Sundays" with no blue-law restrictions on activities; quoted in *With Walt Whitman in Camden* by Horace Traubel

"I see great things in baseball. It's our game—the American game. It will take our people out-of-doors, fill them with oxygen, give them a larger physical stoicism. Tend to relieve us from being a nervous, dyspeptic set. Repair these losses, and be a blessing to us."

> —Unearthed by Douglass Wallop, it appears in his book *Baseball: An Informal History,* 1989

"In our sun-down perambulations, of late, through the outer parts of Brooklyn, we have observed several parties of youngsters playing 'base,' a certain game of ball."

—*Brooklyn Daily Eagle,* July 1846

WIEDER, ROBERT S.

"Baseball fans are junkies, and their heroin is the statistic."

—Widely quoted

WILCOX, F. B.

"Progress always involves risks. You can't steal second base and keep your foot on first."

—Widely attributed

WILEY, MARK

"Pitchers tend to blow things out of proportion because they're not in the game every day. You have to explain to them that they're not as bad as they think they are—and not as good as they think they are."

—As Kansas City pitching coach, *Kansas City Star,* June 17, 1999

WILHELM, HOYT

"It takes no effort at all to pitch a knuckleball. No windup is necessary. It's so simple that very little warmup in the bullpen is required. That's why I can pitch so often without being overworked. I learned the knuckler myself. Fooled around with it in high school. I used to read about Fred Fitzsimmons and Dutch

Leonard, but nobody showed me anything. I developed it myself."

—As a Giant, *Sporting News,* March 30, 1955

WILKIE, WENDELL

"If the America way of life is to survive, let baseball survive. And too, if the game should perish, then in my opinion, the largest part of what we are fighting to protect will end."

—Republican candidate for president, 1940; during World War II

Hoyt Wilhelm (*Society for American Baseball Research; SABR*)

WILKINSON, CHARLES B. "BUD"

"One of the most significant statistics of our time is that stadium seats are being made four inches wider."

> —As special consultant to the President's Council on Youth Fitness; quoted in the *World Book Annual* 1962

WILL, GEORGE F.

"All I remember about my wedding day in 1967 is that the Cubs lost a double-header."

> —A line written in 1977; quoted in a Will profile, *USA Weekend*, April 1, 1990. Another line from the same article, on his youth: "Baseball stuck. Sunday school didn't."

"Baseball's best teams lose about sixty-five times a season. It is not a game you can play with your teeth clenched."

> —Quoted in the *Washington Post Book World*, November 29, 1987

"Correct thinkers think that 'baseball trivia' is an oxymoron: nothing about baseball is trivial."

> —From his column of April 8, 1990

"Football combines the two worst features of modern American life; it's violence punctuated by committee meetings."

> —On Ken Burns's *Baseball*, PBS, 1994

"He is the thinking person's writer about the thinking person's sport."

> —On Tom Boswell, the *Washington Post*, March 28, 1982

"It has no clock, no ties and no Liberal intrusions into the organized progression."

> —His often-quoted political line on baseball

"Night baseball isn't an aberration. What's an aberration is a team that hasn't won a World Series since 1908. They tend to think of themselves as a little Williamsburg, a cute little replica of a major league franchise. Give me the Oakland A's, thank you very much. People who do it right."

> —On the Cubs; quoted by Tom Weir, *USA Today*, April 27, 1990

"Of all the silly and sentimental things said about baseball, none is sillier than the description of the game as 'unhurried' or 'leisurely.' Or (this from folks at the serious quarterlies) that baseball has 'the pace of America's pastoral past.' This is nonsense on stilts."

> —From his *Men at Work: The Craft of Baseball*

"People say we should be paying our nurses more. I agree, but don't blame Don Mattingly because we're not paying our nurses more."

> —Quoted by Tom Weir in his *USA Today* column of April 27, 1990

"Since 1946, the Cubs have had two problems: They put too few runs on the scoreboard and the other guys put too many. So what is the new management improving? The scoreboard."

> —In the *Washington Post*, 1982

"Spring is the winter of the Cub fan's soul."

> —Quoted in the April 1, 1990, *USA Weekend*, which terms it his "immortal line"

"The game is a constantly humbling experience."

> —Quoted by Rick Wolff in *USA Today*, April 10, 1990

"Umpires should be natural Republicans—dead to 'human feelings.'"

> —From *Men at Work;* quoted in *USA Today*, May 29, 1990

WILLIAMS, BERNIE

"Yankee Stadium is the House That Ruth Built, but Jeter is redecorating."

> —Yankees center fielder on teammate Derek Jeter, *Chicago Sun-Times*, April 25, 2000

WILLIAMS, BILL

"A slump starts in your head and winds up in your stomach. You know that eventually it will happen, and you begin to worry about it. Then you know you're in one. And it makes you sick."

> —The Cub great; quoted in *Insight*, June 18, 1990

WILLIAMS, DICK

"I don't want to mellow. I'd rather be known as a winner and a poor loser."

> —As Red Sox manager, on whether he was mellowing with age, *Baseball Digest*, April 1969

"It's the most over-used word in baseball. When my teams have gone well, it has been said I'm a good communicator. When they have gone bad, it has been said I've lost the ability to communicate. But the truth is, through all of it, I have been my same 'obnoxious' self. People confuse 'communication' with execution. Once a team has been taught to play, it starts losing only because it stops executing."

> —On manager/player communications; quoted in the *Los Angeles Herald-Examiner*, July 4, 1982, as manager of the Padres

"I've always gone back to the belief that you don't win—that the other team usually beats itself. That's why I'll continue to emphasize pitching and defense. You get those two things straightened out and the offense will take care of itself."

> —As Angels manager, in the *Christian Science Monitor*, July 17, 1974

"The manager started me in this one game and I thought I was doing all right. But after seven innings I was taken out and replaced by some kid . . . what was his name? . . . Roberts, Robbens, something like that? Oh yeah, now I remember. It was Brooks Robinson."

> —When Oakland A's manager; quoted in the *Sporting News*, July 17, 1971, on how he lost his job as Orioles third baseman

WILLIAMS, EDWARD BENNETT

"I believe there are certain things that cannot be bought: loyalty, friendship, health, love and an American League pennant."

> —On new owner of the Orioles on why he was initially inactive in the free-agent market; quoted in *Sports Illustrated*, November 26, 1979

WILLIAMS, GLUYAS

"One of the hard things for parents to understand is how—if it takes the whole family one hour to get junior up and dressed and off to school in time, with only a slim chance of his remembering everything he's supposed to take—he can get dressed for a ball game, with no prompting, in ten minutes, and be off without forgetting the minutest detail of his equipment."

—Caption for the cartoonist's "Difficult Decisions" for July 24, 1946

WILLIAMS, JOE

"Cobb's immediate project is a story of his life. . . .

"Mostly I'm interested in setting the record straight. A lot of things that have been written about me aren't true. I played the game for keeps, all right, but I never provoked a fight or deliberately spiked a man.

"Just the other day a fellow wrote how I'd tear into home plate with my spikes high as if I intended to cut the catcher in half. What he didn't mention was that the catcher would put his mask in front of the plate, and the bat, too, if he had time to reach for it. Paul Krichell of the Browns did that once too often.

"What happened?

"I slid in high, scissored him between my legs, a bone snapped in his shoulder and the guy never caught another ball game in his life."

—From *The Joe Williams Baseball Reader*, edited by Peter Williams

"They tell a story on Babe Herman which I always thought typified the gay mental abandon of his club. Mr. Herman approached one of the newspapermen in a hotel lobby and complained of the personal character of his writings.

"'I wish you would lay off'n me,' said Mr. Herman. 'I don't mind so much on my account, but the missus has funny ideas.'

"While he was talking, Herman reached into his coat pocket and took out the stub of a cigar.

"'Got a match?' he asked. But before the newspaperman could come up with a match Mr. Herman, who had proceeded meantime to puff, experimentally and with vigor, cried out 'Never mind. It's lit!'"

—*The Joe Williams Baseball Reader*, edited by Peter Williams

WHY ONE SCRIBE DIDN'T VOTE THIS YEAR

"To be named to the Hall is supposedly the highest honor you can bestow on a ball player. Do they appreciate it? Well, last year we voted four of them into the shrine—Frank Frisch, Lefty Grove, Carl Hubbell and Mickey Cochrane—and not a single one showed up. They just couldn't be bothered. So this year Mr. Ken Smith and this fellow historian can include me out. If being immortalized means nothing to the majestic heroes of the diamond, it means incomparably less to me. The only player to show at Cooperstown last year was Ed Walsh, who had been voted in by a special old-timers' committee. Walsh, a 40-game winner for the White Sox in 1908, composed and read a poem for the occasion. In Walsh's day, you see, the ball player had a great respect for the game he lived on and with."

—From the *New York World-Telegram;* quoted in the *Sporting News*, February 18, 1948

WILLIAMS, MATT

"When you think about it, a home run is a mistake. The idea is to hit the ball hard, on a line, so the defense can't react to it. Hit it high in the air, which is how most home runs are hit, and most of the time it will be caught. It's a mistake."

—As Indians third baseman

WILLIAMS, MITCH

"I pitch like my hair's on fire."

—The unorthodox Cub pitcher, 1989

"I'm a firm believer that being wild has its advantages, but I'd give my big toe to throw the ball over the plate like Frank Tanana."

—The twenty-year-old Mitch Williams, on his 127 walks in 164 innings in the California League; quoted in the April 10, 1975, issue of *Baseball America*

"There *are* Cubs fans."

—The Cub and former Ranger reliever on the difference between the fans at Wrigley Field and Arlington Stadium; quoted in the *Philadelphia Inquirer,* April 11, 1989

"They can't wear me out. That's never been a worry of mine. I don't ever get stiff from pitching."

—On making 100 relief appearances; quoted in the *Washington Post,* August 22, 1989

WILLIAMS, STAN

"Oscar is so old that when he broke into the majors he was still a Negro."

—The Yankees coach on veteran outfielder Oscar Gamble; widely quoted, it appeared in the April 13, 1989 *Sports Illustrated*

WILLIAMS, TED

A man has to have goals—for a day, for a lifetime—and that was mine, to have people say, 'There goes Ted Williams, the greatest hitter who ever lived.'"

—*My Turn at Bat*

"All managers are losers; they are the most expendable pieces of furniture on earth."

—Just before being made manager of the Washington Senators in 1968

"Baseball gives every American boy a chance to excel, not just to be as good as someone else but to be better than someone else. This is the nature of man and the name of the game."

—"Scorecard," *Sports Illustrated,* August 8, 1966

"Baseball is crying for good hitters. Hitting is the most important part of the game; it is where the big money is, where much of the status is, and the fan interest. The greatest name in American sports history is Babe Ruth, a hitter."

—The man with a lifetime .344 batting average; quoted several years after his retirement

"Baseball is the only field of endeavor where a man can succeed three times out of ten and be considered a good performer."

—Widely quoted

"But I'll tell you this—I made up my mind a long time ago not to get too excited, no matter which way the crowd goes. I get paid for playing left field and for hitting that baseball. I am not a participant in a popularity contest."

—*Saturday Evening Post*, April 10, 1954

"Circumstances make a career—a man being at the right place at the right time with the right material. Circumstances can make a .400 hitter."

—*My Turn at Bat*

"He could do a lot for the Atlantic salmon."

—On John Updike, after reading "Hub Fans Bid Kid Adieu." Reflective of his dedication as a sports fisherman and conservationist. Writing in the *Boston Globe*, Alexander Theroux said that Williams "impressively but inadvertently displayed his own self-effacing grace along with that novelist's great influence."

1. Hit only strikes.
2. Never swing at a ball you're fooled on or have trouble hitting.
3. After two strikes, concede the long ball to the pitcher; shorten up on the bat and try to put the head of the bat on the ball.

—Advice to young batters; quoted in *Sport*, December 1954

Ted Williams (*Society for American Baseball Research; SABR*)

"Hitting is 50 percent above the shoulders."

—As Washington Senators manager

"I don't care to be known as a .400 hitter with a lousy average of .39955. If I'm going to be a .400 hitter, I want to have more than my toenails on the line."

—Regarding an offer to let him sit out a season-ending doubleheader to maintain his .400 average in 1941, *The Sporting News Chronicle of 20th Century Sport*.

"I felt nothing. Nothing."

—Asked how he felt when he hit his last home run in the last game in the major leagues.

"I hope somebody hits .400 soon. Then people can start pestering that guy with questions about the last guy to hit .400."

—As a former outfielder, 1980

"I keep a couple of phony-baloney clip-on ties in the drawer just in case, but I never dress up anymore. The worst thing I can think of is to have to put on a coat and tie every day and go to work. The last time I wore a tuxedo was in 1940. It was a rental."

—*My Turn at Bat*

"I know—I know all about you. Look, kid, don't ever—y'understand me?—don't *ever* let anyone monkey with your swing."

—To Carl Yastrzemski; quoted in *Yaz*

"If I was being paid $30,000 a year, the very least I could do was hit .400."

—On hitting .406 in 1941

"If there was ever a man born to be a hitter it was me."

—*My Turn at Bat*

"I'm so grateful for baseball—and so grateful I'm the hell out of it as a player."

—*My Turn at Bat*

"My name is Ted fucking Williams and I'm the greatest hitter in baseball."

—According to several accounts, the very words he used to psych himself up for batting.

"Oh, I hated that Boston press. . . . I can still remember the things they wrote, and they still make me mad: How I was always trying to get somebody's job . . . or how I didn't hit in the clutch. . . . I was a draft dodger. I wasn't a team man. I was 'jealous.' I 'alienated' the players from the press. I didn't hit to left field. I took too many bases on balls. I did this, I did that. And so on. And so unfair."

—*My Turn at Bat*

"Oh, so you're a baseball writer! I never met you before, but you're no good. No good till you prove otherwise.

"I didn't always feel like that about baseball writers. I used to open my heart to those guys. Then boom—they'd give me a lousy story."

—On being introduced to Lou Miller of the *New York World-Telegram and Sun;* quoted in the *Sporting News,* August 8, 1951

"One of the silliest things I ever read is that hitters should do better late in the season because the pitchers are tired. How can pitchers be that tired, with the bullpen picking them up in more than three quarters of their games? Also, why shouldn't the hitters be just as tired?"

—Quoted in a *Christian Science Monitor* interview, June 12, 1978

"There has always been a saying in baseball that you can't make a hitter. But I think you can improve a hitter. More than you can improve a fielder. More mistakes are made hitting than in any other part of the game."

—On being asked if you can make a .300 hitter out of a .250 hitter; quoted in *Sport Magazine's All-Time All Stars*

"There's just one thing I can say. Every pitcher is working the outside corner on me. Day in and day out, they keep throwing their best stuff out there—outside and low, outside and high. When the pitch is waist high, it's still outside."

> —During the 1948 season, while hitting .400; quoted in the *Sporting News*

"Those wolves in left field baffle me. One day, they started to holler, 'We want Olson, drop dead, Williams. We want Olson.' I shouted back, 'You'll get Olson, the next inning, you lousy so-and-sos. I'm through after I hit next.' So I took my turn at bat and then Karl Olson went out to left field. He's a big, strong, nice kid. But he came back to the dugout, dazed and rattled. 'What goes on out there, Ted?' he asked. 'No sooner had I taken your place than the fans began to holler that they wanted Williams and I should drop dead.'"

> —Quoted in the *Sporting News,* April 6, 1955

"To hit .400 you've got to have power to keep the defense back and spread out. And you've got to be fast."

> —Quoted by Bill Gutman in *Heavy Hitters*

"You are the perfect example of what I said about writers for a long time, that they're not always right. Because, in your case, they were 10 years late in getting you in here."

> —To Duke Snider on Snider's induction into the Hall of Fame, August 3, 1980

"You can't mention this fresh pitcher business enough. It used to be that a pitcher finished his games because he was expected to finish. In the late innings he was tired, and you could figure on getting to him. But now when he gets tired, you don't see him. I have batted four times in games against four different pitchers. How are you going to get a chance to figure them out? I don't want to take anything away from the old-timers, but you take a player years ago who made more than 3,000 hits. How many do you suppose were made against tired pitchers?"

> —Quoted by Lee Allen on why batting averages have dropped, in his *Sporting News* column of July 15, 1967

"You have to hit the fastball to play in the big leagues."

> —*Sox: From Lane and Fain to Zisk and Fisk* by Bob Vanderberg

"You know what Rogers Hornsby told me forty-five years ago? It was the best batting advice I ever got. 'Get a good ball to hit.' What does that mean? It means a ball that does not fool you, a ball that is not in a tough spot for you. Think of trying to hit it back up the middle. Try not to pull it every time."

> —*Words of Wisdom* by William Safire and Leonard Safir

WILLS, MAURY

"I must have quit baseball a million times in my mind. I had plugged away for eight years [1951–58] without getting anywhere.

"When Bobby [Bragan] became manager at Spokane, I was a right-handed hitter and I was still in my eight-year slump. One of the first things he did was suggest I try hitting left-handed. When I did okay at it, he said, 'Fine you're now a switch-hitter."

—On becoming a switch-hitter, while receiving the Frederick C. Miller Award as best male athlete of 1962, February 7, 1963

"In baseball, a right-fielder can go out to his position and never have a ball hit to him. And then, when he gets to the plate as a batter, he can go 0-for-4 and literally the extent of his exertion is walking from the dugout to the plate and back again . . . and maybe of course a strenuous kick at the water cooler."

—On physical exertion; quoted in *Lately* (magazine) February 1976

"It used to be very prestigious, managing in the major leagues. That was when it was up to the player to make the manager like him. The manager was the boss, a real authority figure. But all that has changed. Now it's the manager who has to make the players happy. He's the one who's always walking on thin ice."

—As an announcer, in the *Los Angeles Herald-Examiner*, June 24, 1977

"It's just as important to know when not to go as it is to know when to go."

—On base stealing

"OK, now, everyone inhale and . . . dehale."

—The Dodger shortstop, leading the team through calisthenics, 1962

"Sure, he's looking right at you but I'm looking at him, too. I can see everything he's doing. The right-handed pitcher turns his back to first base and you aren't able to tell what he may be up to."

—On why it is easier to steal against a left-handed pitcher even though they're looking at each other face-to-face; quoted in the September 1964 *Baseball Digest*

"The only thing he has to do to steal more is hit more singles."

—How a player could improve his number of stolen bases

"The years we got along well, walked hand in hand, were the years the Dodgers did poorly. The years we won were the years we had these fights. To me, that means we cared. Everyone was emotionally involved with the pennant race. Tempers will flare when that happens. When you get so passive that nothing bothers you—whether you win or lose—that means even your own production doesn't bother you. That's bad."

—On his Dodger years; quoted in a *Los Angeles Times* interview, March 27, 1978

WILSON, BERT

"We don't care who wins—as long as it's the Cubs."

—As Cubs announcer

WILSON, EARL

"For the parents of a Little Leaguer, a baseball game is simply a nervous breakdown into innings."

—From his column, December 31, 1979

WILSON, GLENN

"That's the first game I ever played in that had all four seasons."

> —The Pirates outfielder, after a game that was delayed by rain, then snow and finally ended in sunshine; quoted in the *Sporting News*, April 24, 1989

WILSON, HACK

"It starts out like a baseball and when it gets to the plate it looks like a marble."

> —On Satchel Paige's fastball. Paige's comeback: "You must be talkin' about my slow ball. My fastball looks like a fish egg."

"Yes, if you drink liquor, you won't have worms."

> —After manager Joe McCarthy attempted to teach him an object lesson by dropping a worm in a glass of gin and asking him if he had learned anything

WILSON, JIMMY

"Throwing at a batter may be okay for some folks, but when it's done at night it's downright reprehensible. At night, the ball player is full of tensions. It is difficult to see the ball."

> —Quoted in *The Sporting News Chronicle of 20th Century Sport*

WILSON, WILLIE

"When I was a little kid, teachers used to punish me by making me sign my name 100 times."

> —On why he refused to sign autographs; quoted in *Sports Illustrated*, October 6, 1980

WILSON, WOODROW

"To my friend Ty Cobb—1913."

> —Inscription on a photo from the president which Cobb told a reporter in 1942 was his most prized memento; quoted in *Ty Cobb* by Charles Alexander, 1984

Hack Wilson, Rogers Hornsby, and Kiki Cuyler *(Prints and Photographs Division Library of Congress)*

President Woodrow Wilson (*Library of Congress Prints and Photographs Division*)

WINFIELD, DAVE

"Everyone has a breaking point, turning point, stress point. The game is permeated with it. The fans don't see it because we make it look so efficient. But internally, for a guy to be successful, you have to be like a clock spring—wound but loose at the same time."

—As a Yankee; quoted in a *New York Times* interview, July 18, 1982

"These days baseball is different. You come to spring training, you get your legs ready, your arms loose, your agents ready, your lawyer lined up."

—Quoted in *Baseball . . . a Laughing Matter* by Warner Fusselle

WISE, MATT

"I don't have any problems eating salad. I just have problems getting it out of the bowl."

—Milwaukee Brewers reliever Matt Wise, who was sidelined after he cut his finger on a pair of salad tongs. Recorded by Dan Connolly of the *Baltimore Sun* (July 16, 2006), who added that Wise was the 2006 season's early leader to win the "Marty Cordova Dumbest Injury Award." Cordova, the former Orioles outfielder, missed a few games in 2002 because he fell asleep in a tanning bed and burned his face.

WITT, WHITEY

"I'm conservative. My thirty-two hits, placed end to end would probably fall short of one of Babe Ruth's homers. But he got only four

bases on that distance while I got thirty-two. Yes, my lad, science pays."

—As a Yankee after getting thirty-two bunt hits close to the end of the 1923 season; quoted in *Baseball Banter*

WOHLFORD, JIM

"Ninety percent of this game [baseball] is half mental."

—As a San Francisco Giant outfielder, 1982

WOLFE, THOMAS

"One reason I have always loved baseball so much is that it has been not merely 'the great national game,' but really a part of the whole weather of our lives, of the thing that is our own, of the whole fabric, the million memories of America. For example, in the memory of almost every one of us, is there anything that can evoke spring—the first fine days of April—better than the sound of the ball smacking into the pocket of the big mitt, the sound of the bat as it hits the horsehide: for me, at any rate, and I am being literal and not rhetorical—almost everything I know about spring is in it—the first leaf, the jonquil, the maple tree, the smell of grass upon your hands and knees, the coming into flower of April. And is there anything that can tell more about an American summer than, say, the smell of the wooden bleachers in a small town baseball park, that resinous, sultry and exciting smell of old dry wood."

—From a February, 1938, letter to Arthur Mann, included in *The Letters of Thomas Wolfe*, edited by Elizabeth Nowell, 1956

WOLFE, TOM W.

"If somebody had offered me a Class D professional contract, I would have gladly put off writing for a couple of decades."

—*Time*, November 8, 2004

WOOD, SMOKY JOE

"I threw so hard I thought my arm would fly right off my body."

—Comment made after the ninth inning of the first game of the 1912 World Series, when Wood struck out Art Fletcher and Doc Crandall

"The smaller the town the more important the ball club was. Boy if you beat a bigger town they'd practically hand you the key to the city. And if you lost a game by making an error in the ninth or something like that— well, the best thing to do was just pack your grip and hit the road, 'cause they'd never let you forget it."

—Quoted in Harold Seymour's *Baseball: The People's Game*

WOODEN, JOHN

"Baseball. The Boston Celtics and the Los Angeles Lakers could be playing for the championship, and I'd rather be here watching the Angels and Yankees."

—The legendary basketball coach on his favorite sport, from the *Los Angeles Times*, cited by John Erhardt in *Baseball Prospectus* for the "Year in Quotes, 2006"

WOODLING, GENE

"Brownie, if I ever get sick, don't you dare show up. You have such bad hands, I never want you operating on me."

—To infielder Bobby Brown, MD

WOODS, TIGER

"I'd like to be a pitcher, you have four days off to play golf. That's a dream job."

—*Cape Cod Times*, August 5, 2002

"I'd make a bet on that."

—Responding to Ozzie Guillen's contention that Guillen could par a hole at a PGA Tour event quicker than Woods could get a major-league base hit, *Chicago Sun-Times*, December 31, 2006

WOOLF, ROB

"When I negotiated Bob Stanley's contract with the Red Sox, we had statistics demonstrating he was the third-best pitcher in the league. They had a chart showing he was the sixth-best pitcher on the Red Sox."

—The agent; widely quoted

WOOLF, VIRGINIA

"Ring Lardner writes the best prose that has come our way. . . . That this should be true of *You Knew Me, Al*, a story about baseball, a game which is not played in England, a story written often in a language which is not English, gives us pause. To what does he owe his success? . . . We gaze into the depths of a society which goes its ways intent on its own concerns. Games give Lardner what society gives his English brother—a clue, a centre, a meeting place for the diverse activities of people whom a vast continent isolates, whom no tradition controls."

—From the essay "American Fiction"; quoted in Elinor Nauen, ed., *Diamonds Are a Girl's Best Friend: Women Writers on Baseball*

WOOTEN, JAMES T.

"I'd had joy for a while anyway—the kind of joy that rises from that favorite fantasy of all foolish men, the dream of going back to a place they've never been."

—From "Rookies," in Donald Hall, et al., *Playing Around* (Boston, Little, Brown, 1974)

WRIGLEY, PHILIP

"Baseball is too much of a sport to be a business and too much of a business to be a sport."

—Widely attributed

"He has full authority [to buy players and make trades], but he always checks with me. I guess maybe if he didn't check with me, he might not have the authority."

—On his Chicago Cubs director of personnel, Wid Matthews; quoted in *Baseball Digest*, May 1953

"My gum company made a $40-million profit last year, and I can't get the financial writers to say a word about it. But I fire a manager and everybody shows up."

—Quoted in the *New York Times*, April 13, 1977

"The future of major league baseball is in the day time."

—Quoted in the *Sporting News*, February 25, 1953

"This night ball is like a drug. I recall that Sam Breadon first had the Cardinals scheduled for seven night games. Then he found daytime attendance fell off so he had to play more night ball to make up for it. Finally we'll get to the point where it's practically all night ball."

—Quoted in the *Sporting News*, February 20, 1952

WULF, STEVE

"I have never once felt threatened or uncomfortable in the shadows of Yankee Stadium. It is a fortress, not only for those who come to it, but for baseball itself as well. Inside, the game is safe from change, preserved as it was 70 years and several generations ago. The House That Ruth Built, DiMaggio Graced, Mantle Lifted and Reggie Rocked feels like home to me."

—"A Holdup in the Bronx," *Sports Illustrated*, August 2, 1993

"When he punched Keith Hernandez in spring training last season, it was the only time that Strawberry would hit the cutoff man all year."

—The *Sports Illustrated* writer, after Hernandez and Strawberry got into a scuffle during a team photo session in spring training, in the magazine, January 1990

WYATT, WHITLOW

"It's just getting the right picture, the proper perspective, the mental slant, I believe. For instance, I have a set of rules for myself every time I go on the mound. The cardinal rule is never let down for a moment. You can't, to be a consistent winner. To accomplish that I make it a rule:

"To pitch to every batter as though I were facing him the first time. That helps make you careful.

"The second rule is to pitch to every hitter as though you were trying to keep him from getting a long hit. That makes you cut corners or watch weaknesses more carefully.

"The third idea I keep in mind is that no matter how low a batter's average may be you cannot afford to show him too much of even your Sunday pitch or he'll hit it.

"Fourth and final, spoil the batter's timing by changing pace. I did not get back up here until I learned to throw a slow curve to left-handed hitters and after that I added a slider to make my fast one more difficult to distinguish."

—The Brooklyn ace; quoted by Fred Bendel of the *Newark News* in *Baseball Digest*, August 1942

WYNN, EARLY

"A pitcher has to look at the hitter as his mortal enemy."

—As a White Sox pitcher

"A pitcher is only as good as his legs."

—Quoted by Walter Alston in his *Complete Baseball Handbook*

"A pitcher will never be a big winner until he hates hitters!"

—Quoted by Jim Brosnan in *The Long Season*

"It would depend on how well she was hitting."

—What he supposedly answered when asked if he would even throw at his own mother. In the April 1970 *Baseball Digest*, Arthur Daley labels the quote as "apocryphal" before repeating it. In another version Wynn answers the question by answering: "Only if she was digging in." In still another (*Baseball Is a Funny Game* by Joe Garagiola) he is asked if he would blow her down on Mother's Day, and he replies, "I would if she were crowding the plate."

Early Wynn (*Chicago White Sox*)

"I've got a right to knock down anybody holding a bat."

> —After dusting his son; quoted in Roger Kahn, *A Season in the Sun*, 1977

"Somebody will have to come and tear the uniform off me, and the guy who comes better have help."

> —On retirement; quoted in *The Baseball Card Engagement Book*, 1987

"That space between the white lines—that's my office. That's where I conduct my business."

> —Widely attributed

"You can't get enjoyment out of hate. I wish I could live by this 100 per cent but every fourth or fifth day during the summer, I go into a Jekyll-and-Hyde act. Every time a player gets a hit or home run off me, I get strange notions and ideas of things I would like to do to him. Then after the game I feel ashamed and think to myself, 'This guy is a nice fellow and I wonder what's happening to you, Early?' So I'll call him up and invite him to be my guest at dinner and spend the evening talking shop."

> —In his column for the *Cleveland News;* requoted in *Sport*, March 1956

WYNN, JIMMY

"There's magic in the Dodger uniform."

> —Explaining why he, a star with the Dodgers, was a flop at Houston the year before; quoted in *Everything You Always Wanted to Know About Sports and Didn't Know Where to Ask* by Mickey Herskowitz and Steve Perkins

"Winning makes you happy all day."

> —As a Dodger center fielder; quoted by Roger Angell in *Five Seasons*

607

XYZ

YANASE, KOJI

"If an American is hit on the head by a ball at the ballpark, he sues. If a Japanese person is hit on the head he says, 'It's my honor. It's my fault. I shouldn't have been standing there.'"

—Japanese bar association official explaining why there are half as many lawyers in his country than the greater Washington area. *Newsweek*, February 26, 1996

YASTRZEMSKI, CARL

"And if I have my choice between a pennant and a triple crown, I'll take the pennant every time."

—*Yaz*

"Ed, you're the second-best umpire in the league. The other 23 are tied for first."

—To umpire Ed Runge, who credited Yaz with the best barb ever handed to an ump by a player; quoted by Harry Sheer of *Chicago Today* in the July 1973 *Baseball Digest*

"I remember in 1961 when I was a scared rookie, hitting .220 after the first three months of my baseball season, doubting my ability. A man was fishing up in New Brunswick. I said, 'Can we get a hold of him? I need help. I don't think I can play in the big leagues.' He flew into Boston, worked with me for three days, helped me mentally and gave me confidence that I could play in the big leagues. I hit .300 for the rest of the season. I'd like to thank Ted Williams."

—On his induction into the Hall of Fame, July 23, 1989

"I've always hit well in September. I don't know why. Maybe the fans make a difference—I don't know. . . . This is a strange game."

—Quoted in *Late Innings* by Roger Angell

"The biggest thing I've found in hitting is not to get discouraged and change something that gets you completely messed up—even though the tendency is often overwhelming.

But you just can't do it and survive. I was a lousy hitter in May doing exactly the same things that made me a great hitter in June."

—Quoted in the *Christian Science Monitor,* August 20, 1975

"They can talk about Babe Ruth and Ty Cobb and Rogers Hornsby and Lou Gehrig and Joe DiMaggio and Stan Musial and all the rest, but I'm sure not one of them could hold cards and spades to Williams in his sheer knowledge of hitting. He studied hitting the way a broker studies the stock market, and could spot at a glance mistakes that others couldn't see in a week."

—*Yaz*

YAVERBAUM, ERIC

"Owners get rich, players get rich. We don't take either side. We don't care. All we want is baseball."

—The founder of Strike Back, a fan organization; quoted in *USA Today,* March 2, 1990, during the lockout

YAWKEY, TOM

"I never look back. I love baseball and you have to be patient and take the good with the bad. After all, it's only a game."

—Often-quoted summary of baseball which was suggested as his epitaph. Yawkey (1897–1976) was the owner of the Boston Red Sox for forty-three years

"Listen, if trying to treat the players as human beings is spoiling them, then I spoil them.

But I was brought up to treat a human being as a human being until he proves unworthy of himself."

—After being accused of paying too much for players. Before his death he estimated that he had lost ten million dollars trying to develop championship teams.

"Players are the most helpless people in the world. If you told them to get to San Francisco by themselves, they might end up in Mexico City."

—Widely quoted

YOST, EDDIE

"You would think that more pitchers would realize just how much they can help their winning average by their fielding ability. By being a good fielder, a pitcher can cut the man down at third in the two-on, no-out situation and help himself win those 1 to 0 and 2 to 1 games."

—Quoted in the *Sporting News,* February 11, 1953

YOUNG, CHIC

"Baseball, my son, is the cornerstone of civilization."

—Dagwood Bumstead in the cartoon *Blondie*

YOUNG, CURT

"He hit it a lot further than it went."

—Said by the Oakland A's southpaw on Yankee Rickey Henderson's homer, May 1986, *Sports Illustrated,* June 2, 1986

"A pitcher's got to be good and he's got to be lucky to get a no-hit game."

> —Quoted by Francis J. Powers in *My Greatest Day in Baseball*

"Gosh, all a kid has to do these days is spit straight and get $40,000 for signing."

> —August 3, 1948, at a luncheon in Philadelphia

"His trouble is he takes life too seriously. Cobb is going at it too hard."

> —On Ty Cobb, Hall of Fame Collection

"Too many pitchers, that's all, there are just too many pitchers. Ten or 12 on a team. Don't see how any of them get enough work. Four starting pitchers and one relief man ought to be enough. Pitch 'em every three days and you'd find they'd get control and good, strong arms."

> —Quoted in the *Sporting News*, February 14, 1951

Cy Young (*Library of Congress Prints and Photographs, Bain Collection*)

"As Dr. Dafoe said when he handed the fourth Dionne baby to the nurse, 'This thing ain't over yet.'"

> —On the fact that the 1960 World Series would go into a seventh game, in the *New York Daily News*. The allusion is to the Dionne quintuplets.

"Fans are the only ones who really care. There are no free-agent fans. There are no fans who say, 'Get me out of here. I want to play for a winner.'"

> —SABR Collection

"Hold a Met at third and the next thing you know, you're taking his glove out to him."

> —In the *New York Daily News*, back in the mid-1960s when the Mets were dreadful and rarely got the hit that would drive in the runner at third; quoted by Whitey Herzog in *White Rat*

"If Jesus Christ were to show up with his old baseball glove some guys wouldn't vote for him. He dropped the cross three times, didn't he?"

> —On Hall of Fame voting in general and, specifically, on Willie Mays not being elected unanimously; 1979, the *New York Daily News*

"I'm glad you didn't take it personally."

> —To Jim Bouton on May 29, 1970, the day after he had written a review of Bouton's *Ball Four* in the *New York Daily News*. The review said in part, "I feel sorry for Jim Bouton. He is a social leper. He didn't catch it, he developed it. Leonard Schecter is a social leper. People like this, embittered people, sit down in their time of deepest rejection and write. They write, oh hell, everybody stinks,

everybody but me, and it makes them feel much better." Bouton used the Young line as the title for the sequel to *Ball Four*, from Bouton's *I'm Glad You Didn't Take It Personally*

"Is the sound of my typing disturbing your conversation?"

—While working on deadline in the press box, this is what he snarled to gossipers; quoted by Stan Isaacs, *Newsday,* April 9, 1990

"It's not that Billy drinks a lot. Its just that he fights a lot when he drinks a little."

—On Billy Martin; quoted in the *National Review,* January 22, 1990

"My God, they've hired the unknown soldier."

—The sportswriter, expressing the sentiments of many of his colleagues when the owners unexpectedly hired the totally unknown retired general William D. Eckert as the commissioner of baseball

"The San Francisco Giants will draw in New York as long as Willie Mays comes in with them, because Willie Mays is still the New York Giants."

—In the New *York Daily News,* April 1965

"Too many things seem to upset the lords of baseball, or at least the majority of them. They love to see their names in print but want their names preceded by the adjective 'great.' In that, they are not unlike the players."

—From "Diamond Quotes," in *Nine,* 2006 edition

"You and Durocher are on a raft. A wave comes and knocks him into the ocean. You dive in and save his life. A shark comes and takes your leg. Next day, you and Leo start out even."

—His assessment of the ruthless "win at any cost" Leo Durocher, who supposedly said that he would trip his own granddaughter when rounding third if it meant victory

ZACHARY, TOM

"I gave Ruth a curve, low and outside. It was my best pitch. The ball just hooked into the right field seats and I instinctively cried 'foul.' But I guess I was the only guy who saw it that way. Even when Ruth and I were teammates later, we never agreed on that point. If you really want to know the truth, I'd rather have thrown at his big, fat head."

—On serving up Babe Ruth's sixtieth home run; quoted in his *Sporting News* obituary after his death on January 24, 1969, at age seventy-two

ZIEGLER, RON

"He will now have to look at the California Angels as his home team."

—On President Nixon transferring his loyalties as it became clear that the Senators were leaving Washington, *Washington Post,* September 21, 1971.

ZIMMER, DON

"All you see in Red Sox—Yankees games are fights and cops dragging people out by the hair. You rarely see fights here. These are nice people."

—On the Cardinals-Cubs rivalry; quoted by Dan Shaughnessy in the *Boston Globe,* July 30, 1989

"Buy one and send it to my mother. It's her fault I look like this."

> —Chicago Cubs manager Don Zimmer, speaking by phone to his wife in Florida after seeing a *USA Today* photo of himself looking like an old bulldog, *USA Today*, July 5, 1989.

"I agree it's a nasty habit, and I would not advocate that any youngster take up chewing tobacco or snuff. But chewing does cause excessive saliva. You cannot swallow tobacco juice, and here's where spitting comes into the picture.

"Players and coaches in the dugout often eat sunflower seeds, and they spit out the shells, which may look like they are just spitting. Also, I can tell you that a great many more players chew gum than tobacco, so some of those guys spit from habit rather than necessity. I should also tell you that the majority of players who are seen spitting on TV have no idea that the camera is on them.

"Thanks for giving me a chance to bring the facts to the public. Sincerely, Don Zimmer, field manager for the Chicago Cubs."

> —Letter appearing in Ann Landers's advice column, written "in response to your correspondent who wrote about excessive spitting by baseball players," *Chicago Tribune*, October 29, 1990.

"It's what I hate most about this job. Monkeying around with people's lives is never fun. On the other hand, when I've picked the team, 24 players are monkeying around with my life."

> —On making his final cuts at spring training; quoted in the *Major League Baseball Newsletter*, May 1989

Don Zimmer (*Boston Red Sox*)

"The first thing that young, impressionable country boys learn to do in Major League Baseball is speak profanity."

> —From *Coach and Athletic Director*, August 2003

"The game has to be fun if you're going to be any good at all."

> —As Padres manager

"The weather's cold, my club stinks, we can't win, my knees are killing me, I'm off my diet, I can't putt anymore, my wife's nagging me. Other than that, life's great."

> —A note left by the Cubs manager on a plane that would be used by former Dodger pal Roger Craig and his San Francisco Giants; quoted by Steve Fainaru in the *Boston Globe*, April 29, 1990

ZINSSER, WILLIAM

"I am uneasy with stadiums that are too perfect and too removed from their city. Imperfection is a tonic in baseball—the uninvited guest who never runs out of surprises for the fan who thinks he has seen it all. I'm also uneasy with efforts to improve a game that needs no improving: to hype its rhythm with organ music, to alter its subtle balance with designated hitters, to replace with carpeting the very grass it's played on."

—*Spring Training* (New York: Harper & Row, 1989)

"Memory was the glue that held baseball together as the continuing American epic."

—*Spring Training*

"The Mississippi (River) is one of America's four central myths, the others being Abraham Lincoln, the Civil War and baseball."

—*Spring Training*

ZOLDAK, SAM

"You won't find it in the box scores. I did my work in the bull pen. Both Series went six games and I pitched every one of them—went the whole nine innings in most—and never got called on. That's how I got the nickname of Sad Sam. Who wouldn't be sad after all that wasted labor?"

—Recalling his role in the 1944 and 1948 World Series (with Browns and Indians). The quote appeared in his *Sporting News* obituary. Zoldak died on August 25, 1966.

ACKNOWLEDGMENTS

Four individuals were absolutely essential to the researching of this book. Collectively, their influence and inspiration are felt on practically every page.

These are, in alphabetical order:

Joseph C. Goulden, who has fed me (1) clippings, (2) unqualified support

Robert "Skip" McAfee, for access to his sterling collection of baseball quotations

The late Charles D. Poe of Houston, to whom the original version of this book was dedicated

William C. Young, who helped sort through years of clippings and scribblings for for gems

Institutionally, I am obliged to the Society for American Baseball Research whose members chipped in big time, and to the staff of the National Baseball Library at Cooperstown, New York, who have got to be the best in the business of specialized information. I also thank SABR for the use of photographs and for access to the sixty boxes and ten scrapbooks of clippings constituting the lifetime collection of Russell Euper.

And . . .

Paul D. Adomites, editor and writer, for his help with quotes and pictures

Peter Andrijeski of Seattle for his sizable personal collection of quotations

The Reverend Gerry Beirne

Peter C. Bjarkman

John S. Bowman

Bob Brown

Patrick Brown

Larry W. Bryant

William L. Chambers

William Cole, poet, writer, and anthologist

Mary Corliss of the Museum of Modern Art Film Still Archives

Raymond V. Curiale

Everett J. Daniels

The late James Darling

Bill Deane

Martin Gardner

The late Mike Gershman, with special thanks for the use of the
    quotes from his *Baseball Card Engagement Books*

Walt Gianchi

Tom Gill of TGI

Mike Green

Robert S. Greenman

Jerry H. Gregory, Society for American Baseball Research–ite and
    helpmate

R.G. Harding

Thomas Heitz, National Baseball Library

J. Thomas Hetrick

Brigg Hewitt

Craig Steven Hirsch

Steve Hirsch

W. Lloyd Johnson

Dave Kaplan

Peter Kaplan

Keirn Keerane

Dave Kelly, Library of Congress sports specialist, the only person I
    know of who can come up with a baseball quotation in *A Guide to
    Hemingway's Paris*

Pat Kelly, National Baseball Library

Bobby Kraft

Norbert Kraich

Nancy Jo Leachman, librarian and Society for American Baseball
    Research–ite

Norman Macht
Scott D. Maddock
S. M. Martin
Robert J. Mayer
Bill Mead, for great quotations and much more
Ron Menchine
Paul Metcalf
Eldon Meyers
Kenneth B. Miller
Peter Miller
Peter Morris
Bill Moushey
Joe Naiman, for a major assist on finding the unexpected
Jim O'Donnell
Murray R. Pearce
Dr. Howard Pollock
The Prints and Photographs Department, the Library of Congress
Marty Pulvers, who once had this idea himself and graciously turned
    over all his A material
Lawrence Ritter
Randy Roberts
Walter Robertson
Marion Rogers
Sam Sass
David Shulman
Fred Shapiro, the compiler of the magnificent *Yale Book of Quotations*
Lee Sinins
Bob Skole, for his continuing advice and support
Jim Small, of the Baseball Commissioner's Office.
The late Robert Smith of Lenox, Massachusetts, the man who wrote
    the book on baseball
Brad Snyder
Lyle Spatz
Michael A. Stackpole
Bob Staples
Norman Stevens
Ted Sweetland Jr.
Ralph P. Testa
the late James Thorpe III

Donald. E. Toma
David Vincent, of the Society for American Baseball Research biographical committee
Tim Wiles, National Baseball Library
Peter Williams
Tom Wiswell
Irving Zeiger
Linda Ziemer, Chicago Historical Society

BIBLIOGRAPHY

—※·∈—

I. Works That Are Specifically Related to Quotations

Abel, Bob, and Michael Valenti. *Sports Quotes: The Insider's View of the Sports World.* New York: Facts on File, 1983.

Adams, A. K. *The Home Book of Humorous Quotation..* New York: Dodd, Mead, 1969.

Adams, Franklin Pierce. *FPA's Book of Quotations.* New York: Funk and Wagnalls, 1952.

Andrews, Robert, Mary Biggs, and Michael Seidel. *The Columbia World of Quotations* New York, Columbia University Press, 1966.

Associated Press. "Memories of Casey—and Stengelese." *San Francisco Examiner,* September 30, 1975.

Beilenson, Peter. *Grand Slams and Fumbles: Sports Quotes.* White Plains, N.Y.: Peter Pauper Press, 1989.

Bennett, Arnold. *Your United States.* New York: Harper and Brothers, 1912.

Berra, Yogi, and Tom Horton. *Yogi: It Ain't Over . . .* New York: McGraw-Hill, 1989.

Boller, Paul F., and John George. *They Never Said It.* New York: Oxford University Press, 1989.

Carruth, Gorton and Eugene Ehrlich. *The Harper Book of American Quotations.* New York: Harper and Row, 1988.

Cerf, Bennett. *Good for a Laugh.* Garden City, N.Y.: Hanover House, 1952.

———. The *Laugh's on Me.* Garden City, N.Y.: Doubleday, 1959.

Cerf, Christopher, and Victor Navasky. *The Experts Speak.* New York: Pantheon Books, 1984.

Charlton, James. *The Writer's Quotation Book.* New York: Penguin Books, 1980.

Cherry, Jack. *All Star "Quotes."* Houston: All Star Books, no date.

Chieger, Bob. *The Cubbies: Quotations on the Chicago Cubs.* New York: Atheneum, 1987.

———. *Voices of Baseball: Quotations on the Summer Game.* New York: Atheneum, 1983.

Fadiman, Clifton. *The American Treasury, 1455–1955.* New York: Harper and Brothers, 1955.

Fusselle, Warner. *Baseball . . . a Laughing Matter.* St. Louis: Sporting News, *1987.*

Kenin, Richard, and Justin Wintle. *The Dictionary of Biographical Quotation.* New York: Knopf, 1978.

Lardner, John. "With the Bases More Than Full" *New Yorker,* May 20, 1950.

Liddle, Barry. *Dictionary of Sports Quotations.* New York: Routledge and Kegan Paul, 1987.

Maikovich, Andrew. *Sports Quotations.* Jefferson, N.C.: McFarland, 1984.

McAfee, Skip. "Quoting Baseball: The Intellectual Take on our National Pastime," *Nine,* Spring 2005.

Metcalf Fred. *The Penguin Dictionary of Modern Quotations.* New York: Viking, 1986.

Miner, Margaret and Hugh Rawson. *American Heritage Dictionary of American Quotations*. New York: Penguin Reference, 1997.

Monteleone, John J., ed. *Branch Rickey's Little Blue Book*. New York: Macmillan, 1995.

Murphy, Edward F. "Quote: The Subject Was Baseball." *New York Times*, April 25, 1976.

Nathan, David H. *The McFarland Baseball Quotations Dictionary*. Jefferson, N.C., McFarland, 2000.

Nelson, Kevin. *Baseball's Greatest Insults*. New York: Fireside Books, Simon and Schuster, 1984.

———. *Baseball's Greatest Quotes*. New York: Fireside Books, Simon and Schuster, 1982.

Shapiro, Fred R., *The Yale Book of Quotations*. New Haven, Conn.: Yale University Press, 2006.

Simpson, James B. *Simpson's Contemporary Quotations*. New York: HarperCollins Thomas Y. Crowell, 1997.

Sugar, Bert Randolph. *The Book of Sports Quotes*. New York: Quick Fox Books, 1979.

II. Works on Baseball and Sports That Were Especially Useful in Preparing This Collection. Many More Books Were Consulted.

Alexander, Charles C. *Ty Cobb*. New York: Oxford University Press, 1984.

Allen, Ethan. *Baseball: Major League Technique and Tactics*. New York: Macmillan Co., 1953.

———. *Baseball Play and Strategy*. New York: Ronald Press, 1953.

———. *Baseball Techniques Illustrated*. New York: A. S. Barnes, 1951.

Allen, Lee. *Cooperstown Corner: Columns from the Sporting News, 1962–1969*. Cleveland: Society for American Baseball Research, 1990.

Allen, Lee, and Tom Meany. *Kings of the Diamond*. New York: G. P. Putnam, 1965.

Allen, Maury. *Baseball's 100: A Personal Ranking of the Best Players in Baseball History*. New York: A & W Publishers, 1981.

———. *Bo: Pitching and Wooing*. New York: Bantam, 1973.

———. *The Incredible Mets*. New York: Paperback Library, 1969.

———. *You Could Look It Up: The Life of Casey Stengel*. New York: Times Books, 1979.

Allen, Mel, and Frank Graham Jr. *It Takes Heart*. New York: Harper and Brothers, 1959.

Andreano, Ralph. *No Joy in Mudville: The Dilemma of Major League Baseball*. Cambridge, Mass.: Schenkman, 1965.

Angell, Roger. *Five Seasons*. New York: Simon and Schuster, 1977.

———. *Late Innings*. New York: Simon and Schuster, 1982.

———. *The Summer Game*. New York: Popular Library, 1972.

Archibald, Joe. *Baseball Talk for Beginners*. New York: Julian Messner, 1969.

Asinof, Eliot. *Eight Men Out*. New York: Ace Books, 1963.

Baker, Russell. "Come Back, Dizzy." *New York Times*, October 9, 1979.

Bancroft, Jessie H., and William Dean Pulvermacher. *Handbook of Athletic Games*. New York: Macmillan, 1917.

Barber, Red. *1947–When All Hell Broke Loose in Baseball*. New York: Doubleday, 1982.

Barber, Red, and Robert Creamer. *Rhubarb in the Catbird Seat*. New York: Doubleday, 1968.

Bennett, Bob. *On the Receiving End: The Catcher's Guidebook*. Fresno, Cal.: Mid-Cal Publisher, 1982.

Benson, Michael. *Ballparks of North America*. Jefferson, N.C.: McFarland, 1989.

Bergman, Ron. *The Mustache Gang*. New York: Dell, 1973.

Boswell, Tom. *How Life Imitates the World Series*. Garden City, N.Y.: Doubleday, 1982.

———. *My Time Begins on Opening Day*. Garden City, N.Y.: Doubleday, 1984.

Bouton, Jim. *Ball Four: My Life and Hard Times Throwing the Knuckleball in the Big Leagues*. Edited by Leonard Schecter. New York: Dell. 1970.

Breslin, Jimmy. *Can't Anybody Here Play This Game?* New York: Avon Books, 1963.

Brondfield, Jerry. *Hank Aaron . . . 714 and Beyond*. New York: Scholastic Books, 1974.

Brosnan, Jim. *The Long Season*. New York: Harper and Row, 1960.

———. *Pennant Race*. New York: Harper & Row, 1962.

Campanella, Roy. *It's Good to Be Alive*. New York: Signet, 1959.

Carmichael, John P., et. al. *My Greatest Day in Baseball*. New York: Tempo, 1968.

Clark, Steve. *The Complete Book of Baseball Cards*. New York: Grosset & Dunlap, 1976.

Cobb, Ty, with Al Stump. *My Life in Baseball: The True Record*. Garden City, N.Y.: Doubleday, 1961

Cochrane, Gordon S. *Baseball: The Fan's Game*. New York: Funk and Wagnalls Company, 1939.

Coffin, Tristram Potter. *The Old Ball Game: Baseball in Folklore and Fiction*. New York: Herder and Herder, 1971.

Cohen, Marvin. *Baseball the Beautiful*. New York: Links Books, 1974.

Conner, Anthony J. *Baseball for the Love of It*. New York: Macmillan, 1982.

Couzens, Gerald Secor. *A Baseball Album*. New York: Lippincott and Crowell, 1980.

Craig, Roger, with Vern Plagenhoef. *Inside Pitch*. Grand Rapids, Mich.: Eerdsman Publishing, 1984.

Creamer, Robert W. *Babe: The Legend Comes to Life*. New York: Simon and Schuster, 1974.

———. *Stengel: His Life and Times*. New York: Simon and Schuster, 1984.

Crepeau, Richard C. *Baseball: America's Diamond Mind, 1919–1941*. Orlando: University of Central Florida, 1980.

Curry, Jack. "Way with Words Helps Jones in His Second Job." *New York Times*. October 27, 2006.

Day, Laraine. *Day with the Giants*. Garden City, N.Y.: Doubleday, 1952.

Dean, Jerome H. "Dizzy." *Dizzy Baseball: A Gay and Amusing Glossary of Baseball Terms Used by Radio Broadcasters, with Explanations to Aid the Uninitiated*. New York: Greenberg, 1952.

———. *The Dizzy Dean Dictionary*. Rev. ed. St. Louis: Falstaff Brewing Company, 1949.

Deming, Richard. *Vida*. New York: Lancer, 1972.

Dolan, Edward F., Jr. *Calling the Play*. New York: Atheneum, 1982.

Dravecky, Dave, with Tim Stafford. *Comeback*. Grand Rapids, Mich.: Zondervan, 1990.

Durocher, Leo, with Ed Linn. *Nice Guys Finish Last*. New York: Simon and Schuster, 1975.

Durso, Joseph. *Baseball and the American Dream*. St. Louis: The Sporting News, 1986.

———. *Casey*. Englewood Cliffs, N.J.: Prentice-Hall, 1967.

Einstein, Charles. *The Fireside Book of Baseball*. 3 vols. New York: Simon and Schuster, 1956, 1962, 1968.

———. *Willie's Time*. New York: J. P. Lippincott, 1979.

Evans, Billy. *Simplified Base Ball Rules*. N.p., 1923.

Feller, Bob. *Strikeout Story*. New York: Bantam, 1948.

Fleming, G.H. *The Unforgettable Season*. New York: Penguin, 1981.

Flexner, Stuart Berg. *Listening to America*. New York: Simon and Schuster, 1982.

Flood, Curt. *The Way It Is*. New York: Trident Press, 1971.

Ford, Whitey, with Phil Pepe. *Slick*. New York: Dell, 1987.

Frank, Lawrence. *Playing Hardball: The Dynamics of Baseball Folk Speech*. New York: Peter Lang Publishers, 1984.

Freehan, Bill. *Behind the Mask*. New York: World Publishing, 1970.

Frick, Ford C. *Games, Asterisks, and People*. New York: Crown, 1973.

Frommer, Harvey. *New York City Baseball*. New York: Macmillan, 1980.

———. *Rickey and Robinson*. New York: Macmillan, 1982.

———. *Sports Lingo*. New York: Atheneum, 1979.

Fullerton, Hugh S. "The Baseball Primer." *American Magazine*, June 1912.

Garagiola, Joe. *Baseball Is a Funny Game*. New York: Bantam Books, 1960.

Gardner, Martin. *The Annotated "Casey at the Bat."* New York: Bramhall House, 1967.

Garvey, Steve, with Skip Rozin. *Garvey*. New York: Times Books, 1986.

Gehrig, Eleanor, with Joe Durso. *My Luke and I*. New York: Signet, 1976.

Gerlach, Larry R. *The Men in Blue*. New York: Viking, 1980.

Gershman, Michael. *The Baseball Card Engagement Calendar*. Dallas: Taylor, 1987, 1988, 1989, and 1990 editions.

Gibson, Bob, with Phil Pepe. *From Ghetto to Glory*. New York: Popular Library, 1968.

Gordon, Peter, with Sydney Walle and Paul Weinman. *Diamonds Are Forever*. San Francisco: Chronicle Books, 1987.

Graham, Frank. *Baseball Extra*. New York: A. S. Barnes, 1954.

Graham, Frank, and Dick Hyman. *Baseball Wit and Wisdom*. New York: David McKay, 1962.

Grey, Zane. *The Shortstop*. 1909. Reprint, New York: Grosset and Dunlap, 1937.

Gutman, Bill. *Giants of Baseball*. New York: Tempo, 1975.

———. *Heavy Hitters: Lynn, Parker, Carew, Rose*. New York: Tempo, 1974.

Hano, Arnold. *A Day in the Bleachers*. New York: Crowell, 1955.

———. *Willie Mays*. New York: Grosset and Dunlap, 1966.

Hartt, Rollin Lynde. "The National Game." *Atlantic*, August 1908.

Heck, Henry J. "Baseball Terminology." *American Speech*, April 1930.

Henderson, Robert W. *Ball, Bat and Bishop*. New York: Rockport Press, 1947.

Hicks, Raymond L. *Pitching to Win*. New York: Harper and Row, 1973.

Higgins, George V. *The Progress of the Seasons*. New York: Henry Holt, 1989.

Hill, Art. *I Don't Care If I Never Come Back*. New York: Simon and Schuster, 1980.

Howarth, Jerry. *Baseball Lite*. Toronto: Protocol Books, 1986.

Huddle, Franklin P. "Baseball Jargon," *American Speech*, April 1943.

Humber, William. *Let's Play Ball*. Toronto: Lester and Orpen Dennys/Royal Ontario Museum, 1989.

Hynd, Noel. *The Giants of the Polo Grounds*. New York: Doubleday, 1988.

Jackson, Reggie, with Bill Libby. *Reggie*. Chicago: Playboy Press, 1975.

Jackson, Reggie, with Mike Lupica. *Reggie*. New York: Ballantine, 1984.

Johnstone, Jay, with Rick Talley. *Temporary Insanity*. New York: Bantam, 1985.

Jordan, Pat. *A False Spring*. New York: Dodd, Mead, 1975.

———. *The Suitors of Spring*. New York: Dodd, Mead, 1973.

Kahn, Roger. *The Boys of Summer*. New York: Harper and Row, 1971.

———. *Good Enough to Dream*. New York: Doubleday, 1985.

———. *How the Weather Was*. New York: Signet, 1973.

———. *A Season in the Sun*. New York: Harper and Row, 1977.

Kinsella, W. P. *Shoeless Joe*. New York: Ballantine Books, 1983.

Kirschner, Allen. *Great Sports Reporting*. New York: Dell, 1969.

Kluger, Steve. *Changing Pitches*. New York: St. Martin's Press, 1984.

Koppett, Leonard. *A Thinking Man's Guide to Baseball*. New York: Dutton, 1967, the revised and enlarged edition of the original now titled *All About Baseball* was published in 1974 by Quadrangle.

Koufax, Sandy, with Ed Linn. *Koufax*. New York: Viking, 1966.

Krich, John. *El Béisbol: Travels Through the Pan-American Pastime*. New York: Prentice Hall, 1989.

Lardner, Ring. *You Know Me, Al*. Cleveland: World Publishing, 1945.

Lasorda, Tommy, with David Fisher. *The Artful Dodger*. New York: Avon Books, 1985.

Lawson, Thomas W. *The Krank: His Language and What It Means*. Boston: Rand Avary, 1888.

Lee, Gretchen. "In Sporting Parlance." *American Speech*, April 1926.

Libby, Bill, and Vida Blue. *Vida: His Own Story*. Englewood Cliffs, New Jersey: Prentice Hall, 1972.

Lieb, Frederick G. *Baseball as I Have Known It*. New York: Tempo, 1977.

Lindop, Al. "The Names of Summer." *Indianapolis Star*, April 5, 1981.

Lomax, Stan, and Dave Stanley. *A Treasury of Baseball Humor*. New York: Lantern Press, 1950.

Lowenfish, Lee, and Tony Lupien. *The Imperfect Diamond*. New York: Stein and Day, 1980.

Lowry, Phillip J. *Green Cathedrals*. Cooperstown, New York: Society for American Baseball Research, 1986.

Luciano, Ron, and Dave Fisher. *Strike Two*. New York: Bantam, 1984.

———. *The Umpire Strikes Back*. New York: Bantam, 1982.

Lukas, J. Anthony. "How Mel Allen Started a Lifelong Love Affair," *New York Times Magazine*, September 12, 1971.

Lyle, Sparky, and Peter Golenbock. *The Bronx Zoo*. New York: Crown, 1979.

Mack, Connie. *From Sandlot to Big League: Connie Mack's Baseball Book*. New York: Alfred A. Knopf, 1950.

Malamud, Bernard. *The Natural*. New York: Pocket Books, 1952.

Mantle, Mickey, with Herb Gluck. *The Mick*. New York: Jove, 1986.

Marazzi, Rich. *The Rules and Lore of Baseball*. New York: Stein and Day, 1980.

Martin, Billy, and Peter Golenbock. *Number 1*. New York: Dell, 1980.

Masin, Herman L. *Baseball Laughs*. New York: Scholastic Books, 1964.

Mathewson, Christy. *Pitching in a Pinch*. New York: Putnam, 1912.

McBride, Joseph. *High* and *Inside: The Complete Guide to Baseball Slang*. New York: Warner Books, 1980.

McCabe, Neal, and Constance McCabe. *Baseball's Golden Age: The Photographs of Charles M. Conlon*. New York: Harry N. Abrams, 1993.

McCarver, Tim. *Oh, Baby, I Love It*. New York: Dell, 1988.

McCue, Andy. *Baseball by the Books*. Dubuque, Iowa: Brown and Benchmark, 1991.

McDonald, Jack. "Sandwiches and Flies." *San Francisco Examiner*, April 11, 1966.

McGraw, Tug, and Joseph Durso. *Screwball*. Boston: Houghton Mifflin, 1974.

Mead, William B. *Even the Browns*. Chicago: Contemporary Books, 1978.

———. *The Official New York Yankee Hater's Handbook*. New York: Perigee Books, 1983.

———. *Two Spectacular Seasons*. New York: Macmillan, 1990.

Mitchell, Gary, with Gary Matthews. *They Call Me Sarge*. Chicago: Bonus Books, 1985.

Mitchell, Jerry. *The Amazing Mets*. New York: Grosset and Dunlap, 1970.

Mungo, Raymond. *Confessions from Left Field*. New York: Dutton, 1983.

Murnane, T. H. *How to Umpire, How to Captain a Team, How to Manage a Team, How to Coach, How to Organize a League, How to Score, and the Technical Terms of Base Ball*. New York: Spalding Athletic Library, American Sports Publishing, Co., 1915.

Murray, Jim. *The Best of Jim Murray*. Garden City: Doubleday, 1965.

Murray, Tom, ed. *Sport Magazine's All-Time All Stars*. New York: Signet, 1977.

Nash, Bruce, and Allan Zullo. *The Baseball Hall of Shame*, vols. 1–4. New York: Pocket Books, 1985, 1986, 1987, 1990.

Nelson, Kevin. *The Greatest Stories Ever Told About Baseball*. New York: Perigee Books, 1986.

Nichols, Edward J. *Historical Dictionary of Baseball Terminology*. Ann Arbor, Mich.: University Microfilms, 1939.

Novak, Michael. *The Joy of Sports*. New York: Basic Books, 1976.

Nugent, William Henry. "The Sports Section." *American Mercury*, March 1929.

Obojski, Robert. *Bush League: A History of Minor League Baseball*. New York: Macmillan, 1975.

Offit, Sidney, ed. *The Best of Baseball*. New York: Putnam, 1956.

Okrent, Daniel, and Harris Lewine. *The Ultimate Baseball Book*. Boston: Houghton Mifflin, 1979.

Okrent, Daniel, and Steve Wulf. *Baseball Anecdotes*. New York: Oxford University Press, 1989.

Paige, Leroy "Satchel," with David Lipman. *Maybe I'll Pitch Forever*. Garden City, N.Y.: Doubleday, 1962.

Pepe, Phil. *No-Hitter*. New York: Scholastic Books, 1972.

———. *The Wit and Wisdom of Yogi Berra*. New York: Hawthorne, 1974.

Pepitone, Joe, with Berry Stainback. *Joe, You Coulda Made Us Proud*. New York: Dell, 1975.

Perry, Gaylord, with Ed Sudyk. *Me and the Spitter*. New York: Dutton, 1974.

Peterson, Harold. *The Man Who Invented Baseball*. New York: Scribner's, 1973.

Plimpton, George. *Out of My League*. New York, Harper and Row, 1961.

Polner, Murray. *Branch Rickey*. New York: Atheneum, 1982.

Quigley, Martin. *The Crooked Pitch: The Curveball in American Baseball History*. Chapel Hill, N.C: Algonquin Books, 1984.

Rice, Grantland. *The Tumult and the Shouting*. New York: A. S. Barnes, 1954.

Rickey, Branch. *The American Diamond*. New York Simon and Schuster, 1965.

Ritter, Lawrence S. *The Glory of Their Times*. New York: Macmillan, 1966.

Robinson, Brooks. *Third Base Is My Home*. Waco, Tex.: Word Books, 1974.

Robinson, Jackie, with Charles Dexter. *Baseball Has Done It*. Philadelphia: J. B. Lippincott, 1964.

Robinson, Jackie, with Alfred Duckett. *I Never Had It Made*. New York: Putnam, 1972.

Rothan, Martin. *New Baseball Rules and Decision Book*. Lexington, Ky.: Baseball Decisions, 1947.

Ruth, George Herman. *Babe Ruth's Own Book of Baseball*. New York: Putnam, 1928.

———. *How to Play Baseball*. New York: Cosmopolitan Book, 1931.

Ruth, George Herman, with Bob Considine. *The Babe Ruth Story*. New York: Dutton, 1948.

Schecter, Leonard. *The Jocks*. New York: Paperback Library, 1969.

Schiffer, Michael. *Ballpark*. New York: Signet, 1982.

Schlossberg, Dan. *The Baseball Book of Why*. Middle Village, N.Y.: Jonathan David Publishers, 1984.

———. *The Baseball Catalog*. Middle Village, New York: Jonathan David Publishers, 1980.

———. *Hammerin' Hank*. New York: Stadia Sports Publishing, 1974.

Schwed, Fred, Jr. *How to Watch a Baseball Game*. New York: Harper and Brothers, 1957.

Seymour, Harold. *Baseball: The Early Years*. New York: Oxford University Press, 1960.

———. *Baseball: The Golden Age*. New York: Oxford University Press, 1971.

———. *Baseball: The People's Game*. New York: Oxford University Press, 1990.

Shea, Thomas P. *Baseball Nicknames*. Hingham, Massachusetts: Cates-Vincent Publications, 1946.

Shirts, Morris A. *Warm Up for Little League Baseball*. New York: Pocket Books, 1971.

Shulman, David. "Baseball's Bright Lexicon." *American Speech*, February 1951.

Smith, Curt. *America's Dizzy Dean*. St. Louis: Bethany, 1978.

Smith, H. Allen. *Low and Inside*. New York: Doubleday, 1949.

Smith, Ken. "How They Express Themselves." *Baseball Magazine*, August 1939.

Smith, Myron J. *Baseball: A Comprehensive Bibliography*. Jefferson, North Carolina: McFarland, 1986.

Smith, Red. "Sportspeak and Stuff." *New York Times*, July 1, 1981.

———. *To Absent Friends from Red Smith*. New York: Atheneum, 1982.

Smith, Robert. *Babe Ruth's America*. New York: Thomas Y. Crowell, 1974.

———. *Baseball*. New York: Simon and Schuster, 1947.

———. *Baseball's Hall of Fame*. New York: Bantam, 1965.

Smith, Ron. *The Sporting News Chronicle of 20th Century Sport*. New York: Mallard Press, New York, 1991.

Snyder, Brad. *A Well-Paid Slave: Curt Flood's Fight for Free Agency in Professional Sports*. New York: Viking, 2006.

Sperling, Dan. *A Spectator's Guide to Baseball*. New York: Avon Books, 1983.

Spink, Alfred H. *The National Game*. 2nd ed. St. Louis: National Game Publishing, 1911.

Spink, C. C. & Son. *The Sporting News Record Book*. St. Louis: various editions.

Spink, C. C. Johnson. "Sports in Our Language." *Sporting News*, June 10, 1978.

Spink, J. G. Taylor, et al. *Comedians of Baseball Down the Years*. St. Louis: Charles C. Spink and Son, 1958.

Stockton, J. Roy. *The Gashouse Gang and a Couple of Other Guys*. New York: A. S. Barnes, 1945.

Stern, Bill. *Bill Stern's Favorite Baseball Stories*. New York: Pocket Books, 1949.

Stewart, Wayne. "Some Baseball Quotes Can Be Downright Embarrassing." *Baseball Digest*, March 1990.

Sullivan, Frank. "The Cliché Expert Testifies on Baseball." *New Yorker*, August 27, 1949.

Tamony, Peter. "Baseball." *Newsletter and Wasp,* April 14, 1939.

———. "Championship of the World." *Newsletter and Wasp,* October 13 and October 20, 1939.

———. "Sandlot Baseball." *Western Folklore,* October 1968.

Thierry, Edward M. "Slang of the Sporting Writers," *Baseball Magazine,* September 1909.

Thompson, Fresco. *Every Diamond Doesn't Sparkle.* New York: David McKay, 1964.

Torrez, Danielle Gagnon, and Ken Lizotte. *High Inside: Memoirs of a Baseball Wife.* New York: Putnam, 1983.

Turkin, Hy. *The Baseball Almanac.* New York: A. S. Barnes, 1955.

Uecker, Bob, with Mickey Herskowitz. *Catcher in the Wry.* New York: Jove, 1982.

United States Congress, House of Representatives, Committee on the Judiciary. *Organized Baseball.* Washington, D.C.: Government Printing Office, 1952.

Vanderberg, Bob. *Sox: From Lane and Fain to Zisk and Fisk.* Chicago: Chicago Review Press, 1982.

Vecsey, George. *The Baseball Life of Sandy Koufax.* New York: Scholastic Books, 1968.

———. "The Best of Casey Stengel." *Newsday,* August 31, 1965.

———. *Joy in Mudville.* New York: McCall, 1970.

Veeck, Bill, with Ed Linn. *The Hustler's Handbook.* New York: Berkley Books, 1965.

———. *Veeck—As in Wreck.* New York: New American Library, 1962.

Voight, David Q. *American Through Baseball.* Chicago: Nelson-Hall, 1976.

Waggoner, Glen, ed. *Rotisserie League Baseball.* New York: Bantam Books, 1984.

Wallop, Douglass. *Baseball: An Informal History.* New York: Norton, 1969.

———. *The Year the Yankees Lost the Pennant.* New York: Norton, 1954.

Weaver, Earl. *It's What You Learn After You Know It All That Counts.* New York: Pocket Books, 1969.

———. *Winning!* New York: William Morrow, 1972.

West, Harwell E. *The Baseball Scrap Book.* Chicago: Diamond Publishing, 1938.

Whiteford, Mike. *How to Talk Baseball.* New York: Dembner Books, 1983.

Williams, Peter. *The Joe Williams Baseball Reader.* Chapel Hill, N.C.: Algonquin, 1989.

Williams, Ted, with John Underwood. *My Turn at Bat.* New York: Simon and Schuster, 1970.

———. *The Science of Hitting.* New York: Simon and Schuster, 1970.

Wills, Maury, with Don Freeman. *How to Steal a Pennant.* New York: Putnam, 1976.

Yastrzemski, Carl, with Al Hirshberg. *Yaz.* New York: Tempo, 1968.

Zinsser, William. *Spring Training.* New York: Harper and Row, 1989

Zoss, Joel, and John Bowman. *Diamonds in the Rough.* New York: Macmillan, 1989.

PERMISSIONS

———◆———

G rateful acknowledgment is made to the following for formal permission to reprint selections included in this book:

Maury Allen and Bo Belinsky, *Bo: Pitching and Wooing* (New York: Dial, 1973). Excerpts used by permission of Maury Allen.

Roger Angell, "Up the Hall" (*The New Yorker*, "The Sporting Scene," 8/31/87). Excerpt used by permission of Roger Angell.

Ira H. Berkow, "For Jackson, What Choice?" (*The New York Times*, 6/24/86). Copyright © 1986 by The New York Times Company. Reprinted with permission.

John K. Hutchens, "Confessions of a Baseball Fan" (*The New York Times Magazine*, 7/14/46). Excerpts reprinted courtesy of the Estate of John K. Hutchens.

W. P. Kinsella, *Shoeless Joe* (New York: Houghton Mifflin Company: 1982). Copyright © 1982 by W. P. Kinsella. Reprinted by permission of Houghton Mifflin Company. All rights reserved.

Philip Roth, "My Baseball Years" (*The New York Times*, 4/2/73). Copyright © 1973 by The New York Times Company. Reprinted with permission.

Robert W. Service, "Low-Brow," from *Songs of Myself* (New York: Dodd Mead, 1952). Excerpt used by permission of the Estate of Robert W. Service.

Mark Shields permission to quote extensively from his newspaper columns.

The Sporting News, permission to quote excerpts from the newspaper, granted by Steven P. Geitschier, archivist.

Bill Veeck with Ed Linn, *The Hustler's Handbook* (New York: Putnam, 1965). Excerpts used by permission of Mary Francis Veeck.

Bill Veeck with Ed Linn, *Veeck—As in Wreck* (Chicago: University of Chicago Press, 2001). Excerpts used by permission of Mary Francis Veeck.

INDEX

American League Championship Series (ALCS), 39, 40, 120, 333, 427
amphetamines, 431
Anaheim Stadium, 497
Ancient Baseball Celebrities, 323–24
Anderson, Bruce, **13**
Anderson, Dave, **13**
Anderson, George "Sparky," xi, **13–16**, *14*, 387, 496; Ackerman on, 5; Al Clark and, 105; Herzog on, 242
Andrews, Mike, 412
Andrews, Shane, 326
Andujar, Joaquin, **16–17**, *17*
Angell, Roger, **17–20**
Angelos, Peter, **20**
announcers, sports, *see* broadcasters, broadcasting
anonymous quotes, 21–27; from press box, 27–29
anonymous verse, 29–30
Anson, Cap, 30, *30*, 107
Apple, Max, **31**
Appling, Luke, **31**, *31*, 395, 569
Araton, Harvey, **32**
Arizona Diamondbacks, 482
Armstrong, Neil, 129, 212
Aronson, Harvey, **32**
Arthur, Chester A., **32**
artificial turf, 12, 151, 287, 339, 481, 613; D. Allen on, 10; Lee on, 316; P. Richmond on, 438; T. McGraw on, 362
Ashburn, Richie, **32–33**
Asinof, Eliot, **33**
Aspromonte, Bob, **33**
Aspromonte, Ken, **33**
Astrodome, 421, 569
AstroTurf, 438; *see also* artificial turf
Atlanta Braves, 47, 115, 171, 559; bumper sticker on, 39; fans of, 39; Tanner on, 545
Augustine, Saint, **33**
Austen, Jane, **33**
autographs, 23, 372; Blue on, 63; Hornsby on, 249; Lasorda on, 314; Ott on, 411; Puckett on getting paid for, 428; Stengel on, 518, 520; Willie Wilson on, 602
Autry, Gene, **34**, 49, 264, 355
Averill, Earl, **34**, 211, 389, 395, 396
awards, H. Greenberg on, 220

Babitz, Eve, **35**
Backman, Wally, **35**

Baer, Arthur "Bugs," **35–36**
Bagley, Eli, **36**
Bagwell, Jeff, 384
Bailey, F. Lee, 192
Baker, Dusty, 221
Baker, Frank "Home Run," 108, 109, 390, 394
Baker, Kevin, **37**
Baker, Russell, **37**
Balboni, Steve, 387
Baldwin, Charles, 391–92
balk rule, 272, 532, 557; in Knickerbocker rules, 300; Luciano on, 337
Ballard, Jeff, **37**
ballparks, 74, 86, 89, 101, 113, 115, 166, 167, 200, 210, 287, 377, 491, 523, 562; artificial turf in, 10, 12, 151, 287, 316, 339, 362, 438, 481; attendance at, 56, 146, 176, 185, 235, 252, 343, 568, 573; Bogart on going to, 65; Bombeck on, 65–66; Borsch on, 67; Boswell on building of, 68; commercials to encourage attendance at, 65, 185; cookie-cutter, 236, 285; Coover on, 120; crowds at, 30, 191, 193, 235, 252, 255, 362, 372, 476, 590, 598; dimensions in, 5, 14, 113; with domes, 68, 144, 338, 481; Frost on, 188; Harrison on, 234; Hebner on, 236; Hutchens on atmosphere of, 256–57; integration of, 24; Kaat on, 285; Kinsella on, 295; Luciano on, 338–39; playing fields in, 87, 101, 126, 233, 234, 333, 422; Sheed on, 491; stadium seats in, 594; Thomas Wolfe on, 603; Veeck on, 574, 575; women at, 252, 581; Zinsser on, 613; *see also specific ballparks*
ballplayers, 37, 117, 123, 152, 261, 429, 562, 612; agents of, 317, 404; aging of, 50, 169, 211, 223, 230, 270, 286, 352, 361, 413, 417, 435, 457, 475; alcohol and, *see* alcohol; Arthur on, 32; average age of, 183; Beaumont on, 47; Bobby Valentine on intelligence of, 566; Broeg's list of ten most colorful, 330; Brosnan on, 81, 82; C. Crawford on, 123; cheapness of, 436; childhood of, 142, 144, 174, 188, 206, 211, 266, 352, 379; children of, 53, 284, 348, 463; controversy and, 495; death and illness of, 165, 208; D. Green

on egos of, 219; from Dominican Republic, 432; Durocher on, 152, 153; Eakins on, 158; Eisenberg on, 165; ejections and umpire arguments of, 53, 221, 231, 295, 298, 338, 457; fraternization of, 455; gambling of, 11, 249; Garagiola on, 192, 193; Garvey on expendability of, 196; Gehrig on tempers and, 197; Gehringer on, 198; Gent on, 199; Giles on superstars vs., 206; H. Wagner on, 581; H. Walker on aggressive vs. dissention, 584; as idols and role models, 66, 96, 205; James on marks left by, 270; from Japan, 8; Johnstone on mooning of, 275; McGeehan on habits of, 361; misbehavior of, 372; models vs., 123; modern vs. old-time, 42, 46, 110, 136, 137, 152, 172, 371, 414, 576–77; money spending of, 23; M. Smith on, 503; Murtaugh on ideal, 375; nicknames of, 321, 382–401, 512; Paige on modern-day, 414; parents of, 1, 4, 144, 150, 266, 512–13; Paul on controversy and, 421; Phillips on modern-day, 425; physical appearance of, 158, 493, 570, 573; R. Bridges on, 77; Rickey on leisure time of, 441; Rickey on the making of great, 439, 442; Ring Lardner on happiness and, 312; salaries of, *see* contract signings; salaries; schedule of, 82; scouting of, *see* scouting, scouts; selfishness in, 15, 499; Sewell on modern-day, 487; sex and courting of, 11, 12, 64, 69, 103, 236, 362, 363, 519; Shields on physical appearance of, 493; Short on controversy and, 495; Skowron on individual vs. team, 499; Spahn on modern-day, 509; Steinbrenner on, 514; Stengel on modern-day, 519, 534, 539; superstars vs., 172, 206, 225, 576; superstitions of, 153, 178, 179; Tebbetts on vengeance and, 547; training rules for, 322–23; T. Simmons on, 498; Veeck on modern-day, 576–77; Veeck on size of, 570, 573; wearing down of, 11; Winfield on modern-day, 603; wives of, 21, 69, 103, 195, 236, 252, 369, 406, 492, 556, 564; Yawkey on helplessness of, 609; youthful exuberance in, 93–94

Brock, Lou, 71, **79–80**, *79*, 307, 385
Broderick, Bishop Edwin, **80**
Brodkey, Harold, **80**
Broeg, Bob, **80**, 161, 330, 393
Brooke, Rupert, 81
Brooklyn, N.Y., 490, 537
Brooklyn Dodgers, 18, 22, 95, 104, 118,
    123, 141, 148, 186, 217, 245, 261,
    286, 313, 325, 398, 406, 459, 492,
    521, 535, 553; Bankhead on, 38;
    Barber as announcer for, 41–43; fans
    of, 22, 141, 155, 214, 418, 492, 549;
    Giants' rivalry with, 25; Goodwin
    on, 214; Hamill on, 230–31; Murphy
    on, 373; nicknames of, 385, 388;
    relocation of, 28, 38, 154, 206, 507;
    Roeder on, 458; slogan and rallying
    cry of, 501; Stengel on, 529; Terry
    on, 548, 549; in World Series, 455,
    456, 533
Brooklyn Eagle headlines, 324
Brosnan, Jim, **81–83**, *81*, 219, 256
Broun, Heywood, **83**
Brown, Bobby, 55, **83**, 604
Brown, Chester A., **83**
Brown, Joe, **84**
Brown, Mordecai, 399
Brown, Norman O., 224
Browning, Pete, **84**
Brundage, Avery, **84**
Brundidge, Harry, **84**
Bryan, Mike, 240
Buck, Jack, **84**
Buckley, William F., **84**
Buckner, Bill, **84**, 386
Buffett, Warren, **85**
Bulger, Bozeman, **85**
bullpens, 53, 56, 81, 115, 236, 241, 599,
    613
Bumbry, Al, 587, 589
bunting, 113, 166; of Keeler, 581;
    Lowenstein on, 336; by Mantle, 415;
    Paige on, 416; Weaver on, 588
Burdette, Lew, **85**, *85*, 94
Burke, Michael, **86**, 571; Veeck on, 571
Burkett, Jesse, 387
Burleson, Rick, 192
Burnes, Bob, **85**
Burnett, W. R., **86**
Burns, Britt, **86**
Burns, George, **86**
Burns, Ken, **86–87**
Busby, Jim, **87**
Busby, Steve, **87**

Busch, Noel F., **87**
Busch Stadium, 40, 568
Bush, Barbara, **88**
Bush, George H. W., 59, **88–89**, *88*, 397;
    Adair on, 5; as ballplayer, 88, 118;
    LaPoint to, 310
Bush, George W., 58, **89**, 555; Costas
    on, 121; as Rangers owner, 88,
    120–21
Bush, Guy, **90**
Bush, Joe, 254
Bush, Vannevar, **90**
Butcher, John, **90**
Byrd, Sammy, 384
Byrne, Tommy, 386, 520
Byron, Bill, 392

Cabell, Enos, 114
Cadore, Leon, **91**
Cady, Steve, **91**
Caen, Herb, **91**
Cahan, Abraham, **91**
California Angels, 98, 611
Callahan, Tom, **92**
Cambria, Joe, **92**
Camden Yards, 43, 568
Cameron, Mike, **92**
Camilli, Lou, **92**
Camp, Walter, **92**
Campanella, Roy, **92–94**, *93*, 348, 379,
    389, 406
Campanis, Al, **94**
Campbell, Bill, 40
Canada, 306, 558
Candlestick Park, 81, 171, 372, 398,
    400, 424
Canel, Buck, **94**
Cannizzaro, Chris, 520, 521
Cannon, Jimmy, **95**
Canseco, Esther, **96**
Canseco, José, 9, **96**, 328, 420
Cantwell, Mary, **96**
Cape Cod Baseball League, 501
Capone, Al, Veeck on, 575
Capote, Truman, **96**
Caray, Harry, **96–97**, *97*, 246, 375,
    378
Carew, Rod, **97**, 217, 270, 422
Carey, Skip, 203
Carlin, George, **97**
Carlton, Steve, **97**, *97*, 273, 360, 513,
    586
Carlyle, Thomas, 591
Carmen, Don, 331

Carpenter, Ruly, **98**
Carroll, Clay, **98**
Carson, Johnny, **98**
Carter, Gary, **98**, *98*
Carter, Jimmy, **98–99**, 99
Cartwright, Alexander J., **99–100**, *99*,
    299
Carty, Rico, **100**, 385
Casals, Pablo, 261
Case, George, **100**
"Casey at the Bat," 500, 550–52; M.
    Gardner on, 194; Phelps on, 425;
    Rice on, 437; Service on, 487;
    Stengel's nickname and, 537
Cash, Norm, **100**, *100*
Cashen, Frank, **101**
Castro, Fidel, 31, 92, 94, 306
catchers, catching, 14, 22, 79, 110, 167,
    171, 211, 252, 342, 422; Angell on,
    18; base stealing and, 336; Bench on,
    50; in Bible, 45; Boone on, 67; calling
    of games by, 335; Campanella on,
    92, 93; Cashen on, 101; equipment
    of, 26, 205, 410; E. R. Greenberg
    on, 220; Huggins on, 254; Luciano
    on, 337; in Negro Leagues, 428; R.
    Jackson on, 266; Stengel on, 531,
    539; Stengel on Mets' staff of, 533;
    Torborg on, 555; wear and tear on,
    74, 337; W. Ewing on, 169
Cater, Danny, 400
Catton, Bruce, **101**
Caudill, Bill, Elia on, 166
Causey, Wayne, 101
Cavarretta, Phil, 101
Cedeño, Cesar, 141, 153
celebrity: Blue on, 63, 64; of Mantle, 72;
    Ruth on, 475
center fielders, 220; *see also specific center
    fielders*
Cepeda, Orlando, **102**, 384
Cey, Ron, **102**, 395
Chabot, Dan, **102**
Chadwick, Henry, **102–3**, *102*, 329
Chambliss, Audrey, **103**
Chance, Dean, **103**, *103*
Chance, Frank, 395
Chandler, Happy, **103**
Chapman, Jack, 388
Chapman, Ray, **103–4**, 356, 468
Charboneau, Joe, 398
Charles, Ed, **104**, 389
Charles, Ray, **104**
Charleston, Oscar, 386, 390

Chase, Hal, 5, **104**, 395
cheating, 37, 341, 524, 588; Boswell
    on, 68; Broun on, 83; Burdette and,
    85; Chylak on, 105; Grace on, 218;
    Hornsby on, 250; Kubek, Sr. on, 304;
    Lasorda on, 315; of umpires, 338; W.
    Ford on, 181; *see also* illegal pitches;
    spitballs; steroids
Chesbro, Jack, 211, 390
chewing tobacco, Bouton on, 70
Chicago, Ill., 164, 254
Chicago Cubs, 30, 38, 113, 131, 148,
    156, 178, 189, 218, 257, 310, 433,
    467, 475, 480, 500, 570, 594, 601;
    Banks on, 39; Dark on playing for,
    128; Durocher on, 154; fans of, 97,
    107, 193, 216, 386, 467, 545, 594,
    597; Garagiola on, 193; Paretsky on,
    418; slogans and rallying cries for,
    501; Will on, 594; in World Series,
    27, 424, 461, 473, 476–77; Wrigley
    as owner of, 27
Chicago White Sox, 127, 176, 257, 335,
    493, 585; fan banner on, 40; fans of,
    164, 493, 572; in French exhibition
    game, 318; nicknames of, 390, 395,
    397; Richards on, 437; slogans and
    rallying cries of, 500, 501; S. Stone
    on fielding of, 540; Vanderberg on,
    568; Veeck on, 574; *see also* Black Sox
    scandal
Chicago White Stockings, 290
Chiles, Pearce, 400
China, 229
Chisholm, Shirley, **105**
Churchill, Winston, 53
Chylak, Nestor, **105**
Cicotte, Eddie, **105**
Cincinnati Reds, 13, 22, 26, 96, 115,
    176, 385, 390, 464, 469, 506
City Slickers, 244
Civil War, U.S., 87
Clark, Al, **105**
Clark, Jack, 27, **106**, 380
Clark, Will, **106**, 227, 369
Clary, Ellis, **106**
Cleaver, Eldridge, **106**
Clemens, Roger, **106**, *106*, 304, 328, 396
Clement, Amanda, **107**
Clemente, Roberto, **107**, *107*, 141, 384,
    390, 404; Cannon on, 95; Kuhn on,
    305; T. Gorman on, 215
Cleveland, Grover, **107**
Cleveland, Ohio, 276, 482

Cleveland Indians, 103, 111, 217, 335,
    454, 585; Camilli on, 92; nicknames
    of, 388, 393, 399; numbers added to
    uniforms of, 23; Veeck's commercial
    for, 571; in World Series, 26, 367,
    403
Click, Bob, 435
Clinton, Hillary Rodham, **107**
Clinton, William J., **108**
clubhouses, 42, 72, 83, 192, 314, 354,
    403, 566; Bouton on, 69; credo of,
    496; R. Bridges on, 76; R. Jackson
    on, 266
coaches, coaching, 181, 494, 612; Bouton
    on, 70; Brosnan on, 81; Clary on,
    106; Merrill on, 366; Mize on, 370;
    Morgan on, 371; Paige on, 416;
    Weaver on, 587
Coates, Jim, 540
Coates, Joe, 394
Cobb, Irvin S., **108**
Cobb, Ty, **108–11**, *160*, 302, 326, 346,
    415, 522, 535, 609; Averill on,
    34; Bauer on, 35–36; Broun on,
    83; Bulger on, 85; Caen on, 91;
    Cannon on, 95; Cy Young on, 610;
    disagreeable and aggressive character
    of, xi, 35–36, 91, 95, 108, 109, 111,
    596; hits records of, 436; Hornsby
    on criticisms of, 249; inscription at
    Tiger Stadium for, 260; J. Jackson to,
    268; J. Williams on, 596; MacArthur
    on, 340; Morris on, 371; nicknames
    of, 389, 391; Ring Lardner on, 312;
    Ruth on, 473; sign on, 497; Stengel
    on, 519, 522, 528; Woodrow Wilson's
    inscribed photo to, 602
Cobbledick, Gordon, **111**
Cochrane, Gordon S. "Mickey," **112**,
    133, 536, 543, 596
Coffin, Tristram Potter, **112**
Cohane, Tim, **113**
Cohen, James, **113**
Cohen, Marvin, **113**
Cohn, Lowell, **113**
Colander, Pat, **113**
Colavito, Rocky, **113**
Cole, Nat "King," **114**
Coleman, Choo Choo, **114**, 122, 525,
    534
Coleman, Jerry, **114–15**, *114*
Coleman, Ken, 247
Coleman, Len, **116**
Coleman, Vince, **116**, 399

Coletti, Ned, **116**
Collins, Eddie, **116**, 256
Collins, James A. "Rip," **116**, 137, 389
Collins, Tom, **116**
Colorado Rockies, 47
Coluccio, Bob, 392
Combs, Earl, 391, 393, 394
Comiskey, Charlie, 272, 394, 395
Comiskey Park, 41, 164, 308
competition, competitiveness, 124, 172,
    360; Brock on, 79; Durocher on, 152,
    153, 154, 155
Conan Doyle, Arthur, **116–17**
concentration, in baseball, 2–3
Concepcion, Dave, **117**
Cone, David, **117**
Congress, U.S., 443, 559; 1950's anti-
    trust investigations in, 289, 346,
    516–17, 519, 520, 532
Congressional Baseball Game, 118
Coniff, Frank, **117**
Conlan, Charles M., **117**
Conlan, Jocko, **117**
Conners, Jimmy, 51
Connolly, Dan, x
Connolly, Tommy, **117**
Connor, Roger, 388
Connors, Billy, **118**
Connors, Kevin "Chuck," **118**
Considine, Bob, 209
Conte, Silvio, **118**
Continental League, 439, 443
contract negotiations, 192, 207; Alderson
    on, 9; Barry Bonds on, 66; Belinsky
    on, 48; Berra and, 56; Blue on, 63; D.
    Dean and, 131, 138; DiMaggio and,
    87, 142; G. Carter on, 98; Landreaux
    on, 309; Lasorda on Valenzuela's,
    314; Mack on, 340; Marion in, 347;
    Musial on, 375; Rickey and, 118; R.
    Woolf on, 604; Torre on, 556; W.
    Cooper on, 120
contract signings, 21, 24, 49, 51, 96,
    123, 139, 186, 212, 270, 420, 504;
    A. MacPhail on, 343; Barfield on,
    43; Bench on, 51; Darwin on, 129;
    of Gamble, 191; Kaline on, 288;
    Koosman on, 300; Leyland on, 321;
    Quisenberry on his own, 431; of R.
    Jackson, 264; Ruppert on, 470; *see
    also* salaries
Cook, Beano, **118**
Cooke, Alistair, **118**
Cooke, Bob, **119**

Farmer, Mike, 47
Farnsworth Television & Radio Corp. ad, 8
Farrell, Eddie "Doc," 250
Farrell, Jack, **171**
Farrell, James T., **172**
Farrell, Turk, **172**
Farrell, Wes, 26
fastballs, 136, 219, 254, 304, 353, 361, 442, 509, 558; Chapman killed by, 356; Foytack on lacking, 184; of Gullett, 462; of N. Ryan, 263; of Paige, 342, 416, 602; of Quisenberry, 430; Seaver on, 486; of Spahn, 552; T. Williams on, 600; W. Johnson on his, 275
fear, 301, 302, 353, 456
Feather, William, **172**
Feeney, Chub, **172**
Fehr, Don, **172**
Felix, Junior, 171
Feller, Bob, **173**, 342; nicknames of, 387, 396, 399; W. Johnson on, 274
Felton, Terry, 592
Fenway Park, 150, 177, 214, 317, 386, 390, 398, 489, 555; advertisements and billboards at, 495, 497; banners at, 40; Halberstam on, 229; H. Johnson on, 274; Paige on, 416; Stuart on, 541; Updike on, 565; Washington on falling into seats of, 586
Ferber, Edna, **174**
Ferguson, Andrew, **174**
Ferguson, Robert V., **174**, 388
Fetzer, John E., **174–75**
Fewster, Chick, 207
Fidrych, Mark, **175**, *175*, 386
fielding, 22, 213; B. Gibson on, 204; DiMaggio on, 143; errors in, *see* errors, fielding; Freehan on, 185; Henrich on, 238; J. J. Gibson on, 205; J. Robinson on, 456; Lopez on, 335–36; Mays on, 356, 357; Piersall on, 426; Quisenberry on Royals and, 431; R. Jackson on, 267; R. Miller on, 369; S. Stone on White Sox and, 540; Stengel on, 528, 531; Stuart on, 541; W. Cooper on, 120; Yost on pitchers and, 609
Field of Dreams, 20, 88
fights, 77, 295, 526, 601, 605, 611; Hegan on, 236; J. McGraw on, 362; McCarthy on umpires and, 359;

Ruth on, 475; Veeck on, 571
Figueroa, Ed, 319
Fimrite, Ron, **175**
fines, 367, 378, 580
Fingers, Rollie, 538
Finley, Charles, 21, 101, **175–77**, 562; Blue on, 63; Giles on, 205; Kuhn on, 304; McCatty on, 360; Murray on, 374; Red Smith on, 504–5; R. Jackson on, 267
first base, first basemen, 122, 230, 239, 270, 585; best of, 5; Foxx on playing, 184; Lockman on, 333; Spalding on, 510
Fishel, Robert O., **177**
Fisher, Jack, 519
Fisk, Carlton, **177**, 329, 392, 396, 555
Fitzgerald, F. Scott, xvi, **177–78**, *178*
Fitzgerald, Ray, **178**
Fitzsimmons, Fred, 239, 593
Flanagan, Mike, **178**, 398
Flannery, Tim, **179**
Fletcher, Art, **179**
Flick, Elmer, L. Allen on, 11
Flood, Curt, **179**, 179, 495; Snyder on, 507–8; suit filed by, 61, 507, 508
Florida Marlins, 116, 403
Foch, Marshal, 475
Foli, Tim, 387
Folkers, Rich, 115
Folsom, Lowell Edwin, **180**
football, 25, 53, 70, 84, 93, 95, 105, 108, 118, 136, 139, 160, 171, 176, 182, 222, 286, 303, 320, 402, 455, 477, 554, 570, 573, 575, 589; baseball vs., *see* baseball vs. football; Blue on, 62–63; Quindlen on, 429; Rickey on growing popularity of, 441; Ruth on betting on, 474; Will on, 594
Forbes, Gordon, 549
Ford, Gerald R., 118, **180**, *180*
Ford, Richard, 180
Ford, Whitey, **181**, *181*, 322, 345, 387, 399; Angell on, 19; Berra and, 59; endorsements of, 37; Mantle on, 346; Shor on, 494; Stengel on, 520, 527
Foreman, Frank, **182**
Forman, Al, **182**
Fosse, Ray, **182**
Foster, George, **182**, 326, 501
Foster, Rube, 389
Fowler, Art, 398
Fowler, Wyche, **182**
Fowles, John, **182**

Fox, Charlie, **183**
Fox, Nellie, **183**, *183*, 576
Fox Sports, 244
Foxx, Jimmie, **183–84**, 385, 388; L. Gomez on, 209, 210, 212
Foytack, Paul, **184**
France, 318, 476
François, Comte de Barbé-Marbois, **184**
Frank, Lawrence, **184**
Frank, Stanley, **184**
Frankfurter, Felix, **185**
Frawley, William, **185**
Frazee, Harry, 474, 477
Frazier, George, **185**
free agency, 34, 40, 242, 265, 304, 610; Devine on, 139; E. B. Williams on, 595; F. Robinson on, 454; Kuhn on, 305; Samuelson on, 479–80; S. Anderson on, 15; Steinbrenner on, 514; Veeck on, 574
Freehan, Bill, **185**, 276
Freeman, Mark, 532
Fregosi, Jim, **185–86**
Frey, Jim, **186**
Frick, Ford C., 28, 76, **186–87**, 325, 326, 443, 575
Frisch, Frank, 132, 137, **187**, *187*, 249, 389, 596
Frost, Robert, **188**
Fuchs, Emil, **188**, 250
Fuentes, Tito, **188**
Fuller, Mark, **188**
Fullerton, Hugh S., **188**
fungo bats, 81, 427
Furillo, Carl, 396

Gabler, Frank, 390
Gabler, Neal, **189**
Gabor, Eva, **189**
Gaedel, Eddie, 571
Gaetti, Gary, **189**
Galan, Augie, **189–90**
Galbraith, John Kenneth, **190**
Galbreath, John W., **190**
Gallagher, Dave, **190**
Gallico, Paul, **190–91**
Galvin, Pud, 392
Gamble, Oscar, **191**, 597
gambling, 289; Chase on, 104; Cicotte and, 105; Hornsby on, 249; Klem and, 297; Kuhn on, 305; M. Allen on, 11; and Rose scandal, 202, 462, 463, 464; *see also* Black Sox scandal
Game of the Week, 131

Hamilton, Bill, 397
Hamilton, Milo, **231**
Hamman, Ed, **231**
Hamner, Granville, 113
Hampton, Mike, **231**
Haney, Fred, 94
Hanks, Tom, **231**
Hanlon, Ned, **231**
Hano, Arnold, 211, **231–21**
Hanson, Erik, **232**
Harding, Warren G., *472*
Hargrove, Mike, 349, 391
Harrelson, Ken, **232**
Harridge, Will, **232–33**
Harris, Art, **233**
Harris, Bucky, 57, **233**, 386
Harris, Lenny, **233**
Harris, Mark, **233**
Harshman, Jack, **234**
Hartman, Harry, 246
Hartnett, Gabby, **234**
Hartsfield, Roy, **234**
Hartung, Clint, 365
Harvey, Bryan, 497
Harvey, Doug, **234**
Harwell, Ernie, **234–35**
Hawkins, Andy, **235**
Hayes, Von, 50
headlines, 161–64
Healy, Fran, **235**
Hearst, William Randolph, Sr., 36
Hebner, Richie, **235–36**, *236*
Hecht, Henry, **236**
heckling, 8, 96, 218, 256, 268
Heffner, Don, 521
Hegan, Mike, **236**
Held, Woodie, **236**
Hemingway, Ernest, 59, **236–37**
Hemond, Roland, **237**
Hemus, Solly, 207
Henderson, Dave, **237**
Henderson, Rickey, 54, **237–38**, 354, 384, 609
Hendrick, George, 114
Hendricks, Elrod, **238**
Henrich, Tommy, **238**, *238*, 395, 450, 536
Herman, Babe, **238–39**, *239*, 310, 395, 552, 596
Herman, Billy, **239**
Hern, Gerald V., **239**
Hernandez, Keith, **240**, 605
Hernandez, Orlando, 389
Hernandez, Roberto, 449

Hernandez, Willie, **240**
Hershiser, Orel, 328
Hervey, Mary Lepell, **240**
Herzog, Whitey, **240–42**, *241*, 400
Higgins, George V., **242–430**
Higgins, Mike, **243**
high school baseball, 19, 99, 308, 434
Hill, Albert G., **243**
Hill, Art, **243**
Hill, Calvin, **243–44**
Hill, David, **244**
Hiller, Chuck, 388
Hirschbeck, Mark, 60
hit and run: in Bible, 45; Richards on stealing signs for, 438; Rickey on, 444; Wambsganss's recollection of significant, 585
Hitchcock, Billy, **244**
hitters, hitting, 92, 125, 270; Aaron on, 1, 2–3; Berra on, 57; B. Gibson on, 204; Biittner on, 60; Boggs on, 65; Bouton on, 70; Campanella on, 93; Carew on, 97; Carl Hubbell on, 254; Carroll on, 98; Cash on, 100; fear in, 301; Foster on, 182; .400 average in, 60, 70, 80, 110, 157, 216–17, 550, 598, 599, 600; Foxx on, 184; Frey's advice on, 186; Garagiola on his poor, 193; Hanlon on confrontations between umpires and, 231; Hornsby on, 249; Johnstone on, 276; Keeler on, 289; K. Hernandez on, 240; Koppett on, 301; Lasorda on, 314; Lau on, 315; Lavagetto on, 315; L. Gomez on, 212; Lowenstein on, 336; L. Wagner on, 581; Mays on, 357; McCarthy on, 359; Mize on, 370; Musial on, 375; Phillips on, 425; Rivers on, 451; R. Jackson on, 264, 265, 267; Rose on, 463, 513; Rudi on, 467; Schmidt on, 482; Scott on, 484; Shamsky on, 489; S. J. Gould on, 216–17; slumps in, *see* slumps, batting; Spahn on, 508; Stargell on, 513; Stengel on, 520, 538; switch, 2; Templeton on, 548; Terry on, 550; Throneberry on, 554; T. Williams on, 597, 598, 599, 600; Vaughn on, 569; Veale on, 569; W. Cooper on, 120; Yastrzemski on, 608–9; *see also* batting, batters
Hoagland, E., **244**
Hoagland, Jim, **244**
Hoak, Don, **244**

Hobson, Butch, **245**
hockey, 235, 237, 286, 320, 498, 554, 558, 575
Hodapp, Johnny, **245**
Hodges, Gil, **245**, *245*; Alston on, 12; Dressen on, 148; Rickey on, 441; Stengel on, 520
Hodges, Russ, **245–46**
Hoffman, Abbie, **246**
Hoffman, Art, 387
Holke, Walter, 399
Hollander, Zander, x
Holloman, Bobo, 330
Holmes, Tommy, **246**
home plate, 122, 201
Homer, **247**
home run records: Aaron's chase for all-time, 1, 2, 3, 4, 231, 266, 328, 478, 501; Bonds as breaking all-time, 4, 66, 266, 410, 487; Maris's single-season, 2, 147, 328, 347, 348, 410, 433, 451, 480, 577; McGwire and Sosa chase for, 272, 363, 410, 577; of Ruth, 90, 177, 190–91, 433, 436, 476, 478, 547, 611; steroids and, 266
home runs, 182, 222, 232, 476, 529, 583; Aaron on, 4; Aker on, 9; in Bible, 45; Blefary on, 62; broadcasting calls for, 231, 245, 246–47, 451, 466; decade-by-decade firsts of, 325–26; Dykstra on hitting game-winning, 157; Easter on, 159; Eisenhower on, 166; F. Sullivan on, 542; grand-slam, 343, 377; Hornsby on glorification of, 250; Hunter on giving up, 255; J. Gibson on money and, 205; L. Allen on, 11; Lowenstein on, 336; Maddox on, 343; Matt Williams on, 597; Mays on hitting four in game, 357; Niedenfuer on Clark's game-winning, 380; Otis on hitting of, 410; Peterman on Haas's World Series, 424; P. Niekro on Aaron's ability to hit, 380; proliferation of, 9, 11; Raper on, 432; Rosen on game-ending, 465; Ruth on hitting of, 474; Saroyan on, 481; Shields on triples vs., 494; Thomson's pennant-winning, 154, 245, 261, 293, 504, 505, 553
Hood, Thomas, **247**
Hooper, Harry, **248**
Hoover, Herbert, **248**, *248*, 475, 497
Hope, Bob, **248**
Horlen, Joe, 501